# MAN'S
## QUESTION

# GOD'S
## ANSWER

# PROOFREADERS

Abel, Sue
Abbott, Bill
Albritton, Connie
Aycock, Eugene
Aycock, Marcia
Bloss, Deane
Bloss, Saunda
Bonham, Judy
Bransby, Don
Brinker, Fred
Buckley, Margaret
Copeland, Peggy
Dionne, Mary Jane
Dorow, Carol, M.D.
Dorow, Stuart, M. D.
Dunnam, Reba
Elrod, Jim
Esquivias, Teresea
Felton, Betsy
Felton, Dewey
Felton, Mary
Felton, Randy
Fennell, Zack
Frazier, Martha
Gabel, Richard
Garvin, Louise

Gentle, Barbara
Gill, Jerry
Gill, MaryAnn
Griffin, Gwen
Guyton, Glenda
Hartman, Georgia
Hartman, Orbie
Higgins, Brenda
Higgins, Gary
Howerton, Ken
Jones, Bob
Jones, Sandra
Keenman, James
King, Dolores
King, Kevin
Leonard, Ruth
Lewis, Eileen
Lewis, Royal, M.D.
Mapes, Don
Maurer, Jenny
Moen, Adel
Mosley, Bill
Mosley, Lillie
Mosley, Miles
Myers, Barbara
Newby, Mildred

Owens, Jerry
Owens, Linda
Palmer, Mayredean
Reed, David
Reed, Pat
Reid, Allene
Reid, Dail
Richmond, Rev. Walt
Ross, Jeannie
Ross, Willis
Samaripa, Verna
Scott, Leenetta
Scott, Rev. S. J.
Scribner, Van
Self, Emma Jean
Self, Gladys
Self, S. L.
Settle, Jean
Sheaffer, Rev. Daniel T.
Shelton, Lois
Southern, Rami
Steadley, Miller
Stillwell, Carol
Stimson, Karolyn
Stockdale, Jerry
Story, Virginia

Tarver, Sallie
Tarver, Sidney
Taylor, Tammy
Thomas, Kawana
Thomas, Neoma
Thomas, Ron
Vanderburg, Arlene
Vanderburg, Carl
Vandeventer, Neva
Viar, George
Vickers, Margaret
Vickers, Ron
Walton, Joy
Walton, Woodrow
Warren, Frank
Weatherford, Nean
Wilmoth, Debbie
Willis, Treva
Witcher, Shirley
Witcher, Wayne
Young, Dianna

# MAN'S
## QUESTION

# GOD'S
## ANSWER

## LU ANN BRANSBY

WHITAKER
HOUSE

First edition published by Lord & Bransby, forty printings. *Fortieth printing, July 2001.*

Unless otherwise indicated, all Scripture quotations are taken from the King James Version (KJV) of the Bible.

Scripture quotations marked (AMP) are from the *Amplified New Testament,* © 1954, 1958, 1987, by the Lockman Foundation, and are used by permission; or are from the *Amplified Bible, Old Testament,* © 1962, 1964 by Zondervan Publishing House, and used by permission.

Scripture quotations marked (TLB) are from *The Living Bible,* © 1971 by Tyndale House Publishers, Wheaton, Illinois. Used by permission.

Scripture quotations marked (NIV) are from the Holy Bible, *New International Version,* © 1973, 1978, 1984 by the International Bible Society. Used by permission.

Scripture quotations marked (NAS) are from the *New American Standard Bible,* © 1960, 1962, 1968, 1971, 1973, 1975, 1977 by The Lockman Foundation. Used by permission.

Additional references include the following: Dake's Annotated Reference Bible, New World Translation of the Holy Scriptures, Good News Bible, New Scofield Reference Edition, Strong's Exhaustive Concordance, Concordia Self-Study Commentary, Smith's Bible Dictionary, Random House Dictionary of the English Language, Webster's New Collegiate Dictionary, Handbook of Denominations in the United States, The Kingdom of the Cults, St. Martin's Roget's Thesaurus of English Words and Phrases, Handy Dictionary of the Bible, The Impending Hour, Take a Bite out of Crime, U.S. Department of Justice, Washington D.C., National Youth Work Alliance, Washington D.C., The American Social Health Association, U.S. Public Health Service Center for Disease Control, Humanist Manifestos 1 & 2.

## MAN'S QUESTION, GOD'S ANSWER
*Second edition*

Lu Ann Bransby
Lord & Bransby
P.O. Box 60544
Oklahoma City, OK 73106

ISBN: 0-88368-571-X
Printed in the United States of America
© 1982 by Lu Ann Bransby

Whitaker House
30 Hunt Valley Circle
New Kensington, PA 15068
Visit our web site at: www.whitakerhouse.com

Library of Congress Cataloging-in-Publication Data

Bransby, Lu Ann, 1936–
  Man's question, God's answer / by Lu Ann Bransby.
    p. cm.
  ISBN 0-88368-571-X (pbk. : alk. paper)
  1. Sins. 2. Christian life. I. Title.
  BV4625 .B73 2002
  241'.3—dc21                                    2002002117

1 2 3 4 5 6 7 8 9 10 11 / 09 08 07 06 05 04 03 02

**Dr. Daniel T. Sheaffer**

Pastor
Crossroads
Cathedral
*Oklahoma City*

# FOREWORD
## BY
## DR. DANIEL T. SHEAFFER

"MAN'S QUESTION—GOD'S ANSWER" CONTAINS AN ALPHABETICAL LIST OF HABITS, ADDICTIONS, FEARS, PHOBIAS, SINS, CIRCUMSTANCES, PHILOSOPHIES, QUESTIONS, AND PERSONAL PROBLEMS THAT SEPARATE US FROM THE PERFECT WILL OF GOD!

IT IS AN EXCELLENT BOOK FOR COUNSELLING! It contains many Biblical answers to complex subjects which are rarely dealt with in print. It is designed to be a vital witnessing tool! The entire concept of the book is unique and is beneficial as a self-help guide book.

THE WORLD IS SILENTLY SCREAMING FOR THE TRUTH.

"MAN'S QUESTION—GOD'S ANSWER" contains the CONSEQUENCES OF SIN plus THE BLESSINGS OF GOD to those who overcome!

"MAN'S QUESTION—GOD'S ANSWER" EXPOSES MANY DEVICES THAT SATAN USES TO HOLD MANKIND IN BONDAGE. IT FOILS SATAN'S MASTER PLAN TO PREVENT US FROM SPENDING ETERNITY WITH JESUS!

IT'S HIGH TIME FOR CHRISTIANS TO COME OUT OF THE CLOSET AND LEARN THE PROPER SCRIPTURES TO USE WHEN APPROACHED WITH QUESTIONS ON NUMEROUS SEXUAL SINS THAT PLAGUE MANKIND! *". . .It is high time to awake out of sleep. . ."* Romans 13:11

"MAN'S QUESTION—GOD'S ANSWER" IS A SIN VERSUS SOLUTION BOOK! It's an easy-to-use dictionary that will help you take total control over your life and circumstances! *"And ye shall know the truth, and the truth shall make you free."* John 8:32

Every Christian should keep one copy of "Man's Question — God's Answer" in his home, one in his automobile, and one at his place of business. Let's all do our part to win the world to Christ!

---

## A MESSAGE FROM THE AUTHOR:

God created the desire in me to research and write "MAN'S QUESTION—GOD'S ANSWER" during the writing of "THE IMPENDING HOUR" (my recent book on Bible Prophecy). The Holy Spirit and I formed a joint partnership to write this book. We thus became: LORD and BRANSBY! Together we put in over 3,000 hours during a period of fourteen months!

**TIME IS SHORT . . . JESUS IS COMING VERY SOON!** *"Therefore to him that knoweth to do good, and doeth it not, to him it is sin."* James 4:17

We pray this **ANATOMY OF SIN** and the **PRESCRIBED CURE** will help all who search for the right answer to a difficult situation (or sin)!

*"So then every one of us shall give account of himself to God."*
Romans 14:12

My prayers and love go with YOU!!

**Lu Ann Bransby**

# CONTENTS:

"I have spread out my hands all the day unto a rebellious people, which walketh in a way that was not good, after their own thoughts." Isaiah 65:2

# ABORTION

**DEFINITION:** The expulsion of a human fetus during the first 12 weeks of gestation.

**GOD WILL PUNISH THE PERSON WHO IS GUILTY OF TAKING ANOTHER PERSON'S LIFE!** *"Deliver those who are being taken away to death, And those who are staggering to slaughter (those going to abort a fetus) O hold them back. If you say, "See, we did not know this (was wrong)," does He (God) not consider it who weighs the hearts (of us)? And does He (God) not know it who keeps your soul? And will He not render to man according to his work?"* **Proverbs 24:11-12** (New American Standard)

**SINCE A BABY IN THE WOMB IS ALIVE (or there wouldn't be a need for an abortion), IT HAS AN ETERNAL SOUL AND A SPIRIT AS WELL! WHEN A BABY IS ABORTED, ITS SOUL AND SPIRIT GO TO BE WITH GOD!** *"For just as the body without the spirit is dead, so also faith without works is dead."* **James 2:26** (New American Standard)

**PREGNANT MOTHER ... IF ANY PERSON, CHURCH, OR PASTOR GIVES YOU ADVICE ABOUT HAVING AN ABORTION, DON'T LISTEN! TRUST IN JESUS! PRAY! READ THE BIBLE! GOD WILL SEE YOU AND YOUR LITTLE BABY THROUGH YOUR CIRCUMSTANCES, NO MATTER HOW DIFFICULT THEY SEEM TO YOU, NOW!** Jesus said: *"It would be better for him (you) if a millstone were hung around his (your) neck and he (you) were thrown into the sea, than that he (you) should cause one of these little ones to stumble."* **Luke 17:2** (New American Standard)

**POOR LITTLE DEAD ABORTED BABIES ... THEY WERE PUT TO DEATH WITHOUT BENEFIT OF A TRIAL OR DEFENSE!** Up to 55 million abortions will be performed this year world-wide. What a terrible thing to die without being given a chance to live!

**MOTHER-FATHER ... IF YOU HAVE ALREADY HAD AN ABORTION OR YOU'RE THINKING ABOUT HAVING ONE: PRAY, PRAY, PRAY, REPENT, REPENT, REPENT! ASK GOD TO FORGIVE YOU! IF YOU READ YOUR BIBLE YOU WILL DECIDE TO KEEP YOUR BABY! YOU WILL END UP LOVING AND CARING FOR YOUR BABY!**

**THANK GOD! ABORTED BABIES GO TO HEAVEN!** **Psalm 8:2 says:** *"Out of the mouth of babes and sucklings (nursing babies) hast thou (God) ordained strength because of thine enemies (those who seek to destroy them), that thou (God) mightest still (stop) the enemy and the avenger."* ALSO READ: **2 Samuel, chapter 12**

**GOD KNEW SAMSON AND JOHN THE BAPTIST IN THEIR MOTHERS' WOMBS, AND HE KNOWS YOUR UNBORN BABY, TOO!**

**TO ABORT A BABY IS TO REGRET IT THE REST OF YOUR LIFE!** The baby belongs to **God**, even though you carry it in your womb. Give life! Never destroy it!

**PREGNANT MOTHER ... WED OR UNWED ... YOU HAVE ALTERNATIVES! CONSIDER ADOPTION THROUGH A LEGAL CHRISTIAN AGENCY.** There are thousands of Christian families just praying and waiting to adopt a precious little boy or girl. You could give the most precious gift to them, the gift of life! OR, ... You could choose to pray and let the Lord direct you and your unborn baby into a beneficial surrounding where you could keep your baby. Please don't commit the crime of murder! **ABORTION = MURDER!!**

**GOD WILL HELP YOU CHOOSE LIFE FOR YOUR UNBORN INFANT, IF YOU WILL CALL ON HIM AND BELIEVE IN HIM! GOD REALLY LOVES YOU! GOD CERTAINLY LOVES YOUR BABY, TOO!** Jesus said: *"The thief (Satan) cometh not (came for only one reason), but for to steal (life), and to kill (people), and to destroy: I (Jesus) am come that they (people) might have life, and that they might have it more abundantly."* **John 10:10**

**QUESTION: "DID YOU KNOW THAT DOCTORS PERFORM 1.2 MILLION ABORTIONS EACH YEAR? THAT 4,000 BABIES ARE KILLED EACH DAY THROUGH ABORTION? THAT'S 1 EVERY 22 SECONDS!" WHY?... ANSWER: NORMALLY THE REASON IS THAT A FEMALE DOESN'T WANT THE EXTRA BURDEN, OR INCONVENIENCE OF A BABY. SHE (he) FEELS HER FREEDOM AND HAPPINESS WILL BE DESTROYED IF THE BABY IS BORN! ANOTHER EXCUSE IS THAT A GIRL IS NOT MARRIED!**

**MAY GOD HELP US! ABORTION HAS BECOME A**

(Continued)

**POPULAR NEW FORM OF BIRTH CONTROL!** Statistics prove that 75% of the women are unmarried, 32% are teenagers, and 20% are repeat customers.

**TO PERFORM AN ABORTION IS TO COMMIT MURDER! GOD SAID:** *"THOU SHALT NOT KILL!"* **Exodus 20:13 and Deuteronomy 5:17. THAT IS ONE OF THE TEN COMMANDMENTS GOD GAVE US TO ABSOLUTELY OBEY!**

**THIS VERSE SOUNDS LIKE THE CRY OF AN UNBORN BABY, DOESN'T IT?** *"Why did the knees prevent me: (from being born)? or why the breasts that I should suck?"* **Job 3:12** *"Or as a hidden untimely birth (abortion) I had not been; as infants which never saw light."* **Job 3:16**

**IDOLS ARE CREATED BY THE WORK OF MEN'S HANDS! BUT ONLY GOD CAN CREATE A PRECIOUS BABY!** The aborted babies say: *"They have mouths, but they speak not; eyes have they, but they see not; they have ears, but they hear not; neither is there any breath in their mouths."* **Psalm 135:16-17**

**DID YOU KNOW THAT AFTER AN ABORTION A WOMAN FACES AN INCREASED POSSIBILITY OF FUTURE MISCARRIAGES, TUBULAR PREGNANCIES, PREMATURE BABIES, STERILITY, PSYCHIATRIC DIFFICULTIES?**

**POOR LITTLE ABORTED BABIES! THEIR HEART STARTED BEATING ON THE 28th DAY AFTER CONCEPTION! ON THE 30th DAY ALMOST EVERY ORGAN WAS BEGINNING TO FORM! EACH STAGE OF DEVELOPMENT FROM THE FERTILIZED EGG TO OLD AGE REQUIRES ONLY TIME AND NUTRITION TO MATURE TO AN ADULT! EVERYTHING WAS THERE IN THE BEGINNING TO BRING THIS ABOUT!**

**INNOCENT, UNBORN BABIES AREN'T SOMETHING YOU KILL AND THROW AWAY — TO COVER UP YOUR SIN!** *"...Shall I give my first-born for my transgression (sin), the fruit of my body for the sin of my soul?"* **Micah 6:7**

**HERE IS PROOF THAT LIFE BEGINS IN THE WOMB!** *"Now the word of the Lord came to me saying Before I (God) formed you in the womb, I (God) knew you, and before you were born I consecrated you;"* **Jeremiah 1:4-5** (The New American Standard)

In **Luke 1:11-17** God sent His angel to Zacharias to tell him that his wife would give birth to a son and even told him what his name would be. The Bible also tells us that John the Baptist was filled with the Holy Spirit, in his mother's womb. Again, the angel Gabriel announced to Mary: *"BEHOLD, YOU WILL CONCEIVE IN YOUR WOMB AND BEAR A SON, AND YOU SHALL NAME HIM JESUS. HE WILL BE GREAT, AND WILL BE CALLED THE SON OF THE MOST HIGH."* **Luke 1:31-32** (The New American Standard)

**CHILDREN ARE A GIFT FROM GOD! THE FACT THAT A WOMAN CAN EVEN GET PREGNANT IS A BLESSING — NOT A CURSE!** *"Behold, children are a gift of the Lord: the fruit of the womb is a reward."* **Psalm 127:3** (New American Standard)

**GOD RESCUES THE UNBORN, THE INNOCENT, THE HELPLESS! Exodus 23:7 says:** *"Do not kill the innocent ... for I (God) will not acquit the guilty."*

*"When my father and my mother forsake me, then the Lord will take me up."* **Psalm 27:10**

**PRAYER:**

Dear God, I repent that I have **aborted** my baby! I never quite realized that the fetus inside me was a real living human being. I was told it was only a glob and not a real baby! I ask You from the bottom of my heart to forgive me. Help me also to forgive myself. I want to go to heaven and I know I will see my baby there. I thank You for this! I will keep my body under subjection from this moment forward. I will pray for guidance along this line. I will pray and read my Bible daily! With Your help I will not let this terrible thing I've done keep me from going to church and from witnessing to others about becoming a born-again Christian! Lead me to some other lady who is thinking about getting an **abortion**. Help me to witness to her that **abortion** is a sin, and that we must answer to God for the things we do to our bodies! Again, I thank You, God for forgiving me, and for forgetting my sins! I will do only those things which will glorify You, from this moment on. In Jesus' name I pray. AMEN!

# ABSTINENCE

**DEFINITION:** To refrain from indulging in any action which will physically, emotionally, or spiritually cause you real problems.

For example: Eating certain foods or taking certain drugs might be harmful to you. This also includes **smoking cigarettes, drinking intoxicating beverages,** or committing **sinful acts.** A good formula to follow is to ask yourself in every situation, **"What would God want me to do?"**

God commands us to **abstain** from all acts which will not glorify our Heavenly Father. **1 Corinthians 6:19-20 says:** *"What? know ye not that your body is the temple of the Holy Ghost which is in you, which ye have of God, and ye are not your own? For ye are bought with a price: therefore glorify God in your body, and in your spirit, which are God's."*

**1 Thessalonians 4:3 says:** *"For this is the will of God, even your sanctification, that ye should **abstain** from **fornication:** That every one of you should know how to possess his vessel (body-mind) in sanctification and honour."*

**I Thessalonians 5:22 says:** *"ABSTAIN FROM ALL APPEARANCE OF EVIL."*

## PRAYER

Dear God, I ask You to forgive me for not **abstaining** from those things in my life which are not pleasing to You. I now turn away from those things which would not be Your perfect will for my mind, my body, and my soul. I give up these habits. I ask You to change my desires into good ones that will glorify You in my body and in my spirit. Please forgive me if I have been a stumbling block to another person because of my old habits. With Your help I will **abstain** forever from the former things and I now claim the victory over them. AMEN!

**Repeat this verse 10 times a day:** *"I CAN DO ALL THINGS THROUGH CHRIST WHICH STRENGTHENETH ME."* **Philippians 4:13**

# ABUSE

**DEFINITION:** To take unfair advantage of a person or thing, deceitful acts, physical or emotional maltreatment, profane or obscene **abuse,** harshness, verbal attack, to shame and disgrace.

## ABUSE IS AMONG THE SINS THAT WILL PREVENT US FROM INHERITING THE KINGDOM OF GOD.

**1 Corinthians 6:9-10 says:** *"Know ye not that the unrighteous shall not inherit the kingdom of God? Be not deceived: neither fornicators, nor idolaters, nor adulterers, nor effeminate, nor **abusers** of themselves with mankind, nor thieves, nor covetous, nor drunkards, **nor revilers, nor extortioners,** shall inherit the kingdom of God."*

*"Let all bitterness, and wrath, and anger, and clamour, and evil speaking, be put away from you, with all malice: and be ye kind one to another, tenderhearted, forgiving one another, even as God for Christ's sake hath forgiven you."* **Ephesians 4:31-32**

*"FOR THE WAGES OF SIN IS DEATH; BUT THE GIFT OF GOD IS ETERNAL LIFE THROUGH JESUS CHRIST OUR LORD."* **Romans 6:23**

*Just as we are not to **abuse** another person, nor any thing, we are not to **abuse** (destroy, litter) our world.* **1 Corinthians 7:31**

*"And walk in love, as Christ also hath loved us, and hath given himself for us an offering and a sacrifice to God. . . ."* **Ephesians 5:2**

*"Husbands, love your wives, even as Christ also loved the church, and gave himself for it."* **Ephesians 5:25**

*"Be ye angry, and sin not: Let not the sun go down upon your wrath."* **Ephesians 4:26**

### PRAYER
Dear God, please forgive me if I have bruised or **abused** another person's feelings, body, or personal property. I am sorry I have sinned. I will go to the person I have **abused** and will ask him to forgive me. I will make matters right with those I have **abused.** With your help I will no longer commit this sin. Make me aware of other people's feelings. When I act hastily, slow me down. Teach me patience and compassion. Thank you for hearing my plea and for setting me straight. *"Create in me a clean heart, O God; and renew a right spirit within me. . ."* **Psalm 51:10** AMEN!

# ACCUSE FALSELY

God's laws forbid us to **falsely accuse** another person! If we do this we must pay the penalty for that crime, and must always ask God's forgiveness. There are also civil laws in every land which require the guilty **accuser** to pay the penalty for his crime.

**In Luke 3:12-14** when the publicans (tax collectors who were despised) came to be baptised by John, they asked him this question, *"Master what shall we do?" And he said unto them, "Exact no more than that which is appointed (due) you." And the soldiers asked him the same question. And he said, "Do violence to no man, neither accuse any falsely; and be content with your wages."*

**God commanded Christians to follow these standards of behavior as outlined in 1 Peter 3:8-16.** *"Finally, be ye all of one mind, having compassion one of another, love as brethren, be pitiful, be courteous: Not rendering evil for evil, or railing for railing; but contrariwise blessing; knowing that ye are thereunto called, that ye should inherit a blessing. For he that will love life, and see good days, let him refrain his tongue from evil, and his lips that they speak no guile: Let him eschew (shun) evil, and do good; let him seek peace, and ensue it. For the eyes of the Lord are over the righteous, and his ears are open unto their prayers: but the face of the Lord is against them that do evil. And who is he that will harm you, if ye be followers of that which is good? But and if ye suffer for righteousness' sake, happy are ye: and be not afraid of their terror, neither be troubled; But sanctify the Lord God in your hearts: and be ready always to give an answer to every man that asketh you a reason of the hope that is in you with meekness and fear: Having a good conscience; that, whereas they speak evil of you, as of evildoers, they may be ashamed that falsely accuse your good conversation in Christ."*

**GOD COMMANDS THESE THINGS FOUND IN PROVERBS 4:20-27: 1.** Hear God's words **2.** See God's words and keep them in the midst of your heart **3.** God's words are life when you find them, and health to all flesh **4.** Avoid evil **Proverbs 4:15**

Why risk God's wrath and punishment and deny yourself God's richest blessings by **falsely accusing** another person? Why risk the punishment of the law of the land in order to go about **falsely accusing** another person? There is a price tag attached to this crime and you have to pay it. Why not repent of this sin and receive blessings instead of punishment? It's up to you!!

### PRAYER

Heavenly Father, I know that I have **falsely accused** other people many times in my life! I regret this and I now ask You to forgive me. Dear God, help me to control my tongue each time I open my mouth. Help me to say words of encouragement instead of words of **accusation**. Quicken my mind to recall scriptures that will be appropriate to any given situation, instead of loose talk which I will soon regret! *"Let the words of my mouth, and the meditation of my heart, be acceptable in thy sight, O Lord, my strength, and my redeemer."* **Psalm 19:14** AMEN!

# ACID TEST of a BORN AGAIN CHRISTIAN

**LOVE IS THE GREATEST THING GOD GAVE US — NEXT TO ETERNAL LIFE! 1 Corinthians, chapter 13 says:** *"If I had the gift of being able to speak in other languages without learning them, and could speak in every language there is in all of heaven and earth, but didn't love others, I would only be making noise. If I had the gift of prophecy and knew all about what is going to happen in the future, knew everything about everything, but didn't love others, what good would it do? Even if I had the gift of faith so that I could speak to a mountain and make it move, I would still be worth nothing at all without love. If I gave everything I have to poor people, and if I were burned alive for preaching the Gospel but didn't love others, it would be of no value whatever. Love is patient and kind, never jealous or envious, never boastful or proud, never haughty or selfish or rude. Love does not demand its own way. It is not irritable or touchy. It does not hold grudges and will hardly even notice when others do it wrong. It is never glad about injustice, but rejoices whenever truth wins out. If you love someone you will be loyal to him no matter what the cost. You will always believe in him, always expect the best of him, and always stand your ground in defending him. All the special gifts and powers from God will someday come to an end, but love goes on forever. Someday prophecy, and speaking in unknown languages, and special knowledge — those gifts will disappear. Now we know so little, even with our special gifts, and the preaching of those most gifted is still so poor. But when we have been made perfect and complete, then the need for these inadequate special gifts will come to an end, and they will disappear. It's like this: when I was a child I spoke and thought and reasoned as a child does. But when I became a man (grew up) my thoughts grew far beyond those of my childhood, and now I have put away the childish things. In the same way, we can see and understand only a little about God now, as if we were peering at his reflection in a poor mirror; but someday we are going to see him in his completeness, face to face. Now all that I know is hazy and blurred, but then I will see everything clearly, just as clearly as God sees into my heart right now. There are three things that remain — faith, hope, and love — and the greatest of these is love."* **1 Corinthians 13 (The Living Bible)**

**YOU CANNOT HATE ANY PERSON ON EARTH WHETHER HE IS ALIVE OR DEAD: 1 John 3:15 says:** *"Whosoever hateth his brother is a murderer: and ye know that no murderer hath eternal life abiding in him."*

**YOU CANNOT LIKE SOME PEOPLE AND DISLIKE OTHERS ... YOU MUST LOVE ALL PEOPLE! Jesus said in John 13:34-35:** *"A new commandment I give unto you, That ye love one another; as I have loved you, that ye also love one another. By this shall all men know ye are my disciples, if ye have love one to another."*

**Jesus said:** *"This is my commandment, That ye love one another, as I have loved you."* **John 15:12**

"O Lord, correct me, but with judgement; not in 'Thine anger, lest Thou bring me to nothing."

Jeremiah 10:24

**PRAYER:**
Dear God, "How could You love us so much, when we are so guilty of mistreating other people?" Please help me, Dear God, to feel love for every person I encounter. Help me to remain loving even when faced with an uncomfortable situation. Help me express love to others in the way I walk, talk and conduct my everyday affairs. Let me never forget that You created me, and that You created me to love You, and every person in the world. Let me never forget that I am not on this earth to condemn, discriminate, or judge! Everywhere I go, let me be reminded that You loved me so much that You sent Your only son to pay the price for my sins, so that I could receive eternal life. AMEN!

# Adultery

**DEFINITION:** sexual unfaithfulness of a husband or wife in thought or act.

**GOD ABSOLUTELY FORBIDS ADULTERY! Exodus 20:14 says:** *"THOU SHALT NOT COMMIT ADULTERY."* **Deuteronomy 5:18 says:** *"Neither shalt thou commit adultery."* **2 Peter 2:14 says:** *"Having eyes full of adultery, and that cannot cease from sin; beguiling unstable souls. . ."* ALSO READ: **Romans 13:9**

**GOD BLESSES MARRIAGE, BUT JUDGES ADULTERERS!** *"Marriage is honorable in all, and the bed undefiled; but whoremongers and adulterers God will judge."* **Hebrews 13:4**

**DID YOU KNOW THAT WE LIVE IN AN ADULTEROUR GENERATION?** Jesus said: *"Whosoever therefore shall be ashamed of me and of my words in this adulterous and sinful generation; of him also shall the Son of man (Jesus) be ashamed, when he cometh in the glory of his Father with the holy angels."* **Mark 8:38**

**WHEN THE RAPTURE TAKES PLACE, OR WHEN A PERSON DIES, IF HE IS COMMITING ADULTERY IN HIS LIFE JUST PRIOR, HE WILL NOT INHERIT ETERNAL LIFE WITH JESUS!** *"And a certain ruler asked him (Jesus) saying, Good Master what shall I do to inherit eternal life?* **Luke 18:8** JESUS ANSWERED: *"Thou knowest the commandments, Do not commit adultery, Do not kill, Do not steal, Do not bear false witness (lie) Honour thy father and thy mother!"* **Luke 18:20 and Matthew 19:18**

**IF YOU DESIRE IN YOUR HEART TO HAVE SEX WITH A PERSON WHO IS NOT YOUR WIFE OR HUSBAND — ACCORDING TO GOD'S WORD YOU HAVE ALREADY COMMITTED ADULTERY!** Jesus said: *"Ye have heard that it was said of them of old time, Thou shalt not commit adultery: But I say unto you, That whosoever looketh on a woman (or man) to lust after her hath committed adultery with her (or him) already in his heart."* **Matthew 5:27-28**

**WHERE DOES ADULTERY BEGIN? IT BEGINS WITH LUST IN YOUR HEART FOR A PERSON WHO DEFINITELY IS NOT YOUR WIFE OR HUSBAND!** *"Lust not after her beauty in thine heart; neither let her take thee with her eyelids. For by means of a whorish woman a man is brought to a piece of bread: and the adulteress will hunt for the precious life."* **Proverbs 6:25-26**

**IF YOU DON'T WANT TO END UP COMMITTING ADULTERY, DON'T LET SIN REIGN IN YOUR BODY!** *"Let not sin therefore reign in your mortal body, that ye should obey it in the lusts thereof. Neither yield ye your members (body parts) as instruments of unrighteousness unto sin: but yield yourselves unto God, as those that are alive (saved) from the dead (unsaved), and your members as instruments of righteousness unto God. For sin shall not have dominion over you: for ye are not under the (Old Testament) law, but under grace."* **Romans 6:12-14**

**IF YOU LIVE AFTER THE FLESH, YE SHALL DIE:** *"For if ye live after the flesh, ye shall die (be eternally separated from God): but if ye through the (Holy) Spirit do mortify the deeds of the body, ye shall live."* **Romans 8:13**

**PEOPLE WHO COMMIT ADULTERY HOPE NO ONE WILL EVER FIND OUT ABOUT THEIR SIN. . . THEY HIDE THEIR FACE!** *"The eye also of the adulterer waitheth for the twilight, saying, No eye shall see me: and disguiseth his face."* **Job 24:15**

**YOU DEFILE YOUR OWN BODY WHEN YOU COMMIT ADULTERY!** *"Moreover thou shalt not lie carnally (sexually) with thy neighbour's (anyone's) wife, to defile thyself with her."* **Leviticus 18:20**

**IT WAS THE LAW OF THE LAND THAT PERSONS WHO COMMITTED ADULTERY WERE TO BE PUT TO DEATH PRIOR TO JESUS' COMING TO EARTH TO MAKE FULL RESTITUTION FOR OUR SINS!** *"And the man that committeth adultery with another man's wife, even he that committeth adultery with his neighbour's wife, the adulterer (man) and the adulteress (female) shall surely be put to death."* **Leviticus 20:10**

**GOD CALLS OUR BODY "THE TEMPLE OF GOD!"** *"Know ye not that ye are the temple of God, and that the Spirit of God dwelleth in you? If any man defile the temple of God, him shall God destroy; for the temple of God is holy, which temple ye are."* **1 Corinthians 3:16-17**

**Isaiah 5:20 says:** *"Woe unto them that call evil good, and good evil; that put darkness (sin-lies) for light (truth-knowledge) and light for darkness; that put bitter (wrong) for sweet (right) and sweet for bitter!"*

(Continued)

**IF YOU ARE SEXUALLY AROUSED BY ANOTHER PERSON — STAY AWAY FROM THAT PERSON — LEST YOU BE TEMPTED BY SATAN TO COMMIT ADULTERY!** *"Can a man take fire in his bosom and his clothes not be burned? Can one go upon hot coals, and his feet not be burned? So he that goeth in to his neighbour's wife (has intercourse with her); whosoever toucheth her shall not be innocent."* **Proverbs 6:27-29** *"But whoso committeth **adultery** with a woman lacketh understanding: he that doeth it destroyeth his own soul."* **Proverbs 6:32**

**WHEN YOU COMMIT ADULTERY. . . YOU WILL REAP SORROW IN DUE TIME!** *"Be not deceived; God is not mocked; for whatsoever a man soweth, that shall he also reap. For he that soweth to his flesh shall of the flesh reap corruption; But he that soweth to the (Holy) Spirit shall of the (Holy) Spirit reap life everlasting."* **Galatians 6:7-8**

**QUESTION: CAN A BORN-AGAIN CHRISTIAN OBEY ALL OF GOD'S COMMANDMENTS EXCEPT THE ONE ABOUT COMMITTING ADULTERY AND STILL GO TO HEAVEN?**
**ANSWER: NO!** *"For whosoever shall keep the whole law, and yet offend (abuse, break) in one point, he is guilty of all. For he (God) that said, Do not commit **adultery**, said also, Do not kill. Now if thou commit no **adultery**, yet if thou kill, thou art become a transgressor of the law."* **James 2:10-11**

**EXACTLY WHO DOES INHERIT THE KINGDOM OF GOD?** *"This I say then, Walk in the (Holy) Spirit, and ye shall not fulfil the lust of the flesh. For the flesh lusteth against the (Holy) Spirit, and the (Holy) Spirit against the flesh: and these are contrary the one to the other: so that ye cannot do the things that ye would (should). But if ye be led of the Spirit, ye are not under the (Old Testament) law. Now the works of the flesh are manifest (made known) which are these: **Adultery**, fornication, uncleanness, lasciviousness, idolatry, witchcraft, hatred, variance, emulations, wrath, strife, seditions, heresies, envyings, murders, drunkenness, revellings, and such like: of the which I tell you before as I have also told you in time past, that they which do such things shall not inherit the kingdom of God."* **Galatians 5:16-21**

*"Know ye not that the unrighteous shall not inherit the kingdom of God? Be not deceived: neither fornicators, nor idolaters, nor **adulterers**, nor effeminate, nor abusers or themselves with mankind, nor thieves, nor covetous, nor drunkards, nor revilers, nor extortioners, shall inherit the kingdom of God."* **1 Corinthians 6:9-10**

**IN CLOSING: FOR WHATEVER THINGS WE DO IN OUR BODY WE WILL HAVE TO ANSWER TO GOD!**
*"For we must all appear before the judgement seat of Christ; that every one may receive the things done in his body, according to that he hath done, whether it be good or bad."* **2 Corinthians 5:10**

## PRAYER

Dear God, You know that I am guilty of committing **adultery**! I admit that I have sinned. Dear God, I am so sorry that I broke Your laws. I sincerely ask You to forgive me and to create in me a clean mind, heart and body. I will not go where I might be tempted, by Satan, to commit this sinful act again! I will keep my mind on You! I will keep my eyes on the scriptures in my Bible. I will not go to bars and clubs where I could be tempted again. I will stay away from anyone I have sinned with before. I am not strong in this area of my life, so I will need Your help, daily! Help me to bind Satan in this area of my mind when he whispers lustful things in my ears. From this day forward I will live for You. I will dress according to your standards. I will keep my mind on how loving and forgiving You are to me. I will not betray Your kindness! In Jesus' name. AMEN!

## A Text . . .

He that covereth his
sins shall not prosper;
but whoso confesseth
and forsaketh them shall
have mercy.
PROVERBS 28:13

# ALCOHOLISM

**ALCOHOLISM IS AMERICA'S #1 DRUG PROBLEM!**

**ALCOHOL BRINGS SORROW AND DESOLATION.** *"Thou shalt be filled with drunkenness and sorrow, with the cup of astonishment and desolation. . . . "* **Ezekiel 23:33**

**ALCOHOL CAUSES YOU TO WEEP AND HOWL.** *"Awake, ye drunkards, and weep; and howl, all ye drinkers of wine. . . . "* **Joel 1:5**

**ALCOHOL AFFECTS YOUR VISION; CAUSES YOU TO STUMBLE AROUND AND BECOME FILTHY.** *"But they also have erred through wine, and through strong drink are out of the way . . . they err in vision, they stumble in judgement."* **Isaiah 28:7**

**ALCOHOLISM IS A SERIOUS DISEASE!** National statistics tell us that out of the 60,000 deaths that will occur this year as a result of alcohol, ⅓ will be caused by teenage drivers under the influence of **alcohol!**

**ALCOHOL MAKES YOU LOSE YOUR SENSE OF BALANCE.** *"They grope in the dark without light, and he maketh them to stagger like a drunken man."* **Job 12:25**

**GOD CAUTIONS US NOT TO KEEP COMPANY WITH DRUNKARDS.** *". . . if any man that is called a brother be a fornicator, or covetous, or an idolater, or a railer, or a drunkard, or an extortioner; with such an one no not to eat."* **1 Corinthians 5:11**

**ALCOHOLISM IS ONE OF THE SINS THAT IF CONTINUED, WILL CAUSE YOU NOT TO INHERIT ETERNAL LIFE WITH JESUS.** *"Know ye not that the unrighteous shall not inherit the kingdom of God? Be not deceived: neither fornicators, nor idolaters, nor adulterers, nor effeminate, nor abusers of themselves with mankind, nor thieves, nor covetous, nor drunkards, nor revilers, nor extortioners, shall inherit the kingdom of God."* **1 Corinthians 6:9-10**

**ALCOHOL CAUSES STUBBORNNESS, REBELLION, DISOBEDIENCE, GLUTTONY.** *". . . this our son is stubborn and rebellious, he will not obey our voice; he is a glutton, and a drunkard."* **Deuteronomy 21:20**

**Isaiah 5:22-23 says:** *"Woe unto them that are mighty to drink wine, and men of strength to mingle strong drink: which justify the wicked for reward, and take away the righteousness of the righteous from him!"*

**ALCOHOL CAUSES YOU TO STUMBLE AROUND IN YOUR OWN VOMIT, ACCORDING TO ISAIAH 19:14**

**ALCOHOL DECEIVES!** *"Wine is a mocker, strong drink is raging: and whosoever is deceived thereby is not wise."* **Proverbs 20:1**

**ALCOHOL CAUSES RIOTS AND THE GLUTTON FOR ALCOHOL WILL COME TO POVERTY!** *"Be not among winebibbers; among riotous eaters of flesh: For the drunkard and the glutton shall come to poverty: and drowsiness shall clothe a man with rags."* **Proverbs 23:20-21**

**ALCOHOL CAUSES WOES, SORROWS, CONTENTIONS, BABBLINGS, WOUNDS WITHOUT CAUSE, AND REDNESS OF THE EYES.** *"Who hath woe? who hath sorrow? who hath contentions? who hath babbling? who hath wounds without cause? who hath redness of eyes? They that tarry long at the wine; they that go to seek mixed wine. Look not thou upon the wine when it is red, when it giveth his colour in the cup, when it moveth itself aright. At the last it biteth like a serpent, and stingeth like an adder (snake)."* **Proverbs 23:29-32**

**GOD'S ADVICE:** *"Be sober, be vigilant; because your adversary the devil, as a roaring lion, walketh about, seeking whom he may devour."* **1 Peter 5:8**

**GOD'S ADVICE TO YOUNG PEOPLE:** *"Young men likewise exhort to be sober minded."* **Titus 2:6**

**THE END RESULT OF DRINKING ALCOHOL IS TO COME TO YOUR WIT'S END.** *"They reel to and fro, and stagger like a drunken man, and are at their wit's end. Then they cry unto the Lord in their trouble, and he bringeth them out of their distresses."* **Psalm 107:27-28**

(Continued)

**GOD'S REMEDY FOR VICTORY OVER ALCOHOL:**
*"This I say then, Walk in the Spirit, and ye shall not fulfil the lust of the flesh. For the flesh lusteth against the Spirit, and the Spirit against the flesh! and these are contrary the one to the other: so that ye cannot do the things that ye would (should). But if ye be led of the Spirit, ye are not under the law. Now the works of the flesh are manifest (obvious), which are these: adultery, fornication, uncleanness, lasciviousness, idolatry, witchcraft, hatred, variance, emulations, wrath, strife, seditions, heresies, envyings, murders, drunkenness, revellings and such like: of the which I tell you before, as I have also told you in time past, that they which do such things shall not inherit the kingdom of God. But the fruit of the Spirit is love, joy, peace, longsuffering, gentleness, goodness, faith, meekness, temperance: against such there is no law."*
**Galatians 5:16-23**

God can and will forgive anyone who decides to stop drinking. He will heal this sickness and restore the **alcoholic** to a normal functioning person if he will humble himself and pray. Then he must change his old habits and friendships which caused him to drink in the first place: this includes his old drinking buddies! He will need to read his Bible daily and make Christian friends. He will need to ask the Lord each day for strength.

God said: *"Whether therefore ye eat, or drink, or whatsoever ye do, do all to the glory of God."* **1 Corinthians 10:31**

After you have sincerely and honestly confessed to God that you need deliverance, ask God to baptize you with the precious power of the Holy Spirit. Ask Him to give you peace and happiness. Then tell others what God has done for you!

*"For the Lord knoweth the way of the righteous: but the way of the ungodly shall perish."*

Psalm 1:6

### PRAYER
Dear Father in Heaven, You know that I am weak. You know that I **drink.** I am not happy with my life because **alcohol** has brought me much pain and embarrassment. I need Your strength to stop drinking. I need You to forgive me. I need You to change my life! I need You to change my taste buds so that I no longer desire **alcohol!** Please forgive me and help me. Make me become a better person! Help me overcome this filthy habit, and in return I will tell others that our only source of help comes from God! Help me to not backslide after You mercifully help me "kick" the habit. I ask this in the precious name of Jesus and I will give You all the glory for this miracle. I thank You in advance. AMEN!

Therefore I say unto you, What things soever ye desire, when ye pray, believe that ye receive them; and ye shall have them. —MARK 11:24.

# ALIENATION

**DEFINITION: ALIEN:** Belonging or owing allegiance to another country or government, foreign, different in nature, character, race or nation. **ALIENATE:** To make unfriendly, hostile or indifferent where attachment formerly existed; to cause to be withdrawn, estrange.

**A PERSON MAY FEEL ALIENATED AND TOTALLY REJECTED AMONG HIS FRIENDS AND FAMILY WITHOUT EVER HAVING LEFT HIS COUNTRY OR HIS HOME. LONELINESS AND FEELINGS OF ISOLATION SET IT.** In **Job 19:14-19** we read how **alienated** Job felt. He says: *"My relatives have failed me; my friends have all forsaken me. Those living in my home, even my servants, regard me as a stranger. I am like a foreigner to them. I call my servant, but he doesn't come; I beg him! My own wife and brothers refuse to recognize me. Even young children despise me. When I stand to speak, they mock. My best friends abhor (hate) me. Those I loved have turned against me. I am skin and bones and have escaped death by the skin of my teeth."* (Living Bible)

People who **alienate** others do an evil deed! We must repent to God and ask His forgiveness! Next, we must go to those we have **alienated** and confess our sin and ask their forgiveness!

**TO MAKE RESTITUTION TO THOSE WE HAVE ALIENATED, AND TO GOD, WE MUST FOLLOW WHAT GOD SAYS IN MATTHEW 5:23-24.** *"Therefore if thou bring thy gift to the altar, and there rememberest that thy brother hath aught against thee; Leave there thy gift before the altar, and go thy way; first to be reconciled to thy brother, and then come and offer thy gift."*

**JESUS SAID:** *"And when ye stand praying, forgive, if ye have aught against any: that your Father (God) also which is in heaven may forgive you your trespasses. But if ye do not forgive, **neither** will your Father which is in heaven forgive your trespasses."* **Mark 11:25**

To those who have been **alienated** against, God knows your misfortune and will judge those who are guilty and will repay them if they do not repent. God will also give comfort and create new surroundings for you if you remain faithful to Him! In **Colossians 1:21-22** says: *"And you, that were sometime **alienated**, and **enemies** in your **mind** by **wicked works,** yet now hath he (Christ) reconciled in the body of his flesh through death (on the cross) to present you holy and unblameable and unreproveable in his sight."*

**PRAYER:**
**IF YOU ARE GUILTY OF ALIENATING ANOTHER PERSON PLEASE PRAY THIS PRAYER:**
Dear God, I come to You now confessing that I have **alienated** another person. I repent of this unkind act. I ask You to forgive me. I will confess my sin to the party whose happiness or reputation I destroyed. I will not be guilty of repeating this sin. I ask You to have mercy on me and to give me new directions, so that I may please You in my actions. In Jesus' name, I thank You for Your love, tender kindness, and for answering my prayer. AMEN!

**IF YOU ARE THE PERSON WHO HAS BEEN ALIENATED PLEASE PRAY THIS PRAYER:**
Heavenly Father, please come very close to me as I feel You are my only one true friend. I ask You to forgive those who have forsaken me. I forgive them whether they ask me to or not because You have forgiven me of my sins. I want to be like You. Please replace my life with fullness where I have been dealt bitterness! Draw close to me and send angels to surround me and I will praise You forever more. In Jesus' name, AMEN!

# ANARCHY

**Definition:** Absence of government, a state of lawlessness; political disorder due to the absence of governmental authority; rebellion against authority.

**ANARCHY OPPOSES GOD'S PLAN FOR OUR LIVES: LAWLESSNESS IS THE SAME THING AS ANARCHY.**

Why do we have to have laws, anyway? Why can't we have a perfect Utopia where everyone enjoys total freedom without laws? Because laws are for our protection! They were invented by God, not man!

**1 Timothy 1:8-10** Paul writes to Timothy and says: *"But we know that the law is good, if a man use it lawfully; knowing this, that the law is not made for a righteous man, but for the lawless and disobedient, for the ungodly and for sinners, for unholy and profane, for murderers of fathers and murderers of mothers, for manslayers, for whoremongers, for them that defile themselves with mankind, for mensteaters, for liars, for perjured persons, and if there be any other thing that is contrary to sound doctrine."*

**Exodus 22:28 says:** *"Thou shalt not revile the gods* (God, Christ, Holy Spirit or The Trinity)), *nor curse the ruler* (government) *of thy people."*

What causes people to turn hostile toward leaders of governments and seek to destroy them? Why do people prefer a rebellious state of **anarchy?**

Perhaps people become rebellious when their needs are not being met, or when their leaders become corrupt. **Proverbs 14:28 says:** *"In the multitude of people is the king's honour: but in the want of people is the destruction of the prince."* This means that as long as a leader, king, governor, president, etc., is popular his position and life is secure. But, when people's needs are not met, they rebel and cause their leaders to be overthrown or perhaps killed! Often, Satan has possessed a person, or group, to actually assassinate a leader.

**Proverbs 20:28 says:** *"Mercy and truth preserve the king* (leader): *and his throne is upholden by mercy."* This means that when a leader is truthful and believes in fairness and justice his followers can believe in him and uphold him. Then they obey his laws!

**GOD SAID WE ARE NOT TO CURSE OUR GOVERNMENT OR ITS LEADERS: Ecclesiastes 10:20**

**GOD SAID WE ARE TO PAY ALL OUR TAXES: Romans 13:1-7/Matthew 22:17-21**
**GOD SAID WE ARE TO HONOR AND OBEY ALL OUR CIVIC RULERS: Exodus 22:28/Acts 23:5/1 Peter 2:13-17**
**GOD SAID WE ARE TO OBEY ALL LAWS OF GOVERNMENT: Romans 13:1-7/Ezra 7:26**

**GOD SAID WE SHOULD BE AFRAID TO DISOBEY CIVIC RULERS BECAUSE HE GIVES THEM THE AUTHORITY TO MAINTAIN LAW AND ORDER: Proverbs 24:21/Romans 13:3**
**GOD SAID WE ARE TO PAY WHATEVER WE OWE TO EVERY MAN: Romans 13:7**
**GOD SAID WE ARE TO PRAY FOR OUR LEADERS: 1 Timothy 2:1-2**

**GOD SAID WE ARE TO OBEY CIVIL LAWS, NOT ONLY TO ESCAPE PUNISHMENT, BUT TO HAVE A CLEAR CONSCIENCE:** *"Wherefore ye must needs be subject* (to the laws of the land, and of God), *but also for* (your) *conscience sake."* **Romans 13:5**

**GOD ORDERED US TO PAY OUR SHARE OF TAXES!** Our taxes help pay the salaries of our civil servants, who are authorized by God, to protect and defend us! Even if they are ungodly men, but are faithful in carrying out their duties, they are to be respected, supported and obeyed. Remember, God loves them! He loves law and order! It is God's design for our lives that we have human government. That fact will never change! We should pray for and witness to our leaders, and for everyone who breaks our civil laws, and of course, God's laws! *"For for this cause* (law, order) *pay ye tribute* (taxes, respect, etc.,) *also: for they are God's ministers* (servants), *attending continually upon this very thing. Render* (do, pay) *therefore to all their dues* (what's owed them): *tribute to whom tribute is due; custom* (rules) *to whom custom; fear to whom fear; honour to whom honour* (is due)." **Romans 13:6-7**
**TITUS 3:1-2 SAYS:** *"Put them* (us) *in mind to be subject* (obedient) *to principalities* (civil authority) *and powers, to obey magistrates, to be ready to* (do) *every good work* (obey the law), *To speak evil of no man, to be no brawlers* (rebellious to authority, strikers, etc.,), *but gentle, shewing all meekness unto all men."*

(Continued)

When **anarchy** occurs, there is only one solution and that is to turn to God for help! **Luke 19:10** and **Matthew 18:11** says: *"For the Son of Man (Jesus) is come (to this earth) to save that which was lost."*

**Psalm 9:9 says:** *"The Lord also will be a refuge for the oppressed, a refuge in times of trouble."*

**GOD DOES NOT MERELY SUGGEST WE BE LAW-ABIDING CITIZENS. HE COMMANDS US TO OBEY THE LAWS OF OUR LAND! TO REBEL AGAINST GOVERNMENTAL AUTHORITY IS TO REBEL AGAINST ALMIGHTY GOD! GOD HAS GIVEN THE LEADERS IN GOVERNMENT THE AUTHORITY TO PUNISH THOSE WHO RESIST OBEYING LAWS!** *"Let every soul be subject unto the higher powers (of government). For there is no power but (except) of God: the powers that be (exist) are ordained of God. Whosoever therefore* **resisteth** *the power (rulers of government), resisteth the ordinance (laws) of God: and they that* **resist** *shall receive to themselves damnation."* **Romans 13:1-2**

**THE DUTIES OF CIVIC LEADERS ARE NOT TO TERRORIZE MEN WHO OBEY THE LAW, BUT TO PUNISH THOSE WHO SIN AGAINST SOCIETY! IF WE OBEY THE LAWS, WE HAVE NOTHING TO FEAR!** *"For rulers are not a terror to good works (to law abiding citizens), but to the evil (law breakers). Wilt (will) thou then not be afraid of the power (of our rulers or of God)? Do that which is good, and thou shalt have praise of the same (government officials and God)."* **Romans 13:3**

**GOD HAS DELEGATED AUTHORITY TO OUR LEADERS TO PUNISH EVIL AND TO DEFEND THE JUST. THIS INCLUDES CAPITAL PUNISHMENT, WHEN NECESSARY.** *"For he (our leaders) is the minister (servant) of God to thee for good (law, order). But if thou do that which is evil, be afraid; for he (our leaders) beareth not the sword (of justice, punishment) in vain: for he is the minister (servant ordained by God to do his civic, legal duty) of God, (and is given permission to be) a revenger to execute wrath (sentence) upon him that doeth evil."* **Romans 13:4**

**EVERY CHRISTIAN IS WITHOUT EXCUSE IF HE DISOBEYS HUMAN GOVERNMENT!** *"Submit yourselves to every* **ordinance** *of man for the Lord's sake: whether it be to the* **king** *(or president), as* **supreme** *(final authority of human government); Or unto* **governmors**, *as unto* **them that are sent by him** *(the final authority of human government) for the* **punishment of evildoers**, *and for the praise of them that do well (beyond the call of duty). For so is the will of God, that with well doing ye may put to silence the ignorance of foolish (law-breaking) men: as free, and not using your liberty for a cloke of maliciousness, but as the servants of God. Honour all men. Love the brotherhood. Fear God. Honour the king (president, governor, chief of police, etc.)."* **1 Peter 2:13-17**

**IN CLOSING:** *"I exhort (invite, urge, caution) therefore, that,* **first of all**, *supplications,* **prayers**, *intercessions, and* **giving of thanks**, *be made for all men; For kings (highest human government officials),* **and for all that are in authority**; *that* **we may lead a quiet and peaceable life in all godliness and honesty. For this is good and acceptable in the sight of God our Saviour who will have all men to be saved, and come unto the knowledge of the truth."* **1 Timothy 2:1-4**

> **"**
> Everybody wants peace—or at least, so we profess! We work for peace! The pope pleads for peace! Prime ministers strive for peace! Yet there is no peace!
> **"**

*"If my people, which are called by my name (Christians), shall humble themselves, and pray, and seek my face, and turn from their wicked ways; then will I hear from heaven and will forgive their sin, and will heal their land."* **2 Chronicles 7:14**

> **"**
> The peace negotiations are not going to bring peace—only the intervention of God Almighty himself can.
> **"**

**PRAYER**

Dear God, in our land there is currently an evil spirit of **anarchy**. I ask You to bring peace to my home, my family, my friends, my neighbors. Please restore law and order for I know this is Your divine plan! Please forgive me, Lord, if I have willingly or ignorantly participated in the downfall of our government! I repent to You, now! Please protect us all and keep us safe wherever we go by sending angels to surround us! Please let no harm come to those who are innocent. In Jesus' precious name I pray. AMEN!

# ANGER

*"A soft answer turneth away wrath: but grievous words* (meant to hurt, destroy) *stir up anger."* **Proverbs 15:1**

*"Wherefore, my beloeved brethren, let every man be swift to hear, slow to speak, slow to wrath."* **James 1:19**

*". . .put off all these: anger, wrath, malice, blasphemy* (cursing), *and filthy communication out of your mouth."* **Colossians 3:8**

*"Forebearing one another, and forgiving one another, if any man have a quarrel against any: even as Christ forgave you, so also do ye* (you)." **Colossians 3:13**

Jesus said: *". . .I say unto you, that whosoever is **angry** with his brother **without a cause shall be in danger of the judgement. . .**"* **Matthew 5:22**

*"He that is soon **angry** dealeth foolishly* (makes mistakes). . . ." **Proverbs 14:17**

**Proverbs 14:29 says:** *"He that is slow to **wrath** is of great understanding: but he that is hasty of spirit* (hot headed) *exalteth folly."*

*"He that is slow to **anger** is better than the mighty; and he that ruleth his spirit* (uses self control) *than he that taketh a city."* **Proverbs 16:32**

*"A wrathful man stirreth up strife: but he that is slow to **anger** appeaseth* (soothes) *strife.* **Proverbs 15:18**

*"The Lord is merciful and gracious, slow to **anger**, and plenteous in mercy."* **Psalm 103:8. LADIES, HERE'S A REMINDER FOR US!!!!** *"It is better to dwell in the wilderness, than with a contentious* (argumentative) *and **angry** woman."* **Proverbs 21:19**

**MEN, HERE'S A REMINDER FOR YOU!!!!** *"An **angry** man stirreth up strife* (trouble), *and a furious man aboundeth in transgression."* **Proverbs 29:22**

*"For his **anger** endureth but a moment; in his favour is life: weeping may endure for a night, but joy cometh in the morning."* **Psalm 30:5**

**QUESTION: HOW DO YOU CONTROL YOUR ANGER???**
**ANSWER: "KICK THE HABIT," NOW! STOP GETTING ANGRY! Psalm 37:8 says:** *"Cease from **anger**, and forsake wrath; fret not thyself in any wise to do evil."*

*"Let all bitterness, and wrath, and **anger**, and clamour, and evil speaking, be put away from you, will all malice: And be ye kind one to another, tenderhearted, forgiving one another, even as God for Christ's sake hath forgiven you."* **Ephesians 4:31-32**

**GOOD ADVICE: NEVER GO TO BED ANGRY! Ephesians 4:26 says:** *"Be ye **angry**, and sin not: let not the sun go down upon your wrath."*

### PRAYER:

Dear God, I know You see me when I'm **angry.** I know You hear every word I say. I know this displeases You. I need Your help to overcome this sin. Make me aware of my bad habit to speak hurtful things before I open my mouth, so I will not say them! I repent of every **angry** word I have ever spoken. I will make a conscious effort to control my thoughts and tongue each day. If I slip, I will quickly repent and ask Your forgiveness. I will ask those I've been **angry** with to forgive me. I will kick the **anger** habit, with Your help! AMEN!

# ANTI-SEMITISM

**DEFINITION:** Hostility to or discrimination against the Jews.

*"Pray for the peace of Jerusalem: they shall prosper that love thee."* **Psalm 122:6**

*"Give none offence, neither to the Jews, nor to the Gentiles, nor to the church of God."* **1 Corinthians 10:32**

If you love Jesus, and you love the Holy Bible, **you are commanded by God Almighty to also love all Jews! Jesus** was a **Jew!** All of the books of the Bible were written by **Jews,** except the books of Acts and Luke. Luke was a gentile.

Since the beginning of time the **Jews** have been **persecuted.** This grieves God! The Bible says, *"For there is no difference between the Jew and the Greek* (gentiles) *for the same Lord over all is rich unto all that call upon him."* **Romans 10:12**

**QUESTION: "WHAT IS YOUR HEART'S DESIRE?"**
**ANSWER:** *"My heart's desire and prayer to God for Israel is: 'THAT THEY MIGHT BE SAVED.'"* **Romans 10:1**

In Zephaniah we read that Jerusalem was, in times past, morally filthy and polluted, full of oppression, disobedient, rebellious, and unbelieving. They had forsaken God. Their judges were wicked. They were treacherous. Their priests polluted the sanctuary, and they violated all civil and religious laws.

We also read in Zephaniah that **things are going to change!** Today we see good changes taking place. Israel is eternal. Zephaniah says that in the future Israel will sing, shout, be glad, rejoice. They will be ashamed of their past sins. All rebels will be purged. They will no longer be haughty. They will be meek and lowly. **THEY WILL TRUST IN THE NAME OF THE LORD JESUS.** They will sin no more. They will be eternally secure. Their judgement will be over. They will have no enemies. **Jesus will be their Messiah and will reside in their midst, as will God the Father.** They will never see evil again, nor fear. They will prosper financially. God will save them. No one will be able to afflict them. All **Jews** will be regathered to Israel, their homeland! **God will reward them with praise and fame wherever they go to compensate for the shame and discrimination they formerly received.** All people of earth will praise them!!

From cover to cover the Bible clearly states that **the Jews are God's chosen people.** He knows their sins, and He knows ours. **God forgives Jews!** He forgives Gentiles! All a person needs to do is to ask for forgiveness and turn away from sin. Read: **Matthew 24:9-22/Jeremiah 30:6-7/Romans 1:16-17/Romans 11/Zephaniah 13**

The most gifted evangelists the world will ever know will be the 144,000 Jewish evangelists that will preach to the entire world during the soon to come 7 year tribulation period.

**WARNING:** If you ridicule, mistreat or hate a Jew, you are obeying exactly what Satan tells you to do! **Satan is the founder of hatred for the Jews.** God says Satan is a liar! If you love God, you are commanded to pray for and love all Jews. **Failure to obey this commandment jeopardizes your chance to spend eternity with God.** Think about it!!

**PRAYER:**
Dear God, I repent that I have not loved all Jews before now! I never knew it was a commandment that I pray for and love them. Beginning now, I accept them as my brother. I pray for their peace, prosperity and their safety. I pray they will soon realize that Jesus is their Messiah, and will become born-again Christians, as I have done. I pray for their leaders. I sincerely and humbly ask You to forgive me of this sin. AMEN!

**Start today and decide to live at peace with all Jews. Then, you will be able to live with Jesus, and all born-again Christians, in New Jerusalem after Christ returns!!**

# APOSTASY

**DEFINITION:** Desertion of one's faith or religion. Renunciation of religion.

**APOSTASY IS DANGEROUS!** It will take you to hell if you do not turn away from this sin and become a born-again Christian! **Romans 1:22 says:** *"Professing themselves to be wise, they became fools."*

**APOSTATES SERVE SATAN! Romans 1:25 says:** *"Who* (speaking of apostates) *changed the truth of God into a lie, and worshipped and served the creature* (Satan) *more than the Creator* (God), *who is blessed for ever."*

**APOSTATES ARE EVIL!** *"Being filled with all unrighteousness, fornication, wickedness, covetousness, maliciousness; full of envy, murder, debate, deceit, malignity; whisperers, backbiters, haters of God, despiteful, proud, boasters, inventors of evil things, disobedient to parents, without understanding, covenant breakers, without natural affection, implacable, unmerciful: who knowing the judgement of God, that they which commit such things are worthy of death, not only do the same, but have pleasure in them that do them."* **Romans 1:29-32**

*"For it is impossible for those who were once enlightened* (believed in God), *and have tasted of the heavenly gift, and were made partakers* (joint-heirs) *of the Holy Ghost, and have tasted the good word of God* (believed and been saved), *and the powers of the world to come, if they shall fall away, to renew them again unto repentance; seeing they crucify to themselves the Son of God afresh* (all over again) *and put him* (Christ) *to an open shame."* **Hebrews 6:4-6**

**Hebrews 10:26 says:** *"For if we sin wilfully after that we have received the knowledge of the truth* (that God is our Creator and Jesus died to pay for our sins), *there remaineth no more sacrifice* (Jesus was our sacrifice when he was crucified for our sins)."

## WHAT ARE THE CHARACTERISTICS OF AN APOSTATE?

**According to 2 Peter 2:1-19** Apostates are false teachers, false prophets. They deny the Lord. They invite God's swift destruction. They speak evil. They covet. They blaspheme God, Christians and the church. They are presumptuous. They are self-willed. They are not afraid to speak evil things of dignitaries. They speak of things that they don't even understand. They shall perish in their own corruption. They think they are good sports in their own deceit concerning you. They have eyes full of adultery. They can not cease from sin. They are unstable. They curse children. They are full of vanity. They lust. They speak liberty though they are corrupt. They live constantly in sinful bondage.

**God says about apostates:** *"For if after they have escaped the pollutions of the world through the knowledge of the Lord and Saviour Jesus Christ, they are again entangled* (forget and turn against God) *therein, and overcome, the latter end is worse with them than the beginning. For it had been better for them not to have known the way of righteousness, than, after they have known it, to turn from the holy commandment delivered unto them. But it is happened unto them according to the true proverb . . . The dog is turned* (returns) *to his own vomit again; and the sow* (pig) *that was washed* (returns) *to her wallowing in the mire* (slusk, mud)." **2 Peter 2:20-22**

**WHERE AND HOW DOES THIS HATRED FOR GOD CALLED APOSTASY START?** It starts in the mind! **Romans 8:7 says:** *"Because the carnal mind is enmity against God: for it is not subject to the law of God, neither indeed can be."* **NOTE:** Read entire chapter **ROMANS 8**

**ARE YOU SURE YOU WANT TO CONTINUE BEING AN APOSTATE? DO YOU LOVE DEATH? In Proverbs 8:36 God said:** *"But he that sinneth against me wrongeth his own soul: all they that hate me love death."*

**God has already cast all angels who sinned to hell. God has already brought on a flood that utterly destroyed all wickedness of the old world. God loves you very much and wishes that none should perish. God, however, will not violate his own word. He must punish apostates! Unless they repent, they will spend eternity in hell!**

**IN CLOSING: Galatians 6:7 says:** *"BE NOT DECEIVED; GOD IS NOT MOCKED: FOR WHATSOEVER A MAN SOWETH, THAT SHALL HE ALSO REAP."*

**URGENT REMINDER:** *"Know therefore that the Lord thy God, he is God, the faithful God, which keepeth covenant* (His promise) *and mercy with them that love him and keep his commandments to a thousand generations: And repayeth them that hate him to their face, to destroy them: He will not be slack to him that hateth him, he will repay him to his face."* **Deuteronomy 7:9-10**

## PRAYER

Dear God, I now realize and confess that I am guilty of hatred for God, the church and for Christians. I am so sorry. I ask You to forgive me and to forget my sins. I turn away from this sin, I will never hate You again! Please come into my life and change me. Please do not forsake me. I know if I should die this day that I would go to hell if I did not confess my sins and ask Your forgiveness. I ask You now to forgive me. Come into my heart forever. I want to live for You. I will read the Holy Bible. I will go to church services where they welcome the Holy Spirit. From this day forward I will live for You. In Jesus' name I pray. AMEN!

# ARGUING

*"A brother offended is harder to be won (to Christ) than a strong city: and their contentions are like the bars of a castle."* **Proverbs 18:19**

*"A wicked doer giveth heed to false lips; and a liar giveth ear to a naughty tongue."* **Proverbs 17:4**

*"The wise in heart shall be called prudent: and the sweetness of the lips increaseth learning."* **Proverbs 16:21**

*"The heart of the wise teacheth (controls) his mouth, and addeth learning to his lips." "Pleasant words are as an honeycomb, sweet to the soul, and health to the bones."* **Proverbs 16:23-24**

*"AN UNGODLY MAN DIGGETH UP EVIL: AND IN HIS LIPS THERE IS AS A BURNING FIRE* (hot temper)." **Proverbs 16:27**

*"Seest thou a man that is hasty in his words? there is more hope of a fool than of him."* **Proverbs 29:20**

*"An **angry** man stirreth up strife (trouble), and a furious man aboundeth in transgression (sin)."* **Proverbs 29:22**

*". . . Speak evil of no man, to be no brawlers, but gentle, shewing (showing) all meekness unto all men. For we ourselves also were sometimes foolish, disobedient, deceived, serving divers (different) lusts and pleasures, living in malice and envy, hateful, and hating one another. But after that the kindness and love of God our Saviour toward man appeared, Not by works of righteousness which we have done, but according to his mercy he saved us, by the washing of regeneration* (saved us through the crucification of Jesus shed blood), *and (by the) renewing of the Holy Ghost; which he shed on us abundantly through Jesus Christ our Saviour; that (our) being justified by his* (God's) *grace, we should be made heirs (of God) according to the hope of eternal life."* **Titus 3:2-7**

**DO WE EVER NEED TO BE ANGRY OR TO QUARREL. . . NO!! Philippians 2:14 says:** *"Do all things without murmurings and disputings."*

**GOD CAN AND WILL TEACH US HOW TO STOP ARGUING — IF WE WILL ASK HIM!** *"Teach me, and I will hold my tongue: and cause me to understand wherein I have erred* (made mistakes)." **Job 6:24**

**ARGUMENTS NEVER ACHIEVE THE RIGHT RESULTS! Job 6:25 says:** *"How forcible are right words! but what doth your arguing reporve (prove)?"*

**A PERSON WHO RESORTS TO ARGUING KNOWS NOTHING! 1 Timothy 6:4-5 says:** *"He* (or she) *is proud, knowing nothing, but doting about questions and strifes of words, whereof cometh envy, strife, railings, evil surmisings, perverse disputings of men of corrupt minds, and destitute (void) of the truth, supposing that gain* (material or an **argument** ) *is godliness: from such withdraw thyself."*

**GOOD ADVICE: Jesus said:** *'Blessed are the peacemakers: for they shall be called the children of God."* **Matthew 5:9**

**HOW SHOULD WE ANSWER A PERSON WHEN HE MAKES US ANGRY?** *"A soft answer turneth away wrath: but grievous words stir up anger."* **Proverbs 15:1**

**GUARD YOUR ANGER!** *"Devise not evil against thy neighbour* (anyone), *seeing he dwelleth securely by thee. Strive not with a man without cause, if he have done thee no harm."* **Proverbs 3:29-30**

**THINK BEFORE YOU SPEAK!** *"Be not **rash** with thy mouth, and let not thine heart be hasty to utter any thing before God: for God is in heaven, and thou upon earth: therefore let thy words be few."* **Ecclesiastes 5:2-3**

*"Suffer not* (don't allow) *thy mouth to cause thy flesh to sin; neither say thou before the angel, that it was an error* (give a false apology): *wherefore should God be angry at thy voice, and destroy the work of thine hands?"* **Ecclesiastes 5:6**

(Continued)

# before it happens

**JESUS SAID FOR US TO APOLOGIZE!** *"Agree with thine adversary* (enemy) *quickly, whiles thou art in the way with him; lest at any time the adversary deliver thee to the judge, and the judge deliver thee to the officer, and thou be cast into prison."* **Matthew 5:25**

**THERE ARE 6 THINGS GOD HATES, TO ARGUE IS ONE OF THEM! ACCORDING TO Proverbs 6:17-19 GOD HATES:** *"A proud look, a ling tongue, and hands that shed innocent blood, an heart that deviseth* (thinks) *wicked imaginations, feet that be swift in running to mischief, a false witness that speaketh lies, and he that soweth discord* (stirs up trouble and anger) *among brethren."*

**IT IS A COMMANDMENT THAT WE CEASE FROM ARGUING AND LOVE ONE ANOTHER!** *"For all the law is fulfilled in one word, even in this: THOU SHALT LOVE THY NEIGHBOUR AS THYSELF. BUT IF YE BITE AND DEVOUR ONE ANOTHER, TAKE HEED THAT YE BE NOT CONSUMED ONE OF ANOTHER."* **Galatians 5:14-15**

**GOD WARNS US NOT TO ARGUE! ACCORDING TO Leviticus 26:25 GOD WILL NOT TOLERATE A QUARRELSOME PERSON!** God is love! God gives us peace if we will let him! However, if we continue to **argue** after we have been saved He may have to send a pestilence upon us and deliver us over to our enemies in order to make us repent and seek His help!

**WHERE DOES ARGUING START ANYWAY? IT STARTS IN THE HEART!** Jesus said: *"For from within, out of the heart of men, proceed evil thoughts, adulteries, fornications, murder, thefts, covetousness, wickedness, deceit, lasciviousness, an evil eye, blasphemy* (cursing), *pride, foolishness: All these evil things come from within, and defile the man."* **Mark 7:21**

**ARGUING CAUSES HEARTACHES, HEART BREAKS, HEART ATTACKS!**

**GOD'S ADVICE TO PARENTS:** *". . . Provoke not your children to* **anger**, *lest they be discouraged."* **Colossians 3:21**

**GOD PROMISES TO PUNISH ANYONE WHO DOES NOT OBEY HIS INSTRUCTION:** *"But he that doeth wrong shall receive for the wrong which he hath done: and there is no respect of persons."* **Colossians 3:25**

### PRAYER

Dear God, please forgive me for being instrumental in causing an **argument**! I know how to prevent **arguments** from starting. I know how to refrain from keeping one going that someone has started. I repent! I am guilty of this sin! I will use self control! I will turn the other cheek instead of seeking revenge! I will show the world that I am a Christian through my patience, my understanding, and my love for others. Please forgive me if I have been the stumbling block to an unsaved person. When I am tempted to say an unkind word, please refresh my memory with the verse *"a kind word turneth away wrath"*. Thank You for giving me victory over this sin. In Jesus' name I claim the victory. AMEN!

# ARROGANCE

I know
I'm better
than you.
I'm
Arrogant!

**DEFINITION:** Haughtiness; a feeling of superiority manifested in an overbearing manner; exaggerating one's own worth or importance in an overbearing manner; being exceedingly proud (and pride is a sin according to the Bible).

**GOD WARNS US ABOUT BEING ARROGANT!** Isaiah **13:11 says:** *"And I (God) will punish the world for their evil, and the wicked for their iniquity (sins); and I will cause the arrogancy of the proud to cease, and will lay low the haughtiness of the terrible."*

**QUESTION: HOW DO YOU BREAK THE HABIT OF BEING ARROGANT?**
**ANSWER: CONTROL YOUR MIND AND YOUR TONGUE!**

*"Whoso keepeth his mouth and his tongue keepeth his soul from troubles. Proud and haughty scorner is his name, who dealeth in proud wrath."* **Proverbs 21:23-24**

*"Talk no more so exceeding proudly; let not arrogancy come out of your mouth: for the Lord is a God of knowledge, and by him (our) actions are weighed (judged)."* **1 Samuel 2:3**

**REPEAT THIS VERSE 10 TIMES A DAY!** *"Let the words of my mouth, and the meditation of my heart, be acceptable in thy sight, O Lord, my strength, and my redeemer."* **Psalm 19:14**

**IF A PERSON PERSISTS IN BEING ARROGANT HE SHOULD FEAR THE LORD!** *"The fear of the Lord is to hate evil: pride, and arrogancy, and the evil way, and the froward (sulking) mouth, do I (God) hate."* **Proverbs 8:13**

**AN ARROGANT PERSON TELLS HIMSELF HE IS SPECIAL! THE BIBLE SAYS: GOD IS NO RESPECTER OF PERSONS!** Jesus said: *". . .for every one that exalteth (praises) himself shall be abased (humbled); and he that humbleth himself shall be exalted (raised in power and praise)."* **Luke 18:14/14:11**

**ONLY JESUS IS WORTHY TO BE PRAISED!** *"Great is the Lord, and greatly to be praised. . ."* **Psalm 48:1**

**STOP LOOKING AT YOUR FACE IN THE MIRROR! SEEK THE FACE OF JESUS IN YOUR MIRROR!** *"If my people, which are called by my name (Christians), shall humble themselves, and pray, and seek my face (Christ's), and turn from their wicked ways; then will I hear from heaven, and will forgive their sin, and will heal their land."* **2 Chronicles 7:14**

## PRAYER

Dear God in heaven, I know that I am all "puffed-up" with my own self-image! I know, in my heart, that you love me; but that I am not better than anyone else. I ask You to forgive me for being so vain! I ask you to forgive others who have heaped compliments upon me and have helped support my feelings of superiority. I humble myself as I pray to You. Please help me conquer my overly-exaggerated impression of myself. Please humble me! I will no longer worship my looks, my body, my success, nor my intelligence. I know that You are my Creator and that I have disappointed You! I will change with Your help. AMEN!

# ASHAMED OF GOD?

**BETTER BE CAREFUL NOT TO SPEAK IDLE WORDS ABOUT GOD, CHRISTIANS OR CHURCHES!** Jesus said: *"But I say unto you, that every idle word that men shall speak, they shall give account thereof in the day of judgement. For by thy (your) words thou shalt be justified (qualified, made righteous), and by thy words thou shalt be condemned."* **Matthew 12:36-37**

**IF YOU JOKE AND MOCK CHRISTIANS YOU MOCK GOD: Galatians 6:7 says:** *"Be not deceived; God is not mocked: for whatsoever a man soweth (does and says) that shall he also reap (receive)."*

**Jesus said:** *"For there is nothing covered, that shall not be revealed; neither hid, that shall not be known. Therefore whatsoever ye have spoken in darkness (secret) shall be heard in the light; and that which ye have spoken in the ear in closets shall be proclaimed upon the housetops (for the world to hear)."* **Luke 12:2-3**

**ARE YOU DOUBLE-MINDED? WILL YOU LOVE GOD AND THE BIBLE AND BE WILLING TO CONFESS IT OR REMAIN ASHAMED? James 1:8 says:** *"A double-minded man is unstable in all his ways."*

**WHY NOT GO ALL THE WAY WITH GOD AND SERVE HIM? Luke 11:23 says:** *"He that is not with me is against me:"*

**IF YOU ARE ASHAMED TO SERVE GOD . . . YOU MAY BE SERVING SATAN, WITHOUT REALIZING IT!**

**Matthew 6:24 & Luke 16:13 says:** *"No man can serve two masters: for either he will hate the one, and love the other; or else he will hold to the one (whether he serves him or not), and despise the other. . ."*

**NOW IS THE TIME TO CONFESS YOU LOVE GOD AND THE BIBLE WITH YOUR MOUTH AND YOUR ACTIONS! Romans 10:9-10 says:** *If thou shalt confess with thy mouth the Lord Jesus, and shalt believe in thine heart that God hath raised him from the dead, thou shalt be saved. For with the heart man believeth unto righteousness; and with the mouth confession is made unto salvation."*

**1 Peter 4:16 says:** *"Yet if any man suffer as a Christian, let him not be ashamed; but let him glorify God on his behalf."*

**REPEAT 10 TIMES A DAY:** *"O my God, I trust in thee: let me not be ashamed, let not mine enemies (false friends) triumph over me."* **Psalm 25:2**

**FORMULA:** *"Study to show thyself approved unto God, a workman (student of the Bible) that needeth not to be ashamed, rightly dividing the word of truth."* **2 Timothy 2:15**

**IN CLOSING:** *"FOR THE SCRIPTURE SAYETH, WHOSOEVER BELIEVETH ON HIM* (CHRIST) *SHALL NOT BE ASHAMED."* **Romans 10:11**

*"For I am not ashamed of the gospel of Christ: for it is the power of God unto salvation to everyone that believeth; to the Jew first, and also to the Greek (Gentile)."* **Romans 1:16**

*"For whosoever shall be ashamed of me and of my words, of him shall the Son of man (Jesus) be ashamed, when he (Jesus) shall come (back to earth) in his own glory, and in his Father's (God's) and of the holy angels."* **Luke 9:26**

**YOU ARE IN DANGER IF YOU ARE ASHAMED OF GOD AND THE BIBLE: Job 15:6 says:** *"Thine own mouth comdemneth thee, and not I: yea (yes), thine own lips testify against thee."*

*"Let them (you) be ashamed and brought to confusion together that rejoice at mine hurt: let them be clothed with shame and dishonour that magnify themselves against me."* **Psalm 35:26**

**Jesus said:** *". . . Whosoever shall confess me before men, him (you) shall the Son of man (Jesus) also confess before the angels of God: But he that denieth me before men shall be denied before the angels of God. And whosoever shall speak a word against the Son of man (Jesus), it shall be forgiven him: but unto him that blasphemeth (curses) against the Holy Ghost it shall not be forgiven."* **Luke 12:8-10**

**QUESTION: IN YOUR HEART DO YOU BELIEVE IN GOD BUT ARE ASHAMED OR EMBARRASSED TO TALK ABOUT GOD AND THE BIBLE? Titus 1:16 says:** *"They profess that they know God; but in works they deny him, being abominable (disgusting), and disobedient, and unto every good work reprobate (corrupt)."*

### PRAYER

Dear God, I know you love me. I am **ashamed** that I have not let the world know that I am a Christian. Please forgive me. As of today, I will read my Bible daily! As of today I will attend church regularly. As of today I will praise you wherever I go. The world will see this miracle that has taken place in me. I will praise you each day and will thank you for your love and forgiveness. I claim the victory over this sin. In Jesus' name. AMEN!

# ASSAULT & BATTERY

**Exodus 21:18-19 says:** *"If two men are fighting, and one hits the other with a stone or with his fist and injures him so that he must be confined to bed, but doesn't die, if later he is able to walk again, even with a limp, the man who hit him will be innocent except that he must pay for the loss of his time until he is thoroughly healed, and pay any medical expenses."* (The Living Bible)

**Exodus 21:22-27** *"If two men are fighting, and in the process hurt a pregnant woman so that she has a miscarriage, but she lives, then the man who injured her shall be fined whatever amount the woman's husband shall demand, and as the judges approve. But if any harm comes to the woman and she dies, he shall be executed (through the civil court system). If her eye is injured, injure his; if her tooth is knocked out, knock out his; and so on — hand for hand, foot for foot, burn for burn, wound for wound, lash for lash. If a man hits his slave in the eye, whether man or woman, and the eye is blinded, then the slave shall go free because of his eye. And if a master knocks out his slave's tooth, he shall let him go free to pay (him back) for the tooth."* (The Living Bible)

**NOTE: THE ABOVE LAW IS FROM THE OLD TESTAMENT. JESUS HAD NOT YET BEEN BORN. MAN WAS GIVEN PERMISSION BY GOD TO PROTECT HIMSELF AND HIS FAMILY WITH THIS OLD LAW. AFTER JESUS WAS BORN AND THEN DIED ON THE CROSS TO PAY FOR OUR SINS, MAN NO LONGER WAS UNDER THE OLD LAW. BELOW YOU WILL READ THE LAW WE ARE COMMANDED TO FOLLOW TODAY:**

**Jesus said:** *"Don't resist violence! If you are slapped on one cheek, turn the other too. If you are ordered to court, and your shirt is taken from you, give your coat too. If the military demand that you carry their gear for a mile, carry it two. Give to those who ask, and don't turn away from those who want to borrow. There is a saying, "Love your friends and hate your enemies!", BUT I SAY: Love your enemies!*

*Pray for those who persecute you! In that way you will be acting as true sons of your Father in heaven. For he gives his sunlight to both the evil and the good, and sends rain on the just and on the unjust too. If you love only those who love you, what good is that? Even scoundrels do that much. If you are friendly only to your friends, how are you different from anyone else? Even the heathen do that. But you are to be perfect, even as your Father in heaven is perfect."* **Matthew 5:39-48** (The Living Bible)

**IF ASSAULT AND BATTERY OCCURS TO AN INNOCENT VICTIM WE ARE NOT TO SEEK VENGEANCE! VENGEANCE BELONGS TO GOD! IF YOU SEEK VENGEANCE GOD MAY PUNISH YOU!**

**IT IS A SIN AGAINST GOD TO ASSAULT ANYONE, BUT THINGS REALLY GET TOUGH WHEN YOU ASSAULT ONE OF GOD'S BORN-AGAIN CHRISTIANS! Deuteronomy 32:39 says:** *"See now that I (God), even I, am he (the only one true living God), and there is no god with (besides) me: I kill, and I make alive; I wound, and I heal: neither is there any that can deliver (himself) out of my hand."*

**Romans 12:14 says:** *"Bless them which persecute you: bless, and curse not."*

**Romans 12:17 says:** *"Recompense to no man evil for evil..."*

**Romans 12:19 says:** *"Dearly beloved, avenge not yourselves, but rather give place (patience) unto wrath: for it is written, Vengeance is mine (God's); I will repay, saith the Lord."*

**NOT ONLY IS ASSAULT A CRIME AGAINST GOD, THE LAW OF THE LAND MAY CARRY A PRISON OR DEATH SENTENCE FOR ASSAULT AND BATTERY!**

**NEVER COMMIT ASSAULT AND BATTERY! IF ASSAULTED, NEVER SEEK REVENGE! GOD HATES SIN, BUT HE LOVES THE SINNER! IF YOU ARE A CHRISTIAN, AND YOU ARE ASSAULTED, DO NOT SEEK REVENGE! THE GUILTY PERSON MAY BE LED TO CHRIST BECAUSE OF THE FORGIVENESS YOU DISPLAY! THINK ABOUT IT?**

### PRAYER
Dear God, There are many ways to **assault** another person. I am guilty of having **assaulted** others through my uncontrolled tongue. I have accused others. I have hurt others. I have abused others. I ask You to forgive me and give me another chance. I will not commit this sin again. I know that You love me and I thank You for forgiving me. I will go to those I have **assaulted** either physically or emotionally and seek their forgiveness. In Jesus' name I thank you for setting me on the right path. AMEN!

# ASTROLOGY

**DEFINITION:** The divination (attempting to foresee or foretell future events) of the supposed influences of the stars upon human affairs and terrestrial events by their positions and aspects.

**ASTROLOGERS DON'T KNOW THE FUTURE! ONLY GOD KNOWS!** God said: *"Can you hold back the stars? Can you restrain Orion or Pleiades? Can you ensure the proper sequence of the seasons, or guide the constellation of the Bear with her satellites across the heavens? Do you know the laws of the universe and how the heavens influence the earth? Can you shout to the clouds and make it rain? Can you make lightning appear and cause it to strike as you direct it?*

*Who gives intuition and instinct? Who is wise enough to number all the clouds? Who can tilt the water jars of heaven* (rain), *when everything is dust and clods?"* **Job 38:31-38. In chapter 40, verse 1, God said:** *"Do you still want to argue with the Almighty? Or will you yield? Do you — God's critic — have the answers?"* (Living Bible)

**GOD CALLED PEOPLE WHO BELIEVE IN OR PRACTICE ASTROLOGY, "HEATHENS"!** *"Thus saith the Lord, Learn not the way of the heathen, and be not dismayed at the signs of heaven; for the heathen are dismayed at them."* **Jeremiah 10:2**

**ASTROLOGY IS FORBIDDEN BY GOD!** People who make predictions based on cycles of the moon, planets, sun, and signs of a zodiac practice witchcraft. Whether they know it or not, they traffic with demons while they call it

astrology. This is strictly condemned in the Bible.

**GOD COMMANDED US NOT TO WORSHIP THE SUN, MOON, OR STARS!** *"Lest ye corrupt yourselves, and make you a graven image, the similitude of any figure, the likeness of male or female, the likeness of any beast that is on the earth, the likeness of any winged fowl that flieth in the air, the likeness of any thing that creepeth on the ground, the likeness of any fish that is in the waters beneath the earth: And lest thou lift up thine eyes unto heaven, and when thou seest the sun, and the moon, and the stars, even all the host of heaven, shouldest be driven to worship them, and serve them, which the Lord thy God hath divided unto all nations under the whole heaven."* **Deuteronomy 4:16-19**

**GOD COMMANDED THAT WE HAVE NO OTHER GODS! ASTROLOGY HAS BECOME A GOD TO MANY PEOPLE.** *"Thou shalt have no other gods before me. Thou shalt not make unto thee any graven image* (zodiac charms, statues), *or any likeness of any thing that is in heaven above, or that is in the earth beneath, or that is in the water under the earth: Thou shalt not bow down thyself to them,* **nor serve them:** *for I the Lord thy God am a jealous God, visiting the iniquity of the fathers upon the children unto the third and fourth generation of them that hate* (disobey) *me; And shewing* (showing) *mercy unto thousands of them that love me, and keep my commandments."* **Exodus 20:3-6**

**GOD CALLED ASTROLOGY "BAAL" WORSHIP:** *"And they* (Israelites Moses had delivered out of Egypt) *left all the commandments of the Lord their God, and made them molten images, even two calves, and made a grove, and worshipped all the host*

(Continued)

*of heaven* (stars, moon, **astrology**), *and served Baal* (Satan).'' **2 Kings 17:16 God punished them severely!** God also punished Manasseh for the very same thing in **II Chronicles 33**

In Leviticus God said: ''. . . *neither shall ye use enchantment, nor* **OBSERVE TIMES** (astrology).''

**JUST A REMINDER: OUR ANSWERS AND HELP ARE NOT FOUND IN THE STARS, THE SUN, THE MOON!** *''Our help is in the name of the Lord, who made heaven and earth.''* **Psalm 124:8**

*''Ye observe days, and months, and times (seasons, moons) and years. I am afraid of you, lest I have bestowed upon you labor in vain.''* **Galatians 4:10-11**

**BELOW IS A LIST OF FORBIDDEN PRACTICES WHICH GOD CALLED HEATHEN: ENCHANT-MENT:** (practice of magical arts) **Exodus 7:11, 22; 8:7, 18/ Leviticus 19:26/Deuteronomy 18:10/2 Chronicles 33:6/2 Kings 17:17; 21:6/Isaiah 47:9, 12/Jeremiah 27:9/Daniel 1:20. WITCHCRAFT:** (practice of dealing with evil spirits) **Exodus 22:18/Deuteronomy 18:10/I Samuel 15:23/2 Chronicles 33:6/2 Kings 9:22/Micah 5:12/Nahum 3:4/Galatians 5:19-21. SORCERY:** (same as witchcraft) **Exodus 7:11/Isaiah 47:9; 57:3/Jeremiah 27:9/Daniel 2:2/Malachi 3:5/Acts 8:9-11; 13:6-8/Revelation 9:21; 18:23; 21:8; 22:15. SOOTH-SAYING** (fortune telling) **Isaiah 2:6/Daniel 2:27; 4:7; 5:7, 11/Micah 5:12. DIVINATION:** (the art of mystic insight or fortune-telling) **Numbers 22:7; 23:23/Deuteronomy 18:10-14/2 Kings 17:17/I Samuel 6:2/Jeremiah 14:14; 27:9; 29:8/Ezekiel 12:24; 13:6-7, 23; 21:22-29; 22:28/Micah 3:7/Zechariah 10:2/Acts 16:16. WIZAR-DRY:** (same as witchraft; a wizard is a male who practices witchraft) **Exodus 22:18/Leviticus 19:31; 20:6, 27/Deuteronomy 18:11/I Samuel 28:3, 9/2 Kings 21:6; 23:24/2 Chronicles 33:6/Isaiah 19:3. NECROMANCY:** (calling on or pretending to call on the dead for communications) **Deuteronomy 18:11/Isaiah 8:19/I Samuel 28/I Chronicle 10:13. MAGIC:** (any pretended supernatural act) **Genesis 41:8, 24/Exodus 7:11, 22; 8:7, 18-19; 9:11/Daniel 1:20; 2:2, 10, 27; 4:7, 9; 5:11/Acts 19:19. CHARM:** (to put a spell upon, same as enchantment) **Deuteronomy 18:11/Isaiah 19:3. PROGNOSTICA-TION:** (to foretell by indications, omens, signs, etc.) **Isaiah 47:13. OBSERVING TIMES:** (same as prognostication; Astrologers) **Leviticus 19:26/Deuteronomy 18:10/2 Kings 21:6/2 Chronicles 33:6. ASTROLOGY AND STAR GAZING:** (divination by stars, sun, moon) **(Isaiah 47:13/Jeremiah 10:2/Daniel 1:20; 2:2, 10; 4:7; 5:7-15.**

**NOTE: All of the above practices were and still are being used in connection with demon activity. These demons are called ''familiar spirits''. All who forsook God and sought help from the above sources were to be destroyed! If you believe in astrology or any of the above practices, turn away from them! They are demon worship! God forbids born-again Christians to partake in these pagan rites! No matter how innocent you feel it is to read your horoscope or have your fortune told, you are mistaken!**

**HERE ARE SOME OF THE SUBJECTS THAT FALL INTO BAAL (SATAN) WORSHIP: ASTROLOGY,** YOGA, Transcendental Meditation, Hypnosis, Palm Reading, Fortune Telling, Seances, Ouija Boards, Tarot Cards, Magic, ESP, Water Witching, Spirit Mediums, Witchcraft, Crystal Balls, Familiar Spirits, Wizards.

# ASTROLOGY

### PRAYER

Dear God in heaven, I had no idea that **astrology**, fortune telling, and so forth, were absolutely forbidden by You! I saw no harm in them, but now I know differently. I will no longer read, think, or be interested in any of these things! I ask You to forgive me for my interest and participation! I am not willing to spend eternity in hell for practicing and believing in **astrology**, or any heathen acts. Please create in me a desire to read my Bible and to go to church. I want to be a child of Yours and spend eternity with You. Satan is a liar! He made me believe these things were harmless! I now know differently! Thank You for forgiving me and setting me on the right path. In Jesus' name I turn away from all occult activity in my life! AMEN!

**DEFINITION:** The denial of the existence of Almighty God.

**ATHEISTS SHOUT "THERE IS NO GOD!" BORN-AGAIN CHRISTIANS SHOUT** *"But to us there is but one God, the Father, of whom are all things, and we* (are) *in him* (a part of him); *and one Lord Jesus Christ, by* (through) *whom are all things, and we by* (are a part of) *him."* **1 Corinthians 8:6**

**NO OTHER PERSON OR FALSE GOD COULD HAVE CREATED THE EARTH AND ALL ITS FULLNESS!** *"In the beginning God created the heaven and the earth."* **Genesis 1:1** *"For the earth is the Lord's, and the fullness thereof."* **1 Corinthians 10:26** *"Thou, even thou, art Lord alone; thou hast made heaven, the heaven of heavens, with all their host, the earth, and all things that are therein, the seas, and all that is therein, and thou preservest them all; and the host of heaven worshippeth thee."* **Nehemiah 9:6**

**ONLY A FOOL WOULD SAY THERE IS NO GOD!** *"The fool hath said in his heart, There is no God. They* (atheists) *are corrupt, they have done abominable* (disgusting) *works, there is none* (not one Atheists) *that doeth good."* **Psalm 14:1 and Psalm 53:1**

**THE CHRISTIAN PRAYER FOR THE ATHEIST SHOULD BE:** *"Put them in fear, O Lord: that the nations may know themselves to be* (mere) *men* (who are powerless without God)." **Psalm 9:20**

**ATHEISTS ARE IGNORANT!** *"Having the* (their) *understanding darkened* (having closed minds), *being alienated from the life of God through the ignorance that is in them, because of the blindness of their heart: who being past feeling* (cold hearted) *have given themselves over unto lasciviousness* (selfish lusts) *to work all uncleanness* (mischief, sin) *with greediness."* **Ephesians 4:18-19**

**THE ATHEIST IS LOST! HE DOESN'T HAVE THE POWER OF GOD IN HIS LIFE! HE DOESN'T UNDERSTAND OR COMPREHEND HOW POWERFUL GOD IS! HE HAS NO SUBSTITUTE HE CAN CALL ON FOR HELP AND COMFORT!** *"But the Lord is the true God, he is the living God, and an everlasting king: at his wrath the earth shall tremble, and the nations shall not be able to abide his indignation."* **Jeremiah 10:10**

*"He* (God) *hath made the earth by his power, he hath established the world by his wisdom, and hath stretched out the heavens by his discretion. When he uttereth his voice, there is a multitude of waters in the heavens, and he causeth the vapours to ascend from the ends of the earth; he maketh lightnings with rain, and bringeth forth the wind out of his treasures."* **Jeremiah 10:12-13**

**ATHEISTS HAVE NO FEAR OF GOD HEARING WHAT THEY SAY!** *"Thus with your mouth ye have boasted against me, and have multiplied your words against me: I have heard them."* **Ezekiel 35:13**

**WHAT WILL HAPPEN TO AN ATHEIST IF HE DOES NOT BECOME A CHRISTIAN? Proverbs 13:13** says: *"Whoso despiseth the word* (God and the Bible) *shall be destroyed: but he that feareth the commandment* ("THOU SHALL HAVE NO OTHER GOD BEFORE ME") *shall be rewarded."*

**THE ATHEISTS DO NOT KNOW THAT ONLY GOD COULD CREATE MAN!** *"Behold, I am the Lord, the God of all flesh: is there any thing too hard for me?"* **Jeremiah 32:27**

**IF A BORN-AGAIN CHRISTIAN CANNOT WIN AN ATHEIST TO CHRIST, HE SHOULD NOT MARRY HIM!** *"Be ye not unequally yoked together with unbelievers: for what fellowship* (happiness, peace) *hath righteousness with unrighteousness? and what communion hath light* (knowledge, truth) *with darkness* (ignorance, sin)?" **2 Corinthians 6:14** (AND) *"Wherefore come out from among them* (leave them), *and be ye separate, saith the Lord, and touch not the unclean thing; and I will receive you, and will be a Father unto you, and ye shall be my sons and daughters, saith the Lord Almighty."* **2 Corinthians 6:17-18**

**THE THEORY OF THE ATHEIST, THAT THERE IS NO GOD, IS POWERLESS! GOD ALONE HAS ALL POWER! Romans 13:1-3** says: *"Let every soul be subject unto the higher powers* (God, Jesus, the Holy Spirit). *For there is no power but of God: the powers that be* (exist) *are ordained of God. Whosoever therefore resisteth the power* (of God), *resisteth the ordinance* (laws) *of God: and they that resist shall receive to themselves damnation. For rulers are not a terror to good works, but to the evil. Wilt thou then not be afraid of the power* (of God)? *do that which is good, and thou shalt have praise of the same* (God)."

**WHAT ATHEIST CAN MAKE THIS CLAIM?** *"Behold,* (look, listen), *the heaven and the heaven of heavens is the Lord's thy God, the earth also, with all that therein is."* **Deuteronomy 10:14** *"Of old* (thousands of years ago) *hast thou* (God) *laid the foundation of the earth: and the heavens are the work of thy hands."* **Psalm 102:25**

**THERE IS NO HAPPINESS AND PEACE TO THE ATHEIST BECAUSE HE KNOWS NOT GOD!** *"... happy is that people, whose God is the Lord."* **Psalm 144:15**

(Continued)

**ATHEISTS ARE ANTI-CHRISTS!** *"For many deceivers are entered into the world, who confess not that Jesus Christ is (has) come in the flesh. This (person, people) is a deceiver and an anti-christ."* **2 John:7**

**TO DISCOVER GOD IS TO INHERIT ETERNAL LIFE WITH HIM!** *"For whoso findeth me (Christ) findeth life, and shall obtain favour of the Lord. But he (the atheist) that sinneth against me wrongeth his own soul: all they that hate me love death (both physical and eternal separation from God)."* **Proverbs 8:35-36**

**THE ATHEIST GIVES MORE CREDIT TO COLUMBUS, FOR DISCOVERING THE EARTH WAS ROUND, THAN TO GOD WHO CREATED A ROUND EARTH AND FORETOLD IT: Isaiah 40:21-25!** *"Have ye not known? have ye not heard? hath it not been told you from the beginning? have ye not understood from the foundations of the earth? It is he (God) that sitteth upon the circle of the earth, and the inhabitants thereof are as grasshoppers; that stretcheth out the heavens as a curtain, and spreadeth them out as a tent to dwell in: that bringeth the princes (kings, leaders) to nothing; he maketh the judges of the earth as vanity. Yea (yes), they shall not be planted (totally secure); yea, they shall not be sown: yea, their stock shall not take root in the earth: and he shall also blow upon them, and they shall wither, and the whirlwind shall take them away as stubble. To whom then will ye liken me, or shall I be equal? saith the Holy One."*

**IN THE END, EVERY ATHEIST WILL BOW HIS KNEE TO GOD!** *"Look unto me, and be ye saved, all the ends of the earth: for I am God, and there is none else. I have sworn by myself, the word is gone out of my mouth in righteousness, and shall not return, That unto me every knee shall bow, every tongue shall swear."* **Isaiah 45:22-23**

**IT IS FOOLISH FOR ATHEISTS TO SPEAK THEIR UNFOUNDED THEORIES IN AN EFFORT TO RECRUIT OTHERS! THEY HAVE NOTHING TO OFFER A PERSON! WITH THEM THERE IS NO PEACE! PRAY FOR THEM!** *"The tongue of the wise useth knowledge aright (in the right way): but the mouth of fools poureth out foolishness. The eyes of the Lord are in every place, beholding the evil and the good."* **Proverbs 15:2-3** *"By the blast of God they perish, and by the breath of his (God's) nostrils are they consumed."* **Job 4:9** *"The paths of their way are turned aside (wrong); they go to nothing, and perish."* **Job 6:18**

By humility and the fear of the Lord are riches, and honour, and life. PROVERBS 22:4

**THE ATHEIST WRONGFULLY THINKS, "THIS LIFE IS ALL THERE IS"!** *"For the word of the Lord is right; and all his works are done in truth. He loveth righteousness and judgement: the earth is full of the goodness of the Lord. By the word of the Lord were the heavens made; and all the host of them by the breath of his mouth. He gathered the waters of the sea together as an heap: he layeth up the depth in storehouses. Let all the earth fear the Lord: let all the inhabitants of the world stand in awe (respect) of him. For he spake, and it was done; he commanded, and it stood fast (permanent). The Lord bringeth the counsel of the heathen to nought (nothing): he maketh the devices (theories) of the people of none effect. The counsel of the Lord standeth for ever, the thoughts of his heart to all generations. Blessed is the nation whose God is the Lord; and the people whom he hath chosen for his own inheritance. The Lord looketh from heaven; he beholdeth all the sons of men. From the place of his habitation he looketh upon all the inhabitants of the earth. He fashioneth their hearts alike; he considereth all their works. There is no king (person) saved by the multitude of an host: a mighty man is not delivered by much strength. An horse is a vain thing for safety: neither shall he deliver any by his great strength. Behold, the eye of the Lord is upon them that fear him, upon them that hope in his mercy; to deliver their soul from death, and to keep them alive in famine. Our (Christians) soul waiteth for the Lord: he is our help and our shield. For our heart shall rejoice in him, because we have trusted in his holy name. Let thy mercy, O Lord, be upon us, according as we hope in thee."* **Psalm 33:4-22**

**ATHEISTS ARE WITHOUT EXCUSE IN NOT BELIEVING IN GOD!** *"For the invisible things of him (God) from the creation of the world are clearly seen, being understood by the things that are made, even his eternal power and Godhead; so that they are without excuse."* **Romans 1:20**

**ATHEISTS. . . HERE IS A MESSAGE FOR YOU Deuteronomy 4:39 says:** *"Know therefore this day, and consider it in thine heart, that the Lord he is God in heaven above, and upon the earth beneath: there is none else."*

**IN CLOSING:** *"As for me, I will call upon God; and the Lord shall save me. Evening, and morning, and at noon, will I pray, and cry aloud: and he shall hear my voice."* **Psalm 55:16-17**

### PRAYER

Dear God, I no longer choose to be an **atheist!** I want to become a Christian. I confess that I have sinned. I ask You to forgive me for my sins and to remember them no more. I believe that You are the one and only true God. I believe that You sent your only son to die on the cross to pay for my sins. I believe He lives today! I believe You will hear my prayer and forgive me. Please come into my heart and make yourself a living part of my life, my conscience, my actions and my thoughts. I will love You! I will serve You! I will never be ashamed of You agani! In Jesus' name I pray. AMEN!

# BACKBITING

**DEFINITION:** Malicious gossip, slandering another person.

"What is man, that thou art mindful of him?..."

hebrews 2:6

**GOD BELIEVES IN JUSTICE AND FAIRNESS! HIS POWER CAN BRING JUDGEMENT AGAINST BACKBITERS!** *"For I fear, lest, when I come, I shall not find you such as I would* (like to find you), *and that I shall be found unto you such as ye would not* (want to find me): *lest, there be debates, envyings, wraths, strifes,* **backbitings,** *whisperings, swellings* (boastings, ego, intense anger), *tumults* (uproar, confusion, riots)." **2 Corinthians 12:20**

**ARE BACKBITERS ALLOWED TO ENTER HEAVEN IF THEY DON'T REPENT? NO!! NOT ONE BACKBITER! Psalm 15:1-3 says: QUESTION:** *"Lord, who shall abide in thy tabernacle* (heaven)? *Who shall dwell in thy* (God's) *holy hill* (New Jerusalem—a new heaven which will descend down to earth after the Second coming of Christ)? **ANSWER:** *He that walketh uprightly, and worketh righteousness, and speaketh the truth in his heart. He that* **backbiteth not with his tongue,** *nor doeth evil to his neighbor, nor taketh up a reproach* (reason to blame) *against his neighbour."*

**AS THE OLD "SAGE ADVICE" GOES: "IF YOU CAN'T SAY SOMETHING NICE ABOUT SOMEONE, SAY NOTHING AT ALL!"**

**REPEAT 10 TIMES A DAY:** *"Let the words of my mouth, and the meditation of my heart, be acceptable in thy sight, O Lord, my strength, and my redeemer."* **Psalm 19:14**

**GOD DESCRIBES BACKBITING WORDS AS STABBING A PERSON IN THE BACK WITH A SWORD!** *"The words of his mouth were smoother than butter, but war was in his heart: his words were softer than oil, yet were they drawn swords."* **Psalm 55:21**

**1 Peter 2:1 says:** *"Wherefore laying* (lay) *aside all malice* (intended harm without excuse), *and all guile* (deceit-trickery), *and hypocrisies, and envies, and all evil speakings."*

**REMEDY FOR DEALING WITH A BACKBITER: SHOW COMPLETE DISAPPROVAL ON YOUR FACE!** *"The north wind driveth away rain: so doth an* **angry countenance** (expression on your face drive away) *a* **backbiting** *tongue."* **Proverbs 25:23**

### PRAYER

Dear God in heaven, You know that I am guilty of **backbiting.** Many times I have been guilty of this crime against another person. Forgive me, God! Much of my **backbiting** has been against the very people I claim to love the most. I am sorry I have opened my mouth to discredit another. I ask Your forgiveness! Please create in me a wholesome tongue. Please remind me before I open my mouth to be careful of what I'm about to say, lest I have to answer to You for those words! Help me to think, "What would Jesus say if He were here?" Help me to never forget that You love me and want the very best for me. I won't disappoint You! In Jesus' name I pray. AMEN!

# BACKSLIDING

**DEFINITION:** To lapse, fall away morally and spiritually from God and religion.

*". . .no man having put his hand to the plough, and looking back, is fit for the kingdom of God."*

**Luke 9:62**

**BACKSLIDERS SOON REGRET TURNING AWAY FROM GOD!** *"Your own wickedness shall chasten and correct you, and your backslidings and desertion of faith shall reprove (correct, rebuke) you. Know therefore and recognize that this is an evil and bitter thing (you have done): first, you have forsaken the Lord your God; second, you are indifferent to Me (God), and the fear of Me (God) is not in you, says the Lord of hosts."* **Jeremiah 2:19** (The Amplified Bible)

**BACKSLIDERS NEED TO ASK FOR FORGIVENESS FOR THIS SIN!** *"Return, ye backsliding children, and I will heal your backslidings. . ."* **Jeremiah 3:22** *"The backslider in heart* (cold hearted toward God, no fear of rejecting God) *shall be filled with* (the fruit of) *his own ways, and a good man shall be satisfied from himself* (with the holy thoughts and actions which his heart prompts, and in which he delights)." **Proverbs 14:14** (The Amplified Bible)

**CHRISTIANS SHOULD HELP BACKSLIDERS TO RETURN TO THE LORD! Galatians 6:1 says:** *"Brethren, if any person is overtaken in misconduct or sin of any sort, you who are spiritual—who are responsive to and controlled by the Spirit—should set him right and restore and reinstate him, without any sense of superiority and with all gentleness, keeping an attentive eye on yourself, lest you should be tempted also* (to **backslide**)." The Amplified Bible

**CHRISTIANS, DO NOT BE TAKEN IN BY PHILOSOPHY AND INTELLECTUALISM WHICH WOULD CAUSE YOU TO DOUBT GOD AND CAUSE YOU TO BACKSLIDE! Colossians 2:8 says:** *"See to it that no one carries you off as spoil or makes you yourselves captive by his so-called philosophy and intellectualism, and vain deceit* (idle fancies and plain nonsense), *following human tradition—men's ideas of the material* (rather than the spiritual) *world—just crude notions following the rudimentary and elemental teachings of the universe, and disregarding* (the teachings of) *Christ, the Messiah."* (The Amplified Bible)

**A BACKSLIDER MUST REPENT IN ORDER TO GO TO HEAVEN!** In **Revelation 3:5** Jesus said: *"He that overcometh* (sin, **backsliding**), *the same shall be clothed in white raiment* (shining light of God when you go to heaven); *and I will not blot out his name out of the book of life, but I will confess his name before my Father, and before his angels."*

**WHEN A CHRISTIAN HELPS A BACKSLIDER RETURN TO THE LORD, HE SAVES THAT PERSON'S SOUL FROM DEATH! James 5:20 says:** *"Let him know, that he which converteth the sinner from the error of his way* (sin, **backsliding**) *shall save a soul from death* (eternal separation from God), *and shall hide a multitude of sins* (from God's memory)."

**WHEN GOD FORGIVES BACKSLIDERS, HE FORGETS THEIR SINS!** *"I* (God speaking) *will heal their backsliding, I will love them freely: for mine anger* (at their **backsliding**) *is turned away from him."* **Hosea 14:4**

**A CHRISTIAN BECOMES A SINNER AGAIN IF HE CONTINUES IN HIS SIN AFTER HE HAS EARLIER RETURNED TO THE LORD FROM BACKSLIDING!** *"Let not sin therefore reign in your mortal body, that ye should obey it in the lusts thereof. Neither yield ye your members* (parts of your body) *as instruments of unrighteousness unto sin: but yield yourselves unto God, as those that are alive from the dead, and your members as instruments of righteousness unto God. For sin shall not have dominion over you: for ye are not under the law, but under grace. What then? shall we sin, because we are not under the law, but under grace? God forbid. Know ye not, that to whom ye yield yourselves servants to obey, his servants ye are to whom ye obey; whether of sin unto death, or of obedience unto righteousness? But God be thanked, that ye were servants of sin, but ye have obeyed from the heart that form of doctrine which was delivered you. Being then made free from sin, ye became the servant of righteousness. I speak after the manner of men because of the infirmity of your flesh: for as ye have yielded your members servants to uncleanness and to iniquity unto iniquity; even so now yield your members servants to righteousness unto holiness. For when ye were the servants of sin, ye were free from righteousness. What fruit had ye then in those things whereof ye are now ashamed? for the end of those things is death. But now being made free from sin, and become servants to God, ye have your fruit unto holiness, and the end everlasting life. For the wages of sin is death; but the gift of God is eternal life through Jesus Christ our Lord."* **Romans 6:12-23**

27

(Continued)

**IF THE CHRISTIAN CONTINUES ON IN SIN, HE INCURS THE DEATH PENALTY WHICH IS ETERNAL SEPARATION FROM GOD! Ezekiel 18:24 says:** *"But when the righteous turneth away from his righteousness, and committeth iniquity* (sin), *and doeth according to all the abominations* (hatred, lust, evil) *that the wicked man doeth, shall he live? All his righteousness that he hath done shall not be mentioned: in his trespass* **(backsliding)** *that he hath trespassed, and in his sin that he hath sinned, in them shall he die."*

**HOW DOES A CHRISTIAN KEEP FROM BACKSLIDING? Galatians 5:16-25 says:** *"This I say then, Walk in the Spirit, and ye shall not fulfil the lust of the flesh. For the flesh lusteth against the Spirit, and the Spirit against the flesh: and these are contrary the one to the other: so that ye cannot do the things that ye would* (should). *But if ye be led of the Spirit, ye are not under the law. Now the works of the flesh are manifest, which are these:* **Adultery** (married but having sex with another), **fornication** (pre-marital sex), **uncleanness, lasciviousness** (lewdness, lust), **idolatry, witchcraft, hatred, variance** (not able to get along with people), **emulations** (trying to be better than another), **wrath** (angry all the time), **strife, seditions** (resisting authority), **heresies** (denial of the truth about God and religion), **envyings, murders, drunkenness, revellings** (rioting), *and such like: of the which I tell you before, as I have also told you in time past, that* **they which do such things shall not inherit the kingdom of God.** *But the fruit of the* (Holy) *Spirit is love, joy, peace, longsuffering* (patience), *gentleness, goodness, faith, meekness, temperance: against such there is no law. And they that are Christ's* (born-again Christians) *have crucified the flesh* (taken control over lust) *with the affections and lusts. If we live in the Spirit, let us also walk in the Spirit."*

**IF THE BACKSLIDING CHRISTIAN REPENTS AND GETS SAVED FROM THE ERROR OF HIS WAYS, HIS SOUL WILL BE SAVED ALL OVER AGAIN FROM THE DEATH PENALTY ACTION! 1 John 1:9-10 says:** *"If we confess our sins, he* (God) *is faithful and just to forgive us our sins, and to cleanse us from all unrighteousness. If we say that we have not sinned, we make him a liar, and his word is not in us."* **1 John 5:16-21 says:** *"If any one sees his brother* (Christian) *committing a sin that does not* (lead to) *death* (physical), *he will pray and* (God) *will give him life—yes, He* (God) *will grant life to all those whose sin is not* (one leading) *to death. There is a sin* (that leads) *to death; I do not say that one should pray for that. All wrongdoing is sin, and there is sin which does not* (involve) *death—that may be repented of and forgiven. We know that any one born of God does not* (deliberately and knowingly) *practice committing sin, but the One Who was begotten of God carefully watches over and protects him—Christ's divine presence within him preserves him against the evil—and the wicked one* (Satan) *does not lay hold* (get a grip) *on him or touch* (him). *We know* (positively) *that we are of God, and the whole world* (around us) *is under the power of the evil one* (Satan). *And we* (have seen and) *know* (positively) *that the Son of God* (Jesus) *has come to this world and has given us understanding and insight progressively to perceive* (recognize) *and come to know better and more clearly Him* (God) *Who is true; and we are in Him Who is true, in His Son Jesus Christ, the Messiah. This is the true God and Life eternal. Little children, keep yourselves from idols—false gods,* (from anything and everything that would occupy the place in your heart due to God, from any sort of substitute for Him that would take first place in your life). *Amen. So let it be."* (The Amplified Bible)

**In Revelation 2:5 Jesus said:** *"Remember then from what heights you have fallen. Repent—change the inner man to meet God's will—and do the works you did previously* (when first you knew the Lord). . ."* (The Amplified Bible)

**WHAT IF A BACKSLIDER NEVER REPENTS? HE WILL BE LOST FOREVER AND WILL HAVE TO PAY THE PENALTY FOR SIN! 2 Timothy 2:12 says:** *"If we endure, we shall also reign with Him. If we deny and disown and reject Him, He will also deny and disown and reject us."* (The Amplified Bible)
**Hebrews 6:4-8 says:** *"For it is impossible* (to restore and bring again to repentance) *those who have been once for all enlightened, who have consciously tasted the heavenly gift, and have become sharers of the Holy Spirit. And have felt how good the Word of God is and the mighty powers of the age and world to come, if they then deviate from the faith and turn away from their allegiance,* (it is impossible) *to bring them back to repentance, for* (because, while, as long as) *they nail up on the cross the Son of God afresh, as far as they are concerned, and are holding* (Him-Christ) *up to contempt and shame and public disgrace. For the soil which has drunk the rain that repeatedly falls upon it, and produces vegetation useful to those for whose benefit it is cultivated, partakes of a blessing from God. But if* (that same soil) *persistently bears thorns and thistles, it is considered worthless and near to being cursed, whose end is to be burned."* (The Amplified Bible)

**IT IS A MOST SERIOUS SIN TO TURN ONE'S BACK ON GOD AND COMMENCE TO BACKSLIDE! 2 Peter 2:20-21 says:** *"For if after they have escaped the pollutions of the world through the knowledge of the Lord and Saviour Jesus Christ,* (and) *they are again entangled therein,* **(backslide),** *and overcome* (turn completely away from the Lord), *the latter end is worse with* (for) *them than the beginning* (before they were saved). *For it had been better for them not to have known the way of righteousness than, after they have known it, to turn from the holy commandment delivered unto them."*

**EACH INDIVIDUAL HAS A RESPONSIBILITY NOT TO BACKSLIDE! READ: EZEKIEL 18:1-32**

**GOD WILL RECLAIM THE BACKSLIDERS INTO THE FOLD WHEN THEY REPENT! Romans 11:23 says:** *"And even those others* (the Jews), *if they do not persist in* (clinging to) *their unbelief, will be grafted in, for God has the power to graft them in again."* (The Amplified Bible)

**FINAL WARNING ABOUT BACKSLIDING:** *"Let me warn you therefore, beloved, that knowing these things beforehand, you should be on your guard lest you be carried away by the error of lawless and wicked* (persons and) *fall from your own* (present) *firm condition* (as a Christian)—*your own steadfastness* (of mind). *But grow in grace* (undeserved favor, spiritual strength) *and recognition and knowledge and understanding of our Lord and Saviour Jesus Christ, the Messiah. To him* (be) *glory* (honor, majesty and splendor) *both now and to the day of eternity. Amen. . .so be it!"* **2 Peter 3:17-18** (The Amplified Bible)

**PRAYER**

Forgive me God for **backsliding** from You. Please take me back! I want to come home! I regret that I went away from Your protection! I will read my Bible! I will go to church! I will turn over a new leaf! I ask You to forgive me and forget my sin. In Jesus' name, I pray. AMEN!

# BEGGARS

Frequently in the Bible beggars were called ''sluggards'',
''slothful'', and ''lazy'' by God!

**Proverbs 20:4 says:** *"The **sluggard** will not plow when winter sets in; therefore shall he **beg** in harvest, and have nothing."* (The Amplified Bible)

**YOU WON'T BECOME A BEGGAR IF YOU WON'T LAY UP IN BED AND WILL WORK WHILE THE SUN SHINES!** *"Love not sleep, lest thou come to poverty; open thine eyes, and thou shalt be satisfied with bread."* **Proverbs 4:13** *"The desire of the **slothful** kills him, for **his hands refuse to labor**. He covets greedily all the day long, but the (uncompromisingly) righteous gives and does not withold."* **Proverbs 21:25-26** (The Amplified Bible)

*"The soul of the sluggard* (beggar) *desireth, and hath nothing: but the soul of the diligent* (worker) *shall be made fat."* **Proverbs 13:4** *"Slothfulness* (beggars, lazy people) *casteth into a deep sleep* (are sleepy-heads); *and an idle* (lazy) *soul shall suffer hunger."* **Proverbs 19:15**

**GOD HAS NO TOLERANCE FOR LAZY PEOPLE WHO COULD WORK—BUT WON'T WORK—BECAUSE THEY PREFER TO BEG FROM OTHERS! In 2 Thessalonians 3:10-12** Paul wrote: *". . .this we commanded you, that **if any would not work, neither should he eat**. For we hear that there are some which walk among you disorderly, **working not at all**, but are busybodies. Now them that are such* **(beggars)** *we command and exhort by our Lord Jesus Christ, that with quietness they work, and eat their own bread."*

**THE BORN-AGAIN CHRISTIAN WHO OBEYS GOD'S COMMANDMENTS WILL NEVER HAVE TO BEG! NOR WILL HIS CHILDREN!** David wrote in **Psalm 37:25** *"I have been young, and now am old; yet have I not seen the righteous forsaken, nor his seed* (descendents) ***begging bread.''***

**IN CLOSING: JESUS SAID WE ARE TO OCCUPY (WORK) UNTIL HE RETURNS TO EARTH!** *"And he* (Jesus) *called his ten servants, and delivered them ten pounds and said unto them, Occupy till I come."* **Luke 19:13**

**GOD HAS COMPASSION ON BEGGARS IF THERE IS NO OTHER POSSIBLE WAY THEY CAN HELP THEMSELVES, AND IF THEY ARE SADDENED BECAUSE THEY ARE FORCED TO BEG.** *"He* (God) *raiseth up the poor out of the dust, and lifteth up the **beggar** from the dunghill, to set them among princes, and to make them* (let them) *inherit the throne of glory; for the pillars of the earth are the Lord's, and he hath set the world upon them."* **1 Samuel 2:8**

### PRAYER

Dear God, I must confess that I have been guilty of **begging** for money, clothes and personal favors which I could have worked for! I repent I have been so lazy! I repent for using other people's money instead of earning my own! Please forgive me and let me be worthy of meriting Your good favor! I will get up in the morning and will work to feed myself! I will not depend on the government, or family, to support me! I will discipline myself and my work! I will never again be hungry, with Your help and guidance! Please forgive me for failing myself and You! In Jesus' name, I pray. AMEN!

# BESTIALITY
## (SEX WITH ANIMALS)

**DEFINITION:** Any sexual act committed between a human and an animal.

DURING MOSES' DAY THE LAW OF THE LAND REQUIRED THE "DEATH PENALTY" FOR BOTH THE PERSON AND THE BEAST! BESTIALITY IS AN ANCIENT SEX CUSTOM. IT IS STILL PRACTICED BY PEOPLE TODAY! AS THE BIBLE SAYS, "THERE IS NOTHING NEW UNDER THE SUN"! BESTIALITY IS A CRIME AGAINST GOD AND REQUIRES TOTAL REPENTANCE OR IT WILL ETERNALLY SEPARATE MAN FROM GOD!

**Exodus 22:19** says: *"Whosoever lieth* (has intercourse) *with a beast shall surely be utterly destroyed."*

OUR BODY IS THE TEMPLE OF GOD! TO COMMIT BESTIALITY IS TO DEFILE OUR BODY, AND THUS TO DEFILE ALMIGHTY GOD! *"Neither shalt thou lie with any beast to defile thyself therewith; neither shall any woman stand before a beast to lie down thereto: it is confusion."* **Leviticus 18:23**

*"Cursed be he that lieth with any manner* (kind) *of beast. And all the people shall say, AMEN* (we agree)." **Deuteronomy 27:21**

BESTIALITY HAS ALWAYS BEEN PRACTICED IN PAGAN NATIONS BY BOTH MEN AND WOMEN! FOR THIS AND OTHER SINS THE PEOPLE OF CANAAN WERE DESTROYED! READ: Leviticus 18:19-25 and 20:22-24. IN THE EYES OF GOD A MAN'S RELATIONSHIP WITH A WOMAN, WHETHER IT BE HIS WIFE THROUGH MARRIAGE OR COMMON LAW MARRIAGE OR EVEN WITH A HARLOT, WHEN IT COMES TO INTERCOURSE, THEY BECOME ONE FLESH! *"Know ye not that your bodies are the members of Christ? shall I then take the members of Christ, and make them the members of an harlot? God forbid. What? know ye not that he which is joined to an harlot is* **one body?** *for two, saith he, shall be* **one flesh.** *But he that is joined unto the Lord is one spirit. Flee fornication. Every sin that a man* (person) *doeth is without the body, but he that committeth fornication sinneth against his own body. What? know ye not that your body is the temple of the Holy Ghost which is in you, which ye have of God, and ye are not your own? For ye are bought with a price: therefore glorify God in your body, and in your spirit, which are God's."* **I Corinthians 6:15-20**

WITH THIS PRINCIPLE OF "BEING ONE FLESH" IN GOD'S EYES, YOU CAN SEE WHY THE ACT OF BESTIALITY IS NOT ONLY DISGUSTING TO US, BUT A SINFUL CRIME AGAINST GOD! THE VERY ACT OF HAVING SEX WITH AN ANIMAL LOWERS THE DIVINE AND HOLY IMAGE OF GOD TO THE SINFUL IMAGE OF BEING ONE FLESH WITH AN ANIMAL! WHAT A TERRIBLE INSULT TO ALMIGHTY GOD WHO CREATED US IN HIS OWN IMAGE! IT IS GOD'S PLAN FOR MAN TO BE HIGHER IN MORALS AND PRINCIPALS THAN TO COHABIT WITH DUMB ANIMALS! WHAT A SENSELESS WASTE TO SELL OUR SOUL TO SATAN THROUGH TOTAL DISOBEDIENCE TO GOD IN SUCH A DISGUSTING SIN! BESTIALITY IS THE SIN OF A DEPRAVED MIND IN A DEPRAVED MAN OR WOMAN! BESTIALITY LOWERS THE PERSON WHO WAS GIVEN HIS VERY LIFE BY ALMIGHTY GOD, AND GOD, HIMSELF, DOWN TO THE SAME LEVEL AS A BEAST! THE REASON THE ANIMAL WAS TO BE DESTROYED BY MAN, (NOT GOD), WAS TO PUT AN END TO THE POSSIBILITY OF THE SAME ANIMAL ATTEMPTING TO COMMIT THE SEX ACT AGAIN WITH ANOTHER PERSON! *"And if a man lie* (has sex) *with a beast, he shall surely be put to death: and ye shall slay the beast. And if a woman approach unto any beast, and lie down thereto* (to have sex), *thou shalt kill the woman, and the beast: they shall surely be put to death: their blood shall be upon them* (the people shall kill them both)." **Leviticus 20:15-16**

IN THE EVENT YOU'RE AS NAIVE AS I WAS AND THINK THAT BESTIALITY NO LONGER EXISTS, JUST THUMB THROUGH MAGAZINES, ETC., IN THE SUPERMARKET AND YOU WILL DISCOVER DIFFERENTLY!

WHAT SHOULD A PERSON DO IF HE HAS COMMITTED BESTIALITY? GET ON YOUR KNEES THIS INSTANT AND REPENT AND ASK GOD TO FORGIVE YOU. NEVER BE GUILTY OF COMMITTING THIS CRIME AGAINST YOURSELF AND GOD AGAIN.

**PRAYER:**

Dear God, I am so ashamed. I am guilty of committing the sin of **bestiality.** I am embarrassed to even share this with You, but I know that You already know. I can't understand how You could love me so much and be willing to forgive me, but I believe You will forgive me. Please blot this sin from Your memory as I will never do such a terrible sin again as long as I live! I will forgive myself and not look back on this disgusting thing I have done against my own body and against You. I am so sorry. I humble myself and confess I am a sinner! I want to be forgiven. I love You, God! Come into my life and dwell in me. In Jesus' name I thank You. AMEN!

# BETRAYED

**DEFINITION:** To lead astray, to fail or desert especially in time of need; to prove false, to violate a confidence.

**Isaiah 16:3 says:** *". . .betray not the fugitive to his pursuer."* (The Amplified Bible)

**NOTE:** Of the 32 times **betray** is used in Scripture, 28 are used in connection with the **betrayal** of Christ.

**In Luke 12:52-53 Christ gave us a clear picture as to the extent people will betray each other just before he returns.** *"For from henceforth there shall be five in one house divided, three against two, and two against three. The father shall be divided against the son, and the son against the father; the mother against the daughter, and the daughter against the mother; the mother-in-law against her daughter-in-law, and the daughter-in-law against her mother-in-law."*

**SINCE THE BEGINNING OF TIME PEOPLE HAVE BETRAYED EACH OTHER AND GOD.** Adam **betrayed** God's law in the Garden of Eden. I times past, **betrayal** was not an everyday occurence so much as it is today. Our nation was at one time built upon honesty. Lies and **betrayal** did not go unpunished! Parents corrected and punished their children for lies. Our police system punished people for **betraying** and lying through the court system. I am not implying that we no longer punish for this crime, however never has **betrayal**, cheating, and lying been so rampant! Did you know that **betrayal** is one of the end time prophecies Christ said would be so prevalent in our world before He returns to earth? Christ said in the last days (before His return) people will **betray** one another! *"Then shall they deliver you up to be afflicted, and shall kill you: and ye shall be hated of all nations for my name's sake. And then shall many be offended, and shall betray one another, and shall hate one another."* **Matthew 24:9-10**

**CHRIST SAID:** *"Now the brother shall betray the brother to death, and the father* (will betray) *the son; and children shall rise up against their parents, and shall cause them to be put to death."* **Mark 13:12**

**CHRIST SAID:** *"And ye shall be betrayed both by parents, and brethren, and kinsfolks, and friends; and some of you shall they cause to be put to death."* **Luke 21:16**

If you are guilty of betraying another person, now is the time to ask his forgiveness. Now is the time to get right with God! Many have betrayed the laws of the land! Many have betrayed another person's complete confidence! Many have betrayed their children and many children have betrayed their parents! Many employers have betrayed their employees, and vice-versa! It's bad enough when a sinner betrays another person. But, it's a crime against God when a Christian betrays himself, another person, or God! "Now is the time to ask God for forgiveness, and to have those sins forgiven and forgotten by Him!" Do it now!

## PRAYER

Dear God in heaven, I confess to You that I am guilty of **betraying** those I love the most. I am also guilty of **betraying** people who put their confidence in me. I ask Your forgiveness. I need to forgive myself. You promise in the Bible that You will not only forgive, but You will forget my sins! I humble myself before You and ask You to forgive and forget my sins. I thank You and praise You for being so merciful to me! I want to please You! I pray that I have not kept another person from coming to know the Lord because he was watching my life! Please give me the knowledge to measure my words before I speak them, and to be honest in all my dealings! In Jesus' name, I pray. AMEN!

# BIGOTRY

**DEFINITION:** Total intolerance of any idea, theory, party, belief, or opinion that differs from one's own. The bigot glories in his own self-conceit.

**A BIGOT HAS A "HOLIER THAN THOU" OPINION OF HIMSELF!** *". . .they say to one another, 'Don't come too close, you'll defile me! For I am holier than you'. . ."* **Isaiah 65:5** (The Living Bible)

**A BIGOT IS INTOLERANT, STUBBORN, PREJUDICED! Galatians 6:3 says:** *"For if a man think himself to be something* (great), *when he is nothing* (to brag about), *he deceiveth himself."*

**Romans 12:3 says:** *"For I say, through the grace given unto me, to every man that is among you,* **not to think of himself more highly than he ought to think;** *but to think soberly* (realistically), *according as God hath dealt to every man the measure of faith."*

**JESUS TAUGHT AGAINST BIGOTRY WHEN HE TOLD THIS PARABLE:** *"And he spake this parable unto certain which* **trusted in themselves that they were righteous, and despised others:** *Two men went up into the temple to pray; the one a Pharisee, and the other a publican. The Pharisee stood and prayed thus with himself, 'God, I thank thee, that I am not as other men are, extortioners, unjust, adulterers, or even as this publican. I fast twice in the week, I give tithes of all that I possess.' And the publican, standing afar off, would not lift up so much as his eyes unto heaven, but smote upon his breast, saying, God be merciful to me a sinner. I tell you, this man went down to his house justified rather than the other* (man): **for every one that exalteth himself shall be abased; and he that humbleth himself shall be exalted."** **Luke 18:9-15**

**GOD IS NO RESPECTER OF PERSONS! Acts 10:34 says:** *"Then Peter opened his mouth, and said, Of a truth I perceive that God is no respecter of persons."* *"For there is no respect of persons with God."* **Romans 2:11**

**Colossians 3:25 says:** *"But he that doeth wrong shall receive for the wrong which he hath done: and there is no respect of persons* (where God is concerned)."

**BIGOTS (EGOTISTS) HAVE NO FEAR, OR RESPECT, FOR GOD!** *"They are all gone out of the way* (side-stepped God's plan for their lives), *they are* (have) *together become unprofitable* (useless); *there is none that doeth good, no, not one. Their* **throat** *is an open sepulchre* (tomb); *with their* **tongues** *they have used deceit; the poison of asps* (snakes) *is under their* **lips;** *whose* (their) **mouth** *is full of cursing and bitterness: their* **feet** *are swift to shed blood: destruction and misery are in their ways; and the way of peace have they not known:* **There is no fear of God before their eyes."** **Romans 3:12-18**

**BIGOTRY-PREJUDICE-BOASTING! ALL THREE ARE DISGUSTING TO GOD AND EXCLUDED FROM HIS PLAN FOR OUR LIVES! Romans 3:27 says:** *"Where is boasting then? It is excluded. . ."*

**THERE IS ONLY ONE GOD TO THE JEW AND TO THE GENTILE! QUESTION:** *"Is he the God of the Jews only? is he not also* (the God) *of the Gentiles?* **ANSWER:** *YES, of the Gentiles also:"* **Romans 3:29** ALSO READ: **Deuteronomy 10:17 and 2 Chronicles 19:7**

**JESUS SAID: "JUDGE NOT, THAT YE BE NOT JUDGED." Matthew 7:1**

**BIGOTRY IS DISGUSTING AND INEXCUSABLE TO GOD!** A person must humble himself and repent and God will forgive him! **Romans 2:1 says:** *"Therefore thou are inexcusable, O man, whosoever thou art that judgest: for wherein thou judgest another, thou condemnest thyself; for thou that judgest doest the same things."*

## PRAYER

Dear God, I have just come to realize that I am a **bigot!** I have always been overly self-confident! I have sung my own praises, instead of letting others compliment me! Please help me overcome this terrible and selfish trait! Please teach me to keep an open mind when it comes to another's opinion, belief or understanding. Please teach me patience. Please help me to stop thinking I'm the only person in the world who is right! Please teach me tolerance! Help me to learn what it means to love my neighbor as I do myself! Please forgive me for having worshipped my own mind and intelligence! Only You have all the answers and can make no mistakes! Help me to always remember this! In Jesus' name, I pray. AMEN!

# BITTERNESS

# KNOW YOUR ENEMY!

**BITTERNESS STARTS IN THE HEART:** *"The heart knoweth his own* **bitterness;** *and a stranger doth not intermeddle (interrupt) his joy."* **Proverbs 14:10**

**BITTERNESS GETS INTO OUR SPIRIT:** Ezekiel wrote: *"So the Spirit lifted me up, and took me away, and I went in* **bitterness,** *in the heat of my spirit; but the hand of the Lord was strong upon me."* **Ezekiel 3:14**

**IT GRIEVES THE HOLY SPIRIT WHEN WE ARE BITTER! Ephesians 4:30-32 says:** *"And grieve not the Holy Spirit of God, whereby ye are sealed unto the day of redemption. Let all* **bitterness,** *and wrath, and anger, and clamour (loud accusations), and evil speaking, be put away from you, with all malice (hatred): and be ye kind one to another, tenderhearted, forgiving one another, even as God for Christ's sake hath forgiven you."*

**WORDS CAN BE BITTER: Read Psalm 64:3 COMPLAINTS CAN BE BITTER: Read Job 23:2**

**BACKSLIDING CAN BRING BITTER RESULTS:** *"Thine own wickedness shall correct thee, and thy backslidings shall reprove thee: know therefore and see that it is an evil thing and* **bitter,** *that thou hast forsaken the Lord thy God, and that my (God's) fear is not in thee (you), saith the Lord God of hosts."* **Jeremiah 2:19**

**WEEPING CAN BE BITTER:** *"Thus saith the Lord; A voice was heard in Ramah, lamentation (mourning) and bitter weeping; Rachel weeping for her children refused to be comforted for her children, because they were not (they were dead)."* **Jeremiah 31:15**

**A PERSON'S LIFE MAY SOMETIMES BE BITTER!** Example: The Israelites lived **bitter** lives in Egypt before Moses took them out of the land. **Exodus 1:14 says:** *"And they made their lives* **bitter** *with hard bondage (slavery), in mortar, and in brick, and in all manner of service in the field: all their service, wherein they made them serve, was with rigour."*

**A PERSON MAY PROVOKE ANOTHER TO BITTERNESS: Hosea 12:14 says:** *"Ephraim proved him to anger most* **bitterly:** *therefore shall he leave his blood upon him, and his reproach shall his Lord return unto."*

**THERE IS BITTERNESS OF SOUL:** *"And she was in* **bitterness** *of soul, and prayed unto the Lord, and wept sore (until she couldn't cry any more)."* **1 Samuel 1:10**

**BITTERNESS TAKES ROOTS IN OUR LIVES IF WE LET IT!** *"Follow peace with all men, and holiness, without which no man shall see the Lord: looking diligently lest any man fail of the grace of God; lest any root of* **bitterness** *springing up trouble you, and thereby many be defiled;"* **Hebrews 12:14-15**

**HOW CAN A PERSON OVERCOME BITTERNESS? PRAY, PRAY, PRAY, PRAY! Psalm 86:7 says:** *"In the day of my trouble I will call upon thee: for thou (God) wilt answer me."* **Psalm 102:2 says:** *"Hide not thy (God's) face from me in the day when I am in trouble; incline thine ear unto me: in the day when I call answer me speedily."*

### PRAYER

Dear God, I am a **bitter** person. I have had many things take place in my life which have left me with a heart full of **bitterness.** I ask you to forgive me for becoming **bitter** when I should have turned to You for help. I ask You to soften my heart. I ask You to forgive me for all the misery I have dished out to other people. I know that my **bitterness** never solved anything. I regret all the time I have lost by being so **bitter.** Please help me get healed of this sin. I know I have hurt others. I have also hurt myself. I am sure I have hurt You. I turn my **bitter** spirit over to You. God, clean up my heart, my life, my relationships. Help me love others and even my enemies. I know justice belongs to You, only. I repent of my sin and I thank You for answering my prayer, in Jesus' name. AMEN!

# Blasphemy

**DEFINITION:** The act of insulting or showing contempt or lack of reverence for God; the act of claiming the attributes of deity; irreverence toward something considered sacred.

**BLASPHEMY IS AS OLD AS TIME ITSELF!** Lucifer blasphemed God. In **Psalm 74:10** the question was asked: *"O God, how long shall the adversary* (enemy) *reproach* (rebuke you)? *shall the enemy* **blaspheme** *thy name for ever?"*

**BLASPHEMING AGAINST THE HOLY GHOST-THE UNPARDONABLE SIN!** Jesus said: *"Verily I say unto you, All sins shall be forgiven unto the sons of men* (if they ask God to forgive them), *and* **blasphemies** *wherewith soever they shall* **blaspheme:** *But he that shall* **blaspheme** *against the Holy Ghost hath never forgiveness, but is in danger of eternal damnation."* **Mark 3:28-29**

**IF YOU BLASPHEME GOD, YOUR ALLEGIANCE IS NOT TO GOD! IT IS SATAN WHO CAUSES PEOPLE TO BLASPHEME OUR CREATOR. GOD SAID SATAN IS A LIAR AND THE INVENTOR OF LIES!**

**JESUS SAID:** *"He that is not with me* (all the way) *is against me; and he that gathereth not with me scattereth abroad. Wherefore I say unto you, all manner of sin and* **blasphemy** *shall be forgiven unto men: but the* **blasphemy** *against the Holy Ghost shall not be forgiven unto men. And whosoever speaketh a word against the Son of man, it shall be forgiven him: but whosoever speaketh against the Holy Ghost, it shall not be forgiven him, neither in this world, neither in the world to come."* **Matthew 12:30-32**

**CHRIST IS COMING BACK TO EARTH SOON:** *"To execute judgement upon all, and to convince all that are ungodly among them of all their ungodly deeds which they have ungodly committed, and of all their* **hard speeches** (abusive language, swearing against God) *which ungodly sinners have spoken against him."* **Jude 15**

**NOTE:** God will forgive you if you speak against Christ, but not if you attribute the works of the Holy Spirit as having come from Satan! For instance: If you say or believe that God can no longer heal the sick; or if you say that the gift of speaking in tongues comes from Satan rather than the Holy Spirit (regardless of what the Scriptures say,) you **blaspheme** the Holy Spirit, because all gifts come from Him!

**JESUS SAID:** *"And whosoever shall speak a word against the Son of man* (Jesus), *it shall be forgiven him:* **but unto him that blasphemeth against the Holy Ghost it shall not be forgiven."** **Luke 12:10**

**IF A PERSON BLASPHEMES IGNORANTLY IN UNBELIEF, HE CAN BE FORGIVEN IF HE WILL ASK GOD!** (Paul describes himself) *"Who was before a* **blasphemer,** *and a persecutor, and injurious; but I obtained mercy, because I did it* (blasphemed) *ignorantly in unbelief* (before I was a believer in Jesus as my saviour)." **1 Timothy 1:13**

**A PERSON IS FOOLISH TO EVER BLASPHEME GOD! FOR ONLY GOD CAN FORGIVE HIS SINS AND GRANT HIM ETERNAL LIFE THROUGH JESUS!** A **blasphemer** who does not ask for forgiveness is headed straight to hell! **Mark 2:7 says:** *"Why doth* (does) *this man thus speak* **blasphemies?** *who can forgive sins but God only?"* *"Do not they* **blaspheme** *that worthy name* (Christ) *by which ye are called* (Christians)?" **James 2:7**

**DID YOU KNOW THAT THE SIN OF BLASPHEMY IS PROPHESIED AS A SIGN OF THE LAST DAYS BEFORE CHRIST RETURNS?** *"This know also, that in the last days perilous times shall come. For men shall be lovers of their own selves, covetous, boasters, proud,* **blasphemers,** *disobedient to parents, unthankful, unholy, without natural affection* (homosexuals, bestiality, lesbians, etc.), *trucebreakers, false accusers, incontinent, fierce, despisers of those that are good, traitors, heady, highminded, lovers of pleasures more than lovers of God, having a form of godliness, but denying the power* (of the Holy Spirit) *thereof: from such turn away."* **2 Timothy 3:1-5**

**NEVER FORGET THAT GOD HEARS EVERY WORD OF BLASPHEMY SPOKEN BY A PERSON!** *"And thou shalt know that I am the Lord, and that I have heard all thy* **blasphemies** *which thou hast spoken . . . thus with your mouth ye hae boasted against me, and have multiplied your words against me: I have heard them."* **Ezekiel 35:12-13**

**BLASPHEMY STARTS IN THE HEART:** *"But those things which proceed out of the mouth come forth from the heart; and they defile the man. For out of the heart proceed evil thoughts, murders, adulteries, fornications, thefts, false witness,* **blasphemies:** *These are the things which defile a man: but to eat with unwashen hands defileth not a man."* **Matthew 15:18-20**

## PRAYER

Dear God, I need Your help, and I really need it now! I have **blasphemed** You, as You already know! I truly am sorry I ever spoke Your name in vain! I regret I ever used Your name in cursing. I regret I ever told jokes which made sport of You! I know I owe my life to You! I am full of guilt and shame! Please come into my life and forgive me for all my sins! Please love me, and forgive me, and I will not do this terrible thing again! I confess I have sinned! I turn away from sin, I ask you to come into my life and make me aware of who You are! Help me to make the right choices in friends, so I will not be tempted to **blaspheme** You in order to be a fun sport. I am not ashamed of You, God! And, I hope You will not be ashamed of me! I made mistakes through my own ignorance. Now I know I have done You wrong, and have wronged the Holy Spirit! I sincerely and humbly ask Your forgiveness! In Jesus' name I pray. I will give You the glory for Your loving kindness forevermore! AMEN!

# BOASTING

ANNOUNCEMENT: "WE, THE PEOPLE OF THE WORLD, HAVE NOTHING WE CAN BOAST ABOUT IN OURSELVES!" *"Do not boast about tomorrow, For you do not know what a day may bring forth. Let another praise you, and not your own mouth; a stranger, and not your own lips."* **Proverbs 27:1-2** (New American Standard Bible)

BOASTING IS SINFUL AND IT SEEMS TO GO ON FOREVER! *"How long shall they utter and speak hard things? and all the workers of iniquity (sin) boast themselves?* **Psalm 94:4**

THERE IS ONLY ONE PERSON IN THE ENTIRE UNIVERSE WE CAN BOAST ABOUT. . .ONLY GOD IS WORTHY OF OUR BOASTING! *"In God we have boasted all day long, and we will give thanks to Thy name forever."* **Psalm 44:8** (New American Standard Bible)

IF A PERSON WILLFULLY CHOOSES TO BE BOASTFUL, GOD WILL SEPARATE HIMSELF FROM HIM. HE WILL NOT RECEIVE GOD'S BLESSINGS UNTIL HE REPENTS! *"And even as they did not like to retain God in their knowledge, God gave them over to a reprobate (confused) mind, to do those things which are not convenient; being filled with all unrighteousness, fornication, wickedness, covetousness, maliciousness; full of envy, murder, debate, deceit, malignity, whisperers, backbiters, haters of God, despiteful, proud, boasters, inventors of evil things, disobedient to parents, without understanding, covenantbreakers, without natural affection, implacable, unmerciful: Who knowing the judgement of God, that they which commit such things are worthy of death, not only do the same, but have pleasure in them that do them."* **Romans 1:28-32**

QUESTION: IF AN UNSAVED PERSON DOES GOOD WORKS SUCH AS: TITHING, READING THE BIBLE, GIVING TO THE POOR, IS A GOOD NEIGHBOR, GOES TO CHURCH, ETC., WILL HE GO TO HEAVEN? ANSWER: ONLY IF HE REPENTS OF HIS SINS AND BECOMES A BORN-AGAIN CHRISTIAN! He can **boast** about his good works all he chooses, but he will only be allowed to enter heaven after he repents of his sins! Christ paid the debt for each person's sins, when He died on the cross and was resurrected. There is nothing that we can do to merit our salvation. We receive forgiveness of sins through our faith that God will forgive and forget. This is called the "law of faith" as mentioned in the above paragraph.

IN ROMANS 3:27 THE QUESTION IS ASKED: *"WHERE IS BOASTING THEN?"* ANSWER: *"IT IS EXCLUDED."* QUESTION: "BY WHAT LAW? OF WORKS?" ANSWER: *"NAY* (no) *BUT BY THE LAW OF FAITH."*

DID YOU KNOW THAT BOASTERS ARE FULFILLING PROPHECY ABOUT THE LAST DAYS BEFORE CHRIST RETURNS? 2 Timothy 3:1-5 says: *"But realize this, that in the last days difficult times will come. For men will be lovers of self, lovers of money, boastful, arrogant, revilers, disobedient to parents, ungrateful, unholy, unloving, irreconcilable, malicious gossips, without self-control, brutal, haters of good, treacherous, reckless, conceited, lovers of pleasure rather than lovers of God; holding on to a form of godliness, although they have denied its power; and avoid such men (people) as these."* (New American Standard Bible)

### PRAYER

Dear God, I don't know why I **boast**! I guess I want people to notice me more. I have developed a habit of **boasting** which may be hard to break. God, I am going to need Your help. Please help me control my thoughts and tongue so I will not continue in this sin. Help me to remember that You hear every word I say! Help me to remember that You love me no matter how many sins I have committed. Help me break the habit of **boasting.** I will spend more time reading my Bible. I will change my lifestyle so I am not put in a position where I can be tempted to **boast**! I want to please You! I want You to be pleased with me! I can and will change, but I need your help. In Jesus' name, I pray. AMEN!

# Body Exercise

TODAY, BODY EXERCISE (WHICH IS A GOOD HEALTH PRACTICE) HAS SUDDENLY BECOME MORE THAN MERE PHYSICAL FITNESS! IT HAS BECOME A SUBSTITUTE FOR READING THE BIBLE, OR GOING TO CHURCH, IN MANY CASES! EXERCISE IS GOOD; BUT TO LOOK TO BODY EXERCISE FOR SELF-FULFILLMENT IS SINFUL! WHY? BECAUSE, WHEN TOO MUCH ATTENTION IS PAID TO JOGGING, RUNNING, SWIMMING, TENNIS, SOCCER, HEALTH SPAS, ETC., IT TURNS A PERSON'S ATTENTION TOWARD SELF—AND AWAY FROM GOD! OUR GREAT COMMISSION (GIVEN US BY GOD) IS TO TEACH, PREACH, PRAY AND WITNESS TO ALL THE WORLD THAT A PERSON MUST BE BORN AGAIN. 1 Timothy 4:8 says: *"For bodily exercise profiteth little: but godliness is profitable unto all things, having promise of the life that now is, and of that which is to come."*

INSTEAD OF DIRECTING ALL YOUR ATTENTION TO SPORTS, BODY EXERCISE, WEIGHT-LIFTING, JOGGING, OR RUNNING, IN ORDER TO REACH YOUR GOAL OR PRIZE. . . WHY NOT PRESS TOWARD THE PRIZE OF JESUS? Philippians 3:14 says: *"I press toward the mark for the prize of the high calling of God in Christ Jesus."*

PUT PRAYER, READING YOUR BIBLE, AND WITNESSING TO THE LOST, BEFORE BODY EXERCISE, AND GOD WILL BLESS YOU! *"Then shalt thou (you) walk (or run—jog) in thy way safely, and thy foot shall not stumble."* Proverbs 3:23 (AND) *"When thou goest, thy steps shall not be straitened; and when thou runnest, thou shalt not stumble."* Proverbs 4:12

SURE, YOU FOLLOW THE DISCIPLINES FOR JOGGING AND RUNNING BY PACING YOUR STEPS. . . BUT DO YOU ALSO FOLLOW GOD'S DISCIPLINES BY PACING YOUR STEPS IN THE WORD OF GOD, BY READING THE BIBLE EVERY DAY? Psalm 119:133 says: *"Order my steps in thy (God's) word (the Bible): and let not any iniquity (sin) have dominion over me."*

BODY EXERCISE IS GOOD AND WILL INCREASE YOUR STRENGTH, BUT IS NOTHING COMPARED TO WHAT THE LORD CAN DO! Isaiah 40:29-31 says: *"He (God) giveth power to the faint; and to them that have no might he increaseth strength. Even the youths shall faint and be weary, and the young men shall utterly fall: But they that wait upon the Lord shall renew their strength; they shall mount up with wings as eagles; they shall run and not be weary; and they shall walk, and not faint."*

GOD OWNS OUR BODY (AFTER WE BECOME BORN-AGAIN CHRISTIANS)! WHAT WE DO WITH OUR BODY IS HIS BUSINESS! 1 Corinthians 6:19-20 says: *"What? know ye not that your body is the temple of the Holy Ghost which is in you, which ye have (been given) of God, and ye*

*are not your own? For ye are bought with a price: therefore glorify God in your body, and in your spirit, which are God's."*

WHO SHOULD RECEIVE THE TROPHY IN A RACE? *"Know ye not that they which run in a race run all (everyone runs), but one receiveth the prize? So run, that ye may obtain (try to win). And every man (person) that striveth for the mastery (trophy) is temperate in all things. Now they do it to obtain a corruptible crown (one that is temporary); but we (that are Christians) an incorruptible (eternal crown). I therefore so run, not as uncertainly; so fight I, not as one that beateth the air: But I keep under my body, and bring it into subjection (Godly disciplines): lest that by any means, when I have preached to others, I myself should be a castaway."* 1 Corinthians 9:24-27

WHAT SHOULD YOU DO WHEN YOU PULL A MUSCLE, OR SPRAIN AN ANKLE IN DOING BODY EXERCISE, RUNNING OR JOGGING? PRAY THIS VERSE: *"But as for me, I will walk in mine integrity: redeem (help) me, and be merciful unto me. My foot standeth in an even place: in the congregations (to the public) will I bless the Lord."* Psalm 26:11-12

## PRAYER

Dear God, Please forgive me if I have put my **exercise** or **sport** above my interest in worshipping You. Forgive me for those times I remembered to **run** and **exercise** but didn't remember to pray and read my Bible. Help me to get my priorities straight. Let me never forget that although **exercise** strengthens my body, that prayer and meditating on the word of God strengthens my spirit, my life, and my testimony! Remind me to witness to those I meet when I walk, run, swim, and talk. Set me on the right path that You would have me take. In Jesus' name, I pray. AMEN!

# BODY WORSHIP

**JESUS COMMANDED US NOT TO BE SO CON-CERNED AND PRE-OCCUPIED WITH OUR BODY!**
Jesus said: *". . . Therefore I say unto you, Take no thought for your life, what ye shall eat; neither for the **body**, what ye shall put on. The* (your) *life is more than meat* (food), *and the **body** is more than **raiment*** (clothes). *Consider* (think about) *the ravens: for they neither sow* (plant) *nor reap; which neither have storehouse nor barn; and God feedeth them: how much more are ye better than the fowls? ANd which of you with taking thought can add to his stature* (height) *one cubit* (18 inches)? *If ye then be not able to do that thing which is least, why take ye thought for the rest? Consider the lilies how they grow: they toil* (work) *not, they spin not; and yet I say unto you, that* (King) *Solomon in all his glory was not arrayed like one of these* (lily flowers). *If then God so clothe the grass, which is to-day in the field* (wheat, corn, etc.,), *and to-morrow is cast into the oven; how much more will be clothe you, O ye of little faith? And seek not ye what ye shall **eat**, or what ye shall **drink**, neither be ye of doubtful mind. For all these things do the nations of the world seek after: and your Father* (God) *knoweth that ye have need of these things. But rather seek ye the kingdom of God; and all these things shall be added unto you. Fear not, little flock* (children of mine); *for it is your Father's* (God's) *good pleasure to give you the kingdom."* **Luke 12:22-32**

**GOD ASKED US A FAVOR! HE ASKED US TO PREPARE OUR BODIES TO HOLINESS, AS A REASONABLE SERVICE, IN GRATITUDE AND APPRECIATION, FOR WHAT HE HAS DONE FOR US! HE SENT HIS ONLY SON TO DIE ON THE CROSS FOR US, AS A SACRIFICE, IN ORDER THAT WE MIGHT BE SAVED! NOW, ALL WE HAVE TO DO IS ASK FOR OUR SINS TO BE FORGIVEN, AND THEN REPAY GOD BY LIVING A HOLY LIFE! THIS INCLUDES OUR BODIES, OUR SERVICE, OUR TESTIMONY!** *"I beseech you therefore, brethren, by the mercies of God, that ye present your **bodies** a living sacrifice, holy, acceptable unto God, which is your reasonable service. And be not conformed to this world: but be ye transformed* (changed) *by the renewing of your mind, that ye may prove* (in your body-life) *what is that good, and acceptable, and perfect, will of God."* **Romans 12:1-2**

**WE MUST KEEP OUR BODIES UNDER SUBJECTION! THIS INCLUDES SEX DRIVES, ALCOHOL, WEIGHT, SMOKING, DRUGS, EGO ABOUT SIZE, SHAPE, LOOKS, ETC.! WE SHOULD BE CAREFUL TO ALWAYS WEAR DECENT CLOTHING! WE SHOULD BE CAREFUL TO WATCH OUR LANGUAGE! 1 Corinthians 9:27 says:** *"But I keep under my **body*** (I control all my appetites), *and bring it into **subjection**: lest that by any means, when I have preached to others, I myself should be a castaway."*

**MAN IS MUCH MORE PRE-OCCUPIED WITH THE PHYSICAL BODY THAN GOD IS!! GOD COMMANDS US TO LOVE ALL PEOPLE, INSTEAD OF SPENDING SO MUCH TIME TRYING TO IMPRESS OTHERS WITH OUR LOOKS! 1 Corinthians 13:3 says:** *"And though I bestow* (give) *all my goods to feed the poor, and though I give my **body** to be burned, and have not charity* (love) *it profiteth me nothing."*

**HERE IS SOUND ADVICE:** *"Whether* (whatever) *therefore ye **eat**, or **drink**, or whatsoever ye **do**, do **all** to the **glory** of God."* **1 Corinthians 10:31**

*"For our conversation* (citizenship) *is in heaven; from whence also we look for the Saviour, the Lord Jesus Christ: who shall change our vile body, that it may be fashioned like unto his glorious body, according to the working whereby he is able even to subdue all things unto himself."* **Philippians 3:20-21**

### PRAYER
Dear God, I am guilty of adoring my **body**, my **mind**, my **looks!** When I have received compliments, they have gone to my head! I wanted to believe all the wonderful things people said about me. Without realizing it, I began to **worship myself,** and my intellect! I know there is no other God! Yet, I have been worshipping myself! I know I am nothing! I know You created me, and that You created me to serve You! I know that only Christ is perfect, and compared to Him, I am nothing! I ask You to forgive all my sins. I ask You to humble me! I want to please You! Thank You for answering my prayer! AMEN!

# BOREDOM

There are many reasons for **boredom!!** Any person who has not had a born-again experience with the Lord is more apt to suffer **boredom!** Any person who does not pray, and go to church, and develop Christian friends, is apt to suffer **boredom!** Any person who back-slides from God becomes restless! Sometimes even good Christians get **bored!** But there is a cure for **boredom.** You can spend time reading the Scriptures, and praying, and witnessing to your neighbors. You can fast, pray, and ask God to give you a special assignment to do for Him. You can get a church hymnal and sing some favorite songs. You can volunteer some free time to work in a hospital where your Christian influence, and words of kindness will be much appreciated. You can **volunteer some free time to work in a retirement or nursing home. You can read the Bible to senior citizens whose** eyesight is failing! Here's an idea for curbing **boredom,** even when you're on a job. Learn one of these short verses listed below, each day. Repeat it until it is memorized! Each day learn one more short verse. At the end of the week you will know 7 new verses. At the end of each month you will have memorized 30 new verses. God will make the verses start working for you. He will open doors, if you first start occupying your mind with wholesome things instead of "self!" **HERE GOES:** *"BE OF GOOD COURAGE, AND HE SHALL STRENGTHEN YOUR HEART, ALL YE THAT HOPE IN THE LORD."* **Psalm 31:24**
*"WHAT TIME I AM AFRAID, I WILL TRUST IN THEE."* **Psalm 56:3**

*"I SHALL NOT DIE, BUT LIVE, AND DECLARE THE WORKS OF THE LORD."* **Psalm 118:17**
*"IN THE DAY OF MY TROUBLE I WILL CALL UPON THEE: FOR THOU WILT ANSWER ME."* **Psalm 86:7**
*"OUR HELP IS IN THE NAME OF THE LORD, WHO MADE HEAVEN AND EARTH."* **Psalm 124:8**
*"BELIEVE ON THE LORD JESUS CHRIST, AND THOU SHALT BE SAVED, AND THY HOUSE."* **Acts 16:31**
*"GIVE US HELP FROM TROUBLE: FOR VAIN IS THE HELP OF MAN."* **Psalm 60:11**

*". . .EXCEPT YE REPENT, YE SHALL ALL LIKEWISE PERISH."* **Luke 13:3**
*". . .I* (Jesus) *AM THE WAY, THE TRUTH, AND THE LIFE: NO MAN COMETH UNTO THE FATHER, BUT BY ME."* **John 14:6**
*"FOR THE SON OF MAN* (Jesus) *IS COME TO SAVE THAT WHICH WAS LOST."* **Matthew 18:11**
*"FOR IF YE FORGIVE MEN THEIR TRESPASSES, YOUR HEAVENLY FATHER WILL ALSO FORGIVE YOU."* **Matthew 6:14**
*"ASK, AND IT SHALL BE GIVEN YOU: SEEK, AND YE SHALL FIND: KNOCK, AND IT SHALL BE OPENED UNTO YOU:"* **Matthew 7:7**
*"COME UNTO ME, ALL YE THAT LABOUR AND ARE HEAVY LADEN, AND I* (Jesus) *WILL GIVE YOU REST."* **Matthew 11:28**
*"FOR ALL HAVE SINNED, AND COME SHORT OF THE GLORY OF GOD."* **Romans 3:23**

### PRAYER

Dear God, I confess that I stay **bored** most of the time! I do not have enough interesting things to keep my mind and my hands busy. Dear God, perhaps You have some ideas for me? Dear God, please let me know if there is some study course You would like for me to take. Or, if there is some job that You would like for me to do. Let me know if I should spend my time doing for others. Help me to rise above my situation. I feel so shallow complaining about being **bored,** when there are so many people who are paralyzed and can't work! Teach me what You would have me do! Help me to overcome thinking about myself so much, and to think of others more! Dear God, open the door that will lead me to do something productive for You, and I will praise You for it! Until I receive an answer from You, I will show my faith in this prayer, by praying and reading my Bible. In Jesus' name, I thank You for an answer to this prayer. AMEN!

# BORROWING
# SELLING
# BUYING

**THERE ARE MANY WHO BORROW AND NEVER PAY BACK!** *"The wicked **borroweth**, and **payeth** not again: but the righteous sheweth* (shows) *mercy, and giveth* (knowing they lost their loan, yet they do not resort to hatred)." **Psalm 37:21**

**IT IS BEST NOT TO OWE ANYTHING (AS IN BORROWING)!** *"Owe no man anything, but to love one another: for he that loveth another hath fulfilled the law* (Thou shalt love thy neighbor as thy self)." **Romans 13:8**

**IF YOU OWE A PERSON SOMETHING. . . DON'T MAKE THEM WORRY IF, OR WHEN, THEY'LL BE PAID BACK!** *"Withold not good* (your loan) *from them to whom it is due, when it is in the power of thine hand to do it."* **Proverbs 3:27**

**DON'T MAKE EXCUSES OR ANTAGONIZE THE PERSON YOU OWE, BY MAKING HIM WAIT TO BE PAID BACK! AFTER ALL, HE LOANED TO YOU WHEN YOU NEEDED HELP!** *"Say not unto thy neighbour* (anyone), *Go, and come again, and tomorrow I will give; when thou hast it* (have the money) *by* (with) *thee."* **Proverbs 3:28**

**IF YOU AREN'T FORCED TO BORROW. . . DON'T BORROW!! WHEN YOU DO BORROW, YOU BECOME A SERVANT TO THE LENDER!** *"The rich ruleth over the poor, and the **borrower** is servant to the lender."* **Proverbs 22:7**

**Jesus said: IF YOU KNOW A PERSON WHO DESPERATELY NEEDS YOUR TEMPORARY FINANCIAL HELP, DON'T TURN HIM AWAY!** *"Give to him that asketh thee and from him that would **borrow** of thee turn not thou away* (don't turn him away)." **Matthew 5:42**

**BEFORE YOU BORROW, BUY, OR SELL ANYTHING. . . BE HONEST IN ALL YOUR DEALINGS, OR YOU MAY LOSE A FRIENDSHIP OVER IT! FREQUENT BUYING, SELLING, OR BORROWING, HAS SPLIT UP FRIENDS AND FAMILY MEMBERS. YOU COULD END UP IN COURT HATING EACH OTHER!** *"And if thou* (you) *sell ought* (anything) *unto thy neighbour* (anyone), *or **buyest** ought* (anything) *of thy neighbour's hand, ye shall not oppress one another."* **Leviticus 25:14**

**CAUTION! DON'T OVER-SPEND — AND YOU WON'T BE FORCED TO BORROW!** *"There is treasure to be desired and oil* (heat) *in the dwelling* (house) *of the wise; but a foolish man* (person) *spendeth it up."* **Proverbs 21:20**

## PRAYER

Dear God, I have been less than honest in my pattern of **borrowing, buying or selling!** I ask You to forgive me. I will repay those I owe on a regular basis, even though I can not **repay** them all at once. I will go and explain this to them. When I **sell** anything I will be cautious to **charge** correctly. I will not abuse another person's pocket-book! When I **sell** anything I will make my product, and word, good to the best of my ability! When I must **borrow**, I will **pay** all that is due and on time! If **I owe interest** I will cheerfully **pay** it! I will arrange my **finances** better, so that I do not have to constantly jeopardize my **credit!** I will establish **good credit** by not **over-spending!** I will tell the truth in all my personal and business ventures. I ask You to forgive me in all the areas where I have previously failed You! Help me in the area of **honesty** and **finances.** Help me restore those friendships I have abused in times past! In Jesus' name, I pray. AMEN!

# BREAKING COMMANDMENTS

THE 10 COMMANDMENTS GOD GAVE MOSES TO PASS ON TO US ARE FOUND IN EXODUS 20 AND IN DEUTERONOMY 7:21. THEY READ: *"THOU SHALT HAVE NONE OTHER GODS BEFORE ME — THOU SHALT NOT MAKE UNTO THEE ANY GRAVEN IMAGE — THOU SHALT NOT TAKE THE NAME OF THE LORD THY GOD IN VAIN — REMEMBER THE SABBATH DAY, TO KEEP IT HOLY — HONOUR THY FATHER AND THY MOTHER — THOU SHALT NOT KILL — THOU SHALT NOT COMMIT ADULTERY — THOU SHALT NOT STEAL — THOU SHALT NOT BEAR FALSE WITNESS AGAINST THY NEIGHBOUR — THOU SHALT NOT COVET."* NOTE: Please read the above Scripture references, because God goes into specific details.

**IF WE OBEY GOD'S COMMANDMENTS HE PROMISES TO BLESS OUR LAND!** *"And it shall come to pass, if ye shall hearken diligently unto my **commandments** which I command you this day, to love the Lord your God, and to serve him with all your heart and with all your soul, That I will give you the **rain** of your land in his **due season**, the first rain and the latter rain, that thou mayest gather in thy **corn**, and thy **wine**, and thine **oil**. And I will send **grass** in thy fields for thy cattle, that thou mayest **eat** and be **full**."* Deuteronomy 11:13-15

**GOD PROMISED CURSES FOR DISOBEDIENCE!** *"Take heed to yourselves, that your heart be not deceived, and ye turn aside* (away), *and serve other gods, and worship them; And then the Lord's wrath be kindled against you, and he shut up the heaven, that there be no rain, and that the land yield not her fruit; and lest ye perish quickly from off the good land which the Lord giveth you."* Deuteronomy 11:16-17

**CONDITION OF BLESSING UPON THE HOME:** *"Therefore shall ye lay up these my words in your **heart** and in your **soul**, and bind them for a sign upon your **hand**, that they may be a frontlets between your **eyes*** (in everything you say, think, do, or see). *And ye shall **teach** them your children, **speaking of them** when thou **sittest** in thine house, and when thou **walkest** by the way, when thou **liest down** and when thou **risest up**. And thou shalt **write them** upon the door posts of thine house, and upon thy gates: **That your days may be multiplied, and the days of your children**, in the land which the Lord sware unto your fathers to give them, as the days of heaven upon the earth."* Deuteronomy 11:18-21

**THE CHOISE IS OURS, TO CHOOSE A BLESSING OR CURSE!** *"Behold, I set before you this day a **blessing** and a **curse**; A blessing, if ye **obey** the **commandments** of the Lord your God, which I command you this day: And a **curse**, if ye will **not** obey the **commandments** of the Lord your God, but turn aside* (away) *out of the way which I command you* (not to do) *this day, to go after other gods, which ye have not known."* Deuteronomy 11:26-28

**HOW LONG DID GOD COMMAND US TO OBEY HIS COMMANDMENTS? . . . ALWAYS!** *"Therefore thou shalt love the Lord thy God, and keep his charge, and his statutes, and his judgements, and his **commandments**, always."* Deuteronomy 11:1

**GOD CAREFULLY EXPLAINED WHY BREAKING THE SABBATH IS AGAINST HIS WILL FOR US:** *"Six days thou shalt labour, and do all thy work: But the seventh day is the **sabbath** of the Lord thy God: in it thou shalt not do any work, thou, nor thy son, nor thy daughter, nor thy manservant* (male employee), *nor thy maidservant* (female employee), *nor thine ox, nor thine ass, nor any of thy cattle, nor thy stranger that is within thy gates* (your property); *that thy manservant and thy maidservant may rest as well as thou* (you). *"* Deuteronomy 5:13-14

**IN CLOSING: GOD SAID. . .** *"O that there were such an heart in them* (all people), *that they would fear me* (respect and obey), *and keep all my commandments always, that it might be well with them, and with their children for ever!"* Deuteronomy 5:29

### PRAYER

Dear God, I am guilty of having broken most of Your **commandments**! I know how to obey them. I know when I do wrong. Chasten me, dear God. Help me to grow in strength, and wisdom, so that I might do the things that please You! I repent of all the sins I have committed in my lifetime! I ask You to forgive me. I will praise You, obey you, and honor You from this day forward! Teach me, Lord, what You would have me do! AMEN!

# BRIBERY

**DEFINITION:** To induce or influence for money or favor from another person; gifts given or promised to a person in a position of trust in order to pervert his judgement or corrupt his conduct; anything that serves to entice or influence a person to change his conduct to insure that you get what you desire.

---

**In Psalm 26:9-10 David prayed:** *"Gather not my soul with sinners* (protect me from sinners), *nor my life with bloody men* (cruel, mean): *In whose hands is mischief, and their right hand is full of bribes."*

**GOD WROTE LAWS AGAINST BRIBERY: QUESTION:** *"Lord, who shall abide in thy tabernacle* (God's house)? *Who shall dwell in thy holy hill?"* **Psalm 15:1 ANSWER:** *"He that putteth not out his money to usury* (unusually high interest), *nor taketh reward against the innocent* (cannot be bribed). *He that doeth these things shall never be moved* (will be eternally secure)." **Psalm 15:5**

**GOD SAID . . . "WOE UNTO THEM THAT DO TAKE BRIBES".** *"Woe unto them that are wise in their own eyes, and prudent in their own sight!"* *"Which justify the wicked* (deeds) *for reward* (bribery), *and take away the righteousness of the righteous from him!"* **Isaiah 5:21, 23**

**A PERSON WHO ACCEPTS A BRIBE BECOMES A SLAVE TO THE GIVER:** *"And thou shalt take no gift: for the gift blindeth the wise, and perverteth the words of the righteous."* **Exodus 23:8**

**WHY DO PEOPLE GIVE BRIBES? ANSWER: TO GAIN SPECIAL UNMERITED AND SOMETIMES UNLAWFUL, FAVORS WHICH THEY ARE NOT ENTITLED TO RECEIVE!** *"A man's gift* (bribe) *maketh room for him* (gets him in the door), *and bringeth him before great men."* **Proverbs 18:16**

**ACCEPTING BRIBES BRINGS UNHAPPINESS TO YOUR HOME!** *"He that is greedy of gain* (will accept a bribe) *troubleth his own house; but he that hateth gifts* (bribes) *shall live."* **Proverbs 15:27**

**EVIL PEOPLE BRIBE OTHERS TO GET WHATEVER THEY WANT!** *"A wicked man taketh a gift out of the bosom* (breast pocket) *to pervert the ways of judgement."* **Proverbs 17:23**

**THE PERSON WHO OFFERS AND GIVES YOU A BRIBE IS NOT YOUR FRIEND!** *"To have respect of persons is not good: for for a piece of bread that man will transgress* (break moral-civic laws)." **Proverbs 28:21**

**GIFTS EARNED DISHONESTLY DON'T ALWAYS MAKE THE PERSON WHO RECEIVES THEM HAPPY!** *"Surely oppression* (hard times, guilt) *maketh a wise man mad* (worried, scared); *and a gift destroyeth the heart* (conscience won't let you enjoy the gift, **bribe**)." **Ecclesiastes 7:7**

**Isaiah 33:15-16 says:** *"He that walketh righteously, and speaketh uprightly; he that despiseth the gain of oppressions* (oppressing the poor), *that shaketh his hands from holding of bribes, that stoppeth his ears from hearing of blood, and shutteth his eyes from seeing evil; He shall dwell on high* (with God); *his place of defence shall be the munitions of rocks: bread shall be given him; his waters shall be sure."*

**ACCEPTING BRIBES IS A SIN AGAINST YOURSELF, AGAINST THE OTHER PERSON AND AGAINST GOD!** *"For I know your transgressions* (sins) *are many and your sins are great, You who distress the righteous and accept bribes, and turn aside the poor in the gate* (at the door)." **Amos 5:12** (New American Standard Bible)

**OFFERING AND ACCEPTING BRIBES IS A CIVIL CRIME AND A CRIME AGAINST GOD'S LAWS!** *"Thou shalt not wrest* (buy-off) *judgement; thou shalt not respect persons, neither take a gift: for a gift doth blind the eyes of the wise, and pervert the words of the righteous."* **Deuteronomy 16:19**

**IF AN EVIL PERSON ACCEPTS A BRIBE TO KILL AN INNOCENT PERSON, GOD WILL PUT A CURSE ON HIM!** *"Cursed be he that taketh reward to slay an innocent person. And all the people shall say Amen* (yes, we agree)." **Deuteronomy 27:25**

**UNLESS A PERSON (WHO IS GUILTY OF GIVING AND RECEIVING BRIBES) REPENTS — HE WILL RECEIVE GOD'S JUDGEMENTS UPON HIM!** *"For the congregation of hypocrites shall be desolate, and fire shall consume the tabernacles* (places of business, churches, government, etc.) *of bribery."* **Job 15:34**

## PRAYER

Dear God in heaven, I know You have eyes and have seen and heard me offer and receive **bribes!** I knew it was wrong then, and I'm more aware that it is wrong, now! I ask You to forgive me. I repent of this sin. I pray You will forgive and forget just as You promise in Your Word. I will also forgive myself. I will not do business with those I've done this evil deed with, again! I will go about my business with peace, and the knowledge that I have received your forgiveness! I will not put myself in a position to lie, cheat or swear! I will cultivate new friends, who are godly! I will read my Bible. I will go to church! With Your help, and Your confidence in me, I will strive daily to be more like Jesus! I accept Your forgiveness. I praise You for loving me when I was so sinful! In Jesus' name. AMEN!

# BROKEN HEART

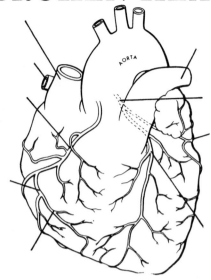

**DEAR FRIEND: FOR WHATEVER REASON YOUR HEART FEELS BROKEN, GOD KNOWS YOUR HURTS AND HE CARES FOR YOU!**

**Psalm 31:24** says: *"Be strong, and let your heart take courage, All you who hope in the Lord."* (New American Standard Bible)

*"The Lord is near to the brokenhearted, And saves those who are crushed in spirit."* **Psalm 34:18** (New American Standard Bible)

*"Reproach has broken my heart, and I am so sick. And I looked for sympathy, but there was none, and for comforters, but I found none."* **Psalm 69:20** (New American Standard Bible)

**PRAISE THE LORD! HE HEALS THE BROKEN-HEARTED!** *"He heals the brokenhearted, And binds up their wounds."* **Psalm 147:3** (New American Standard Bible)

**GOD HAS A GOOD MEMORY; HE WILL NOT LET THE PERSON WHO HAS BROKEN YOUR HEART GO UNPUNISHED!** *"Because he did not remember to show lovingkindness, but persecuted the afflicted and needy man (person), and the despondent in heart, to put them to death (which may bring on death)."* **Psalm 109:16** (New American Standard Bible)

**DAVID FELT SICK, NEEDY AND BROKEN-HEARTED . . . DO YOU FEEL LIKE DAVID???** *"For I am afflicted and needy, and my heart is wounded within me."* **Psalm 109:22** (New American Standard Bible)

*"The (Holy) Spirit of the Lord God is upon me, because the Lord has anointed me to bring good news to the afflicted; He has sent me to bind up the brokenhearted, to proclaim liberty to captives and freedom to prisoners."* **Isaiah 61:1** (New American Standard Bible)

Jesus said: *"The Spirit of the Lord is upon Me, Because He* (God) *anointed Me to preach the gospel to the poor. He* (God) *has sent Me* (Jesus) *to proclaim release to the captives, and recovery of sight to the blind, to set free those who are down-trodden, to proclaim the favorable year of the Lord* (when Jesus will return to earth the second time)." **Luke 4:18-29** (New American Standard Bible)

**YOU'VE HEARD THE OLD EXPRESSION . . . "PUT ON A HAPPY FACE" . . . WELL, IT CAME FROM THE BIBLE!** *"A joyful heart makes a cheerful face, but when the heart is said, the spirit is broken."* **Proverbs 15:13** (New American Standard Bible)

**HOW DO YOU KEEP FROM BREAKING SOMEONE'S HEART? . . . HOW DO YOU KEEP FROM GETTING YOUR OWN HEART BROKEN?** *"A gentle answer turns away wrath, but a harsh word stirs up anger."* **Proverbs 15:1** (New American Standard Bible)

**WHEN TEMPTED TO LASH BACK AT SOMEONE WHO HAS JUST OFFENDED YOU:** *"Stand in awe, and sin not: Commune with your own heart upon your bed, and be still."* **Psalm 4:4**

**HERE IS A VERSE YOU WILL NEED TO MEMORIZE! IT WILL GIVE YOU GREAT RESULTS:** *"Create in me a clean heart, O God; and renew a right spirit within me."* **Psalm 51:10**

**TAKE INVENTORY:** *"Search me, O God, and know my heart: Try me, and know my thoughts: And see if there be any wicked way in me, and lead me in the way everlasting."* **Psalm 139:23-24**

## PRAYER

Dear God, I am guilty on two charges! I have hurt others. I have caused them to feel **brokenhearted.** I have also had my feelings and pride, hurt so that I too became **broken-hearted!** In both cases I should have turned to You for the help, strength and courage I needed! Please forgive me for turning inward, when You were there all the time to help me! Please forgive me Lord, for those I have alienated through not controlling my tongue! And for not giving careful attention to the person's needs. Please forgive me for not running to You when my **heart was broken** by another! I know You are just a prayer away and that You love me! Please help me to remember that I have sinned, but that You are waiting lovingly, to forgive me! Please forgive me now! In Jesus' name. AMEN!

# BROKEN PROMISES

PROMISES START IN THE BRAIN — THEN GO DIRECTLY TO THE TONGUE — AND ON OUT THROUGH THE MOUTH. WOULDN'T IT BE A BLESSING AND SOLVE A LOT OF PROBLEMS IF PEOPLE THOUGHT LONG AND HARD BEFORE THEY MADE A PROMISE? MAYBE THEN, THERE'D BE NO BROKEN PROMISES!

Ecclesiastes 5:2-7 says: *"Be not rash with thy mouth, and let not thine heart be hasty to utter any thing before God: for God is in heaven, and thou upon earth: therefore let thy words be few. For a dream cometh through the multitude of business; and a fool's voice is known by multitude of words. When thou vowest a vow* (swear to keep a promise) *unto God, defer not to pay it; for he* (God) *hath no pleasure in fools: pay that which thou has vowed* (promised). *Better is it that thou shouldest not vow* (promise), *than that thou shouldest vow and not pay* (break your promise). *Suffer not* (don't allow) *thy mouth to cause thy flesh to sin; neither say thou before the angel, that it was an error: wherefore should God be angry at thy voice, and destroy the work of thine hands? For in the multitude of dreams and many words there are also divers* (various) *vanities* (desires of ego) *but fear thou God."*

JUST BECAUSE SOMEONE HAS BROKEN A PRO-MISE TO YOU DOES NOT GIVE YOU LICENSE TO BREAK A PROMISE! *"Be of the same mind one toward another. Mind not high things, but condescend to men of low estate. Be not wise in your own conceits. Recompense to no man evil for evil. Provide things honest in the sight of all men. If it be possible, as much as lieth in you, live peaceably with all men. Dearly beloved, avenge not yourselves, but rather give place unto wrath; for it is written, Vengeance is mine; I will repay, saith the Lord. Therefore if thine enemy hunger, feed him; if he thirst, give him drink: for in so doing thou shalt heap coals of fire on his head. Be not overcome of evil, but overcome evil with good."* **Romans 12:16-21**

WHAT CAN WE DO ABOUT A PERSON WHO CON-STANTLY MAKES PROMISES AND THEN BREAKS THEM?? PRAY WITHOUT CEASING FOR THAT PERSON! RECRUIT THE PRAYER CHAIN IN YOUR CHURCH TO PRAY FOR THAT PERSON! FIND COMFORT IN THOSE VERSES OF SCRIPTURE WHICH BRING YOU CLOSER TO GOD! *". . .If God be for us, who can be against us?"* **Romans 8:31**

WHEN YOUR CLOSEST FAMILY MEMBER BREAKS A PROMISE TO YOU, JUST REMEMBER THAT GOD IS THE ONE WHO WILL STICK BY US NO MATTER WHAT SITUATION PREVAILS! *"A man that finds friends must shew himself friendly: and there is a friend that sticket closer than a brother* (and that is Jesus Christ)." **Pro-verbs 18:24**

## PRAYER

Dear God, I am guilty of making **promises** and then **break-ing** them! I don't know why I do this, but I frequently do! Please forgive me and help me! I have lost many friends because of this terrible habit. I have turned my family away from me because of this, also! I can't even respect myself for what I have done. What a terrible world this would be if You were like me! I know I can put my trust in You! **I know You can't lie!** That's what I've been doing! Please help me con-trol this tendency. Help me to restore lost friendships. Create in me a person who can be trusted, and loved, for my good qualities! Please change my image! I will do my part! I will put a "brake" on my tongue, so that I am careful what I say! Come into my life and make me a better person. In Jesus' name, I pray. AMEN!

# BURDENS

*"FOR ALL THE LAW IS FULFILLED IN ONE WORD, EVEN IN THIS; THOU SHALL LOVE THY NEIGHBOR AS THYSELF."* **Galatians 5:14**

IF YOU KNOW A PERSON WHO IS "LOADED-DOWN" WITH BURDENS, HERE'S WHAT YOU SHOULD DO! *"Bear ye one another's burdens, and so fulfill the law of Christ."* **Galatians 6:2**

WHERE DO BURDENS NORMALLY COME FROM? MOST OFTEN A PERSON BRINGS THEM UPON HIMSELF! *"For every man shall bear his own burden."* **Galatians 6:5** This means that even when a person wants to help you carry your load, you must do everything in your power to overcome your **burden** in the way that God would have you do!

PERSONS IN POSITIONS OF LEGAL AUTHORITY OFTEN PUT BURDENS ON MAN THAT ARE EXTREMELY DIFFICULT TO BEAR . . . AS IN COURTS OF LAW! Jesus said: *"Woe unto you also, ye lawyers! for ye lade* (load-down) *men with burdens grievous to be borne* (difficult to carry out), *and ye yourselves touch not the burdens with one of your fingers."* **Luke 11:46**

HOW CAN A PERSON GET OUT FROM UNDER A HEAVY BURDEN? *"Cast thy burden upon the Lord, and he shall sustain thee: he* (God) *shall never suffer* (allow) *the righteous to be moved."* **Psalm 55:22**

GOD WILL TAKE THE LOAD OFF YOUR SHOULDERS AND BACK — IF YOU OBEY HIS COMMANDMENTS — ASK HIM FOR STRENGTH — PRAISE HIM — AND WALK IN HIS WILL FOR YOUR LIFE! *"For thou* (God) *hast broken the yoke of his* (your) *burden, and the staff of his shoulder,* (and) *the rod of his oppressor. . ."* **Isaiah 9:4** Here's another Scripture that promises God will see you through the load of **burdens** you're carrying. God will never desert you!

**Isaiah 10:27 says:** *"And it shall come to pass in that day, that his* (your) *burden shall be taken away from off thy shoulder, and his yoke from off thy neck, and the yoke shall be destroyed because of the anointing."*

GOD'S PLAN = EQUALITY AMONG ALL! GOD DOESN'T WANT ANYONE TO BURDEN ANOTHER PERSON. GOD DOESN'T WANT YOU TO BE A BURDEN TO ANYONE, EITHER! *"Of course, I don't mean that those who receive your gifts should have an easy time of it at your expense* (making themselves **burdensome**), *but you should divide with them. Right now you have plenty and can help them; then at some other time they can share with you when you need it. In this way each will have as much as he needs."* **2 Corinthians 8:13-14** (The Living Bible)

MANY PEOPLE (FALSELY) BELIEVE GOD HAS PUT A HEAVY BURDEN, SICKNESS, OR TRIAL, ON THEM — IN ORDER TO TRY (TEST) THEIR FAITH! THEY BELIEVE WRONG! *"Let no man say when he is tempted* (or **burdened**), *I am tempted of God: for God cannot be tempted with evil, neither tempteth he any man: But every man is tempted, when he is drawn away of his own lust* (backslides), *and enticed. Then when lust hath conceived, it bringeth forth sin: and sin, when it is finished, bringeth forth death* (eternal separation from God)." **James 1:13-15**

### PRAYER

Dear God, I have a **burden** on my heart, but I know I am not alone! I know You are there just waiting for me to have enough faith to call on You, for help! I need Your help! I am weak! I feel lonely! I feel unloved and unloveable! I have no other direction in which I can turn! Please come into my heart and help me. Please forgive me if I have done things which brought **burdens** upon myself. Please forgive me if I have been a **burden** to others! Please help me to walk hand in hand with You, and to look only to You for my strength! Please bring me some happiness! Please help me overcome my problems, both the big ones, and the smaller ones! Please help me to remember not to look to others for comfort, but to come straight to You through prayer! Rather than dwelling on my problems I will pray and read my Bible. I know You will be in the room with me! I thank You in advance for an answer to my prayer! I claim the victory over my **burdens**! In Jesus' name I pray. AMEN!

# BUSYBODY

**A CHRISTIAN IS COMMANDED BY GOD NOT TO BE A BUSYBODY!** *"But let none of you suffer* (be found guilty) *as a murderer, or as a thief, or as an evildoer, or as a busybody in other men's matters."* **1 Peter 4:15**

**GOD WROTE FAIR AND JUST RULES FOR CHRISTIAN CONDUCT! GOD SAYS IDLENESS PROMOTES A PERSON TO BECOME A BUSYBODY!** *"And withal they learn to be idle, wandering about from house to house; and not only idle, but tattlers also and busybodies, speaking things which they* (we) *ought not* (to speak)." **1 Timothy 5:13**

**BUSYBODIES ARE USUALLY PEOPLE WHO DO NOT WORK! THEY ARE IDLE ... AND ... IDLENESS HAS ALWAYS BEEN THE DEVIL'S WORKSHOP!** *"For we hear that there are some which walk among you disorderly, working not at all, but are busybodies: Now them that are such* (disorderly, **busybodies**) *we command and exhort* (warn, advise) *by our Lord Jesus Christ, that with quietness they work, and eat their own bread."* **2 Thessalonians 3:11-12**

**A BUSYBODY WHO SPREADS WHAT HE HEARS IS A FOOL!** *"The lips of the righteous feed many: but fools die for want of wisdom."* **Proverbs 10:21** *"Wise men lay up knowledge: but the mouth of the foolish is near destruction."* **Proverbs 10:14**

**A GOOD RULE TO FOLLOW: LET YOUR SPEECH BE BETTER THAN SILENCE! OTHERWISE, BE SILENT!**

**DEATH AND LIFE ARE IN THE POWER OF THE TONGUE!** *"Death and life are in the power of the tongue: and they that love it shall eat the fruit thereof."* **Proverbs 18:21**

**BUSYBODIES ... "DO YOU REMEMBER THE GOLDEN RULE"? IT GOES LIKE THIS:** (Jesus speaking) *"Therefore all things whatsoever ye would that men should do to you, do ye even so to them: for this is the law and the prophets."* **Matthew 7:12**

**WOULD YOU WANT PEOPLE TO GET INTO YOUR PERSONAL BUSINESS AND REPEAT ANYTHING YOU MIGHT NOT WANT REPEATED? THEN MEMORIZE THAT VERSE AND LIVE BY IT!**

**IF A BUSYBODY HAS DONE YOU AN INJUSTICE, FIRST: FORGIVE HIM WHETHER HE ASKS YOU TO OR NOT! SECOND: PRAY FOR HIM AND LOVE HIM, ANYWAY! YOUR LOVING AND FORGIVING EXAMPLE MAY LEAD HIM TO THE LORD, IF HE IS A SINNER. YOUR GENTLENESS MAY LEAD HIM TO RETURN TO THE LORD IF HE IS A BACKSLIDER!** Jesus said: *"But if ye do not forgive, neither will your Father which is in heaven forgive your trespasses* (sins)." **Mark 11:26**

**HOW MANY TIMES SHOULD WE FORGIVE?** *"Then came Peter to him* (Jesus) *and said, Lord, how oft* (often) *shall my brother sin against me, and I forgive him? till seven times? Jesus saith unto him, I say not unto thee, Until seven times: but, Until 70 times seven."* **Matthew 18:21-22**

**GOD'S ADVICE TO THE BUSYBODY:** *"Whether therefore ye eat, or drink, or whatsoever ye do, do all to the glory of God."* **1 Corinthians 10:31**

**BUSYBODY, "BE CAREFUL WHAT YOU HEAR AND SAY"!** *". . . Take heed what ye hear: with what measure ye mete* (repeat what you heard), *it shall be measured* (out) *to you. . ."* **Mark 4:24**

**HERE IS A GOOD VERSE FOR THE BUSYBODY TO MEMORIZE:** *"Let the words of my mouth, and the meditation of my heart, be acceptable in thy sight, O Lord, my strength, and my redeemer."* **Psalm 19:14**

### PRAYER

Dear God, I admit I am a **busybody!** I am so ashamed! I want to quit this evil habit! I ask You to forgive me. I ask You to help me mind my own business! I know my tongue has gotten me into a lot of trouble. Remind me when I start to ask questions and gossip that I should be repeating Scriptures, instead! Give me wisdom to mind my own affairs! Teach me to control my curiosity and my tongue! In Jesus' name I pray. AMEN!

# CAPITAL PUNISHMENT

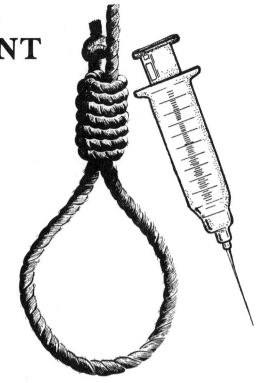

**MAN REAPS WHAT HE SOWS. THIS IS GOD'S LAW OF RECIPROCITY!** *"Be not deceived; God is not mocked: for whatsoever a man soweth, that shall he also reap. For he that soweth to his flesh* (sinful nature, actions) *shall of the flesh reap corruption; but he that soweth to the* (Holy) *Spirit shall of the* (Holy) *Spirit reap life everlasting."* **Galatians 6:7-8**

GOD ESTABLISHED A SYSTEM OF **"LAW AND ORDER"** TO PROTECT THE RIGHTEOUS MAN! GOD NEVER WANTED MAN TO SIN OR TO HAVE TO BE PUNISHED! EVER SINCE THE FALL OF ADAM GOD HAS FOUND IT NECESSARY TO PUNISH SIN SO RIGHTEOUS PEOPLE COULD DWELL UPON THE EARTH IN PEACE AND SAFETY!

GOD CREATED HUMAN GOVERNMENT! *"Let every soul be subject unto the higher powers* (human government). *For there is no power but* (is ordained) *of God: the powers that be are ordained of God. Whosoever therefore resisteth the power, resisteth the ordinance of God: and they that resist shall receive to themselves damnation. For rulers are not a terror to good works, but to the evil. Wilt thou then not be afraid of the power? do that which is good, and thou shalt have praise of the same: For he* (rulers of human government) *is the minister of God to thee for* (your) *good. But if thou do that which is evil, be afraid; for he* (rulers) *beareth not the sword in vain; for he is the minister of God, a revenger to execute wrath upon him that doeth evil. Wherefore ye must needs be subject, not only for wrath* (punishment that you will receive if you break God's laws and the laws of human government), *but also for conscience sake."* **Romans 13:1-5** *"For this, Thou shalt not commit adultery, Thou shalt not kill, Thou shalt not steal, Thou shalt not bear false witness, Thou shalt not covet; and if there be any other commandment, it is briefly comprehended in this saying, namely, Thou shalt love thy neighbour as thyself. Love worketh no ill to his neighbour: therefore love is the fulfilling of the law."* **Romans 13:9-10** *"Whosoever committeth sin transgresseth also the law: for sin is the transgression of the law."* **1 John 3:4** *"He that committeth sin is of the devil: for the devil sinneth from the beginning. For this purpose the Son of God* (Jesus) *was manifested, that he might destroy the works of the devil. Whosoever is born of God doth not commit sin; for his seed remaineth in him: and he cannot sin, because he is born of God."* **1 John 3:8-9**

*"GOD JUDGETH THE RIGHTEOUS, AND GOD IS ANGRY WITH THE WICKED EVERY DAY. IF HE TURN NOT, HE WILL WHET HIS SWORD; HE HATH BENT HIS BOW, AND MADE IT READY. HE HATH ALSO PREPARED FOR HIM THE INSTRUMENTS OF DEATH; HE ORDAINETH HIS ARROWS AGAINST THE PERSECUTORS. BEHOLD, HE TRAVAILETH WITH INIQUITY, AND HATH CONCEIVED MISCHIEF, AND BROUGHT FORTH FALSEHOOD. HE MADE A PIT, AND DIGGED IT, AND IS FALLEN INTO THE DITCH WHICH HE MADE. HIS MISCHIEF SHALL RETURN UPON HIS OWN HEAD, AND HIS VIOLENT DEALING SHALL COME DOWN UPON HIS OWN PATE* (SKULL)." **Psalm 7:11-16**

**BECAUSE OF MAN'S SINFUL NATURE AND DISOBEDIENCE TO GOD AND HUMAN GOVERNMENT, GOD CREATED CAPITAL PUNISHMENT! IF YOU SIN, STOP NOW AND ASK FORGIVENESS BECAUSE SIN DOES NOT PAY!** *"Because sentence against an evil work is not executed speedily, therefore the heart of the sons of men is fully set in them to do evil. Though a sinner do evil an hundred times, and his days be prolonged, yet surely I know that it shall be well with them that fear God, which fear before him: But it shall not be well with the wicked, neither shall he prolong his days, which are as a shadow; because he feareth not before God."* **Ecclesiastes 8:11-13**

**GOD REALIZED THE NEED FOR CAPITAL PUNISHMENT:** *"Whoso sheddeth man's blood, by man shall his blood be shed: for in the image of God made he man."* **Genesis 9:6**

**FOR THIS PURPOSE GOD ESTABLISHED THE LOWER COURT SYSTEM!** *"Judges and officers shalt thou make thee in all thy gates* (towns, cities, counties, states), *which the Lord thy God giveth thee, throughout thy tribes* (in all nations): *and they shall judge the people with just judgment."* **Deuteronomy 16:18**

**GOD ESTABLISHED THE SUPREME COURT!** *"And thou shalt teach them ordinances and laws, and shalt shew* (show) *them the way wherein they must walk, and the work that they must do. Moreover thou shalt provide out of all the people able men, such as fear God, men of truth, hating covetousness; and place such over them, to be rulers of thousands, and rulers of hundreds, rulers of fifties, and rulers of tens: And let them judge the people at all seasons: and it shall be, that every great matter they shall bring unto thee, but every small matter they shall judge: so shall it be easier for thyself, and they shall bear the burden with thee. If thou shalt do this thing, and God command thee so, then thou shalt be able to endure, and all this people shall also go to their place in peace."* **Exodus 18:20-23**

**GOD COMMANDED JUDGMENT BE OPEN AND FAIR!** *"Thou shalt **not wrest judgment**; thou shalt **not respect persons**, **neither take a gift*** (bribe): *for a gift* (bribe) *doth blind the eyes of the wise, and **pervert the words** of the righteous."* **Deuteronomy 16:19**

**BY THE SPOKEN COMMANDMENT OF GOD—NO PERSON IS TO BE CONVICTED WITHOUT THE WITNESS OF TWO-THREE PERSONS!** *"At the mouth of two witnesses, or three witnesses, shall he that is worthy of death be put to death; but at the mouth of one witness he shall not be put to death. The hands of the witnesses shall be first upon him to put him to death, and afterward the hands of all the people. So thou shalt put the evil away from among you."* **Deuteronomy 17:6-7**

**LET JUDGMENT BE EXECUTED SPEEDILY!** *"And whosoever will not do the law of thy God, and the law of the king* (human government), *let judgment be executed speedily upon him, whether it be unto death, or to banishment, or to confiscation of goods, or to imprisonment."* **Ezra 7:26**

(Continued)

**GOD ALLOWS CAPITAL PUNISHMENT IN ORDER TO CLEANSE THE LAND FROM EVIL PEOPLE!** *"Whoso killeth any person, the murderer shall be put to death by the mouth of witnesses: but one witness shall not testify against any person to cause him to die. Morever ye shall take no satisfaction for the life of a murderer, which is guilty of death: but he shall be surely put to death."* **Numbers 35:30-31** *"One witness shall not rise up against a man for any iniquity* (wrong doing), *or for any sin, in any sin that he sinneth: at the mouth of two witnesses, or at the mouth of three witnesses, shall the matter be established."* **Deuteronomy 19:15/Matthew 18:16/2 Corinthians 13:1/1 Timothy 5:19/Hebrews 10:28**

# Capital Punishment

# It's a Life -or-Death Question

Christ bore our sins on the cross because He loves us, and because He knew mortal man could do nothing to save himself! The Bible says all men have sinned from the very beginning and need to ask for forgiveness. **Capital punishment was created to protect the righteous person from the wilful lawbreaker.** God gives both blessings and curses. Blessings are available to those who love and obey His commandments, and curses are available for those who willfully reject Him by breaking His laws, and the laws of human government! Read: **Galatians 3:13** *"And if a man have committed a sin worthy of death, and he be to be put to death, and thou hang him on a tree: his body shall not remain all night upon the tree, but thou shalt in any wise bury him that day; (for he that is hanged is accursed of God); that thy land be not defiled, which the Lord thy God giveth thee for an inheritance."* **Deuteronomy 21:22-23**

**Jesus said:** *"The thief* (Satan) *cometh not (to earth), but for to steal, and to kill, and to destroy: I am come that they might have life, and that they might have it more abundantly."* **John 10:10**

**EVERY PERSON SPENDS ETERNITY EITHER WITH GOD OR SATAN! EACH PERSON CHOOSES HIS OWN DESTINY WHILE HE LIVES IN HIS PHYSICAL BODY. AFTER HE DIES HE NO LONGER HAS THE PRIVILEGE OR RIGHT TO CHOOSE. WHY NOT CHOOSE TO LIVE FOR GOD? HE LOVES YOU AND CREATED YOU IN HIS OWN IMAGE. HE LONGS TO SPEND ETERNITY WITH YOU IN PEACE, LOVE AND COMPANIONSHIP!**

*"But we know that **the law is good,** if a man use it lawfully; knowing this, that the law is not made for a righteous man, but for the lawless and disobedient, for the ungodly and for sinners, for unholy and profane, for murderers of fathers and murderers of mothers, for manslayers, for whoremongers, for them that defile themselves with mankind, for menstealers, for liars, for perjured persons, and if there be any other thing that is contrary to sound doctrine."* **1 Timothy 1:8-10**

**PRAYER**

Dear God, Please forgive me for all my sins. I repent of my sins and ask you to come into my life to live. I know that if I died this day I would not go to heaven. I know that I want to spend eternity with You. I am so sorry for my sins. I turn away from all sinful activity in my life. Please let me feel Your presence. Become a part of my thoughts all through the day and night. I will study the scriptures and pray for wisdom to know Your will for my life. I love You because You first loved me. In Jesus' name, I pray. AMEN!

# CARNAL MIND

**DEFINITION:** Marked by sexuality; given to crude bodily pleasures; temporal, wordly, sensual, fleshly, self-gratification of bodily desires, pleasures, appetites, intellect; physical rather than godly; spiritual desires of lust.

**Romans 8:6-8 says:** *"For to be carnally minded is death; but to be spiritually minded is life and peace. Because the carnal mind is enmity against God: for it is not subject to the law of God, neither indeed can be. So then they that are in the flesh cannot please God."*

**DOES THIS VERSE DESCRIBE YOU?** *"For we know that the law is spiritual: but I am carnal, sold under* (sold out to) *sin."* **Romans 7:14** *"For I know that in me* (that is, in my flesh) *dwelleth no good thing: for to will* (desire to do good) *is present with me; but how to perform that which is good I find not* (the courage to do)." **Romans 7:18**

**DO YOU NEED A WEAPON TO FIGHT AGAINST BEING CARNALLY MINDED? GOD OFFERS YOU ALL THE WEAPONS YOU'LL EVER NEED WHEN YOU BECOME A BORN-AGAIN CHRISTIAN!** *"For the weapons of our warfare are not* **carnal** *(flesh and blood), but mighty through God to the pulling down of strongholds* (ego, lust, sin, etc.); *Casting down imaginations* (evil thoughts, sex sins, occult theories, etc.), *and every high thing* (intellect, etc.) *that exalteth itself against the knowledge* (truth) *of God, and bringing into captivity every thought to the obedience of Christ."* **2 Corinthians 10:4-5**

**ALL SEX SINS FALL INTO THE CATEGORY OF CARNALITY!** *"Moreover thou shalt not lie* **carnally** *with thy neighbour's wife, to defile thyself with her."* **Leviticus 18:20** *"And whosoever lieth* **carnally** *with a woman, that is a bondmaid* (servant), *betrothed* (engaged) *to an husband, and not at all redeemed* (married), *nor freedom given her; she shall be scourged* (punished); *they shall not be put to death, because she was not free."* **Leviticus 19:20** *"And a man lie with her* **carnally,** *and it be hid from the eyes of her husband* (not known to him), *and be kept close* (secret), *and she be defiled, and there be not witness against her, neither she be taken with the manner;"* **Numbers 5:13**

**THE CARNAL MAN'S GREATEST DESIRE IS TO BE "FIRST" IN IMPORTANCE AMONG PEOPLE!** Even the disciples experienced this **carnal desire.** Read Mark 9:33/Luke 9:46/Luke 22:24/Matthew 20:20-23.

**TO HAVE AN "EGO PROBLEM" IS TO BE CARNALLY MINDED!** *"For if a man think himself to be something, when he is nothing, he deceiveth himself."* **Galatians 6:3/Romans 12:3**

**HOW CAN A PERSON KEEP FROM BEING CARNALLY MINDED? WALK IN THE SPIRIT OF GOD!** *"This I say then, Walk in the Spirit, and ye shall not fulfil the* **lust of the flesh.** *For the flesh lusteth against the Spirit, and the Spirit against the flesh: and these are contrary the one to the other: so that ye cannot do the things that ye would* (should). *But if ye be led of the Spirit, ye are under the law. Now the works of the flesh are manifest, which are these:* **Adultery, fornication, uncleanness, lasciviousness, Idolatry, witchcraft, hatred, variance, emulations, wrath, strife, seditions, heresies, envyings, murders, drunkenness, revellings, and such like:** *of the which I tell you before, as I have also told you in time past, that* **they which do such things shall not inherit the kingdom of God.** *But the fruit of the Spirit is love, joy, peace, longsuffering, gentleness, goodness, faith, meekness, temperance: against such there is no law."* **Galatians 5:16-23** *"If we live in the* (Holy) *Spirit, let us also walk in the Spirit. Let us not be desirous of vain glory* (ego), *provoking one another, envying one another."* **Galatians 5:25-26**

*"Lay hands suddenly on no man, neither be partaker of other men's sins: keep thyself pure."* 1 Timothy 5:22

**PRAYER**

Dear God, please forgive me for being **carnally minded.** I have been **jealous.** I have **envied** other people. I have **committed sex sins.** I have felt **hatred.** I have believed in **occult teachings.** I have enjoyed movies and TV which sexually excited me. Please forgive all my sins! Help me be a new person in Your eyes and in the eyes of the world! Teach me love and patience! Teach me not to glory in my own body, friends, job, looks, talents or intellect! Let my rely on You totally for my wisdom and peace of mind! I want to be a better person! I want to be a Christian! Thank You for waking me up about the way I was conducting my life! In Jesus' name, I pray. AMEN!

48

# CHEATING

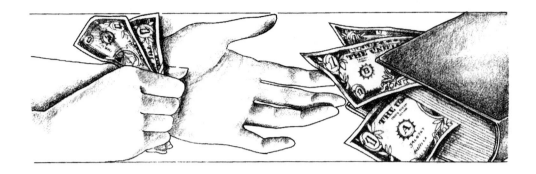

**THERE ARE MANY KINDS OF CHEATING. ALL CHEATING IS SINFUL!**

**GOD WROTE LAWS AGAINST CHEATING IN BUSINESS ... AGAINST KEEPING 2 SETS OF BOOKS AND SEPARATE PRICE LISTS FOR PREFERRED CUSTOMERS, OR IN ORDER TO CHEAT ON TAXES, ETC.** *"Thou shalt not have in thy bag divers* (various) *weights, a great and a small* (large and small). *Thou shalt not have in thine house* (or business) *divers measures, a great and a small. But thou shalt have a perfect and just weight, a perfect and just measure shalt thou have: that thy days may be lengthened in the land which the Lord thy God giveth thee. For all that do such* (dishonest) *things, and all that they do unrighteously, are an abomination unto the Lord thy God."* **Deuteronomy 25:13-16**

**HERE IS GOD'S ABSOLUTE LAW WRITTEN AGAINST CHEATING!** *"Ye shall not steal, neither deal falsely, neither lie one to another. And ye shall not swear by my name falsely, neither shalt thou profane the name of thy God: I am the Lord."* **Leviticus 19:11-12**

**GOD COMMANDED US TO USE ACCURATE MEASUREMENTS AND IMPARTIAL JUDGEMENTS TOWARD ALL:** *"You must be impartial in judgement. Use accurate measurements — lengths, weights, and volumes — and give full measure, for I am Jehovah your God ..."* **Leviticus 19:35-36** (The Living Bible)

**CHILDREN ARE COMMANDED BY GOD TO BE HONEST!** *"Even a child is known by his doings, whether his work be pure, and whether it be right."* **Proverbs 20:11**

**LYING SCALES, WEIGHTS, PAPERS, BALANCES ... GOD HATES!** *"Divers weights are an abomination unto the Lord; and a false balance is not good."* **Proverbs 20:23**

**GOD WILL BLESS YOUR BUSINESS IF YOU ARE HONEST!** *"Seest thou a man diligent in his business? he shall stand before kings; he shall not stand before mean men."* **Proverbs 22:29**

**IF A PERSON CHEATS YOU, DO NOT CHEAT HIM BACK!** *"Recompense to no man evil for evil. Provide things honest in the sight of all men. If it be possible, as much as lieth in you, live peaceably with all men."* **Romans 12:17-18**

**A PERSON WHO GETS RICH BY CHEATING OTHERS IS NEVER HAPPY WITH HIS RICHES!** *"For your sins are very great — is there to be no end of getting rich by* **cheating**? *The homes of the wicked are full of ungodly treasures and lying scales. Shall I say "Good"! to all your merchants with their bags of false, deceitful weights? How could God be just while saying that? Your rich men are wealthy through extortion and violence; your citizens are so used to lying that their tongues can't tell the truth! Therefore I will wound you! I will make your hearts miserable for all your sins. You will eat but never have enough; hunger pangs and emptiness will still remain. And though you try and try to save your money, it will come to nothing at the end, and what little you succeed in storing up, I'll give to those who conquer you!"* **Micah 6:10-14** (The Living Bible)

**CHEATERS EVENTUALLY BECOME POOR!** *"He becometh poor that dealeth with a slack hand: but the hand of the diligent maketh rich!"* **Proverbs 10:4**

**IT'S BETTER NOT TO HAVE VERY MUCH AND BE HONEST THAN TO BE RICH AND DISHONEST!** *"Better is a little with righteousness than great revenues* (money, assets) *without right* (honesty)." **Proverbs 16:8**

**IF A PERSON CHEATS YOU ... DON'T JUDGE HIM! FORGIVE HIM!** Jesus said: *"Judge not, and ye shall not be judged: condemn not, and ye shall not be condemned: forgive, and ye shall be forgiven."* **Luke 6:37**

**IF YOU CHEAT ... YOU WILL GET CHEATED IN RETURN! IF YOU ARE HONEST, MUCH GAIN WILL COME YOUR WAY ... (IF) YOU GIVE TO THE LORD!** Jesus said: *"Give, and it shall be given unto you; good measure, pressed down and shaken together, and running over, shall men give into your bosom. For with the same measure that ye mete* (measure, give) *withal it shall be measured to you again."* **Luke 6:38**

**GOD LOVES HONEST PEOPLE!** *"A false balance is abomination to the Lord: but a just weight is his delight."* **Proverbs 11:1**

**CHEATERS SET THEIR OWN TRAPS!** *"The righteousness of the perfect shall direct his way: but the wicked shall fall by his own wickedness."* **Proverbs 11:5**

**CHEATERS: HERE'S HOW YOU CAN OVERCOME YOUR CHEATING HABIT. HANDLE ALL MATTERS HONESTLY AND TRUST IN THE LORD FOR DIRECTION!** *"He that handleth a matter wisely shall find good: and whoso trusteth in the Lord, happy is he."* **Proverbs 16:20**

**AS YOU KNOW, THERE ARE CHEATERS IN MARRIAGE, CHEATERS IN SCHOOL, CHEATERS ON THE JOB, ETC., AND GOD SAYS ALL CHEATING IS SIN!**

## PRAYER

Dear God, I have **cheated** in every area of my life, it seems! The list would fill up a book! I ask You to forgive me for **cheating** in all areas of my life. I especially ask You to forgive me for **cheating** You. Your commandment says, "thou shalt not steal," and I have stolen from You by not obeying and doing the things You asked me to do! Please forgive me for all my sins. I will apologize to those I have **cheated** and will ask forgiveness of all whose names come to my mind. Now that I am saved, I turn away from this sin! AMEN!

# CHILD ABUSE

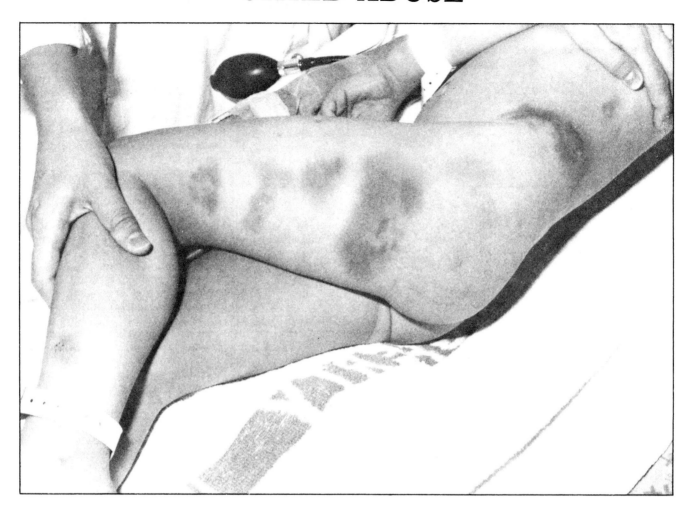

**CHILDREN ARE A BLESSING GIVEN US BY GOD!** Jesus said: *"And whoso shall receive one such little child in my name receiveth me."* **Matthew 18:5**

**IF ANYONE OFFENDS AND ABUSES A CHILD HE WILL BE PUNISHED BY GOD!** Jesus said: *"But whoso shall offend* (or abuse) *one of these little ones which believe in me, it were* (would be) *better for him that a millstone were hanged about his neck, and that he were drowned in the depth of the sea."* **Matthew 18:6 and Mark 9:42**

**NEVER DESPISE A LITTLE CHILD! GOD LOVES THEM SO MUCH HE ASSIGNS ANGELS OVER THEM!** Jesus said: *"Take heed* (be advised) *that ye despise not one of these little ones; for I say unto you, That in heaven their angels do always behold* (see) *the face of my Father* (God) *which is in Heaven."* **Matthew 18:10**

**IT IS NEVER GOD'S WILL THAT A LITTLE CHILD SHOULD DIE!** Jesus said: *"Even so it is not the will of your Father which is in heaven, that one of these little ones should perish."* **Matthew 18:14**

**NEVER FORBID A CHILD TO GO TO CHURCH OR BECOME A CHRISTIAN!** Jesus said: *"Suffer* (allow) *little children, and forbid them not, to come unto me: for of such is the kingdom of heaven."* **Matthew 19:14 and Mark 10:14**

**WHEN YOU ARE KIND AND GOOD TO A LITTLE CHILD, YOU ARE ACTUALLY BEING GOOD TO JESUS!** *"And he* (Jesus) *took a child; and set him in the midst of them: and when he had taken him in his* (Christ's) *arms, he said unto them* (disciples), *Whosoever shall receive one of such children in my name, receiveth me: and whosoever shall receive me, receiveth not me, but him* (God) *that sent me."* **Mark 9:36-37**

**WHO IS REALLY RESPONSIBLE FOR CHILD ABUSE? SATAN!!!**

**NOTE TO THE CHILD ABUSER:** You need to become a born-again Christian, now! Humble yourself on your knees. Repent and tell God what you've done. Ask Him to forgive you and mean it with all your heart! Believe God will forgive you. Go and sin no more. **Next,** go to church regularly. Join the church and be baptised. Support your church with your tithe and with your time. Pray all the time! Read your Bible! Live a Christian life in everything you say and do!

**UNDER NO CIRCUMSTANCE DOES GOD GIVE US PERMISSION TO TAKE THE LAW IN OUR OWN HANDS!** *"Recompense to no man evil for evil. Provide things honest in the sight of all men. If it be possible, as much as lieth in you, live peaceable with all men. Dearly beloved, avenge not yourselves, but rather give place unto wrath: for it is written, Vengeance is mine; I will repay, saith the Lord."* **Romans 12:17-19**

### PRAYER

Dear God, You know I am guilty of **child abuse!** I repent of this terrible crime against a child, against myself, and against You! Please forgive me. I will not commit this sin ever again. Teach me to forgive myself. Teach me to love little children. Teach me patience. Teach me to control my thoughts and anger! I will go to church! I will pray for myself and others! I will become a born-again Christian! I will work and mind my own business! I will read my Bible every spare moment when I'm not working or asleep! I know You love me and can forgive me! I accept Your forgiveness! In Jesus' name, I thank You! and I receive You as my Lord, my master, and my saviour! AMEN!

# CHILD MOLESTERS

**CHILD MOLESTERS WILL NOT INHERIT THE KINGDOM OF GOD UNLESS THEY REPENT AND RECEIVE FORGIVENESS!** *"Know ye not that the unrighteous shall not inherit the kingdom of God? Be not deceived: neither fornicators, nor idolaters, nor adulterers, nor effeminate, nor* **ABUSERS OF THEMSELVES WITH MANKIND** (grownups or children), *nor thieves, nor covetous, nor drunkards, nor revilers, nor extortioners, shall inherit the kingdom of God."* **1 Corinthians 6:9-10**

**CHILD MOLESTERS CAN BE FORGIVEN IF THEY TRUTHFULLY REPENT AND ASK FORGIVENESS!** *"And such were some of you: but ye are washed, but ye are sanctified, but ye are justified in the name of the Lord Jesus, and by the* (Holy) *Spirit of our God."* **1 Corinthians 6:11**

**PARENTS: TEACH YOUR CHILDREN NOT TO TAKE CANDY FROM STRANGERS!** Whether a person exposes himself, fondles a child, or commits rape, the psychological damage may greatly depend on how you, the parent, react! The same holds true for teachers, relatives, counselors, and ministers. *"Little children, let no man deceive you: he that doeth righteousness is righteous, even as he* (Jesus) *is righteous. He that committeth sin is of the devil; for the devil sinneth from the beginning. For this purpose the Son of God was manifested, that he might destroy the works of the devil. Whosoever is born of God doth not commit sin; for his seed remaineth in him: and he cannot sin, because he is born of God. In this the children of God are manifest, and the children of the devil* (child abusers, sex offenders): *whosoever doeth not righteousness* (sins) *is not of God, neither he that loveth not his brother* (any person)." **1 John 3:7-10**

**THE PERSON WHO MOLESTS INNOCENT CHILDREN MAY BE MALE OR FEMALE; MARRIED OR UNMARRIED; OVERSEXED OR SEXUALLY FRUSTRATED! STATISTICS TELL US THAT ATTEMPTS TO HAVE SEX WITH CHILDREN IS USUALLY MOTIVATED BY LACK OF SELF-ESTEEM IN THE OFFENDER!** Jesus said: *"The thief* (Satan) *cometh not, but for to steal, and to kill, and to destroy: I* (Christ) *am come that they* (me, you) *might have life, and that they might have it more abundantly."* **John 10:10**

**SEX OFFENDERS MAY NOT SHOW OBVIOUS SYMPTOMS OF BEING MENTALLY DISTURBED! THEY MAY, IN FACT, COMPARE IN INTELLIGENCE TESTS WITH THE MOST NORMAL PERSON!** *"Let the wicked forsake his way, and the unrighteous man his thoughts: and let him return unto the Lord, and he* (God) *will have mercy upon him, and to our God, for he will abundantly pardon."* **Isaiah 55:7**

**PARENTS SHOULD BE EXTREMELY CAUTIOUS ABOUT LEAVING A CHILD ALONE OR WITH ANYONE!** Be cautious of boy babysitters who have no friends their own age and who prefer the company of younger children, for instance!

**HOW CAN A PARENT TEACH A CHILD ABOUT A POTENTIAL CHILD ABUSER, KIDNAPPER, SEX OFFENDER, ETC,?** **1.** Tell them not to open the door to any stranger. **2.** Tell them not to accept a ride or go into any person's house without your express consent. **3.** Teach them to say "no" to anyone who wants to touch the private parts of their body and if a person does touch them in that way . . . they should scream for help! **4.** Tell them to come straight to you and tell you if any person says or does anything or they see anything that makes them feel uncomfortable or embarrassed. Tell them you will not be angry with them under any circumstances.

**ALL SEX OFFENDERS ARE DISCIPLES OF SATAN!** Jesus said: *"Take heed* (watch out) *that ye despise not one of these little ones; for I say unto you, That in heaven their angels do always behold the face of my Father* (God) *which is in heaven."* **Matthew 18:10**

**CHILDREN ARE NEVER RESPONSIBLE FOR AN OLDER CHILD'S ACTIONS, OR FOR ADULTS! A CHILD IS NOT PHYSICALLY, EMOTIONALLY OR INTELLECTUALLY EQUAL!**

**TEACH CHILDREN THAT ANY PERSON WHO TRICKS, DECEIVES, LIES OR EXPLOITS THEM IS A BAD PERSON!** *"Train up a child in the way he should go: and when he is old, he will not depart from it."* **Proverbs 22:6**

**CHILD ABUSE/PORNOGRAPH RAPE/INCEST IS DAMAGING TO THE CHILD, TO THE FAMILY, AND TO THE PERSON WHO COMMITTED THE SINFUL ACT!** A responsible parent should report any suspected abuser to the police, not only for your child's sake but also for the sake of other children, even if it is a relative! It's unlikely your child was the first victim! Jesus said: *"But whoso shall offend* (use, abuse) *one of these little ones which believe in me, it were* (would be) *better for him that a millstone were hanged about his neck, and that he were drowned in the depth of the sea."* **Matthew 18:6/Mark 9:42**

**HOW CAN A LOVING PARENT DEAL WITH THE SITUATION WHEN HIS CHILD HAS BEEN MOLESTED? ACCORDING TO GOD, YOU HAVE NO CHOICE BUT TO PRAY AND FORGIVE THAT PERSON!** Jesus said: *"For if ye forgive men their trespasses* (sin), *your heavenly Father will also forgive you: But if ye forgive not men their trespasses, neither will your Father* (God) *forgive your trespasses."* **Matthew 6:14-15**

**HERE IS A MESSAGE TO THE PERSON WHO IS GUILTY OF SEXUALLY LUSTING FOR, OR WHO HAS ALREADY MOLESTED A CHILD:** You need to fall on your knees and repent to God exactly what you have done! Mean it in your heart when you ask God to forgive you! Really humble yourself and acknowledge that you are a sinner, and that you want God to forgive you and to save you from spending eternity in hell! Ask God to come into your life and clean you up! Ask God to change your sinful desires into healthy ones! Ask God to erase your past from your memory! Ask God to help you to always say and do the right things! Thank God for saving you! Tell Him you love Him! Tell Him you will live for Him from this moment on! Pray all through the day and night as long as you live! Go to church as long as you live! Thank God daily for His tender mercy and for loving you!

### PRAYER

Heavenly Father, I have committed the heinous crime of **molesting children.** I am so ashamed. Will You forgive me? I will never be guilty of doing this sinful act again! I ask you with all sincerity to believe me and forgive me. Wash me in the precious blood of Jesus. I will keep my body pure from this moment on. I will pray, fast, and read my Bible! I will go to church. **I will never be guilty of touching a child in a suggestive and sexual manner again!** Come into my heart to stay. I know that Satan was the founder of my unclean desires and actions. Therefore from this day forward I will rebuke him in the name of Jesus. Thank You for loving and forgiving me. In Jesus' name. AMEN!

# CHILDREN

**JESUS BLESSES LITTLE CHILDREN!** *"Then were there brought unto him* (Jesus) *little children, that he should put his hands on them, and pray: and the disciples rebuked them. But Jesus said, Suffer* (allow) *little children, and forbid them not, to come unto me: for of such is the kingdom of heaven. And he laid his hands on them, and departed thence* (went his way)." **Matthew 19:13-15**

**PARENTS: NEVER FORBID YOUR CHILDREN TO BELIEVE IN GOD, TO GO TO CHURCH, OR TO PRAY!** Jesus said: ". . .*Suffer* (allow) *little children to come unto me, and forbid them not: for of such is the kingdom of God. Verily I say unto you, Whosoever shall not receive the kingdom of God as a little child shall in no wise enter therein."* **Luke 18:16-17 and Mark 10:13-16**

**GOD SAID WE ARE TO TEACH AND CORRECT OUR CHILDREN IN HIS PRINCIPLES!** *"He* (parent) *that spareth his rod hateth his son: but he that loveth him chasteneth him betimes* (speedily)." **Proverbs 13:24**

*"Chasten thy son while there is hope* (while he is young), *and let not thy soul spare* (give-in) *for his crying."* **Proverbs 19:18** ". . .*a wise son* (daughter) *maketh a glad father; but a foolish son is the heaviness* (heartache) *of his mother."* **Proverbs 10:1**

**PARENTAL CORRECTION SHOULD BEGIN WHEN THE CHILD IS AN INFANT AND CONTINUE UNTIL HE IS AN ADULT!** *"Train up a child in the way he should go: and when he is old, he will not depart from it."* **Proverbs 22:6**

*"Foolishness is bound in the heart of a child; but the rod of correction shall drive it far from him."* **Proverbs 22:15**

**CHILDREN: YOU ARE COMMANDED TO HONOR YOUR PARENTS AS LONG AS YOU LIVE!** *"Hearken* (listen) *unto thy father that begat thee, and despise not thy mother when she is old."* **Proverbs 23:22** *"Thy father and thy mother shall be glad, and she that bare thee shall rejoice."* **Proverbs 23:25** *"My son, hear the instruction of thy father, and forsake not the law of thy mother."* **Proverbs 1:8** *"My son, if sinners entice* (tempt, tease) *thee, consent thou not."* **Proverbs 1:10** *"Children, obey your parents in the Lord: for this is right. Honour thy father and mother; which is the first commandment with promise; that it may be well with thee, and thou mayest live long on the earth."* **Ephesians 6:1-3** *"Children, obey your parents in all things: for this is well pleasing unto the Lord."* **Colossians 3:20**

**CHILDREN: WHEREVER YOU GO, REMEMBER TO FOLLOW THE INSTRUCTIONS YOUR PARENTS GAVE YOU!** *"My son* (daughter), *keep thy father's commandment, and forsake not the law of thy mother: Bind them continually upon thine heart, and tie them about thy neck. When thou goest, it shall lead thee; when thou sleepest, it shall keep thee; and when thou awakest, it shall talk with thee."* **Proverbs 6:20-22**

**CHILDREN: DO YOU WANT TO LIVE A LONG LIFE?** *"Honour thy father and thy mother: that thy days may be long upon the land which the Lord thy God giveth thee."* **Exodus 20:12** *"Honour thy father and thy mother, as the Lord thy God hath commanded thee; that thy days may be prolonged, and that it may go well with thee, in the land which the Lord thy God giveth thee."* **Deuteronomy 5:16**

**CHILDREN: NEVER CURSE YOUR PARENTS, EVEN IN YOUR THOUGHTS!** Jesus said: *"For God commanded, saying, Honour thy father and mother: and, he that curseth father or mother, let him die the death."* **Matthew 15:4**

**CHILDREN: YOU ARE COMMANDED TO LOVE ALL PEOPLE, JUST AS YOU LOVE YOURSELF!** *"Honor your father and your mother, and, you shall love your neighbor as yourself."* **Matthew 19:19** (The Amplified Bible) Also read: **Leviticus 19:18**

**CHILDREN: WATCH OUT FOR YOUR "EGO". IT WILL GET YOU INTO TROUBLE!** *"A self-confident and foolish son* (daughter) *is a grief to his father, and bitterness to her who bore him* (gave birth to him)." **Proverbs 17:25** (The Amplified Bible)

**KIDS: MAKE SURE YOUR FRIENDS ARE THE RIGHT KIND THAT GOD WOULD CHOOSE FOR YOU!** *"Whoever keeps the law* (of God and man) *is a wise son, but he who is a companion of gluttons and the carousing, self-indulgent and extravagant shames his father."* **Proverbs 28:7** (The Amplified Bible)

**CHILDREN: NEVER MOCK, LAUGH, MAKE JOKES ABOUT, OR TALK BACK TO YOUR PARENTS! NEVER GOSSIP OR REVEAL PERSONAL THINGS ABOUT YOUR FAMILY TO OTHER PEOPLE!** *"A wise son heareth his father's instruction: but a scorner heareth not rebuke."* **Proverbs 13:1** *"For whom the Lord loveth he correcteth; even as a father* (corrects) *the son in whom he delighteth."* **Proverbs 3:12**

**SATAN WANTS ALL CHILDREN TO BE DISOBEDIENT!** *"Wherein in time past ye walked according to the course of this world, according to the prince of the power of the air* (Satan), *the* (evil) *spirit that now worketh in the children of disobedience."* **Ephesians 2:2**

**KIDS: IF YOU KNOW TO DO RIGHT BUT DELIBERATELY DO WRONG, YOU ARE FOLLOWING SATAN'S ORDERS!** *"But he who commits sin is of the devil—takes his character from the evil one* (Satan); *for the devil has sinned from the beginning. The reason the Son of God* (Jesus) *was made manifest* (visible) *was to undo* (destroy) *the works the devil* (has done)." **1 John 3:8** (The Amplified Bible)

**KIDS: GOD SENT HIS ONLY SON JESUS TO DIE ON THE CROSS TO PAY FOR YOUR SINS! JESUS IS ALIVE AND WELL TODAY! HE LOVES YOU! YOU NEED TO BECOME A BORN-AGAIN CHRISTIAN BY: 1. REPENTING OF YOUR SINS. 2. ASKING GOD TO FORGIVE YOU. 3. GOING TO CHURCH AND READING YOUR BIBLE. 4. PRAYING, PRAISING GOD!**

### PRAYER

Dear God, Even though I'm a kid I've always known that I should mind my mother, my daddy, and even my grandparents! I know I should also mind my teachers and parents of my friends. I am thankful that I live in a country where we are free to go to public schools. I'm not the best kid in the world but I know how to be a better kid than I have been. I ask You to forgive me for all the things I have said that were wrong! Help me to be a better child! Forgive me for my sins. Thank You, Jesus, for loving me! AMEN!

# CLEANLINESS

THERE ARE ALL KINDS OF UNCLEANLINESS: THERE IS THE DIRTY MIND, DIRTY BODY, DIRTY SPIRIT, DIRTY HOUSE, DIRTY DEALINGS WITH DIRTY PEOPLE OR ANIMALS, TO MENTION A FEW!

TO BE UNCLEAN IN YOUR BODY, MIND, AND SPIRIT IS TO DESTROY GOD'S TEMPLE! *"Know ye not that ye are the temple of God, and that the (Holy) Spirit of God dwelleth in you? If any man defile the temple of God, him shall God destroy; for the temple of God is holy, which temple ye are."* **1 Corinthians 3:16-17**

WE CAN BATHE OUR BODY, BUT IT REALLY TAKES A LOVING GOD TO CLEANSE OUR SOUL! *"Who can bring a* **clean** *thing out of an* **unclean?** *not one (person)."* **Job 14:4**

SINNER OR CHRISTIAN: IF YOU WANT TO BE MORE HOLY IN THE SIGHT OF THE LORD, MEMORIZE THIS: *"Having therefore these promises (of God), dearly beloved, let us* **cleanse** *ourselves from all filthiness of the flesh and spirit, perfecting holiness in the fear (and respect) of God."* **2 Corinthians 7:1**

GOD LOVES EVERY PERSON ON EARTH! BUT, IF A PERSON REBELS AGAINST GOD AND LUSTS FOR SEX WITH OTHER THAN HIS MARRIAGE PARTNER . . . GOD WILL LET HIM SIN, BECAUSE HE GAVE US FREE WILL! *"Wherefore God also gave them up to* **uncleanness** *through the lusts of their own hearts, to dishonour their own bodies between themselves."* **Romans 1:24**

WHEN A PERSON SINS THROUGH UNCLEANNESS, HE OBEYS HIS MASTER WHOSE NAME IS SATAN! *"For this cause God gave them up unto vile (repulsive) affections: for even their women did change the natural use (marital sex with a male) into that which is against nature (sex with a female): And likewise also the men, leaving the natural use of the woman (sex with a female), burned in their lust one toward another; men with men working (doing) that which is unseemly, and receiving in themselves that recompence (just reward for sin) of their error (sin) which was meet (deserved and proper)."* **Romans 1:26-27**

IS IT TOO MUCH TO ASK THAT WE PRESENT OUR BODIES ACCEPTABLE TO GOD IN RETURN FOR THE LOVING SACRIFICE GOD MADE FOR US? *"I beseech you therefore, brethren, by the mercies of God, that ye present your bodies a living sacrifice, holy, acceptable unto God, which is your reasonable service."* **Romans 12:1**

IF WE KEEP OUR EYES, HANDS, MIND AND BODY FREE FROM SIN, GOD WILL REWARD US FOR OBEDIENCE! *"The Lord rewarded me according to my righteousness; according to the* **cleanness** *of my hands hath he recompensed (lovingly repaid) me."* **Psalm 18:20**

GOD REMINDED US IN NUMBERS 8:7 to shave and wash our clothes to make our physical bodies clean!

UNCLEANNESS IS SIN AND CAN PREVENT A PERSON FROM INHERITING THE KINGDOM OF GOD! *"Now the works of the flesh are manifest (recognized and evident), which are these: Adultery, fornication,* **uncleanness,** *lasciviousness (lewdness, lust), idolatry, witchcraft, hatred, variance (discord), emulations (ego, rivalry), wrath, strife, seditions (wresting authority), heresies (false doctrines), envyings, murders, drunkenness, revellings (wild parties), and such like: of the which I tell you before, as I have told you in time past, that they which do such things shall not inherit the kingdom of God."* **Galatians 5:19-21**

PRACTICAL ADVICE: *"So get rid of all* **uncleanness** *and the rampant outgrowth of wickedness, and in a humble (gentle, modest) spirit receive and welcome the Word (God, Bible) which implanted and rooted (in your hearts) contains the power to save your souls."* **James 1:21** (The Amplified Bible)

NOW . . . ASK GOD TO DELIVER YOU FROM ALL UNCLEANNESS! *"The Lord knoweth how to deliver the godly out of temptations, and to reserve the unjust unto the day of judgement to be punished: But chiefly them that walk after the flesh in the lust of* **uncleanness,** *and despise government. Presumptuous are they, self-willed, they are not afraid to speak evil of dignities."* **2 Peter 2:9-10**

HERE ARE SOME SELECTED SCRIPTURES WHICH WILL HELP YOU CLEAN UP YOUR LIFE, BODY, AND SOUL. *"Come close to God and He will come close to you. (Recognize that you are) sinners, get your soiled hands* **clean;** *(realize that you have been disloyal) wavering individuals with divided interests, and purify your hearts. As you draw near to God be deeply penitent and grieve, even weep (over your disloyalty). Let your laughter be turned to grief and your mirth to dejection and heartfelt shame (for your sins). Humble yourselves — feeling very insignificant — in the presence of the Lord, and He will exalt you. He will lift you up and make your lives significant."* **James 4:8-10** (The Amplified Bible)

Ephesians 5:4-8 says: *"Let there be no* **filthiness** *(obscenity, indecency) nor foolish and sinful (silly and corrupt) talk, nor coarse jesting, which are not fitting or becoming; but instead voice your thankfulness (to God). For be sure of this, that no person practicing sexual vice or impurity in thought or in life, or one who is covetous — that is, who has lustful desire for the property of others and is greedy for gain (for) that (in effect) is an idolater, has any inheritance in the kingdom of Christ and of God. Let no one delude and deceive you with empty excuses and groundless arguments (for these sins), for through these things the wrath of God comes upon the sons of rebellion and disobedience. So do not associate or be sharers with them. For once you were in darkness, but now you are light in the Lord; walk as children of light — lead the lives of those native-born to the Light (of Jesus)."* **Ephesians 5:4-8**

### PRAYER

Dear God, I am 100 percent guilty of being **unclean** in my body. With my eyes I have coveted **unclean** things which would disappoint You! I have used my hands to commit **unclean** acts! I have let my entire body and my soul go **unclean.** I ask You to forgive me! Give me every opportunity to **clean** up my life! I want to be like Jesus in every way! I will need Your help! Please create in me a **clean heart, clean thoughts,** and **clean speech.** Help me organize myself in such a way that at no time can it be said that my house, car or place of business is **unclean.** I repent of every sin I have committed! I thank You for Your loving kindness! In Jesus' name I pray. AMEN!

# COMPLAINING

**COMPLAINING IS A SIN OF THE FLESH AND THE SPIRIT!** *"These are murmurers, **complainers**, walking after their own lusts; and their mouth speaketh great swelling words, having men's persons in admiration because of advantage."* **Jude 16**

**COMPLAINERS ARE SELFISH!** *"Therefore I will not refrain my mouth; I will speak in the anguish of my spirit; I will **complain** in the bitterness of my soul."* **Job 7:11**

**COMPLAINING CAN MAKE YOU SICK!** *". . .my bed shall comfort me, my couch shall ease my **complaint**."* **Job 7:13**

**JOB SAID:** *"Even today is my **complaint** bitter: my stroke is heavier than my groaning."* **Job 23:2**

**COMPLAINERS USUALLY LIKE TO "DUMP" THEIR COMPLAINTS ON YOU! THEY SHOULD BE GIVING THEIR COMPLAINTS TO THE LORD! HE CAN CHANGE THEM INTO VICTORIES!** *"My soul is weary of my life; I will leave my **complaint** upon myself; I will speak in the bitterness of my soul."* **Job 10:1**

**COMPLAINERS USUALLY WANT AN AUDIENCE AND WILL GO TO ANY LENGTHS TO FIND ONE!** *"Attend unto me, and hear me: I mourn in my **complaint**, and make a noise;"* **Psalm 55:2**

**IF YOU MUST COMPLAIN . . . TELL GOD YOUR PROBLEMS! ONLY GOD CAN BRING YOU PEACE AND HAPPINESS! LISTEN TO WHAT DAVID SAID WHEN HE WAS IN A CAVE!** *"I cried unto the Lord with my voice; with my voice unto the Lord did I make my supplication. I poured out my **complaint** before him; I shewed (showed) before him my trouble."* **Psalm 142:1-2**

**I DON'T LIKE MYSELF WHEN I COMPLAIN! NOBODY ELSE WANTS TO BE AROUND ME, EITHER! SO, HOW DO I GO ABOUT "KICKING THE HABIT"? HERE ARE SOME VERSES THAT WILL FIX YOU UP IF YOU WILL TRY THEM!** *"Oh, what a wonderful God we have! How great are his wisdom and knowledge and riches! How impossible it is for us to understand his decisions and his methods! For who among us can know the mind of the Lord? Who knows enough to be his own counselor and guide? And who could ever offer to the Lord enough to induce him to act? For everything comes from God alone. Everything lives by his power, and everything is for his glory. To him be glory evermore. And so . . . I plead with you to give your bodies to God. Let them be a living sacrifice, holy—the kind he can accept. When you think of what he has done for you, is this too much to ask? Don't copy the behavior and customs of this world, but be a new and different person with a fresh newness in all you do and think. Then you will learn from your own experience how his ways will really satisfy you. As God's messenger I give each of you God's warning: Be honest in your estimate of yourselves, measuring your value by how much faith God has given you. Just as there are many parts to our bodies, so it is with Christ's body. We are all parts of it, and it takes every one of us to make it complete, for we have different work to do. So we belong to each other, and each needs all the others. God has given each of us the ability to do certain things well. So if God has given you the ability to prophesy, then prophesy whenever you can — as often as your faith is strong enough to receive a message from God. If your gift is that of serving others, serve them well. If you are a teacher, do a good job of teaching. If you are a preacher, see to it that your sermons are strong and helpful. If God has given you money, be generous in helping others with it. If God has given you administrative ability and put you in charge of the work of others, take the responsibility seriously. Those who offer comfort to the sorrowing should do so with Christian cheer. Don't just pretend that you love others: really love them. Hate what is wrong. Stand on the side of good. Love each other with brotherly affection and take delight in honoring each other. Never be lazy in your work but serve the Lord enthusiastically. Be glad for all God is planning for you. Be patient in trouble, and prayerful always. When God's children are in need, you be the one to help them out. And get into the habit of inviting guests home for dinner or, if they need lodging, for the night. If someone mistreats you because you are a Christian, don't curse*

*him; pray that God will bless him. When others are happy, be happy with them. If they are sad, share their sorrow. Work happily together. Don't try to act big. Don't try to get into the good graces of important people, but enjoy the company of ordinary folks. And don't think you know it all! Never pay back evil for evil. Do things in such a way that everyone can see you are honest clear through. Don't quarrel with anyone. Be at peace with everyone, just as much as possible. Dear friends, never avenge yourselves. Leave that to God, for he has said that he will repay those who deserve it (don't take the law into your own hands). Instead feed your enemy if he is hungry. If he is thirsty give him something to drink and you will be heaping coals of fire on his head. In other words, he will feel ashamed of himself for what he has done to you. Don't let evil get the upper hand but conquer evil by doing good. Obey the government, for God is the one who has put it there. There is no government anywhere that God has not placed in power. So those who refuse to obey the laws of the land are refusing to obey God, and punishment will follow. For the policeman does not frighten people who are doing right; but those doing evil will always fear him. So if you don't want to be afraid, keep the laws and you will get along well. The policeman is sent by God to help you. But if you are doing something wrong, of course you should be afraid, for he will have you punished. He is sent by God for that very purpose. Obey the laws, then, for two reasons: first, to keep from being punished, and second, just because you know you should. Pay your taxes too, for these same two reasons. For government workers need to be paid so that they can keep on doing God's work, serving you. Pay everyone whatever he ought to have: pay your taxes and import duties gladly, obey those over you, and give honor and respect to all those to whom it is due. Pay all your debts except the debt of love for others — never finish paying that! For if you love them, you will be obeying all of God's laws, fulfilling all his requirements. If you love your neighbor as much as you love yourself you will not want to harm or cheat him, or kill him or steal from him. And you won't sin with his wife or want what is his, or do anything else the Ten Commandments say is wrong. All ten are wrapped up in this one, to love your neighbor as you love yourself. Love does no wrong to anyone. That's why it fully satisfies all of God's requirements. It is the only law you need. Another reason for right living is this: you know how late it is; time is running out. Wake up, for the coming of the Lord is nearer now than when we first believed. The night is far gone, the day of his return will soon be here. So quit the evil deeds of darkness and put on the armor of right living, as we who live in the daylight should! Be decent and true in everything you do so that all can approve your behavior. Don't spend your time in wild parties and getting drunk or in adultery and lust, or fighting, or jealousy. But ask the Lord Jesus Christ to help you live as you should, and don't make plans to enjoy evil.* **Romans 11:33-13:14** (The Living Bible)

## PRAYER

Dear God, I don't know how I ever got into the habit of **complaining,** but now it has become a way of life for me! I want to break this ugly habit. I want others to enjoy being with me, instead of dreading to see me coming! Please forgive me for my constant **complaining.** It sounds awful to me and to others! You must be so disappointed in me! Please forgive me for **complaining** when there are many people less fortunate than I! In Jesus' name, I pray. AMEN!

# COVETING

**DEFINITION:** To wish for what belongs to another; to crave to possess another's possessions; to be greedy, grasping, having lack of restraint; eagerness to possess and ability to acquire and keep.

**EXODUS 20:17 LISTS SIX THINGS NOT TO BE COVETED OF YOUR NEIGHBOR:** *"Thou shalt not **covet** thy neighbour's wife, nor his manservant, nor his maidservant, nor his ox, nor his ass, nor any thing that is thy neighbour's."* **Deuteronomy 5:21** says we are not to **covet** our neighbour's property!

**EXODUS 22:29-30 SAYS WE ARE NOT TO COVET ANYTHING THAT IS GOD'S!**

**WARNING: COVETOUSNESS = IDOLATRY! IDOLATRY AND COVETOUSNESS = SIN AND GOD HATES SIN!** *"Take heed and beware of **covetousness**: for a man's life consisteth not in the abundance of the things which he possesseth."* **Luke 12:15**

**COVETOUSNESS = EVILNESS = VIOLENCE!** *"Woe to them that devise iniquity, and work evil upon their beds! when the morning is light, they practice it, because it is in the power of their hand. And they **covet** fields, and take them by violence; and houses, and take them away: so they oppress a man and his house, even a man and his heritage."* **Micah 2:1-2**

**COVETING BRINGS ABOUT BONDAGE! COVETING IS LUSTING FOR WHAT IS NOT YOURS** Paul said: *". . .for I had not known lust, except the law said, Thou shalt not **covet**."* **Romans 7:7**

**COVETING IS LISTED IN THE SAME CATEGORY AS MURDER ACCORDING TO THE HOLY BIBLE!** *"Thou shalt not commit adultery, Thou shalt not kill, Thou shalt not steal, Thou shalt not bear false witness, Thou shalt not **covet;** and if there be any other commandment, it is briefly comprehended in this saying, namely, Thou shalt love thy neighbour as thy self. Love worketh no ill to his neighbour: therefore love is the fulfilling of the law."* **Romans 13:9-10**

**LISTED BELOW ARE 23 SINS THAT WILL SEPARATE US FROM GOD IF WE DO NOT REPENT AND RECEIVE GOD'S LOVING FORGIVENESS.** *"Being filled with all unrighteousness, fornication, wickedness, **covetousness,** maliciousness; full of envy, murder, debate, deceit, malignity; whisperers, backbiters, haters of God, despiteful, proud, boasters, inventors of evil things, disobedient to parents, without understanding, covenant-breakers, without natural affection, implacable, unmerciful: Who knowing the judgement of God, that they which commit such things are worthy of death (separation from God), not only do the same (things), but have pleasure in them that do them."* **Romans 1:29-32**

**NEVER LET IT BE SAID THAT THE TEMPTATION TO COVET COMES FROM GOD! SATAN IS THE ONE WHO PLANTS THIS IDEA IN MAN'S HEART!** *"Let no man say when he is tempted, I am tempted of God: for God cannot be tempted with evil, neither tempteth he any man: But every man is tempted, when he is drawn away (from God) of his own lust, and enticed. Then when lust hath conceived, it bringeth forth sin: and sin, when it is finished, bringeth forth death."* **James 1:13-15**

COVETING BEGINS WHEN OUR EYES SEE SOMETHING THEY LONG FOR. THEN OUR EYES TAKE THE MESSAGE DIRECTLY TO OUR HEART. IF THE LONGING BECOMES TOO INTENSE IT CAN LEAD A PERSON TO GO SO FAR AS TO KILL TO GET WHAT IS DESIRED! *"But thine eyes and thine heart are not but for thy **covetousness,** and for to shed innocent blood, and for oppression, and for violence, to do it."* **Jeremiah 22:17**

**COVETING IS A NATURAL EMOTION WHETHER RICH OR POOR, RELIGIOUS OR NOT! WE NEED TO RECOGNIZE THIS TRAIT AND ASK GOD TO FORGIVE US WHEN WE COMMIT THIS SIN!** *"For from the least of them even unto the greatest of them every one is given to **covetousness;** and from the poorest even unto the priest every one dealeth falsely."* **Jeremiah 6:13**

**DO YOU WANT TO BE FREE FROM THE SIN OF COVETOUSNESS?** *"If ye then be risen with Christ, seek those things which are above, where Christ sitteth on the right hand of God. Set your affection on things above, not on things on the earth."* **Colossians 3:1-2**

**HOW DO YOU BEGIN?** *"Mortify therefore your members (of your body and spirit) which are upon the earth; fornication, uncleanness, inordinate affection, evil concupiscence (sexual desire), and **covetousness,** wich is idolatry: For which things; sake the wrath of God cometh on the children of disobedience:"* **Colossians 3:5-6**

**IN CLOSING:** *"For we brought nothing into this world, and it is certain we can carry nothing out."* **1 Timothy 6:7**

### PRAYER

Dear God, I am guilty of wanting things that belong to other people! I know this is wrong! I know I have all I need to supply my needs for this day. Please forgive me for always wanting things. This is a terrible trait in me. I ask You to help me overcome this sin. I know that whatever my actual needs are You will meet! I also know that I don't need every thing I see in order to make me happy! I ask You to forgive me of this sin. Help me to become a sweeter person. Please forgive me. I want to set my sights on You and not on the things of the world. In Jesus' name I pray. AMEN!

# CREMATION

Jesus said: *"He is not the God of the dead, but the God of the living: ye therefore do greatly err* (are mistaken to think otherwise).*"* **Mark 12:27**

**WHY DO SOME PEOPLE CREMATE? TO CUT DOWN EXPENSES . . . TO SAVE MONEY . . . TO SAVE TIME AND HASSLE.**

**HOW DID CREMATION BEGIN?** In ancient times Israelites buried bodies, whereas other nations surrounding them burned their dead bodies. Cremation originated when people died in a land that didn't belong to them. They didn't own the land and couldn't be buried on it, but the land had been promised them and they very much wanted to be buried on it, so they cremated the dead bodies. You see, the people wanted their bones buried in the land that would some day belong to them. Joseph ordered his skeleton be transported from Egypt, as an act of his faith in the same promise. As a result of this burial began a Jewish tradition! Jews have always respected their traditions.

**CREMATION IS NOT PAGAN. BURIAL IS NOT PAGAN. EITHER PLAN IS OKAY!** Today American funerals are sometimes shocking and heathen. No other country in the world carries on like we do at funerals. We doll up dead bodies with expensive cosmetics, we purchase expensive coffins, we insist on beautiful burial sites (with a view), ornate vaults, and high-priced head stones. The price tag runs into millions, perhaps billions. America with its lavish burials has become more pagan than righteous! Whereas pagans cremated in Old Testament times, THEY BURY NOW!

**OBVIOUSLY IT'S HOW YOU GO ABOUT CONDUCTING THE AFFAIRS OF DISPOSING OF A DEAD BODY THAT CREATES A SPIRITUAL EVENT OR A PAGAN RITUAL!**

**MAN IS NOT A BODY—HE ONLY WEARS ONE JUST AS A PERSON WEARS CLOTHES!** The way to grasp this truth is to stand in front of a casket and look down into its contents! As you observe the body it becomes apparent—**THE PERSON IS GONE!** The whole physical body is there . . . brains and all. Nothing is missing. Then it suddenly strikes you. **MAN IS NOT A BODY,** he only uses one to get around on earth. His body is his earthsuit, and nothing more! Paul said: *"Therefore we are always confident, knowing that, whilst we are at home in the body, we are absent* (our spirit is absent) *from the Lord."* **2 Corinthians 5:6** *"We are confident, I say, and willing rather to be absent from the body, and to be present with the Lord. Wherefore we labour* (for the Lord), *that whether present or absent, we may be accepted of him. For we must all appear before the judgment seat of Christ; that every one may receive the things done in his body, according to that* (those things) *he hath done, whether it be good or bad."* **2 Corinthians 5:8-10**

**MAN IS THE IMAGE OF GOD. THEREFORE MAN IS A SPIRIT BEING!** Naturally the image has to be like the object, and since God is spirit then man himself is a spirit being. *"God is a Spirit: and they that worship him must worship him in spirit and in truth."* **John 4:24**

**A MAN AND HIS BODY ARE TWO DIFFERENT CREATURES, EACH HAVING ITS OWN LIFE! THUS THE PHYSICAL BODY CAN DIE BUT THE MAN'S SPIRIT WILL CONTINUE TO LIVE ON! AMAZING BUT TRUE!!** Now that you know that a man's life is totally independent of his body, it gives you the freedom of choice to select burial or cremation. The body has no connection with man himself, and this hopefully will relieve your mind.

**WHAT WE REFER TO AS DEATH IS NOT THE DEATH OF GOD'S IMAGE — BUT OF MAN'S PHYSICAL EARTHSUIT!** It is a biblical fact that the image of God in man's body never dies, only his physical body!

**ALL MEN LIVE FOREVER WHETHER IN HEAVEN OR HELL!** When God created man in His image, He designed man's spirit to live forever. Only man's animal body dies and returns to dust. **Read: Genesis 1:27/Genesis 2:7/Genesis 3:19**

**BURIAL OR CREMATION SHOULD NEVER BE A MATTER OF SUPERSTITION, GUILT FEELINGS, OR EVEN REVERENCE — BUT A MATTER OF DISPOSAL AND PREFERENCE!** When it comes to burial here is the primary message from God. *"In the sweat of thy face thou shalt eat bread, till thou* **RETURN TO THE GROUND;** *for out of it wast thou taken: for dust thou art, and unto dust shalt thou return."* **Genesis 3:19**

**•••••••••••••••••••••••••••••••••••••••••••••••••••••**
### BURIAL OR CREMATION? IT'S UP TO YOU!
**•••••••••••••••••••••••••••••••••••••••••••••••••••••**

Jesus said: *"For he is not a God of the dead, but of the living: for all live unto him."* **Luke 20:38**

**GOD CREATED THE LAW OF DECAY!** Whether we bury dead bodies in the ground in a box or reduce them to ashes, is of no concern to God. Man makes a big thing of it, but God's Word does not! The burial process or cremation process still means one thing: the body returns to dust!

**GOD'S LAW OF DECAY IS FULFILLED WHEN THE BODY RETURNS TO DUST. HOW IT HAPPENS IS NOT IMPORTANT TO HIM, OR HE WOULD HAVE BEEN SPECIFIC!**

**HOW SHOULD WE DISPOSE OF DEAD BODIES?** As conveniently and respectfully as possible. Decide on burial or cremation because God's law of decay takes place either way. In both cases the body oxidizes. The only difference between either method is a matter of speed. In a box in the ground the body oxidizes slowly, in a crematorium it oxidizes fast.

**BUT, IS CREMATION EVER A FITTING WAY TO TREAT THE TEMPLE OF THE HOLY SPIRIT?** It makes no difference! The body is the Spirit's temple only so long as the image of God is in it. Once the body dies and the spirit is gone, the physical body is no longer the temple of the spirit any longer.

**THE HOLY SPIRIT RESIDES IN THE BELIEVER, NOT IN HIS BODY!** God's spirit is no more connected to our bodies than is our spirit. The Holy Spirit is married to our spirit, not to our physical body. **Romans 8:16-17 says:** *"The* (Holy) *Spirit itself beareth witness with our spirit, that we are the children of God: and if children, then* (we are) *heirs; heirs of God, and joint-heirs with Christ; if so be that we suffer with him, that we may be also glorified together."*

**WHILE WE ARE ALIVE IN OUR PHYSICAL BODIES THEY ARE SACRED AND ARE THE TEMPLES OF GOD. BUT ONCE WE'RE OUT OF THEM, THEY ARE WORTHLESS TO GOD OR ANYONE!** Unless you pickle (embalm) it, the odor is awful. Those who ignorantly argue that burying the body in a box and covering the box with dirt somehow preserves it as the temple of the Holy Spirit are misinformed. The Holy Spirit can never be buried! To assume that theory is reading something into the Scriptures that isn't there!

**FUNERALS ARE A MATTER OF PREFERENCE!** Cremation costs around $300. The average funeral with a coffin costs $2400. Some people prefer not to go through the grief of seeing the corpse. Some people prefer to shift the focus away from the dead body to the person who is alive in Christ. Some people are desirous of eliminating the routine funeral ceremony. Some people feel corpse-centered ceremonies are carnal, and featuring the body is unscriptural. Some funerals on the other hand are joyful with singing and testimonies and praise to the Lord. When the unsaved see Christians joyful at a time of bereavement, it's a powerful testimony!

# CURSING

**THE BIBLE SAYS A WHOLESOME TONGUE IS A TREE OF LIFE!** *"A wholesome tongue is a tree of life: but perverseness therein is a breach in the spirit."* **Proverbs 15:4**

**IT MAKES NO DIFFERENCE IF YOU CURSE SOMEONE OR SOMETHING UNDER YOUR BREATH! GOD KNOWS AND HEARS AND YOU WILL HAVE TO ANSWER FOR IT!** Jesus said: *"For there is nothing covered, that shall not be revealed; neither hid, that shall not be known. Therefore whatsoever ye have spoken in darkness shall be heard in the light; and that which ye have spoken in the ear in closets shall be proclaimed upon the housetops."* **Luke 12:2-3**

**TALK ABOUT A MOUTHFUL . . . DOES THIS VERSE APPLY TO YOU? IT CONTAINS: CURSING, DECEIT, FRAUD, MISCHIEF, VANITY! I PERSONALLY BELIEVE THAT BAD BREATH AND HEARTBURN GOES ALONG WITH CURSING!** *"His mouth is full of* **cursing** *and deceit and fraud: under his tongue is mischief and vanity."* **Psalm 10:7**

**IT IS POSSIBLE TO PRAISE GOD AND CURSE MEN WITH THE SAME TONGUE!** *"Therewith bless we God, even the Father; and therewith* **curse** *we men, which are made after the similitude of God. Out of the same mouth proceedeth blessing and* **cursing.** *My brethren, these things ought not so to be."* **James 3:9-10**

**HOW SHOULD WE REACT WHEN SOMEONE CURSES US?** *"Bless them which persecute you: bless, and* **curse** *not."* **Romans 12:14**

**CURSING STARTS WITH PRIDE AND PRIDE IS SIN! PEOPLE WHO CURSE USUALLY LIE!** *"For the sin of their mouth and the words of their lips let them even be taken in their pride: and for* **cursing** *and lying which they speak."* **Psalm 59:12**

**BE CAREFUL WHAT YOU WISH FOR! YOU JUST MIGHT GET YOUR WISH!** David prayed this prayer about the wicked people around him: *"As he loved* **cursing,** *so let it come unto him: as he delighted not in blessing, so let it be far from him. As he clothed himself with* **cursing** *like as with his garment, so let it come into his bowels like water* (diarrhea), *and like oil into his bones* (cancer of the bone?)." **Psalm 109:17-18**

**HOW MANY TIMES SHOULD WE FORGIVE A PERSON WHO CURSES US? FOREVER!!!** Jesus said: *"I say not unto thee, Until seven times: but, Until seventy times seven* (forever)." **Matthew 18:22**

**WHY DO PEOPLE WHO BEGAN BY LOVING OTHER PEOPLE END UP CURSING EACH OTHER?** Because this fulfills prophecy regarding the overwhelming power of Satan in our thoughts, hearts, minds and actions. Jesus said: *"And because iniquity* (sin) *shall abound, the love of many shall wax* (grow) *cold."* **Matthew 24:12**

**A CURSING TONGUE NEEDS GOD THE "GREAT PHYSICIAN" TO RECREATE IT AND HE WILL IF YOU ASK!** *"Create in me a clean heart, O God; and renew a right spirit within me."* **Psalm 51:10**

### PRAYER

Dear God, will You please forgive me for **cursing?** I truly repent of this sin! I ask Your forgiveness. I also ask You to recreate my heart so that I will not desire to **curse!** Each day, O God, I will pause and offer my prayer to You. Please accept my prayer and help me to always remember that it is much sweeter to praise than to **curse!** It is sweeter to give than to get, to love than to lambast. I thank You for sending Jesus to pay for my sins in order that I can come to You and ask forgiveness and receive it! I thank You for hearing my prayer and for answering it! I will live for You. AMEN!

# CURSING YOUR PARENTS

THE OLD MOSIAC LAW SAID IF A PERSON CURSED HIS PARENTS HE WAS TO BE PUT TO DEATH! THANK GOD JESUS CAME INTO THIS WORLD SO THAT OUR SINS COULD BE FORGIVEN IF WE REPENTED AND TURNED AWAY FROM THEM! *"Whoso **curseth** his father or his mother, his lamp (life) shall be put out in obscure darkness."* **Proverbs 20:20** *"For everyone that **curseth** his father or his mother shall be surely put to death: he hath **cursed** his father or his mother; his blood shall be upon him."* **Leviticus 20:9**

WHERE DOES THE DESIRE TO CURSE COME FROM? Jesus said: *"For out of the heart proceed evil thoughts, murders, adulteries, fornications, thefts, false witness, blasphemies (cursing): These are the things which defile a man (person): but to eat with unwashen hands defileth not a man."* **Matthew 15:18-20 & Mark 7:20-23**

JESUS SAID: *"Thou knowest the commandments, Do not commit adultery, Do not kill, Do not steal, Do not bear false witness, Defraud not, Honour thy father and mother."* **Mark 10:19**

DID YOU KNOW THAT WE HOLD THE POWER OF LIFE OR DEATH IN OUR TONGUE? *"Death and life are in the power of the tongue: and they that love it (life) shall eat the fruit thereof."* **Proverbs 18:21**

SATAN INVENTED CURSING. IF YOU LOVE GOD NEVER BE GUILTY OF CURSING! SAY "GET THEE BEHIND ME, SATAN!" Jesus said: *". . .Get thee behind me, Satan: thou art an offence unto me: for thou savourest (desire) not the things that be of God, but those that be of men."* **Matthew 16:23**

GOD WILL FORGIVE YOU WHEN YOU CURSE YOUR PARENTS, IF YOU REPENT AND DO NOT CURSE THEM (OR ANYONE) AGAIN! TRUE REPENTANCE MEANS TURNING AWAY FROM THE SIN! *"Let the words of my mouth, and the meditation of my heart, be acceptable in thy sight, O Lord, my strength, and my redeemer."* **Psalm 19:14**

WHAT IS THE COST OF CURSING YOUR PARENTS AND NOT REPENTING? *"For the wages of sin is death (eteranl separation from God), but the gift of God is eternal life through Jesus Christ our Lord."* **Romans 6:23**

WHY DOES SATAN WANT YOU TO CURSE YOUR PARENTS? BECAUSE HE HATES YOUR "GUTS!"! HE WANTS YOU TO BE ETERNALLY SEPARATED FROM GOD! HE WANTS YOU TO SPEND ETERNITY WITH HIM! *"For God sent not his Son into the world to condemn the world; but that the world through him might be saved."* **John 3:17**

HOW DO YOU BREAK THE CURSING HABIT? FIRST: YOU REPENT! *"Except ye **repent**, ye shall all likewise perish."* **Luke 13:3, 5.**

SECOND: YOU CONFESS YOUR SIN! *"If we **confess** our sins, he is faithful and just to forgive us our sins, and to cleanse us from all unrighteousness."* **1 John 1:9**

THIRD: FORSAKE THE IMPULSE TO CURSE, FOREVER! *"Let the wicked **forsake** his way, and the unrighteous man his thoughts: and let him return unto the Lord, and he will have mercy upon him; and to our God, for he will abundantly pardon."* **Isaiah 55:7** *"If my people, which are called by my name, shall humble themselves, and pray, and seek my face, and turn from their wicked ways; then will I hear from heaven, and will forgive their sin, and will heal their land."* **2 Chronicles 7:14**

### PRAYER

Dear God, I am guilty of **cursing my parents** and others! I repent of this sin! I sincerely ask you to forgive me. I will never **curse** anyone again! I do not want to spend eternity with Satan! I love You, God! I want to be the kind of person who has a clean mouth, thoughts and actions. Help me get control of my thoughts, lest I be tempted. Please blot out my sins and I will praise You as long as I live. In Jesus' name, I pray! AMEN!

# DANCING

DANCING IS SPOKEN OF IN THE BIBLE AS A SYMBOL OF REJOICING. DANCING WAS A PART OF THE RELIGIOUS CEREMONIES OF THE EGYPTIANS. FOR THE MOST PART WOMEN DID THE DANCING AND MALES AND FEMALES SELDOM INTERMINGLED!

IN THE EARLY PERIOD OF THE JUDGES, THE VIRGINS OF SHILOH DANCED AS A PART OF THE RELIGIOUS FESTIVITIES (Judges 21:19-23). DANCING WAS ALSO USED FOR FESTIVE AMUSEMENTS APART FROM ANY RELIGIOUS CEREMONIES. READ: Jeremiah 31:4, 13/Mark 6:22

THERE IS A TIME AND A PLACE IN EVERY PERSON'S LIFE FOR EVERYTHING, INCLUDING A TIME TO DANCE! Ecclesiastes 3:1-8 LISTS 28 THINGS THAT MAN WILL DO WHEN THE SEASON IS RIGHT. *"To every thing there is a season, and a time to every purpose under the heaven: A time to be born, and a time to die; a time to plant, and a time to pluck up that which is planted; A time to kill, and a time to heal; a time to break down, and a time to build up; A time to weep, and a time to laugh; a time to mourn, and a time to **dance**; A time to cast away stones, and a time to gather stones together; a time to embrace, and a time to refrain from embracing; A time to get, and a time to lose; a time to keep, and a time to cast away; A time to rend, and a time to sew; a time to keep silence, and a time to speak; A time to love, and a time to hate; a time of war, and a time of peace."*

DAVID PRAISED GOD FOR TURNING HIS GRIEF AND MOURNING INTO DANCING AND PRAISING GOD! *"Thou hast turned for me my mourning into **dancing**: thou (God) hast put off my sackcloth, and girded me with gladness;"* Psalm 30:11

PRAISING GOD AND WALKING AND LEAPING WAS A FORM OF DANCING WHICH GOD APPROVED IN THE BIBLE! In **Acts 3:6-9** Peter and John were going into the temple around 3:00 in the afternoon to pray when they came across a man lame from birth. As Christ had previously taught them to do, they said to the man, "In the name of Jesus Christ of Nazareth rise up and walk!" Then Peter took him by the right hand, and lifted him up: and immediately his feet and ankle bones received strength. And he leaped up, stood and walked and entered with Peter and John into the temple, walking and leaping, and praising God. And all the people saw him walking and praising God.

DANCING USED TO BE SACRED IN THE EYES OF THE LORD, BEFORE SATAN DISTORTED IT! In 2 Samuel 6:14-16 David **danced** before the Lord with all his might.

THERE ARE MANY SCRIPTURES IN THE BIBLE DESCRIBING "PRAISE DANCING"! *"Let them praise his name in the **dance**: let them sing praises unto him with the timbrel (tambourine) and harp. For the Lord taketh pleasure in his people: he will beautify the meek with salvation."* **Psalm 149:3-4** *"Praise him (God) with the timbrel and **dance**: praise him with stringed instruments and organs. Praise him upon the loud cymbals: praise him upon the high sounding cymbals. Let every thing that hath breath praise the Lord. Praise ye the Lord."* **Psalm 150:4-6**

PEOPLE USED TO DANCE IN SPITE OF PERSECUTION, AS AN ACT OF THEIR FAITH THAT GOD WAS WITH THEM! Jesus said: *"And he lifted up his eyes on his disciples, and said, Blessed be ye poor: for yours is the kingdom of God. Blessed are ye that hunger now: for ye shall be filled. Blessed are ye that weep now: for ye shall laugh. Blessed are ye, when men shall hate you, and when they shall separate you from their company, and shall reproach you, and cast out your name as evil, for the Son of man's (Christ) sake. Rejoice ye in that day, and leap (dance) for joy: for, behold, your reward is great in heaven: for in the like manner did their fathers unto the prophets."* **Luke 6:20-23** NOTE: Would you feel like dancing if you were hated, rejected and slandered?

IF THE ONLY REASON PEOPLE DANCED TODAY WERE TO PRAISE GOD, THERE WOULD BE NO NEED FOR GOD TO EVER BE DISPLEASED WITH DANCING! HOWEVER, NOWADAYS MEN AND WOMEN, AND BOYS AND GIRLS SQUEEZE AND HOLD EACH OTHER IN SEXUAL EMBRACES! IN NO WAY DO THEY PRAISE GOD WHEN THEY DANCE! FOR THE MOST PART DANCING IS DONE IN BARS AND NIGHT CLUBS! DANCING IS A WAY TO GIVE IN TO THE "LUST" OF THE FLESH! EROTIC EMOTIONS USUALLY ARISE IN ONE PERSON OR THE OTHER! TEMPTATIONS TO TOUCH AND FEEL GOES BEYOND DECENT MORAL CONVICTIONS! EMOTIONS GET CONFUSED AS THE MUSIC SWELLS AND SLOWS DOWN! MUSIC STIRS THE SOUL, SO SAY THE POETS! TOUCHING ANOTHER PERSON'S BODY TURNS INTO LUSTFUL DESIRES! DANCING CAN ALSO BRING OUT JEALOUSY THAT MIGHT NEVER HAVE OCCASION TO SURFACE, IF THE PEOPLE WERE SITTING IN CHURCH! DANCING IN CLUBS AND BARS IS USUALLY DONE WHEN THE LIGHTS ARE LOW OR TURNED OUT! WHEN PEOPLE ARE DANCING THE DARKNESS COVERS A MULTITUDE OF SINS THAT ARE TAKING PLACE! WHERE THERE IS ROCK MUSIC THERE IS SMOKING, PERHAPS DRUGS, AND ALMOST ALWAYS LIQUOR! MIX TOGETHER SUGGESTIVE LANGUAGE, SOME TOUCHING, KISSING, NECKING, FOREPLAY, DIRTY JOKES AND SEXUAL ADVANCES AND YOU CAN SEE HOW FAR REMOVED DANCING IS FROM PRAISING GOD!

(Continued)

# "Everything you've always wanted to know about Dancing, but didn't know who to ask..."

MANY BELIEVE THAT SATAN IS THE ORIGINATOR OF ROCK AND ROLL! NEVER BEFORE IN THE HISTORY OF THE WORLD HAVE PEOPLE TAKEN OFF SO MANY CLOTHES AND LET SO MUCH "HANG-OUT" AS ON THE DANCE FLOOR! RUBBING BODIES TOGETHER TO EXCITE THE SEXUAL DESIRES IS NOT PRAISING GOD!

TODAY, THERE ARE GAY DANCE BARS FOR MEN AND WOMEN ACROSS THE UNITED STATES AND THERE ARE NUDE DANCERS! THERE IS USUALLY SOMEONE WORKED-OVER WITH A KNIFE, BEAT UP OR KILLED EVERY NIGHT IN A BAR, OR DANCE HALL, ACROSS THE WORLD! WHY? BECAUSE DANCING IS NO LONGER DONE FOR THE SOLE PURPOSE OF PRAISING GOD! SATAN CHANGED DANCING, WHICH USED TO BE A WAY OF REJOICING AND PRAISING GOD, INTO A DISGUSTING EVENT WHICH PRAISES ONLY HIM!

THERE IS NO REFERENCE IN THE BIBLE WHICH SAYS THAT BUMPING, GRINDING, HUNCHING, TWISTING AROUND EACH OTHER, LOCKING BODIES, RUBBING TOGETHER, NECKING AND SHAKING HIPS AND BREASTS IS PLEASING IN THE EYES OF GOD! SO. . .GIVE UP DANCING!

AS A CHRISTIAN I DO NOT BELIEVE THAT PEOPLE CAN ENGAGE IN THIS KIND OF DANCE WITHOUT BECOMING SEXUALLY AROUSED! SINCE DANCING IS NOT FOR THE PURPOSE OF REJOICING AND PRAISING GOD (AS IT ONCE WAS) THEN WE MUST ASSUME IT IS NOT PLEASING TO GOD! PRAY ABOUT IT AND GOD WILL REVEAL TO YOU IF IT IS HIS WILL FOR YOU TO DANCE!

JUST A REMINDER: PERHAPS THE GREATEST PREACHER WHO EVER LIVED (OTHER THAN JESUS CHRIST) GOT HIS HEAD CHOPPED OFF AND PLACED ON A DINNER PLATTER BECAUSE OF A YOUNG GIRL WHO DANCED SO GOOD THAT THE KING GRANTED HER A WISH IN EXCHANGE FOR HER DANCING FOR HIM! THE PREACHER'S NAME WAS JOHN THE BAPTIST. THE KING WAS NAMED HEROD.

### PRAYER

Dear God, I repent if I have displeased You by **dancing.** I cannot say that I have ever **danced** to praise and glorify You! I cannot say that when I **danced** the people around me were praying and praising You! I cannot say that when I **danced** my mind was solely on You! I cannot say that when I **danced** I showed others that I was a Christian! I cannot say that while I **danced** others saw Jesus in me! I repent of having done anything that would not be a testimony to others that Jesus is foremost in my life! I ask You to forgive me for not keeping my body untouched and pure in your sight! I pray for forgiveness if I have caused another person to question my morals! I do not need to **dance** to have peace and happiness! I do not need to **dance** to feel fulfilled and happy! I do need You in my life! I can be satisfied with wholesome body exercise and Christian entertainment which cannot be questioned! Please come into my heart and forgive me. I will not go **dancing** again because I do not believe in my heart that it is best for my life, or my testimony! In Jesus' name I pray. AMEN!

# DEATH

**HEBREWS 9:27 SAYS IT IS APPOINTED UPON MEN TO DIE!** *"And as it is appointed unto men once to **die**, but after this the judgement:"*

**ECCLESIASTES 3:1-2 SAYS THERE IS A TIME TO BE BORN AND A TIME TO DIE!** *"To every thing there is a season, and a time to every purpose under the heaven: A time to be born, and a time to **die**; a time to plant, and a time to pluck up that which is planted;"*

**BECAUSE OF THE SIN OF ADAM ALL MEN ARE APPOINTED TO DIE!** *"For as in Adam all **die**, even so in Christ shall all be made alive."* **1 Corinthians 15:22**

**BECAUSE OF WILLFUL SIN DEATH CAME INTO EXISTENCE!** *"For the wages of sin is **death** (not physical or spiritual but eternal which is the penalty for sin); but the gift of God is eternal life through Jesus Christ our Lord."* **Romans 6:23**

**WHEN WE RECEIVE FORGIVENESS FOR OUR SINS, WE RECEIVE ETERNAL LIFE WITH JESUS! IF DEATH OCCURS WHILE THERE IS SIN IN OUR LIFE WE WILL BE ETERNALLY SEPARATED FROM GOD!** *"For the law of the (Holy) Spirit of life in Christ Jesus hath made me free from the law of sin and **death**."* **Romans 8:2**
**TO BE CARNALLY (SINFULLY) MINDED IS DEATH (SEPARATION FROM GOD)!** *"For to be carnally minded is **death**; but to be spiritually minded is life and peace. Because the carnal mind is enmity (hatred) against God: for it is not subject to the law of God, neither indeed can be (the carnal mind serves Satan). So then they that are in the flesh cannot please God."* **Romans 8:6-8**

*"For if ye live after the flesh, ye shall **die**: but if ye through the (Holy) Spirit do mortify the deeds of the body, ye shall live."* **Romans 8:13**

**ONLY OUR PHYSICAL (OUTER) BODY DIES! OUR SPIRIT LIVES ON ETERNALLY!** *"For the body without the spirit is **dead**, so faith without works is **dead** also."* **James 2:26**

**WHEN OUR EARTHLY BODIES ARE CHANGED AND BECOME IMMORTAL, DEATH BECOMES SWALLOWED UP IN VICTORY!** Paul wrote: *"Behold, I shew (show) you a mystery; We shall not all sleep, but we shall all be changed, In a moment, in the twinkling of an eye, at the last trump: for the trumpet shall sound, and the **dead** shall be raised incorruptible, and we shall be changed. For this corruptible (body) must put on incorruption, and this mortal (body) must put on immortality. So when this corruptible (body) shall have put on incorruption (not subject to death, again), and this mortal (body) shall have put on immortality (your eternal spirit), then shall (it) be brought to pass the saying that is written, **Death** is swallowed up in victory. O **death**, where is thy sting? O grave, where is thy victory? The sting of **death** is sin; and the strength of sin is the law. But thanks be to God, which (who) giveth us the victory through our Lord Jesus Christ."* **1 Corinthians 15:51-57**

**PHYSICAL DEATH WILL BE DESTROYED FOREVER AT THE END OF THE MILLENNIUM!** *"Then cometh the end, when he (Christ) shall have delivered up the*

*kingdom (of born again Christians) to God, even the Father; when he shall have put down all rule and all authority and power. For he (Christ) must reign, till he hath put all enemies under his feet. The last enemy that shall be destroyed is **death**."* **1 Corinthians 15:24-26**

**"AND GOD SHALL WIPE AWAY ALL TEARS FROM THEIR EYES; AND THERE SHALL BE NO MORE DEATH, NEITHER SORROW, NOR CRYING, NEITHER SHALL THERE BE ANY MORE PAIN: FOR THE FORMER THINGS ARE (WILL BE) PASSED AWAY."** Revelation 21:4

**DEATH NEVER ENDS THE CONSCIOUS EXISTENCE OF THE SOUL AND SPIRIT! DEATH ONLY PUTS AN END TO THE "BODY-SUIT" WE WEAR HERE ON PLANET EARTH IN ORDER TO GET AROUND! OUR SOUL AND SPIRIT CONTINUE ETERNALLY EITHER WITH GOD, IN HEAVEN, OR WITH SATAN IN HELL!**

**AT THE END OF THE 1,000 YEAR PERIOD (CALLED THE MILLENNIUM) WILL BE THE GREAT WHITE THRONE JUDGEMENT. GOD WILL JUDGE THE WICKED DEAD (WHO NEVER MADE IT TO HEAVEN) AND THEY WILL HAVE TO GIVE ACCOUNT OF THEIR PREVIOUS LIFE!** John said: *"And I saw a great white throne, and him (God) that sat on it, from whose face the earth and the heaven fled away; and there was found no place for them. And I saw the **dead**, small and great, stand before God; and the books were opened: and another book was opened, which is the book of life: and the **dead** were judged out of those things which were written dead which were in it; and **death** and hell delivered up the **dead** which were in them: and they were judged every man according to their works. And **death** and hell were cast into the lake of fire. This is the second **death**. And whosoever was not found written in the book of life was cast into the lake of fire."* **Revelation 20:11-15**

**MANY PEOPLE FOOLISHLY DIE WITHOUT THE WISDOM THAT ONLY GOD CAN GIVE!** Read Job 4:21

**IF WE DON'T OBEY GOD'S COMMANDMENTS AND REPENT OF OUR SINS WE WILL DIE WITHOUT KNOWLEDGE!** *"But if they obey not, they shall perish by the sword, and they shall **die** without knowledge."* **Job 36:12**

(Continued)

**ADAM BROUGHT DEATH TO US AS HIS HEIRS! JESUS BRINGS ETERNAL LIFE TO US WHEN WE BECOME HEIRS OF HIS!** *"For if by one man's offence (Adam's) **death** reigned by one; much more they which receive abundance of grace and of the gift of righteousness shall reign in (eternal) life by one, Jesus Christ. Therefore as by the offence of one (Adam) judgment came upon all men to condemnation (to die); even so by the righteousness of one (Jesus) the free gift came upon all men unto justification of life. For as by one man's disobedience many were made sinners, so by the obedience of one (Jesus) shall many be made righteous."* **Romans 5:17-19**

**SINCE SIN BRINGS US A REWARD OF DEATH (ETERNAL SEPARATION FROM GOD) SO DOES JESUS BRING US LIFE (ETERNAL) WHEN WE REPENT OF OUR SINS!** *". . .But where sin abounded, grace did much more abound: That as sin hath reigned unto **death**, even so might grace reign through righteousness unto eternal life by Jesus Christ our Lord."* **Romans 5:20-21**

**PAUL LOVED JESUS SO MUCH THAT HE SAID:** *"For to me to live is Christ, and to **die** is gain."* **Philippians 1:21**

**THE MOST TRAGIC DEATH HISTORY EVER RECORDED WAS WHEN JESUS DIED FOR OUR SINS IN ORDER THAT WE MIGHT RECEIVE ETERNAL LIFE!** *"For I delivered unto you first of all that which I also received, how that Christ **died** for our sins according to the Scriptures; and that he (Christ) was buried, and that he rose again the third day according to the Scriptures:"* **1 Corinthians 15:3-4**

**CHRIST'S DEATH WOULD HAVE BEEN IN VAIN HAD HE NOT ARISEN TO NEW LIFE. PRAISE GOD HE'S ALIVE TODAY!** *"But I would not have you to be ignorant, brethren, concerning them which are asleep (dead), that ye sorrow not, even as others which have no hope. For if we believe that Jesus **died** and rose again, even so them also which sleep in Jesus (died a Christian) will God bring with him."* **1 Thessalonians 4:13-14** *"For the Lord himself shall descend from heaven with a shout, with the voice of the archangel, and with the trump of God: and the **dead** in Christ shall rise first: Then we which are alive and remain shall be caught up together with them in the clouds, to meet the Lord in the air: and so shall we ever be with the Lord. Wherefore comfort one another with these words."* **1 Thessalonians 4:16-18**

**THE ONLY WAY TO DIE IS AS A CHRISTIAN!** John wrote: *"And I heard a voice from heaven saying unto me, Write, Blessed are the **dead** which die in the Lord from henceforth: Yea (yes), saith the (Holy) Spirit, that they may rest from their labours; and their works do follow them (live on)."* **Revelation 14:13. READ: Acts 24:15**

**OUR SOUL AND SPIRIT ARE IMMORTAL AND LEAVE OUR BODY AT DEATH! Read: Luke 16:22 and 2 Corinthians 5:8**

**SATAN HAS THE POWER OVER DEATH! JESUS HAS THE POWER OVER LIFE! THE DECISION IS OURS TO SPEND ETERNITY WITH SATAN OR WITH JESUS!** *"Forasmuch then as the children are partakers of flesh and blood, he (Christ) also himself likewise took part of the same (flesh and blood life); that through **death** he (Christ) might destroy him (Satan) that had the power of **death**, that is, the devil; and deliver them who through fear of **death** were all their lifetime subject to bondage."* **Hebrews 2:14-15**

**THE RESURRECTION WILL BRING FORTH NEW "GLORIFIED" BODIES TO THE CHRISTIANS, JUST LIKE CHRIST HAS. OUR SOULS ARE ALREADY IMMORTAL! GOD IS NOT THE GOD OF THE DEAD, BUT OF THE LIVING! Matthew 22:30-32 and Luke 20:27-38**

**THE SOUL AND SPIRIT ARE IMMORTAL AND LEAVE THE BODY AT DEATH! Read Luke 16:20-31**

**DEATH IS PAINFUL! Read Acts 2:24**

**DEATH IS ONLY A CHANGE OF STATE!** *"If a man **die**, shall he live again? All the days of my appointed time will I wait, till my change come."* **Job 14:14**

**OUR EARTHLY BODY IS LIKE A SUIT OF CLOTHES WE WEAR! WHEN WE DIE WE SIMPLY SLIP OUT OF OUR SUIT OF CLOTHES (OUR BODY) AND OUR SOUL AND SPIRIT GO TO BE WITH EITHER JESUS OR SATAN! WE CAN ONLY CHOOSE WHERE WE WILL SPEND ETERNITY WHILE WE LIVE! AFTER WE DIE IT'S TOO LATE! Read 2 Peter 1:14**

**GOD'S DESIGN FOR OUR PHYSICAL BODY IS FOR IT TO RETURN TO DUST FROM WHENCE IT CAME. IT REALLY MAKES NO DIFFERENCE WHETHER OUR PHYSICAL BODY IS BURIED OR CREMATED!** *"In the sweat of thy face shalt thou eat bread, till thou return unto the ground; for out of it wast thou taken: for dust thou art, and unto dust shalt thou return."* **Genesis 3:19**

**IN DEATH THERE IS NO REMEMBRANCE!** *"For in **death** there is no remembrance of thee (God): in the grave who shall give thee thanks?"* **Psalm 6:5** *"For he that is **dead** is freed from sin. Now if we be **dead** with Christ (a deceased Christian), we believe that we shall also live with him: knowing that Christ being raised from the **dead dieth no more; death** hath no more dominion over him. For in that he (Christ) **died**, he died unto sin once: but in that he liveth, he liveth unto God. Likewise reckon ye also yourselves to be **dead** indeed unto sin, but alive unto God through Jesus Christ our Lord. Let not sin therefore reign in your mortal body, that ye should obey it in the lusts thereof."* **Romans 6:7-12**

**IN CLOSING:** *"But God commendeth (gave without merit) his love toward us, in that, while we were yet sinners, Christ **died** for us."* **Romans 5:8**

*"I SHALL NOT **DIE** (BE SEPARATED FROM GOD), BUT LIVE (ETERNALLY), AND DECLARE THE WORKS OF THE LORD."* **Psalm 118:17**

## PRAYER

Dear God, Please forgive me for all my sins. I know that someday I will face death just as the Bible teaches. When I die I want to go to heaven to be with You for all eternity. Please forgive me for all my sins. Come into my life and cleanse me and live in me. Please help me conquer the fear of death. I know that the Scriptures say that to die is gain, yet the thought of death scares me. Please remove this fear. In Jesus' name, AMEN!

(Continued)

# DEATH DREAM—AT AGE 17

I dreamt **I died** on an ordinary school day. How I wish I had taken the bus! But I was too cool for the bus. I remember how I wheedled the car out of Mom. I pleaded, "all the kids drive!" My dream started out a normal dream and ended in a horrible nightmare. I'll continue. . .

I dreamt the 2:50 bell rang and I threw all my books in the locker. I was free until 8:40 tomorrow morning! I ran to the parking lot excited at the thought of driving a car and being my own boss . . . Freedom!. . .

I dreamt I was goofing off—going too fast and taking crazy chances. I was enjoying my freedom and having fun. The last thing I remember was passing an old lady who seemed to be going awfully slow. I heard the crash and felt a terrific jolt. Glass, steel, and blood flew everywhere! My whole body seemed to be turning inside out. I heard myself scream.

I dreamt I suddenly awakened and it was very quiet. A police officer was standing over me. Then I saw a doctor. My body was mangled. I was saturated with blood. Pieces of jagged glass were sticking out all over. Strange, but I couldn't feel anything!

I dreamt I screamed . . . Hey, don't pull that sheet over my head . . . I can't be **dead.** I'm only 17. I've got a date tonight. I'm supposed to grow up and have a wonderful life. I haven't lived enough yet. I can't be **dead**!

Later I was placed in a drawer. My folks had to identify me. Why did they have to see me like this? Why did I have to look at Mom's eyes when she faced the most terrible ordeal of her life? Dad suddenly looked like an old man. He told the man in charge, "Yes, he is my son. He was a good boy. But he never became a born-again Christian! We prayed for him and we witnessed to him, but now it's too late.

I dreamt my funeral was a weird experience. I saw all my relatives and friends walk toward the casket. They passed by, one by one, and looked at me with the saddest eyes I've every seen. Some of my buddies were crying. A few of the girls touched my hand and sobbed as they walked away. They all said, "We won't see him in heaven . . . he waited too late to get saved!"

I Dreamt I screamed, "Please . . . somebody . . . wake me up! Get me out of here. I can't bear to see my Mom and Dad so broken up. My grandparents are so racked with grief they can barely walk. My brothers and sisters are like zombies. They move like robots. Everyone's in a daze. No one can believe this, and I can't believe it, either.''

In hell I screamed, "I'm not **dead!**" I have a lot of living to do! I want to laugh and run again. I want to sing and talk. All I want is one more chance. I will give my heart and life to you. I know you didn't kill me but if I was a Christian everything would be alright. I see fires burning, and people screaming and horrible images coming to take me away. Oh no, God! I'm only 17! BUT IT WAS TOO LATE!

**END OF DREAM!** Guess what! I became a born again Christian today. It was the best decision I ever made. I'm the happiest 17 year old in the world! How about you???

# DEBATING

**DEFINITION:** Fight, contend, engage an opponent in an argument, regulated discussion of a proposition between two matched sides.

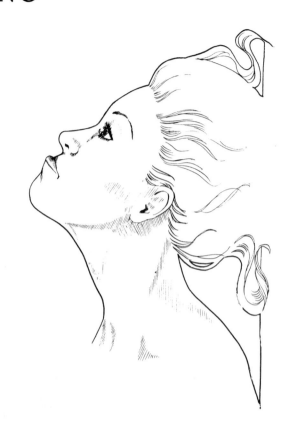

**THE BIBLE SAYS TO BE CAREFUL NOT TO START A DEBATE BECAUSE YOU WILL PROBABLY BE THE LOSER! GOD SAYS WE ARE TO LOVE OUR NEIGHBOR AS OURSELF! Proverbs 25:8-10 says:** *"Go not forth hastily to strive* (debate), *lest thou know not what to do in the end thereof, when thy neighbour hath* (has) *put thee to shame.* ***Debate*** *thy cause with thy neighbour himself; and discover not* (don't repeat) *a secret to another: lest he that heareth it put thee to shame, and thine infamy* (disgrace) *turn not away."*

**DEBATING GOES HAND IN HAND WITH ENVY, WRATH, STRIFE, BACKBITING, WHISPERING, SWELLINGS (BOASTING), TUMULTS (VIOLENT OUTBURSTS)! Paul wrote in 2 Corinthians 12:20** *"For I fear, lest, when I come, I shall not find you such as I would* (like to find you), *and that I shall be found unto you such as ye would not* (like to find me): *lest there be* ***debates,*** *envyings, wraths, strifes, backbitings, whisperings, swellings, tumults, and lest, when I come again, my God will humble me among you, and that I shall bewail* (regret) *many which have sinned already, and have not repented of the uncleanness and fornication* (sex between people who are not married to each other) *and lasciviousness* (lust) *which they have committed.*

**GOD'S LAW IS FOR US TO LOVE EACH OTHER AND LIVE IN PEACE! SATAN'S LAW IS FOR US TO HATE EACH OTHER AND TO DEBATE, ENVY AND FIGHT AGAINST GOD'S LAWS! GOD WILL NOT TOLERATE THIS FOREVER!** *"But God shows his anger from heaven against all sinful, evil men who push away the truth from them. For the truth about God is known to them instinctively; God has put this knowledge in their hearts. Since earliest times men have seen the earth and sky and all God made, and have known of his existence and great eternal power. So they will have no excuse* (when they stand before God at Judgement Day). *Yes, they knew about him all right, but they wouldn't admit it or worship him or even thank him for all his daily care. And after awhile they began to think up silly ideas of what God was like and what he wanted them to do. The result was that their foolish minds became dark and confused. Claiming themselves to be wise without God, they became utter fools instead. And then, instead of worshiping the glorious ever-living God, they took wood and stone and made idols for themselves, carving them to look like mere birds and animals and snakes and puny men. So God let them go ahead into every sort of sex sin, and do whatever they wanted to—yes, vile and sinful things with each other's bodies. Instead of believing what they knew was the truth about God, they deliberately chose to believe lies. So they prayed to the things God made, but wouldn't obey the blessed God who made these things. That is why God let go of them and let them do all these evil things, so that even their women turned against God's natural plan for them and indulged in sex sin with each other. And the men, instead of having a normal sex relationship with women, burned with lust for each other, men doing shameful things with other men and, as a result, getting paid within their own souls with the penalty they so richly deserved. So it was that when they gave God up and would not even acknowledge him, God gave them up to doing everything their evil minds could think of. Their lives became full of every kind of wickedness and sin, of greed and hate, envy, murder, fighting, lying, bitterness, and gossip. They were backbiters, haters of God, insolent, proud braggarts, always thinking of new ways of sinning and continually being disobedient to their parents. They tried to misunderstand, broke their promises, and were heartless—without pity. They were fully aware of God's death penalty for these crimes, yet they went right ahead and did them anyway, and encouraged others to do them, too. "Well", you may be saying, "what terrible people you have been talking about!" But wait a minute! You are just as bad. When you say they are wicked and should be punished, you are talking about yourselves, for you do these very same things. And we know that God, in justice, will punish anyone who does such things as these. Do you think that God will judge and condemn others for doing them and overlook you when you do them, too? Don't you realize how patient he is being with you? Or don't you care? Can't you see that he has been waiting all this time without punishing you, to give you time to turn from your sin? His kindness is meant to lead you to repentance."* **Romans 1:18-Romans 2:4** (The Living Bible)

### PRAYER

Dear God, please forgive me for all the **debates** I've gotten myself into through my own selfish ego! I do not know everything! I know that only You have all the answers! Please forgive me for my foolish arrogance. Please help me gain control of my thoughts, my tongue and my actions. Help me to break the habit of **debating!** Please help me to become more like You. In Jesus' name I pray. AMEN!

# DEBTS

WHEN YOU PROMISE GOD YOU WILL PAY A DEBT DON'T NEGLECT TO PAY IT. GOD CANNOT BE FOOLED! *"When thou vowest a vow* (debt) *unto God, defer not to pay it; for he hath no pleasure in fools: pay that which thou hast vowed* (promised). *Better is it that thou shouldest not vow* (promise), *than that thou shouldest vow* (owe) *and not pay."* **Ecclesiastes 5:4-5**

JESUS SAID: IF YOU OWE ANYONE YOU MUST PAY YOUR DEBTS, LEST THE PERSON YOU OWE TURNS YOU OVER TO THE JUDGE AND YOU END UP IN PRISON! *"Agree with thine adversary quickly, whiles thou art in the way with him; lest at any time the adversary deliver thee to the judge, and the judge deliver thee to the officer, and thou be cast into prison. Verily I say unto thee, Thou shalt by no means come out thence* (from prison), *till thou hast paid the uttermost farthing* (amount)." **Matthew 5:25-26**

THE LORD'S PRAYER SAYS: *"And forgive us our **debts**, as we forgive our **debtors**."* **Matthew 6:12**

NOT ONLY ARE WE TO PAY OUR DEBTS TO GOD, WE ARE TO PAY ALL OUR DEBTS TO THE CITY, COUNTY, STATE AND GOVERNMENT! GOD ESTABLISHED GOVERNMENTAL LAWS AND NEVER DOES HE EXCUSE MANKIND FROM PAYING HIS LEGAL DEBTS! Jesus said: *". . . Render therefore unto Caesar* (government) *the things which are Caesar's; and unto God the things that are God's."* **Matthew 22:21 and Mark 12:17, Luke 20:22-25**

THE BIBLE CLEARLY STATES THAT WE ARE TO PAY OUR DEBTS FIRST BEFORE WE SPEND ANY MONEY ON OURSELVES! *"Then she* (a woman) *came and told the man of God* (Elisha, the prophet). *And he said, Go, sell the oil, and pay thy **debt**, and live thou and thy children on the rest."* **2 Kings 4:7**

WHEN YOU LEND MONEY TO A FRIEND DON'T CHARGE HIM INTEREST OR ATTEMPT TO PUNISH HIM! *"If you lend money to a needy fellow-Hebrew* (or anyone), *you are not to handle the transaction in an ordinary way, with interest. If you take his clothing as a pledge* (collateral) *of his repayment, you must let him have it back at night. For it is probably his only warmth; how can he sleep without it? If you don't return it, and he cries to me for help, I will hear and be very gracious to him* (at your expense), *for I am very compassionate."* **Exodus 22:25-27** (The Living Bible) *"And if thou sell ought* (anything) *unto thy neighbour, or buyest ought* (anything) *of thy neighbour's hand* (that belongs to him), *ye shall not oppress one another."* **Leviticus 25:14**

WHEN YOU GO INTO DEBT YOU BECOME THE SERVANT TO THE ONE WHO LENT TO YOU! *"Just as the rich rule the poor, so the borrower is servant to the lender."* **Proverbs 22:7** (The Living Bible)

BE VERY CAUTIOUS BEFORE YOU COUNTERSIGN FOR ANOTHER PERSON, LEST YOU LOSE ALL YOU HAVE! ALWAYS PRAY FIRST AND SEEK GOD'S WILL IN THESE MATTERS! *"Unless you have the extra cash on hand, don't countersign a note. Why risk everything you own? They'll even take your bed.!"* **Proverbs 22:26-27** (The Living Bible)

IF YOU KEEP ANY ANIMAL, PROPERTY, OR ANY OTHER THING FOR ANOTHER PERSON AND IT GETS STOLEN YOU MUST REPAY THE OWNER! *"If a man asks his neighbor to keep a donkey, ox, sheep, or any other animal* (or anything) *for him, and it dies, or is hurt, or gets away, and there is no eyewitness to report just what happened to it, then the neighbor must take an oath that he has not stolen it, and the owner must accept his word, and no restitution shall be made for it. But if the animal or property has been stolen, the neighbor caring for it must repay the owner."* **Exodus 22:10-12** (The Living Bible)

*"BUT IF A MAN IS JUST AND DOES WHAT IS LAWFUL AND RIGHT . . . AND IS A MERCIFUL CREDITOR, HOLDING ON TO THE ITEMS GIVEN TO HIM IN PLEDGE BY POOR DEBTORS, AND IS NO ROBBER, BUT GIVES FOOD TO THE HUNGRY AND CLOTHES TO THOSE IN NEED, AND GRANTS LOANS WITHOUT INTEREST, AND STAYS AWAY FROM SIN, AND IS HONEST AND FAIR WHEN JUDGING OTHERS, AND OBEYS MY LAWS — THAT MAN IS JUST, SAYS THE LORD, AND HE SHALL SURELY LIVE."* **Ezekiel 18:5-9.** (The Living Bible)

*IN CLOSING: "WITHHOLD NOT GOOD FROM THEM TO WHOM IT IS DUE, WHEN IT IS IN THE POWER OF THINE HAND TO DO IT. SAY NOT UNTO THY NEIGHBOUR, GO, AND COME AGAIN, AND TOMORROW I WILL GIVE; WHEN THOU HAST* (HAVE) *IT BY* (WITH) *THEE."* **Proverbs 3:27-28** ALSO READ: **Luke 7:41-43/Matthew 18:23-35**

## PRAYER

Dear God, forgive me for always going into **debt**. Forgive me for my **debts** which I never repayed to You and to others. Help me in the arena of my finances and to be more honest. In Jesus' name I pray. AMEN!

# DECEIVE

*"BE NOT **DECEIVED**; GOD IS NOT MOCKED: FOR WHAT-SOEVER A MAN SOWETH, THAT SHALL HE ALSO REAP."* **Galatians 6:7**

*"THE WISDOM OF THE PRUDENT IS TO UNDERSTAND HIS (GOD'S) WAY: BUT THE FOLLY OF (SELF-CONFIDENT) FOOLS IS **DECEIT**."* **Proverbs 14:8**

*"BREAD OF **DECEIT** IS SWEET TO A MAN; BUT AFTER-WARDS HIS MOUTH SHALL BE FILLED WITH GRAVEL."* **Proverbs 20:17**

*"THE WICKED WORKETH A **DECEITFUL WORK**: BUT TO HIM THAT SOWETH RIGHTEOUSNESS SHALL BE A SURE REWARD."* **Proverbs 11:18**

*"A TRUE WITNESS DELIVERETH SOULS: BUT A **DECEIT-FUL WITNESS** SPEAKETH LIES."* **Proverbs 14:25**

*"HE THAT HATETH DISSEMBLETH WITH HIS LIPS, AND LAYETH UP **DECEIT** WITHIN HIM; WHEN HE SPEAKETH FAIR, BELIEVE HIM NOT: FOR THERE ARE SEVEN ABOMINATIONS IN HIS HEART. WHOSE HATRED IS COVERED BY **DECEIT**, HIS WICKEDNESS SHALL BE SHEW-ED BEFORE THE WHOLE CONGREGATION."* **Proverbs 26:24-26**

*"FAITHFUL ARE THE WOUNDS OF A FRIEND; BUT THE KISSES OF AN ENEMY ARE **DECEITFUL**."* **Proverbs 27:6**

*"**FAVOUR IS DECEITFUL**, AND BEAUTY IS VAIN: BUT A WOMAN THAT FEARETH THE LORD, SHE SHALL BE PRAIS-ED."* **Proverbs 31:30**

*"THE **HEART IS DECEITFUL** ABOVE ALL THINGS, AND DESPERATELY WICKED: WHO CAN KNOW IT?"* **Jeremiah 17:9**

*"SHALL I (GOD) COUNT THEM PURE WITH THE WICKED BALANCES, AND WITH THE BAG OF **DECEITFUL WEIGHTS**?"* **Micah 6:11**

**WE ARE COMMANDED (AFTER WE BECOME SAVED) TO CHANGE OUR CONVERSATIONS FROM DECEITFUL ONES! Ephesians 4:22-23.**

*"THEN IT SHALL BE, BECAUSE HE HATH SINNED, AND IS GUILTY, THAT HE SHALL RESTORE THAT WHICH HE TOOK VIOLENTLY AWAY, OR THE THING WHICH HE HATH **DECEITFULLY** GOTTEN, OR THAT WHICH WAS DELIVERED HIM TO KEEP, OR THE LOST THING WHICH HE FOUND."* **Leviticus 6:4**

*"WILL YE SPEAK WICKEDLY FOR GOD? AND TALK **DECEITFULLY** FOR HIM?"* **Job 13:7**

*"WHO SHALL ASCEND INTO THE HILL OF THE LORD? OR WHO SHALL STAND IN HIS HOLY PLACE? HE THAT HATH CLEAN HANDS, AND A PURE HEART; WHO HATH NOT LIFTED UP HIS SOUL INTO VANITY, NOR SWORN **DECEIT-FULLY**."* **Psalm 24:3-4**

*"THY TONGUE DEVISETH MISCHIEFS; LIKE A SHARP RAZOR, **WORKING DECEITFULLY**."* **Psalm 52:2** *"THOU LOVEST ALL DEVOURING WORDS, O THOU **DECEITFUL TONGUE**."* **Psalm 52:4**

*"CURSED BE HE THAT DOETH THE WORK OF THE LORD **DECEITFULLY**, AND CURSED BE HE THAT KEEPETH BACK HIS SWORD FROM BLOOD."* **Jeremiah 48:10**

*"THEREFORE SEEING WE HAVE THIS MINISTRY, AS WE HAVE RECEIVED MERCY, WE FAINT NOT; BUT HAVE RE-NOUNCED THE HIDDEN THINGS OF DISHONESTY, NOT WALKING IN CRAFTINESS, NOR HANDLING THE WORD OF GOD **DECEITFULLY**; BUT BY MANIFESTATION OF THE TRUTH COMMENDING OURSELVES TO EVERY MAN'S CON-SCIENCE IN THE SIGHT OF GOD."* **2 Corinthians 4:1-2**

**JESUS SAID:** *"HE ALSO THAT RECEIVED SEED AMONG THE THORNS IS HE THAT HEARETH THE WORD; AND THE CARE OF THIS WORLD, AND THE **DECEITFULNESS OF RICHES**, CHOKE THE WORD, AND HE BECOMETH UN-FRUITFUL."* **Matthew 13:22/Mark 4:19**

*"TAKE HEED, BRETHREN, LEST THERE BE IN ANY OF YOU AN EVIL HEART OF UNBELIEF, IN DEPARTING FROM THE LIVING GOD. BUT EXHORT ONE ANOTHER DAILY, WHILE IT IS CALLED TODAY; LEST ANY OF YOU BE HARDENED THROUGH THE **DECEITFULNESS OF SIN**."* **Hebrews 3:12-13**

*"FOR THEY SPEAK NOT PEACE: BUT THEY DEVISE **DECEITFUL MATTERS** AGAINST THEM THAT ARE QUIET IN THE LAND."* **Psalm 35:20**

*"THEY ALSO THAT SEEK AFTER MY (DAVID'S) LIFE LAY SNARES FOR ME: AND THEY THAT SEEK MY HURT SPEAK MISCHIEVOUS THINGS, AND **IMAGINE DECEITS** ALL THE DAY LONG."* **Psalm 38:12**

*"...THIS IS A REBELLIOUS PEOPLE, LYING CHILDREN, CHILDREN THAT WILL NOT HEAR THE LAW OF THE LORD: WHICH SAY TO THE SEERS (FORTUNE-TELLERS), SEE NOT; AND TO THE PROPHETS (PREACHERS), PRO-PHESY NOT UNTO US RIGHT THINGS, SPEAK UNTO US SMOOTH THINGS, **PROPHESY DECEITS**."* **Isaiah 30:9-10**

*"BE NOT A WITNESS AGAINST THY NEIGHBOUR WITHOUT CAUSE; AND **DECEIVE NOT WITH THY LIPS**."* **Proverbs 24:28**

 (Continued)

"...TAKE HEED THAT NO MAN **DECEIVE** YOU. FOR MANY SHALL COME IN MY NAME, SAYING, I AM CHRIST; AND SHALL **DECEIVE** MANY." **Matthew 24:4-5/Mark 13:5-6/Luke 21:8**

"LET NO MAN **DECEIVE** HIMSELF. IF ANY MAN AMONG YOU SEEMETH TO BE WISE IN THIS WORLD, LET HIM BECOME A FOOL, THAT HE MAY BE WISE. FOR THE WISDOM OF THIS WORLD IS FOOLISHNESS WITH GOD. FOR IT IS WRITTEN, HE TAKETH THE WISE IN THEIR OWN CRAFTINESS." **1 Corinthians 3:18-19**

"KNOW YE NOT THAT THE UNRIGHTEOUS SHALL NOT IN-HERIT THE KINGDOM OF GOD? **BE NOT DECEIVED:** NEITHER FORNICATORS, NOR IDOLATERS, NOR ADULTERERS, NOR EFFEMINATE, NOR ABUSERS OF THEMSELVES WITH MANKIND, NOR THIEVES, NOR COVETOUS, NOR DRUNKARDS, NOR REVILERS, NOR EX-TORTIONERS, SHALL INHERIT THE KINGDOM OF GOD." **1 Corinthians 6:9-10**

"**BE NOT DECEIVED:** EVIL COMMUNICATIONS CORRUPT GOOD MANNERS." **1 Corinthians 15:33**

"BUT EVIL MEN AND SEDUCERS SHALL WAX WORSE AND WORSE, **DECEIVING**, AND BEING **DECEIVED**." **2 Timothy 3:13**

"WITH HIM (GOD) IS STRENGTH AND WISDOM: THE **DECEIVED** AND THE **DECEIVER** ARE HIS." **Job 12:16**

"FOR MANY **DECEIVERS** ARE ENTERED INTO THE WORLD, WHO CONFESS NOT THAT JESUS CHRIST IS COME IN THE FLESH. THIS IS A **DECEIVER** AND AN ANTICHRIST." **2 John :7**

"AS A MAD MAN WHO CASTETH FIREBRANDS, ARROWS, AND DEATH, SO IS THE MAN THAT **DECEIVETH** HIS NEIGHBOUR, AND SAITH, AM NOT I IN SPORT?" **Proverbs 26:18-19**

"AND THERE WAS MUCH MURMURING AMONG THE PEO-PLE CONCERNING HIM (JESUS): FOR SOME SAID, HE IS A GOOD MAN: OTHERS SAID, NAY (NO); BUT HE **DECEIVETH** THE PEOPLE." **John 7:12**

"FOR IF A MAN THINK HIMSELF TO BE SOMETHING, WHEN HE IS NOTHING, HE **DECEIVETH** HIMSELF." **Gala-tians 6:3**

"IF ANY MAN AMONG YOU SEEM TO BE RELIGIOUS, AND BRIDLETH NOT HIS TONGUE, BUT **DECEIVETH** HIS OWN HEART, THIS MAN'S RELIGION IS VAIN." **James 1:26**

"AND THE GREAT DRAGON WAS CAST OUT, THAT OLD SERPENT, CALLED THE DEVIL, AND SATAN, WHICH **DECEIVETH** THE WHOLE WORLD: HE WAS CAST OUT IN-TO THE EARTH, AND HIS ANGELS WERE CAST OUT WITH HIM." **Revelation 12:9**

"BUT BE YE DOERS OF THE WORD, AND NOT HEARERS ONLY, **DECEIVING** YOUR OWN SELVES." **James 1:22**

"FOR AMONG MY PEOPLE ARE FOUND WICKED MEN: THEY LAW WAIT, AS HE THAT SETTETH SNARES; THEY SET A TRAP, THEY CATCH MEN. AS A CAGE IS FULL OF BIRDS, SO ARE THEIR HOUSES FULL OF **DECEIT:** THEREFORE THEY ARE BECOME GREAT, AND WAXEN RICH." **Jeremiah 5:26-27**

"TAKE HEED TO YOURSELVES, THAT YOUR HEART BE NOT **DECEIVED**, AND YE TURN ASIDE, AND SERVE OTHER GODS, AND WORSHIP THEM." **Deuteronomy 11:16**

"BEWARE LEST ANY MAN SPOIL YOU THROUGH PHILOSOPHY AND VAIN **DECEIT**. AFTER THE TRADITION OF MEN, AFTER THE RUDIMENTS OF THE WORLD, AND NOT AFTER CHRIST." **Colossians 2:8**

"HE THAT SPEAKETH TRUTH SHEWETH FORTH RIGHTEOUSNESS: BUT A FALSE WITNESS **DECEIT**." **Pro-verbs 12:17**

"**DECEIT** IS IN THE HEART OF THEM THAT IMAGINE EVIL: BUT TO THE COUNSELLORS OF PEACE IS JOY." **Pro-verbs 12:20**

"HOW LONG SHALL THIS BE IN THE HEART OF THE PRO-PHETS THAT PROPHESY LIES? YEA, THEY ARE PROPHETS OF THE **DECEIT** OF THEIR OWN HEART." **Jeremiah 23:26**

"FOR FROM WITHIN, OUT OF THE HEART OF MEN, PRO-CEED EVIL THOUGHTS, ADULTERIES, FORNICATIONS, MURDERS, THEFTS, COVETOUSNESS, WICKEDNESS, **DECEIT**, LASCIVIOUSNESS, AND EVIL EYE, BLASPHEMY, PRIDE, FOOLISHNESS: ALL THESE EVIL THINGS COME FROM WITHIN, AND DEFILE THE MAN." **Mark 7:21-23**

"THOU SHALT DESTROY THEM THAT SPEAK LEASING: THE LORD WILL ABHOR THE BLOODY AND **DECEITFUL** MAN." **Psalm 5:6**

"JUDGE ME, O GOD, AND PLEAD MY CAUSE AGAINST AN UNGODLY NATION: O DELIVER ME FROM THE **DECEIT-FUL** AND UNJUST MAN." **Psalm 43:1**

"BUT THOU, O GOD, SHALT BRING THEM DOWN INTO THE PIT OF DESTRUCTION: BLOODY AND **DECEITFUL** MEN SHALL NOT LIVE OUT HALF THEIR DAYS; BUT I WILL TRUST IN THEE." **Psalm 55:23**

"HOLD NOT THY PEACE, O GOD OF MY PRAISE; FOR THE MOUTH OF THE WICKED AND THE **MOUTH OF THE DECEITFUL** ARE OPENED AGAINST ME; THEY HAVE SPOKEN AGAINST ME WITH A LYING TONGUE." **Psalm 109:1-2**

"DELIVER MY SOUL, O LORD, FROM LYING LIPS, AND FROM A **DECEITFUL TONGUE**." **Psalm 120:2**

"FOR THE RICH MEN THEREOF ARE FULL OF VIOLENCE, AND THE INHABITANTS THEREOF HAVE SPOKEN LIES, AND THEIR **TONGUE IS DECEITFUL** IN THEIR MOUTH." **Micah 6:12**

"THE REMNANT OF ISRAEL SHALL NOT DO INIQUITY, NOR SPEAK LIES; NEITHER SHALL A **DECEITFUL TONGUE** BE FOUND IN THEIR MOUTH: FOR THEY SHALL FEED AND LIE DOWN, AND NONE SHALL MAKE THEM AFRAID." **Zephaniah 3:13**

**NOTE: DECEIT IS ALSO CALLED CRAFT, CRAFTINESS, CRAFTY IN Job 5:12-13/2 Corinthians 12:16/Job 15:5**

"LET NOT HIM THAT IS **DECEIVED** TRUST IN VANITY: FOR VANITY SHALL BE HIS RECOMPENSE." **Job 15:31**

"THEY CONCEIVE MISCHIEF, AND BRING FORTH VANITY, AND THEIR BELLY PREPARETH **DECEIT**." **Job 15:35**

**PRAYER**

Dear God, Please forgive me for **deceiving others,** myself, and most of all for trying to **deceive** You! I had no idea that **deceiving** anyone was such a sin! I now know that it is the same thing as lying! I repent of this sin and I will be 100 percent honest from this moment on! I now turn over a new way of life. I will no longer **deceive** myself or You. Forgive me, Lord. In Jesus' name, I pray. AMEN!

# DEFRAUD

**DEFINITION:** To deprive of a right or property by fraud;

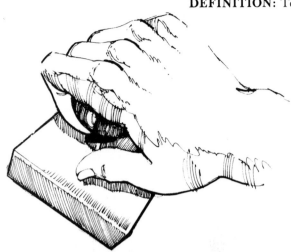

BE CAREFUL WHAT YOU WISH FOR! THE PRICE YOU PAY FOR DEFRAUDING ANOTHER PERSON WILL BE CHARGED AGAINST YOU (IN THE END) BY ALMIGHTY GOD! *"Behold, the hire of the labourers who have reaped down your fields, which is of you kept back by **fraud**, crieth: and the cries of them which have reaped are entered into the ears of the Lord of sabaoth."* **James 5:4**

IF YOU OWE SOMEONE BE PROMPT TO PAY, FOR SLEEPLESS NIGHTS MAY COME TO YOU IF YOU DON'T! *"Thou shalt not **defraud** thy neighbour, neither rob him: the wages of him that is hired shall not abide with thee all night until the morning."* **Leviticus 19:13**

WALK IN THE FOOTPRINTS OF THE LORD AND YOU WILL FIND PEACE, CONTENTMENT AND ETERNAL SECURITY! *"Thou knowest the commandments, Do not commit adultery, Do not kill, Do not steal, Do not bear false witness, **Defraud not**, Honour thy father and mother."* **Mark 10:19**

WE ARE WAITING FOR THE RAPTURE, LORD! *"Receive us: we have wronged no man, we have corrupted no man, we have **defrauded** no man."* **2 Corinthians 7:2**

YOU CAN HELP KEEP OTHERS' SIDEWALKS CLEAN ONLY AFTER YOURS IS MAINTAINED! *"Behold, here I am: witness against me before the Lord, and before his anointed: Whose ox have I taken? or whose ass have I taken? or whom have I **defrauded**? Whom have I oppressed? or of whose hand have I received any bribe to blind mine eyes therewith? and I will restore it you. And they said, Thou hast not **defrauded** us, nor oppressed us, neither hast thou taken ought (any possessions) of any man's hand. And he said unto them, The Lord is witness against you, and his anointed is witness this day, that ye have not found ought in my hand. . . ."* **1 Samuel 12:3-5**

YOU'VE HEARD THE SAYING, WHEN YOU CAN BE HONEST WITH YOURSELF, THEN YOU CAN BE HONEST WITH OTHERS. *"Wherefore putting away lying, speak every man truth with his neighbour: for we are members one of another."* **Ephesians 4:25**

DON'T WORRY ABOUT THE RICHES YOU HAVE OR MAY ACQUIRE! SET YOUR SIGHTS ON THE RICHES YOU WILL HAVE FOR ALL ETERNITY THROUGH JESUS CHRIST (IF YOU ARE A BORN-AGAIN CHRISTIAN)! ALL OF THE RICHES OF THIS EARTH ARE ONLY TEMPORARY! *"While we look not at the things which are seen, but at the things which are not seen: for the things which are seen are temporal; but the things which are not seen are eternal."* **2 Corinthians 4:18**

WE ARE COMMANDED NEVER TO DEFRAUD ANOTHER PERSON, BUT IF YOU HAVE ALREADY DEFRAUDED SOMEONE, QUICKLY ASK GOD TO FORGIVE YOU! *"That no man go beyond and **defraud** his brother in any matter: because that the Lord is the avenger of all such, as we also have forewarned you and testified."* **1 Thessalonians 4:6** *"Recompense to no man evil for evil, provide things honest in the sight of all men. If it be possible, as much as lieth in you, live peaceably with all men."* **Romans 12:17-18**

# FRAUD

FRAUD MAY CONTAIN CURSING, DECEIT, MISCHIEF AND VANITY! *"His mouth is full of cursing and deceit and **fraud**: under his tongue is mischief and vanity."* **Psalm 10:7**

GOD HEARS THE CRIES OF VICTIMS OF FRAUD! *"Behold, the hire of the labourers who have reaped down your fields, which is of you kept back by **fraud**, crieth: and the cries of them which have reaped are entered into the ears of the Lord of sabaoth."* **James 5:4**

### PRAYER

Dear Lord, please forgive me for **defrauding** other people. I now realize how much I was cheating! Forgive me for **defrauding** in business and in my dealings with the government! Please help me keep my mind pure and my heart on You. Help me to react as Jesus would, in every area of my life! If I have caused others to follow in my footsteps please forgive me. I will go to those I have **defrauded** and will make full restitution. I thank You for Your loving forgiveness. I will be honest from this moment on. Help me every day as I grow. In Jesus' name, AMEN!

# DELINQUENCY

**DEFINITION:** A psychological tendency to commit offenses against the law whether it be man's laws or God's.

**DELINQUENCY WAS FORETOLD AS EVIDENCE OF THE LAST DAYS BEFORE CHRIST RETURNS!** *"This know also, that in the last days perilous times shall come. For men shall be lovers of their own selves, covetous, boasters, proud, blasphemers, disobedient to parents, unthankful, unholy, without natural affection, trucebreakers, false accusers, incontinent, fierce, despisers of those that are good, traitors, heady, highminded, lovers of pleasures more than lovers of God; having a form of godliness, but denying the power thereof: from such (people) turn away."* **2 Timothy 3:1-5**

**DELINQUENTS ARE:** *". . . filled with all unrighteousness, fornication, wickedness, covetousness, maliciousness; full of envy, murder, debate, deceit, malignity, whisperers, backbiters, haters of God, despiteful, proud, boasters, inventors of evil things, disobedient to parents, without understanding, covenantbreakers, without natural affection, implacable, unmerciful: Who knowing the judgment of God, that they which commit such things are worthy of death* (both physical and eternal separation from God), *not only do the same* (things), *but have pleasure in them that do them."* **Romans 1:29-32**

**DELINQUENTS USUALLY THINK THEY ARE THE SMARTEST THING WALKING ON THE FACE OF THE EARTH!** *"Because that, when they knew* (there was a) *God, they glorified him not as God, neither were thankful; but became vain in their imaginations, and their foolish heart was darkened. Professing themselves to be wise, they became fools."* **Romans 1:21-22** *"Wherefore God also gave them up to uncleanness through the lusts of their own hearts, to dishonour their own bodies between themselves: Who changed the truth of God into a lie, and worshipped and served the creature* (mankind) *more than the Creator* (God), *who is blessed for ever. Amen. For this cause God gave them up unto vile affections: for even their women did change the natural use into that which is against nature* (they became lesbians or committed sex with animals). *And likewise also the men, leaving the natural use of the woman, burned in their lust one toward another* (became homosexuals); *men with men working that which is unseemly, and receiving in themselves that recompence* (reward) *of their error which was meet* (only fair that they receive). *And even as they did not like to retain God in their knowledge, God gave them over to a reprobate mind, to do those things which are not convenient* (natural and lawful)." **Romans 1:24-28**

**PARENTS ARE COMMANDED BY GOD TO TRAIN A CHILD IN GODLY PRINCIPLES SO HE WILL NOT BECOME A DELINQUENT!** *"Train up a child in the way he should go: and when he is old, he will not depart from it."* **Proverbs 22:6** *"And thou shalt love the Lord thy God with all thine heart, and with all thy soul, and with all thy might. And these words, which I command thee this day, shall be in thine heart: And thou shalt teach them diligently unto thy children, and shalt talk of them when thou sittest in thine house, and when thou walkest by the way, and when thou liest down, and when thou risest up."* **Deuteronomy 6:5-7**

**GOD SAID TO USE DISCIPLINE** (AS NEEDED) **TO PROPERLY TRAIN A CHILD!** *"Withhold not correction from the child: for if thou beatest him with the rod, he shall not die. Thou shalt beat him with the rod, and shalt deliver his soul from hell."* **Proverbs 23:13-14** *"Foolishness is bound in the heart of a*

*child; but the rod of correction shall drive it far from him."* **Proverbs 22:15**

**PARENTS ARE RESPONSIBLE TO TEACH THEIR CHILDREN GOD'S LAWS!** *"And, ye fathers, provoke not your children to wrath: but bring them up in the nurture and admonition of the Lord."* **Ephesians 6:4**

**CHILDREN ARE COMMANDED TO OBEY THEIR PARENTS. THIS IS GOD'S PLAN!** *"Children, obey your parents in the Lord: for this is right. Honour thy father and mother; which is the first commandment with promise; that it may be well with thee, and thou mayest live long on the earth."* **Ephesians 6:1-3**

**PARENTS, CHILDREN, AND THE WHOLE WORLD, REAP THE BENEFITS OF LEARNING GOD'S REQUIREMENTS!** Jesus said: *"And this is life eternal, that they might know thee the only true God, and Jesus Christ, whom thou hast sent."* **John 17:3**

**DELINQUENCY IS THE END RESULT OF WHAT SATAN DOES TO A PERSON BECAUSE HE IS MISERABLE, AND MISERY LOVES COMPANY!** *"The thief* (Satan) *cometh not* (would not have come to earth), *but* (except) *for to steal, and to kill, and to destroy: I* (Christ) *am come* (to earth) *that they* (me, you) *might have life, and that they* (me, you) *might have it more abundantly."* **John 10:10**

## PRAYER

Dear God in heaven, please forgive me for not listening to my parents, and teachers. Please forgive me for turning away from those things that I knew were good and decent. Please forgive me for lying, stealing, cheating and abusing others. Forgive me for almost destroying myself and others. Thank You for loving me enough to send Your only son to die on the cross for my sins. Thank You, God! I know Jesus is alive today and is coming back. Dear God, I don't want to go to hell. I want to live forever with You. Please forgive me for every sin I have ever committed and blot them from your memory. I will live a good clean life from this moment on. I will confess with my mouth to others that Jesus saved me. I will try my best to lead others to Christ. I will go to church and read my Bible. I will pray each day and memorize the verses which help me, so I can repeat them to others who are in the shape I was in. Thank You for saving my soul from the pit of hell. In Jesus' name. AMEN!

# DEMANDING

**PLACE NO DEMAND ON OTHERS THAT YOU WOULD NOT PLACE ON YOURSELF! UNFORTUNATELY, WOMEN SEEM TO BE MORE GUILTY THAN MEN ABOUT DEMANDING!** *"A foolish woman is clamorous* (noisy, demanding, insistent): *she is simple, and knoweth nothing."* **Proverbs 9:13**

**YOU'VE HEARD THE OLD SAYING, "SPEAK SHORT AND SWEET, FOR YOUR WORDS MAY BE EASIER TO EAT!"** *"The wise in heart will receive commandments; but a prating fool* (one who talks too long or rattles on and on) *shall fall."* **Proverbs 10:8**

**SPEAK SOFTLY. LIVE PEACEFULLY. WALK IN THE PATH OF THE LORD. DEMAND NOTHING!** *"Let no corrupt communication proceed out of your mouth, but that which is good to the use of edifying* (to improve spiritually), *that it* (what you speak) *may minister grace unto the hearers. And grieve not the Holy Spirit of God, whereby ye are sealed unto the day of redemption. Let all bitterness, and wrath, and anger, and clamour* (loud talk), *and evil speaking, be put away from you, with all malice* (desire to see another suffer): *And be ye kind one to another, tenderhearted, forgiving one another, even as God for Christ's sake hath forgiven you."* **Ephesians 4:29-32**

**YOUR FIRST RESPONSE TO ANY DEMAND PUT ON YOU SHOULD BE TO FOLLOW GOD'S COMMANDMENTS!** *"Trust in the Lord with all thine heart; and lean not unto thine own understanding. In all thy ways acknowledge him, and he shall direct thy paths. Be not wise in thine own eyes: fear the Lord, and depart from evil."* **Proverbs 3:5-7**

**ALL OF US ARE GUILTY OF DEMANDING AT SOME TIME OR ANOTHER!** *"And the soldiers likewise demanded of him* (John), *saying, And what shall we do? And he* (John) *said unto them, Do violence to no man, neither accuse any falsely; and be content with your wages."* **Luke 3:14**

**THE PHARISEES DEMANDED THAT JESUS TELL THEM WHEN HE WOULD COME BACK TO EARTH. WHAT NERVE!!** *"And when he was demanded of the Pharisees, when the kingdom of God should* (would) *come, he answered them and said, The kingdom of God cometh not with* (by) *observations* (on a certain date that I will tell you): *Neither shall they say, Lo* (look) *here! or, lo* (look) *there! for, behold, the kingdom of God is within you."* **Luke 17:20-21**

### PRAYER

Dear Lord, Please forgive me for being a **demanding** person. I have no right to **demand** anything of others since I am not perfect! Let me hear Your **demands** and I will follow! Help me overcome the tendency to **demand** things of others. I know You have commanded us to love one another. Help me to remember to always be forgiving when others place **demands** on me. Let me never forget that people's **demands** are shallow and that the only things You **demand** of me are loving and heavenly. You are my creator; therefore I thank You for giving me the wisdom to know that I can always come to You and seek guidance and forgiveness. I thank You for this. In Jesus' name, I pray. AMEN!

# DESPISE

**DO NOT DESPISE YOUR NEIGHBOUR!** *"He that is void of wisdom **despiseth** his neighbour; but a man of understanding holdeth his peace."* **Proverbs 11:12**

**DO NOT DESPISE GOD'S STATUTES!** God said: *"And if ye shall **despise** my statutes, or if your soul abhor my judgements, so that ye will not do all my commandments, but that ye break my covenant: I also will do this unto you; I will even appoint over you terror, consumption, and the burning ague (chills, fever), that shall consume the eyes, and cause sorrow of heart: and ye shall sow your seed in vain, for your enemies shall eat it."* **Leviticus 26:15-16**

**WOMEN ARE COMMANDED NOT TO DESPISE THEIR HUSBANDS! Esther 1:17**

**FOOLS DESPISE WISDOM AND INSTRUCTION!** *"The fear of the Lord is the beginning of knowledge: but **fools despise wisdom** and instruction."* **Proverbs 1:7**

**DO NOT DESPISE GOD'S NAME!** *"A son honoureth his father, and a servant his master: if then I be a father, where is mine honour? and if I be a master, where is my fear? saith the Lord of hosts unto you, O priests, that despise my name. . . ."* **Malachi 1:6**

**DO NOT DESPISE THE GOVERNMENT!** *"The Lord knoweth how to deliver the godly out of temptations, and to reserve the unjust unto the day of judgment to be punished: but chiefly them that walk after the flesh in the lust of uncleanness, and **despise** government. Presumptuous are they, self-willed, they are not afraid to speak evil of dignities."* **2 Peter 2:9-10** *"Likewise also these filthy dreamers defile the flesh, **despise** dominion, and speak evil of dignities."* **Jude:8**

**DO NOT DESPISE CHASTENING!** *"Behold, happy is the man whom God correcteth: therefore **despise** not thou the chastening of the Almighty."* **Job 5:17** *"My son, **despise** not the chastening of the Lord; neither be weary of his correction: For whom the Lord loveth he correcteth; even as a father the son in whom he delighteth."* **Proverbs 3:11-12** *"And ye have forgotten the exhortation which speaketh unto you as unto children, My son, **despise** not thou the chastening of the Lord, nor faint when thou art rebuked of him: For whom the Lord loveth he chasteneth, and scourgeth every son whom he receiveth."* **Hebrews 12:5-6**

**DO NOT DESPISE THE WORK OF GOD'S HANDS!** *"Is it good unto thee that thou shouldest oppress, that thou shouldest **despise** the work of thine hands, and shine upon the counsel of the wicked?"* **Job 10:3**

**DO NOT DESPISE SOMEONE WHO STEALS FROM YOU IF HE IS STARVING!** *"Men do not **despise** a thief, if he steal to satisfy his soul when he is hungry."* **Proverbs 6:30**

**DO NOT DESPISE YOUR PARENTS WHEN THEY ARE OLD!** *"Hearken unto thy father that begat thee, and **despise** not thy mother when she is old."* **Proverbs 23:22**

**DO NOT DESPISE CHILDREN!** Jesus said: *"Take heed that ye **despise** not one of these little ones; for I say unto you, That in heaven their angels do always behold the face of my Father which is in heaven."* **Matthew 18:10**

**DO NOT DESPISE CHRISTIANS!** *"We are fools for Christ's sake, but ye are wise in Christ; we are weak, but ye are strong; ye are honourable, but we are **despised**."* **1 Corinthians 4:10**

**JESUS SAID WE ARE NOT TO DESPISE OTHERS! Luke 18:9**

**YOU ARE A FOOL IF YOU DESPISE YOUR FATHER'S INSTRUCTION!** *"A fool **despiseth** his father's instruction: but he that regardeth reproof is prudent."* **Proverbs 15:5**

**YOU ARE A FOOL TO DESPISE YOUR MOTHER!** *"A wise son maketh a glad father: but a foolish man **despiseth** his mother."* **Proverbs 15:20**

**DO NOT DESPISE YOUR OWN SOUL!** *"He that refuseth instruction **despiseth** his own soul: but he that heareth reproof getteth understanding. The fear of the Lord is the instruction of wisdom; and before honour is humility."* **Proverbs 15:32-33**

**IF PEOPLE DESPISE CHRISTIANS, REMEMBER THEY DESPISED CHRIST AND GOD ALSO!** Jesus said: *"He that heareth you heareth me; and he that **despiseth** you **despiseth** me; and he that **despiseth** me **despiseth** him (God) that sent me."* **Luke 10:16** *"He therefore that **despiseth**, **despiseth** not man, but God, who hath also given unto us his Holy Spirit."* **1 Thessalonians 4:8**

**DO NOT DESPISE AND TURN AWAY THE WORDS OF A POOR MAN!** *". . . Wisdom is better than strength: nevertheless the poor man's wisdom is **despised**, and his words are not heard."* **Ecclesiastes 9:16**

**JOB 36:5 SAYS THAT GOD DOESN'T DESPISE ANYONE!** *"Behold, God is mighty, and **despiseth** not any: he is mighty in strength and wisdom."*

### PRAYER

Dear God, I humble myself before You and ask You to forgive me for having **despised** others in the past. Forgive me for **despising** my parents, and myself. Most of all I ask You to forgive me for those times when I've been so miserable and somehow thought it was Your fault and **despised** You. God help me for making this horrible assumption. I know that You love me and want what's best for me. Thank You for being a God who forgives sin or we'd have no hope. In Jesus' name I pray. AMEN!

# DESTITUTE

**DEFINITION:** Suffering extreme want, extreme poverty.

**BEFORE YOU THINK OF TURNING AWAY A DESTITUTE PERSON, REMEMBER THAT GOD HEARS THE PRAYERS OF THE DESTITUTE!** *"He* (God) *will regard the prayer of the **destitute**, and not despise their prayer."* **Psalm 102:17**

**HAVE YOU EVER FELT YOUR HEART WAS BROKEN AND YOUR LIFE WAS DESTITUTE?** David said: *". . .My eyes are toward You* (God), *O God the Lord; in You do I trust and take refuge, pour not out my life nor leave it **destitute** and bare. Keep me from the trap which they have laid for me, and the snares of evildoers."* **Psalm 141:8-9** (The Amplified Bible)

**HAVE YOU EVER BEEN DESTITUTE OF WISDOM?** *"Folly is joy to him that is **destitute** of wisdom: but a man of understanding walketh uprightly."* **Proverbs 15:21**

**IF YOUR SISTER OR BROTHER NEEDS CLOTHES, FOOD, AND IS DESTITUTE — DON'T TURN THEM AWAY!** *"If a brother or sister be naked, and **destitute** of daily food, and one of you say unto them, Depart in peace* ("Bye-Bye, see you later"), *be ye warmed and filled* (with food); *notwithstanding* (and if) *ye give them not those things which are needful to the body; what doth it profit? Even so faith, if it hath not works, is dead, being alone."* **James 2:15-17**

**BE CAREFUL WHEN YOU TURN YOUR BACK ON A DESTITUTE PERSON, BECAUSE IT COULD BE AN ANGEL!** *"Be not forgetful to entertain strangers: for thereby some have entertained angels unawares."* **Hebrews 13:2**

**MANY TIMES GOD HAS PUNISHED A NATION FOR NOT ACCEPTING HIM, BY MAKING IT DESTITUTE!** *"When I shall make the land of Egypt desolate* (barren), *and the country shall be **destitute** of that whereof it was* (previously) *full, when I* (God) *shall smite all them that dwell therein, then shall they know that I am the Lord."* **Ezekiel 32:15**

**THE BIBLE SAYS WE ARE NOT TO DENY THE TRUTH OR BE DISHONEST (DESTITUTE OF THE TRUTH)!** *"He is proud, knowing nothing, but doting about questions and strifes of words, whereof cometh envy, strife, railings, evil surmisings, perverse disputings of men of corrupt minds, and **destitute** of the truth, supposing that gain is godliness: from such* (people) *withdraw thyself. But godliness with contentment is great gain. For we brought nothing into this world, and it is certain we can carry nothing out. And having food and raiment let us be therewith content."* **1 Timothy 6:4-8** *"He that saith, I know him* (God), *and keepeth not his commandments, is a liar, and the truth is not in him."* **1 John 2:4**

**IF YOU ARE DESTITUTE AND OPPRESSED CALL ON THE LORD, HE LOVES YOU AND WILL HELP YOU!** *"The Lord also will be a refuge for the oppressed, a refuge in times of trouble."* **Psalm 9:9**

**WHEN A PERSON BELIEVES IN GOD AND SATAN COMES AGAINST HIM TO MAKE HIM DESTITUTE OF CLOTHES, FOOD, EMPLOYMENT, GOD WILL SEND ANGELS TO PROTECT AND GUIDE HIM!** *"For He* (God) *shall give his angels charge over thee, to keep thee in all thy ways."* **Psalm 91:11**

### PRAYER

Dear God, I ask You to forgive me for those times I was **destitute** of You in my life! I ask You to forgive me for not helping people who were less fortunate than I am. Please forgive our nation as a whole for not accepting You. Please forgive me for turning inward when I had problems, instead of turning to You for my help! Please come into my heart and forgive my sins. Forgive me for feeling I was **destitute** of friends when You are the one true friend I need! In Jesus' name I pray. AMEN!

# DEVIL-DEMONS

DEMONS WERE ONCE ANGELS WHO WERE CAST OUT OF HEAVEN: Revelation 12:9-10/2 Peter 2:4/Jude 6

SATAN AND HIS DEMONIC ANGELS ARE AS REAL AS GOD AND HIS HEAVENLY ANGELS: Matthew 4:1, 11/Job 1:6

HOW TO OVERCOME DEMONS: 1 John 4

DEMONS ARE UNCLEAN SPIRITS: Mark 5:1-19

BORN-AGAIN CHRISTIANS HAVE POWER OVER DEMONS: Mark 6:7, 12-13

MARK 9:17-27, TELLS OF 10 AFFLICTIONS DEMONS CAUSED!

WE ARE NOT BORN EVIL, WE ONLY BECOME EVIL IF DEMONS ENTER: 2 Timothy 2:26

DEMONS FLEE FROM THOSE WHO RESIST THEM! James 4:7/Ephesians 6:11, 16/4:27

DEMONS HAVE HIGH INTELLIGENCE: 2 Corinthians 11:14-15

MYRIADS OF DEMONS JOINED SATAN (LUCIFER) BEFORE THE FLOOD: Genesis 6:1-2/1 Peter 3:19-20

DEMONS FIGHT AGAINST GOD TO OPPRESS MANKIND: Luke 8:27-29/Revelation 16:13-14

DEMONS WILL BE THROWN INTO THE LAKE OF FIRE WITH SATAN AND DESTROYED FOREVER: Revelation 20:2-3, 10/Luke 8:31/Ezekiel 28:18-19/Matthew 25:41

IF DEMONS OPERATE FROM OUTSIDE OUR BODY WE MUST RESIST THEM: James 4:7/1 Peter 5:8-9

DEMONS ARE RESPONSIBLE FOR ALL WORLD DISTRESS AND CAUSE SIN AND DEATH: Genesis 3:1-5/John 8:44

DEMONS ALWAYS OPPRESS MANKIND: Hebrews 2:14-15/2 Corinthians 4:4/Luke 13:16

DEMONS ARE THE CAUSE OF MOST OF OUR TROUBLES: Revelation 12:12, 17/16:14, /1 Peter 5:8

IF DEMONS OPERATE FROM INSIDE OUR BODY, WE MUST HAVE THEM CAST OUT: Matthew 8:16/Mark 1:39

DEMONS BELIEVE IN AND TREMBLE AT GOD'S PRESENCE: James 2:19

HOW TO DESTROY THE WORKS OF THE DEVIL: 1 John 3:8

DEMONS CAN CAUSE WOUNDS AND POSSESS MEN: Acts 19:16

THERE IS ONE CHIEF DEVIL (SATAN) BUT MANY DEMONS: Matthew 9:33-34/Matthew 12:24-28/Mark 3:15-22/Luke 11:15-20

DEMONS CAN CAUSE SICKNESS: Mark 9:17-27/Acts 10:38

DEMONS SEEK OUT WAYS TO ENTER ALL HUMAN LIFE: Ephesians 6:11-17

DEMONS HAVE POWER OVER DEATH: Hebrews 2:14-15

DEMONS MUST BE RESISTED FOR TOTAL VICTORY: James 4:7/1 Peter 5:8-9

DEMONS DECEIVE THE WHOLE WORLD: Revelation 12:9

DEMONS WILL BE CONFINED TO ETERNAL HELL: Revelation 20:7-10

A DEVIL/DEMONS MAY POSSESS A PERSON AND CAUSE DUMBNESS: Matthew 9:32-33/Matthew 12:22
A DEVIL/DEMONS MAY POSSESS A PERSON AND CAUSE BLINDNESS: Matthew 12:22
A DEVIL/DEMONS MAY POSSESS A PERSON AND CAUSE GREVIOUS VEXATIONS: Matthew 15:22/Mark 7:24-30

(Continued)

A DEVIL/DEMONS MAY POSSESS A PERSON AND CAUSE CONVULSIONS AND SUICIDAL MANIA: Luke 9:37-43

A DEVIL/DEMONS MAY POSSESS A PERSON AND CAUSE INSANITY: Mark 5:1-18/Luke 8:26-39

A DEVIL/DEMONS MAY POSSESS A PERSON AND CAUSE UNCLEANNESS: Luke 4:35-36

DEMON POSSESSION: Matthew 7:22/8:16, 28-33/Mark 1:32

SATAN IS THE SUPREME RULER OVER HIS DEMONS: Matthew 9;34/12:24-28

DEMONS CONVERSE WITH MEN: 1 Corinthians 10:20-21

DEMONS TEACH DOCTRINES: 1 Timothy 4:1

DEMONS CAN WORK FALSE MIRACLES: Revelation 16:14/Matthew 24:24/2 Thessalonians 2:8-12/Revelation 13:12-17

DEMONS STALK ABOUT MEN AS ROARING LIONS: 1 Peter 5:8

JESUS NEVER SENT ANYONE OUT TO PREACH WITHOUT FIRST COMMISSIONING THEM TO CAST OUT DEMONS: Matthew 10:1-8/Luke 10:17/Mark 3:14-15/6:12-13/16:15-18/John 14:12

THE SIX MOST COMMON FORMS OF DEMON ACTIVITY IN MAN ARE: OUR EMOTIONS (attitudes, relationships)/OUR THOUGHTS/OUR TONGUE/OUR SEX/OUR ADDICTIONS/OUR PHYSICAL BODIES (infirmities).

SATAN IS THE INVENTOR OF LIES, TROUBLE, FEAR: John 8:44

SATAN BECAME EVIL WHEN HE TRIED TO BECOME GOD: Ezekiel 28:13-17/Isaiah 14:12-15

SATAN IS ALLOWED TO REMAIN ON EARTH UNTIL THIS ISSUE IS SETTLED: John 12:31

SATAN WAS CAST OUT OF HEAVEN WHEN THE KINGDOM RULE BEGAN: Revelation 12:9-10

SATAN ATTEMPTS TO CONTROL THE WORLD AS GOD OF THIS WORLD: 1 John 5:19/2 Corinthians 4:4/Revelation 12:9

SPIRITUAL SICKNESS DESTROYS MAN: Isaiah 1:4-6/Hosea 4:6

SPIRITUAL HEALING IS A COMMISSION GIVEN BY GOD: John 6:63/Luke 4:18

SPIRITUAL HEALING REMOVES SIN AND GIVES US A HAPPY LIFE: James 5:19-20/Revelation 7:14-17

DEMON SPIRITS CONSTANTLY FIGHT AGAINST GOD: 2 Peter 2:4/Jude 6

JESUS CURES OUR INFIRMITIES IF WE HAVE FAITH TO BELIEVE HE CAN AND WE'RE A CHRISTIAN: Matthew 4:23

SPIRITISM IS THE WORK OF DEMONS: Isaiah 8:19-20/Leviticus 19:31/20:6, 27/Deuteronomy 18:10

ASTROLOGY IS THE WORK OF DEMONS: Isaiah 47:13/Daniel 1:20/2:2, 27/4:7/5:7-15/Jeremiah 10:2

NECROMANCY IS THE WORK OF DEMONS: Deuteronomy 18:11

FORTUNE TELLING IS DEMONISM: Acts 16:16-18/1 Samuel 28:3

CLAIRVOYANCE IS THE WORK OF DEMONS: 1 Samuel 28:13-14

## PRAYER

Dear God, I cannot ignore that Satan or demons exist because I believe in the entire Bible. I know that the Bible is the living Word of God. I now humble myself and ask You to forgive me for all my sins. I take authority in the name of Jesus over every area of my life. I rebuke Satan and all of his followers from oppressing me, my family, my home, and my business. I will not give place to the devil in any area of my life. I will feed my spirit on the Word of God. I will pray daily for wisdom and guidance. I know that You love me and that no weapon formed against me shall prosper as long as I keep my faith in You. I will obey Your commandments. I will stay strong in my faith and belief and together we will spend eternity. I thank You for this. In Jesus' precious name, I pray. AMEN!

# DISCRIMINATE

**DEFINITION:** To make a difference in treatment or favor on a basis other than individual merit.

**THE BIBLE SAYS WE ARE TO SHOW NO PREJUDICE, NO PARTIALITY!** *"My brethren, pay no servile regard to people—show no* **prejudice,** *no* **partiality.** *Do not (attempt to) hold and practice the faith of our Lord Jesus Christ (the Lord) of glory together with—snobbery! For if a person comes into your congregation whose hands are adorned with gold rings and who is wearing splendid apparel, and also a poor (man) in shabby clothes comes in, And you pay special attention to the one who wears the splendid clothes and say to him, Sit here in this preferable seat! while you tell the poor (man), Stand there! or, Sit there on the floor at my feet! Are you not* **discriminating** *among your own, and becoming critics and judges with wrong motives? Listen, my beloved brethren. Has not God chosen those who are poor in the eyes of the world to be rich in faith and in their position as believers, and to inherit the kingdom which He has promised to those who love Him? But you (in contrast) have insulted—humiliated, dishonored and shown your contempt for—the poor. Is it not the rich who domineer over you? Is it not they who drag you into the law courts? Is it not they who slander and blaspheme that precious name by which you are distinguished and called (the name of Christ invokved in baptism)? If indeed you (really) fulfill the royal Law, in accordance with the Scripture, You shall love your neighbor as (you love) yourself, you do well.* **Leviticus 19:18.** *But if you show servile regard (prejudice, favoritism) for people, you commit sin and are rebuked and convicted by the Law as violators and offenders."* **James 2:1-9** (The Amplified Bible)

**JESUS GAVE A NEW COMMANDMENT TO US AND IT SAYS WE ARE NEVER TO DISCRIMINATE AGAINST ANOTHER!** *"A new commandment I give unto you, That ye love one another; as I have loved you, that ye also love one another. By this shall all men know that ye are my disciples, if ye have love one to another."* **John 13:34-35**

**THE WORLD DISCRIMINATES AGAINST THE CHRISTIANS AND HATES THEM!** *"For this is the message that ye heard from the beginning, that we should love one another. Not as Cain, who was of that wicked one (Satan), and slew his brother. And wherefore (why?) slew he him? Because his own works were evil, and his brother's righteous.* **Marvel not, my brethren, if the world hate you.** *We know that we have passed from death (eternal separation from God) unto life (eternal union with God), because we love the brethren. He that loveth not his brother abideth in death. Whosoever hateth his brother is a murderer: and ye know that no murderer hath eternal life abiding in him. Hereby perceive we the love of God, because he laid down his life for us: and we ought to lay down our lives for the brethren. But whoso hath this world's good, and seeth his brother have need, and shutteth up his bowels of compassion from him, how dwelleth the love of God in him? My little children, let us not love in word, neither in tongue; but in deed and in truth."* **1 John 3:11-18**

*If we spend 16 hours a day dealing with tangible things and only 5 minutes a day dealing with God, is it any wonder that tangible things are 200 times more real to us than God?*

**LISTED BELOW ARE 20 REASONS WE SHOULD LOVE OTHERS:**
1. To prove that we are of God. **1 John 4:7**
2. It proves sonship. **1 John 4:7/5:1-2**
3. It is proof of knowing God. **1 John 4:7-8**
4. God is love and we should imitate him. **1 John 4:8,16**
5. God has imparted love to us. **1 John 4:9/Rom 5:5**
6. God sent His son to make it all possible. **1 John 4:9/1 Peter 2:21**
7. That we might live. **1 John 4:9-10,14**
8. Because God first loved us. **1 John 4:10,19**
9. We have been loved and forgiven so much. **1 John 4:10/John 3:16**
10. It is our duty. **1 John 4:11**
11. God loved us when we were unlovable. **1 John 4:11/Romans 5:6-10**
12. God dwells in us. **1 John 4:12**
13. God's love is perfected in us. **1 John 4:12**
14. Because of the indwelling Spirit. **1 John 4:13**
15. We believe in love. **1 John 4:16**
16. We dwell in God. **1 John 4:16**
17. We are like Him. **1 John 4:17**
18. It proves we love God. **1 John 4:20**
19. It is a command. **1 John 4:21/5:2**
20. It is natural as sons of God. **1 John 5:1-2**

**PRAYER**

Dear God, please forgive me for **discriminating** against other people. This was a result of my pride and my vanity. I know that pride is sin. Please forgive me. I know that I am not better than anyone else. I repent of my superior feelings against others who are not as fortunate as I am. Humble me in Your eyes. Save me, forgive me and blot out my sins. In Jesus' name I pray. AMEN!

# DISOBEDIENCE

**DO YOU KNOW PEOPLE WHO CLAIM THEY LOVE GOD BUT DISOBEY HIS COMMANDMENTS?** *"They profess that they know God; but in works they deny him, being abominable* (disgusting), *and **disobedient,** and unto every good work reprobate* (condemned, corrupt.)" **Titus 1:16**

**GOD SAID THAT IN THE LAST DAYS BEFORE CHRIST RETURNS CHILDREN WILL BE DISOBEDIENT TO THEIR PARENTS!** *"Backbiters, haters of God, despiteful, proud, boasters, inventors of evil things, **disobedient to parents;"** Romans 1:30*

**BECAUSE OF ADAM'S DISOBEDIENCE WE WERE BORN INTO SIN!** *"For as by one man's **disobedience** (Adam's) many were made sinners, so by the **obedience** of one (Jesus Christ) shall many be made righteous." Romans 5:19*

**THE NATION ISRAEL HAS ALWAYS BEEN DISOBEDIENT TO GOD!** *"But to Israel he saith, All day long I have stretched forth my hands unto a **disobedient** and gainsaying* (contradicting, disputing) *people." Romans 10:21*

**DISOBEDIENT PEOPLE REFUSE TO RECEIVE CORRECTION! EVEN WHEN IT COMES FROM GOD!** *"O Lord, do not your eyes look on the truth? (They have meant to please you (God) outwardly, but You look on their hearts.) You have stricken them, but they have not grieved; You have consumed them, but they have refused to take correction or instruction; they have made their faces harder than a rock, they have refused to repent and return to You." **Jeremiah 5:3** (The Amplified Bible)*

**BEFORE JOHN WAS BORN IT WAS FORETOLD THAT HE WOULD TEACH THE DISOBEDIENT THE WAY TO BE JUST!** *"And many of the children of Israel shall he turn to the Lord their God. And he shall go before him in the spirit and power of Elias, to turn the hearts of the fathers to the children, and the **disobedient** to the wisdom of the just; to make ready a people prepared for the Lord." Luke 1:16-17*

**ACTS 5:29 SAYS WE OUGHT TO OBEY GOD RATHER THAN MEN!**

**THE BIBLE LISTS CURSES FOR DISOBEDIENCE!**
*Cursed be the man that maketh any graven image.* **Deuteronomy 27:15**
*Cursed be the one who dishonors his father and mother.* **Deuteronomy 27:16**
*Cursed be the one who moves his neighbor's landmark.* **Deuteronomy 27:17**
*Curses be to the one who misleads a blind man from his way.* **Deuteronomy 27:18**
*Cursed be he who perverts the justice due to strangers, the fatherless and widows.* **Deuteronomy 27:19**

**ALL ARE SERVANTS OF SATAN AND DISOBEDIENT TO GOD UNTIL WE BECOME BORN-AGAIN CHRISTIANS!** God said to: *"Put them in mind to be subject to principalities* (governments), *and powers, to obey magistrates, to be ready to every good work, to speak evil of no man, to be no brawlers, but gentle, shewing all meekness unto all men. For we ourselves also were sometimes foolish, **disobedient,** deceived, serving divers lusts and pleasures, living in malice and envy, hateful, and hating one another. But after that the kindness and love of God our Saviour toward man appeared." Titus 3:1-4*

**IT IS IMPOSSIBLE TO DISOBEY GOD IN SECRET!** *"Be not deceived; God is not mocked: for whatsoever a man soweth, that shall he also reap. For he that soweth to his flesh shall of the flesh reap corruption; but he that soweth to the* (Holy) *Spirit shall of the* (Holy) *Spirit reap life everlasting. And let us not be weary in well doing: for in due season we shall reap, if we faint not." **Galatians 6:7-9***

**LAWS ARE MADE FOR THE DISOBEDIENT—NOT FOR THE OBEDIENT!** *"Knowing this, that the law is not made for a righteous man, but for the lawless and **disobedient,** for the ungodly and for sinners, for unholy and profane, for murderers of fathers and murderers of mothers, for manslayers. For whoremongers, for them that defile themselves with mankind, for menstealers, for liars, for perjured persons, and if there be any other thing that is contrary to sound doctrine." **1 Timothy 1:9-10***

**DISOBEDIENCE FULFILLS END TIME PROPHECY ABOUT THE LAST DAYS BEFORE CHRIST RETURNS!** *"This know also, that in the last days perilous times shall come. For men shall be lovers of their own selves, covetous, boasters, proud, blasphemers, **disobedient to parents,** unthankful, unholy, without natural affection, trucebreakers, false accusers, incontinent, fierce, despisers of those that are good, traitors, heady, highminded, lovers of pleasures more than lovers of God; Having a form of godliness, but denying the power thereof: from such turn away. For of this sort are they which creep into houses, and lead captive silly women laden with sins, led away with divers lusts, Ever learning, and never able to come to the knowledge of the truth." **2 Timothy 3:1-7***

**READ ABOUT THE WRATH OF GOD UPON THE CHILDREN OF DISOBEDIENCE: Colossians 3:1-10/Ephesians 5:1-7/Ephesians 2:1-2.**

## PRAYER

Dear God, I have been **disobedient** to others and most especially to You! I ask You to forgive me and to cleanse me from all my sins. Please come into my life and give me a brand new beginning. I am not happy being **disobedient!** I want You to be pleased with me. Please cover me with the blood of Jesus and send guardian angels to surround me, lest I fall! Thank You for giving me a new lease on life! In Jesus' name I pray. AMEN!

# DIVORCE

MEN AND WOMEN ARE COMMANDED NOT TO DIVORCE THEIR SPOUSE IF THERE IS ANY POSSIBLE WAY THEY CAN RECONCILE THEIR MARRIAGE! BEING "INCOMPATIBLE" IS NOT A GOOD EXCUSE TO GET A DIVORCE. PRAYING TOGETHER, FASTING, READING THE BIBLE, GOING TO CHURCH AND RECEIVING CHRISTIAN COUNSELING WILL HELP YOU BECOME COMPATIBLE, AGAIN!

ACCORDING TO THE BIBLE, A MAN OR WOMAN SHOULD NOT GET A DIVORCE SIMPLY BECAUSE HE (OR SHE) IS NO LONGER SEXUALLY ATTRACTED TO HIS (OR HER) SPOUSE—OR BECAUSE HE (OR SHE) IS SEXUALLY ATTRACTED TO ANOTHER PERSON! IN GOD'S EYES MARRIAGE IS VERY SERIOUS. MANY PEOPLE TREAT IT AS IF IT IS A CASUAL THING YOU MAY KEEP OR DISCARD!

IF A MAN DIVORCES HIS WIFE, (OR A WOMAN DIVORCES HER HUSBAND) WHEN HIS (OR HER) MATE IS NOT GUILTY OF HAVING SEX OUTSIDE THE MARRIAGE, IT MAY CAUSE THE PERSON WHO IS BEING DIVORCED TO COMMIT ADULTERY! WHY? BECAUSE, WHEN A MAN OR WOMAN WAS MARRIED HE (OR SHE) WAS ACCUSTOMED TO HAVING INTERCOURSE! AFTER EITHER MARRIAGE PARTNER RECEIVES A DIVORCE IT DOES NOT NECESSARILY MAKE THE SEX DRIVE SUDDENLY GO AWAY! THEREFORE, THE TEMPTATION TO HAVE SEX MIGHT TAKE PLACE IF THE TEMPTATION IS TOO GREAT! *"It hath been said, Whosoever shall put away his wife, let him give her a **writing of divorcement:** But I* (Christ) *say unto you, That whosoever shall put away* (divorce) *his wife, saving* (except) *for the cause of fornication* (sex without marriage), *causeth her to commit adultery: and whosoever shall marry her that is **divorced** committeth adultery."* **Matthew 5:31-32**

The Pharisees tempted Jesus by asking him, *"Is it lawful for a man to put away* (divorce) *his wife for every cause? And he answered and said unto them, Have ye not read, that he which made them at the beginning made them male and female, And said, For this cause* (reason) *shall a man leave father and mother, and shall cleave to his wife: and they twain* (two) *shall be one flesh? Wherefore they are no more twain* (two separate people), *but one flesh. What therefore God hath joined together, let no man put asunder. They say unto him, Why did Moses then command to give a **writing of divorcement** and to put her away? He* (Jesus) *saith unto them, Moses because of the hardness of your hearts suffered* (allowed) *you to put away your*

*wives: but from the beginning it was not* (God's plan to do) *so. And I say unto you, Whosoever shall put away* (divorce) *his wife, except it be for fornication* (sex without marriage), *and shall marry another, committeth adultery: and whoso marrieth her which is put away* (divorced) *doth commit adultery."* **Matthew 19:3-9/Matthew 5:31-32/Mark 10:2-12**

**Luke 11:17 says:** *"Every kingdom divided against itself is brought to desolation; and a house divided against a house falleth."*

**Luke 16:18 says:** *"Whosoever putteth away his wife, and marrieth another, committeth adultery: and whosoever marrieth her that is put away from her husband committeth adultery."*

**Mark 3:25 says:** *"And if a house be divided against itself, that house cannot stand."*

BEFORE YOU GET ENGAGED BE SURE TO ASK GOD TO REVEAL TO YOU IF THE PERSON YOU ARE DATING IS THE PERSON HE PREFERS THAT YOU MARRY! DON'T GET IN A BIG HURRY TO GET MARRIED! WAIT FOR GOD TO GIVE YOU AN ANSWER! HE WILL NEVER LEAVE YOU DANGLING AND HE WILL ANSWER YOUR PRAYER!

BEFORE YOU EXCHANGE WEDDING VOWS, AND SAY . . . "I DO" . . . MAKE SURE THE PERSON YOU ARE ABOUT TO MARRY IS THE ONE GOD WOULD CHOOSE FOR YOU TO MARRY! AFTER YOU HAVE EXCHANGED THE VOWS AND THE MINISTER ANNOUNCES YOU TO BE HUSBAND AND WIFE . . . HONOR THOSE VOWS AS LONG AS YOU LIVE! *"When you make a vow to the Lord, Be prompt in doing whatever it is you promised him, for the Lord demands that you promptly fulfill your vows; it is a sin if you don't. (But it is not a sin if you refrain from vowing!) Once you make the vow, you must be careful to do as you have said, for it was your own choice, and you have vowed to the Lord your God."* **Deuteronomy 23:21** (The Living Bible)

**1 Corinthians 7:1-17** (The Living Bible) says: *"If you do not marry, it is good. But usually it is best to be married, each man having his own wife, and each woman having her own husband, because otherwise you might fall back into sin. The man should give his wife all that is her right as a married woman, and the wife should do the same for her husband: for a girl who marries no longer has full right to her own body, for her husband then has his rights to it, too; and in the same way the husband no longer has full right to his own body, for it belongs also to his wife. So do not refuse these rights to each other. The only exception to this rule would be the agreement of both husband and*

(Continued)

wife to refrain from the rights of marriage for a limited time, so that they can give themselves more completely to prayer. Afterwards, they should come together again so that Satan won't be able to tempt them because of their lack of self-control. I'm not saying you must marry; but you certainly may if you wish. I wish everyone could get along without marrying, just as I do. But we are not all the same. God gives some the gift of a husband or wife, and others he gives the gift of being able to stay happily unmarried. So I say to those who aren't married, and to widows—better to stay unmarried, if you can, just as I am. But if you can't control yourselves, go ahead and marry. It is better to marry than to burn with lust. Now, for those who are married I have a command, not just a suggestion. And it is not a command from me, for this is what the Lord himself has said: A wife must not leave her husband. But if she is separated from him, let her remain single or else go back to him. And the husband must not divorce his wife. Here I want to add some suggestions of my own. These are not direct commands from the Lord, but they seem right to me: If a Christian has a wife who is not a Christian, but she wants to stay with him anyway, he must not leave her or divorce her. And if a Christian woman has a husband who isn't a Christian, and he wants her to stay with him, she must not leave him. For perhaps the husband who isn't a Christian may become a Christian with the help of his Christian wife. And the wife who isn't a Christian may become a Christian with the help of her Christian husband. Otherwise, if the family separates, the children might never come to know the Lord; whereas a united family may, in God's plan, result in the children's salvation. But if the husband or wife who isn't a Christian is eager to leave, it is permitted. In such cases the Christian husband or wife should not insist that the other stay, for God wants his children to live in peace and harmony. For, after all, there is no assurance to you wives that your husbands will be converted if they stay; and the same may be said to you husbands concerning your wives. But be sure in deciding these matters that you are living as God intended, marrying or not marrying in accordance with God's direction and help, and accepting whatever situation God has put you into. . .''

1 Corinthians 6:13-20 (The Living Bible) says: ''. . .Sexual sin is never right: our bodies were not made for that, but for the Lord, and the Lord wants to fill our bodies with himself. And God is going to raise our bodies from the dead by his power just as he raised up the Lord Jesus Christ. Don't you realize that your bodies are actually parts and members of Christ? So should I take part of Christ and join him to a prostitute? Never! And don't you know that if a man joins himself to a prostitute she becomes a part of him and he becomes a part of her? For God tells us in the Scripture that in his sight the two become one person. But if you give yourself to the Lord, you and Christ are joined together as one person. That is why I say to run from sex sin. No other sin affects the body as this one does. When you sin this sin, it is against your own body. Haven't you yet learned that your body is the home of the Holy Spirit God gave you, and that he lives within you? Your own body does not belong to you. For God has bought you with a great price. So use every part of your body to give glory back to God, because he owns it.

Psalm 124:8 says: ''Our help is in the name of the Lord, who made heaven and earth.''

Acts 16:31 says: ''Believe on the Lord Jesus Christ, and thou shalt be saved, and thy house.''

''The wife is part of her husband as long as he lives; if her husband dies, then she may marry again, but only if she marries a Christian.''
1 Corinthians 7:39 (The Living Bible)

**GOD DOES NOT MERELY ASK US IN A CORDIAL WAY TO CLEAN UP OUR LIVES AND HEARTS. WE ARE COMMANDED TO!**

**"It doesn't look like a broken home."**

**"AH, WHAT A TANGLED WEB WE WEAVE, WHEN FIRST WE PRACTICE TO DECEIVE!"**

**GOD IS NOT MOCKED!** ''God is not mocked, for whatsoever a man (person) soweth (does), that shall be also reap (receive).''
**Galatians 6:7**

### PRAYER
Dear God, Please help me do everything in my power to keep my marriage together. I know that you bless those marriages which put Jesus in the center of them. I do not want to end up in the divorce courts. Help me and help my spouse realize that this is not Your divine will for our lives. Come into my heart and please forgive me for my sins. Forgive me for not doing all I could to make my marriage a blessing. I will read my Bible each day and pray for wisdom and instruction. I will go to church and worship with other believers. I will tithe and fast as You have instructed we should do. I will obey Your commandments to the very best of my ability. Come live in me and let me feel Your presence. In Jesus' name, I pray. AMEN!

# DOUBLE-MINDED

**DEFINITION:** A set of principles that applies differently to one group of people or circumstances than to another, wavering or undecided in mind.

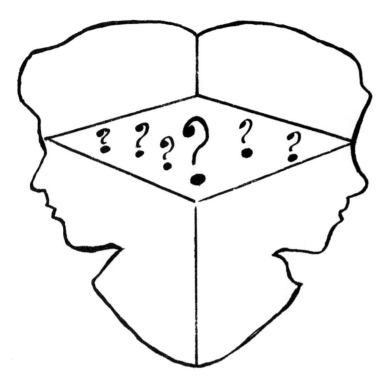

**YOU ARE ONLY AS GOOD AS THE FRIENDS YOU KEEP!** Jesus said: *"NO SERVANT CAN SERVE TWO MASTERS: FOR EITHER HE WILL HATE THE ONE, AND LOVE THE OTHER: OR ELSE HE WILL HOLD TO THE ONE, AND DESPISE THE OTHER. YE CANNOT SERVE GOD AND MAMMON* (bad influences, money, anything other than God).*"* **Luke 16:13**

**IF YOU ARE UNDECIDED ABOUT JESUS AND CANNOT GIVE YOUR ALL, THEN YOU ARE NOT GIVING AT ALL!** *"Now the just shall live by faith: but if any man draw back, my soul shall have not pleasure in him* (that is undecided).*"* **Hebrews 10:38**

**JESUS SAID HE'D RATHER WE LOVE HIM OR HATE HIM. TO BE DOUBLE-MINDED MAKES HIM WANT TO VOMIT. DOUBLE-MINDEDNESS IS THE MOST DISGUSTING TRAIT A PERSON CAN HAVE!** Jesus said: *"I know thy works* (thoughts, actions) *that thou art neither cold nor hot* (neither believe in me, nor disbelieve in me): *I would* (wish) *thou wert* (were) *cold or hot. So then because thou art lukewarm* (double-minded, indifferent, changeable) *and neither cold nor hot* (neither love nor hate me), *I will spue* (vomit) *thee out of my mouth."* **Revelation 3:15-16**

**WHAT MAKES A PERSON DOUBLE-MINDED ABOUT WHETHER OR NOT TO BELIEVE IN JESUS? BECAUSE SATAN IS THE AUTHOR OF CONFUSION!** Jesus said: *"Behold, I stand at the door* (of your heart), *and knock: if any man hear my voice, and open the door, I will come in to him, and will sup* (be with him when he eats, sleeps and in everything he does) *with him, and he with me. To him that overcometh* (being double-minded, holding onto Satan while not quite sure of believing in God) *will I grant to sit with me in my throne, even as I also overcame, and am set down with my Father in his throne."* **Revelation 3:20-21**

**IF YOU HAVE A PROBLEM WITH BEING DOUBLE-MINDED ABOUT GOD, IN BUSINESS AFFAIRS, OR WHATEVER, MEMORIZE THIS VERSE. REPEAT IT TEN TIMES A DAY! IT WILL HELP YOU OVERCOME!** *"A double minded man is unstable in all his ways."* **James 5:8**

**YOU CAN COVER MORE DISTANCE IN ONE DIRECTION THAN YOU CAN IF YOU GO OFF IN FOUR!** *"If any of you lack wisdom, let him ask of God, that giveth to all men liberally, and upbraideth not; and it shall be given him. But let him ask in faith, nothing wavering* (not changing from one choice to another). *For he that wavereth is like a wave of the sea driven with the wind and tossed. For let not that man think that he shall receive any thing of the Lord. A **double minded** man is unstable in all his ways."* **James 1:5-8**

**YOU CAN'T HAVE IT EVERY WHICH WAY! WHEN YOU WERE A CHILD AND ALL CLEANED UP, SOMETIMES YOU WOULD DELIBERATELY PLAY IN THE MUD IN TOTAL DISOBEDIENCE TO YOUR PARENTS. AS BORN-AGAIN CHRISTIANS ONCE CHRIST HAS FORGIVEN US AND WE ARE CLEAN IN HIS EYES, WE ARE NEVER TO DELIBERATELY JUMP BACK INTO THE MUD (SINS) OF LIFE!** *"Ye adulterers and adulteresses, know ye not that the friendship of the world is enmity* (deep-seated dislike) *with God, whosoever therefore will be a friend of the world is the enemy of God. Do ye think that the scripture saith in vain, The spirit that dwelleth in us lusteth to envy? But he* (God) *giveth more grace* (than Satan does). *Wherefore he saith God resisteth the proud, but giveth grace unto the humble. Submit yourselves therefore to God. Resist the devil, and he will flee from you. Draw nigh* (close) *to God, and he will draw nigh to you. Cleanse your hands, ye sinners; and purify* (clean up) *your hearts, ye **double minded.**"* **James 4:4-8**

We can communicate an idea around the world in 70 seconds, but it sometimes takes years for one of God's commands to penetrate one-fourth of inch of human skull!

### PRAYER

Dear God, Please forgive me for being **double-minded.** No one can trust a person who is always "wishy-washy"! I am changeable, therefore, people can never depend on what I might do or say! Please help me overcome this failing. Please help me be firm and honest in all my affairs. Give me the wisdom to know the difference between right and wrong. Please help me to become known as a trustworthy Christian. Come into my life and give me directions that are godly. Quicken my mind to think before I speak! Forgive me if I have disappointed others and for disappointing You. In Jesus' name, I pray. AMEN!

# DREAMS

## A FILTHY DREAM WILL DEFILE YOUR OWN FLESH!

*"Even as Sodom and Gomorrha, and the cities about them in like manner* (also), *giving themselves over to fornication* (sex without marriage, homosexuality, etc.), *and going after strange flesh* (sex between two men, demon angels with women, women with women, bestiality, orgies, etc.), *are set forth for an example* (of God's vengeance), *suffering the vengeance of eternal fire* (in hell). *Likewise also these **filthy dreamers** defile the flesh, despise domonion* (authority), *and speak evil of dignities."* Jude 7-8

## FILTHY DREAMS CAN BE A FORM OF IDOLATRY! GOD CREATED US TO LOVE HIM WHEN WE'RE AWAKE AND ASLEEP!

*"Mortify* (destroy the strength and vitality) *therefore your members* (body parts) *which are upon the earth* (while you live); *fornication* (sex without marriage), *uncleanness* (all sex perversions), *inordinate affection* (unnatural, excessive passion and lust), *evil concupiscence* (evil, depraved lust, passion, appetite to sexually harm), *and covetousness* (greed), *which is idolatry: For which things' sake the wrath of God cometh on the children of disobedience."* Colossians 3:5-6

## MANY PEOPLE ACCUSE GOD OF SENDING THEM A SCARY DREAM, WHEN GOD IS NOT GUILTY! JOB DID THAT VERY THING! Job 7:13-14

## IF WE LIVE A HOLY LIFE WE WON'T BE THE VICTIM OF FILTHY DREAMS AND TERRIBLE NIGHTMARES! IN GENESIS 37 WE READ ABOUT JOSEPH AND HIS TWO DREAMS. WHEN HE TOLD THEM TO HIS BROTHERS, THEY HATED HIM! DREAMS ARE DREAMS! BUT THEY SOMETIMES HAVE A WAY OF SEEMING VERY REAL TO THE EXTENT OF AFFECTING OUR WAKING LIVES!

*"For a dream cometh through the multitude of business. . ."* Ecclesiastes 5:3

*"For in the multitude of dreams and many words there are also divers* (various) *vanities: but fear thou God."* Ecclesiastes 5:7

NOT ALL DREAMS ARE FALSE! NOR DO THEY ALL COME FROM SATAN! THERE ARE 34 DREAMS RECORDED IN SCRIPTURES. GOD GAVE DANIEL SKILL, UNDERSTANDING, AND WISDOM TO INTERPRET DREAMS AND VISIONS! READ: Daniel 1, 2 and 5.

IN THE LAST DAYS GOD SAID HE WOULD POUR OUT OF HIS SPIRIT UPON ALL LIVING PEOPLE THROUGH PROPHESY, VISIONS AND DREAMS! *"And it shall come to pass in the last days* (before Christ returns to earth), *saith God,* (that) *I will pour out of my Spirit upon all flesh: and your sons and your daughters shall **prophesy**, and your young men shall see **visions**, and your old men shall **dream dreams**: And on my servants and on my handmaidens I will pour out in those days of my Spirit; and they shall prophesy: And I will shew* (show) *wonders in heaven above, and signs in the earth beneath; blood, and fire, and vapour of smoke: The sun shall be turned into darkness, and the moon into blood, before that great and notable day of the Lord come* (before the actual day Christ returns): *And it shall come to pass, that whosoever shall call on the name of the Lord shall be saved."* Acts 2:17-21

Are there any "Godly" truths contained in those dream analysis books? or the theories taught by the late Edgar Cayce? What about auras, visions, familiar spirits, esp, dreams, etc.? None of the above are based on Biblical teachings! All dreams and visions come from a person's vivid imagination, from Satan or from God! The things of God are perfect and can be proven through the Scriptures! The manifestations from Satan are deceptive and lies. They're meant to confuse or destroy! A Christian can easily tell what is from God and what is from Satan!

DON'T PUT TOO MUCH STOCK INTO DREAMS. NOT ALL DREAMS AND VISIONS ARE SACRED, OR TRUE! DREAMS CAN COME FROM SATAN, AND HE FULLY INTENDS TO CONFUSE AND LEAD YOU ASTRAY! HE MAY APPEAR AS GOD, BUT GOD ALMIGHTY SAYS NOT TO HEARKEN TO OUR DREAMS! *"For thus saith the Lord of hosts, the God of Israel; Let not your prophets and your diviners* (fortune-tellers), *that be in the midst of you, deceive you, neither hearken* (listen, pay attention) *to your **dreams** which ye cause to be **dreamed**. For they prophesy falsely unto you in my* (God's) *name: I have not sent them, saith the Lord."* Jeremiah 29:8-9

A CHRISTIAN NEVER HAS TO RELY ON DREAMS OR VISIONS FOR AN ANSWER TO A PRAYER! *"For I know the thoughts that I think toward you, saith the Lord, thoughts of **peace**, and not of evil, to give you an expected end* (answer). *Then shall ye call upon me, and ye shall go and pray unto me, and I will hearken* (listen and answer) *unto you. And ye shall **seek me**, and **find me**, when ye shall search for me with all your heart."* Jeremiah 29:11-13

### PRAYER

Dear God, I have been very foolish to think You were appearing to me in dreams when I was **not** receiving special revelations! I know that Satan appears as an angel of light! Please give me a peaceful night's rest each time I lie down. I will say my prayers each night and praise You when I awake! I know that no weapon that is formed against me will prosper! Forgive me for my sins! Forgive me for claiming to be something special when I know that You are no respector of persons! Help me clean up my life, my thoughts, and my actions! Help me to control my tongue! I praise You and thank You for loving me! In Jesus' name, I pray. AMEN!

# DRUGS

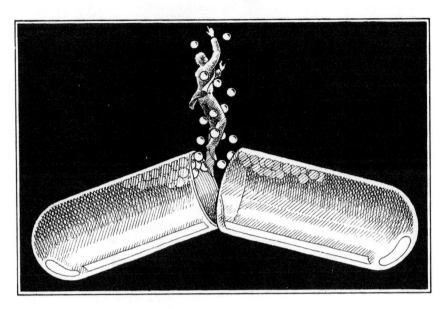

**WHY DO PEOPLE TAKE DRUGS?** Over 25% of American women take drugs to fight tension, anxiety, insomnia, depression. They do not consider the dangerous side effects, the possibility of addiction, or overdose. They take **"uppers"**, **"downers"**, and other potent mind-altering drugs! They experience "mood" changes. They take tranquilizers and whatever other drugs their doctor prescribes and feel completely safe and secure because they were prescribed by a licensed physician.

Between ⅔ to ¾ of psychoactive prescriptions are issued to women and girls. Drugs intended to elevate or decrease activity may also affect pain, mood or tension. A person's tolerance level increases as he attempts to reach the desired result. There can be unpleasant emotional and physical responses to the cessation of use, i.e., **withdrawal symptoms.**

Minor tranquilizers (**Miltown, Equanil**) remain in the bloodstream in higher than normal amounts for a longer time. Tranquilizers or painkillers, mixed with alcohol is often the cause of **accidental deaths** or **suicides.** There is another dangerous aspect. Drugs stored in the body's fatty tissues do not leave the system easily. When a person stops taking medication the drugs stored in body tissue continue to be released into the system for some time and can cause complications. Since women generally have more fatty tissue through their bodies than men, they are likely to retain greater amounts of a drug for a longer time. NEVER FORGET ... THE BRAIN IS THE SINGLE LARGEST FATTY ORGAN IN THE BODY!

The most popular minor tranquilizers in recent years are **Librium, Valium** and **Quaaludes.** Their purpose is intended to relax muscles. Many of these drugs are also used extensively in the treatment of **alcoholism** in an effort to reduce the unpleasant effects of abstinence. In many cases the "cure" becomes the problem! Diet pills referred to as

"speed" are used as stimulants. However, they make it very difficult to stabilize life and behavior! More often than not users develop **erratic patterns** of daily medication. They alternate between **stimulation** and **sedation.** Often they find themselves behaving in a schizophrenic manner upon cessation of these drugs! Hospitalization may follow and in some severe cases **convulsions,** a sense of **persecution, illusions, hallucinations.** In any event the central nervous system (spinal cord, brain) are altered.

**ANY DRUG CAPABLE OF INFLUENCING YOUR MIND WILL ALSO AFFECT YOUR PHYSICAL STATE. ALTERATIONS IN YOUR BODY WILL TRIGGER MENTAL RESPONSES!** During times of stress our tendency to "lose our temper" or cry a lot does not mean we are neurotic! Nor does it mean we need a tranquilizer! **Psalm 124:8** says: *"Our help is in the name of the Lord, who made heaven and earth."*

**ALL TOO OFTEN MOOD-ALTERING DRUGS ARE UNIVERSALLY PRESCRIBED TO MALES AND FEMALES WITHOUT EVER DISTINGUISHING THE DIFFERENCES IN ANATOMY, NUTRITION, FEMALE CYCLES OF HORMONAL CHANGES, IN ORDER TO CORRECTLY DETERMINE DOSAGE!** This is a real hazard when people depend on their doctor for safe therapy.

**MEN, WOMEN, BOYS & GIRLS SELL THEIR SOULS TO SATAN DAILY IN ORDER TO ACQUIRE MARIJUANA, COCAINE, HEROIN, AMPHETAMINES, HASHISH, BARBITURATES, PIPES & OTHER DRUG PARAPHERNALIA!**

**FATHERS ON DRUGS CAN CAUSE BIRTH DEFECTS!** Drug exposure before conception, particularly to **Methadone, Darvon, Caffeine, Thaledomide, Alcohol,**

(Continued)

Anesthetic gases & Nicotine can result in reduced birth weight, learning ability, and increased infant mortality. Many ingredients in "over-the-counter drugs", such as mercury, can cross the placenta and concentrate in the fetus. It has been discovered that: marijuana smoking may reduce sperm and testosterone levels, damage alterations in brain waves and may cause driving accidents.

**THE AGE OF MARIJUANA USERS STARTS AS EARLY AS 8 YEARS OF AGE IN THE UNITED STATES!** The percentage of high school seniors using marijuana daily would boggle our minds! Marijuana creates a temporary euphoria, mellowness and relaxation. It distorts perception, weakens critical judgement, interferes with the ability to concentrate. Prolonged heavy use in adolescents affects motivation, school performance, adds feelings of alienation, strains family relationships. Withdrawal can be very serious if the supply is cut off! Although it is yet to be proven that marijuana smokers become heroin addicts, they are more likely than non-users to experiment with other drugs. **Marijuana smoke contains more cancer-causing substances than an equivalent amount of tobacco smoke.** It has more immediate effect on the lungs. Heavy use can product bronchial irritation. It reduces the amount of air the lungs can move following a deep breath, not to mention the inability to expel bacteria and other foreign substances!

**MARIJUANA QUICKENS THE HEART RATE AND MAY CAUSE IRREGULAR HEART RHYTHM!** It affects the body's endocrine system, the glands, and the hormones that affect normal growth, energy and reproduction. **Genetic damage may occur!** Marijuana may impair the body's immunity system, which provides protection against disease. As research continues, there are reports of chromosome damage.

**IN MALES, HEAVY MARIJUANA USE REDUCES SPERM PRODUCTION!** Sperm mobility may cause abnormalities. These abnormalities seem to disappear once marijuana use has been discontinued. Heavy use can **reduce the male sex drive.** Statistics show that heavy users for 5 years or more tend to develop impotence!

**IN FEMALES, MARIJUANA USE CAN RESULT IN FAILURE TO RELEASE A RIPENED EGG DURING THE MONTHLY REPRODUCTIVE CYCLE!** Most experts agree that pregnant women should definitely avoid drugs. Like alcohol, marijuana may cause birth defects!

**MARIJUANA CAN SERIOUSLY INTERFERE WITH SUCCESS IN SCHOOL OR ON THE JOB!** Heavy use can impair short-term memory, reading comprehension, mathematical problem-solving and overall capacity to think! Marijuana can alter a person's judgment and self-perception.

**DRUGS INTERFERE WITH DRIVING & OPERATING MACHINERY!** Being "high" interferes with the necessary skills to drive or operate equipment. It slows down your reactions, dulls the sense of visual perception, interferes with coordination. The effects may linger for hours, even after a person no longer feels "high". **Teenage drivers are notorious for causing accidents while under the influence of drugs, alcohol or both!**

**MARIJUANA IS GLORIFIED IN MUSIC AND IN**

POPULAR PUBLICATIONS. SATAN SEES TO THIS THROUGH HIS OVERWHELMING POWER OF SUGGESTION. DRUGS BRING BONDAGE TO THE MIND, BODY, SPIRIT. THEY AFFECT YOUR FUTURE. THEY CAN SEPARATE YOU FROM GOD ETERNALLY UNLESS YOU GET SMART!

**WHAT DOES GOD HAVE TO SAY ABOUT USING DRUGS?** *"Be sober* (don't use drugs, alcohol), *be vigilant* (alert, wise); *because your adversary* (enemy) *the devil, as a roaring lion, walketh about, seeking whom he may devour."* **1 Peter 5:8**

**KIDS, WHEN YOU FEEL "PEER PRESSURE" TO SMOKE MARIJUANA OR TAKE "SPEED", ETC., DON'T GIVE IN! DON'T TRUST ANYTHING THEY SAY. THEY WILL LIE TO YOU!** *"It is better to trust in the Lord than to put confidence in man* (any person)." **Psalm 118:8**

**NEVER PUT ANYTHING IN YOUR MOUTH STRONGER THAN MILK, COCA-COLA, COFFEE! 1 Thessalonians 5:22** says: *"Abstain from all appearance of evil."*

**DRUGS ARE A SIGN OF THE LAST DAYS BEFORE CHRIST RETURNS!** *"This know also, that in the last days perilous times shall come. For men* (people) *shall be lovers of their own selves, covetous, boasters, proud, blasphemers, disobedient to parents, unthankful, unholy. Without natural affection* (homosexuals), *trucebreakers, false accusers, incontinent, fierce, despisers of those that are good, traitors, heady* (drug "highs" & ego) *highminded, lovers of pleasures* (drugs, sex, money) *more than lovers of God; having a form of godliness* ("I'm Okay, You're Okay), *but denying the power* (of the Holy Spirit) *thereof: from such* (people & things) *turn away."* **2 Timothy 3:2-5**

**DRUGS ARE DECEIVING. PEOPLE WHO USE THEM OR SELL THEM ARE DECEIVED!** *"But evil men* (people) *and seducers* (those who talk you into taking drugs, alcohol, sex, etc.) *shall wax* (grow) *worse and worse, deceiving and being deceived."* **2 Timothy 3:13**

**THE DRUG PUSHER IS AN EVIL WOLF DRESSED UP IN A NICE SHEEP'S CLOTHING!** *"Beware of false prophets, which come to you in sheep's clothing* (pretending to help you), *but inwardly they are ravening* (wild, hungry, out to destroy you) *wolves."* **Matthew 7:15**

**THOSE WHO SCOFF AND SAY THERE'S NOTHING WRONG WITH MARIJUANA, OR TRANQUILIZERS, FULFILL BIBLE PROPHECY ABOUT THE LAST DAYS!** *". . . There shall come in the last days scoffers, walking after their own lusts."* **2 Peter 3:3**

**IN CASE YOU THINK YOUR BODY BELONGS ONLY TO YOU, THINK AGAIN! YOU HAD NOTHING TO DO WITH BEING BORN AND YOU WERE CREATED BY GOD!** *"Know ye not that ye are the temple* (body) *of God, and that the* (Holy) *Spirit of God dwelleth in you?"* **1 Corinthians 3:16**

**WARNING:** *"If any man* (person) *defile the temple of God, him shall God destroy; for the temple of God is holy, which temple ye are."* **1 Corinthians 3:17**

**WE ARE COMMANDED TO GLORIFY GOD IN OUR BODY & THAT MEANS "NO DRUGS!"** *"What? know ye not that your body is the temple of the Holy Ghost which is in you,* which ye have of God, and ye are not your own? For ye are bought with a price: therefore glorify God in your body, and in your spirit, which are God's.'' **1 Corinthians 6:20**

**WE ARE COMMANDED TO KEEP OUR BODIES UNDER SUBJECTION (CONTROL)!** ''But I keep under my body, and bring it into subjection: lest that by any means, when I have preached to others, I myself should be a castaway.'' **1 Corinthians 9:27**

**EVERYTHING WE DO TO OUR BODIES WILL BE JUDGED BY GOD AND THERE'S NO ESCAPING THAT!** ''For we must all appear before the judgement seat of Christ; that every one may receive the things done in his body, according to that (thing) he hath done (to his body), whether it be good or bad.'' **2 Corinthians 5:10**

**WE ARE COMMANDED TO PRESENT OUR BODIES A LIVING SACRIFICE!** ''I beseech (beg) you therefore, brethren, by the mercies of God, that ye present your bodies a living sacrifice, holy, acceptable unto God, which is your reasonable service.'' **Romans 12:1**
**OUR BODIES ARE MEMBERS OF CHRIST!** Read: **1 Corinthians 6:15-17**

**IF YOU LIVE ONLY TO FULFILL YOUR FLESHLY NEEDS AND WANTS (WHICH INCLUDES DRUGS, SEX, ALCOHOL, ETC.), YOU SEPARATE YOURSELF ETERNALLY FROM GOD!** ''For if ye live after (for) the flesh, ye shall die (be eternally separated from God): but if ye through the (Holy) Spirit do mortify the deeds of the body, ye shall live.'' **Romans 8:13**

**ARE DRUGS ACTUALLY MENTIONED IN THE BIBLE???** **ABSOLUTELY!** ''Sorcery'' is Greek for ''pharmakeia'', which is derived from the word ''pharmakeus'' and from ''pharmakon'' which is drugs, i.e., spell-giving potions. *Strong's Exhaustive Concordance of The Bible. **OUR WORD ''PHARMACY'' IS THE ENGLISH WORD FROM THE GREEK WORD!** *Also read: **Exodus 7:11/Jeremiah 27:9/Daniel 2:2/Malachi 3:5/Revelation 21:8**

**INVENTORS OF EVIL THINGS = DRUGS, DRUG PARAPHERNALIA, SEX DEVICES, ETC.: Romans 1:30**

**YOU MAY SECRETLY TAKE DRUGS & THINK NO ONE KNOWS, BUT GOD DOES KNOW. HE LOVES YOU BUT HE HATES SIN. NOTHING CAN BE HIDDEN FROM GOD!** ''He (God) revealeth the deep and secret things: he knoweth what is in the darkness, and in the light (truth) dwelleth with him.'' **Daniel 2:22**

**HOW CAN YOU KICK THE DRUG HABIT?** Pray and humble yourself and be honest to God. Confess your sin to him and ask his forgiveness. he will help you overcome! ''He that overcometh shall inherit all things (that God has in store for you); and I will be his God, and he shall be my son.'' **Revelation 21:7**

**WHAT HAPPENS IF A PERSON DOES NOT GIVE UP DRUGS? WILL HE GO TO HEAVEN WHEN HE DIES, OR WHEN THE RAPTURE TAKES PLACE WILL HE BE ''CAUGHT UP'' TO BE WITH JESUS IN THE CLOUDS? ACCORDING TO THE BIBLE HE WILL SPEND ETERNITY WITH SATAN IF HE DOES NOT REPENT AND FORSAKE THEM FOREVER! GOD HATES DRUGS SO MUCH THAT HE LISTS THEM IN THE SAME CATEGORY AS MURDER!** ''But the fearful, and unbelieving, and the abominable, and murderers, and whoremongers, and sorcerers (drug users and pushers) and idolaters (those who worship anything other than the one true living God), and all liars shall have their part in the lake which burneth with fire and brimstone...'' **Revelation 21:8**

**JESUS SAID:** ''And, behold, I come quickly; and my reward is with me, to give every man according as his work shall be.'' **Revelation 22:12** ''Blessed are they that do his commandments, that they may have right to the tree of life, and may enter in through the gates into the (Holy) city. For without (outside the city) are dogs and sorcerers (false teachers, homosexuals, drug pushers, users), and whoremongers, and murderers, and idolaters, and whosoever loveth and maketh a lie.'' **Revelation 22:14-15**

**BELOW IS A SAMPLE LIST OF SOME OF THE MOST POPULAR DRUGS USED BY PEOPLE TODAY. IT IS NOT A COMPLETE LIST, BUT MAY HELP YOU BECOME SOMEWHAT FAMILIAR WITH SOME OF THE NAMES.**

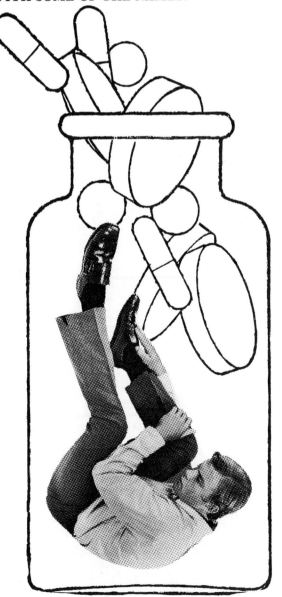

(Continued)

## UPPERS-DOWNERS-TRANQUILIZERS
## PHARMACEUTICAL PAIN KILLERS:

Black mollies/Los Angeles Turnarounds
White Crosses
Cocaine (very popular, expensive, movie stars inhale through the nose), Coke, Girl, Snow
Reds/rainbows/Tuinal/Seconal/Amytal/Mexican Reds/ Amies/Barbs/Blues
Valium/Librium (most commonly used by housewives)
Quaaludes/Mequin/Sopors/Ludes/714's
Yellow Jackets
Demerol/Morphine/Fiorinal/Percodan/Coedine
Marijuana (pot, grass, joints)

## HALLUCINOGENIC:

LSD (Acid) (window pane, orange sunshine, blotter acid, purple haze, orange barrel )
Mescaline (chocolate)
D.M.T./D.E.T./D.P.T.
Morphine/Coedine

## HEAVY DRUGS:

Angel Dust (P.C.P.) (used in marijuana, very dangerous, may cause death) (peace pills, bog)
Morphine/Coedine/Methadone/Percodan
Heroin (Smack, Skag, Junk, Horse, Boy)
Dilaudid/Opium/Cocaine

## PRAYER:

Dear God, I am a **drug** user. I want to be forgiven of this sin which is affecting my body, mind, and spirit. I did not know that my body belongs to you. Please forgive me for doing things that you do not want me to do. Please help me clean up my act. Please help me break this terrible habit. Please change my craving for **drugs** into what you would have me to do. I want to become a born again Christian. Please come into my heart and forgive all my sins. I do not want to go to hell. I want to be with Jesus each day of my life. I need to sense his presence in all that I think or do. Thank you for loving me so much that you gave your only son to die on the cross for my sins. Thank you for raising him from the dead to new life. I know that he lives today and that you can help me. I ask you to help me, now! I need your help. I need your forgiveness. Thank you for giving me another chance. I will try real hard to please you. Beginning this moment, I claim the victory over **drugs.** I lay the **drugs** down and I will never be guilty of taking them again. Please give me strength and heal me from this awful desire. Give me strength and I will praise you forever. In Jesus' name, I pray. AMEN!

# EATING AND DRINKING

*"For the kingdom of God is not meat and drink; but righteousness, and peace in the Holy Ghost."* **Romans 14:17**

**JESUS SAID:** *"Blessed are they which do hunger and thirst after righteousness: for they shall be filled."* **Matthew 5:6**

**JESUS SAID:** *"It is written, Man shall not live by bread alone, but by every word that proceedeth out of the mouth of God."* **Matthew 4:4**

**BORN-AGAIN CHRISTIANS SHOULDN'T WORRY TOO MUCH ABOUT WHETHER THEY WILL HAVE GROCERIES TO EAT TOMORROW!** Jesus said: *". . .Take no thought for your life, what ye shall eat, or what ye shall drink; nor yet for your body, what ye shall put on. Is not the life more than meat, and the body (more) than raiment (clothes)? Behold (look at) the fowls (birds) of the air: for they sow (plant) not, neither do they reap (harvest), nor gather into barns; yet your heavenly Father feedeth them. Are ye not much better than they?"* **Matthew 6:25-26**

*"Whether (whatever) therefore ye eat or drink, or whatsoever ye do, do all to the glory of God."* **1 Corinthians 10:31**

**STOP THINKING ABOUT FOOD SO MUCH AND THE COST OF FOOD, AND YOUR WAISTLINE! SPEND MORE TIME IN PRAYER, FASTING, AND LEADING OTHERS TO CHRIST! ONE DAY SOON WE'LL HAVE NO NEED FOR FOOD, SO START CONCENTRATING MORE ON GOD! FOOD IS NOT SO IMPORTANT AND WE ALL NEED TO FAST MORE!** *"Food (is intended) for the stomach and the stomach for food, but God will finally end (the functions of) both and bring them to nothing. . ."* **1 Corinthians 6:13** (The Amplified Bible)

*"The meek shall eat and be satisfied: they shall praise the Lord that seek him: your heart shall live for ever."* **Psalm 22:26**

**FOOD TASTES BETTER WHEN YOU EARN IT THROUGH YOUR OWN LABOR! WELFARE PROGRAMS FOR LAZY PEOPLE ARE AGAINST GOD'S PLAN FOR OUR LIVES!** *"There is nothing better for a man, than that he should eat and drink, and make himself enjoy good in his labor."* **Ecclesiastes 2:24** (The Amplified Bible)

**FOOD IS NEVER ENOUGH TO SATISFY. ONLY THE PEACE OF GOD SATISFIES OUR APPETITE!** *"All the labour of man is for his mouth, and yet the appetite is not filled."* **Ecclesiastes 6:7**

**MOST PEOPLE GET TOO HUNG UP ON MATERIAL POSSESSIONS, FOOD, AND CLOTHES! THIS IS WRONG!** *"For we brought nothing into this world, and it is certain we can carry nothing out. And having food and raiment (clothes) let us be therewith content."* **1 Timothy 6:7-8**

**HOW MUCH MORE CLEAR COULD JESUS HAVE BEEN IN THIS STATEMENT ABOUT HOW UNIMPORTANT THE SUBJECT OF FOOD IS?** *". . .It is written, That man shall not live by bread alone, but by every word of God."* **Luke 4:4** *". . .Therefore I say unto you, Take no thought for your life, what ye shall eat; neither for the body, what ye shall put on. The life is more than meat, and the body is more than raiment (clothes). Consider the ravens: for they neither sow (plant) nor reap (harvest); which neither have storehouse nor barn; and God feedeth them: how much more are ye better than the fowls (birds)?"* **Luke 12:22-24** *"And seek not ye what ye shall eat, or what ye shall drink, neither be ye of doubtful mind. For all these things do the nations of the world seek after; and your Father (God) knoweth that ye have need of these things. But rather seek ye the kingdom of God; and all these things shall be added unto you. Fear not, little flock (of Christians); for it is your Father's good pleasure to give you the kingdom."* **Luke 12:29-32**

**GOD FEEDS HIS SERVANTS AND LETS OUR ENEMIES EAT VIOLENCE!** *"A man shall eat good by the fruit of his mouth: but the soul of the transgressors shall eat violence."* **Proverbs 13:2** *"The righteous eateth to the satisfying of his soul: but the belly of the wicked shall want."* **Proverbs 13:25** *"Better is a dinner of herbs where love is, than a stalled ox and hatred therewith."* **Proverbs 15:17**

**WHEN SOMEONE INVITES YOU OUT TO EAT — BE SURE OF HIS MOTIVES LEST YOU FIND YOURSELF INDEBTED TO HIM!** *"When you sit down to eat with a ruler, consider who and what are before you; For you will put a knife to your throat, if you are a man given to desire (material gain or recognition). Be not desirous of his dainties (expensive food and atmosphere), for they are deceitful food (offered with questionable motives)."* **Proverbs 23:1-3** *"Will you set your eyes upon wealth, when (suddenly) it is gone? For riches certainly make themselves wings, like an eagle that flies toward the heavens. Eat not the bread (food offered to you) of him who has a hard, grudging and envious eye, neither desire his dainty foods; For as he thinks in his heart, so is he. As one who reckons he says to you, eat and drink, yet his heart is not with you (but is gruding the cost). The morsel (amount) which you have eaten you will vomit up, and your complimentary words will be wasted."* **Proverbs 23:5-8** (The Amplified Bible)

**DO NOT EAT WITH GLUTTONS NOR DRUNKARDS!** *"Do not associate with winebibbers; be not among them nor among gluttonous eaters of meat. For the drunkard and the glutton shall come to poverty, and drowsiness shall clothe a man with rags (because he will be drunk all the time instead of working)."* **Proverbs 23:20-21** (The Amplified Bible)

**ALSO READ: THE CHAPTER ON OBESITY AND THE CHAPTER ON FASTING!**

### PRAYER

Dear God, let me never forget to give thanks for the **food** You have supplied me with before I **eat!** Forgive me for placing so much emphasis on what I'm going to have to **eat** for **dinner** or what I'm going to **feed** my company! Let my conversations about **food costs** and **menus** change into ones about how much You love me and have helped me. Forgive me for my sin of **over-eating** and for being **wasteful with food.** Forgive me for those times when I drank **alcoholic beverages** with my meals! I will spend more time in prayer and less time in the kitchen! I will never neglect to go to church because I have a **roast** on cooking! Come into my life and help me get my perspective back to thinking about You instead of spending so much time thinking about **food** and the **grocery bills.** I know You will never leave me nor forsake me! I know that as long as I obey Your commandments You will furnish me all the **food** that is necessary to fill me! Thank You for loving me. In Jesus' name, I pray. AMEN!

# EFFEMINATE
## -------------------------------

**DEFINITION:** Unmanly, marked by weakness and love of ease; a male having unsuitable feminine qualities; soft or delicate to an unmanly degree in traits, tastes, habits; womanish.

What causes a boy (or man) to be effeminate? Satan does! You see, God's plan is for a man to be a man and a woman to be a woman. He forbids men to have sex with men (homosexuals) and women to have sex with women (lesbians)! Either case is evil and halts God's master plan to have men and women marry and replenish the earth. This is impossible when men have intercourse with men and women with women! Satan hates God. He is the author of confusion and lies and all sin. God calls Satan a thief. When Satan steals a boy's masculinity he loves it because he figures he has one more soul that will live with him in hell. *"The thief* (Satan) *cometh not,* (would not have come to planet earth), *but* (except) *to steal, and to kill, and to destroy: I* (Christ, speaking) *am come* (to earth) *that they* (me, you) *might have life, and that they might have it more abundantly. I am the good shepherd: the good shepherd giveth his life for the sheep."* **John 10:10-11**

How can a young boy (or man) get rid of the appearance and characteristics of being effeminate? Become a born-again Christian by recognizing that you are a sinner! Ask God to forgive you. Turn away from all sin in your life. **Ask God to help you overcome being effeminate!** Go to an uncompromising church which teaches the entire Bible. Ask the minister to pray and cast out the unclean spirit (in you) which causes you to be effeminate.

The worst thing about a young boy (or man) being effeminate is that the person usually becomes a homosexual! This is not a trait any normal boy (or man) would desire for his life if he thinks logically! A man of God will be needed to rebuke Satan and to force the unclean spirit out of the person! All the effeminate traits will gradually vanish if the person stays very close to God! God is all-loving and forgiving! If you have a son (or brother) who has this problem, take him to a spirit-filled minister so he can be delivered!

**GOD'S LAWS ARE NOT UNFAIR! THEY ARE JUST WHEN ONE USES THEM FOR THE PURPOSE FOR WHICH THEY WERE DESIGNED!** *"Now we recognize and know that the Law of God is good, if any one uses it lawfully — for the purpose for which it was designed; Knowing and understanding this: that the Law is not enacted for the righteous — the upright and just, who are in right standing with God; but for the lawless and unruly, for the ungodly and sinful, for the irreverent and profane, for those who strike and beat and* (even) *murder fathers and strike and beat and* (even) *murder mothers; for manslayers, For **impure and immoral persons,** those who **abuse themselves with men,** kidnappers, liars, perjurers and whatever else is opposed to wholesome teaching and sound doctrine."* **1 Timothy 1:8-10** (The Amplified Bible)

**THE BIBLE SAYS THAT IF A MAN IS EFFEMINATE AND DOES NOT GET SAVED HE WILL NOT INHERIT THE KINGDOM OF GOD. GOD HATES THIS TRAIT!** *"Know ye not that the unrighteous shall not inherit the kingdom of God? Be not deceived: neither fornicators* (those who engage in pre-marital sex), *nor idolaters* (those who love anything or anyone more than God), *not adulterers* (married persons having sex with other than their spouse), *nor effeminate* (usually homosexuals), *nor abusers of themselves with mankind* (homosexuals, lesbians, sex perverts), *nor thieves, nor covetous, nor drunkards, nor revilers* (abusers of others), *nor extortioners, shall inherit the kingdom of God."* **1 Corinthians 6:9-10**

*"For God's* (holy) *wrath and indignation are revealed from heaven against all ungodliness and unrighteousness of men, who in their wickedness repress and hinder the truth and make it inoperative. For that which is known about God is evident to them and made plain in their inner consciousness, because God* (Himself) *has shown it to them. For ever since the creation of the world His invisible nature and attributes that is, his eternal power and divinity have been intelligible and clearly discernible in and through the things that have been made — His handiworks. So* (men) *are without excuse — altogether without any defense or justification. Because when they knew and recognized Him as the God, they did not honor and glorify Him as God, or give Him thanks. But instead they became futile and godless in their thinking with vain imaginings, foolish reasoning and stupid speculations — and their senseless minds were darkened. Claiming to be wise, they became fools —professing to be smart, they made simpletons of themselves. And by them the glory and majesty and excellence of the immortal God were exchanged for and represented by images, resembling mortal man and birds and beasts and reptiles. Therefore God gave them up in the lusts of their* (own) *hearts to sexual impurity, to the dishonoring of their bodies among themselves, abandoning them to the degrading power of sin. Because they exchanged the truth of God for a lie and worshiped and served the creature rather than the Creator* (God), *Who is blessed forever. For this reason God gave them over and abandoned them to vile affections and degrading passions. For their women exchanged their natural function for an unnatural and abnormal one* (they became lesbians). ***And the men also turned from natural relations with women and were set ablaze*** (consumed) *with lust for one another, men committing shameful acts with men and suffering in their own bodies and personalities the inevitable consequences and penalty of their wrong doing and going astray, which was* (their) *fitting retribution. And so, since they did not see fit to acknowledge God or approve of Him or consider Him worth the knowing, God gave them over to a base and condemned mind to do things not proper or decent but loathsome; Until they were filled — permeated and saturated — with every kind of unrighteousness, iniquity, grasping and covetous greed and malice. They were full of envy and jealousy, murder, strife, deceit and treachery, ill will and cruel ways. They were secret backbiters and gossipers, slanderers, hateful to and hating God, full of insolence, arrogance and boasting; inventors of new forms of evil, disobedient and undutiful to parents. They were without understanding, conscienceless and faithless, heartless and loveless and merciless. Though they are fully aware of God's righteous decree that those who do such things deserve to die, they not only do them themselves but approve and applaud others who practice them.* **Romans 1:18-32** (The Amplified Bible)

**SINCE FEMININE TRAITS AND CLOTHING ARE APPEALING TO THE EFFEMINATE MAN, THEY SOMETIMES LIKE TO DRESS LIKE A WOMAN. GOD FORBIDS THIS!** *"The woman shall not wear that which pertains to a man, **neither shall a man put on a woman's garment;** for all that do so are an abomination* (totally disgusting) *to the Lord your God."* **Deuteronomy 22:5**

### PRAYER

Dear God, I am **effeminate!** I want to be rid of this problem in my life once and for all! Please forgive me of all my sins and come into my life to stay! Help me to know that with You all things are possible! I want to be free. I want to change my life from an unhappy one to a happy one! Please help me. I turn away from those things which make me appear **effeminate.** I will go to church. I will confess to others that I am a born-again Christian. I will be baptised. I will seek the aid of a minister who believes in casting out unclean spirits in the name of Jesus. I love You God and I thank You for answering my prayer. In Jesus' name, I pray. AMEN!

# EMERGENCY SCRIPTURES

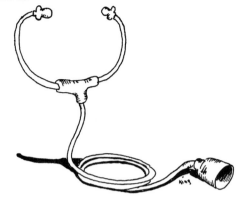

**ACCIDENTS:**
Psalm 91:10-12/Mark 3:5/Isaiah 43:2/Psalm 34:7

**BACK PROBLEMS:**
Luke 13:11-13

**BLEEDING:**
Ezekiel 16:6/Mark 5:25-29

**BURNS:**
Job 33:25/Isaiah 43:2

**CANCER**
Exodus 23:25/Psalm 91:10/1 Peter 2:24/Isaiah 53:4-5
    Matthew 8:17

**DEATH:**
Psalm 33:18-19/Psalm 118:17

**DEPRESSION:**
Isaiah 53:4-5/61:3/51:11/Psalm 34:18/16:11/128:2/147:3/30:11
Jeremiah 31:13

**EARS:**
Mark 7:34-35/Isaiah 35:5-6/Proverbs 20:12

**EPIDEMICS:**
Psalm 91:10

**EYES:**
Isaiah 35:5/42:16/Psalm 146:8/Proverbs 20:12/Mark
8:23/Deuteronomy 34:7

**FATIGUE:**
Isaiah 40:29

**FEAR:**
Psalm 91:5, 11/136:11-12/34:7/Isaiah 26:3/Deuteronomy
33:27/John 14:27

**FEVER:**
Matthew 8:14-15/Acts 28:8-9/John 4:50-53

**FIRE—FLOOD:** Isaiah 43:2

**FINANCES:**
Philippians 4:19/Proverbs 11:31/15:6/8:21/Psalm 68:19/Matthew
6:24-25, 33

**GLANDULAR DEFICIENCIES:**
Philippians 4:19/Exodus 23:25

**HEART:**
Psalm 31:24/51:10

**INSOMNIA:**
Psalm 4:8/127:2/Ecclesiastes 5:12/Proverbs 3:24

**JOINTS:**
Psalm 22:14

**KNEES:**
Isaiah 35:3/Hebrews 12:12

**LAMENESS:**
Isaiah 35:5-6/Zephaniah 3:19/Micah 4:5

**LEARNING DISABILITIES:**
1 Corinthians 2:16/Proverbs 4:13/Nehemiah 9:20/John 14:26/Job
32:8/2 Timothy 1:7/Exodus 31:3, 6/Daniel 1:17/Psalm
19:7/138:8/Isaiah 54:13

**LONG LIFE:**
Proverbs 9:11

**MENTAL SOUNDNESS:**
Luke 4:18-19/Isaiah 35:3-4/54:14, 17/Psalm
31:22-24/9:9-10/146:8/42:5, 11/Hebrews 12:12-13/Jeremiah
29:11-13/2 Timothy 1:7/Nehemiah 8:10/Philippians 2:5/1 Corinthians 2:16

**MISCARRIAGE:**
Psalm 113:9/128:3/147:13/Exodus 23:26/Isaiah 65:20-23

**PESTS AND PLAGUES:**
Psalm 91:10

**PRE-MATURE BABIES:**
Isaiah 65:20

**STUTTERING:**
Isaiah 32:4/Exodus 4:11-12

**SKIN DISORDERS:**
Psalm 42:11

**SMOKING—DRINKING—DRUGS:**
2 Corinthians 7:1/Philippians 4:13/Psalm 27:1/Romans 8:35-37

**TEETH:**
Isaiah 58:11

**ULCERS—VIRUS:**
Exodus 23:25

**WITHERED LIMBS—ARTHRITIS:**
Mark 3:5

**WEIGHT CONTROL:**
Luke 21:34/Romans 6:6-7, 14/14:17-18/13:14/Galatians 5:1,
16/6:8-9/2:21/2 Corinthians 10:4-5/5:21/Matthew 4:4/5:6/6:25,
33/Psalm 23/Proverbs 25:16/23:1-3/13:20, 25/Job 23:12/1 John
5:21/John 4:32, 34/1 Corinthians 6:12-13

**EMERGENCY HEALING SCRIPTURES:**
3 John 2
1 Peter 2:24
John 15:3, 7/14:6
Mark 3:15/16:17-20
Hebrews 4:12

Colossians 1:13
Psalm 107:13, 20/103:1-4
Proverbs 4:20-24
Acts 3:16
Deuteronomy 7:15

Jeremiah 1:12
Malachi 4:2
Isaiah 53:4-5/55:11
Matthew 24:35/8:17

# EMPLOYEES EMPLOYERS

**GOD COMMANDED US TO OBEY OUR EMPLOYERS! HOWEVER, IF AN EMPLOYER ORDERS HIS EMPLOYEE TO DO ANY THING THAT WOULD BE A SIN IN THE EYES OF GOD, THE PERSON SHOULD NOT DO SO, BUT SHOULD FIND A DIFFERENT JOB!** *"Servants, you must respect your masters and do whatever they tell you — not only if they are kind and reasonable, but even if they are tough and cruel. Praise the Lord if you are punished for doing right! Of course, you get no credit for being patient if you are beaten for doing wrong; but if you do right and suffer for it, and are patient beneath the blows, God is well pleased. This suffering is all part of the work God has given you. Christ, who suffered for you, is your example. Follow in his steps: He never sinned, never told a lie, never answered back when insulted; when he suffered he did not threaten to get even; he left his case in the hands of God who always judges fairly. He personally carried the load of our sins in His own body when He died on the cross, so that we can be finished with sin and live a good life from now on. For his wounds have healed ours!"* **1 Peter 2:18-24** (The Living Bible)

**CHRISTIAN EMPLOYEES: NEVER LET IT BE SAID THAT CHRIST'S PEOPLE ARE POOR WORKERS!** *"Christian slaves (employees) should work hard for their owners (employers) and respect them; never let it be said that Christ's people are poor workers. Don't let the name of God or his teaching be laughed at because of this. If their (your) owner (employer) is a Christian, that is no excuse for slowing down; rather they should work all the harder because a brother in the faith is being helped by their (your) efforts."* **1 Timothy 6:1-2** (The Living Bible)

**EMPLOYEES SHOULD TRY HARD TO PLEASE THEIR EMPLOYERS — NOT JUST TO TRY TO GET A RAISE BUT BECAUSE THIS IS WHAT GOD WANTS YOU TO DO!** *"You slaves (employees) must always obey your earthly masters (employers), not only trying to please them when they are watching you but all the time; obey them willingly because of your love for the Lord and because you want to please him. Work hard and cheerfully at all you do, just as though you were working for the Lord and not merely for your masters (employers), remembering that it is the Lord Christ who is going to pay you, giving you your full portion of all he owns. He is the one you are really working for. And if you don't do your best for him, he will pay you in a way that you won't like — for he has no special favorites who can get away with shirking."* **Colossians 3:22-25** (The Living Bible)

**EMPLOYERS: YOU ARE COMMANDED TO BE JUST AND FAIR TO YOUR EMPLOYEES BECAUSE YOU ARE BEING WATCHED BY GOD!** *"You slave owners (employers) must be just and fair to all your slaves (employees). Always remember that you, too, have a Master in heaven who is closely watching you."* **Colossians 4:1** (The Living Bible)

**EMPLOYEES: YOU ARE COMMANDED TO WORK HARD EVEN WHEN YOUR BOSS ISN'T WATCHING OR ISN'T THERE!** *"Slaves (employees), obey your masters; be eager to give them your very best. Serve them as you would Christ. Don't work hard only when your master is watching and then shirk when he isn't looking; work hard and with gladness, all the time, as though working for Christ, doing the will of God with all your hearts. Remember, the Lord will pay you for each good thing you do, whether you are slave (owned) or free (to quit a job)."* **Ephesians 6:5-8** (The Living Bible)

**EMPLOYERS: NEVER THREATEN YOUR EMPLOYEES OR YOU MAY HAVE TO ANSWER TO GOD!** *"And you slave owners (or employers) must treat your slaves right, just as I have told them to treat you. Don't keep threatening them; remember, you yourselves are slaves to Christ; you have the same Master they do, and he has no favorites."* **Ephesians 6:9** (The Living Bible)

**EMPLOYEES: YOU MUST NEVER TALK BACK TO YOUR EMPLOYERS NOR STEAL FROM THEM! YOU MUST BE TRUSTWORTHY!** *"Urge slaves (employees) to obey their masters and to try their best to satisfy them. They must not talk back, nor steal, but must show themselves to be entirely trustworthy. In this way they will make people want to believe in our Savior and God."* **Titus 2:9-10** (The Living Bible)

**ANY EMPLOYER OR EMPLOYEE WHO CAN'T TAKE CRITICISM CAN'T KEEP A GOOD JOB!** *"The man who is often reproved but refuses to accept criticism will suddenly be broken and never have another chance. With good men in authority, the people rejoice; but with the wicked in power, they groan."* **Proverbs 29:1-2** (The Living Bible)

**WHEN YOU WORK YOUR VERY BEST, YOU WON'T FEEL THE NEED TO COMPARE YOURSELF TO ANOTHER PERSON!** *"Let everyone be sure that he is doing his very best, for then he will have the personal satisfaction of work well done, and won't need to compare himself with someone else. Each of us must bear some faults and burdens of his own. For none of us is perfect!"* **Galatians 6:4-5** (The Living Bible)

**EMPLOYER: WHEN YOU HIRE A MAN WHO IS POOR AND HUNGRY, DON'T WITHHOLD HIS WAGES! BECAUSE IF HE CRIES OUT TO GOD THROUGH HUNGER, YOU WILL HAVE TO ANSWER FOR IT!** *"Never oppress a poor **hired man,** whether (he is) a fellow Israelite or a foreigner living in your town. Pay him his wage each day before sunset, for since he is poor he needs it right away; otherwise he may cry out to the Lord against you and it would be counted as a sin against you."* **Deuteronomy 24:14-15** (The Living Bible)

**EMPLOYERS AND EMPLOYEES SHOULD LOVE EACH OTHER AND HELP EACH OTHER!** *"Don't just pretend that you love others: really love them. Hate what is wrong. Stand on the side of the good. Love each other with brotherly affection and take delight in honoring each other. Never be lazy in your work but serve the Lord enthusiastically. Be glad for all God is planning for you. Be patient in trouble, and prayerful always. When God's children are in need, you be the one to help them out. And get into the habit of inviting guests home for dinner or, if they need lodging, for the night. If someone mistreats you because you are a Christian, don't curse him; pray that God will bless him. When others are happy, be happy with them. If they are sad, share their sorrow. Work happily together. Don't try to act big. Don't try to get into the good graces of important people, but enjoy the company of ordinary folks. And don't think that you know it all! Never pay back evil for evil. Do things in such a way that everyone can see you are honest clear through. Don't quarrel with anyone. Be at peace with everyone, just as much as possible. Dear friends, never avenge yourselves. Leave that to God, for he has said that he will repay those who deserve it. Don't take the law into your own hands. Instead, feed your enemy if he is hungry. If he is thirsty give him something to drink and you will be "heaping coals of fire on his head." In other words, he will feel ashamed of himself for what he has done to you. Don't let evil get the upper hand but conquer evil by doing good."* **Romans 12:9-21** (The Living Bible)

### PRAYER

Dear God, please forgive me for not being a proper **employee (or employer)!** I know how to be a **better worker!** I have not loved others, and I have disappointed You! Forgive me for wasting time on my job! Forgive me for stealing! Forgive me for being unkind! Forgive all my sins and I will become the kind of person that You want me to be! I thank You for loving me and for giving me another chance! I will make every effort to make things right with those I have offended. In Jesus' name, I pray. AMEN!

# EMPLOYMENT

**JESUS SAID WE ARE TO OCCUPY (WORK) UNTIL HE RETURNS!** Luke 19:13

**GOD WANTS US TO ENJOY OUR WORK AND TO CONSIDER IT A GIFT FROM GOD!** *". . .It is good and comely* (fitting) *for one to eat and to drink and to **enjoy** the good of all his **labour** that he taketh under the sun all the days of his life, **which God giveth him:** for it is his portion. Every man also to whom God hath given riches and wealth, and hath given him power to eat thereof, and to take his portion, and to rejoice in his **labour;** this is the **gift of God.**"* **Ecclesiastes 5:18-19/8:15/3:13**

**THE BIBLE SAYS WE ARE NOT TO LABOR JUST TO BE RICH — FOR MONEY IS NOT ETERNAL!** *"**Labour not to be rich:** cease from thine own wisdom. Wilt* (will) *thou set thine eyes upon that which is not* (eternal)? *for riches certainly make themselves wings; they **fly away** as an eagle toward heaven."* **Proverbs 23:4-5**

*"For what shall it profit a man, if he shall gain the whole world, and lose his own soul?"* **Mark 8:36**

**A PERSON SHOULD NEVER LET HIS JOB BECOME HIS WHOLE LIFE!** *"Ye have sown much, and bring in little; ye eat, but ye have not enough; ye drink, but ye are not filled with drink; ye clothe you, but there is none warm; and he that earneth wages earneth wages to put it into a bag with holes."* **Haggai 1:6**

*"In all labour there is profit: but the talk of the lips tendeth only to penury."* **Proverbs 14:23**

**MONEY CAN NEVER BRING TRUE HAPPINESS!** *"Lay not up for yourselves treasures upon earth, where moth and rust doth corrupt, and where thieves break through and steal: But lay up for yourselves treasures in heaven, where neither moth nor rust doth corrupt, and where thieves do not break through nor steal: For **where your treasure is, there will your heart be also.**"* **Matthew 6:19-21** *"**Labour not for the meat which perisheth,** but for that meat* (the Word of God) *which endureth unto everlasting life, which the Son of man* (Jesus) *shall give unto you: for him hath God the Father sealed* (gave the Holy Spirit)." **John 6:27**

**MAN SHOULD ENJOY HIS LABOR BUT NEVER EXPECT IT TO SATISFY, LIKE GOD CAN SATISFY HIM!** *"All things are full of **labour;** man cannot utter* (even imagine) *it: the eye is not satisfied with seeing, nor the ear filled with hearing."* **Ecclesiastes 1:8** *"Go to now, ye rich men, weep and howl for your miseries that shall come upon you. Your riches are corrupted, and your garments are moth-eaten. Your gold and silver is cankered* (rusted); *and the rust of them shall be a witness against you . . . Ye have heaped treasure together for the last days."* **James 5:1-3**

Man's work is soon forgotten! No job is worthy of spending so much time on that you neglect your family, your church and God! Ecclesiastes 1:8-11

**THE PROFIT FROM ALL YOUR LABOUR IS LEFT BEHIND, SO IT'S BEST TO KEEP YOUR JOB IN PROPER PERSPECTIVE — NEVER PUT YOUR JOB BEFORE YOUR SERVICE TO GOD!** *"Yea* (yes), *I hated all my **labour** which I had taken under the sun: because I should leave it unto the man that shall be after me. And who knoweth whether he shall be a wise man or a fool? yet shall he have rule over all my **labour** wherein I have **laboured,** and wherein I have shewed* (showed) *myself wise under the sun. . ."* **Ecclesiastes 2:18-19**

**WHAT GOOD IS IT TO WORK ALL OF YOUR LIFE IF YOU'RE ONLY GOING TO PUT IT IN THE BANK?** *"For what hath man of all his **labour,** and the vexation of his heart, wherein he hath **laboured** under the sun? For all his days are sorrows, and his travail grief, yea* (yes), *his heart taketh not rest in the night."* **Ecclesiastes 2:22-23**

*"The sleep of a labouring man is sweet, whether he eat little or much: but the abundance of the rich will not suffer* (allow) *him to sleep."* **Ecclesiastes 5:12**

**PERSONAL MESSAGE TO EMPLOYEES:** *"Servants, obey in all things your **masters** according to the flesh; not with eyeservice, as menpleasers; but in singleness of heart, fearing* (obeying) *God: And whatsoever ye do, do it heartily, as to the Lord* (as you would if you worked for Christ, in person), *and not unto men; knowing that of the Lord ye shall receive the reward of the inheritance* (born-again Christians are joint-heirs with Christ); *for ye serve the Lord Christ. But he that doeth wrong shall receive for the wrong which he hath done: and there is no respect of persons* (with God)." **Colossians 3:22-25**

**PERSONAL MESSAGE TO EMPLOYERS:** *"Masters, give unto your **servants** that which is just and equal; knowing that ye also have a Master* (God) *in heaven."* **Colossians 4:1** *"Fret not thyself because of evildoers, neither be thou envious against the workers of iniquity* (don't envy those employers, employees who get away with sin and don't get caught, or you have to do more work than they, and get less pay). *For they shall soon be cut down like the grass, and wither as the green herb. **Trust in the Lord, and do good;** so shalt thou dwell in the land, and verily thou shalt be fed. Delight thyself also in the Lord; and he shall give thee the desires of thine heart. Commit thy way unto the Lord; trust also in him; and he shall bring it* (the desires of your heart) *to pass."* **Psalm 37:1-5**

## PRAYER

Dear God, Please forgive me for being late to **work.** Forgive me for all my sins! I have done less than my best efforts in my **employment.** Teach me to be more courteous to those I **work** for and with! Help me to keep my hands and my mind busy! Help me to learn to mind my own business and not to gossip! Forgive me for being jealous when others got promotions before I received mine! Forgive me for envying others who seem to receive special favors! Help me to do a good day's **work** as if I were **working** directly for You! Help me become known as a peace maker, and not one who disrupts others! Let others see Jesus in my face and in my **work.** I will not steal even a pencil! I will be completely honest in all my **work habits!** I will be completely honest, in my conversations. I will not complain. I do love You, and I want to be with You someday. Therefore, I realize how important it is to be the kind of Christian You want me to be. Please come into my heart to stay. Let me feel Your presence! Thank You for forgiving all my sins! I praise You and I will live for You! In Jesus' name, AMEN!

# ENCHANTMENTS (MAGIC)

All forms of sorcery (occult practices) are sin! Satan is the inventor of the occult! Anyone who puts any trust in enchantments, astrology, dreams, star-gazing, crystal balls, ouija boards, fortune tellers, reincarnation, palmistry, tarot cards, etc., is doomed (by his own choice) to go to hell — unless he totally turns away from all interest and participation in these things and becomes a born-again Christian! *"But these two things shall come to thee in a moment in one day, the loss of children, and widowhood: they shall come upon thee in their perfection* (full measure) *for the multitude of thy sorceries, and for the great abundance of thine enchantments. For thou hast trusted in thy* (occult) *wickedness: thou hast* (have) *said, None seeth me. Thy wisdom and thy knowledge, it hath perverted* (turned your mind away from) *thee* (God) *and thou hast said in thine heart, I am* (great, superior, safe, I don't need God), *and none else beside me. Therefore shall evil come upon thee; thou shalt not know, from whence* (where) *it riseth: and mischief* (accidents) *shall fall upon thee; thou shalt not be able to put it off: and desolation shall come upon thee suddenly, which thou shalt not know* (in advance). *Stand now with thine enchantments, and with the multitude of thy sorceries, wherein thou hast* (have) *laboured from thy youth; if so be thou shalt be able to profit, if so be mayest prevail. Thou art wearied* (totally confused) *in the multitude of thy counsels. Let now the astrologers, the stargazers, the monthly prognosticators* (foretelling events through omens, signs), *stand up, and save thee from these things that shall come upon thee."* **Isaiah 47:9-13**

**EVER SINCE ADAM AND EVE SINNED, WERE CAST OUT OF THE GARDEN OF EDEN, MAN HAS PRACTICED OCCULT ACTIVITIES. GOD HATES ANYTHING CONNECTED WITH THE OCCULT!** *"There shall not be found among you anyone that maketh his son or his daughter to pass through the fire, or that useth divination* (fortune telling) *or an observer of times* (charting sun, moon, planets, fortune telling), *or an enchanter* (one who casts spells, magic, voodoo), *or a witch, or a charmer* (casting spells or hypnotising), *or a consulter* (spirit medium) *with familiar spirits* (demon spirits), *or a wizard* (male witch), *or a necromancer* (one who communicates with the dead). *For all that do these things are an abomination* (disgusting, evil, sin) *unto the Lord: and because of these abominations the Lord thy God doth* (does) *drive them out from before thee."* **Deuteronomy 18:10-12/2 Kings 17**

**Leviticus 19:26 says:** *". . .neither shall ye use enchantment* (magic, casts spells, charm snakes), *nor observe times* (astrology)," *"And the soul* (person) *that turneth* (goes) *after such* (people) *as have familiar spirits* (demon spirits), *and after wizards* (male witches), *to go a-whoring after them, I will even set my face against that soul* (person), *and will cut* (separate) *him off from among his people. Sanctify* (cleanse) *yourselves therefore, and be ye holy: for I am the Lord your God."* **Leviticus 20:6-7**

**GOD SAYS NOT TO LISTEN TO (OR BELIEVE) ANYTHING THAT HAS TO DO WITH THE OCCULT! HERE ARE FIVE CATEGORIES OF PEOPLE WE SHOULD STAY AWAY FROM ALL CONTAINED IN THIS ONE VERSE:** *"Therefore hearken not ye* (don't listen) *to your PROPHETS, nor to your DIVINERS, nor to your DREAMERS, nor to your ENCHANTERS, nor to your SORCERERS."* **Jeremiah 27:9**

**MANASSEH WAS ONLY 12 YEARS OLD WHEN HE BEGAN HIS 55-YEAR REIGN OVER JERUSALEM. HE WAS EVIL AND VERY MUCH INVOLVED IN THE OCCULT ARTS.** *"And he* (Manasseh) *made his sons pass through the fire, and observed times* (suns, moons), *and used enchantments, and dealt with familiar* (demon) *spirits and wizards* (male witches): *he wrought* (did) *much wickedness in the sight of the Lord, to provoke him to anger."* **2 Kings 21:6/2 Chronicles 33:6**

When you read to the word "light" in the Bible it always means truth, wisdom, holy. Christ is always associated with light! "Darkness" is always symbolic of evil, sin, bondage, death and hell! Satan is always associated with darkness! All occult practice is called darkness!

**CHRISTIANS ARE COMMANDED TO NOT BE COMPANIONS WITH ANYONE (OR ANYTHING) TO DO WITH THE OCCULT!** *"Be ye not unequally yoked together with unbelievers: for what fellowship hat righteousness with unrighteousness? and what communion hath light* (Christ) *with darkness* (Satan)?" **2 Corinthians 6:14** *"Wherefore come out* (get away) *from among them, and be ye separate, saith the Lord, and touch not the unclean thing; and I will receive you and will be a Father unto you, and ye shall be my sons and daughters, saith the Lord Almighty."* **2 Corinthians 6:17-18**

**WARNING:** If you are dabbling with psychics, black magic, ouija boards, tarot cards, crystal balls, palmistry, astral projection, automatic writing, hypnosis, mind control, dream analysis, seances, astrology, thought transferrence, voodo, etc., stop it now! Give it up forever! Ask Jesus to forgive you. Then turn away from these sinful practices forever! God forbids them! God faithfully promises to forgive our sins and to blot them from his memory, if we will humble ourselves and ask forgiveness and turn away from them. He will help you overcome! *"He that overcometh shall inherit all things; and I will be his God, and he shall be my son. But the fearful, and unbelieving, and the abominable, and murderers, and whoremongers, and sorcerers, and idolaters, and all liars, shall have their part in the lake which burneth with fire and brimstone: which is the second death."* **Revelation 21:7-8** Jesus said: *"And, behold, I come* (back to earth) *quickly; and my reward is with me, to give every man according as his work shall be. I am Alpha and Omega, the beginning and the end, the first and the last. Blessed are they that do his commandments, that they may have right to the tree of life, and may enter in through the gates into the city* (God's holy city). *For without* (the gates) *are dogs* (homosexuals), *and sorcerers, and whoremongers, and murderers, and idolaters, and whosoever loveth and maketh a lie."* **Revelation 22:12-15**

**NOT SINCE THE BOOK OF GENESIS WAS WRITTEN HAS THERE BEEN SUCH A WORLDWIDE FASCINATION WITH THE OCCULT AS THERE IS TODAY! DID YOU KNOW THAT OCCULT ACTIVITY IS AN END TIME PROPHECY ABOUT THE LAST DAYS JUST BEFORE CHRIST RETURNS?** Jesus said: *"For there shall arise false Christs, and false prophets, and shall shew great signs and wonders, insomuch that, if it were possible, they shall deceive the very elect."* **Matthew 24:24** Hitler used **mind control** to cause the murder of 5 million jews. **Jim Jones** used **mind control** to cause the suicides of 900 men, women, boys and girls. **Uri Geller** uses **mind control** to bend metal objects and to **levitate** through space for distances as far as 30 miles. There are thousands of examples about how **magic** is used in the film, TV industry, etc. **Astrology** has never been so popular! Twenty-four hours a day, across the world, people are asking, "What's your sign?"

## PRAYER

Dear God, I confess I am interested in **occult practices** and have participated in them. I didn't know they were forbidden, until now! I don't want to give allegiance to things Satan has created to destroy my mind and soul. I turn away from any fascination or activity to do with the **occult**. I ask You to come into my heart and forgive me. Change my directions and hobbies away from **extra-sensory perception** to realistic Bible reading and praying. Help me overcome the power Satan has over me. I rebuke all **occult** activity in my life in the name of Jesus! Thank You for loving me and for warning me about the wrong direction I was taking. I turn away from these sinful practices. In Jesus' name, I pray. AMEN!

# ENEMIES

IF AN UNSAVED PERSON SEEKS TO ABUSE OR DISCREDIT A BORN-AGAIN CHRISTIAN, HIS CHANCES AT BEING SUCCESSFUL ARE "NIL"! THE LORD IS ALWAYS ON THE SIDE OF THE CHRISTIAN WHO OBEYS THE COMMANDMENTS! ALL CHRISTIANS SHOULD LEARN THIS VERSE AND REPEAT IT AS OFTEN AS NEEDED! *"Do not rejoice against me, O my enemy, for though I fall, I will rise again! When I sit in darkness, the Lord himself will be my Light."* **Micah 7:8** (The Living Bible)

HERE IS A LIFETIME GUARANTY WHICH CAN NEVER BE REVOKED NOR CANCELLED! IT IS ADDRESSED TO BORN-AGAIN CHRISTIANS, ONLY! *"When a man is trying to please God, God makes even his worst enemies to be at peace with him."* **Proverbs 16:7** (The Living Bible)

IF YOU PUT FORTH EVERY EFFORT TO LIVE A GOOD CHRISTIAN LIFE, AND YOU DISCOVER YOU HAVE AN ENEMY WHO WISHES TO DISCREDIT OR DESTROY YOU, WHAT SHOULD YOU DO? MEMORIZE THIS VERSE AND REPEAT IT OVER AND OVER UNTIL YOU GET DELIVERANCE! GOD WILL COME TO YOUR RESCUE! *"O Lord my God, in thee do I put my trust: save me from all them that persecute me, and deliver me."* **Psalm 7:1**

HAVE YOU EVER FELT THAT YOUR ENEMIES OUT-NUMBERED YOUR FRIENDS AND THAT THEY WERE STRONGER THAN YOU?* David wrote: *"But mine enemies are lively, and they are strong: and they that hate me wrongfully are multiplied. They also that render evil for good are mine adversaries* (enemies); *because I follow the thing that good is. Forsake me not, O Lord: O my God, be not far from me. Make haste to help me, O Lord my salvation."* **Psalm 38:19-22**

GOD IS OUR SHELTER AND A STRONG TOWER FROM ALL OUR ENEMIES! *"For thou hast been a shelter for me, and a strong tower from the enemy."* **Psalm 61:3** *"Thou* (God) *through thy commandments hast made me wiser than mine enemies: for they are ever with me."* **Psalm 119:98**

A CHRISTIAN IS COMMANDED NOT TO REJOICE WHEN HIS ENEMY FALLS. THIS KIND OF BEHAVIOR OPPOSES THE GREATEST COMMANDMENT OF ALL — WHICH IS TO LOVE OUR NEIGHBOR! *"Rejoice not when thine enemy falleth, and let not thine heart be glad when he stumbleth: Lest the Lord see it, and it displease him, and he turn away his wrath from him."* **Proverbs 24:17**

WE ARE COMMANDED TO DO GOOD TO OUR ENEMIES! THIS IS NOT JUST A SUGGESTION, IT IS A COMMANDMENT! *"If thine enemy be hungry, give him bread to eat; and if he be thirsty, give him water to drink."* **Proverbs 25:21**

THE JEWS HAVE ALWAYS HAD ENEMIES . . . WHY? . . . BECAUSE OF THEIR SINS AGAINST GOD! *"And thy lovers* (friends) *have forgotten thee; they seek thee not; for I* (God) *have wounded thee with the wound of an enemy, with the chastisement of a cruel one, for the multitude of thine iniquity; because thy sins were increased."* **Jeremiah 30:14**

JESUS COMMANDS THAT WE LOVE OUR ENEMIES AND PRAY DILIGENTLY FOR THEM! Jesus said: *"Ye have heard that it hath been said, Thou shalt love thy neighbour, and hate thine enemy. But I say unto you, Love your enemies, bless them that curse you, do good to them that hate you, and pray for them which despitefully use you, and persecute you;"* **Matthew 5:43-44/Luke 6:27-28** *"But love ye your enemies, and do good, and lend, hoping for nothing again; and your reward shall be great, and ye shall be the children of the Highest* (God): *for he is kind unto the unthankful and to the evil."* **Luke 6:35**

IT MAY BE VERY DIFFICULT TO THINK OF YOUR ENEMY AS A BROTHER — BUT THAT'S WHAT WE ARE ASKED TO DO! *"Yet count him* (your enemy) *not as an enemy, but admonish him as a brother."* **2 Thessalonians 3:15**

IF WE LIVE A GODLY LIFE, GOD PROMISES TO MAKE OUR ENEMIES HIS FOOTSTOOL WHEN CHRIST RETURNS TO EARTH! Read: **Psalm 110:1/Hebrews 10:13**

ALSO, WHEN CHRIST COMES BACK TO EARTH HE WILL PUT ALL ENEMIES UNDER HIS FEET. THE LAST ENEMY TO BE DESTROYED IS DEATH! *"Then cometh the end, when he* (Christ) *shall have delivered up the kingdom to God, even the Father; when he shall have put down all rule and all authority and power. For he must reign, till he hath put all enemies under his feet. The last enemy that shall be destroyed is death."* **1 Corinthians 15:24-26**

WHEN ENEMIES KNOCK AT YOUR DOOR RUN GET YOUR BIBLE AND BEGIN READING THE 23rd Psalm!

### PRAYER

Dear God, please forgive me for being an **enemy** to another person when I should have been a friend. Please protect me from those who might be my **enemies**! Teach me to love others just as You love me! I know that it is better to love than to hate! I know that I am happiest when I am giving out love! I pray for my **enemies** and ask You to forgive them as You forgive me. Help me to be more like Christ in my thoughts and in my actions. Please forgive me for all my sins and I will praise You forever! In Jesus' name, I pray. AMEN!

91

# ENVY

**ENVY BRINGS CONFUSION. IT IS AN EVIL SIN THAT GRIPS HOLD OF A PERSON SUCH AS A CANCER WOULD!**

*"Who is a wise man and endued* (gifted) *with knowledge among you? let him shew* (show) *out of a good conversation his works with meekness of wisdom. But if ye have bitter **envying** and strife in your hearts, glory not and lie not against the truth. This wisdom* (to evny) *descendeth not from above, but is earthly, sensual, devilish. For where **envying** and strife is, there is confusion and every evil work.''* **James 3:13-16**

**ENVY = LUST = ENEMY OF GOD!** *"Do ye think that the scripture saith in vain, The* (evil) *spirit that dwelleth in us* (from Satan) *lusteth* (craves) *to **envy?''*** **James 4:5**

**DO NOT ENVY YOUR NEIGHBOR! ENVY = VANITY = SIN! Read: Ecclesiastes 4:4**

**INSTEAD OF ENVYING ANYONE (OR ANYTHING) WHY NOT LAY ASIDE THIS ATROCIOUS SIN AND LEARN WHAT THE WORD OF GOD HAS TO SAY! THE BIBLE WILL HELP YOU OVERCOME ENVY!** *"Wherefore laying* (lay) *aside all malice* (hatred), *and all guile* (wickedness), *and hypocrisies* (fault finding), *and **envies**, and all evil speakings,* (and) *as newborn babes* (would need milk) *desire the sincere milk of the word* (the Bible) *that ye may grow thereby.''* **1 Peter 2:1-2** *"Love worketh no ill to his neighbour: therefore love is the fulfilling of the law.''* **Romans 13:10**

Many people today are like the evil Romans in Paul's day who changed the truth of God into lies! They did things that Satan told them to do such as: worshipping idols and defiling their bodies! They became homosexuals and lesbians! God became so disgusted with them that he eventually gave up on trying to get them to change! *"And even as they did not like to retain God in their knowledge, God gave them over to a reprobate* (corrupt) *mind, to do those things which are not convenient* (natural); *Being filled with all unrighteousness, fornication* (having sex without marriage), *wickedness, covetousness, maliciousness* (meanness); *full of **envy**, murder, debate* (arguing), *deceit* (trickery), *malignity* (injurious statements), *whisperers* (gossips), *backbiters, haters of God, despiteful, proud, boasters, inventors of evil things* (sex devices, torture instruments, etc.), *disobedient to parents, without understanding, covenant-breakers, without natural affection, implacable* (unmoveable), *unmerciful: who knowing the judgement of God, that they which commit such things are worthy of death, not only do the same, but have pleasure in them that do them.''* **Romans 1:28-32**

**ENVY = A WORK OF DARKNESS AND DARKNESS = SIN!**
*"The night is far spent* (it's time to repent), *the day is at hand* (of Christ's return) *let us therefore cast off the works of **darkness**, and let us put on the armour of **light** (Christ). Let us walk honestly, as in the day; not in rioting and drunkenness, not in chambering and wantonness* (undisciplined, merciless), *not in strife and **envying**. But put ye on the Lord Jesus Christ, and make not provision for the flesh, to fulfil the lusts thereof.''* **Romans 13:12-14**

**IF YOU SINCERELY LOVE PEOPLE: YOU WON'T ENVY THEM, THEIR POSSESSIONS, OR ANY OTHER THING!**
*"Charity* (love) *suffereth long* (is patient), *and is kind; Charity* (love) *envieth not; charity* (love) *vaunteth* (boasts) *not itself, is not puffed up* (does not have an ego problem.)''* **1 Corinthians 13:4**

**AS CHRISTIANS, WE ARE COMMANDED NOT TO FRET OVER OTHERS WHO ARE ENVIOUS! AS CHRISTIANS WE SHOULD RISE ABOVE THEIR IMMORAL STANDARDS AND LET OTHERS SEE JESUS IN US!** *"Fret not thyself because of evildoers, neither be thou **envious** against the workers of iniquity.''* **Psalm 37:1/Proverbs 24:19**

**DID YOU KNOW THAT GOD HATES ENVY SO MUCH THAT HE CLASSIFIES IT IN THE SAME CATEGORY WITH MURDER?** *"Now the works of the flesh are manifest* (made known), *which are these: Adultery, fornication, uncleanness, lasciviousness* (lust), *idolatry, witchcraft, hatred, variance, emulations* (trying to imitate, or excel), *wrath, strife, seditions* (resisting lawful authority), *heresies* (religious opinion contrary to God's will), ***envyings**, murders, drunkenness, revellings* (wild parties), *and such like: of the which I tell you before, as I have also told you in time past, that they which do such things shall not inherit the kingdom of God.''* **Galatians 5:19-21**

**IT'S A TRUE STATEMENT FROM THE BIBLE: "YOU CAN'T TAKE IT WITH YOU", SO WHY LOWER YOURSELF TO CHILDISH ENVY?** *"For we brought nothing into this world, and it is certain we can carry nothing out. And having food and raiment* (clothes) *let us be therewith content.''* **1 Timothy 6:7-8**

*"For wrath killeth the foolish man, and envy slayeth the silly one!''* **Job 5:2**

*"Be not thou envious against evil men, neither desire to be with them. For their heart studieth destruction, and their lips talk of mischief.''* **Proverbs 24:1-2**

**ENVY WILL EVENTUALLY ROT YOUR BONES. . . SO SAYS THE BIBLE!** *"A sound heart is the life of the flesh: but **envy*** (becomes) *the rottenness of the bones.''* **Proverbs 14:30**

*"Strive not with a man without cause, if he have done thee no harm. **Envy** thou not the oppressor, and choose none of his ways.''* **Proverbs 3:30-31**

*"Wrath is cruel, and anger is outrageous; but who is able to stand before envy?''* **Proverbs 27:4**

**WHEN THE APOSTLE PAUL CAME ON HIS THIRD VISIT TO SEE THE CORINTHIANS HE WAS AFRAID THEY WOULD NOT BE CONDUCTING THEMSELVES AS CHRISTIANS. Paul wrote:** *"For I fear, lest, when I come, I shall not find you such as I would* (like to find you), *and that I shall be found unto you such as ye would not* (like to find me): *lest there be debates, **envyings**, wraths, strifes, backbitings, whisperings, swellings, tumults.''* **2 Corinthians 12:20**

## PRAYER

Dear God, I am guilty of being **envious** of other people and of people's things! I know this is wrong! It makes me sick to my heart that I am this way! Please forgive me. I know I can change! I will need Your help to overcome. Please help me! I realize that **envy** is like an infectious disease and I want to be free. Please forgive me for all of my sins and I will praise You forever! In Jesus' name, I pray. AMEN!

# EVOLUTION

The evolutionist believes that all things evolved through a gradual process in which the whole universe progressed through interrelated phenomena. The entire concept of evolution is unscriptural! History has proven the Bible to be correct! Science has been unable to prove their theory of evolution, because it cannot be done! The Holy Bible is very clear on the subject of creation!

**GOD DOES EXIST AND IS OUR LOVING CREATOR!** *"The heavens declare* (certify) *the glory of God; and the firmament sheweth* (proves beyond doubt) *his handywork* (creation).*"* **Psalm 19:1**

**WHY WAS OUR UNIVERSE CREATED ANYWAY? WHY WAS MAN CREATED?** *"Thou art worthy, O Lord, to receive glory and honour and power: for thou hast created all things, and for thy pleasure they are and were created."* **Revelation 4:11** *"He that loveth not* (God) *knoweth not God; for God is love."* **1 John 4:8**

**GOD CREATED EACH "KIND" TO FIT A SPECIFIC PURPOSE!** *"And God created great whales, and every living creature that moveth, which the waters brought forth abundantly, after their kind, and every winged fowl after his kind: and God saw that it was good. And God blessed them, saying, Be fruitful, and multiply, and fill the waters in the sea, and let fowl multiply in the earth."* **Genesis 1:21-22** *"And God said, Let the earth bring forth the living creature after his kind, cattle, and creeping thing, and beast of the earth after his kind: and it was so. And God made the beast of the earth after his kind, and cattle after their kind, and every thing that creepeth upon the earth after his kind and God saw that it was good."* **Genesis 1:24-26** *"The hearing ear, and the seeing eye, the Lord hath made even both of them."* **Proverbs 20:12**

**GOD'S UNFAILING LAW OF "KINDS" ALWAYS HOLDS TRUE!** *"And God said, Let the earth bring forth grass, the herb yielding seed, and the fruit tree yielding fruit after his kind, whose seed is in itself, upon the earth; and it was so. And the earth brought forth grass, and herb yielding seed after his kind, and the tree yielding fruit, whose seed was in itself, after his kind: and God saw that it was good."* **Genesis 1:11-12**

**MAN WAS CREATED IN GOD'S PERFECT IMAGE!** *"And God said, Let us* (God, Christ, The Holy Spirit) *make man in our image, after our* (own) *likeness: and let them* (all men) *have dominion over the fish of the sea, and over the fowl of the air, and over the cattle, and over all the earth, and over every creeping thing that creepeth upon the earth. So God created man in his own image, in the image of God created he him* (man); *male and female created he them. And God blessed them, and God said unto them, Be fruitful, and multiply, and replenish the earth, and subdue it: and have dominion over the fowl of the air, and over every living thing that moveth upon the earth."* **Genesis 1:26-28**

**MAN NEVER EVOLVED FROM A FOUR-FOOTED BEAST! GOD MADE MAN TO WALK UPRIGHT!** *"Lo, this only have I found, that God hath made man upright, but they* (all men) *have sought out many inventions* (devices, ways of sinning).*"* **Ecclesiastes 7:29**

**THE THEORY OF MAN EVOLVING FROM AN AMOEBA IS STUPID!** *"Ever learning* ("Big Bang" theories), *and never able to come to the knowledge of the truth."* **2 Timothy 3:7**

**THE BIBLE AGREES WITH TRUE SCIENCE! THE ACCOUNT AND ORDER OF CREATION IS CONFIRMED IN GENESIS 1:3-26.**

**HERE IS A SIMPLE QUESTION FOR THE SCIENTISTS WHO CAME UP WITH THE RIDICULOUS THEORY OF EVOLUTION!** *"Where wast thou when I* (God speaking) *laid the foundations of the earth? declare, if thou hast understanding. Who hath laid the measures* (dimensions) *thereof, if thou knowest? or who hath stretched the line upon it? Whereupon are the foundations thereof fastened? or who laid the corner stone thereof; When the morning stars sang together, and all the sons of God shouted for joy? Or who shut up the sea with doors, when it brake forth, as if it had issued out of the womb?"* **Job 38:4-8** *"Hast thou entered into the springs of the sea? or hast thou walked in the search of the depth?"* **Job 38:16** *"Hast thou perceived the breadth of the earth? declare if thou knowest it all. Where is the way where light dwelleth? and as for darkness, where is the place thereof."* **Job 38:18-19** *"By what way is the light parted, which scattereth the east wind upon the earth? Who hath divided a watercourse for the overflowing of waters, or a way for the lightning of thunder; To cause it to rain on the earth, where no man is; on the wilderness, wherein there is no man; To satisfy the desolate and waste ground; and to cause the bud of the tender herb to spring forth? Hath the rain a father? or who hath begotten the drops of dew? Out of whose womb came the ice? and the hoary* (grey) *frost of heaven, who hath gendered it? The waters are hid as with a stone, and the face of the deep is frozen* (icebergs).*"* **Job 38:24-30** *"Knowest thou the ordinances of heaven? canst thou set the dominion thereof in the earth? canst thou lift up thy voice to the clouds, that abundance of waters may cover thee? canst thou send lightnings, that they may go, and say unto thee, Here we are? who hath put wisdom in the inward parts? or who hath given understanding to the heart? who can number the clouds in wisdom? or who can stay the bottles of heaven, when the dust groweth into hardness, and the clods cleave fast together?"* **Job 38:33-38** *"Who provideth for the raven his food? when his young ones cry unto God, they wander for lack of meat."* **Job 38:41** *"Professing themselves* (the scientists) *to be wise, they became fools."* **Romans 1:22**

(Continued)

**SCIENCE AGREES WITH THE SCRIPTURAL RECORD OF THE EARTH'S CYCLES OF OPERATION!** *"The sun also ariseth, and the sun goeth down, and hasteth (goes quickly) to his place where he arose. The wind goeth toward the south, and turneth about unto the north; it whirleth about continually, and the wind returneth again according to his circuits. All the rivers run into the sea, yet the sea is not full; unto the place from whence the rivers come, thither (there) they return again."* **Ecclesiastes 1:5-7** *"While the earth remaineth, seedtime and harvest, and cold and heat, and summer, and winter, and day and night shall not cease."* **Genesis 8:22**

**PHILOSOPHY AND SCIENCE ARE DESIGNED TO TURN MAN AWAY FROM THE SPIRITUAL TEACHINGS OF GOD! Read: Colossians 2:8/1 Timothy 6:20**

**SCIENCE AGREES THAT THE EARTH IS ROUND AND IS SUSPENDED IN SPACE JUST AS THE HOLY BIBLE STATES!** *"It is he (God) that sitteth upon the circle of the earth, and the inhabitants thereof are as grasshoppers; that stretcheth out the heavens as a curtain, and spreadeth them out as a tent to dwell in."* **Isaiah 40:22** *"He (God) stretcheth out the north over the empty place, and hangeth the earth upon nothing."* **Job 26:7**

**SCIENTISTS CANNOT SAVE MAN FROM DEATH! Read: John 5:28-29/11:23-25/Psalm 49:7**

**SCIENCE AGREES WITH THE BIBLICAL ACCOUNT OF DISEASE AND QUARANTINING! Read: Leviticus 13:9-11, 21 and Leviticus 14:34-42**

**MAN CAN NEVER PROVE "THE BIG BANG" THEORY! NEITHER CAN MAN BRING TOTAL CONTROL TO THE TIDE OF DELINQUENCY AND WORLD PROBLEMS! Read: 2 Timothy 3:1-5/Luke 21:25**

**OBVIOUSLY, THE ENTIRE CONCEPT OF EVOLUTION IS STRAIGHT FROM THE PIT OF HELL! SATAN LOVES IT WHEN HE IS ABLE TO PULL A SCAM THAT GULLIBLE PEOPLE WILL FALL FOR, ESPECIALLY WHEN IT'S A RIDICULOUS ONE THAT TRIES TO DENY GOD AS BEING OUR LOVING CREATOR!**

**SCIENCE CANNOT SAVE MAN'S SOUL NOR OFFER HIM ETERNAL LIFE! Read: Isaiah 43:11/Revelation 21:3-5/ Matthew 6:10**

**IN CLOSING:** *"God forbid: yea, let God be true, but every man (evolutionist) a liar."* **Romans 3:4**

### PRAYER

Dear God, I am guilty of believing in **evolution.** Now, I realize it is a lie! I know that mortal man could never match Your creation and that we can do nothing for ourselves! I know You created me and gave me free will to choose good or evil, I now make my choice! I choose to believe in You! I turn away from all theories of science and psychology which disagree with Your Word! I will study the Bible to gain understanding! Please come into my heart and forgive all my sins. I turn away from them! From this moment on I will obey Your commandments! I will pray daily. I will not be a part of any conversation which would deny Your divine creation! I love You and I thank You for saving my soul! In Jesus' name, I pray. AMEN!

# EXCOMMUNICATION

**THE MORAL STANDARD, AS PRESENTED IN THE HOLY BIBLE, MUST BE UPHELD FOR THE WELFARE OF THE ENTIRE BODY OF CHRISTIAN BELIEVERS!**

**A CHRISTIAN'S MORALS AND ACTIONS MUST BE GODLY. HE MUST NOT ENGAGE IN THE "WORKS OF THE FLESH"!** *"Now the works of the flesh are manifest* (made known), *which are these: Adultery, fornication, uncleanness, lasciviousness, idolatry, witchcraft, hatred, variance, emulations, wrath, strife, seditions, heresies, envyings, murders, drunkenness, revellings, and such like: of the which I tell you before, as I have also told you in time past, that they which do such things shall not inherit the kingdom of God."* **Galatians 5:19-21** *"But the fruit of the* (Holy) *Spirit is love, joy, peace, longsuffering, gentleness, goodness, faith, meekness, temperance: against such there is no law."* **Galatians 5:22-23** *"Finally, brethren, whatsoever things are true, whatsoever things are honest, whatsoever things are just, whatsoever things are pure, whatsoever things are lovely, whatsoever things are of good report; if there by any virtue, and if there be any praise, think on these things."* **Philippians 4:8** *"But the fearful, and unbelieving, and the abominable, and murderers, and whoremongers, and sorcerers, and idolaters, and all liars, shall have their part in the lake which burneth with fire and brimstone: which is the second death."* **Revelation 21:8 READ: 1 Peter 5:1-11**

**A CHRISTIAN MUST BE HONEST!** *"Wherefore putting away lying, speak every man truth with his neighbour: for we are members one of another. Be ye angry, and sin not: let not the sun go down upon your wrath: neither give place to the devil. Let him that stole steal no more: but rather let him labour, working with his hands the thing which is good, that he may have to give to him that needeth. let no corrupt communication proceed out of your mouth, but that which is good to the use of edifying, that it may minister grace unto the hearers."* **Ephesians 4:25-29** *"Recompense to no man evil for evil. Provide things honest in the sight of all men. If it be possible, as much as lieth in you, live peaceably with all men."* **Romans 12:17-18**

**A CHRISTIAN MUST OBSERVE CLEANLINESS IN HIS BODY, HIS SPIRIT, AND HIS HOME!** *"Having therefore these promises, dearly beloved, let us cleanse ourselves from all filthiness of the flesh and spirit, perfecting holiness in the fear of God."* **2 Corinthians 7:1** *"That the aged men be sober, grave, temperate, sound in faith, in charity, in patience. The aged women likewise, that they be in behaviour as becometh holiness, not false accusers, not given to much wine, teachers of good things; that they may teach the young women to be sober, to love their husbands, to love their children, to be discreet, chaste, keepers at home, good, obedient to their own husbands, that the word of God be not blasphemed. Young men likewise exhort to be sober minded. In all things shewing thyself a pattern of good works: in doctrine, shewing uncorruptness, gravity, sincerity, sound speech, that cannot be condemned; that he that is of the contrary part may be ashamed, having no evil thing to say of you."* **Titus 2:2-8**

**THE POSSIBILITY OF EXCOMMUNICATION MAY INDUCE REPENTANCE!** *"Now we command you, brethren, in the name of our Lord Jesus Christ, that ye withdraw yourselves from every brother that walketh disorderly, and not after the tradition which he received of us. For yourselves know how ye ought to follow us: for we behaved not ourselves disorderly among you."* **2 Thessalonians 3:6-7** *"And if any man obey not our word by this epistle, note that man, and have no company with him, that he may be ashamed."* **2 Thessalonians 3:14**

**EXCOMMUNICATION IS UNPLEASANT, BUT AT THE SAME TIME IT HELPS OTHERS AVOID TAKING THE WRONG COURSE!** *"Them that sin rebuke before all, that others also may fear* (and respect God's direction in this matter before the church)." **1 Timothy 5:20** *"Be not wise in thien own eyes: fear the Lord, and depart from evil."* **Proverbs 3:7** *"Looking diligently lest any man fail of the grace of God; lest any root of bitterness springing up trouble you, and thereby many be defiled."* **Hebrews 12:15**

**A CHRISTIAN MUST NOT DRINK, BRAWL, OR COVET!** *"Not given to wine, no striker, not greedy of filthy lucre* (dishonest money gain); *but patient, not a brawler, not covetous."* **1 Timothy 3:3** *"And take heed to yourselves, lest at any time your hearts be overcharged with surfeiting, and drunkenness, and cares of this life, and so that day come upon you unawares."* **Luke 21:34**

**THE CONGREGATION MUST BE KEPT CLEAN AND AN HONOUR TO GOD!** *"Know ye not that the unrighteous shall not inherit the kingdom of God? Be not deceived: neither fornicators, nor idolaters, nor adulterers, nor effeminate, nor abusers of themselves with mankind, nor thieves, nor covetous, nor drunkards, nor revilers, nor extortioners, shall inherit the kingdom of God. And such were some of you: but ye are washed, but ye are sanctified, but ye are justified in the name of the Lord Jesus, and by the Spirit of our God."* **1 Corinthians 6:9-11**

**EXCOMMUNICATION (DISFELLOWSHIPING) REMOVES REPROACH TO A GODLY CHURCH AND RETAINS GOD'S FAVOR!** *"In the name of our Lord Jesus Christ, when ye are gathered together, and my spirit, with the power of our Lord Jesus Christ, to deliver such an one unto Satan for the destruction of the flesh, that the spirit may be saved in the day of the Lord Jesus."* **1 Corinthians 5:4-5** *"Moreover if thy brother shall trespass against thee, go and tell him his fault between thee and him alone: if he shall hear thee, thou hast gained thy brother. But if he will not hear thee, then take with thee one or two more, that in the mouth of two or three witnesses every word may be established. And if he shall neglect to hear them, tell it unto the church: but if he neglect to hear the church, let him be unto thee as a heathen man and a publican."* **Matthew 18:15-17**

*"For behold this selfsame thing, that ye sorrowed after a godly sort, what carefulness it wrought in you, yea, what clearing of yourselves, yea, what indignation, yea, what fear, yea, what vehement desire, yea, what zeal, yea, what revenge! In all things ye have approved yourselves to be clear in this matter."* **2 Corinthians 7:11**

**GROUNDS FOR EXCOMMUNICATION ARE SPIRITUAL AND MORAL UNCLEANNESS!** *"But now I have written unto you not to keep company, if any man that is called a brother be a fornicator, or covetous, or an idolater, or a railer, or a drunkard, or an extortioner; with such an one no not to eat."* **1 Corinthians 5:11** For example: If a person is a practicing homosexual, or lesbian, or is involved in any form of occult activity, if he will not repent and forsake these sins, this would be grounds for excommunication!

(Continued)

**GROUNDS FOR EXCOMMUNICATION WOULD BE IF A PERSON IS INVOLVED IN CULTS, SECTS OR ATTEMPTS TO CAUSE A DIVISION AMONG THE BODY OF BELIEVERS!** *"Now I beseech you, brethren, mark them which cause divisions and offences contrary to the doctrine which ye have learned; and avoid them. For they that are such serve not our Lord Jesus Christ, but their own belly; and by good words and fair speeches deceive the hearts of the simple."* **Romans 16:17-18** *"A man that is an heretick after the first and second admonition reject; knowing that he that is such is subverted, and sinneth, being condemned of himself."* **Titus 3:10-11** *"Be ye not unequally yoked together with unbelievers: for what fellowship hath righteousness with unrighteousness? and what communion hath light* (truth) *with darkness* (sin)?*"* **2 Corinthians 6:14**

**APOSTASY IS GROUNDS FOR EXCOMMUNICATION!** *"For it is impossible for those who were once enlightened, and have tasted of the heavenly gift* (of salvation), *and were made partakers of the Holy Ghost, and have tasted the good word of God, and the powers of the world to come, if they shall fall away, to renew them again unto repentance; seeing they crucify to themsevles the Son of God* (Jesus) *afresh, and put him to an open shame."* **Hebrews 6:4-6** *"Let no man deceive you by any means: for that day shall not come, except there come a falling away first, and that man of sin be revealed, the son of perdition."* **2 Thessalonians 2:3** *"For the time will come when they will not endure sound doctrine; but after their own lusts shall they heap to themselves teachers, having itching ears; and they shall turn away their ears from the truth, and shall be turned unto fables."* **2 Timothy 4:3-4** *"For some are already turned aside after Satan."* **1 Timothy 5:15** *"But there were false prophets also among the people, even as there shall be false teachers among you, who privily shall bring in damnable heresies, even denying the Lord that bought them, and bring upon themselves swift destruction. And many shall follow their pernicious ways; by reason of whom the way of truth shall be evil spoken of. And through covetousness shall they with feigned words make merchandise of you: whose judgment now of a long time lingereth not, and their damnation slumbereth not."* **2 Peter 2:1-3**

**GROUNDS FOR EXCOMMUNICATION WOULD INCLUDE REBELLION AGAINST GOD AND THE CHURCH!** *"For rebellion is as the sin of witchcraft, and stubborness is as iniquity and idolatry. Because thou hast rejected the word of the Lord, he hath also rejected thee. . ."* **1 Samuel 15:23** *"Likewise also these filthy dreamers defile the flesh, despise cominion, and speak evil of dignities. Yet Michael the archangel, when contending with the devil he disputed about the body of Moses, durst not bring against him a railing accusation, but said, The Lord rebuke thee. But these speak evil of those things which they know not: but what they know naturally, as brute beasts, in those things they corrupt themselves. Woe unto them! for they have gone in the way of Cain, and ran greedily after the error of Balaam for rewards, and perished in the gainsaying of Core."* **Jude 8-11**

**GENUINE REPENTANCE IS A BASIS FOR MERCY AND COMES FROM A CONTRITE HEART!** *"And David's heart smote him after that he had numbered the people. And David said unto the Lord, I have sinned greatly in that I have done* (he committed adultery and had a man slain); *and now, I beseech thee, O Lord, take away the iniquity of thy servant; for I have done very foolishly."* **2 Samuel 24:10** *"Because thine heart was tender, and thou hast humbled thyself before the Lord, when thou heardest what I spake against this place, and against the inhabitants thereof, that they should become a desolation and a curse, and hast rent thy clothes, and wept before me; I also have heard thee, saith the Lord."* **2 Kings 22:19**

**TRUE REPENTANCE IS NOT A RESULT OF FEAR OR REGRET — BUT A GENUINE HATRED OF SIN!** *"The fear of the Lord is to hate evil: pride, and arrogancy, and the evil way, and the froward mouth."* **Proverbs 8:13** *"Ye that love the Lord, hate evil: he preserveth the souls of his saints; he delivereth them out of the hand of the wicked."* **Psalm 97:10**

**EVIDENCE OF TRUE REPENTANCE MUST EXIST BEFORE A PERSON (WHO HAS BEEN EXCOMMUNICATED) CAN BE REINSTATED INTO THE BODY OF BELIEVERS!** *"Bring forth therefore fruits meet* (appropriate) *for repentance."* **Matthew 3:8/Luke 3:8/Acts 26:20**

The Bible says that all the hypocrites will be swept away! They will be left utterly desolate! **Job 15:34-35**

The Bible says that if hypocrites were allowed to rule and reign, all people would be ensnared! **Job 34:30**

**CHRISTIANS SHOULD HATE LYING BUT LOVE GOD'S LAWS!** *"I hate and abhor lying: but thy law do I love."* **Psalm 119:163**

**FOOLS HATE KNOWLEDGE! Read: Proverbs 1:22** *"For that they hated knowledge, and did not choose the fear of the Lord."* **Proverbs 1:29**

**REPENTANCE IS A BASIS FOR MERCY. IT ALLOWS MERCY TO THE WRONGDOER!** *"So that contrariwise ye ought rather to forgive him, and comfort him, lest perhaps such a one should be swallowed up with overmuch sorrow. Wherefore I beseech you that ye would confirm your love toward him."* **2 Corinthians 2:7-8** *"For godly sorrow worketh repentance to salvation not to be repented of: but the sorrow of the world worketh death."* **2 Corinthians 7:10** *"For he shall have judgment without mercy, that hath shewed no mercy; and mercy rejoiceth against judgment."* **James 2:13**

**BELOW IS A BASIC LIST OF BIBLICAL REASONS FOR EXCOMMUNICATION: 1. Dishonesty 2. Coveting 3. Trouble makers 4. Drunkenness 5. Extortion 6. Idolatry 7. Causing divisions 8. Fornication 9. Unbelief 10. Serious backsliding 11. Turning away from the faith 12. Practicing false doctrines 13. Being a heretic**

### PRAYER

Dear God, Please forgive my ungodly actions. I don't want to be **excommunicated** from my church! Please impress upon my mind that I'm treading in deep waters of sin that will separate me from the body of believers if I don't turn my life around. I want to serve You and obey Your commandments! Please forgive me for all my sins and renew the joy of my salvation. I repent that I have disappointed You! I have also disappointed myself! I never realized that my ungodly conduct could cause me to be disfellowshipped from my local church. I turn my life over to You. Create in me the desire to do what is right in Your eyes. I know that You sent Your son Jesus to die on the cross for my sins. I know that You love me! I turn away from all sinful activity in my life. I will serve You from this moment on! In Jesus' name, I pray. AMEN!

# EXCUSES

LISTED BELOW ARE SOME "PHONY" EXCUSES FOR NOT ACCEPTING CHRIST AS ONE'S PERSONAL SAVIOR!

**1. IT'S TOO NARROW-MINDED TO SAY THERE IS ONLY ONE WAY!** WHY? There's only one way to count money correctly and give correct change. There's only one way to correctly fly an airplane or put complicated machinery together. **Jesus said:** *"I am the way, the truth, and the life: no man cometh unto the Father* (God), *but* (except) *by* (through) *me."* **John 14:6**

**2. THERE ARE TOO MANY HYPOCRITES IN CHURCHES!** Would you burn all your money because you heard there was some counterfeit money floating around? Would you throw away a bushel of delicious apples because one had a blemish? Would you burn all your clothes because one zipper broke? Yes, one of the disciples betrayed Jesus, but that didn't keep the remaining eleven from following and trusting Jesus!

**3. CHRISTIANITY IS TOO HARD TO UNDERSTAND!** Just accept God and the Bible as being true! It works! We may not fully understand how TV works, but we don't refuse to turn on a set because of this. God is more reliable than a TV set because God always works! Our faith makes sense after we completely trust God! Someday we'll understand all things! Meanwhile you are missing tremendous blessings by being left out! *"But the natural* (sinful) *man receiveth not the things of the* (Holy) *Spirit of God: for they are foolishness unto him: neither can he know them, because they are spiritually discerned. But he that is spiritual judgeth all things, yet he himself is judged of no man."* **1 Corinthians 2:14-15**

**4. FAITH IN GOD IS TOO UNSCIENTIFIC!** So, ask yourself how all the planets move in their natural orbits so accurately. And, how is it that they are so perfectly timed that it is possible for man to explore the moon? It's only possible because of God's infinite accuracy. Ask yourself who created the earth (and you) and gave you the ability to have a brain in your head. Who designed it all? Scientists cannot even control nature! They can only accomplish anything within the boundries of God's laws. *"The heavens declare the glory of God; and the firmament* (clouds, sun, moon, heavens, planets, constellations, etc.) *sheweth his* (God's) *handywork."* **Psalm 19:1**

**5. EVERYTHING ABOUT CREATION, GOD AND SALVATION IS TOO INCREDIBLE FOR ME TO ACCEPT!** Why? You accept your parents, your friends, the person who flies the airplane. You accept water to be pure without seeing it tested! You accept teachers and leaders without knowing them personally! You accept history books without having lived when they were written! You accept many things and many people, all of whom can not claim to have a perfect record! Only God is completely trustworthy! Only God has a perfect record! He can never change or die. *"Jesus Christ the same yesterday, and today, and forever."* **Hebrews 13:8**

**6. IF YOU BECOME A CHRISTIAN YOU HAVE TO GIVE TOO MUCH!** Yes! You have to give up your endless search for the truth because the Bible says *"And the truth shall make you free."* **John 8:32** You could also give up searching for who you are, why you are here, and where you will spend eternity. You would also give up all the confusion that comes from all your questions and doubts. You can give up your struggles, and you can get rid of them by trusting in Jesus! Jesus said: *". . .I am come* (to earth) *that they* (you) *might have life, and that they* (you) *might have it more abundantly."* **John 10:10**

**7. EVEN ATHEISTS ARE KNOWN TO CRY OUT TO GOD TO FORGIVE THEM ON THEIR DEATH BEDS!** *"Now we know that God heareth not sinners: but if any man be a worshipper of God, and doeth his* (God's) *will, him he* (God) *heareth."* **John 9:31**

**8. WHY DO PEOPLE BELIEVE IN FALSE RELIGIONS AND GIVE "PHONY" EXCUSES FOR NOT BELIEVING IN THE ENTIRE HOLY BIBLE? BECAUSE THEY ARE BEING DECEIVED BY SATAN! HE IS THE INVENTOR OF LIES! 2 Timothy 3:16 says:** *"All scripture is given by inspiration of God, and is profitable for doctrine, for reproof, for correction, for instruction in righteousness: that the man of God* (the born-again Christian) *may be perfect, throughly furnished unto all good works."* *"Beware of false prophets* (false teachings), *which come to you in sheep's clothing* (using the excuse, pretense that they are righteous), *but inwardly they are ravening wolves."* **Matthew 7:15**

**9. ANOTHER EXCUSE PEOPLE (WHO ARE IGNORANT OF THE SCRIPTURES) USE IS TO LAUGH AND SCOFF AT THE TRUTH! 2 Peter 3:3 says:** *"There shall come in the last days scoffers, walking after their own lusts."* **MANY PEOPLE WON'T TAKE A STAND BECAUSE OF RIDICULOUS "PEER PRESSURE". THEY'RE WEAK AND AFRAID OF BEING RIDICULED! Jesus said:** *"Whosoever therefore shall confess me before men, him will I confess also before my Father which is in heaven. But whosoever shall deny me before men, him will I also deny before my Father which is in heaven."* **Matthew 10:32-33**

**10. ANOTHER EXCUSE THAT KEEPS PEOPLE FROM TRUSTING IN GOD IS THEY'RE UNCONCERNED AND INDIFFERENT "THANKS" TO THEIR INFLATED EGO! Jesus said:** *"I know thy works* (thoughts, actions) *that thou art neither cold* (an atheist) *nor hot* (a born-again Christian). *So then because thou art lukewarm* (indifferent) *and neither cold nor hot* (neither love nor hate me), *I will spue* (vomit) *thee out of my mouth."* **Revelation 3:15-16** *"No man can serve two masters* (God and Satan): *for either he will hate the one, and love the other: or else he will hold to the one and despise the other. Ye cannot serve God and mammon* (money, prestige, intellect, material things)." **Matthew 6:24** *"A double minded man is unstable in all his ways."* **James 1:8**

**11. CHRIST WILL RETURN TO EARTH SOON. MANY PEOPLE DON'T WANT HIM TO RETURN BECAUSE HE IS PURE! THEY DON'T WANT TO BE PURE SO, THEY DON'T WANT HIM TO RETURN!** *"And every man that hath this hope in him* (Christ) *purifieth himself, even as he* (Christ) *is pure."* **1 John 3:3**

(Continued)

**12. MANY PEOPLE EXCUSE THEMSELVES FROM NOT BELIEVING AND ACCEPTING GOD, BECAUSE THEY WORSHIP FALSE GODS SUCH AS: MONEY, SEX, SPORTS, POWER, INTELLECT, DRUGS, ALCOHOL, THEIR BODY, ETC.!** *"For bodily exercise profiteth little. . ."* **1 Timothy 4:8** *"For what shall it profit a man, if he shall gain the whole world, and lose his own soul?"* **Mark 8:36** *"Lay not up for yourselves treasures upon earth, where moth and rust doth corrupt, and where thieves break through and steal: but lay up for yourselves treasures in heaven, where neither moth nor rust doth corrupt, and where thieves do not break through nor steal: for where your treasure is, there will your heart be also."* **Matthew 6:19-21**

**13. MANY PEOPLE USE EXCUSES FOR NOT READING THE BIBLE AND PRAYING! THEIR EGO WON'T LET THEM ADMIT THEIR IGNORANCE AS TO WHAT THE BIBLE DOES (OR DOES NOT) SAY AND THEY'RE LAZY! MANY PEOPLE FEEL INTELLECTUALLY SELF-SUFFICIENT!** *"Study* (the Bible) *to shew thyself approved unto God, a workman* (student) *that needeth not to be ashamed, rightly dividing* (understanding) *the word of truth* (the Bible)." **2 Timothy 2:15** *"Ever learning* (wordly things) *and never able to come to the knowledge of the truth."* **2 Timothy 3:7**

**14. THEY FALSELY BELIEVE THAT IF YOU ARE A GOOD PERSON, OR WERE SPRINKLED AS A BABY, OR YOU'RE A CHURCH MEMBER, OR YOU WERE BAPTIZED THAT YOU WILL BE RAPTURED OR GO TO HEAVEN, IF YOU DIE FIRST! Jesus said:** *"Except a man be born again* (repent and ask God to forgive him), *he cannot see the kingdom of God."* **John 3:3**

**15. THEY USE THE EXCUSE THAT THEY'VE HEARD THAT CHRIST WAS COMING BEFORE AND HE DIDN'T, SO WHY BELIEVE HE'LL RETURN SOON?** If people would study the prophecies in the Bible they would never use that excuse! There were prophecies yet to be fulfilled, and God will not violate His written word! He clearly stated that Israel must first become a nation, which only happened in 1948. God said that the generation which sees this come to pass will also see the second coming of Christ to earth! *"And in the morning, it will be foul weather today: for the sky is red and lowring* (cloudy). *Oh ye hypocrites, ye can discern* (understand) *the face of the sky* (predict the weather); *but can ye not discern* (understand) *the signs of the times?"* **Matthew 16:3** *". . .None of the wicked shall understand: but the wise shall understand."* **Daniel 12:10**

**WHAT'S YOUR EXCUSE?** *". . .LET GOD BE TRUE, BUT EVERY MAN A LIAR."* **Romans 3:4**

Dear God, Please forgive me for putting my career before You. I ask You to forgive me for all my sins! I have neglected reading the Bible! No job should have ever come between me and You! I know You love me and want what's best for my life. I know that You want me to work, but not to go over board and neglect going to church! Please forgive me for my neglect. Quicken my spirit to put my life and affairs in proper order. In Jesus' name, I pray. AMEN!

#### WHAT IS YOUR EXCUSE FOR NOT BELIEVING IN GOD?

*"Because that which may be known of God is manifest* (obvious) *in them; for God hath shewed* (showed) *it unto them* (you). *For the invisible things of him* (God) *from the creation of the world are clearly seen, being understood by the things that are made, even his* (God's) *eternal power and Godhead* (God, Jesus, The Holy Spirit); *so that they* (you) *are without excuse."* **Romans 1:19-20**

Jesus told a parable (earthly story with a spiritual meaning) to his disciples about the many excuses man will use for not following the Lord and believing in him! Luke 14:16-27

#### UNGODLINESS IS INEXCUSABLE!

*"Therefore thou art inexcusable, O man, whosoever* (you) *art* (are) *that judgest: for wherein thou judgest another, thou condemnest thyself; for thou that judgest doest* (does) *the same things."* **Romans 2:1**

**JESUS SAID:** *"Are you a wise and faithful servant of the Lord? Have I given you the task of managing my household, to feed my children day by day? Blessings on you if I return and find you faithfully doing your work. I will put such faithful ones in charge of everything I own! But if you are evil and say to yourself, 'My Lord won't be coming for a while,' and begin oppressing your fellow servants, partying and getting drunk, your Lord will arrive unannounced and unexpected, and severely whip you and send you off to the judgement of the hypocrites; there will be weeping and gnashing of teeth."* **Matthew 24:45-51** (The Living Bible)

# Prepare For Excuses

One of the most profitable things a Christian can do in preparing to witness is to learn how to counter the excuses of the lost. Some of the more common excuses are:

**I want to wait awhile.** The Bible says, *"Boast not thyself of tomorrow, for thou knowest not what a day may bring forth"* (Prov. 27:1). *"Behold now is the accepted time, behold now is the day of salvation"* (I Cor. 6:2). God said TODAY. To say some other time is to say "NO" to Christ. God's spirit will not always strive with man (Gen. 6:3). *"He that being often reproved hardeneth his neck, shall suddenly be destroyed, and that without remedy"* (Prov. 29:1).

**Too many hypocrites in the church.** Make this decision in the light of your own life and not the lives of others. *"So every one of us shall give ACCOUNT OF HIMSELF to God"* (Romans 14:12).

**I'm good enough. I don't need to be saved.** The Bible says, *"There is none righteous, no not one"* (Romans 3:10b). It is not your righteousness that salvation concerns but rather your sin.

**I'm too bad to be saved.** Christ said, *"I am not come to call the righteous, but sinners to repentance"* (Matt. 9:13). *"The Lord is not willing that any should perish but that all should come to repentance"* (2 Pet. 3:9).

**I don't know enough to be saved.** You must exercise simple childlike faith. *"Verily I say unto you, Whosoever shall not receive the kingdom of God as a little child shall in no wise enter therein"* (Luke 18:17).

**I'm afraid I can't hold out.** The Bible says, *"To as many as receive Him to them GAVE HE POWER to become the sons of God, even to them that believe on His name"* (John 1:12). It's God's job to give men power to become His sons and to keep them once they have. ☐

#### PRAYER

Dear God, I have used hundreds of **excuses** for all the mistakes I've made! I've even been guilty of blaming others for my own mistakes. The greatest mistake I've ever made is to not trust in You! Please forgive all my sins and come into my heart and life. I trust in You! I will not be ashamed of You! I will confess You boldly! Take my life and clean it up! I will go to church, and will pray and read my Bible! I will obey Your commandments. I accept You as my Creator! Thank You for sending Jesus Christ to die on the cross for my sins, so that I could be saved! Help me in all areas of my life and I will praise You as long as I live! In Jesus' name. AMEN!

# EXTORTION

**DEFINITION:** A gross overcharge; a swindler; the act or practice of extorting money or other property; to obtain from a person by force or undue or illegal power or ingenuity; excessive; exorbitant.

In the Bible, extortion is referred to as taking excessive interest rates! Extortion stems from greed! Extortion is dishonest gain and is a sin against God and man! In many cases extortion carries not only a prison sentence, but in some cases it carries a death penalty depending on the country where the crime takes place! *"In thee* (speaking of Israel) *have they taken gifts to shed blood; thou hast taken* **usury** *(excessive interest rates) and* **increase,** *and thou hast greedily gained of thy neighbours by* **extortion,** *and hast forgotten me, saith the Lord God. Behold, therefore I* (God) *have smitten mine hand at thy* **dishonest gain** *which thou hast made, and at thy blood which hath been in the midst of thee."* **Ezekiel 22:12**

**EXTORTIONERS ALWAYS SEEM TO APPEAR (ON THE OUTSIDE) AS SOLID CITIZENS WHO ARE PROFESSIONAL AND TRUSTWORTHY. THEY ARE TWO-FACED SINNERS AND ACTORS!** Jesus said: *"Woe* (warning) *unto you, scribes and Pharisees, hypocrites! for ye make clean the outside of the cup and of the platter, but within they are full of* **extortion** *and excess."* **Matthew 23:25**

**DAVID PRAYED:** *"Let the* **extortioner** *catch all that he hath* (coming to him); *and let the strangers spoil his labour* (ruin his business). *Let there be none to extend mercy to him. . ."* **Psalm 109:11-12**

**PAUL WROTE TWO LETTERS TO THE CORINTHIANS REGARDING EXTORTIONERS. THE ADVICE HE GAVE THEM IS STILL GOOD ADVICE TODAY!** *"I wrote unto you in an epistle* (letter) *not to* (keep) *company with fornicators* (those who have sex and are not married to each other): *Yet not altogether* (just) *with the fornicators of this world, or with the covetous* (people who want things that belong to others), *or* **extortioners** *(swindlers), or with idolaters* (those who worship money, sex, intellect, material things); *for then must ye needs* (you would need to) *go out of the world. But now I have written unto you* (in this letter) *not to keep company, if any man that is called a brother be a fornicator, or covetous, or an idolater, or a railer* (person who makes loud, rash accusations), *or a drunkard, or an* **extortioner** *(swindler); with such an one no not to eat* (do not eat with this person)." **1 Corinthians 5:9-11**

**THE BIBLE CLEARLY STATES THAT EXTORTIONERS WILL NOT INHERIT THE KINGDOM OF GOD!** In other words, unless an **extortioner** repents before his death, he will go to hell! The same holds true when the rapture takes place! Unless the **extortioner** has previously repented and turned away from his sins, he will not be raptured with Jesus (for seven years of safety) while the tribulation period takes place! God hates the sin of **extortion,** but He loves the sinner! He wants none of us to perish! He longs for each person on earth to come to a saving grace, and to inherit eternal life with Jesus! But, He gave us free will to choose Him or to choose the ways of Satan. It's up to us! *"Know ye not that the unrighteous shall not inherit the kingdom of God? Be not deceived: neither fornicators* (those who practice sex outside of marriage), *nor idolaters* (those who worship their body, astrology, any occult, gold, football, money, power, etc.), *nor adulterers* (a married person who has sex outside his marriage), *nor effeminate* (boys who submit their body to unnatural sexual sins and who usually become hardened homosexuals), *nor abusers of themselves with mankind* (sex perverts, homosexuals, rape, incest, sex orgies, masochism), *nor thieves, nor covetous, nor drunkards, nor revilers, nor* **extortioners** *(swindlers), shall inherit the kingdom of God."* **1 Corinthians 6:9-10**

**JESUS TOLD HIS DISCIPLES A PARABLE (AN EARTHLY STORY WITH A SPIRITUAL MEANING) ABOUT EXTORTIONERS AND OTHER WICKED PEOPLE WHO WERE VERY SELF-CONFIDENT. THESE PEOPLE THOUGHT THEY WERE CHRISTIANS BECAUSE THEY PAID THEIR TITHES AND FASTED TWICE A WEEK. IF YOU READ Luke 18:1-14 YOU WILL LEARN A VALUABLE LESSON IN HUMILITY!** *"He that saith, I know him* (Christ), *and keepeth not his commandments, is a liar, and the truth is not in him."* **1 John 2:4**

**WHAT CAUSES A PERSON TO COMMIT THE SIN OF EXTORTION? GREED PLUS NO LOVE FOR GOD OR MANKIND!** *"Love not the world, neither the things that are in the world. If any man love the world, the love of the Father* (God) *is not in him. For all that is in the world, the lust of the flesh, and the lust of the eyes, and the pride of life is not of the Father* (God), *but is of the world. And the world passeth away, and the lust thereof: but he that doeth the will of God abideth for ever."* **1 John 2:15-17**

### PRAYER

Dear God, Please forgive me for being guilty of **extortion.** I am guilty of charging extremely high interest. I have been dishonest and I have lied! I am guilty of using other people in order to get what I want! I have abused other people's confidence in me. I have betrayed them. I ask Your forgiveness. I turn away from this sin. I will do an honest day's work for an honest day's pay. I will love others as I know You love me! Come into my life and make me a new person! I will serve You from this day forward! In Jesus' name I pray. AMEN!

# FALSE PROPHETS

**WHAT IS A FALSE PROPHET?** He is a person who intentionally makes claims to having supernatural powers supposedly given him by God. His intentions are to deceive and mislead. Nothing he says is true. He is not loyal. He is treacherous. He is not solid or permanent. He disguises his facts in order to consume innocent people. He usually claims his testimony is of divine origin. Everything a **false prophet** claims will be lies against the Holy Bible. He will generally offer his sceptics a few isolated scriptures in order to sound righteous. He will usually appear wholesome and will have a charming personality. His conversation might include several ''God bless you's'' in order to trick you and deceive you into thinking the deity of Almighty God is fully with him. He is a **false prophet** and a liar! **The god he serves willingly and faithfully is Satan, no matter what he says!**

**Jesus said:** *''Beware of false prophets, which come to you in sheep's clothing* (pretending to be holy, godly), *but inwardly they are ravening wolves. Ye shall know them by their fruits* (works). *Do men gather grapes* (out) *of thorns, or figs* (out) *of thistles? Even so every good tree bringeth forth good fruit; but a corrupt tree* (false prophet) *bringeth forth evil fruit. A good tree cannot bring forth evil, neither can a corrupt tree bring forth good fruit. Every tree that bringeth not forth good fruit is hewn* (cut) *down, and cast into the fire. Wherefore by their fruits* (works) *ye shall know them. Not every one that saith unto me, Lord, Lord, shall enter into the kingdom of heaven; but he that doeth the will of my Father* (God) *which is in heaven. Many will say to me in that day, Lord, Lord, have we not prophesied in thy name? And in thy name have cast out devils? and in thy name done many wonderful works? And then will I profess unto them, I never knew you: depart from me, ye that work iniquity* (wickedness, injustice, sin).'' **Matthew 7:15-23**

**HOW CAN YOU RECOGNIZE A FALSE PROPHET?** Jesus said: *''Take heed that no man deceive you. For many shall come in my name, saying, I am Christ; and shall deceive many.''* **Matthew 24:4-5** *''And then shall many be offended, and shall betray one another, and shall hate one another. And many false prophets shall rise, and shall deceive many. And because iniquity* (sin) *shall abound* (be everywhere), *the love of many* (people) *shall wax* (grow) *cold. But he that shall endure unto the end, the same shall be saved. And this gospel of the kingdom shall be preached in all the world for a witness unto all nations; and then shall the end come.''* **Matthew 24:10-14** *''For there shall arise false Christs, and false prophets, and shall shew* (show) *great signs and wonders; insomuch that, if it were possible, they shall deceive the very elect.''* **Matthew 24:24**

**A FALSE PROPHET DOES NOT TEACH THE ENTIRE HOLY BIBLE! HE DOES NOT BELIEVE IN THE TRINITY (WHICH IS COMPOSED OF GOD THE FATHER, JESUS CHRIST, AND THE HOLY SPIRIT.) 1 John 5:7 A FALSE PROPHET DOES NOT BELIEVE THAT JESUS WAS BORN OF A VIRGIN Matthew 1:23 AND IS THE ONLY BEGOTTEN SON OF GOD John 3:16 NOR DOES HE BELIEVE THAT JESUS DIED ON THE CROSS IN PROPITIATION FOR OUR SINS Romans 3:22-25/5:8 HE DOES NOT BELIEVE THAT CHRIST ROSE ON THE THIRD DAY 1 Corinthians 15:4 AND IS ALIVE AND WELL TODAY! Revelation 1:18 NEITHER DOES HE BELIEVE THAT YOU MUST REPENT OF YOUR SINS AND BECOME A BORN-AGAIN CHRISTIAN TO INHERIT ETERNAL LIFE WITH JESUS! Mark 1:15 A FALSE PROPHET DOES NOT BELIEVE, NOR TEACH, THE REALITY OF EVERLASTING HELL! Matthew 23:33**

**MANY FALSE PROPHETS DERIVE THEIR TEACHINGS FROM THEORIES WHICH ARE OCCULT! AND ALL OCCULT ACTIVITY IS STRAIGHT FROM THE PIT OF HELL!** Here are a few occult activities which a **false prophet** might be involved in: enchantments, voodoo, charms, spells, ouija boards, seances, levitation, seers, diviners, mind control, hypnosis, ESP, false dreams, familiar spirits (which are deceased demon spirits called ''guides''), astrology, stargazing, fortune tellers, palm readers, water witching, automatic writing, astral projection, Transcendental Meditation (TM), Yoga, EST, humanism, and hundreds of other teachings which are modern day versions of the old biblical ''Baal'' worship whose founder is none other than Satan!

**HOW ARE FALSE PROPHETS SUCH AS JIM JONES ABLE TO DECEIVE AND RECRUIT THE MASSES?** They usually begin by prophesying lies while using the name of Jesus. They convince themselves and others they are ''chosen''! Actually they receive their knowledge and the ability to perform miracles from Satan! They present people with their inspired goals to bring peace and justice in a troubled world! They generally know a few scriptures, are very convincing, and appear loving and legitimate! *''I have heard what the prophets said, that prophesy lies in my name, saying, I have dreamed, I have dreamed. How long shall this be in the heart of the prophets that prophesy lies? yea* (yes) *they are prophets of the deceit of their own heart; Which think to cause my people to forget my name by their dreams which they tell every man to his neighbour, as their fathers have forgotten my name for Baal* (Satan worship).'' **Jeremiah 23:25-27**

(Continued)

*"Therefore, behold (listen), I am against the prophets, saith the Lord, that steal my words every one from his neighbour. Behold, I am against the prophets, saith the Lord, that use their tongues, and say, He (God) saith. Behold, I am against them that **prophesy false dreams**, saith the Lord, and do tell them, and cause my people to err by their **lies;** and by their lightness; yet I (God) sent them not, nor commanded them: therefore they shall not profit this people at all, saith the Lord."* **Jeremiah 23:30-32**

**DON'T BE GUILTY OF LISTENING TO FALSE PROPHETS TELL YOU THEIR DREAMS AND VISIONS BECAUSE THEY ARE FROM SATAN. GOD SAYS SATAN IS A LIAR AND A THIEF AND A DESTROYER!** *"Thus saith the Lord of hosts, Hearken not (don't listen) unto the words of the prophets that prophesy unto you: they make you vain: they speak a vision of their own heart, and not out of the mouth of the Lord (God). They say still unto them that despise me, The Lord hath said, Ye shall have peace; and they say unto everyone that walketh after the imagination of his own heart, No evil shall come upon you."* **Jeremiah 23:16-17** *"I have not sent these prophets, yet they ran: I have not spoken to them, yet they prophesied. But if they had stood in my counsel, and had caused my people to hear my words, then they should have turned them from their evil way, and from the evil of their doings."* **Jeremiah 23:21-22**

**COMBINING ALL THE FALSE PROPHETS WHO HAVE EVER LIVED, THE MOST EVIL ONE IS YET TO COME DURING THE SEVEN YEAR TRIBULATION PERIOD. Read: Daniel 11.** He will assist the Anti-Christ who will become the world dictator!

**LISTED BELOW ARE SEVEN WAYS TO TEST FALSE PROPHETS!**
1. By their confession of Jesus, 1 John 4:2-3
2. By their relationship with the world, 1 John 4:5/2:15-17/James 4:4
3. By how they receive Christianity, 1 John 4:6
4. By their attitude toward the commandments of God, 1 John 4:6/3:20-24/John 14:15
5. By the depth of their love for others, 1 John 4:7-21/3:11-16/John 13:34-35/15:12-15
6. By whether or not they are filled with the Holy Spirit, 1 John 4:4-6
7. By the word of God, 1 John 4:6/5:10/2 Timothy 3:16/2 Corinthians 4:4.

**NOTE: SATAN WILL PRODUCE THE FUTURE ANTI-CHRIST AND FALSE PROPHET AND IS VERY MUCH ALIVE IN OUR WORLD!** Read: **1 John 3:2/2 Thessalonians 2:1-12.** Satan has produced many anti-christs before, but the last and most corrupt one is yet to come. He will come after the Christians are raptured (evacuated) from planet earth during the seven-year tribulation period. After the Christians are raptured he will arise and will take control over the world, its money, its religion! The Holy Spirit is the Spirit of truth **John 14:16-17/15:26/16:13** and the spirit of error and lies is Satan. **2 Corinthians 4:4/11:14-15/Matthew 13:19/1 Timothy 4:1-2.**

**A FEW FALSE PROPHETS IN OUR TIME ARE: JIM JONES, REV. MOON, URI GELLER OF ISRAEL, AND PERHAPS EVEN CARL SAGAN!**

**IF YOU ARE A VICTIM OF DECEPTION: GET AWAY FROM YOUR FALSE PROPHET NOW! JOIN A BIBLE-BELIEVING CHURCH AND ATTEND REGULARLY! READ YOUR BIBLE EACH DAY AND PRAY! ASK GOD TO GIVE YOU TRUTH AND WISDOM! ASK HIM TO FORGIVE YOU AND HE WILL! HE LOVES YOU AND WANTS TO GIVE YOU PEACE AND FULFILLMENT! HE WANTS YOU TO LIVE ETERNALLY WITH HIM AND OTHER BELIEVERS! TODAY IS THE DAY TO GET THINGS STRAIGHTENED OUT WITH GOD!**

**PRAYER**

Dear God, please forgive me for I have been deceived by **false prophets.** I didn't know there was anything wrong with the psychology that's been presented to me! From this moment on I will only believe what is in the Holy Bible! I will not put all my confidence in man! I know that Jesus died on the cross to pay for my sins. I confess I am a sinner. I repent and turn away from my sins. I want to live a Christian life. Please come into my heart and give me peace. Let me know that I am forgiven. In Jesus' name, I pray. AMEN!

# FALSE RELIGIONS

**WHAT IS A FALSE RELIGION?** Any religion which **denies** that God Almighty created the universe and sent his only son Jesus Christ, born of a virgin **to die on the cross for our sins** is a **false religion.** Any religion which **denies** that Jesus Christ was **resurrected** on the third day and is **alive** today is a **false religion!** Any religion which teaches that you can go to heaven **without** a born-again experience is a **false religion.** Any religion which teaches out of written materials other than the entire Holy Bible is a **false religion.** A false religion perverts the gospel of the entire Holy Bible into lies! Paul wrote in Galatians chapters 1 and 2 that any doctrine other than the Word of God is "cursed"! And those who teach and preach it are "cursed", also! **False religions** have a price tag that goes along with them. It's called "bondage"! **False religions have always been in existence!** Today we refer to them as **cults. To join a false religion is very dangerous.** Not only will it **confuse** and **deceive** you, there may be serious repercussions if you decide to leave the organization. In some cases people have disappeared or even been murdered when they attempted to leave a cult! **The founder of all false religions is Lucifer (or Satan) as most of us refer to him! He is the author of confusion, deceit and lies! He hates the human race, because God created us for Himself, and because God loves us. Anything God loves, Satan hates!**

**WHY DO FALSE RELIGIONS SUCCEED?** Because they are "pros" in the art of **manipulating** people into believing **lies!** They are **cunning!** Their format is skillfully designed to please people who are not members of orthodox religions! They search out people who want something to hold their attention, without having to face subjects like repentance, salvation, heaven and hell! **False religions** may appear in the beginning to contain good qualities which would benefit all men while appealing to the base passions of men. Their founders usually possess vast knowledge of worldly affairs. And "worldly" means they are successful in influencing others! Like a pestilence, they usually start out small and multiply rapidly overnight! Most of their converts are "rejects" who wander to and fro aimlessly! Many are "drones" who are "psychology freaks"! All these combined are looking for ways to start a new movement that will change the world! Most **false religions** teach that God is within man already, and that he doesn't need to seek and have a personal relationship with his Creator! Their goal is to change the world into a utopia. **Followers willingly forfeit their freedom of choice in any decisions once they join. They become submissive and passive** once they have become indoctrinated. Once they accept the bait, they are hooked! **False religions are usually centered around current existing prejudices, opinions, and world events.** Where there is a loop-hole in racial tension they move in with their **bag of tricks** that will fix everything up with "good-for-all" schemes! **They seek out and recruit drop-outs, misfits, weak people, and morally loose people.** They make these **already-mixed-up people** feel special, wanted, important and much needed! They are convinced they will become important founders and leaders in the movement!

**A FEW FALSE RELIGIONS, PRACTICES AND TEACHINGS ARE:** Scientology, Transcendental Meditation (TM), EST, Hare Krishna, Church of Religious Science, Hinduism, Jainism, Sikhism, Buddhism, Zoroastrianism, Confucianism, Taoism, Shinto, Islam, Judasism, Mormonism, Unity School of Christianity, Theosophy, Witchcraft, Satanism, Astrology, Spiritualism, The Kabbala, The I-Ching, The Tarot, The Unification Church, The Divine Light Mission, The Way International, Urantia, Yoga, Communism, Humanism, I/AM, Atheism, Ku Klux Klan movement, Science of Mind, Rosicrucian Order, Mayan, Edgar Cayce Foundation, The Prophecies of Nostradamus, Mohammedanism, Reincarnation, Baha'ism, Unitarian, and all Metaphysical sciences, theories and religions! Any theory, teaching, or religion which stems from eastern philosophy is occult, and false according to the Holy Bible!

Jones on the day of the massacre

THE NUMBER ONE OBJECT IN LOOKING FOR RECRUITS FOR FALSE RELIGIONS IS TO FIND PEOPLE WHO ARE NOT KNOWLEDGEABLE ABOUT THE BIBLE, AND WHO ARE TOTALLY "OPEN" FOR NEW AND UNFOUNDED SUGGESTIONS!

**FALSE RELIGIONS ARE VAIN RELIGIONS!** *"If any man among you seem to be religious, and bridleth not his tongue, but deceiveth his own heart, this man's religion is vain."* **James 1:26**

**FALSE RELIGIONS DENY THE DEITY OF JESUS AND BRING SWIFT DESTRUCTION UPON THEMSELVES!** *". . .there were **false prophets** also among the people, even as there shall be **false teachers** among you, who privily* (secretly) *shall bring in damnable heresies* (opinions contrary to church dogma), *even denying the Lord that bought them* (through his death on the cross to pay for their sins), *and bring upon themselves swift destruction. And many shall follow their pernicious* (destructive) *ways; by reason of whom the way of truth* (God, the Bible) *shall be evil spoken of."* **2 Peter 2:1-2**

*"The Lord knoweth how to deliver the godly out of temptations, and to reserve the unjust* (followers of false religions) *unto the day of judgement to be punished."* **2 Peter 2:9** *"Take heed to yourselves, that your heart be not deceived, and ye turn aside, and serve other gods* (false religions), *and worship them."* **Deuteronomy 11:16**

Do not heed or follow false prophets: **Deuteronomy 13:1-4**
Do not fear them: **Deuteronomy 18:20-22**
Do not provide places of worship for them: **Deuteronomy 16:21-22**

**LISTED BELOW ARE IDOLATROUS THEORIES AND PRACTICES WHICH GOD COMMANDS WE NOT FOLLOW!** Astrology, witchcraft, reincarnation, geneology, enchantments, hypnosis, casting spells, consorting with familiar spirits, fortune tellers, mystics, psychics, sorcery, soothsayers, card readers; using mantras, charms, poltergeist (ghosts), astral projection (occult out of the body space travel), mind control, automatic writing, thought transference, prognostications, etc. **Leviticus 19**

(Continued)

**WHY CAN'T PEOPLE WORSHIP IN THEIR OWN WAY WHEN THERE ARE SO MANY RELIGIONS TO CHOOSE FROM?** Because many people falsely assume that no one religion has the full truth about God, therefore it doesn't really matter what you believe as long as you're sincere. They are totally wrong! God has revealed himself to us throughout the entire Bible. No born-again Christian ever gropes in the dark wondering who God is! He has a personal relationship with God from the moment he becomes born again! God came down to earth in the person of Jesus Christ. **Jesus said:** *"I am the way, and the truth and the life. No one comes to the Father except through me."* **John 14:6 CHRIST IS THE VISIBLE IMAGE OF THE INVISIBLE GOD!** All the fullness of the deity of God lives in the bodily form of Jesus **Colossians 1:15, 19/2:9.** Only through having a personal experience with Christ will you ever know the truth about God. The Bible says until we become born-again Christians, we are separated from God because of our sins. Christ died to take away our sins and reconcile us to God. I pray you will investigate Jesus, learn who He is, and what He has done for you! Then, yield your life to Him without reserve! It will be the happiest decision you will ever make! Furthermore, you will escape eternal hell which is reserved for people who willfully refuse to accept Christ. God is love. God loves you. He wants you to be happy, at peace, and to live eternally in a perfect existence with Him!

**DID YOU KNOW THAT THE RISE IN FALSE RELIGIONS FULFILLS END TIME PROPHECY ABOUT THE LAST DAYS BEFORE CHRIST RETURNS TO EARTH?** *"This know also, that in the last days perilous times shall come. For men shall be lovers of their own selves, covetous, boasters, proud, blasphemers, disobedient to parents, unthankful, unholy, without natural affection, trucebreakers, false accusers, incontinent, fierce, despisers of those that are good, Traitors, heady, highminded, lovers of pleasures more than lovers of God;* **Having a form of godliness, but denying the power** (of the Holy Spirit) **thereof:** *from such turn away."* **2 Timothy 3:1-5**

**GOD HAS THIS TO SAY ABOUT THOSE WHO SPEND THEIR TIME STUDYING PSYCHOLOGY, HUMANISM, EVOLUTION, AND OTHER FALSE TEACHINGS!** *"Ever learning, and* **never able to come to the knowledge** *of the truth."* **2 Timothy 3:7** *"But evil men and seducers* (leaders who get people to join false religions) *shall wax* (grow) *worse and worse, deceiving, and being deceived."* **2 Timothy 3:13**

**IN 2 Corinthians Chapter 11 FALSE RELIGIONS ARE CALLED "FALSE APOSTLES"!**

**Luke 12:29-32 SAYS:** *"And seek not ye what ye shall eat, or what ye shall drink, neither be ye of doubtful mind. For all these things do the nations of the world seek after: and your Father* (God) *knoweth that ye have need of these things. But rather* **seek ye the kingdom of God;** *and all these things shall be added unto you. Fear not, little flock* (of born-again Christians); *for it is your Father's* (God's) *good pleasure to give you the kingdom."* **NOTE:** The word **"doubtful"** in the above verse means **suspended, anxious, to be carried about as meteors move about, tossed up and down between hope and fear. Superstition that comes from seeking guidance by meteors, planets, signs of the zodiac, magic, witchcraft, traffic with demons under the guise of astrology, is strictly condemned by God!**

**PRAYER**

Dear God, I am guilty of believing the garbage that has been presented me through a **false religion!** I know that no man created the universe! I know that science does not have all the answers! I know that when I am confused You still love and care for me! Please come into my heart and cleanse me from all my sins! I give myself to You and You alone! I turn away from all **false teachings.** I accept only the Holy Bible! I will pray and go to a Bible believing church from this moment forward! Stay close by me and let me feel Your presence! I love You and praise You for setting me straight! In Jesus' name, AMEN!

# FAMILIAR SPIRITS

**DEFINITION:** A supernatural spirit or **demon** supposed to attend on or serve a person. They are **demon spirits** who possess psychic mediums! The medium surrenders his or her free will over to these **demon spirits** in order to enlist their assistance in getting desired answers to their questions. These **demon spirits** imitate the deceased relative or friend and they give fake messages which falsely comforts those who are mixed up and confused already. The **demon spirits** make predictions and give other supposed messages.

In **Acts 16:16** a girl had a **familiar spirit.** When **familiar spirits** could not be conjured up, many times counterfeit demonstrations would be given by ventriloquists by using a bottle or large water skin. Everything to do with mediums, and **familiar spirits** is straight from the pit of hell! **God will not tolerate any occult activity in the life of a Christian!** All occult practices, teachings, and theories are from Satan!

Listed below are 12 heathen practices which were and still are carried on in connection with demons, called "familiar spirits"! All who forsake God and seek help from these demons will be destroyed unless they willingly repent and turn away from any interest and participation in such! 1. Enchantments (magical arts) 2. Witchcraft 3. Sorcery 4. Sooth-saying 5. Divination (fortune telling) 6. Wizardry (males = wizards, females = witches) 7. Necromancy (fortune telling through communicating with deceased persons) 8. Magic 9. Charms (to put a spell or hypnotise) 10. Prognostication (to foretell the future by omens, signs) 11. Observing times (foretelling the future by watching clouds, flocks of birds, lucky-unlucky days, etc.) 12. Astrology and Star-gazing (foretelling the future by stars, sun, moon, planets). (Dake's Annotated Reference Bible)

**GOD SAYS IN LEVITICUS 19:31: REGARD NOT THEM WITH SPIRIT MEDIUMS!** *"And the soul* (person) *that turneth after such* (persons) *as have **familiar spirits,** and after wizards, to go a whoring after them, I* (God) *will even set my face against that soul, and will cut him off* (separate him) *from among his people."* **Leviticus 20:6** *"A man also or woman that hath a **familiar spirit,** or that is a wizard, shall surely be put to death* (be eternally separated from God): *they shall stone them with stones: their blood shall be upon them."* **Leviticus 20:27**

**KING MANASSEH OF JUDAH USED MEDIUMS WITH FAMILIAR SPIRITS AND COMMITTED NUMEROUS SINS TO ANGER GOD! Read: 2 Kings 21:6/2 Chronicles chapter 33** Josiah put away all the workers with **familiar spirits,** wizards, and idol worshippers in Judah, and in Jerusalem. Read: **2 Kings 23:24**

**THESE EIGHT PAGAN PRACTICES WERE FORBIDDEN IN ISRAEL AND ARE STILL FORBIDDEN TODAY, BY GOD!** *"There shall not be found among you any one that maketh his son or his daughter to pass through the fire, or that useth divination* (fortune tellers), *or an observer of times, or an enchanter, or a witch. Or a charmer* (using charms on others), *or a **consulter with familiar spirits** (a medium goes into a trance and conjures up demon spirits who will talk through his or her voice and send messages to the living), or a wizard, or a necromancer* (communicating with the dead). *For all that do these things are an abomination unto the Lord: and because of these abominations the Lord thy God doth drive them out from before thee."* **Deuteronomy 18:10-12**

God commands us not to consult people with familiar spirits because those spirits belong to Satan! Why seek guidance for your troubles from the dead? God has all the answers that will help you. He loves you! But Satan wants to kill you! He wants you to go to hell! It's up to you! Read: Isaiah 8:19-22/19:3

**DID YOU KNOW THAT THE VOICES FROM FAMILIAR SPIRITS COMES FROM THE GRAVES OF THE WICKED DEAD?** Read: Isaiah 29:4

**THE FACT THAT ALL OCCULT PRACTICES ARE ON THE INCREASE FULFILLS END TIME PROPHECY ABOUT THE LAST DAYS BEFORE CHRIST RETURNS!** *"Now the* (Holy) *Spirit speaketh expressly, that in the latter times some shall depart from the faith* (in God), *giving heed to seducing spirits, and doctrines of devils; Speaking lies in hypocrisy; having their conscience seared with a hot iron."* **1 Timothy 4:1-2/Matthew chapter 24/Revelation chapter 13/Revelation chapter 16 and chapter 20.** *"For the time will come when they will not endure sound doctrine; but after their own lusts shall they heap to themselves teachers, having itching ears; And they shall turn away their ears from the truth* (of God), *and shall be turned unto fables."* **2 Timothy 4:3-4**

**WHAT WILL HAPPEN TO PEOPLE WHO CONSULT MEDIUMS WITH FAMILIAR SPIRITS? OR TO THOSE PEOPLE WHO ARE POSSESSED WITH FAMILIAR SPIRITS? THEY WILL ALL BE DESTROYED ALONG WITH SATAN AND HIS DEMON SPIRITS UNLESS THEY REPENT AND FORSAKE THIS PRACTICE!** *"And then shall that Wicked* (Anti-Christ) *be revealed, whom the Lord shall consume with the spirit of his mouth, and shall destroy with the brightness of his coming: Even him* (Anti-Christ), *whose coming is after the working of Satan with all power and signs and lying wonders, And with all deceivableness of unrighteousness in them that perish; because they received not the love of the truth* (of God), *that they might be saved. And for this cause* (reason) *God shall send them strong delusion, that they should* (would) *believe a lie: That they all might be damned who believed not the truth* (of God), *but had pleasure in unrighteousness."* **2 Thessalonians 2:8-12**

**TO GAIN BETTER UNDERSTANDING ABOUT HOW MUCH GOD HATES EVERYTHING TO DO WITH SIN (WHICH INCLUDES ALL OCCULT ACTIVITY) READ 2 Peter Chapter 2!**

**IF YOU ARE A BELIEVER IN ANY OCCULT PRACTICE, OR YOU HAVE A FAMILIAR SPIRIT, ASK GOD TO COME INTO YOUR HEART TODAY! ASK HIM TO FORGIVE YOU! BECOME A BORN-AGAIN CHRISTIAN AND YOU WILL SPEND ETERNITY WITH JESUS, NOT IN HELL WITH SATAN! GOD LOVES YOU!**

### PRAYER

Dear God, please forgive me for believing in **E.S.P., fortune telling** and **astrology!** Please forgive me for paying money to **fortune tellers.** I don't know whether they were merely "phonies," or whether they had **a familiar spirit!** I ask You to forgive me for committing this sin! Forgive me for being interested and for believing in **astrology.** I know that all these things are from Satan, now that I have read the above verses! I know that You would never lie to me! It all sounded so harmless, and was just something different to think about! I never realized that it was an evil conspiracy to trap me into going to hell! I will no longer read any books with **occult** theories! I will change my friends, if necessary! I will seek out Christians who do not believe or practice occult activities so I will not be tempted! Come into my heart and forgive me! I know You love me! I will pray and I will go to church! I turn my life, my thoughts, and my actions over to You! In Jesus' name, I pray.

# FASTING

**DEFINITION:** To abstain from food.

FASTING IS A SACRED CUSTOM OF CLEANSING ONE'S SELF AND DRAWING CLOSER TO GOD. FASTING IS AN ACT OF OBEDIENCE TO GOD.

ONE REASON A PERSON FASTS AND PRAYS IS TO CLEANSE HIS BODY AND TO FREE HIS MIND WHEN ASKING GOD TO SUPPLY PROTECTION FROM ENEMIES! Ezra 8:21-23

Under normal circumstances when a person **fasts,** he **humbles himself, prays and repents!** God is impressed and moves events in a person's life when he is truly sincere in his **fast!** If he is **not** sincere in **fasting and praying** but only wants to use God (to gain special favors) God is **not** obliged to accept his **fast** and might send judgment upon him! **GOD CAN NEVER BE MOCKED!** *"Thus saith the Lord unto this people, Thus have they* (Israel) *loved to wander, they have not refrained their feet, therefore the Lord doth not accept them; he will now remember their iniquity* (sins)*, and visit* (recall) *their sins. Then said the Lord unto me* (Jeremiah)*, Pray not for this people for their good* (in their behalf)*. When they fast, I* (God) *will not hear their cry; and when they offer burnt offering and an oblation* (eucharistic elments, a part of sacred rites)*, I will not accept them: but I will consume them by the sword, and by the famine, and by the pestilence."* **Jeremiah 14:10-12**

**BEFORE YOU FAST: HERE IS A CONDITION YOU MUST MEET BEFORE RECEIVING AN ANSWER TO YOUR PRAYERS!** Jesus said: *"For if ye forgive men their trespasses, your heavenly Father will also forgive you: But if ye forgive not men their trespasses, neither will your Father* (God) *forgive your trespasses."* **Matthew 6:14-15**

Jesus said: when you **fast,** you are not to go around with a sad expression in order to impress people or to get attention! He said this is hypocritical! He said not to go around telling people you are **fasting,** for this is bragging! *"Moreover when ye fast, be not, as the hypocrites, of a sad countenance: for they disfigure their faces, that they may appear unto men to fast. Verily I say unto you, They have their reward. But thou, when thou fastest, anoint thy head and wash thy face; That thou appear not unto men* (don't look for an audience) *to* (before you) *fast, but unto thy Father* (God) *which is in secret* (God cannot be seen)*, and thy Father which seeth in secret, shall reward thee openly."* **Matthew 6:16-18**

JESUS SAID THAT WHEN HE WAS WITH THE DISCIPLES THEY HAD **NO** NEED TO **FAST** (BECAUSE THEIR NEEDS WERE ALL BEING FULFILLED) BUT TO **FAST** WHEN HE WOULD BE TAKEN AWAY FROM THEM TO BE CRUCIFIED! JESUS REFERRED TO HIMSELF AS A "BRIDEGROOM". Matthew 9:15/Luke 5:33-35

JESUS SAID WHEN THERE IS AN UNSURMOUNTABLE PROBLEM IN OUR LIFE WE SHOULD FIRST **PRAY AND FAST** BEFORE WE ATTEMPT TO RESOLVE OUR PROBLEMS! THIS ALSO APPLIES IN OUR ATTEMPTS TO ENLIST THE AID OF GOD (THROUGH THE NAME OF JESUS) IN CASTING OUT DEMONS! Matthew 17:14-21

IN ACTS 13:1-3 AN ENTIRE CHURCH FASTED AND PRAYED!

**HERE IS A BIBLE TRUTH ABOUT FASTING:** Fasting is a cure for unbelief! Faith needs prayer for its development and full growth, and prayer needs fasting for the same reason. **Fasting** has done wonders when used in **combination** with prayer and faith!

**FASTING AND PRAYER HUMBLES THE PERSON BEFORE GOD!** Psalm 35:13

**FASTING AND PRAYER CHASTENS THE SOUL!** *"When I wept, and chastened my soul with fasting, that was to my reproach."* Psalm 69:10

**FASTING CRUCIFIES ALL OF THE APPETITES. IT DENIES THEM SO YOU CAN GIVE YOUR ENTIRE TIME AND PRAYER TO GOD!** 2 Samuel 12:16-23/Matthew 4:1-11

**FASTING MANIFESTS SINCERITY BEFORE GOD TO THE EXCLUSION OF ALL ELSE!** 1 Corinthians 7:5

**FASTING SHOWS OBEDIENCE AND MAY GIVE THE DIGESTIVE SYSTEM A REST!** Matthew 6:16-18/9:15/Luke 5:33

**FASTING** DEMONSTRATES THE **MASTERY** OF MAN OVER APPETITES AND **AIDS HIM IN FREEING HIMSELF** OF TEMPTATIONS! **IT HELPS TO ATTAIN POWER OVER DEMONS! IT DEVELOPS FAITH! IT CRUCIFIES UNBELIEF AND AIDS IN PRAYER!** Matthew 4:1-11/17:15-21

ALL BORN-AGAIN BELIEVERS ARE SUPPOSED TO **FAST,** BUT **NO** REGULATIONS OR SET RULES ARE GIVEN AS TO HOW LONG (OR HOW OFTEN) A PERSON SHOULD **FAST!** IT IS DETERMINED BY INDIVIDUAL DESIRE AND NEEDS! Matthew 9:14-15/1 Corinthians 7:5/Acts 13:1-5

PEOPLE SHOULD **FAST** WHEN RECEIVING **CORRECTION** FROM GOD. THIS IS REFERRED TO AS "CHASTENING" *IN THE SCRIPTURES!* 2 Samuel 12:16-23

### WHEN SHOULD A PERSON FAST?
WHEN THEY ARE UNDER JUDGMENT FROM GOD 1 Kings 21:27. WHEN THEY ARE IN NEED Ezra 8:21. WHEN THEY ARE IN DANGER Esther 4. WHEN THEY ARE WORRIED Daniel 6:18. WHEN THEY ARE IN TROUBLE Acts 27:9, 33. WHEN THEY ARE IN SPIRITUAL CONFLICT Matthew 4:1-11. WHEN THEY ARE DESPERATE IN PRAYER TO GOD Acts 9.

**NOTE:** Since **fasting and prayer** are so prominent in the Bible, modern Christians should **fast** more often until they receive power from God over all the powers of the devil! Many things about **fasting** and its benefits are not known to modern men, but through the ages those who have been men of great prayer, **fasted** much!

ISAIAH CHAPTER 58 LISTS **23** THINGS THAT **CONSTITUTES A TRUE FAST.** IT ALSO CONTAINS 10 THINGS THAT DO **NOT CONSTITUTE A FAST.** IT ALSO CONTAINS **20 BLESSINGS** FROM A **TRUE FAST!** BECAUSE OF THE LENGTH OF THIS CHAPTER YOU WILL NEED TO READ IT FOR YOURSELF!

FASTING IS A WHOLESOME AND TREMENDOUS WAY TO DIET AND LOSE THE WEIGHT YOU DESIRE TO LOSE, WHILE PRAYING TO GOD! PLEASE GIVE FASTING SOME SERIOUS CONSIDERATION! IT CERTAINLY GIVES THE DIGESTIVE SYSTEM A REST. A WORD OF CAUTION: IF YOU DESIRE TO FAST, PRAY AND SEEK GOD'S WILL, WHY NOT TRY ONE 24-HOUR DAY A WEEK! THE LENGTH OF TIME A PERSON FASTS SHOULD BE SENSIBLE AT ALL TIMES! UNDER NO CIRCUMSTANCE SHOULD A PERSON OVERDO FASTING (THINKING TO GAIN SPECIAL REWARDS FROM GOD)! HIS PLAN IS NEVER FOR US TO OVERDO—BUT TO BE SINCERE!

# FATHER
# (Earthly)

**GOD SAYS WE ARE TO HONOR OUR EARTHLY FATHER! THIS IS SO IMPORTANT TO GOD THAT HE INCLUDED IT IN THE TEN COMMANDMENTS!** *"Honour thy father and thy mother: that thy days may be long upon the land which the Lord thy God giveth thee."* **Exodus 20:12**

**THIS IS THE FIRST COMMANDMENT OUT OF THE TEN WHICH GIVES US A PROMISE! THE ABOVE VERSE SUGGESTS THAT MAN MORE OR LESS DETERMINES THE LENGTH OF HIS OWN LIFE AND DESTINY!** *"Honour thy father and thy mother, as the Lord thy God hath commanded thee; that thy days may be prolonged, and that it may go well with thee, in the land which the Lord thy God giveth thee."* **Deuteronomy 5:16**

**DO YOU WISH TO LIVE TO BE A RIPE OLD AGE?** *"Honour thy father and thy mother; which is the first commandment with promise; That it may be well with thee, and thou mayest live long on the earth."* **Ephesians 6:2-3**

**FATHERS ARE COMMANDED TO BRING UP THEIR CHILDREN IN THE KNOWLEDGE AND OBEDIENCE TO GOD'S LAWS!** *"And, ye fathers, provoke not your children to wrath: but bring them up in the nurture* (education, discipline, correction) *and admonition* (warning, reproof) *of the Lord."* **Ephesians 6:4** *"Fathers, provoke not your children to anger, lest they be discouraged."* **Colossians 3:21** As a father you are to avoid harshness, anger, favoritism, severity and cruelty toward your children! Cruel parents generally have bad children! Correction is wonderful, if it is administered in love, and godliness. Stern punishment is revenge! Proper correction comes from affectionate concern! A child is to be nourished with wholesome discipline and instruction in an effort to form a strong young Christian mind toward God and peaceful Christian living.

**CHILDREN ARE COMMANDED TO BE OBEDIENT TO THEIR FATHER IN EVERYTHING!** *"Children, obey your parents in all things: for this is well pleasing unto the Lord."* **Colossians 3:20**

**THERE ARE FOUR REASONS WHY CHILDREN ARE TO OBEY THEIR PARENTS: FIRST:** It is not merely a suggestion that children obey their parents, it is a commandment! **SECOND: Ephesians 6:1** says it is the right thing to do! **THIRD:** It is a blessing of well being **Ephesians 6:3 FOURTH:** It promises long life: **Ephesians 6:3**

**GOD COMMANDED US NEVER TO CURSE OUR FATHER OR MOTHER!** *"For God commanded, saying, Honour thy father and mother: and, He that curseth father or mother, let him die the death."* **Matthew 15:4** *"For Moses said, Honour thy father and thy mother; and, whoso curseth father or mother, let him die the death."* **Mark 7:10** In these 2 verses God clearly reveals that He expects us not only to respect and be submissive, but also to support our parents whether it be spiritually or financially. READ: **Exodus 21:17/Proverbs 20:20/Deuteronomy 27:16**

**JESUS SAID:** *Thou knowest the commandments, Do not commit adultery, Do not kill, Do not steal, Do not bear false witness, Defraud not, Honour thy father and mother."* **Mark 10:19/Luke 18:20**

**GOD COMMANDED US TO FEAR, RESPECT AND HONOR OUR FATHER AND MOTHER!** *"Ye shall fear every man his mother, and his father, and keep my sabbaths: I am the Lord your God."* **Leviticus 19:3**
*"Hear ye children, the instruction of a father, and attend to know understanding."* **Proverbs 4:1** *"A wise son heareth his father's instruction: but a scorner heareth not rebuke."* **Proverbs 13:1** *"A fool despiseth his father's instruction: but he that regardeth* (follows) *reproof* (correction) *is prudent* (wise)."* **Proverbs 15:5**

**NO MATTER WHETHER WE AGREE WITH OUR EARTHLY FATHER (OR NOT), WE ARE NEVER TO JUDGE HIM!** *"Judge not, that ye be not judged. For with what judgement ye judge, ye* (also) *shall be judged: and with what measure ye mete* (give out), *it shall be measured to you again."* **Matthew 7:1-2**

**GOD FORETOLD THAT A SON WOULD TURN AGAINST HIS FATHER, AND A DAUGHTER AGAINST HER MOTHER, AND A DAUGHTER IN LAW AGAINST HER MOTHER-IN-LAW: (Matthew 10:34-36) THIS IS BECAUSE OF ABNORMAL AND SATANIC OPPRESSION TO THE GOSPEL!** *"The father shall be divided against the son, and the son against the father; the mother against the daughter, and the daughter against the mother; the mother in law against her daughter in law, and the daughter in law against her mother in law."* **Luke 12:53** *"For the son dishonoureth the father, the daughter riseth up against her mother, the daughter in law against her mother in law; a man's enemies are the men* (people) *of his own house."* **Micah 7:6**

**DID YOU KNOW THAT IT FULFILLS END TIME PROPHECY (ABOUT THE LAST DAYS BEFORE CHRIST RETURNS) THAT CHILDREN WILL BE DISOBEDIENT TO PARENTS? THEY WILL DECEIVE THEMSELVES, AND THEIR PARENTS, AND VICE-VERSA!** *"This know also, that in the last days perilous times shall come. For men shall be lovers of their own selves, covetous, boasters, proud, blasphemers, disobedient to parents, unthankful, unholy, without natural affection, trucebreakers, false accusers, incontinent, fierce, despisers of those that are good, traitors, heady, highminded, lovers of pleasures more than lovers of God; having a form of godliness, but denying the power* (of the Holy Spirit) *thereof; from such turn away."* **2 Timothy 3:1-5**

**IF YOU HAVE DISOBEYED, CURSED, OR ABUSED YOUR FATHER (OR) IF YOUR FATHER HAS DONE ANY OF THESE THINGS TO YOU . . . WHAT SHOULD YOU DO? PRAY AND ASK GOD TO FORGIVE YOU AND HIM! TRY AS BEST YOU CAN TO MAKE AMENDS! FORGIVE . . . FORGIVE . . . FORGIVE EACH OTHER AND YOURSELF! ASK GOD TO HELP YOU!**

### PRAYER

Dear God, I am so sorry I have lied, cursed, disobeyed, and displeased my **father.** I am so sorry I have not obeyed Your commandments! Please forgive me and restore me to the knowledge that You are not a respecter of persons. Please help me overcome finding faults with my father. I will do my best to make things right in the eyes of my **father.** In Jesus' name, I pray.

# FATIGUE

**DEFINITION:** Weariness from labor or exertion; nervous exhaustion whether it stems from manual, or emotional labor; a tendancy to break down under repeated stress; to be weary from labor; tired.

**WHAT IS THE MOST COMMON CAUSE OF FATIGUE? FEAR OF THE UNKNOWN! HOW DO YOU OVERCOME FEAR OF THE UNKNOWN? HERE'S THE ANSWER: YOU NEED TO TRUST GOD AND LET GOD TAKE CARE OF TOMORROW FOR YOU!** Jesus said: *"Take therefore no thought for the morrow: for the morrow (tomorrow) shall take thought for the things of itself. Sufficient unto the day* (more of everything than you need for today) *is the evil thereof."* **Matthew 6:34** *"Thou shalt not be afraid for the terror* (crime) *by night; nor for the arrow* (danger) *that flieth by day."* **Psalm 91:5** *"I will say of the Lord, He is my refuge and my fortress: my God; in him will I trust."* **Psalm 91:2** *"The Lord is on my side; I will not fear: what can man do unto me?"* **Psalm 118:6** *"It is better to trust in the Lord than to put confidence in man."* **Psalm 118:8**

We must learn to depend wholly upon the unlimited power and protection of God! God can change your fatigue into renewed strength! All we have to do is to live in His will, pray and believe He will supply all our needs! God cannot fail! The biggest hinderer of our having a successful and healthy life is in our failure to relinquish our will over to God!

Sometimes only in our weakest moments do we willingly submit ourselves over to God! We limit our creator to do all the wonderful things He wants to do for us!

**WHERE DO YOU GET STRENGTH TO COMBAT FATIGUE? LET GOD BE YOUR STRENGTH! LEAN ON HIM! HE WILL SUPPLY ALL YOUR NEEDS! HE PROMISES THIS AND GOD CANNOT LIE!** *"The Lord is my strength and song, he is* (has) *become my salvation: he is my God, and I will prepare him an habitation* (place to live in my heart, life); *my father's God, and I will exault him."* **Exodus 15:2**

**IF YOU WILL TURN YOUR LIFE OVER TO GOD AND ALLOW HIM TO STRENGTHEN YOU THEN YOU WILL BE MORE THAN A CONQUERER!**

**FATIGUF OPPRESSION!** *"The Lord also will be a refuge for the oppressed, a refuge in times of trouble. And they that know thy name will put their trust in thee: for thou, Lord, hast not forsaken them that seek thee."* **Psalm 9:9-10** Read: **Psalm 18:1-2** *"The Lord executeth righteousness and judgement for all that are oppressed."* **Psalm 103:6**

**FATIGUE = DISTRESS!** *"In my distress I called upon the Lord, and cried unto my God: he heard my voice out of his temple, and my cry came before him, even into his ears."* **Psalm 18:6**

**INSTEAD OF TELLING EVERYONE THAT YOU SUFFER FROM FATIGUE IN ORDER TO GET SYMPATHY AND ATTENTION . . . LEARN THIS VERSE AND PRACTICE IT! GOD WILL BLESS YOU IF YOU DO!** *"Let the words of my mouth, and the meditation of my heart, be acceptable in thy sight, O Lord, my strength, and my redeemer."* **Psalm 19:14**

**AFTER GOD HAS RESTORED YOUR ENERGY LEVEL DON'T FORGET TO PRAISE HIM!** *"The Lord is my strength and my shield; my heart trusted in him, and I am helped: therefore my heart greatly rejoiceth; and with my song will I praise him. The Lord is their strength, and he is the saving strength of his anointed* (Messiah)." **Psalm 28:7-8**

**WHEN WE REPENT OF OUR SINS AND ASK GOD FOR DIVINE PROTECTION HE IS FREE TO HEAL OUR CONDITION OF FATIGUE! OUR TOTAL SUBMISSION TO LET HIM TAKE CHARGE OF OUR AFFAIRS FREES HIM TO SEND ANGELS TO PROTECT US, OUR HOME, OUR JOB, OUR HEALTH!** *"There shall no evil befall thee, neither shall any plague come nigh thy dwelling* (home). *For he* (God) *shall give his angels charge over thee, to keep thee in all thy ways."* **Psalm 91:10-11**

**DO YOU KNOW ANY OTHER WAY YOUR FATIGUE, ILLNESSES, AND DISEASES CAN BE HEALED?** David prayed and sang: *"Bless the Lord, O my soul, and forget not all his* (God's) *benefits: Who forgiveth all thine iniquities; who healeth all thy diseases; Who redeemeth thy life from destruction, who crowneth thee with lovingkindness and tender mercies, who satisfieth thy mouth with good things; so that thy youth is renewed like the eagle's."* **Psalm 103:2-5**

**IF YOU HAVE RECEIVED A COMPLETE PHYSICAL CHECK-UP, AND IT IS DETERMINED THAT YOU ARE NOT ANEMIC, AND YOU ARE GETTING AT LEAST SEVEN HOURS SLEEP AT NIGHT — THEN HERE IS A SOLUTION THAT WILL HELP YOU WHEN YOU FEEL FATIGUED, SAD, SICK OR LIKE YOU NO LONGER WANT TO LIVE! BELIEVE AND SAY:** *"I shall not die, but live, and declare the works of the Lord."* **Psalm 118:17**

Never give in to fatigue! Fight it off by getting busy with your mind and hands! Do something different. Write a letter! Buy some artificial flowers and create a flower arrangement! Clean out your garage and have a garage sale! Volunteer to work a day each week for a hospital — you will spread some cheer to those less fortunate than yourself! Get a "paint by number" set and paint a picture! Read the Bible to someone and let them sit back, relaxed and refreshed! Learn to needlepoint! Paint a room a bright new color! Go fishing! Do anything that comes to your mind that would be different and decent! Keep your hands busy and your mind will be busy too! *"Blessed be the Lord my strength, which teacheth my hands to war, and my fingers to fight (for godly purposes):"* **Psalm 144:1**

(Continued)

# FATIGUE

You can fight fatigue by changing your environment! Move furniture around at home, at work, or for someone who needs a change of scenery! Take a trip! Even a weekend mini trip of 30 miles changes a person's outlook on life!

Breathe deeply! Eat three nourishing meals a day! Eat two meals a week at a cafeteria! It will lift your spirits! Begin an exercise program by taking five minutes just before you start your day and five minutes before you go to bed at night! You will feel better when you change your old routines! You will certainly sleep better at night!

Organize yourself when you are fresh in the morning! List only two top priority items you wish to accomplish and then do them! The first 10 minutes (after you get up in the morning) gives you time to make your bed, exercise five minutes, say a good morning prayer, and brush your teeth! The next hour you can accomplish much! When you pray, ask God each day to renew your spirit! Ask Him to give you direction for each new day! *"Create in me a clean heart, O God; and renew a right spirit within me."* **Psalm 51:10**

**WHEN FEAR, DOUBT, OR FATIGUE COMES TO HAUNT YOU . . . REALIZE THEY ARE DIRECT PRODUCTS OF SATAN! DON'T BE AFRAID! TRUST IN GOD! MEMORIZE THIS VERSE AND REPEAT IT EVERY TIME THE OCCASION CALLS FOR IT!** *"What time I am afraid, I will trust in thee."* **Psalm 56:3**

Last, but extremely important: Bind Satan! He can be the source of fatigue, sickness, depression, sorrows and all trouble! Satan oppresses all mankind, but the born-again Christian is given the authority to destroy his efforts! Say 10 times a day *"Get thee behind me, Satan!"* Read: Mark 9:23-25/5:8/16:17/Luke 10:17-19 to learn how to cast out any demonic spirits which may be oppressing you! Bear in mind that if you are not a born-again Christian, it will not work! The authority to take complete charge over unclean spirits is reserved and given only to the born-again believer! It's a free gift from Jesus! Repeat 10 times a day: *"Our help is in the name of the Lord, who made heaven and earth."* **Psalm 124:8**

"Plug" yourself totally into God! Connect your conversations into other Christians! Ask God to give you a new Christian friend! Don't tell your new friend all your troubles! Let go of trouble, plug into God! He will make real troubles vanish if you live in His will and obey His commandments! Read your Bible each day and pray . . . pray . . . pray and believe . . . believe . . . believe!

CONFESS YOUR NEW STRENGTH, WHICH JESUS GIVES YOU, TO OTHERS! DON'T BE ASHAMED OF JESUS OR HE WILL BE ASHAMED OF YOU! BUY A GOSPEL RECORD AND SING ALONG WITH IT! LIFT UP YOUR VOICE TO GOD ALL DAY LONG! GOD HAS GOOD EARS AND HE WILL BLESS YOU! JOIN A CHURCH CHOIR AND BE FAITHFUL! *"Praise ye the Lord. Sing unto the Lord a new song, and his praise in the congregation* (church choir that you join) *of saints* (born-again believers).*"* **Psalm 149:1**

# Go To Church!

**LET THE WEAK DECLARE . . .** *"I AM STRONG!"*

## PRAYER

Dear God, please forgive all my sins. I humble myself asking and believing! I receive Your forgiveness. I will live for You. I know You have the power to give me strength and good health! Help me become friends with other Christians. I will go to church. I will read my Bible. I will praise You! I will do my part and I believe You will do Yours! In Jesus' name, I pray. AMEN!

# FEAR

FEAR COMES FROM SATAN! FEAR IS THE OPPOSITE OF FAITH! A BORN-AGAIN CHRISTIAN CAN CONQUER FEAR AS HE BUILDS HIS FAITH IN GOD! GOD HELPS US CAST FEAR OUT OF OUR LIVES! *"There is no fear in love; but perfect love casteth out fear: because fear hath torment. He that feareth is not made perfect in love. We love him (God) because he first loved us."* **1 John 4:18-19** JESUS SAID: *". . .Why are ye fearful, O ye of little faith."* **Matthew 8:26**

GODLY FEAR (RESPECT FOR GOD) IS COMMANDED THROUGHOUT THE BIBLE! *"Blessed is everyone that feareth the Lord, that walketh in his (God's) ways."* **Psalm 128:1** *"Praise ye the Lord. Blessed is the man (person) that feareth the Lord, that delighteth greatly in his commandments."* **Psalm 112:1**

*"The fear of the Lord is the beginning of knowledge: but fools despise wisdom and instruction."* **Proverbs 1:7**

JESUS' DISCIPLES WERE JUST AS HUMAN AS WE! WHEN THEY SAW JESUS WALKING ON THE SEA, THEY THOUGHT IT WAS A SPIRIT AND THEY CRIED OUT WITH FEAR! JESUS SAID: *"It is I; be not afraid."* **Mark 6:50**

IF WE TRUST GOD FOR OUR SAFE KEEPING THERE IS NOTHING WE SHOULD EVER FEAR! FEAR CAN "SAP" YOUR STRENGTH! THIS VERSE SHOULD GIVE YOU COMFORT: *"The Lord is my light and my salvation; whom shall I fear? the Lord is the strength of my life; of whom shall I be afraid?"* **Psalm 27:1**

DON'T BE AFRAID OF DEATH BECAUSE EVEN IN DEATH GOD IS ALWAYS WITH YOU! HE WILL NEVER LEAVE YOU NOR FORSAKE YOU! HE PROMISES THIS! *"Yea (yes), though I walk through the valley of the shadow of death, I will fear no evil: for thou art with me; thy rod and thy staff they comfort me."* **Psalm 23:4**

IF YOU ARE A BORN-AGAIN CHRISTIAN: YOU NEVER NEED TO FEAR TROUBLES WHICH MIGHT ARISE. GOD IS ALWAYS WITH YOU! GOD WILL ALWAYS TAKE CARE OF YOUR ENEMIES, AND DELIVER YOU UNHARMED! *"For he (God) hath delivered me out of all trouble: and mine eye hath seen his desire upon mine enemies."* **Psalm 54:7**

GOD CAN DELIVER YOU FROM THE FEAR OF DARKNESS AND THE SATANIC POWER OF SATAN! *"(God) hath delivered us from the power of darkness, and hath translated us into the kingdom of his dear Son (Jesus)."* **Colossians 1:13** *"When thou liest down, thou shalt not be afraid: yea (yes), thou shalt lie down, and thy sleep shall be sweet."* **Proverbs 3:24**

NEVER FEAR WARS — NOR FEAR ITSELF! *"Be not afraid of sudden fear, neither of the desolation of the wicked, when it cometh."* **Proverbs 3:25**

To the born-again Christian: never fear anyone who would come against you to sue you or seek to do you an injustice! God will take care of you! Pray the prayer that David prayed and you will get results! *"Deliver me from mine enemies, O my God: defend me from them that rise up against me. Deliver me from the workers of iniquity, and save me from bloody (cruel) men."* **Psalm 59:1-2**

MEMORIZE THESE TWO VERSES SO THEY WILL COME BACK TO YOUR MEMORY WHEN YOU ARE AFRAID: *"In God have I put my trust: I will not be afraid what man can do unto me."* **Psalm 56:11** *"What time I am afraid, I will trust in thee."* **Psalm 56:3**

STAY AWAY FROM FEAR BECAUSE IT CAN BRING ON A HEART ATTACK! DID YOU KNOW THAT THE INCREASE IN FEAR IN THESE LAST DAYS (BEFORE CHRIST RETURNS TO EARTH) WAS PROPHESIED ALMOST 2,000 YEAR AGO? FEAR AND HEART ATTACKS ARE ONE OF THE SIGNS OF THE END TIMES! JESUS SAID: *"Men's hearts failing them (will fail them) for fear, and for looking after those things which are coming on the earth: for the powers of heaven shall be shaken. And then shall they see the Son of man (Jesus) coming in a cloud with power and great glory."* **Luke 21:26-27**

EMPLOYEES ARE COMMANDED TO OBEY THEIR EMPLOYERS IN HONESTY, AND TO FEAR (RESPECT) GOD! *"Servants, obey in all things your masters according to the flesh; not with eye-service, as menpleasers; but in singleness of heart, fearing God. And whatsoever ye do, do it heartily, as to the Lord (as if you were doing work for God), and not unto men."* **Colossians 3:22-23**

SEEK THE LORD DAILY. HE WILL HEAR AND ANSWER YOU! HE WILL DELIVER YOU FROM ALL YOUR FEARS! *"I sought the Lord, and he heard me, and delivered me from all my fears."* **Psalm 34:4**

SOMETIMES GOD ALLOWS SATAN TO BRING FEAR ON WICKED PEOPLE — WHEN THEY WILLFULLY REFUSE TO REPENT AND TURN THEIR LIVES OVER TO GOD! *"I (God) also will choose their delusions, and will bring their fears upon them; because when I called, none did answer; when I spake, they did not hear: but they did evil before mine eyes, and chose that (sin, Satan) in which I delighted not."* **Isaiah 66:4**

LACK OF PROPER REST CAN MAKE A PERSON NERVOUS AND FEARFUL! **2 Corinthians 7:5-7**

SINNERS ARE NATURALLY FEARFUL! BORN-AGAIN CHRISTIANS HAVE A MEDIATOR (JESUS) TO LOVE THEM AND TO FIGHT THEIR BATTLES FOR THEM! JESUS WILL GRANT A PERSON'S WISHES — IF THAT PERSON OBEYS GOD'S LAWS IF HIS WISHES ARE GODLY ONES! *"The fear of the wicked, it shall come upon him (the thing he feared): but the desire of the righteous shall be granted."* **Proverbs 10:24**

You are afraid that if the Rapture comes or if you died this very day, that you would not be instantly in the presence of Jesus? Confess to God that you are a sinner! Repent from the bottom of your heart! Ask God to forgive your sins and to remember them no more! Humble yourself! Then: thank Him for forgiving you! End your prayer with "In Jesus' precious name, I receive forgiveness for my sins, and I praise You!" NEXT: Confess that you are now a born-again Christian to other people! Don't be ashamed of Jesus or he will be ashamed of you!

NO MATTER WHAT YOU MAY FEAR, SUFFER, OR IMAGINE — (IF YOU ARE A BORN-AGAIN CHRISTIAN) BE ASSURED THAT THERE IS NOTHING IN THE ENTIRE UNIVERSE THAT WILL EVER BE ABLE TO SEPARATE YOU FROM THE LOVE AND PROTECTION OF GOD! *"For I am persuaded, that neither death, nor life, nor angels, nor principalities, nor powers, nor things present, nor things to come, nor height, nor depth, nor any other creature, shall be able to separate us from the love of God, which is in Christ Jesus our Lord."* **Romans 8:38-39**

*"Having therefore these promises, dearly beloved, let us cleanse ourselves from all filthiness of the flesh and spirit, perfecting holiness in the fear of God."* **2 Corinthians 7:1**

### PRAYER

DEAR GOD, Please forgive me for being **fearful**. I know that **no harm will come to me as long as I abide in Your perfect will for my life!** Come into my life and take charge of my comings and my goings! I trust in You to protect me! **I will lean on You if I am afraid!** Thank You for forgiving all my sins! In Jesus' name, I pray. AMEN!

# FEEBLENESS

**ONE THING THAT CAN MAKE A WOMAN FEEL FEEBLE IS TO HAVE TOO MANY CHILDREN!** 1 Samuel 2:5

**GOD'S WORDS CAN STRENGTHEN FEEBLE KNEES!** *"Thy words have upholden* (upheld) *him that was falling, and thou hast strengthened the **feeble knees**."* **Job 4:4** *"Strengthen ye the weak hands, and confirm the **feeble knees**. Say to them that are of a fearful heart, Be strong, fear not: behold, your God will come with vengeance, even God with a recompence* (just rewards), *he will come and save you. Then the eyes of the blind shall be opened, and the ears of the deaf shall be unstopped."* **Isaiah 35:3-5**

**TO THOSE WHO ARE FEEBLE: PLEASE KNOW THAT GOD KNOWS YOUR CONDITION! YOU ARE NOT ALONE! IF YOU ARE A BORN-AGAIN CHRISTIAN GOD WILL GIVE YOU STRENGTH TO HELP AND ENCOURAGE YOU!** *"Wherefore lift up the hands which hang down, and the **feeble knees**; And make straight paths for your feet, lest that which is lame be turned out of the way; but let it* (feebleness) *rather be healed."* **Hebrews 12:12-13**

**GOD DOES NOT WANT YOU TO BE FEEBLE! HE WANTS YOU TO BE HEALTHY AND HAPPY! IT WILL TAKE PRAYER AND FAITH! GOD IS STILL IN THE HEALING BUSINESS!**

**ALL OF THE SINFUL PEOPLE LEFT ON EARTH (DURING THE TERRIBLE SEVEN YEAR TRIBULATION) WILL MOURN AND BECOME FEEBLE! THEIR KNEES WILL BE AS WEAK AS WATER!** *"All **hands** shall be **feeble**, and all knees shall be weak as water. They shall also gird* (cover) *themselves with sackcloth, and horror shall cover them; and shame shall be upon all faces, and baldness upon all their heads. They shall cast their silver in the streets, and their gold shall be removed: their silver and their gold shall not be able to deliver* (help) *them in the day of the wrath of the Lord: they shall not satisfy their souls, neither fill their bowels: because it is the stumbling block of their iniquity* (these events are the product of their own sins and rejection of Jesus)." **Ezekiel 7:17-19** *"...And every heart shall melt, and all **hands** shall be **feeble**, and every spirit shall faint, and all knees shall be weak as water: behold, it* (the tribulation period) *cometh, and shall be brought to pass, saith the Lord God."* **Ezekiel 21:7**

**AS A BORN-AGAIN CHRISTIAN YOU ARE COMMANDED TO COMFORT THE FEEBLEMINDED! PATIENCE IS REQUIRED AND PATIENCE IS REWARDED!** *"Now we exhort* (require of) *you, brethren, warn them that are unruly, **comfort** the **feebleminded**, support the weak, be patient toward all men. See that none render evil for evil unto any man; but ever* (always) *follow that which is good, both among yourselves, and to all men."* **1 Thessalonians 5:14-15**

**IF YOU ARE FEEBLE THIS VERSE IS FOR YOU! REPEAT IT OVER AND OVER AND MAKE IT WORK FOR YOU!** *"The Lord is my strength and song, and he is* (has) *become my salvation: he is my God, and I will prepare him an habitation* (place to live in me); *my father's God, and I will exalt him."* **Exodus 15:2**

**WHEN FEEBLENESS OVERTAKES YOUR STRENGTH, AND YOU FEEL HELPLESS TO THE DANGERS THAT MAY SURROUND YOU, AND YOUR FLESH IS TOO WEAK TO HELP YOU PROTECT YOURSELF — LET GO AND LET GOD BECOME YOUR STRENGTH AND YOUR PROTECTION!** *"I will love thee, O Lord, my strength. The Lord is my rock* (foundation), *and my fortress* (safety), *and my deliverer; my God, my strength, in whom I will trust; my buckler, and the horn of my salvation, and my high tower. I will call upon the Lord, who is worthy to be praised; so shall I be saved from mine enemies."* **Psalm 18:1-3**

**WHEN YOU ARE WEAK AND FEEBLE, KEEP TRUSTING IN THE LORD! HE WILL GIVE YOU STRENGTH! DON'T FORGET TO PRAISE HIM FOR HIS GOODNESS!** *"The Lord is my strength and my shield* (from heaven); *my heart trusted in him, and I am helped: therefore my heart greatly rejoiceth; and with my song will I praise him."* **Psalm 28:7** *"The Lord will give strength unto his people; the Lord will bless his people with peace."* **Psalm 29:11** *"The Lord is my strength and song, and is* (has) *become my salvation."* **Psalm 118:14**

**BE PATIENT WHEN YOU PRAY FOR STRENGTH! WAIT ON THE LORD, HE WILL ANSWER!** *"...They that wait upon the Lord shall renew their strength; they shall mount up with wings as eagles; they shall run, and not be weary; and they shall walk, and not faint."* **Isaiah 40:31**

*Jesus came to seek that which was lost, and bring again that which was driven away, and will bind up that which was broken, and will strengthen that which was sick.* **Ezekiel 34:16**

**A FEEBLE PERSON CAN REGAIN HIS STRENGTH IF HIS FAITH IS STRONG AND HE OBEYS GOD'S COMMANDMENTS!** *"Seek the Lord and his strength, seek his face continually."* **1 Chronicles 16:11** *"Seek the Lord, and his strength: seek his face evermore."* **Psalm 105:4** *"Glory and honour are in his presence; strength and gladness are in his place. Give unto the Lord, ye kindreds of the people, give unto the Lord glory and strength."* **1 Chronicles 16:27-28**

**LET THE JOY OF THE LORD BE YOUR STRENGTH!**

**THERE IS SOMETHING MUCH BETTER THAN RECEIVING STRENGTH OVER YOUR FEEBLENESS: IT'S CALLED WISDOM!** *"...Wisdom is better than strength:..."* **Ecclesiastes 9:16**

No matter what the cause of your feebleness is . . . never blame God! Jesus came that we might have life and that we might have it more abundantly! Satan is the destroyer, liar and thief! Rebuke Satan when he attempts to make you weak! Stand strong in your faith in God! He will reward you with a perfect body and mind, one day for we will be just like Him!

### PRAYER

Dear God, please forgive me for whining about my **feeble body**. I know that my strength will come from You. Please forgive me if I have used my **feebleness** to get extra attention. Please forgive me if I have used it as a crutch to receive extra sympathy. Forgive me for my sins, and help me to remember that there are people who are not even as fortunate as I! Help me organize my time so that it will be more productive! While I have eyes, I will read the Bible through! While I have ears, I will call and comfort someone! Teach me to count my blessings! I trust You to give me what I need in my life! I trust You to hear and answer my prayers! I will pray more for others, and less for myself! I will witness to someone new! I will praise You as long as I live! In Jesus' name, AMEN!

# FLIRTING

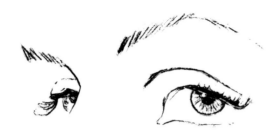

**FLIRTING IS NOT REALLY A SINCERE THING TO DO AND IT CAN ALSO BRING SORROW!** *"He that winketh with the eye causeth sorrow: but a prating fool* (one who talks too long, idle chatter), *shall fall."* **Proverbs 10:10**

**HOW CAN A PERSON OVERCOME THE HABIT OR TEMPTATION TO FLIRT? ASK GOD TO HELP YOU OVERCOME! PRAY:** *"Turn away mine eyes from beholding vanity; and quicken thou me in thy* (God's) *way."* **Psalm 119:37**

**FLIRTING = LUST OF THE FLESH!** *"Love not the world, neither the things that are in the world. If any man love the world, the love of the Father* (God) *is not in him. For all that is in the world, the **lust of the flesh**, and the **lust of the eyes**, and the pride of life, is not of the Father, but is of the world. And the world passeth away, and the lust thereof: but he that doeth the will of God abideth for ever."* **1 John 2:15-17**

**THE EYES OF SINNERS ARE RESTLESS, LUSTFUL, FLIRTY AND NEVER SATISFIED!** *"Hell and destruction are never full; so **the eyes of man** are never satisfied."* **Proverbs 27:20**

**WHAT IS THE BEST WAY TO BREAK THE HABIT OF FLIRTING ONCE IT'S REALLY GOT A HOLD ON YOU? ANSWER: LOOK STRAIGHT AHEAD AT ALL TIMES!** *"Let thine **EYES** look right on, and let thine **EYELIDS** look straight before thee."* **Proverbs 4:25**

**CHRISTIANS SHOULDN'T BE GUILTY OF FLIRTING! A CHRISTIAN CAN FIND WAYS TO EXPRESS HIMSELF IN WORDS, KINDNESS, AND IN HIS ACTIONS, WITHOUT FLIRTING! SINNERS FLIRT WITH THEIR EYES, AND THEY FLIRT WITH DANGER JUST FOR EXCITEMENT! THEY ALSO FLIRT WITH DEATH WITHOUT REALIZING THEY WILL GO TO HELL UNLESS THEY CHANGE THEIR WAYS! ACCORDING TO THE BIBLE, A PERSON WHO FLIRTS IS A "NAUGHTY" PERSON!**

*"A naughty person, a wicked man, walketh with a froward mouth. He **winketh with his eyes**, he speaketh with his feet, he teacheth with his fingers; frowardness is in his heart, he deviseth mischief continually, he soweth discord. Therefore shall his calamity come suddenly; suddenly shall he be broken without remedy* (without being able to save himself)." **Proverbs 6:12-15**

*"Why doth thine heart carry thee away? And **what do thy eyes wink at** that thou turnest thy spirit against God, and lettest such words go out of thy mouth?"* **Job 15:12-13**

**WHY FLIRT? FLIRTING IS TEMPTATION AND TEMPTATION IS SIN!**

**PEOPLE FLIRT WITH FIRE WHEN THEY PLAY WITH MATCHES!**

**PEOPLE FLIRT WITH DEATH WHEN THEY DRINK ALCOHOL AND DRIVE A VEHICLE!**

**PEOPLE FLIRT WITH DEATH WHEN THEY PLAY WITH GUNS, AND THE LIST IS UNENDING! ACCORDING TO THE SCRIPTURES, FLIRTING IS DECEPTIVE AND UNNECESSARY. FLIRTING STEMS FROM THE LUST OF THE FLESH AND LUST OF THE FLESH = SIN!**

**HOW DO YOU GIVE UP WORDLY THINGS?** *"Submit yourselves therefore to God. Resist the devil, and he will flee from you. Draw nigh* (come close) *to God, and he will draw nigh to you. Cleanse your hands, ye sinners; and purify your hearts, ye double minded."* **James 4:7-8**

**MEMORIZE THIS VERSE AND REPEAT IT EVERY TIME YOU FEEL TEMPTATION OF ANY KIND:** Jesus said: *". . .Get thee behind me, Satan: thou art an offence unto me: for thou savourest not the things that be of God, but those that be of* (sinful) *men."* **Matthew 16:23**

## PRAYER

Dear God, please forgive me for **flirting**! I know that **flirting is "game playing"** and is not wholesome! I know that there are fine ways I can express myself without having to resort to flirting! Please come into my heart and forgive all my sins. I want to follow Your principles! I want to be a Christian. Help me to grow each day into the kind of person You want me to be! Help me control all my urges! I thank You for hearing my prayer and for forgiving my sins! In Jesus' name, I pray! AMEN!

# FORNICATION

**DEFINITION:** Human sexual intercourse other than between a man and his wife; sexual intercourse between a spouse and an unmarried person; sexual intercourse between unmarried people; sexual intercourse between a single or married person with a prostitute. **Fornication in the Bible means any sexual intercourse or foreplay outside the legal bounds of (male-female) matrimony!** It also includes incest, prostitution (male or female), and sodomy! All adultery is fornication! All forms of unchastity is fornication!

**FORNICATION IS SIN! CHRISTIANS ARE COMMANDED TO ABSTAIN FROM FORNICATION!** The apostle James said: *". . .abstain from pollutions of idols, and from **fornication**, and from things strangled, and from blood."* **Acts 15:20 (AND)** *". . .abstain from meats offered to idols, and from blood, and from things strangled, and from **fornication:** from which if ye keep yourselves* (sexually pure and spiritually pure), *ye shall do well* (in the sight of God)." **Acts 15:29/21:25**

**THE APOSTLE PAUL SAID:** *"For this is the will of God, even your sanctification* (holiness), *that ye should **ABSTAIN FROM FORNICATION:** That everyone of you should know how to possess* (keep) *his vessel* (his own body) *in sanctification* (holiness) *and honour; Not in the lust of concupiscence* (sexual desire), *even as the Gentiles, which know not God. That no man go beyond and defraud his brother in any matter: because that the Lord is the avenger of all such* (sins), *as we also have forewarned you and testified. **For God hath not called us unto uncleanness, but unto holiness.**"* **1 Thessalonians 4:3-7**

**ONLY AFTER A PERSON (WHO IS GUILTY OF FORNICATION) REPENTS AND TURNS AWAY FROM THIS SIN, IS HE WORTHY OF GOD'S BLESSINGS!** *"If a man therefore purge himself from these* (fornication, other sins), *he shall be a vessel* (body and spirit) *unto honour, sanctified* (holy), *and meet* (useful and proper) *for the master's use* (God's use), *and prepared unto every good work."* **2 Timothy 2:21**

*"Flee also, youthful lusts: but follow righteousness, faith, charity, peace, with them that call on the Lord out of a pure heart."* **2 Timothy 2:22**

**WHY DOES A PERSON HAVE SEX WITHOUT THE BENEFIT OF MARRIAGE? SATAN PUTS THE TEMPTATION IN HIS HEART! THEN, WHEN THE PERSON COMMITS THE ACT—SATAN KNOWS HE HAS TRAPPED THEM!** *"For out of the heart proceed evil thoughts, murders, adulteries, **fornications**, thefts, false witness, blasphemies* (cursing): *These are the things which defile a man* (person): *but to eat with unwashen hands defileth not a man* (person)." **Matthew 15:19-20**

**GOD LONGS FOR US TO RECOVER OURSELVES OUT OF THE TRAPS SATAN SETS FOR US!** *". . .that they may recover themselves out of the snare of the devil, who are taken captive by him* (Satan) *at his will."* **2 Timothy 2:26**

**OUR BODY WAS NOT CREATED TO BE USED FOR FORNICATION!** *"Meats for the belly, and the belly for meats: but God shall destroy both it and them. **Now the body is not for fornication, but for the Lord; and the Lord for the body.**"* **1 Corinthians 6:13**

**TO AVOID THE SIN OF FORNICATION: EACH PERSON SHOULD TOTALLY ABSTAIN FROM SEXUAL INTERCOURSE UNTIL HE HAS HIS OWN WIFE (OR SHE HAS HER OWN HUSBAND).** *"Nevertheless, **to avoid fornication,** let every man have his own wife, and let every woman have her own husband. Let the husband render* (freely give himself) *unto the wife due benevolence* (respect, kindness): *and likewise also the wife unto the husband. The wife hath not power of her own body, but the husband: and likewise also the husband hath not power of his own body, but the wife."* **1 Corinthians 7:2-4**

**A CHRISTIAN'S BODY MUST BE FREE FROM SIN! OUR BODY IS WHERE THE HOLY SPIRIT OF GOD LIVES!** *"What? know ye not that your body is the temple of the Holy Ghost which is in you, which ye have of God, and ye are not your own? For ye **are bought with a price*** (which Christ paid on the cross for our sins): *therefore glorify God in your body, and in your spirit, which are God's."* **1 Corinthians 6:19-20** *"Ye are bought with a price; be not ye the servants of men. Brethren, let every man* (person), *wherein he is called* (to be a Christian), *therein abide with God."* **1 Corinthians 7:23-24**

**A CHRISTIAN'S BODY MUST BE HOLY—IN ORDER FOR THE HOLY SPIRIT TO LIVE IN US!** *"For they that are after* (the sins of) *the flesh do mind* (obey) *the things of the flesh; but they that are after the* (Holy) *Spirit* (do mind or obey) *the things of the* (Holy) *Spirit."* **Romans 8:5**

**FORNICATION DESTROYS A PERSON'S RELATIONSHIP WITH GOD! A CHRISTIAN IS COMMANDED TO PRESENT HIS BODY A LIVING SACRIFICE UNTO GOD, WHICH IS ONLY REASONABLE, CONSIDERING WHAT GOD HAS DONE FOR HIM!** *"I beseech* (beg) *you therefore, brethren, by the mercies of God, that ye present your bodies a living sacrifice, holy, acceptable unto God, which is your reasonable service. And be not conformed to this world* (its lust and sins): *but be ye transformed by the renewing of your mind, that ye may prove what is that good, and acceptable, and perfect will of God."* **Romans 12:1-2**

*"**For to be carnally*** (sexually) ***minded is death*** (an eternal separation from God unless repented), *but to be spiritually minded is life and peace. Because the carnal mind is enmity against God: for it is not subject to the law of God, neither indeed can be. So then they that are in the flesh* (those who fulfill the sinful sexual demands of the flesh) *cannot please God. But ye* (as born-again Christians) *are not in the flesh, but in the* (Holy) *Spirit, if so be that the Spirit of God dwell in you. Now if any man* (person) *have not the Spirit of Christ, he is none of His* (Christ's followers). *And if Christ be in you* (if you are a born-again Christian), *the body is dead* (free from the sins once committed) *because of sin; but the* (Holy) *Spirit is* (eternal) *life* (with Jesus) *because of righteousness."* **Romans 8:6-10**

**IF A CHRISTIAN FALLS BACK INTO SIN AND COMMITS FORNICATION, HE INSTANTLY SEPARATES HIMSELF FROM GOD! HE MUST REPENT ALL OVER AGAIN AND ASK FORGIVENESS AND TURN AWAY FROM SIN!** *"Therefore, brethren, we are debtors* (to Christ for dying on the cross to pay for our sins), *not to the flesh* (sex sins, lusts), *to live after* (for) *the flesh. For if ye live after* (for) *the flesh, ye shall die* (be eternally separated from God): *but if ye through the* (Holy) *Spirit do mortify the deeds of the body, ye shall live. For as many as are led by the Spirit of God, they are the sons of God."* **ROMANS 8:12-14**

(Continued)

**GOD'S PLAN FOR OUR LIVES REQUIRES THAT WE BE FREE FROM FORNICATION AND LUST!** *"Wherefore come out from among them, and be ye separate, saith the Lord, and touch not the unclean thing* (demoniac, moral and physical sins must be cleansed from our body and spirit if one wants the fulfillment of the promises of God): *and I* (God) *will receive you. And will be a Father unto you, and ye shall be My sons and daughters, saith the Lord Almighty."* **2 Corinthians 6:17-18**

**GOD'S PROMISES AND BLESSINGS ARE RESERVED ONLY FOR BORN-AGAIN CHRISTIANS WHO HAVE BEEN SUCCESSFUL IN OVERCOMING SINFUL TEMPTATIONS AND ACTIONS!** *"Having therefore these promises, dearly beloved, **let us cleanse ourselves from all filthiness of the flesh and spirit,** perfecting holiness in the fear* (and respect) *of God."* **2 Corinthians 7:1** *"This I say then, walk in the* (Holy) *Spirit, and ye shall not fulfil the lust of the flesh. For the flesh lusteth against the* (Holy) *Spirit, and the* (Holy) *Spirit against the flesh: and these are contrary the one to the other: so that ye cannot do the things that we would* (should)." **Galatians 5:16-17**

**LISTED BELOW ARE 17 WORKS OF THE FLESH!** *"Now the works of the flesh are manifest* (made known), *which are these, **Adultery, fornication, uncleanness*** (sodomy, homosexuality, lesbianism, pederasty, bestiality and all sex perversion), ***lasciviousness*** (anything that promotes sex and lust), ***idolatry, witchcraft, hatred, variance, emulations, wrath, strife, seditions, heresies, envyings, murders, drunkenness, revellings,*** *and such like: of the which I tell you before, as I have told you in time past, that they which do such things shall not inherit the kingdom of God."* **Galatians 5:19-21 NOTE: DID YOU NOTICE THAT GOD PUTS THE SIN OF FORNICATION RIGHT IN THE SAME VERSE AND CATEGORY AS MURDER?**

**IF A PERSON COMMITS ANY OF THE ABOVE SINS, HE WILL NEVER INHERIT THE KINGDOM OF GOD UNLESS HE REPENTS AND ASKS GOD'S FORGIVENESS AND TURNS AWAY FROM THEM!**

**TO BE ASSURED THAT YOU ARE A BORN-AGAIN CHRISTIAN: YOU MUST REPENT OF FORNICATION AND ALL OTHER SINS, INCLUDING LUST, AND TURN AWAY FROM THEM FOREVER!** *"...they that are Christ's* (born-again Christians) *have crucified* (killed) *the* (lust of) *flesh with the affections and lusts. If we live in the* (Holy) *Spirit, let us also walk in the* (Holy) *Spirit."* **Galatians 5:24-25** *"But **fornication,** and all **uncleanness,** or covetousness, let it not be once named among you, as becometh saints* (born-again Christians); *neither **filthiness,** nor foolish talking, nor jesting, which is not convenient* (pleasing to God): *but rather giving of thanks. For this ye* (you) *know, that no **whoremonger,** nor **unclean person,** nor covetous man, who is an idolater, hath any inheritance in the kingdom of Christ and of God."* **Ephesians 5:3-5**

**DID YOU KNOW THAT THE RISE IN SEX SINS FULFILLS END TIME PROPHECY ABOUT THE LAST DAYS BEFORE CHRIST RETURNS TO EARTH?** *"This know also, that in the last days perilous times shall come. For men* (people) *shall be lovers of their own selves, covetous, boasters, proud, blasphemers, disobedient to parents, unthankful, unholy, **without natural affection,** trucebreakers, false accusers, incontinent, fierce, despisers of those that are good, traitors, heady, highminded, lovers of pleasures more than lovers of God: Having a form of godliness, but denying the power thereof:* (and) *from such* (people) *turn* (get) *away."* **2 Timothy 3:1-5**

# Fornication

**TO KNOW JUST HOW MUCH GOD HATES FORNICATION READ: 1 Corinthians 10:8 WHERE 23,000 PEOPLE DIED IN JUST ONE DAY'S TIME BECAUSE OF THIS SIN!**

**CHRISTIANS ARE NOT TO KEEP COMPANY WITH FORNICATORS—NOR ARE WE TO EVEN EAT WITH THEM!** Paul said: *"I wrote unto you in an epistle* (letter) *not to* (keep) *company with **fornicators:** Yet not* (only) *altogether with the **fornicators** of this world, or with the covetous, or extortioners, or with idolaters; for then must ye needs go out of the world. But now I have written unto you not to keep company, if any man that is called a brother* (Christian) *be a **fornicator,** or covetous, or an idolater, or a railer, or a drunkard, or an extortioner; with such an one no not to eat* (don't eat with anyone who does these things, especially if he professes to be a Christian)." **1 Corinthians 5:9-11**

Fornication

**DID YOU KNOW THAT IF A PERSON DIES AND HAD NOT REPENTED OF HIS SINS HE WILL NOT GO TO HEAVEN?** *"Know ye not that the unrighteous shall not inherit the kingdom of God? Be not deceived: neither **fornicators,** nor idolaters, nor adulterers, nor effeminate* (boys usually on the way to becoming hardened homosexuals), *nor abusers of themselves with mankind* (incest, lesbianism, etc.). *Nor thieves, nor covetous, nor drunkards, nor revilers, nor extortioners, shall inherit the kingdom of God. And such were some of you: but ye are washed* (forgiven of your sins and cleansed if you have repented and turned away from sin), *but ye are sanctified* (holy), *but ye are justified in the name of the Lord Jesus, and by the* (Holy) *Spirit of our God."* **1 Corinthians 6:9-11**

**WHEN YOU COMMIT FORNICATION YOU SIN AGAINST YOUR OWN BODY!** *"But he that is joined unto the Lord is one spirit* (with the Lord). ***FLEE FORNICATION.*** *Every sin that a man* (person) *doeth is without* (outside) *the body; but he that committeth **fornication,** sinneth against his own body."* **1 Corinthians 6:17-18**

**HERE IS A MESSAGE TO UNMARRIED PERSONS AND WIDOWS!** *"I say therefore to the unmarried and widows, it is good for them if they abide even as I* (having no sex). *But if they cannot contain* (stay pure) *let them marry: for it is better to marry than to burn* (give into passion)." **1 Corinthians 7:8-9**

### PRAYER

Dear God, please forgive me for committing **fornication.** I repent of all my sins and ask You to forgive me. I turn away from all sin! I know that Jesus died for my sins, in order that I might come to You and ask forgiveness! I want to be forgiven! I will stay away from those who might tempt me into committing **fornication** again! I will make Christian acquaintances. I will read my Bible! I will go to church regularly! I will need Your help with my thoughts and in all my ways! I know that I can count on You, because You love me! Thank You for giving me eternal life with You! In Jesus' name, I pray. AMEN!

# FORTUNE TELLERS

**FORTUNE TELLERS DO NOT POSSESS A GOD-GIVEN TALENT TO KNOW THE FUTURE OR ANY OTHER EVENT!** God alone knows the future! Only those events which are outlined in the Holy Bible will happen with certainty! **Fortune tellers receive their powers from Satan, not from God!** Fortune tellers deceive their clients by using phrases such as "God told me to tell you this would happen!" Fortune tellers have been around as long as Satan has been around! History tells us that witches (fortune tellers) were once burned at the stake! Today, however, most people don't know that fortune telling is a sin when they place their life and decisions in the hands of one of these charlatans! Some of the "tools" of their trade are crystal balls, tea leaves, palm reading, card reading, tarot cards, the use of familiar spirits (which are demon spirits), and so on! Fortune tellers tell lies to their clients (culprits)! Never forget that God says Satan is a liar and the inventor of lies!

**FORTUNE TELLERS ARE OFTEN CALLED "SEERS" OR "DIVINERS".** Fortune tellers were very famous in Egypt and because of the rebellion of the people to turn away from such practices, God judged them! **God always judges fortune tellers because they prophesy lies!** People ought to turn to God, not to workers of iniquity! *". . . This is a rebellious people* (the Egyptians), *lying children, children that will not hear the law of the Lord. Which say to the seers* (fortune tellers), *See not; and to the prophets, Prophesy not unto us right* (Godly) *things, speak unto us smooth things, prophesy deceits."* **Isaiah 30:9-10**

Fortune telling is associated with sorcery and divination! God hates all such occult activity because it deals with demon spirits, lies and deceit! Fortune telling is sin! God hates the practice of predicting the future but loves the sinner! God wants these people to be saved! He wants them to turn away from these satanic and pagan practices and to turn to Him for their answers! *"You have advisors by the ton—your **astrologers and stargazers**, who try to tell you what the future holds. But they are as useless as dried grass burning in the fire. They cannot even deliver themselves! You'll get no help from them at all. . ."* **Isaiah 47:13-14** (The Living Bible) *"Thou art wearied in the multitude of thy counsels* (fortune tellers' tales). *Let now the astrologers, the stargazers, the **monthly prognosticators** (astrologers, fortune tellers), stand up, and save thee from these things that shall come upon thee."* **Isaiah 47:13-14**

**TO BELIEVE IN (OR PRACTICE) FORTUNE TELLING IS TO DO SATAN'S WORK FOR HIM! IT IS A FORM OF IDOLATRY!** *". . .the Lord testified against Israel, and against Judah, by all the prophets, and by all the **seers** (fortune tellers), saying, Turn ye from your evil ways, and keep my* (God's) *commandments and my statutes, according to all the law which I commanded your fathers, and which I sent you by my servants the prophets."* **2 Kings 17:13**

**GOD WILL JUDGE ALL PEOPLE WHO PRACTICE FORTUNE TELLING!** *"Thus saith the Lord concerning the prophets that make my people err, that bite with their teeth, and cry Peace; and he that putteth not into their mouths* (those who don't pay money), *they even prepare war against him* (by conjuring up evil spirits). *Therefore night shall be unto you, that ye shall not have a vision; and it shall be dark unto you, that ye shall not divine* (be able to cast a speel to remove); *and the sun shall go down over the prophets, and the day shall be dark* (utter darkness) *over them. Then shall the **seers** (fortune tellers) be ashamed, and the **diviners** confounded* (without any answers): *yea* (yes), *they shall all cover their lips; for there is no answer* (help) *of God."* **Micah 3:5-7**

**FORTUNE TELLING = DIVINATION = THE ART OF MYSTIC INSIGHT! THIS GIFT COMES FROM SATAN AND HIS FOLLOWERS!**

**FOR THE RIGHT PRICE, A FORTUNE TELLER WILL PROMISE LIFE TO A WICKED PERSON AND MAKE HIM FEEL A SENSE OF FALSE SECURITY! BOTH SHOULD REPENT AND TURN AWAY FROM SUCH SILLY SIN AND ASK GOD TO FORGIVE THEM!** *"Because with lies ye* (fortune tellers) *have made the heart of the righteous sad, whom I have not made sad; and strengthened the hands of the wicked, that he should not return from his wicked way, by promising him life: Therefore ye shall see no more vanity* (ego, money, fame), *nor **divine divinations** (conjure up predictions): for I* (God) *will deliver my people out of your hand: and ye shall know that I am the Lord."* **Ezekiel 13:22-23**

**GOD CALLED FORTUNE TELLERS "FOOLISH PROPHETS"!** *"They have seen vanity* (believed their own lies) *and lying **divination** (lying predictions), saying, The Lord saith: and the Lord hath not sent them: and they have made others to hope that they would confirm the word. Have ye not seen a vain vision, and have ye not spoken a **lying divination,** whereas ye say, The Lord saith it; albeit* (although) *I* (God) *have not spoken? Therefore thus saith the Lord God; Because ye have spoken vanity, and seen lies, therefore, behold, I am against you, saith the Lord God. And mine hand shall be upon the prophets that see vanity* (visions, have ego problems, tell lies to get money), *and that **divine lies:** they shall not be in the assembly of my people* (born-again Christians), *neither shall they be written in the writing* (history) *of the house of Israel, neither shall they enter into the land of Israel, and ye shall know that I am the Lord God."* **Ezekiel 13:6-9**

**THERE WERE EIGHT PAGAN PRACTICES THAT WERE FORBIDDEN TO CANAAN AND ISRAEL! THESE SAME PRACTICES ARE IN OPERATION TODAY AND GOD STILL FORBIDS THEM! IN THE SCRIPTURES BELOW FORTUNE TELLING IS REFERRED TO AS "OBSERVING TIMES"!** *"There shall not be found among you any one that maketh his son or his daughter to pass through the fire* (to worship an idol god), *or that useth **divination** (fortune telling), or an **observer of times** (fortune telling), or an enchanter* (one who uses charms, mantras, hexes on others), *or a witch, or a charmer* (snake or hypnosis), *or a consulter with familiar* (demon) *spirits, or a wizard* (male witch), *or a necromancer* (divination by means of pretended communication with the dead). *For all that do these things are an abomination unto the Lord: and because of these abominations the Lord thy God doth drive them out from before thee."* **Deuteronomy 18:10-12** *"For these nations, which thou shalt possess, hearkened* (listened) *unto **observers of times** (fortune tellers), and unto **diviners:** but as for thee* (Israel), *the Lord thy God hath not suffered* (allowed) *thee to do so."* **Deuteronomy 18:14**

(Continued)

FORTUNE TELLING IS AN ENEMY TO CHRISTIANITY! GOD'S WILL IS FOR US NEVER TO ENGAGE IN FORTUNE TELLING (OR TO LISTEN TO THOSE WHO PRACTICE IT)! *"For so is the will of God, that with well doing* (obeying God), *ye may put to silence the ignorance of foolish men* (fortune tellers lack the intelligence it takes to give up fortune telling and to accept Christ).*"* **1 Peter 2:15**

UNLESS A FORTUNE TELLER REPENTS, GETS SAVED AND TURNS FROM THIS SINFUL PRACTICE — THE THINGS HE PREDICTS (SUCH AS WAR, DEATH, ETC.) SHALL SURELY COME UPON HIM! GOD WILL NOT TOLERATE FORTUNE TELLERS AND THEIR LIES WITHOUT JUDGING THEM! Jeremiah wrote: *". . .behold the prophets* (fortune tellers) *say unto them, Ye shall not see the sword* (you won't go to war or see death), *neither shall ye have famine* (go hungry); *but I* (fortune teller speaking) *will give you assured peace in this place. Then the Lord said unto me* (Jeremiah), *The prophets prophesy lies in my name: I sent them not, neither have I commanded them* (to speak in my behalf), *neither spake* (I, God) *unto them: they prophesy unto you a false vision and divination* (predicting the future), *and a thing of nought* (no truth), *and the deceit of their heart. Therefore thus saith the Lord concerning the prophets that prophesy in my* (Christ's) *name, and I sent them not, yet they say, Sword and famine shall not be in this land; By sword and famine shall those prophets be consumed."* **Jeremiah 14:13-15**

GOD WARNS US NEVER TO LISTEN TO DREAM ANALYSIS, HYPNOTISTS, PALM READERS, PSYCHICS, ASTROLOGERS, MAGICIANS, FORTUNE TELLERS! ALL OCCULT ACTIVITY IS UNDER THE TOTAL AUTHORSHIP OF SATAN! *"Therefore hearken not* (don't listen) *ye to your prophets, nor to your diviners* (fortune tellers), *nor to your dreamers, nor to your enchanters, nor to your sorcerers . . . for they prophesy a lie unto you, to remove you far from your land; and that I* (God) *should drive you out, and ye should perish."* **Jeremiah 27:9-10**

God wants us to realize the absolute unwavering truth that: ESP, astrology, palmistry, hypnosis, dream interpreters, fortune tellers, etc., do not receive their power from God! They are all false prophets! Anyone who trusts in them falls prey to the tricks of Satan! Don't be gullible! Read your Bible and learn about such sinful practices! *"For thus saith the Lord of hosts, the God of Israel; Let not your prophets and your diviners, that be in the midst of you, deceive you, neither hearken* (pay attention) *to your dreams which ye caused to be dreamed. For they prophesy falsely unto you in my name: I have not sent them, saith the Lord."* **Jeremiah 29:8-9**

SOOTHSAYING = FORTUNE TELLING! Read: Acts 16:16 WHERE PAUL CAST A DEMON SPIRIT OF "SOOTHSAYING" OUT OF A YOUNG GIRL! BECAUSE HE DID, HE WAS CAST INTO PRISON! HOWEVER, GOD MIRACULOUSLY CAUSED A GREAT EARTHQUAKE AND DELIVERED PAUL AND SILAS OUT OF PRISON!

WARNING TO FORTUNE TELLERS! WHEN A FORTUNE TELLER PREDICTS AN EVENT IN A PERSON'S LIFE, HE REPRESENTS HIS PREDICTION TO BE FACT AND TRUTH! HE MOCKS GOD BECAUSE GOD FORBIDS THIS PRACTICE! *"Whoso rewardeth evil for good, evil shall not depart from his house."* **Proverbs 17:13** *"Be not deceived; God is not mocked; for whatsoever a man soweth* (does) *that shall he also reap* (receive).*"* **Galatians 6:7**

To embrace fortune telling, or any other occult activity, is to worship and serve a false god! Fortune telling is idolatry! Idolatry includes anything on which affections are passionately set and which hold a person's complete admiration, attention and belief!

Fortune telling falls into the category of witchcraft! It deals with evil spirits, magical incantations, casting spells and charms upon another person!

FORTUNE TELLING IS A "WORK OF THE FLESH"! THOSE WHO PREDICT THE FUTURE THROUGH THE PRACTICE OF FORTUNE TELLING WILL NOT INHERIT THE KINGDOM OF GOD UNLESS THEY REPENT AND TURN AWAY FROM THIS SINFUL OCCUPATION! *"Now the works of the flesh are manifest* (made known), *which are these: Adultery* (sex by a married person with other than their spouse), *fornication* (sex with no marriage), *uncleanness* (homosexuality, lesbianism, masturbation, bestiality or sex with animals, incest, etc.), *lasciviousness* (lust, filth, sex promotion, pornography, sex devices), *idolatry* (idols, all occult activity, anything worshipped other than Almighty God), *witchcraft* (evil spirits, drugs, spells, fortune tellers, astrology, Satan worship, etc), *hatred, variance* (disputes), *emulations* (ego, jealousy, rivalry), *wrath* (rage), *strife* (vengeance), *seditions* (total disorder, mass confusion), *heresies* (non-comformists against God), *envyings* (to wish another ill-will), *murders, drunkenness, revellings* (riots, obscene music, sinful activities, seances, orgies, etc.), *and such like: of the which I tell you before, as I have also told you in time past, that they which do such things shall not inherit the kingdom of God."* **Galatians 5:19-21**

Fortune tellers make their reputation and income by telling "gullible people" lies! (Zechariah 10:2). Fortune tellers are false prophets! They pretend to have your best interest at heart, but they only want your business for their financial gain! They will tell you anything, (they know you want to hear) so you will come back and spend more money with them! *"Beware of false prophets, which come to you in sheep's clothing* (appearing wholesome, trustworthy, gifted from God), *but inwardly* (inside their heart) *they are ravening* (wild, starving) *wolves."* **Matthew 7:15**

*GOD WILL JUDGE ALL FORTUNE TELLERS FOR THEIR LIES, TRICKS, DECEPTION! THOSE WHO BELIEVE IN FORTUNE TELLERS AND HAVE TAKEN PLEASURE THROUGH THEM WILL ALSO BE JUDGED! FORTUNE TELLING IS NOT JUST FUN AND GAMES! IT'S SERIOUS BUSINESS! FAILURE TO GIVE UP THE PRACTICE OF FORTUNE TELLING COULD RESULT IN A PERSON'S GOING TO HELL!* *"*(Those persons) *who knowing the judgement of God, that they which commit such things are worthy of death* (eternal separation from God), *not only do the same* (sin), *but have pleasure in them that do them."* **Romans 1:32** *"Know ye not* (don't you know?) *that the unrighteous shall not inherit the kingdom of God? Be not deceived: neither fornicators, nor idolaters* (fortune tellers), *nor adulterers, nor effeminate, nor abusers of themselves with mankind, nor thieves, nor covetous, nor drunkards, nor revilers, nor extortioners, shall inherit the kingdom of God."* **1 Corinthians 6:9-10**

GOD SEES AND HEARS WHAT FORTUNE TELLERS PREDICT. AND, IF YOU GO TO FORTUNE TELLERS FOR ADVICE YOU NEED TO REPENT AND RECEIVE FORGIVENESS! THEN, TURN AWAY FOREVER FROM THIS EVIL PRACTICE BECAUSE IT IS A TRICK OF SATAN! *"For there is nothing covered, that shall not be revealed; neither hid, that shall not be known* (to God). *Therefore whatsoever ye have spoken in darkness shall be heard in the light* (before Christ); *and that which ye have spoken in the ear in closets shall be proclaimed upon the housetops."* **Luke 12:2-3**

### PRAYER

Dear God, I repent of the sin of **fortune telling!** I will not be guilty of predicting supposed events in another person's life ever again! I turn away from this wicked practice! I know that God has not given me this talent! Only God knows the future! I know that I cannot save myself! I believe that You are the only one true God! Please forgive me for going to **fortune tellers** and for believing the lies they have told me! I will never be guilty of foolishly spending my money on these fakes! I know that Jesus holds my future in His hands! Please forgive all my sins! I will no longer go to **fortune tellers!** I will read my Bible to learn what events are going to happen. I know that God cannot lie! I know that **fortune tellers** only want my money and I realize they don't love me! I know that You do love me! Therefore, as long as I live I will trust in You! In Jesus' name, I pray. AMEN!

# GAMBLING

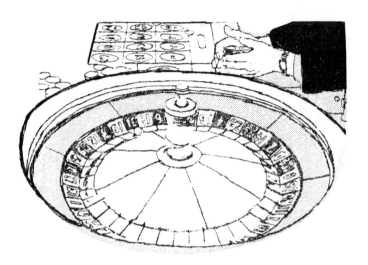

**WHAT CAUSES A PERSON TO BECOME A GAMBLER? SATAN! GOD CALLS SATAN A LIAR AND A THIEF! SATAN LIES, STEALS, AND DESTROYS A PERSON'S LIFE!** *"The thief (Satan) cometh not, but for to steal, and to kill, and to destroy: I (Christ) am come that they might have life, and that they might have it more abundantly."* **John 10:10**

**GOD HATES GAMBLING BUT LOVES THE GAMBLER! HE WANTS THE GAMBLER TO TURN AWAY FROM THIS SINFUL PRACTICE AND GET SAVED!** *"The good man's earnings advance the cause of righteousness. The evil man squanders his on sin."* **Proverbs 10:16** (The Living Bible)

**RICHES ACCUMULATED THROUGH GAMBLING VANISH QUICKLY!** *"The evil man (a gambler) gets rich for the moment, but the good man's reward lasts forever."* **Proverbs 11:18** (The Living Bible) *"A fortune can be made from cheating, but there is a curse that goes with it."* **Proverbs 20:21** (The Living Bible)

**GAMBLING IS A FORM OF IDOLATRY! ANYTHING THAT BECKONS A PERSON'S ATTENTION, AND AFFECTION, MORE THAN GOD DOES, IS IDOLATRY! GOD LISTED 10 VERY IMPORTANT THINGS WE MUST NOT DO IF WE WANT TO LIVE A HAPPY LIFE! THEY ARE THE 10 COMMANDMENTS! THE 1ST COMMANDMENT READS:** *"Thou shalt have no other gods (such as gambling) before me."* **Exodus 20:3**

**GAMBLING IS A SIN! THE SUCCESS OF A GAMBLER IS SHORT-LIVED!** *"Wealth from **gambling** quickly disappears; wealth from hard work grows."* **Proverbs 13:11** (The Living Bible)

**GAMBLING CAN DESTROY A PERSON'S LIFE! THERE IS NO SURE AND QUICK WAY TO RICHES! HARD WORK, DILIGENCE, PRAYER AND RIGHTEOUS LIVING BRING RICHES . . . NOT GAMBLING!** *"Lazy people want much but get little, while the diligent are prospering."* **Proverbs 13:4** (The Living Bible)

**A GAMBLER LOSES HIS SELF-CONTROL WHEN ASKED IF HE WANTS TO STAY IN THE GAME! WHEN HE SAYS "YES", HE STANDS A GOOD CHANCE OF RUINING HIS BUSINESS, LOSING ALL HIS MONEY, AND PERHAPS HIS FAMILY!** *"Self-control means controlling the tongue! A quick retort (answer) can ruin everything."* **Proverbs 13:3** (The Living Bible)

**THE BIBLE SAYS WE SHOULD NEVER LOAN MONEY, OR CO-SIGN A NOTE IF WE KNOW A PERSON IS A CREDIT RISK.** *"Be sure you know a person well before you vouch for his credit! Better refuse than suffer later."* **Proverbs 11:15** (The Living Bible)

**GAMBLERS ALWAYS RUN "SCARED"! THEY KNOW THEIR LUCK MAY RUN OUT AT ANY MOMENT!** *"Crooks are jealous of each other's loot, while good men long to help each other."* **Proverbs 12:12** (The Living Bible)

**REGARDLESS OF HOW MUCH PRACTICAL ADVICE PEOPLE GIVE A GAMBLER, HE USUALLY DECEIVES HIMSELF AND OTHERS, WHEN HE TAKES MONEY AND SETS DOWN TO GAMBLE! GAMBLING IS EVIL!** *"Deceit fills hearts that are plotting for evil; joy fills hearts that are planning for good!"* **Proverbs 12:20** (The Living Bible)

**A GAMBLER WILL LIE TO HIMSELF, HIS FAMILY AND ANYONE ELSE WHO MIGHT TRUST HIM!** *"Lies will get any man into trouble, but honesty is its own defense."* **Proverbs 12:13** (The Living Bible) *"Thou shalt not lie."* **Exodus 20:16**

**WHEN A GAMBLER REFUSES TO REPENT AND TURN AWAY FROM SIN, HE WILL BE JUDGED PERSONALLY, BY GOD, FOR AT LEAST THESE SINS: DENYING THE HOLY SPIRIT, IDOLATRY, LYING, UNRIGHTEOUSNESS, COVERING, DECEIVING, MALIGNING OTHERS, BOASTING, FOR REJECTING THE TRUTH, AND POSSIBLY FOR DRINKING! NOW I ASK YOU, "IS GAMBLING AND ALL THAT GOES WITH IT, WORTH SPENDING ETERNITY IN HELL?"**

**MOST GAMBLING IS AN ILLEGAL WAY OF EARNING MONEY!** *"Dishonest money brings grief to all the family, but hating bribes brings happiness."* **Proverbs 15:27** (The Living Bible) *"A little, gained honestly is better than great wealth gotten by dishonest means."* **Proverbs 16:8** (The Living Bible) *"Better be poor and honet than rich and dishonest."* **Proverbs 19:1** (The Living Bible)

**GAMBLING IS FOLLY!** *"If a man enjoys folly, something is wrong! The sensible stay on the pathways of right."* **Proverbs 15:21** (The Living Bible) *"As a dog returns to his vomit, so a fool repeats his folly."* **Proverbs 26:11** (The Living Bible)

**GAMBLERS MAKE A BAD MISTAKE WHEN THEY PRAY TO GOD TO HELP THEM JUST AS THEY BEGIN TO ROLL THE DICE! GOD DOESN'T HEAR THE PRAYERS OF SINNERS, UNTIL THEY ASK TO BE FORGIVEN FOR THEIR SINS!** *"The Lord is far from the wicked, but he hears the prayers of the righteous."* **Proverbs 15:29** (The Living Bible)

**GAMBLERS BRING EMBARRASSMENT TO THEMSELVES, THEIR FRIENDS AND CERTAINLY TO THEIR FAMILIES! GAMBLING MAKES RICH MEN POOR! THEN, WHEN THEY TURN TO OTHERS FOR FINANCIAL HELP (TO SUPPORT THIS EVIL HABIT) THEY MAY NOT FIND IT AVAILABLE!** *"A poor man's own brothers turn away from him in embarrassment; how much more his friends! He calls after them, but they are gone."* **Proverbs 19:7** (The Living Bible)

**GAMBLING DEALS WITH THE UNKNOWN! IT IS DANGEROUS AND SINFUL!** *"It is dangerous and sinful to rush into the unknown."* **Proverbs 19:2** (The Living Bible)

**GAMBLERS USUALLY END UP IN FIGHTS, BECAUSE OF THEIR DEFEATS!** *"A short tempered man must bear his own penalty; You can't do much to help him. If you try once you must try a dozen times!"* **Proverbs 19:19** (The Living Bible) *"It is hard to stop a quarrel once it starts, so don't let it begin."* **Proverbs 17:14** (The Living Bible) *"Fools start fights everywhere while wise men keep peace."* **Proverbs 29:8** (The Living Bible)

(Continued)

GAMBLERS USUALLY HAVE A "HOT" TEMPER WHEN THEY FOOLISHLY LOSE ALL THEIR MONEY! THEY GET INSULTED EASILY, TOO! *"A fool is quick-tempered; a wise man stays cool when insulted."* **Proverbs 12:16** (The Living Bible) *"A quarrelsome man starts fights as easily as a match sets fire to paper."* **Proverbs 26:21** (The Living Bible) *"There is more hope for a fool than a man of quick temper."* **Proverbs 29:20** (The Living Bible) *"A hot tempered man starts fights and gets into all kinds of trouble."* **Proverbs 29:22** (The Living Bible)

GAMBLERS DON'T SEEM TO REALIZE THEY WILL HAVE TO ANSWER TO GOD ON JUDGEMENT DAY FOR THIS SIN, UNLESS THEY REPENT AND TURN AWAY FROM IT! *"Your riches won't help you on Judgement Day; only righteousness counts then."* **Proverbs 11:4** (The Living Bible)

GAMBLERS ARE LAZY! THEY LIVE TO GAIN RICHES, WITHOUT HAVING TO WORK FOR THEM! THEY COVET! COVETING IS A SIN! *"Some men are so lazy they won't even feed themselves!"* **Proverbs 19:24** (The Living Bible) *"Thou shalt not covet."* **Exodus 20:17**

GAMBLING IS IDOLATRY! *"Thou shalt have no other gods before me."* **Exodus 20:3**

GAMBLERS USUALLY CURSE WHEN THEY MAKE A BAD MOVE  OR LOSE THEIR MONEY! CURSING IS A SIN! *"Thou shalt not take the name of the Lord thy God in vain; for the Lord will not hold him guiltless that taketh his name in vain."* **Exodus 20:7**

GAMBLING IS HASTY SPECULATION WHICH SOONER OR LATER BRINGS POVERTY TO THE GAMBLER! *"Steady plodding brings prosperity; hasty speculation brings poverty."* **Proverbs 21:5** (The Living Bible) *"Dishonest gain will never last, so why take the risk?"* **Proverbs 21:6** (The Living Bible)

WHEN A GAMBLER BORROWS MONEY TO SUPPORT HIS EVIL HABIT AND FINDS HE CANNOT PAY HIS DEBTS, HE IS LIKELY TO END UP DEAD! *"The man who strays away from common sense will end up dead!"* **Proverbs 21:16** (The Living Bible)

GAMBLERS ARE USUALLY DRINKERS AND SPEND-THRIFTS! WITHOUT KNOWING IT THEY PLAY RIGHT INTO THE HANDS OF THE BIGGEST LOSER OF THEM ALL . . . SATAN! WHY WOULD A GAMBLER WANT TO SELL HIS SOUL TO THE DEVIL  JUST FOR ONE MORE ROLL OF THE DICE OR TURN OF THE CARDS? *"Be sober, be vigilant; because your adversary* (enemy) *the devil, as a roaring lion, walketh about, seeking whom he may devour. . ."* **1 Peter 5:8** *"A man who loves pleasure becomes poor; wine and luxury are not the way to riches!"* **Proverbs 21:17** (The Living Bible)

IT IS INEVITABLE THAT A GAMBLER'S "LUCK" WILL SOON RUN OUT! *"The wicked will finally lose, the righteous will finally win."* **Proverbs 21:18** (The Living Bible)

GAMBLERS NEVER CONTEMPLATE THE CONSE-QUENCES WHEN THEY SET ABOUT TO GAMBLE! "THIS GAME WILL MAKE ME A RICH MAN!" THEY SAY! THEY ARE DAY DREAMERS! THEY DECEIVE THEMSELVES! *"A prudent man forsees the difficulties ahead and prepares for them; the simpleton goes blindly on and suffers the consequences."* **Proverbs 22:3** (The Living Bible)

THE GAMBLER STUPIDLY BRAGS THAT THE DECK WAS "STACKED" TODAY! "TOMORROW WILL BE BET-TER!" DON'T COUNT ON IT! *"Don't brag about your plans for tomorrow — wait and see what happens."* **Proverbs 27:1** (The Living Bible) *"Ambition and death are alike in this: neither is ever satisfied."* **Proverbs 27:20** (The Living Bible)

GAMBLERS ARE CHEATERS! *"Better to be poor and honest than rich and a cheater."* **Proverbs 28:6** (The Living Bible)

EVENTUALLY GAMBLERS BECOME DEPRAVED BECAUSE GAMBLING BECOMES A SICKNESS! *"When a poor man oppresses those even poorer, he is like an unexpected flood sweeping away their last hope."* **Proverbs 28:3** (The Living Bible)

How can a gambler overcome the urge to gamble? Acknowledge you are a sinner! Repent! Confess your sins to God! Sincerely ask his forgiveness in your own words! God will forgive you! Then, you must never gamble again! Stay away from the people who would tempt you to gamble! Stay away from the places where you gambled! Make sure you are sincere and God will help give you the strength! If you are not completely sincere and honest with God you will be mocking him! *"He that overcometh shall inherit all things; and I will be his God, and he shall be my son."* **Revelation 21:7**

**Luke 13:5 says:** *"Except ye repent; ye shall all likewise perish."* **John 3:3 says:** *"Except a man be born again he cannot see the kingdom of God."* **2 Corinthians 6:2 says:** *"Now is the accepted time: behold* (listen) *now is the day of salvation."*

IF A GAMBLER REFUSES TO GIVE UP THIS SINFUL PRACTICE AND DIES, HE WILL GO TO HELL, UNLESS HE REPENTED! WHY WAIT? GAMBLING CAN'T POSSIBLY BE WORTH SPENDING ETERNITY IN HELL, WHEN YOU CAN SPEND IT WITH JESUS!

GAMBLERS BET ON EVERYTHING THEY EVER EARN-ED, CAN BORROW, OR STEAL! THE OVERWHELMING URGE TO GAMBLE HAS BROKEN UP MANY HOMES AND FAMILIES! MANY FAMILIES HAVE SUFFERED NEEDLESSLY, BECAUSE A MEMBER IN THE FAMILY GAMBLED AWAY EVERYTHING HE OWNED TO PAY HIS GAMBLING DEBTS! *"The fool who provokes his family to anger and resentment will finally have nothing worthwhile left. He shall be the servant of a wiser man."* **Proverbs 11:29** (The Living Bible)

A GAMBLER THINKS THE MONEY HE JUST WON IS "GOOD LUCK" MONEY! HE SURMISES THAT SINCE HE WAS LUCKY WINNING THIS MONEY, IT WILL SURELY BRING HIM MORE MONEY THE NEXT TIME HE GAMBLES! HE MAY BE SADLY AND FINANCIALLY MISTAKEN! *"Trust in your money and down you go: Trust in God and flourish as a tree!"* **Proverbs 11:28** (The Living Bible)

### PRAYER

Dear God, Please come into my heart and forgive me for all my sins. I humbly ask You to forgive me. **I will never gamble again!** I will not go to the places I use to go  so I will not be tempted to **gamble!** I will make Christian friendships! I believe that Jesus is Your son, and that He died on the cross to pay for my sins! I believe He rose on the third day and lives today! I don't want to go to hell! I want to spend eternity with Jesus! I know You love me, and I love you! I will need Your help to overcome this temptation! I know that I can count on You to help me! Give me strength, Lord! Give me peace of mind! Teach me to be honest and forthright! Forgive me for lying, and everything else I have done to disappoint You! From this moment on, I will be a Christian! I will not be ashamed to tell others what You have mercifully done for me! In Jesus' name, I pray. AMEN!

# GOSSIP

PEOPLE SPREAD GOSSIP TO BE NOTICED AND TO GAIN ATTENTION! GOSSIP IS A NASTY HABIT!

WHEN A PERSON GOSSIPS, HE DECEIVES AND SLANDERS ANOTHER PERSON WHILE PRETENDING TO BE A GOOD SPORT AND FRIEND! THE "GOSSIP" IS AS DANGEROUS AS AN INSANE PERSON WITH A GUN, FIERY DARTS OR A SHARP KNIFE! *"As a mad* (insane) *man who casteth* (throws) *firebrands* (darts, shoots a gun), *arrows, and death, So is the man* (person) *that deceiveth his neighbour, and saith, Am not I in sport* (aren't I your good friend, to tell you these things)?" **Proverbs 26:18-19**

WHERE THERE IS NO GOSSIP, THERE SHOULD BE NO TENSION! *"Where no wood is, there the fire goeth out: so where there is no talebearer, the strife ceaseth."* **Proverbs 26:20**

GOSSIP HURTS AS BAD AS A WOUND! *"The words of a talebearer are as wounds, and they go down in the innermost parts of the belly."* **Proverbs 26:22**

A PERSON WHO HATES ANOTHER PERSON WILL INEVITABLY GOSSIP ABOUT HIM! *"He that hateth* (another person) *dissembleth with his lips, and layeth up deceit within him; When he speaketh fair* (nice things), *believe him not: for there are seven abominations* (disgusting things) *in his heart."* **Proverbs 26:24-25**

IF A PERSON OPENS A CONVERSATION WITH YOU IN ORDER TO GOSSIP ABOUT YOUR FRIEND, WHAT CAN YOU DO? DON'T ANSWER HIM!! DON'T TELL HIM WHAT HE WANTS TO HEAR! *"Answer not a fool according to his folly, lest thou also be like unto him."* **Proverbs 26:4**

GOSSIPERS ARE NOT VERY INTELLIGENT! THEY TELL EVERYTHING THEY KNOW! *"A fool* **uttereth all his mind:** *but a wise man keepeth it in till afterwards."* **Proverbs 29:11**

ACCORDING TO THE BIBLE: IF YOU LISTEN TO A GOSSIPER, YOU ARE JUST AS WICKED AS HE IS! *"A wicked doer giveth heed* (listens) *to false lips; and a liar giveth ear to a naughty tongue."* **Proverbs 17:4**

IDLENESS MAY PROMOTE A PERSON TO GOSSIP — JUST TO HAVE SOMETHING TO DO! *". . .they learn to be* **idle,** *wandering about from house to house; and not only idle, but* **tattlers** *also and* **busybodies,** *speaking things which they ought not."* **1 Timothy 5:13**

TO GOSSIP IS TO BEAR FALSE WITNESS! Jesus said: *". . .Thou shalt do no murder, Thou shalt not commit adultery, Thou shalt not steal, Thou shalt not bear* **false witness.**" **Matthew 19:18**

CHRISTIANS SHOULD NEVER BE GUILTY OF GOSSIP! GOSSIP IS THE OPPOSITE OF GODLINESS! *"An ungodly man* (person) *diggeth up evil: and in his lips there is as a burning fire."* **Proverbs 16:27**

GOSSIP CAN BREAK UP GOOD FRIENDS! *"A froward man* (person) *soweth strife: and a* **whisperer** (gossiper) *separeth chief friends."* **Proverbs 16:28** *"He shutteth his eyes to devise froward things:* **moving his lips** *he bringeth evil to pass."* **Proverbs 16:30**

BE CAREFUL WHO YOU TRUST YOUR INNERMOST SECRETS WITH. BETTER MAKE SURE HE IS A GOD-FEARING BORN-AGAIN CHRISTIAN! *"A talebearer revealeth secrets: but he that is of a faithful spirit concealeth the matter."* **Proverbs 11:13**

WARNING: EVERYTHING WE SAY AND DO WILL BE REVEALED WHEN WE STAND FACE TO FACE WITH GOD! Jesus said: *"For there is nothing covered, that shall not be revealed; neither hid, that shall not be known. Therefore whatsoever ye have spoken in darkness shall be heard in the light; and that which ye have spoken in the ear in closets* (gossip) *shall be proclaimed upon the housetops* (every one will hear)." **Luke 12:2-3**

CHRISTIANS SHOULD STAY AWAY FROM PEOPLE WHO MEDDLE IN OTHER PEOPLE'S AFFAIRS, AND WITH THOSE WHO USE EXCESSIVE FLATTERY! *"He that goeth about as a* **talebearer** *revealeth secrets: therefore* **meddle not** *with him that* **flattereth** *with his lips."* **Proverbs 20:19**

WOULD YOU WANT TO HAVE A REPUTATION AS A GOSSIP — WHEN A GOOD NAME IS BETTER THAN SILVER AND GOLD? *"A good name is rather to be chosen than great riches, and loving favour* (with God) *rather than silver and gold."* **Proverbs 22:1**

PARENTS SHOULD NEVER GOSSIP, BECAUSE THEIR CHILDREN WILL IMITATE THEM! PARENTS NEED TO TRAIN THEIR CHILDREN AT AN EARLY AGE NOT TO GOSSIP! *"Train up a child in the way he should go: and when he is old, he will not depart from it."* **Proverbs 22:6**

IN THE END, THE "GOSSIP" LOSES FRIENDS, LOVE, RESPECT FOR HIMSELF, AND FROM GOD! HE HAS NO ONE TO BLAME BUT HIMSELF! *"Thine own* **mouth** *condemneth thee, and not I: yea, thine own* **lips** *testify against thee."* **Job 15:6**

A GOSSIPER'S PASTIME IS TO MEDDLE SO HE WILL ALWAYS HAVE FRESH GOSSIP TO PASS ON! *"It is an honour for a man* (person) *to cease from strife: but every fool will be* **meddling.**" **Proverbs 20:3**

GOSSIP IS WICKED, MISCHIEF AND SIN! *"A wicked messenger* (gossiper) *falleth into mischief: but a faithful ambassador* (true Christian) *is health* (peace, love, prosperity)." **Proverbs 13:17**

CHRISTIANS ARE COMMANDED NOT TO GOSSIP! *"Thou shalt not go up and down as a* **talebearer** *among thy people: neither shalt thou stand against the blood of thy neighbour: I am the Lord."* **Leviticus 19:16**

## PRAYER

Dear God, please forgive me for all my sins. **I am 100 percent guilty of being a gossip!** I have hurt others through this sin! I have lost respect, good will, and friendship, because of this terrible habit. I ask You to forgive me. Help me clean up my conversation! **I will not gossip any more!** I will diligently try to think what Jesus would say before I open my mouth! Please help me restore faith in myself, and others in me! I know I have disappointed You! No more will I do the things I have done in the past. Come into my life and create in me a clean heart and I will praise You forever. In Jesus' name, I pray. AMEN!

# GOVERNMENT

**THE ORIGINAL CREATOR OF GOVERNMENT WAS ALMIGHTY GOD!** *"For unto us a child* (Jesus) *is born, and unto us a son is given: and the* **government** *shall be upon his shoulder: and his name shall be called Wonderful, Counsellor, The Mighty God, The Everlasting Father, The Prince of Peace. Of the increase of his* (CHRIST) **government** *and peace there shall be no end, upon the throne of David, and upon his kingdom, to order it, and to establish it with judgement and with justice from henceforth even for ever. The zeal of the Lord of hosts will perform this."* **Isaiah 9:6-7**

**GOD ORGANIZED GOOD GOVERNMENT FOR OUR SAFETY!** *"Where no counsel is, the people fall: but in the multitude of counsellors there is safety."* **Proverbs 11:14**

**CHRISTIANS ARE COMMANDED TO OBEY ALL GOVERNMENTAL LAWS, TAXES, REGISTRATIONS, ETC.!** Jesus said: *"Render therefore* (pay debts owed and respect the government) *unto Caesar* (our earthly government) *the things which are Caesar's* (the government); *and unto God the things that are God's."* **Matthew 22:21**

**A CHRISTIAN'S FIRST RESPONSIBILITY MUST BE TO GOD, BEFORE THE GOVERNMENT! GOD'S KINGDOM IS NOT PART OF THIS WORLD!** Jesus said: *"My kingdom is not of this world:. . ."* **John 18:36**

**AS SURELY AS GOD RULES OVER GODLY PEOPLE, SATAN HAS AN ORGANIZED GOVERNMENT WHICH RULES OVER UNSAVED PEOPLE!** *". . .for the prince of this world* (Satan) *cometh, and hath nothing in me* (Christ)." **John 14:30/Matthew 4:8**

**GOD'S REQUIREMENTS MUST ALWAYS COME FIRST BEFORE EARTHLY GOVERNMENT!** *"Then Peter and the other apostles answered and said, We ought to obey God rather than men."* **Acts 5:29** *"But seek ye* **first** *the* **kingdom of God,** *and his righteousness, and all these things shall be added unto you."* **Matthew 6:33**

**CHRISTIANS MUST MAINTAIN NEUTRALITY IN WORLD AFFAIRS — NEITHER DISOBEYING, NOR SUBSTITUTING THEM FOR GOD'S COMMANDMENTS! JESUS WAS NOT ACTIVE IN WORLD AFFAIRS SINCE HE CAME TO DO HIS FATHER'S BUSINESS! JESUS TAUGHT US TO OBEY OUR GOVERNMENT BUT WE ARE TO PUT OUR FULL ATTENTION ON GOD, FIRST!** *"They* (born again Christians) *are not of the world, even as I* (Christ) *am not of the world."* **John 17:16**

**CHRIST, WHO KNEW NO SIN, ENTREATS US TO BE AMBASSADORS FOR HIM! THIS IS MUCH MORE IMPORTANT THAN BEING AN AMBASSADOR IN GOVERNMENT!** *"Now then we are* **ambassadors for Christ,** *as though God did beseech you by us* (through born-again Christians): *we pray you in Christ's stead* (behalf), *be ye reconciled to God. For he* (God) *hath made him* (Jesus) *to be sin for us,* **who knew no sin;** *that we might be made the righteousness of God in him* (Christ)." **2 Corinthians 5:20-21**

**CHRISTIAN WARFARE IS A PROTECTION FOR PEOPLE OF ALL NATIONS!** *"Put on the whole armour of God, that ye may be able to stand against the wiles of the devil. For we wrestle not against flesh and blood, but against principalities, against powers, against the rulers of the darkness of this world, against spiritual wickedness in high places."* **Ephesians 6:11-12**

**WHEN A CHRISTIAN SOLDIER GOES TO WAR, HE IS NOT TO FORSAKE BATTLE FOR OTHER INTERESTS!** *"Thou therefore endure hardness, as a good soldier of Jesus Christ."* **2 Timothy 2:3**

**WHEN A GOVERNMENT DECLARES WAR . . . THE BEST ARMOUR A CHRISTIAN CAN HAVE IS THE TRUTH OF GOD!** *"Wherefore take unto you the* **whole armour of God,** *that ye may be able to withstand in the evil day, and having done all, to stand. Stand therefore, having your* **loins girt about with truth,** *and having on the* **breastplate of righteousness;** *And your feet* **shod with the preparation of the gospel of peace;** *Above all, taking the* **shield of faith** *wherewith ye shall be able to quench* **all the fiery darts** *of the wicked. And take the* **helmet of salvation,** *and the* **sword of the** (Holy) **Spirit,** *which is the word of God."* **Ephesians 6:13-17**

**TODAY, THERE ISN'T ONE GOVERNMENT THAT ATTEMPTS TO OBEY ALL THE COMMANDMENTS OF GOD! ALL NATIONS DO THEIR OWN THING! CHRISTIANITY IS NO LONGER ADMIRED BY GOVERNMENT!** *"If the world hate you* (the born-again Christian), *ye know that it hated me* (God) *before it hated you. If ye were of the world* (worldly), *the world would love his own* (kind): *but because ye are not of the world* (but are a part of the spiritual world of God), *therefore the world* (governments) *hateth you."* **John 15:18-19**

**FOR A CHRISTIAN TO BECOME INVOLVED IN GOVERNMENT, BEFORE HONORING GOD'S LAWS, MAKES HIM AN ENEMY OF GOD!** *"Ye adulterers and adulteresses, know ye not that the friendship of the world is enmity with God? whosoever therefore will be a friend of the world is the enemy of God."* **James 4:4** *"For to be carnally minded is death* (eternal separation from God); *but to be spiritually minded is life and peace. Because the carnal mind is enmity against God: for it is not subject to the law of God, neither indeed can be* (because the carnal mind belongs to those who obey Satan)." **Romans 8:6-7**

**EVERY NATION HAS CORRUPT GOVERNMENT, BECAUSE SATAN REIGNS IN EVERY PERSON WHO IS NOT A FOLLOWER OF GOD! THAT'S NO EXCUSE FOR CHRISTIANS NOT TO PAY THEIR TAXES, TRAFFIC FINES, TO VOTE, ETC.!**

**THANK GOD!! MOST OF US DO NOT WORSHIP GOVERNMENT, AS AN IDOL, LIKE THE JEWS DID DURING THE DAYS WHEN THE BIBLE WAS WRITTEN! READ: Daniel 3:15-18**

**REGARDLESS OF HOW EVIL COMMUNISM IS, AND NO MATTER HOW MANY FAULTS ANY GOVERNMENT HAS, THE GREATEST GOVERNMENT OF ALL WILL WIN IN THE END!** John wrote: *". . .I beheld, and lo, a great* **multitude,** *which* **no man could number,** *of all nations, and* **kindreds,** *and* **people,** *and* **tongues,** *stood before the throne, and before the Lamb* (Christ), *clothed with white robes, and palms in their hands. And cried with a loud voice, saying, Salvation to our God which sitteth upon the throne, and unto the Lamb* (Jesus)." **Revelation 7:9-10**

119

# GRAVES

MAN IS A THREE-FOLD BEING . . . BODY, SOUL, SPIRIT!
READ: 1 Thessalonians 5:23/Hebrews 4:12

### WHY DOES MAN DIE?
**MAN HAD A PERFECT START WITH THE PROSPECT OF AN ENDLESS LIFE.** Genesis 1:28, 31
**BECAUSE OF MAN'S DISOBEDIENCE TO GOD, DEATH CAME INTO BEING.** Genesis 3:19/Deuteronomy 32:5
**THE BODY CAN BE KILLED, BUT NOT THE SOUL.** Matthew 12:28/Luke 12:4-5
**SIN AND DEATH HAVE PASSED ON TO ALL ADAM'S CHILDREN.** Romans 5:12
**AFTER JESUS RETURNS, DEATH WILL BE DESTROYED.** 1 Corinthians 15:26/Revelation 21:4

### WHAT IS THE CONDITION OF THE DEAD?
**ONLY MAN'S PHYSICAL BODY DIES AND IS BURIED. HIS SOUL AND SPIRIT LIVE ON.** Ezekiel 18:4/Isaiah 53:12/Job 11:20
**THE INNER MAN (SOUL, SPIRIT) IS ETERNAL. THE OUTER BODY IS MORTAL.** 2 Corinthians 4:16-18
**THE DEAD OUTER BODY OF MAN IS UNCONSCIOUS AND KNOWS NOTHING.** Ecclesiastes 9:5, 10/Psalm 146:3-4
**THE OUTER DEAD BODY AWAITS RESURRECTION.** John 11:11-14, 23-26/Acts 7:60

### TALKING WITH THE DEAD IS IMPOSSIBLE!
**WE ARE WARNED AGAINST TRYING TO SPEAK WITH THE DEAD.** Isaiah 8:19/Leviticus 19:31
**PRACTICERS OF SPIRITISM WILL NOT INHERIT THE KINGDOM OF GOD.** Galatians 5:19-21
**THE DEAD ARE UNAWARE OF HONORS BESTOWED UPON THEM.** Ecclesiastes 9:10/Job 14:1-2, 21
**DEAD PERSONS HOLD NO POWER OVER THE LIVING.** Romans 7:2-3/1 Corinthians 7:39
**TRUE HONOR BELONGS NOT TO THE DEAD, BUT TO GOD.** Romans 1:25/Isaiah 38:19

### GRAVES
**THE GRAVE IS NOT EVERLASTING HELL, AS SOME PEOPLE BELIEVE! THE HEBREW WORD FOR GRAVE, TOMB, BURYING PLACE, IS "QEBER"! THE HEBREW WORD FOR HELL IS "SHEOL"! THE GRAVE IS ALWAYS THE PLACE OF THE BODY, NEVER THE SOUL AND SPIRIT.** Genesis 35:20/2 Samuel 3:32/19:37/1 Kings 13:30/Psalm 88:5/Isaiah 53:9/John 11:17/12:17
**AT THE TIME OF PHYSICAL DEATH, THE SOUL AND SPIRIT OF THE RIGHTEOUS GO DIRECTLY TO HEAVEN. THE PHYSICAL BODY GOES TO DUST AFTER IT IS PUT INTO THE GRAVE, UNTIL THE RESURRECTION TAKES PLACE.** 2 Corinthians 5:8/Philippians 1:21-24/Hebrews 12:22-23/Revelation 6:9-11
**THE ORIGINAL OUTER BODY NEVER RISES FROM DEATH. IT RETURNS TO ETERNAL DUST.** Job 14:12.
**GOD GIVES EACH PERSON A NEW BODY IN THE RESURRECTION.** 1 Corinthians 15:35-53/Philippians 3:21/2 Corinthians 5:1-8

**MAN HAS A WILL, MAKING HIM A FREE MORAL AGENT AND A RESPONSIBLE BEING!** John 3:16/ 7:17/ Romans 7:18/ 1 Corinthians 7:36-37/ 9:17/ 2 Peter 1:21/ Revelation 22:17

**"SOUL-SLEEP" IS NOT TAUGHT AT ALL IN THE HOLY BIBLE!**

**SOULS OF THE RIGHTEOUS HAVE ETERNAL LIFE, EVEN AFTER THE BODY DIES!** John 3:16/ 5:24/ 6:47, 53, 63/ 11:25-26/ 14:19

### A FEW FACTS PROVING HELL IS NOT THE GRAVE!
**1.** In Scriptures, "sheol-hades" (hell) is never the place of the outer physical body, "qebermnaymion" (grave) is never the place of the soul and spirit. Psalm 16:10/ Acts 2:25-29.
**2.** Sheol is never located on earth; queber (grave) is always located on earth (73 times in the Bible).
**3.** Physical bodies never go to sheol (hell), but go to qeber (graves) (75 times in the Bible).
**4.** An individual's sheol (hell) is never mentioned: individual qebers (graves) mentioned 79 times.
**5.** Man never puts anyone into sheol (hell); man puts bodies into quebers (graves) mentioned 40 times.
**6.** Man never digs, sees, touches, or makes a sheol (hell); Man digs and makes qebers (graves) mentioned 51 times.
**7.** Sheol-hades (hell), unlike the grave, is a place of activity, a place of wrath, torment. Deuteronomy 32:22/ Luke 16:19-31

**THE SOUL AND SPIRIT DESIGN! THE BODY EXECUTES! MAN THROUGH HIS BODY HAS MATERIAL OR WORLD CONSCIOUSNESS . . . THROUGH THE SOUL, SELF-CONSCIOUSNESS, AND THROUGH THE SPIRIT, GOD CONSCIOUSNESS!**

**TOO MUCH HONOR TO THE DEAD, CEMETERY MONUMENTS, CRYPTS, SARCOPHAGUS, MEMORIALS, TOMB STONES, AND A PERSON'S ASHES, MAY BE FORMS OF IDOLATRY! IDOLATRY IS FORBIDDEN IN THE SCRIPTURES!**

**ANY PERSON WHO IS PRE-OCCUPIED WITH GOING TO THE CEMETERY TO VISIT THE GRAVE OF A LOVED ONE IS NOT LETTING GO OF DEATH AND GETTING ON WITH LIFE! GOD DOES NOT LIKE FOR PEOPLE TO LIVE IN THE PAST! GOD TOLD US TO "OCCUPY" (WORK, STAY BUSY) UNTIL HE COMES! TOO MUCH TIME, ATTENTION AND CONVERSATION ABOUT SOMEONE WHO HAS ALREADY DIED IS A FORM OF IDOLATRY AND GOD FORBIDS THIS!**

### PRAYER
Dear God, Please forgive me for all my sins. Please forgive me for living in the past with the memories of a loved one who is already dead and buried! Please help me live in the present and plan for the future! Give me strength to stay away from the **cemetery!** I know the dead have no power over the living! I know the **cemetery** is not where You want me to spend so much time! I know that Your desire for my life is for me to work and witness to the living about the love of Christ! I let go of the bondage that death has held over me! Instead of going to the **cemetery**, I will go to church! Instead of talking so much about someone who has died, I will talk about Christ, who is very much alive! Instead, of honoring the dead so much, I will honor the living by telling them about Your plan of salvation! I know there is nothing I can do about my loved ones, who did not repent of their sins, prior to their death! I will not let this hold me back or grieve me, any longer! There is much work to do to help others get ready for heaven! Therefore, I will do my part in telling others how to become a Christian! I know that for me to be an effective Christian, I must get busy! Thank You for opening my eyes and for encouraging me to look upwards, not downwards towards the **GRAVE,**   In Jesus' name, I pray. AMEN!

# GREED

**GREED IS THE OFFSPRING OF SATAN! WHEN A PERSON HAS NOT REPENTED OF HIS SINS AND RECEIVED SALVATION, HE WILL NATURALLY HAVE ALL KINDS OF PROBLEMS! HIS MASTER IS SATAN AND SATAN WILL EVENTUALLY DESTROY HIM!** *"Having the* (their) *understanding darkened* (by Satan), (and) *being alienated* (separated) *from the love of God through the ignorance that is in them, because of the blindness of their heart: Who being past feeling have given themselves over unto lasciviousness* (lust), *to work all uncleanness* (to commit sins) *with greediness."* **Ephesians 4:18-19**

**GREED OFTEN LEADS TO EXTORTION!** *"Thou hast taken usury* (unusually high interest) *and increase* (material things dishonestly acquired), *and thou hast greedily gained* (prospered) *of thy neighbours by extortion, and hast forgotten me, saith the Lord God."* **Ezekiel 22:12**

**MANY PEOPLE CAN'T BE SATISFIED WITH SUFFICIENCY FOR THE DAY! THEIR GREEDY APPETITE CAN NEVER BE SATISFIED! THEY GREED FOR MORE GAIN — EVEN AT THE OTHER PERSON'S EXPENSE! MANY PEOPLE ARE SO GREEDY THAT THEY KILL, OR HAVE SOMEONE KILLED, IN ORDER TO HAVE THEIR GREED SATISFIED.** *"So are the ways of every one that is greedy of gain; which taketh away the life of the owners thereof!"* **Proverbs 1:19** *"He that is greedy of gain troubleth his own house; but he that hateth gifts* (does not covet or experience greed) *shall live."* **Proverbs 15:27**

**THE BIBLE DESCRIBES PEOPLE WHO ARE GREEDY AS "DOGS"!** *"Yea* (yes), *they are greedy dogs which can never have enough, and they are shepherds that cannot understand: they all look to their own way, every one for his gain, from his quarter."* **Isaiah 56:11**

**GREED IS SIN! IT IS A DISEASE OF THE SPIRIT! A PERSON WHO IS GREEDY CAN NEVER BE HAPPY WITH THE THINGS HE ACCUMULATES THROUGH HIS GREED. HE WILL NEVER BE HAPPY UNTIL HE REPENTS AND GETS SAVED! HE WILL NEED TO ASK GOD TO DELIVER HIM FROM THE UNCLEAN SPIRIT OF GREED! THEN, HE WILL PROSPER THROUGH THE HELP OF GOD!** *"There is no peace, saith my God, to the wicked."* **Isaiah 57:21**

**GREED = IDOLATRY!** God said in the Ten Commandments: *"Thou shalt have no other gods before me."* **Exodus 20:3**

**GREED MAY LEAD A PERSON TO COVET THINGS THAT BELONG TO OTHERS! COVETING IS SIN!** God said in the Ten Commandments: *"Thou shalt not covet thy neighbour's house, thou shalt not covet thy neighbour's wife, nor his manservant* (male employee), *nor his maidservant* (daughter or female employee), *nor his ox* (cattle), *nor his ass* (donkey, horses), *nor any thing that is thy neighbour's."* **Exodus 20:17**

**GREED, WHEN FULLY DEVELOPED, IS AS DANGEROUS AS A HUNGRY LION LURKING IN THE STREETS!** *"Like as a lion that is greedy of his prey* (supper), *and as it were a young lion lurking in secret places* (hidden)." **Psalm 17:12**

**IF AN UNSAVED PERSON DIES WITH GREED STILL IN HIS HEART, HE WILL NOT GO TO HEAVEN! AFTER A PERIOD OF TIME GOD WILL RESURRECT HIM TO LIFE AND HE WILL HAVE TO ANSWER TO GOD FOR HIS GREED AND OTHER SINS! AFTER THIS, HE WILL BE CAST INTO THE ETERNAL LAKE OF FIRE WHERE HE WILL BURN FOREVER AND EVER AND EVER AND EVER AND EVER!** Revelation chapters 20-22

**IS GREED REALLY WORTH IT? WHY GO TO HELL WHEN JESUS LOVES YOU AND WANTS TO SAVE YOU? FIRST: REPENT OF YOUR SINS TO GOD! THEN: ASK HIM TO FORGIVE YOU! NEXT: TURN AWAY FROM SIN AND CONFESS THAT YOU ARE SAVED TO ANOTHER! DON'T BE ASHAMED OF JESUS OR HE WILL BE ASHAMED OF YOU! LAST: SERVE, LOVE AND PRAISE HIM!**

### PRAYER

Dear God, I confess that I am a sinner. I want to be saved. Please forgive me for all my sins. **I turn away from sin and greed in my life!** Please come into my life and create in me a whole new person. I love You and I will serve You from this day forward! In Jesus' name I pray and thank You. AMEN!

# GRIEF

A PERSON TENDS TO FEEL HE IS ALONE IN HIS GRIEF! HE THINKS NO ONE EVER GRIEVED OR WAS AS SAD AS HE IS! IF YOU ARE A BORN-AGAIN CHRISTIAN, YOU HAVE GOD WITH YOU EVERY MOMENT TO COMFORT YOU! GOD PROMISES HE WILL NEVER LEAVE US, NOR FORSAKE US. Hebrews 13:5

Naturally, we worry about our own grief, and that of our families. But, do we ever think about how much we grieve the Holy Spirit? *"And grieve not the Holy Spirit of God, whereby ye are sealed unto the day of redemption."* Ephesians 4:30

THERE ARE ALL KINDS OF GRIEF! GRIEF HURTS! GRIEF SCARES! BUT, WE SHOULD NEVER LET GRIEF TURN INTO BITTERNESS OR DOUBT GOD'S LOVE AND COMPASSION FOR US! WE SHOULD NEVER LET GRIEF HOLD US BACK FROM LIVING A HAPPY, PRODUCTIVE LIFE.

GOD DIDN'T PROMISE US WE'D NEVER GRIEVE! Christians have an edge over lost people, because with the loving help and strength God gives us, we can overcome grief and transcend into new directions!

WHEN GRIEF COMES, A CHRISTIAN CAN TRUST IN THE LORD FOR UNDERSTANDING AND STRENGTH! *"Trust in the Lord with all thine heart; and lean not unto thine own understanding. In all thy ways acknowledge him, and he shall direct thy paths."* Proverbs 3:5-6

ANY CHRISTIAN WHO LIVES IN THE COMPLETE WILL OF THE LORD HAS THE IMMEDIATE STRENGTH AND COMFORT FROM THE LORD AT HIS DISPOSAL! CHRISTIANS SHOULD STUDY THE SCRIPTURES, SO THEY CAN CALL THEM TO MEMORY WHEN THEY NEED JUST THE RIGHT WORDS OF COMFORT TO PASS ON TO THEIR NEIGHBOR!

GRIEF NEED NOT BE OUR ENEMY! FOR WITHOUT GRIEF AND SORROW WE WOULD NEVER NEED TO CALL ON GOD!

GRIEF SHOULD NEVER CAUSE A PERSON TO BLAME GOD AND GET MAD AT HIM! GRIEF IS AN IDEAL TIME TO FEEL HIS EXISTENCE MORE THAN EVER! *"Our help is in the name of the Lord, who made heaven and earth."* Psalm 124:8

Tears wash the eyes as nothing else can, and show us new views of humility, compassion, and priorities. Sorrow strips away superfluities and gets one down to the bone. Grief is an indispensable means of finding out what is important and what is not. We should analize our grief when it comes, and make sure it is not an indulgence! *"Search me, O God, and know my heart: Try me, and know my thoughts: And see if there be any wicked way in me, and lead me in the way everlasting."* Psalm 139:23-24

TO PROLONG GRIEF IS NEUROTIC AND AGAINST GOD'S WILL FOR OUR LIVES! Sometimes people do so because they think their grief is not acknowledged as it should be. Sorrow is the last emotion we can feel about someone. It is a powerful one, and to have it dismissed as unworthy or transient may seem like mockery. However, it is easy to fall into the trap of perpetuating it, either to impress the world with its importance or because letting it go means breaking the last tenuous thread. *"Cast thy burden upon the Lord, and he shall sustain thee: he shall never suffer* (allow) *the righteous to be moved."* Psalm 55:22

THERE IS A VAST DIFFERENCE BETWEEN GRIEF AND GRIEVANCE! We need to keep them clear and far apart, or we shame the love we fancy we are honoring. To be "mad at" God or other people, to imagine we are singled out for trouble, or to cling tenaciously to sorrow and blot out everything else, is not true anguish at all. It is merely using grief as an occasion for indulging grievances. Many people confuse grief with self pity. *"What time I am afraid, I will trust in thee* (God)." Psalm 56:3

OUR SPIRIT IS NOT MADE UP OF ONE EMOTION ONLY, ANY MORE THAN THE HEALTHY BODY CONSISTS OF ONLY ONE FUNCTION! After a period of concentration, the heart and mind reach out for equilibrium. *"O God, be not far from me: O my God, make haste for my help."* Psalm 71:12

GRIEF IS AN ACUTE STAGE OF LOVE . . . AS LEGITIMATE IN ITS TIME AS RAPTURE IS IN LOVE'S BEGINNING! No one knows what the causes of loss and sorrow may be, but we do know that a certain amount of grief is honorable and valuable and just. God is the only person who can deliver us out of our grief. CALL ON HIM! HE LOVES YOU AND CARES ABOUT YOUR HURTS! *"Hear me, O Lord, for thy lovingkindness is good: turn unto me according to the multitude of thy tender mercies."* Psalm 69:16

### PRAYER

Dear God, Please come to me quickly, for I am grief stricken! I need all the comfort and strength You alone can give me! Please forgive me for all my sins! I repent of all the things I have done which were wrong in Your eyes! I want to clean up my life! Forgive me for those I have slighted and offended. I thank You for allowing me to be born. I thank You for saving my soul! I thank You for loving me and for never forsaking me! I need You right now! Please come very close to me and let me sense Your presence. As long as I live I will praise You. I will never blame You for sickness, sorrow or death! I know that Your son, Jesus, was born so that some day He could die on the cross to pay for my sins. I know that He was resurrected and lives today. I know that without Your love and forgiveness I would be lost forever. As much as is within me, I will serve You! I will praise You. I know that my grief can be overcome with Your loving help! I know that You will restore peace in me. I thank You for all Your blessings! In Jesus' name, I pray. AMEN!

# GRUDGES

Holding a grudge is the same thing as judging another! This is totally against God's will for our lives! It's against all the commandments! Neither should we hold a grudge in secret (in our heart), or live ungodly, for the sake of gain or advantage! *"Thou shalt not hate thy brother in thine heart: thou shalt in any wise rebuke thy neighbour (anyone), and not suffer (allow, encourage) sin upon him. Thou shalt not avenge, nor bear any **grudge** against the children of thy people, but thou shalt love thy neighbour as thyself: I am the Lord.''* **Leviticus 19:17-18**

**GOD WILL JUDGE ANYONE WHO HOLDS A GRUDGE AGAINST ANOTHER PERSON!** *"Grudge not one against another, brethren, lest ye be condemned: behold (watch, listen), the judge (God) standeth before the door.''* **James 5:9**

When a person murmurs about another person, he secretly holds a grudge against him! When you share (or give anything) to another person and really don't want to. . .you are holding a grudge! *"Use hospitality one to another **without grudging** (murmuring).''* **1 Peter 4:9 NOTE:** It is better to do nothing, merely because it is expected (or commanded), if you can't do it out of love for God and your fellowman!

*"Do all things without murmurings and disputings.''* **Philippians 2:14**

**TO HOLD A GRUDGE AGAINST ANOTHER PERSON IS TO OBEY SATAN! GOD COMMANDS US TO LOVE ONE ANOTHER!** *"Wherefore putting away lying, speak every man truth with his neighbour: for we are members one of another. Be ye angry (irritated), and sin not: let not the sun go down upon your wrath: Neither give place to the devil.''* **Ephesians 4:25-27**

**WHEN A CHRISTIAN HOLDS A GRUDGE, IT GRIEVES THE HOLY SPIRIT!** *"Let no corrupt communication proceed out of your mouth, but that which is good to the use of edifying, that it may minister grace unto the hearers. And grieve not the Holy Spirit of God, whereby ye are sealed unto the day of redemption.''* **Ephesians 4:29-30**

**NOW IS THE BEST TIME TO REPENT AND GET STRAIGHT WITH GOD AND MAN!** *"Let all bitterness (malice), and wrath (hatred), and anger, and clamour (uproar), and evil speaking (cursing, threats, lies), be put away from you, with all malice (wickedness): And be ye kind one to another, tender-hearted, forgiving one another, even as God for Christ's sake hath forgiven you.''* **Ephesians 4:31-32**

It's sad but true! Many people hold grudges without a reason! Sometimes it's over someone else's wealth, success or education! Sometimes it's a case of prejudice, revenge, or jealousy! Holding a grudge is a sin which must be repented of! *"Be not a witness against thy neighbour (anyone) without cause; and deceive not with thy lips. Say not, I will do so to him as he hath done to me: I will render to the man according to his work.''* **Proverbs 24:28-29**

**CHRISTIANS SHOULD NEVER HOLD A GRUDGE OR "FEEL PUT-UPON" FOR THEIR SERVICE TO THE CHURCH, TO GOD, TO THE POOR, AND TO OTHERS!** *"But ye, brethren, be not weary in well doing.''* **2 Thessalonians 3:13**

Christians should never give money, time, or talent to God (or the Church) if he does it grudgingly! God's blessings only go to liberal heart-felt givers! *"But this I say, He which soweth sparingly (stingy) shall reap also sparingly; and he which soweth bountifully (from the heart) shall reap also bountifully. Every man according as he purposeth in his heart (not in a moment of compulsion, guilt, or to impress others, or God), so let him give; not **grudgingly,** or of necessity (feeling forced to): for God loveth a cheerful giver.''* **2 Corinthians 9:6-7**

**WHEN A PERSON HOLDS A GRUDGE, HE DECEIVES HIMSELF INTO THINKING HE IS WISE OR SUPERIOR! GOD HATES ALL FORMS OF DECEPTION!** *"Let no man deceive himself. If any man among you seemeth to be wise in this world, let him become a fool (make a fool of himself), that he may be wise (see himself as others see him). For the wisdom of this world is foolishness with God. For it is written, He taketh the wise in their own craftiness (deceit). And again, The Lord knoweth the thoughts of the wise, that they are vain.''* **1 Corinthians 3:18-20**

Did you know that people who hold a grudge fulfill end time prophecy, about the last days before Christ returns to earth? Below are 2 prophecies about holding grudges! Paul said: *"But evil men (people) and seducers shall wax (grow) worse and worse, deceiving and being deceived.''* **2 Timothy 3:13** (AND) Jesus said: *"And because iniquity (sins, wickedness) shall abound (multiply all over the world), the love of many shall wax (grow) cold.''* **Matthew 24:12**

**IN CLOSING, JESUS SAID:** *"These things I command you, that ye love one another.''* **John 15:17**

### PRAYER

Dear God, **please forgive me for holding a grudge against another person.** I know this has made my heart turn cold. I know this is not Your will for my life! I ask You to forgive me for all my sins! I want to be the kind of person You want me to be! I want to love all people, just as You do! I will go to the person I have been holding a **grudge** against and ask his forgiveness, even though he doesn't know that I've been doing this! I will think before I speak! I will study my Bible in order to learn wisdom! I will obey Your commandments! I will pray for others, including the person I've been holding a **grudge** against! I will try as best I can to set an example of love and Christianity for others to see! I humble myself and ask You to come into my heart. Forgive me and blot out my sins! In Jesus' name, I pray. AMEN!

# HATRED

**ALL HATRED IS SIN (EXCEPT) HATRED FOR SIN! HATRED IS A WORK OF THE FLESH! ANYONE WHO HATES ANOTHER PERSON WILL NOT INHERIT THE KINGDOM OF GOD — UNLESS HE REPENTS AND GETS SAVED!** *"Now the works of the flesh are manifest* (made known), *which are these:* ***Adultery, fornication*** (sex without marriage), ***uncleanness*** (satanic oppression, occult activity, sex sins, etc.), ***lasciviousness*** (lust, lewdness), ***idolatry*** (worship things other than God), ***witchcraft, hatred, variance, emulations*** (jealousy, ego, envious rivalry), ***wrath, strife, seditions*** (resistance to lawful authority), ***heresies*** (contrary to God's truth), ***envyings, murders, drunkenness, revellings*** (wild parties, sex orgies, drugs, booze, etc.), *and such like: of the which I tell you before, as I have also told you in time past, that* ***they which do such things shall not inherit the kingdom of God."*** **Galatians 5:19-21**

**GOD CONSIDERS HATRED TO BE EQUAL TO MURDER!**

**HATE BREEDS HATE BUT GOD WILL FORGIVE THE SIN OF HATRED IF YOU WILL REPENT AND ASK GOD TO SAVE YOU!** *"**Hatred** stirreth up strifes: but love covereth all sins."* **Proverbs 10:12**

**HATRED CAUSES A PERSON TO LIE!** *"He that hideth **hatred** with **lying lips**, and he that **uttereth a slander, is a fool."*** **Proverbs 10:18**

If you are a Christian and you know another person hates you, how should you treat that person? Tell him you love him! Pray continuously for him! Perhaps you will lead him to Christ through your love! Jesus said: *"Ye have heard that it hath been said, Thou shalt love thy neighbour, and **hate** thine enemy. But I say unto you, **Love your enemies, bless them that curse you, do good to them that hate you, and pray for them which despitefully use you, and persecute you."*** **Matthew 5:43-44** Jesus said: *"But I say unto you which hear, **Love your enemies, do good to them which hate you, bless them that curse you, and pray for them which despitefully use you.** And unto him that smiteth thee on the one cheek offer also the other; and him that taketh away thy cloak* (cape) *forbid not to take thy coat also. Give to every man that asketh of thee; and of him that taketh away thy goods ask them not again. And as ye would that men should do to you, do ye also to them likewise. For if ye love them which love you, what thank* (thanks) *have ye? for sinners also love those that love them. And if ye do good to them which do good to you, what thank* (thanks) *have ye? for sinners also do even the same. And if ye lend to them of whom ye hope to receive, what thank* (thanks) *have ye? for sinners also lend to sinners, to receive as much again. But **love ye your enemies,** and do good, and lend, hoping for nothing again, and your reward shall be great, and ye shall be the children of the Highest* (God); *for he is kind unto the unthankful and to the evil. Be ye therefore merciful, as your Father* (God) *also is merciful."* **Luke 6:27-36**

**WHEN A PERSON BECOMES A CHRISTIAN HE NO LONGER FEELS HATRED!** *"For we ourselves also were sometimes foolish, disobedient, deceived, serving divers* (various) *lusts and pleasures, living in malice and envy, hateful, and **hating one another.** But after that the kindness and love of God our Saviour toward man appeared. Not by works of righteousness which we have done, but according to his mercy he saved us, by the washing of regeneration, and renewing of the Holy Ghost; which he shed on us abundantly through Jesus Christ our Saviour."* **Titus 3:3-6**

**JESUS SAID THAT IN THE LAST DAYS BEFORE HE RETURNS TO EARTH THAT LOVE AMONG PEOPLE WOULD TURN TO HATE!** *"Then shall they deliver you up to be afflicted, and shall kill you: and ye shall be **hated** of all nations for my name's sake. And then shall many be offended, and shall betray one another, and shall **hate one another.** And many false prophets shall rise, and shall deceive many. And because iniquity* (sin) *shall abound* (get completely out of control) *the **love of many shall wax** (grow) **cold."*** **Matthew 24:9-12**

**JESUS SAID:** *"If the world **hate** you, ye know that it **hated** me before it hated you!"* **John 15:18** *"Marvel not, my brethren, if the world **hate** you."* **1 John 3:13**

**THE BIBLE SAYS THAT IF YOU HATE YOUR BROTHER YOU ARE A MURDERER!** *"Whosoever **hateth** his brother is a **murderer:** and ye know that no murderer hath eternal life abiding in him."* **1 John 3:15**

Why does a person grow to hate another person? Because he listens to Satan who hates us all! Satan is a liar and a thief! He wants to destroy us all! He is miserable. He knows that one day he will burn forever in the eternal lake of fire! Misery loves company, and he wants you to join him! He's smart! He knows that you will never inherit eternal life with Jesus if you have any hatred in your heart! Why would you want to be on the losing team when you can find peace, happiness, and eternal life with Jesus? *"The thief* (Satan) ***cometh not*** (to planet earth) *but* (except) *for to steal, and to kill, and to destroy: I* (Christ) *am come that they* (me, you) *might have life, and that they* (me, you) *might have it more abundantly."* **John 10:10**

**DID YOU KNOW THAT THERE ARE SEVEN THINGS THAT GOD HATES?** *"These 6 things doth the Lord hate: yea* (yes), *7 are an abomination unto him: 1. a proud look, 2. a lying tongue, 3. and hands that shed innocent blood, 4. an heart that deviseth wicked imaginations, 5. feet that be* (are) *swift in running to mischief, 6. a false witness that speaketh lies, 7. and he that soweth discord among brethren."* **Proverbs 6:16-19**

**THE FEAR OF THE LORD IS TO HATE EVIL!** *"The fear of the Lord is to **hate evil: pride, and arrogancy, and the evil way, and the froward mouth, do I hate."*** **Proverbs 8:13**

**ANGER MAY LEAD A PERSON TO FEEL HATRED!** *"He that is soon angry dealeth foolishly: and a man of wicked devices* (thoughts, actions) *is **hatred."*** **Proverbs 14:17** *"Ye that love the Lord, **hate evil:** he* (God) *preserveth the souls of his saints; he* (God) *delivereth them out of the hand of the wicked."* **Psalm 97:10**

Through studying the Bible and obeying God's laws a Christian soon grows to hate false ways and vain thoughts (which come from Satan)! *"Through thy* (God's) *precepts* (laws, commandments) *I get understanding: therefore **I hate every false way.**"* **Psalm 119:104** *"**I hate vain thoughts:** but thy* (God's) *law do I love."* **Psalm 119:113** *"Therefore I esteem* (give my highest respect to) *all thy* (God's) *precepts* (laws) *concerning all things to be right, and **I hate every false way.**"* **Psalm 119:128**

**A CHRISTIAN SHOULD NEVER LOWER HIMSELF TO HATRED, EXCEPT TO HATE SIN! THEN GOD WILL BLESS HIM ABOVE THOSE AROUND HIM!** *"Thou hast loved righteousness, and **hated** iniquity* (sin); *therefore God, even thy God, hath anointed thee with the oil of gladness above thy fellows."* **Hebrews 1:9**

Did you ever love another person when all he gave you in return was hatred? We are commanded to love our enemies! With continued prayer and love we may be able to lead a person to Christ! David prayed: *"And they reward me evil for good, and **hatred** for my love."* **Psalm 109:5**

**ALL HATRED COMES FROM SATAN! TO BE DELIVERED YOU MUST REPENT OF YOUR SINS AND ASK GOD TO FORGIVE YOU!**          **PRAYER**

Dear God, I confess that I am a sinner! I want to be saved! I repent of all my sins and I turn away from them. Please come into my heart and life. Please forgive me and I will praise You! I will love my enemies and do good to those who despitefully use me! I will read my Bible and pray! Thank You for saving my soul! In Jesus' name, AMEN!

# HEALTH HEALING

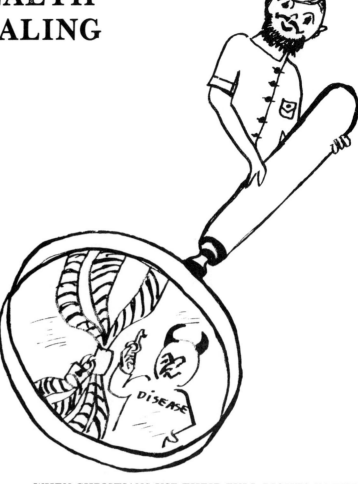

**FOR A SOUND HEART:** *"A sound heart is the life of the flesh: but envy the rottenness of the bones."* **Proverbs 14:30**

God's eternal kingdom will bring permanent physical cures! Each time we pray "The Lord's Prayer" we ask for His Kingdom to come! *"Thy kingdom come. Thy will be done in earth, as it is in heaven."* **Matthew 6:10**

**JESUS IS ALIVE AND WELL! HE HEALS THE SICK TO-DAY JUST AS HE ALWAYS HAS!** *"And Jesus went about all Galilee, teaching in their synagogues, and preaching the gospel of the kingdom, and healing all manner of sickness and all manner of disease among the people. And his fame went throughout all Syria: and they brought unto him all sick people that were taken with divers (various) diseases and torments, and those which were possessed with devils, and those which were lunatick (insane), and those that had the palsy (were paralyzed) and he healed them."* **Matthew 4:23-24**

**PRAYER CAN BRING DIVINE HEALTH TO THE SICK!** *"Is any among you afflicted? let him pray. Is any merry? let him sing psalms. Is any sick among you? let him call for the elders of the church; and let them pray over him, anointing him with oil in the name of the Lord:* **And the prayer of faith shall save the sick, and the Lord shall raise him up; and if he have committed sins, they shall be forgiven him. Confess your faults one to another, and pray one for another, that ye may be heal-ed.** *The effectual fervent prayer of a righteous man (person) availeth much."* **James 5:13-16**

Jesus healed a woman who had an issue of blood for over 12 years — resurrected a girl from the dead — healed 2 blind men — 10 lepers — a dumb man — and cast demons out of others! Matthew 8:16/Chapter 9/20:29/Mark 5:21-23/10:46/Luke 8:36-40/18:35/17:11-19

**IN MATTHEW 12/MARK 3/and LUKE 6 JESUS HEALED MULTITUDES!**

**FAITH COMBINED WITH PRAYER WILL MAKE YOU WHOLE!** Mark 5:34/6:56/10:52/Luke 8:48-56/17:11-19/18:42/ Acts 4:9

DEMONS CAN CAUSE SICKNESS AND INFIRMITIES! DUMBNESS: Mark 9:17, 25 DEAFNESS: Mark 9:25 FOAM-ING OF THE MOUTH: Mark 9:18, 20 FITS: Mark 9:18, 20, 26 GNASHING OF TEETH: Mark 9:18 LIFELESSNESS — COMPLETE EXHAUSTION: Mark 9:18, 26 SUICIDAL TENDENCIES: Mark 9:22 INSANITY: Matthew 17:15.

*"Bu t He was wounded for our transgressions, He was bruised for our iniquities: the chastisement of our peace was upon Him; and with His stripes we are healed."* **Isaiah 53:5**

**PEOPLE WHO OBEY GOD'S COMMANDMENTS, PRAY PROPERLY, AND HAVE TOTAL FAITH THAT GOD CAN AND WILL HEAL THEM, ARE HEALED! HERE ARE SOME SCRIPTURES WHERE VARIOUS DISEASES ARE HEALED: BLINDNESS:** Mark 10:52/Luke 18:42 **LEPROSY:** Luke 17:11-19 **LAMENESS:** Acts 3:1-11/14:8-10 **IM-POTENCE:** Acts 4:9 **HOMOSEXUALITY:** Jude 23

**JESUS COMMISSIONED HIS DISCIPLES TO HEAL THE SICK!** *"And* **heal the sick** *that are therein, and say unto them, The kingdom of God is come nigh (soon) unto you."* **Luke 10:9**

**TO LAY ON HANDS AND ANOUNT WITH OIL:** Mark 16:18/6:13/Acts 9:17/28:8/James 5:14

**WHEN CHRISTIANS USE THEIR FULL RIGHTS IN THE GOSPEL THEY CAN HAVE HEALTH OF BODY AND SOUL!** 3 John 2/1 Peter 2:24/Matthew 8:16-17/James 5:14

**FOR ADDITIONAL RESEARCH: HEALTH:** Proverbs 4:22/12:18/13:17/16:24 **HEALING:** Malachi 4:2 **CURE:** Jeremiah 33:6 **REMEDY:** 2 Chronicles 36:16/Proverbs 6:15/29:1 **SOUND HEART:** Proverbs 14:30 **WHOLESOME:** Proverbs 15:4

**HERE ARE FOUR SECRETS TO PERFECT HEALTH AND ETERNAL LIFE. ALL YOU HAVE TO DO IS FOLLOW THEM!**
1. **Obey** God's words: **Proverbs 4:20**
2. **Listen** to God's words: **Proverbs 4:20**
3. **Read** God's words constantly: **Psalm 1:2-3/James 1:21-27/2 Timothy 3:16**
4. **Keep** God's Word in your heart: **Proverbs 4:20-21/Romans 1:16/10:17**
God's saving health: **Psalm 67:2**
Faith in God will give a healthy countenance: **Psalm 42:11/43:5**
The tongue of the wise is health: **Proverbs 12:18**
Pleasant words bring health to the bones: **Proverbs 16:24**
God will restore health to Israel: **Jeremiah 30:17/33:6**

**SOME HEALING REQUIRES PRAYER AND FASTING!** Mark 9:29 **NOTE:** Fasting should not go beyond the point of im-pairing health! One can fast up to 40 days before starvation begins if he is a healthy person but it's not recommended! For people who are not healthy **fasting must be done with great care, under pro-per supervision, and for short periods of time!**

**GOD'S WILL FOR ALL CHRISTIANS:** *"Beloved, I wish above all things that thou mayest* **prosper** *and be in* **health,** *even as thy soul prospereth."* **3 John:2**

(Continued)

## 35 FACTS ABOUT SICKNESS AND HEALING:

1. **Health was natural and eternal before the fall.** Genesis 1:26-31/2:17

2. **Both death and sickness originated with sin** and are now being propagated by Satan. Romans 5:12-21/Job 2:6-7/Luke 13:16/John 10:10/Acts 10:38/1 John 3:8

3. The first prophecy and promise of redemption **included healing.** Genesis 3:15/Isaiah 53:5/Matthew 8:16-17/1 Peter 2:24

4. **The first recorded healing** was by the prayer of a prophet. Genesis 20:7, 17

5. **The first recorded bodily affliction came through wrongdoing.** Genesis 20:1-18

6. God made covenants with His people to **heal** them. **Exodus 15:26/23:25/Leviticus 26/Deuteronomy 28/Matthew 8:17/1 Peter 2:24/James 5:14**

7. God has always kept His covenants and has **healed multitudes** by spiritual means. **Psalm 103:3/105:37/107:20/Acts 10:38**

8. **Spiritual healing is promised and commanded by God. Exodus 15:26/Psalm 91/Isaiah 58/Matthew 8:17/13:15/James 5:14-16/1 Peter 2:24**

9. Spiritual means for healings were used in the wilderness by Israel. Exodus 15:26/Numbers 11:1-3/12:13-16/21:1-9

10. Healing was promised on condition of obedience. Leviticus 26/Deuteronomy 28/Exodus 15:26/Psalm 91/Isaiah 58/James 5:14-15

11. God permits Satan to afflict sinners (and even His own people) when they go astray, to bring them to repentance. Job 33:12-30/Psalm 38/103:3/Numbers 12:13-16/21:9/1 Corinthians 5:1-5/2 Corinthians 2:6-11/Galatians 6:7-8

12. God always healed when lessons were learned and men repented. Genesis 20:7, 17/Numbers 11:2/12:13-16/21:1-9/Job 33:12-30/42:1-12/Psalm 103:3/James 5:14-15

13. Health, as well as healing, was promised when men met certain conditions. Exodus 15:26/Leviticus 26/Deuteronomy 28/Psalm 91/Proverbs 3:1-8/12:18/13:3/15:4/18:8, 21/Isaiah 58/James 5:14/1 Peter 3:10-11/3 John 2

14. Christ came to redeem from both sin and sickness. Isaiah 53/61:1-2/Matthew 8:17/9:5/Galatians 3:13/Romans 8:11/Acts 10:38/1 Peter 2:24/1 John 3:8

15. Healing is in fulfillment of prophecy. Isaiah 35:3-6/53:5/61:1-12/Matthew 8:17/Acts 10:38/1 Peter 2:24/Matthew 13:15/61:1-2

16. Jesus proved His Sonship by **healing all men. Matthew 4:23-24/11:3-6/Luke 4:16-21/Acts 10:38/1 John 3:8**

17. **Every disciple called of Christ was given power to heal. Matthew 10:1-8/Mark 6:7-13/Luke 10:1-21/Acts 1:8**

18. Jesus commanded His disciples to become endued with power to **heal** before they went out. Luke 24:49/Acts 1:4-8

19. All disciples throughout this age are commanded to observe the same commands Christ gave the first disciples. Matthew 28:20/Acts 1:4-8/Mark 16:15-20

20. Early disciples confirmed the Word by **healing. Mark 16:15-20/Acts 2:43/3:1-12/5:12-16/6:8/8:7-13/11:19-22/14:3, 27/15:4, 12/19:11-12/28:9/Romans 15:18-19, 29/1 Corinthians 16:10/Philippians 1:7/1 Thessalonians 2:13/Hebrews 2:3-4**

21. **The Holy Spirit was sent into the world to carry on the healing ministry. Acts 1:1-8/2:33/1 Corinthians 12/Hebrews 2:3-4**

22. **Jesus promised every believer the power to do the works that He did. Matthew 17:20/21:22/Mark 9:23/11:22-24/16:15-20/John 14:12-15/15:7, 16/16:23-26/Acts 1:4-8**

23. **Gifts of healing (and other gifts) are promised as the spiritual equipment of the church. 1 Corinthians 1:7/12:1-11/Romans 1:11/12:6-8/15:18-19, 29/Hebrews 2:3-4**

24. **Healing is part of the work of the church. Matthew 10:1-8/Luke 10:1-21/24:49/Acts 1:8/1 Corinthians 12/James 5:14-16**

25. **Healing is provided as part of Christ's atonement. Isaiah 53:4-5/Matthew 8:16-17/13:14-15/John 3:14/10:10/Romans 1:16/8:11/1 Corinthians 11:23-32/Galatians 3:13/James 5:14-16/1 Peter 2:24**

26. **Healing is part of the children's bread and their promised right by virtue of redemption. Matthew 7:7-11/15:22-28/17:20/21:22/Mark 9:23/11:22-24/Luke 13:16/John 3:14-16/14:12-15/15:7, 16/16:23-26/1 John 3:8, 20-22/5:14-15/3 John 2**

27. **Healing is one of the signs of the gospel to follow believers. Mark 16:15-20**

28. **Healing was not only for the Old Testament days (Exodus 15:26/Psalm 91/103:3) and for the Millennium (Isaiah 30:26/33:24/35:1-10). It is also for this age, or the gospel is faulty and the new covenant worse than the old one. Matthew 8:17/21:22/Mark 9:23/11:22-24/16:15-20/John 14:12-15/15:7, 16/2 Corinthians 3:6-15/1 Corinthians 12:1-11/Hebrews 2:3-4**

29. **Healing proves that God's promises are true. 2 Corinthians 1:20**

30. **Healing is part of salvation, for the Hebrew and Greek words for salvation all imply the ideas of forgiveness, healing, health, and full deliverance from the curse. Romans 1:16/Galatians 3:13/1 Peter 2:24**

31. **Healing can naturally be expected as part of the infinite care of God over His children. Matthew 6:10/7:7-11/17:20/21:22/Mark 9:23/11:22-24/Luke 11:1-13/18:1-18/John 14:12-15/15:7, 16/16:23-26/Hebrews 11:6/James 1:4-8/5:14-16**

32. **Healing is on the same basis as forgiveness of sins, prayer and faith! Matthew 9:1-7/13:15/21:22/Acts 28:27/James 1:4-8/5:14-16/Hebrews 11:6**

33. **Healing proves the resurrection of Christ and the descent of the Holy Spirit. Acts 1:4-8/2:33/3:16/4:12/Romans 8:11**

34. **God has provided all necessary means of healing and complete defeat of satanic powers. 2 Corinthians 10:4-5/Ephesians 6:10-18/Mark 16:15-20/John 14:12-15/James 4:7/5:14-16/1 Peter 2:24/5:7-9**

35. **Healing is always the will of God for His people who may "ask what ye will" John 15:7; "whatsoever" Matthew 21:22/John 15:12-15/15:16; "anything" John 14:14; "what things soever ye desire" Mark 11:22-24 and "much more" than earthly parents would or could give their children Matthew 7:7-11**

**IT IS CLEAR THAT BODILY HEALING IS PROVIDED FOR IN THE OLD AND NEW TESTAMENTS! THE NEW TESTAMENT ONLY CONTAINS BETTER PROMISES THAN THOSE IN THE OLD TESTAMENT. Hebrews 8:6**

### PRAYER

Dear God, Please forgive me for all my sins! I know Your desire for me is to be healthy, happy, saved, and at peace with all people! I know there have been many times that I have abused my own body through improper diet, lack of exercise, and not enough rest! I have neglected to pray and earnestly believe for my complete healing! I know there have been numerous times You prescribed the proper treatment and cure through my doctor! I know You are there just waiting to give me strength and to revitalize my health! I know You really love me or You wouldn't have sent Jesus to die on the cross so I could be saved! I know that Jesus is alive today, and is the same yesterday, today, and forever! I know that Jesus is still in the healing business! I know that Jesus came so that I might have life, and that I might have it more abundantly! Many illnesses could have been prevented had I obeyed Your commandments and claimed Your promises! I know that You are not responsible for my illnesses nor my infirmities! I left myself wide open for Satan to attack me in the area of my health! I was vulnerable, and totally without the knowledge of the authority given me in the name of Jesus! In order that I might walk in perfect health, I will study my Bible daily and learn to exercise the authority given me as a born-again Christian! I will claim my divine healing! I ask you to forgive my sins and my lack of faith to realize that You can and will heal me, if only I obey Your Word! In Jesus' name, I pray. AMEN!

# HEAVEN

**HEAVEN IS A REAL PLACE!** It is not just a condition or state of being! **Jesus said:** *"In my Father's* (God's) *house are many mansions: if it were not so, I would have told you. I go to prepare a place for you. And if I go and prepare a place for you, I will come again, and receive you unto myself; that where I am, there ye may be also."* **John 14:2-3**

**WE CAN EAT, DRINK, TOUCH, COMMUNICATE . . . ANYTHING EXCEPT BE SAD!**

**WHILE WE LIVE ON EARTH WE CAN STORE UP TREASURES IN HEAVEN!** *". . .Lay up for yourselves treasures in heaven, where neither moth nor rust doth corrupt, and where thieves do not break through nor steal."* **Matthew 6:20**

**GOD PREPARES A PLACE IN HEAVEN FOR YOU — AS SOON AS YOU BECOME A BORN-AGAIN CHRISTIAN!** *"For we know that if our earthly house of this tabernacle were dissolved, we have a building of God, an house not made with hands, eternal in the heavens."* **2 Corinthians 5:1**

**IN HEAVEN THERE ARE NO TEARS, DEATH, SORROW, PAIN, JAILS, HOSPITALS, CEMETERIES!** All things will be perfect, beautiful, peaceful and new! *"And God shall wipe away all tears from their eyes; and there shall be no more death, neither sorrow, nor crying, neither shall there be any more pain: for the former things are passed away."* **Revelation 21:4**

**THERE IS NO NIGHT (OR DARKNESS) IN HEAVEN!** *"And the city had* (has) *no need of the sun, neither of the moon, to shine in it: for the glory of God did* (does) *lighten it, and the Lamb* (Jesus) *is the light thereof. And the nations of them which are saved shall walk in the light of it* (Jesus' glory)*: and the kings of the earth do bring their glory and honour into it."* **Revelation 21:23-24** *"And the gates of it shall not be shut at all by day; for there shall be no night there."* **Revelation 21:25**

**ONLY BORN-AGAIN CHRISTIANS WHO WERE LIVING IN THE WILL OF GOD (AND) OBEYING HIS COMMANDMENTS AT THE TIME OF THEIR DEATH (OR WHEN THE RAPTURE TAKES PLACE) WILL JOIN JESUS IN HEAVEN!** *"And they shall come from the* **east,** *and from the* **west,** *and from the* **north,** *and from the* **south,** *and shall sit down in the kingdom of God."* **Luke 13:29**

**HEAVEN IS A BIG PLACE!** Heaven has "expanses" which refers to the extent of heaven (Deuteronomy 33:26/Job 35:5). This explains Paul's "third" heaven (2 Corinthians 12:2). One heaven is the air or atmosphere where clouds gather. The firmament in which the sun, moon and stars are fixed is another heaven. The upper heaven, the home of Almighty God, His angels, and born-again saints, is the invisible realm of holiness and happiness. (1 Kings 8:30/Daniel 2:28/Matthew 5:45).

**HEAVEN CONTAINS GREAT MULTITUDES OF PEOPLE . . . SO MANY THAT THERE AREN'T ENOUGH NUMBERS IN OUR LANGUAGE TO COUNT THEM!** *". . .I beheld, and lo, a great multitude, which no man could number, of all nations, and kindreds, and people, and tongues, stood before the throne* (of God) *and before the Lamb* (Jesus) *clothed with white robes* (glorified incorruptible bodies), *and palms in their hands."* **Revelation 7:9**

**HEAVEN CONTAINS THOUSANDS (OR MILLIONS) OF LITTLE BABIES WHO NEVER HAD A CHANCE TO KNOW RIGHT FROM WRONG!** God takes care of the little ones who leave this life. They're happily in heaven, now!

**WHAT DOES HEAVEN LOOK LIKE?** It is a giant gold satellite which will eventually suspend above earth. Only born-again Christians will be allowed to flow up to it and back down to the restored earth. **Heaven, which will be renamed "NEW JERUSALEM" after the 1,000 year millennium period, will contain no sea** (Revelation 21:1). **It will contain new water which comes from the fountain of life** (Revelation 21:6/22:17). **We will inherit all things** (Revelation 21:7). **We will be joint heirs with Jesus** (Revelation 21:7/1 John 3:1-2). New Jerusalem will have a wall big and tall with **12 gates made of pearl.** At the 12 gates will be 12 angels. The name of the 12 tribes of the children of Israel will be on the 12 gates. **There will be three gates on each side facing the north, south, east and west.** The wall of the city will have **12 foundations** and in the foundations will be the names of the 12 disciples of Jesus. **The city will be 12,000 furlongs in length, breadth and height** or **1500 miles square** (Revelation 21:16). The wall will be 144 cubits (300 feet high at 25 inches per cubit) (Revelation 21:17). The wall will be made of **JASPER** (diamonds). The city will be made of **PURE GOLD CLEAR AS GLASS** (Revelation 21:18). The 12 foundations of the wall of the city are **JASPER, SAPPHIRE, CHALCEDONY, EMERALD, SARDONYX, SARDIUS, CHRYSOLITE, BERYL, TOPAZ, CHRYSOPRASUS, JACINTH, AMETHYST** (Revelation 21:19-20). The streets are **PURE GOLD** (not paved, but pure gold) and clear as glass (Revelation 21:21). God and Jesus will be **visibly present** to all of us and their presence is the temple we will worship (Revelation 21:22). The city will have **no need of the sun or moon** because the glory of God and Christ will light it (Revelation 21:23). All nations of the earth will travel to New Jerusalem to bring their gifts forever (Revelation 21:24-26). **The gates will not be shut day or night.** There is no night there (Revelation 21:25). There will be **12 great rivers flowing down the middle of 12 great broadways** going through the 12 gates into all parts of the earth, below. There will be many **fountains** of "water of life" throughout the city. **The water will be crystal clear.** On each side of the river will be a tree of life which will bear **12 kinds of fruits** all year long (Revelation 22:2). We're talking about 12 great rivers flowing 1500 miles through 12 great broadways where rows of trees of life are, with each row being 1500 miles long. The **leaves** of each tree will have **healing** qualities for the nations of earth (outside the walls of New Jerusalem) as well as for the resurrected saints (Revelation 2:7/22:2). Since there is no sickness or disease, I believe the leaves will give off health, life and love (Revelation 21:4/22:2-3/Genesis 3:22-24). **We will be able to actually look into the face of God.** We will reign with Him forever (Revelation 22:4-5). All nations who are alive at the end of the 1,000 year millennium will travel to New Jerusalem each year to worship the Lord and to keep the Feast of Tabernacles celebration (Isaiah 66:18/Zechariah 14:16-21). **All Christians will automatically become Kings and Priests forever with Jesus Christ** (Revelation 1:6/5:10/Daniel 7:18). **Can you imagine a city 1500 miles square and 1500 miles high? We're actually talking about 3,375,000,000 cubic miles!!! This makes New Jerusalem (Heaven) over 2 times the size of the moon. We'll ascend (go up) and descend down to earth.** Galatians 4:26 says New Jerusalem is above the earth (not ground level).

### IN THE BIBLE THERE ARE 7 NAMES OF THE CITY OF GOD:

**THE HOLY CITY:** (Revelation 21:2/22:19)
**NEW JERUSALEM:** (Revelation 3:12/21:2)
**THE TABERNACLE OF GOD:** (Revelation 15:5/21:3)
**THE BRIDE, THE LAMB (Jesus) WIFE:** (Revelation 21:2, 9)
**THE HOLY JERUSALEM:** (Revelation 21:10)
**THE HEAVENLY JERUSALEM:** (Hebrews 12:22)
**THE FATHER'S HOUSE:** (John 14:2)

127

(Continued)

**THERE'S NO SIN IN HEAVEN!** In heaven we'll fellowship with all the saints of God and with His angels! We'll talk with Moses, Elijah, Paul, Abraham, John, and all the rest. We'll share all things. We'll sing praises with all our loved ones. There will be much activity in heaven!

**WE WILL HAVE A NEW, PERFECT BODY IN HEAVEN!** *"As we have borne the image of the earthy, we shall also bear the image of the heavenly."* **1 Corinthians 15:49** *"In a moment, in the twinkling of an eye, at the last trump* (trumpet sound): *for the trumpet shall sound, and the dead shall be raised incorruptible, and we shall be changed. For this corruptible* (body) *must put on incorruption* (before it can enter heaven), *and this mortal* (body) *must put on immortality."* **1 Corinthians 15:52-53 (AND) Romans 8:23** says we wait for the redemption of our body! *"When he* (Jesus) *shall appear, we shall be like him; for we shall see him as he is."* **1 John 3:2** In heaven there are no imperfections and flaws! Our body will be brand new, beautiful, perfect and eternal! PRAISE GOD!!!!

**IN HEAVEN WE WILL HAVE UNLIMITED, UNIVERSAL KNOWLEDGE!** On this earth our brain is limited. It's as if we're looking through a clouded glass and we're not able to make out all the details! *". . .Now we see through a glass, darkly; but then* (when we get to heaven) *face to face* (with God): *now I* (we) *know* (only) *in part; but then shall I know even as also I* (we) *am known."* **1 Corinthians 13:12**

**YOUR STOCKS, BONDS, GOOD NAME, CHURCH MEMBERSHIP, CHRISTENING, WATER BAPTISM, PRIEST OR POPE CAN'T GET YOU INTO HEAVEN!** There's only one way a person is allowed to enter heaven and that is to repent of your sins and humbly ask God's forgiveness. Then you must live for God, by obeying His commandments, clear up to your death (or the rapture)!

**JESUS SAID THAT IF A PERSON THINKS HE CAN ENTER HEAVEN WITHOUT HAVING A BORN-AGAIN EXPERIENCE, HE IS THE SAME AS A THIEF AND A ROBBER! John 10:1** Jesus said: *"I am the* (only) *way."* **John 14:6** *"Neither is there salvation in any other: for there is none other name under Heaven given among men whereby we must be saved."* **Acts 4:12**

**GOOD WORKS WILL NOT GUARANTEE YOU ENTRANCE INTO HEAVEN!** *"For by* (God's) *grace are ye saved through faith; and that not of yourselves: it is the gift of God: Not of works, lest any man should boast."* **Ephesians 2:8-9** *"Not by works of righteousness which we have done, but according to his mercy he saved us, by the washing of regeneration, and renewing of the Holy Ghost. Which he* (God) *shed on us abundantly through Jesus Christ our Saviour. That being justified by his grace, we should be made heirs according to the hope of eternal life."* **Titus 3:5-7**

**THERE ARE ONLY TWO CLASSES OF PEOPLE IN THE WORLD . . . SAVED (or) LOST!** The second you die you are instantly in the presence of God (or Satan)! *"He that committeth sin is of* (belongs to) *the devil."* **1 John 3:8** JESUS SAID: *"Except a man* (person) *be born again, he cannot see the kingdom of God."* **John 3:3** *"For God so loved the world, that he gave his only begotten Son* (Jesus), *that whosoever believeth in him* (Jesus) *should not perish* (die in vain, eternally) *but have everlasting life."* **John 3:16**

**TO DIE A BORN-AGAIN CHRISTIAN . . . PLACES YOU INSTANTLY IN HEAVEN IN THE PRESENCE OF JESUS!** *". . .to be absent from the* (earthly) *body, is to be present with the Lord."* **2 Corinthians 5:8** *ALSO READ: Luke 23:43

**WE CAN'T BEGIN TO IMAGINE WITH OUR FINITE MIND HOW BEAUTIFUL, PERFECT, AND PEACEFUL, CONDITIONS ARE IN HEAVEN!** *". . .Eye hath not seen, nor ear heard, neither have entered into the heart of man, the things which God hath prepared for them that love him."* **1 Corinthians 2:9**

**HEAVEN WAS CREATED BY GOD:** Genesis 1:1/2:1/Psalm 8:3/Isaiah 42:5/45:12-18 **Heaven was created before the earth:** Genesis 1:1/Job 38:4-7. **The materials were brought into existence when God spoke and God formed them with His hands. Heaven was created in the dateless past:** Genesis 1:1/Proverbs 8:22-31

**WHY DID GOD CREATE HEAVEN?** For an eternal home of perfection for Himself, His angels, and His born-again believers. **Isaiah 45:18/Psalm 8:3-8/Colossians 1:15-18/Revelation 4:11**

**HEAVEN HAS KINGDOMS:** (Colossians 1:15-18/Ephesians 3:9-10/1 Peter 3:22) . . . **LAWS:** (Job 38:33/Jeremiah 31:35-36/33:25/Ezekiel 28:15) . . . **RULERS:** (Genesis 14:19, 22/24:3, 7/Daniel 4:35/Matthew 6:10/11:25) . . . **HEAVEN IS THE HIGHEST PLANET IN EXISTENCE:** (Ephesians 1:21/4:10/Hebrews 7:26) . . . **PARADISE:** (2 Corinthians 12:1-4/Revelation 2:7) . . . **WHERE GOD LIVES:** (Deuteronomy 26:15/1 Kings 8:30, 39, 43, 49).

**WHERE IS HEAVEN?** In the **northern part of the universe,** in relationship to the earth (Isaiah 14:12-14/Psalm 75:6-7) **ABOVE:** (1 Kings 8:23) in the **highest part of creation** (Job 22:12/Luke 2:14/Ephesians 1:21/4:10. **HEAVEN IS ROUND!** (Job 22:14/Psalm 19:6/Isaiah 40;22/Ecclesiastes 1:6). **HAS REAL CITIES:** (Hebrews 11:10-15/13:14/Revelation 21:2, 9-27). **MANSIONS:** (John 14:1-3). **TEMPLES:** (Revelation 3:12/7:15/11:19/14:17/15:5/16:1, 17/Isaiah 6:1). **CONTAINS THE ARK OF THE TESTAMENT:** (Revelation 11:19). **THRONES:** (Isaiah 6:1/Daniel 7:9-10/Revelation 3:21/4:2, 4/22:3). **BOOKS:** (Luke 10:20/Hebrews 12:23/Revelation 5:1/13:8/20:11-15/22:19). **TABLES:** (Luke 22:30). **FOOD:** (Revelation 2:7, 17/22:1-3). **CHARIOTS:** (2 Kings 2:11/6:17/Zechariah 6:1-8/Ezekiel 1:15-28/Psalm 68:17). **FURNITURE:** (Hebrews 8:5/9:23/Exodus 25:40). **MUSICAL INSTRUMENTS:** (Revelation 4:8-11/5:8-14/7:7-17/14:1-5/15:2-4/19:1-10). **CLOTHING:** (Daniel 7:9/10:5/Matthew 28:3/Acts 1:10/Revelation 4:4/6:9-11/7:9-17/15:6/19:8). **FEASTS:** (Luke 22:16, 30). **DRINKS:** (Luke 22:18/Revelation 7:17). **BREAD:** (Psalm 78:24-25/John 6:31). **ROAST LAMB:** (Luke 22:16). **FRUITS:** (Revelation 2:7/22:2). **ANIMALS:** (2 Kings 2:11/6:17/Zechariah 1:8, 10/6:1-5/Revelation 19:11, 14, 21). **ALL MATERIAL THINGS AS ON EARTH:** (Romans 1:20/Philippians 2:10). **FLOORS, RAINBOWS, LIGHTNINGS, THUNDERS, LAMPS:** (Revelation 4:3, 5-6/15:2.

**AS FOR ME . . . I CAN HARDLY WAIT TO GO TO HEAVEN . . . HOW ABOUT YOU???**

*"And many of them that sleep in the dust of the earth shall awake* (be resurrected), *some to everlasting life, and some to shame and everlasting contempt."* **Daniel 12:2**

**ADDITIONAL SCRIPTURES FOR FURTHER STUDY:** (Revelation chapter 21-22/3:12/John 14:1-3/Hebrews 13:14/Galatians 4:26 **RESTITUTION OF ALL THINGS:** (Acts 3:21/1 Corinthians 13:8-13/15:24-28/Hebrews 1:13/2:5-8

# HELL

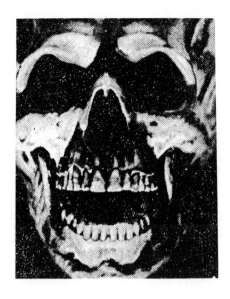

**DEFINITION:** The place and state of punishment of the wicked after death; the abode of evil condemned spirits is Gehenna or Tartarus and the abode of the wicked dead is Sheol or Hades.

**GOD IS WILLING TO FORGIVE EVERY KNOWN SIN EXCEPT BLASPHEMING THE HOLY SPIRIT!** *"But he that shall blaspheme against the Holy Ghost hath never forgiveness, but is in danger of eternal damnation."* **Mark 3:29 *Read: Unpardonable Sin**

**Blasphemy against the Holy Ghost includes any willful, malicious and slanderous word spoken against the person and work of the Holy Spirit, or ascribing the work of the Holy Spirit to Satan!** It is unpardonable because it is willful rejection of light and deliberate insult to the last and only executive of God to man to bring about remission of sins. **When men do away with the only agent of God in redemption and the only method of forgiveness, there is no other person to plead their case before God, so their souls are lost eternally.** One may blaspheme and insult the Spirit in ignorance and be forgiven. *"(Paul) who was before a blasphemer, and a persecutor, and injurious: but I obtained mercy, because I did it ignorantly in unbelief."* **1 Timothy 1:13**

Many times in the Scriptures words like eternal damnation, eternal judgement, eternal punishment, and eternal hell interchange. They all refer to the eternal torment in hell!

**IN HELL THE FIRE CAN NEVER BE QUENCHED! Mark 9:42-48/Isaiah 66:22-24 IN HELL MAN IS REFERRED TO AS A "WORM" AND HIS SPIRIT CAN NEVER DIE! Mark 9:42-48/Job 25:6/Psalm 22:6/Isaiah 41:14/66:24.** *This refers to the remorse of the conscience that each man will receive over his failure to do what was necessary to escape hell. It is the conscious, never dying, part of the human being that will feel eternal torments of fire in eternal hell. **Matthew 8:12/13:42, 50/22:13/24:51/25:30, 46/Revelation 14:9-11/20:10-15/21:8/Isaiah 66:24.** The spirit in hell feels and knows but can never escape!

**BOTH BODY AND SOUL WILL BE CAST INTO HELL AT THE JUDGEMENT: Revelation 20:11-15/Matthew 10:28**

**Did you know that if you are angry with your brother without just cause (or) if you call him a "fool" to his face — you are in danger of hell fire? Matthew 5:22**

**HELL IS THE PLACE OF THE ETERNAL PUNISHMENT OF THE WICKED! Matthew 5:29-30/10:28/18:9/23:15, 33/Mark 9:43-47/Luke 12:5/James 3:6**

Hell is referred to as the Lake of Fire: **Revelation 19:20/20:10-15/21:8** A furnace of fire: **Matthew 13:42, 50** Fire and brimstone: **Matthew 25:41, 46/Revelation 14:9-11/19:20/20:10-15/21:8/Isaiah 66:22-24**

*"Wherefore I say unto you, all manner of sin and blasphemy shall be forgiven unto men: but the blasphmey against the Holy Ghost shall not be forgiven unto men. And whosoever speaketh a word against the Son of man (Jesus), it shall be forgiven him: but whosoever speaketh against the Holy Ghost it shall not be forgiven him, neither in this world (this age), neither in the world to come (the Millennium, after Christ has returned)."* **Matthew 12:31-32**

**TO BLASPHEME THE HOLY GHOST IS TO:** Speak evil of Him **Jude 8/Ephesians 4:31** Rail **1 Timothy 6:4/2 Peter 2:11** Revile **Matthew 27:39** Defame **1 Corinthians 4:13** Slander **Romans 3:8** Insult by blasphemy **Matthew 12:31**

**GOD LOVES US! HE WANTS NONE OF US TO GO TO HELL! BUT, SINCE WE ARE NOT "ROBOTS" WE ARE FREE TO CHOOSE OUR OWN DESTINY!** *"Hell and destruction are before the Lord: how much more then the hearts of the children of men?"* **Proverbs 15:11**

Hell (Sheol) is an **unseen** world. It is the place of departed evil spirits. **HELL IS NOT THE GRAVE WHERE BODIES ARE PLACED! *Read: "GRAVES"**

**ANOTHER PERSON CAN NEVER SEND YOU TO HELL! NO MAN CAN KILL THE SOUL AND SPIRIT BECAUSE THEY ARE IMMORTAL! 1 Peter 3:4. ONLY GOD CAN CAST A PERSON INTO HELL. Revelation 20:11-15/Psalm 9:17** *"And I say unto you my friends, Be not afraid of them that kill the body, and after that have no more that they can do. But I will forewarn you whom ye shall fear: Fear him* (God) *which after he* (another person) *hath killed, you* (God) *hath power to cast* (him) *into hell; yea* (yes), *I say unto you, Fear him* (God)." **Luke 12:4-5**

**THE SAME SENSES A PERSON HAS WHILE HE LIVES WILL BE VERY MUCH ALIVE IN HELL! Luke 16:19-31**

**LISTED BELOW ARE 10 REASONS A PERSON IN HELL IS TORMENTED:**

1. Remorse and despair in seeing the godly whom they despised now in their glorified body, receiving eternal life and happiness with God. **Luke 16:23**
2. Living with the memory of the very sins they know damned their souls to hell. **Luke 16:25**
3. Eternal desire for the good that would have freed them from being in hell. **Luke 16:25**
4. Memory of lost opportunities in life that could have caused them to be with God. **Luke 16:25**
5. Regret over sins committed which can never be recalled. **Luke 16:25**
6. Absolute impossibility of escape from eternal misery and suffering. **Luke 12:26**
7. Eternal separation from loved ones which they can see beyond an impassable gulf. **Luke 16:23-26**
8. Regret over their bad example in life that caused their friends and loved ones to live outside of the perfect will of God. **Luke 16:27-31**
9. Ever deepening remorse for not listening to the Word of God, and for not spending their time, talents, and money to propagate it, so that many others could escape hell. **Luke 16:27-31**
10. Last: The conscious thoughts of eternity in fire and brimstone (sulphur). **Luke 16:23-31/Matthew 25:41, 46/Revelation 14:9-11/20:11-15/21:8/Isaiah 66:22-24**

(Continued)

Blasphemy is to insult, curse, or attribute the works of the Holy Spirit to Satan. It is always unforgiveable if it is done maliciously and knowingly. **Hebrews 6:4-9/10:26-31/1 Timothy 1:13**

## EVERLASTING HELL IS ALSO PREPARED AS PUNISHMENT FOR THE DEVIL AND HIS ANGELS! Matthew 25:41

## HELL IS A PLACE OF TORMENT — NOT A STATE OR CONDITION OF LIFE!

**PRAYING TO (OR FOR) THE DEAD IS USELESS! NOTHING HAPPENS! IT'S TOO LATE!** There is only one verse in Scripture where a person prayed to the dead. Let those who do so remember that prayer to the dead means nothing and gets nothing. **Luke chapter 16.**

Gehenna, the place of future and eternal torment is the same as the "lake of fire." **Revelation 19:20/20:10-15/21:8**

**A PERSON IN HELL LIVES IN EVERLASTING CHAINS! Jude 6-7 AND IS TORMENTED DAY AND NIGHT FOR EVER AND EVER! Revelation 20:10**

**THERE ARE FIVE DEPARTMENTS IN HELL FOR DEPARTED SPIRITS:**
1. **TARTARUS 1 Peter 3:19/2 Peter 2:4/Jude 6-7.** This prison is a special one for **fallen angels** who sinned before the flood. **No human beings or demons ever go to this prison.**
2. **PARADISE Luke 16:19-31/23:43.** This was the abode of the righteous after physical death where they were held captive by the devil against their will until Christ conquered death, hell, and the grave. It is now empty of the righteous who go to heaven at death since Christ captured the captives in hell and took them to heaven with Him when He ascended.
3. **HELL Matthew 16:18/Luke 16:19-31.** This is the **torment compartment** of sheol-hades where wicked souls have always gone and will always go until the end of the Millennium. Then the wicked will be brought out of here to be reunited with their resurrected and immortal bodies and to be cast in to the lake of fire for eternity **Revelation 20:11-15.**
4. **ABYSS OR BOTTOMLESS PIT Luke 8:26-31/Romans 10:7/Revelation 9:1-2/11:7/17:8/20:1-10.** This is the abode of demons and some angelic beings. **No human soul and spirit ever go to the abyss.** The old testament equivalent is Abaddon and is translated destruction **Job 26:5-6/28:22/31:12/Psalm 88:11/Proverbs 15:11/27:20.**
5. **LAKE OF FIRE.** This is the eternal hell and perdition of all fallen angels, demons and wicked men **Revelation 20:10-15/21:8.** This is the same as "gehenna." **It is the final hell prepared for the devil and his angels Matthew 25:41** and is eternal in duration **Matthew 25:46/Revelation 14:9-14/19:20/20:10-15/Isaiah 66:22-24.**

Our word "infernal" means belonging to hell or the eternal regions of hell and fire! Tartarus is defined as the place of punishment in the lower world!

Hell is a place of great pain: Psalm 18:5/116:3/Luke 16:19-31
Hell is a place where a person goes in a moment and quickly: Numbers 16:30-32/Job 21:13/Psalm 55:15

Where is hell located? In the "nether" parts of the earth (Ezekiel 31:14-18/32:24) in the lower parts of the earth (Psalm 63:9/68:18/Ephesians 4:8-10) in the heart of the earth (Matthew 12:40), below the depth of the seas and below the foundations of the mountains (Jonah 2:2-6), beneath, like a pit (Proverbs 15:24/Isaiah 14:9-19/Ezekiel 31:14-18/32:18-31

Hell is a place hidden from man, but naked before God: Job 26:6/Proverbs 15:11/Psalm 139:8/Amos 9:2.
Hell is a place of full consciousness: Isaiah 14:9-15/Ezekiel 32:27-31/Luke 16:19-31.
Hell is a place for the soul and spirit, not the physical body! Psalm 16:10/30:3/49:15/86:13/89:48/Proverbs 23:14/Acts 2:25-29.
Hell is a place where knowledge and memory exist: Isaiah 14:10, 16/Luke 16:19-31.
Hell is a place of regret over mistreatment of others: Luke 16:24-31.
Hell is a place where men still have will power, though it is too late to accept God's terms: Luke 16:24-31.
Hell is a place so terrible that those who are there plead for some means of warning others not to come there: Luke 16:26-31.
Hell is a place where souls are not burned up by the fire: Luke 16:22-31.
Hell is a place of cruelty and a place that enlarges itself: Isaiah 5:14.
Hell is a place that is never full or satisfied: Proverbs 27:20/30:16/Habakkuh 2:5.
Hell is a place which only salvation can deliver you from before you die: Psalm 86:13.
Hell is a place of gates and bars: Job 17:16/Isaiah 38:10/Matthew 16:18/Revelation 1:18.

ALL PEOPLE REMAINING ON EARTH WILL BE PERMITTED TO LOOK DOWN INTO ETERNAL HELL (AT CERTAIN OPENINGS) TO SEE THE PUNISHMENT OF REBELS IS FOREVER (AS A PERPETUAL WARNING AGAINST SIN AND TRANSGRESSION) AFTER THE MILLENNIUM! *"And they shall go forth, and look upon the carcasses of the men that have transgressed against me* (God): *for their worm* (referring to man's soul and spirit) *shall not die, neither shall their fire be quenched: and they shall be an abhorring unto all flesh."* **Isaiah 66:24 NOTE:** The carcasses referred to are the bodies of men in eternal hell which will never be destroyed—bodies that will have been resurrected to immortality (deathlessness) so that they may be punished for deeds done in the body before death. These eternal bodies in hell are considered "dead carcasses" because of being without the life of God, which is given to the resurrected saints. The purpose of having an opening to hell will be to cause coming generations to abhor sin and its consequences! When natural men can actually see into eternal hell it will be a great warning for them to walk in the ways of God! Not only men of the new earth, (after Christ returns and restores it), but angels also, and all other beings will be able to look into this place and see how horrible the punishment of sin can be **Revelation 14:9-11.** Horrifying as the thought may be, the view may be God's best method of keeping eternal generations in line with His laws and commandments as they progress in the new earth in the eternity future.

### PRAYER
"Dear God, I want to become a born-again Christian. I confess to You that I am a sinner. I ask You to forgive me for my sins and to blot them out from Your memory. I believe you sent Your only son Jesus to die on the cross to pay for my sins! I believe He lives today! Come into my life and I will live for You from this moment on! Thank You for allowing me to become a born-again Christian. In Jesus' name, I pray. AMEN!

# HOMOSEXUALS
# LESBIANS

male & female

# Homosexuals

**DEFINITION:** Sexual desire toward a member of one's own sex; Lesbians are female homosexuals.

In America many homosexuals flaunt their lifestyle and beliefs. In big cities they can be seen hugging, kissing, and holding hands. In the Soviet Union the punishment for homosexuality carries a sentence of 8 years in prison.

**WHEN A NATION REFUSES TO LISTEN TO GOD'S STANDARD OF MORALITY, GOD RELEASES THEM OVER TO A REPROBATE MIND!** *"Wherefore God also gave them up to **uncleanness** through the **lusts** of their own hearts, to **dishonour their own bodies** between themselves: Who changed the truth of God into a lie, and worshipped and served the creature (Satan) more than the Creator (God), who is blessed for ever. For this cause God gave them up unto **vile affections:** for even **their women did change the natural use into that which is against nature** (became lesbians): And likewise also the men, leaving the natural use of the woman, burned in their lust one toward another: **men with men** working that which is unseemly (not natural), and receiving in themselves that recompence (just reward) of their error which was meet (only fitting they should receive). And even as they did not like to retain God in their knowledge, God gave them over to a **reprobate mind,** to do those things which are not convenient (unnatural); Being filled with all unrighteousness, fornication, wickedness, covetousness, maliciousness; full of envy, murder, debate,* deceit, malignity; whisperers, backbiters, haters of God, despiteful, proud, boasters, inventors of evil things, disobedient to parents, without understanding, covenantbreakers, **without natural affection,** implacable, unmerciful: **Who knowing the judgement of God, that they which commit such things are worthy of death, not only do the same, but have pleasure in them that do them.** " Romans 1:24-32

**GOD'S PLAN FOR THE HUMAN, AND ANIMAL RACE, IS FOR US TO REPRODUCE! THIS IS IMPOSSIBLE FOR HOMOSEXUALS AND LESBIANS! IT IS AN INGENIUS PLAN, CREATED BY SATAN, TO HALT GOD'S PLAN FOR THE FAMILY!**

**TO COMMIT HOMOSEXUALITY IS TO SIN AGAINST YOUR OWN BODY, THE OTHER PERSON, — AND WORST OF ALL — AGAINST GOD!** *"Know ye not that ye are the temple of God, and that the Spirit of God dwelleth in you? If any man* (person) *defile the temple of God, him shall God destroy; for the temple of God is holy, which temple ye are.* " I Corinthians 3:16-17

131

(Continued)

## HOW CAN A GAY CHANGE AND START OVER?

Only through Jesus! He alone is the key to change! The answer is not going from homosexual activity to straight sexual activity, but by **becoming straight mentally, emotionally and physically without sexual involvement!** A homosexual can only be changed through his own free choice to decide that God's design for all people is right, and brings true happiness! **Homosexuality is a sin.** And, as sure as a liar can become honest, so can the homosexual be freed by Jesus!

## WHEN AND WHERE DID HOMOSEXUALITY BEGIN?

An archangel named **Lucifer** rebelled against the laws of God's government (**Isaiah 14:12-15/Ezekiel 28:12-19**). Lucifer was created to bring truth to the earth. Instead, he swayed ⅓ of God's angels to follow him when God threw him out of heaven (**Revelation 12:4**). Lucifer's angels became demons! They totally rejected God's laws of Christian love, giving, and holy living. Lucifer's rebellion caused his name to be changed to Satan, which means ''the adversary'' (enemy). According to **Genesis 1:3** God gives account of his marvellous purpose for humans. In **Genesis 1:26** we learn that we were created in God's image. God reproduced Himself! Satan **resented** human sexuality and the divine purpose God had in creating humans. According to **Mark 12:25** Satan did not have sex! He hated God because he was cast out of heaven, and because he could not reproduce! So, he devised an evil plan whereby he could sway human minds and behavior away from God!

## GOD CREATED US MALE AND FEMALE (Genesis 1:27).

God called all of His creation, (including sex in humans), ''good'' (**Genesis 1:31**)! Man and woman, in the garden of Eden, were unclothed. They had not sinned, therefore they were unashamed (**Genesis 2:25**). God ordained that man should leave his father and mother and cleave unto his wife and the two would be one flesh (**Genesis 2:24**)!

## GOD'S PLAN REGARDING SEX IS THAT THERE BE A MARRIAGE BETWEEN AN ADULT MALE AND FEMALE.

God knows the emotional and physical needs of human beings! He created us, remember? He said it was ''not good that man should be alone'' (**Genesis 2:18**). God knew that the human male needs to give and receive love, appreciation, and affection from another human to be happy and fulfilled. **That's why God created woman — to fill an emptiness in man!**

God designed the human female with a need to receive appreciation, and love, and to give it! God also instilled in the human male and female a need to appreciate and love other humans. This need was fulfilled when God created the family. **In order to establish a family there is the need for sexual attraction.** That's why God created sex! God ordained sex, (or marital love), as the proper function of the sex drive! **Sex in the bond of marriage is far more than human reproduction!** It's intention is to unite a married couple in love, and respect, in a way shared with no other, and to build stable families!

## GOD'S FIRST SEX LESSON:

God taught that marriage is for persons mature and self-disciplined enough to leave their parents and to successfully establish a separate home. Parents are to teach God's ways to their children through example. That takes maturity of mind! God's plan for all humans is to build godly character! By free moral choice, God had to allow Satan to have contact with the first human couple. He had to see which way they would choose to go! Instantly, Satan planted into the first woman's mind the idea that God had lied to them. The first human couple fell prey to Satan's trick and took something that was not theirs. Instantly their minds were affected. They were embarrassed to discover they were naked. They hid from God. Fear, unknown to them, came into being (**Genesis 3:10**)! Satan convinced them they ought to be ashamed about the way God had created their individual bodies. **Satan is the originator of the idea that sex is evil, dirty, and shameful!** This is how and where sexual attitudes and feelings among humans first began! Ever since, Satan has worked in humans to pervert attitudes, emotions, and relationships! Satan has implanted in human minds selfishness!

During early childhood some human minds accept **WRONG** moods, and feelings of attraction, to the same sex. **Again, ''thanks to Satan'', it may be so early in life that homosexuals and lesbians falsely think they were born that way!**

Adam and Eve were driven from the Garden of Eden and from any further contact with God's Spirit. Ever since, all humanity has been cut off from God's Spirit which would have guided them in godly ways through life. Mankind was given 6,000 years to develop and experience Satan's plan for them. The Bible and history books recorded the terrible consequences. Today, human beings repeat these vulgar experiences, just as did previous generations.

## GOD GAVE US HIS LAWS!

God inspired the Bible (**2 Timothy 3:16**) so mankind would not be ignorant and without knowledge of the way we should live. It contains the cause of human problems, and how we can overcome them, if we choose! Most humans reject knowledge given by God!

## MANY EDUCATED PERSONS DON'T BELIEVE THERE ARE FALLEN SPIRIT BEINGS INFLUENCING AND DECEIVING ALL HUMANITY (Revelations 12:9)!

They don't believe that Satan is the unseen ruler and god of this world (**2 Corinthians 4:4**). Satan is called the ''prince of the power of the air'' and ''the spirit that now worketh in the children of disobedience.'' **Colossians 3:5-6/ Ephesians 2:2**

## SATAN HOLDS CLASS 24 HOURS A DAY TO PROMOTE THE LUSTS OF OUR FLESH!

He works overtime to see that we fulfill all the desires of the flesh and mind (**Ephesians 2:2-3**)! There are no limits, or controls, to the human mind, except those an individual learns or chooses to restrain! *''Now the works of the flesh are manifest* (made known) ... *ADULTERY* (sex between a married person and other than his spouse), *FORNICATION* (sex outside marriage), *UNCLEANNESS* (masturbation, sex devices, foreplay outside of marriage, filthy talk, sexual suggestions, preoccupation with fondling one's own body, dirty minds, physical-moral sexual uncleannes, sex diseases, etc.), *LASCIVIOUSNESS* (lewd, lust), *IDOLATRY* (loving-serving anything other than God), *WITCHCRAFT,*

(Continued)

*HATRED, VARIANCE, EMULATIONS, WRATH, STRIFE, SEDITIONS, HERESIES, ENVYINGS, MURDERS, DRUNKENNESS, REVELLINGS* (wild sex parties, orgies, booze, drugs, sexual deviates) *and such like."* (**Galatians 5:19-21**) Thanks to Satan and his armies, he inspires **rebellion, selfishness** and **lust** in human beings! He puts desires in mind that are vulnerable. This includes young children! An individual's sexual feelings, and values, depend upon what thoughts and emotions are allowed to develop in his mind, from infancy on!

**WRONG AND DAMAGING EMOTIONAL (AND SEXUAL) FEELINGS TAKE ROOT IN EACH HUMAN MIND IF HUMANS DO NOT RESIST THEM!** Some wrong experiences leave deep impressions, emotions, and desires! And, if repeated enough, they become deeply learned and the mind conditioned!

Satan fully understands this deep conditioning in human minds and emotions! He uses this to thwart God's purpose in our lives! Though many deny it, all humans become (in one way or another) the slaves of deceptive sins, pleasures and feelings (**Hebrews 3:13/John 8:34**)! Only through the forgiveness of God can we escape! It takes faith and the power of the Holy Spirit (plus) human effort to break the chains of wrong thinking! Then we must learn that right thinking is revealed in God's laws!

**A PERSON'S MOST IMPORTANT SEX ORGAN IS HIS BRAIN!** If a person is properly guided in youth, by example and teaching to respect the opposite sex, and is prepared to serve and love other human beings, that person can develop a right heterosexual desire! **Sex education and emotional feelings are not learned by formal instruction!** Sex education and emotional feelings start from infancy with the ways parents and other influential persons treat each other and the child. Wrong sexual feelings do not develop merely out of a wrong culture, but also out of ignorance! Many young people are not taught wholesome attitudes about sex at home! They are not taught right standards of sexual conduct! They are not taught that certain sexual practices are wrong, or damaging, and why they are to be avoided!

**MANY YOUNG PEOPLE DON'T UNDERSTAND THEIR FEELINGS AND EMOTIONS!** They lack proper understanding and communication from concerned parents who can help evaluate their feelings! Without proper parental example, wrong or misguided feelings of affection toward others can begin to stir sexual feelings, and start a wrong pattern of association in the mind!

**MILLIONS OF INDIVIDUALS FOLLOW "PEER PRACTICES" OR ANY EXCITING, EROTIC, THOUGHT THAT CROSSES THEIR MINDS!** They seem "natural". What they may not realize is that wrong thoughts and feelings can be learned not only from others, but from their own uncontrolled thoughts! They may be injected into their minds by an evil spirit — by Satan or his demons. A person may have allowed himself to respond to such emotions (or activity) so early in life that they become a "natural" part of the way he has always felt! **They look back on their life and conclude they must have been born a homosexual or lesbian!**

**HUMANS SEEK EXCITEMENT!** Everyone needs a sense of worth — something to defeat routine, emptiness, or loneliness in his life! Whenever sexual (or emotional) seeds are planted, they will grow, — in youth or even after one is married! The Bible warns us, *"Be not deceived; God is not mocked; for whatsoever a man soweth, that shall he also reap* (**Galatians 6:7**)!

**TO SOME, EXTRAMARITAL OR HOMOSEXUAL THOUGHTS (OR ACTS) MAY SEEM A WAY TO FIND AFFECTION, GAIN ATTENTION, RECOGNITION, SECURITY OR MONEY!** Maybe they seem a way of proving sexual "prowess" or the only option available. One wrong thought, uncontrolled, leads to still more! Sometimes a person doesn't know he should resist temptation! Maybe he doesn't care! Minds that feed on wrong emotional or erotic thoughts in various fantasies (especially masturbation or pornography) will eventually have them ingrained as desires and emotions!

**MOST PEOPLE "COP-OUT" AND BLAME OTHERS FOR THEIR HOMOSEXUAL PROBLEM!** It's true that parents may (or may not) have set a right example in their relationships and teachings. Satan may be solely to blame. But individuals also repeatedly allow themselves to respond to wrong ways of living and thinking!

A person, young or old, may choose to rebel to right teaching and example! He or she can decide to go his or her own way. Satan did! The Bible says *"Your adversary* (enemy) *the devil prowls like a roaring lion seeking some one to devour. Resist him."* **1 Peter 5:8-9**

**GODLY SEXUAL BEHAVIOR:** God is very concerned about the cultural and family environments of human beings. Family and environment is where the foundations of human relationships, sexual feelings, values, and ideas are established! God is also concerned about the physical and mental abilities parents pass on to their children! Wrong sexuality opens the door to rapid degeneration! It brings physical and spiritual disease to the human body, mind and spirit!

True happiness, fulfillment and social stability can only be achieved if humans follow God's laws!

**RESEARCH HAS FOUND THAT HOMOSEXUALITY IS NOT BORN INTO A PERSON!** A child's gender is largely influenced by the way parents (and other influential persons) respond to the child; what they name the child, how they treat, handle, clothe the child! Aspects of a child's own personality may affect the attitudes and responses of parents and be reflected back to the child. This is usually obvious by the time a child is 2 years of age! As a child grows it learns its gender role. A male and female come to understand from their culture, and from parental role models, what appropriate values, duties, functions, mannerisms, and attitudes are expected of males and females in their culture. Men and women have different muscular and skeletal structures and usually different metabolisms! They have different sex organs, hormones, and emotional levels! God created some organs, such as men's lungs, to be larger than women's! And the liver and kidneys in women are larger! Men and women's voices, dexterity, perception and psychology usually differ!

(Continued)

# Homosexuals-Lesbians 4

**GOD CREATED ONLY MEN TO IMPREGNATE AND ONLY WOMEN CAN LACTATE, GESTATE AND MENSTRUATE!** Males, in general, are more muscular and physically stronger than females. Females are generally more maternal in their interests, emotions and feelings. Within each sex there are differences in body size and shape, muscular development, temperament, emotional levels, mental abilities, and other things that cause individual personality and appearance. These differences color a person's view of himself or herself — his masculinity or her femininity. These characteristics strongly influence whether a person becomes a homosexual or lesbian and whether he or she is dominant or passive, bold or shy. The direction of a person's sex life is determined primarily by his learning and how he responds to a host of events in his own life.

**MOST MEN AND WOMEN ARE HETEROSEXUAL AS OPPOSED TO BISEXUAL, BECAUSE OF THEIR RELIGIOUS AND SOCIAL TRADITIONS.**

**HORMONES:** Research has uncovered no chromosomal differences between homosexuals and heterosexuals! Effeminate men also have no chromosomal differences with normal heterosexual males. Homosexuals and effiminates have been found to have sex hormone levels within the same ranges as those found in exclusive heterosexuals! Most sex researchers recognize that although sex hormones influence sex organs and glandular development, tissue structure and strength of the sex drive, they are not the primary determinant of sexual interest.

**IF EXTRA MALE SEX HORMONE (TESTOSTERONE) IS GIVEN TO A MAN WHETHER HE IS HETEROSEXUAL OR HOMOSEXUAL, IT WILL MOST LIKELY INCREASE HIS SEX DRIVE, BUT IT HAS NO INFLUENCE ON HIS CHOICE OF SEX OBJECTS.** Injected estrogen (the female sex hormone), will reduce the sex drive in a man, but it will not affect his sexual orientation!

**THE MAJORITY OF MALES IN MOST CULTURES ARE HETEROSEXUALLY ORIENTED.** However, even heterosexuals allow their minds and sexual feelings to be diverted by wrong attitudes and desires. Some heterosexuals develop a degree of homosexual interest! **Feminine heterosexual females are the majority, but there are also masculine-mannered females.** Female homosexuals (lesbians) are often typically feminine in appearance and manner. Others are very mannish ("butch" or "dyke"). There are degrees in both sexes. This is why we need to know what God has to say on the subject!

**ACCORDING TO EPHESIANS 5:12 SOME PEOPLE DO THINGS THAT ARE TOO OBSCENE TO EVEN DESCRIBE!**

EFFEMINATE MANNERISMS IN MALES MAY BE DUE TO BEING REARED IN AN ALMOST EXCLUSIVE FEMALE ENVIRONMENT! EFFEMINATE MANNERISMS MAY ALSO BE A WAY OF PORTRAYING NON-AGGRESSIVENESS! EFFEMINANCY IS HARMFUL BECAUSE IT DAMAGES A MALE'S PROPER LEADERSHIP, AND THINKING, IN A FAMILY UNIT! EFFEMINATES ARE AGAINST GOD'S PLAN FOR A MAN/BOY!

**HUMAN SEXUALITY IS MORE THAN ONE'S GENDER OR A SEXUAL ACT!** Human sexuality is a total way of thinking, acting, and feeling. One's sexuality affects the way one responds to his own sex, the opposite sex, marriage, the family, and every aspect of life! That's why sex has so much impact on human lives and culture. It's the reason why God commands men and women to develop sex rightly!

**GOD SAYS WE MUST KEEP OUR BODY UNDER CONTROL. WE WILL HAVE TO ANSWER FOR THOSE ACTS WE DO IN OUR BODY!** *"For we must all appear before the judgement seat of Christ; that every one may receive the things done in his body, according to that* (which) *he hath done, whether it be good or bad."* **2 Corinthians 5:10**

**HOMOSEXUALITY AND ALL OTHER SEX SINS ARE CALLED "UNCLEANNESS" IN THE SCRIPTURES! Read: 2 Corinthians 12:21** *"Let not sin therefore reign in your mortal body, that ye should obey it in the lusts thereof."* **Romans 6:12** *"Who being past feeling* (sexually corrupt) *have given themselves over unto lasciviousness* (lust), *to work* (commit sex sins, fantasies) *all **uncleanness*** (homosexuality, all sex sins) *with greediness."* **Ephesians 4:19** *"But fornication* (sex without marriage), *and all **uncleanness**, or covetousness, let it not be once named among you, as becometh saints* (born again Christians). *Neither filthiness, nor foolish talking, nor jesting, which are not convenient* (godly): *but rather giving of thanks* (to God). *For this ye know, that no **whoremonger**, nor **unclean person**, nor covetous man, who is an idolater, hath any inheritance in the kingdom of Christ and of God."* **Ephesians 5:3-5** *"Wherefore God also gave them up to **uncleanness** through the lusts of their own hearts, to dishonour their own bodies between themselves."* **Romans 1:24** *"Mortify therefore your members which are upon the earth, fornication, uncleanness, inordinate affection, evil concupiscence, and covetousness, which is idolatry: For which things' sake the wrath of God cometh on the children of disobedience."* **Colossians 3:5-6**

**ALL MANNER OF SEXUAL SIN IS ALSO REFERRED TO AS "INFIRMITY OF THE FLESH!"** *"...for as ye have yielded your members* (body parts) *servants to **uncleanness*** (sex sins) *and to iniquity unto iniquity, even so now yield your members servants to righteousness unto holiness."* **Romans 6:19**

**HOMOSEXUALITY, LESBIANISM, AND ALL OTHER SEX SINS TOTALLY SEPARATE A PERSON FROM GOD. THEY MUST BE REPENTED OF AND PUT OUT OF A PERSON'S LIFE OR ELSE HE WILL NEVER BE TRULY HAPPY OR INHERIT ETERNAL LIFE WITH CHRIST!** *"For the wages of sin is death, but the gift of God is eternal life through Jesus Christ our Lord."* **Romans 6:23**

**ACCORDING TO 2 PETER 2:10 PEOPLE WHO COMMIT SEX SINS ARE PRESUMPTUOUS, SELF-WILLED AND NOT AFRAID TO SPEAK EVIL OF DIGNITIES!**

**HOMOSEXUALS-LESBIANS ARE WITHOUT NATURAL AFFECTION! READ: 2 Timothy 3:3 and Romans 1:25-31**

*(Continued)*

134

**BEING A HOMOSEXUAL OR LESBIAN WILL: 1.** Ruin your reputation **Proverbs 5:9 2.** Will cause you years of trouble **Proverbs 5:9 3.** Will bring material ruin **Proverbs 5:10 4.** Will ruin your health **Proverbs 5:11 5.** Will bring regret, remorse **Proverbs 5:12-13 6.** Will reduce you to wickedness **Proverbs 5:14 7.** Will cause eternal ruin **Proverbs 5:23 8.** Is deceptive **Proverbs 5:3 9.** Brings destruction **Proverbs 5:4 10.** Can bring death **Proverbs 5:5 11.** Is unpredictable **Proverbs 5:6 12.** Is against your parents' guidance **Proverbs 2:17**

**HOMOSEXUALS AND LESBIANS DEFILE THEIR FLESH!** *"Even as Sodom and Gomorrah, and the cities about them in like manner, giving themselves over to **fornication** (sex without marriage), and going after **strange flesh** (homosexuals, lesbians, sex with angels, etc.), are set forth for an example, suffering the vengeance of eternal fire (hell). Likewise also these **filthy dreamers defile the flesh**, despise dominion, and **speak evil of dignities."** **Jude 7-8**

**IN THE OLD TESTAMENT DAYS THE PENALTY FOR HOMOSEXUALITY WAS DEATH!** *"If a man also lie with mankind, as he lieth with a woman, both of them have committed an abomination: they shall surely be put to death; their blood shall be upon them."* **Leviticus 20:13**

**THE BIBLE IS VERY CLEAR ON THE SUBJECT OF HOMOSEXUALITY!** *"Thou shalt not lie with mankind, as with womankind: it is abomination."* **Leviticus 18:22**

**HOMOSEXUALS, LESBIANS AND SODOMITES WERE REFERRED TO AS "DOGS" IN SCRIPTURES. READ: Deuteronomy 23:17-18**

**HOMOSEXUALS AND LESBIANS ARE REFERRED TO AS "WHOREMONGERS" READ: Ephesians 5:5-8**

**HOMOSEXUALITY AND LESBIANISM IS A PHYSICAL AND SPIRITUAL SICKNESS WHICH DESTROYS MANY! READ: Isaiah 1:4-6/6:10**

**HOMOSEXUALS AND LESBIANS DISREGARD GOD'S LAWS REGARDING MARRIAGE VOWS! READ: Proverbs 2:17**

**HOMOSEXUALS AND LESBIANS LEAD OTHERS TO HELL!**

**SEX STARTS AND ENDS IN THE MIND! 1.** The sinful mind is an enemy against God (**Romans 8:7**) **2.** The sinful mind is vain (**Ephesians 4:17**) **3.** The sinful mind is defiled (**Titus 1:15**) **4.** God forbids body worship (**1 Corinthians 6:13, 19-20/9:27/13:3/Luke 12:22/Romans 12:1**)

**ADVICE TO HOMOSEXUALS:** God's plan for man is to have a "helpmeet" (wife)! Read: **Genesis 2:18-23**

**MARRIAGE IS HONORABLE!** Read: **Hebrews 13:4.** When you find a wife or husband you find a "good thing." **Proverbs 18:22**

**LESBIANS ... YOU NEED TO REPENT AND BE DELIVERED! YOUR DESIRE SHOULD BE TO YOUR HUSBAND! READ: Genesis 3:16**

**SPIRITUAL HEALING HAS EXCELLENT BENEFITS! SPIRITUAL HEALING IS A COMMISSION BY GOD! READ: John 6:63/Luke 4:18! SPIRITUAL HEALING REMOVES SIN AND GIVES A HAPPY LIFE! READ: James 5:19-20/Revelation 7:14-17.**

**HOMOSEXUALITY AND LESBIANISM ARE SINS THAT SEPARATE YOU FROM GOD IN THIS LIFE! AND, IF A PERSON HAS NOT REPENTED AND RECEIVED FORGIVENESS, WHEN HE DIES HE WILL GO TO HELL! DOESN'T IT MAKE SENSE THAT SINCE THE MEDICAL PROFESSION HAS DETERMINED THAT A PERSON IS NOT BORN A HOMOSEXUAL THAT HE WOULD DESIRE TO GO STRAIGHT AND RECEIVE GOD'S BLESSINGS IN HIS LIFE? GOD LOVES THE HOMOSEXUAL-LESBIAN! BUT HATES THE SIN HE OR SHE COMMITS! HE WANTS NONE OF US TO PERISH, BUT**

(Continued)

IT IS UP TO THE INDIVIDUAL! GOD GAVE US FREE WILL, REMEMBER? NOW, IF YOU SINCERELY WANT TO RECEIVE FORGIVENESS AND WANT TO BECOME STRAIGHT, YOU WILL NEED TO REPENT AND ASK GOD TO FORGIVE YOU! IT MAY MEAN THAT YOU WILL NEED TO CHANGE YOUR FRIENDS AND SOCIAL ENVIRONMENT!

**UNLESS A HOMOSEXUAL (OR) LESBIAN REPENTS AND GETS SAVED, HE WILL NOT GO TO HEAVEN!**
*"Know ye not that the unrighteous shall not inherit the kingdom of God? Be not deceived: neither fornicators* (sex without marriage), *nor idolaters, nor adulterers, nor effeminate* (earliest stages of homosexuality), *nor abusers of themselves with mankind, nor thieves, nor covetous, nor drunkards, nor revilers, nor extortioners, shall inherit the kingdom of God."* **I Corinthians 6:9-10**
*"...Now the body is not for fornication* (any sex without marriage), *but for the Lord; and the Lord for the body."* **I Corinthians 6:13** *"Know ye not that your bodies are the members of Christ? shall I then take the members of Christ, and make them the members of an harlot? God forbid. What? know ye not that he which is joined to an harlot is one body? for two, saith he, shall be one flesh. But he that is joined unto the Lord is one spirit. Flee fornication. Every sin that a man doeth is without the body; but* **he that committeth fornication sinneth against his own body.** *What? know ye not that* **your body is the temple** *of the Holy Ghost which is in you, which ye have of God, and ye are not your own? For ye are bought with a price: therefore glorify God in your body, and in your spirit, which are God's."* **I Corinthians 6:15-20**

**MOST HOMOSEXUALS-LESBIANS ARE MILITANT TODAY, AND NOT EMBARRASSED TO TALK ABOUT THEIR SEXUAL PREFERENCES! MANY CALL THEMSELVES THE "ORAL MAJORITY". ACCORDING TO THE BIBLE, WHEN A SOCIETY BECOMES LIKE SODOM AND GOMORRAH, IT IS NOT FAR FROM DESTRUCTION! THE PLANS OF THE MILITANT HOMOSEXUALS IS TO CREATE A UNISEXUAL SOCIETY IN THIS COUNTRY! GOD HELP OUR LITTLE CHILDREN!**

**Across the country homosexuals teach children** in classrooms. Some are even **preachers** in pulpits! They greatly influence what is or isn't censored on national TV! However, the same networks don't allow Christian organizations this privilege! Make no doubt about it, "thanks to Satan", there is a massive homosexual revolution taking place, and unless the Lord comes soon our children may be inticed or recruited!

**WE SHOULD PRAY FOR AND WITNESS TO HOMOSEXUALS!** They are living in bondage to Satan. And, may not even know it! In their heart, most are not happy, and do not enjoy life, though they may say, "I'm gay and proud of it!"

IF, AFTER MUCH PRAYER, YOU FIND THAT YOU ARE NOT TOTALLY DELIVERED, THEN YOU MUST ACCEPT THE BIBLE AS THE ABSOLUTE WORD OF GOD AND BELIEVE IT WHEN GOD SAYS THAT DEMONS CAN INHABIT OUR BODIES! SEEK THE AID OF A TRUSTED MINISTER AND HAVE THE UNCLEAN SPIRITS CAST OUT! THEN CAN YOU BE TOTALLY FREE! YOU WILL NEED TO READ YOUR BIBLE, PRAY AND ATTEND CHURCH REGULARLY! YOU WILL NEED TO MAKE SOME CHRISTIAN ACQUAINTANCES! YOU WILL NEED TO CHANGE THE PLACES WHERE YOU GO, SO AS NOT TO BE REMINDED, OR TEMPTED!

**PRAYER:**
Dear God, Please forgive me for all my sins! I have never been more sincere in my life as I am this very moment! I want to be free from the sin of **homosexuality** (or **lesbianism**)! I want to change my life! I truly want to become a Christian! I believe that if I died this very day I would go to hell! I believe exactly what the Holy Bible says! Please come into my life and fill me with Your Spirit! Cleanse me and wash away my sins! I don't want to go to hell! I want to start all over and live the kind of life which You promise brings fulfillment! I am sick at heart for the things I have done. Please forgive me for sinning against my own body, and against You. Please forgive me for sinning and causing other people to sin! I will change my friends! **I will not go to the places where I am known as a homosexual!** I will go to church! I will pray each day and ask for strength to ward off temptation! I will read my Bible daily. I will memorize the verses which help me! I will do everything within my power to live a straight, godly life! I want to find peace and happiness! I know I'm not happy this way! **It is a relief to know that I was not born a homosexual (or lesbian)!** I now realize that Satan has been my master! I realize what a liar and a thief he is! If I begin to weaken, I will say, "get thee behind me, Satan"! I humbly ask Your forgiveness. I declare with my mouth that I am now a born again Christian! I will not be ashamed to tell others that I am saved! I will grow daily in Your word! I thank You for saving my soul, I will praise You as long as I live! In Jesus' name, I pray. AMEN!

# HOROSCOPES

**THE PRACTICE OF ASTROLOGY AND HOROSCOPES ARE FORBIDDEN IN THE BIBLE!** Those who practice the art of star gazing, charting new moons, and studying the positions of the stars and planets, totally disregard God's warnings! These practices are pagan in origin! Your sun sign proves nothing about you! **There is absolutely no validity in the absurd theories of astrology or horoscope charts!** If this were not true then God would have ordained their use instead of blatantly warning us not to believe in or use them! Never forget that God created the sun, moon, and planets as a sign of His creativity and for our beauty! They have no powers of their own nor were they ever given any powers to control our lives and destiny! This is a lie dreamed up by Satan to divert a person's attention away from God as his sole help and comforter! **We are not to observe astrology or read horoscopes!** *"Therefore shall ye observe all my* (God's) *statutes* (laws), *and all my judgements, and do them: I am the Lord."* **Leviticus 19:37**

**It is so ridiculous to put any stock in a horoscope chart because our calendar may be off by many years!** In order to maintain the relationship of the lunar months to the solar years it was periodically necessary to add a 13th month, which was called Second Adar, during the writing of the Bible. Jewish months are generally identified by number instead of names in the Scriptures. Who knows for sure where we are on our modern calendar? No one can prove anything by the calendar, moon, stars, or planets!

In the New Testament, all religious laws regarding days, weeks, months, years, sabbaths, new moons, feasts, and all such forms (which were very much a part of the Old Testament) are completely done away with! Jesus came to put an end to those pagan ideas! Jesus is our life and our future! Jesus has all the help and answers we need for our life! **Horoscope charts do not have the answers to our future, but God does!**

In the New Testament Paul condemns the observance of days, months, times, years and having respect for them as if they were a religion! Read: **Romans 14:5-6/Colossians 2:14-17**

**If you don't know God as your personal Saviour, when all creation clearly declares His handiwork, how can you so gullibly serve the elements in our solar system?** The elements have no special powers apart from God! In the Bible, days, months, new moons, times, years, and seasons were called **"beggarly elements"**! *"But now, after that ye have known God, or rather are known of God, how turn ye again to the weak and **beggarly elements**, whereunto ye desire again to be in bondage* (to Satan, false belief)? *ye observe days, and months, and times, and years. I am afraid of you, lest I have bestowed upon you labour in vain."* **Galatians 4:9-11**

In the Bible, astrologers were sometimes called scientists! They divided the heavens for the purpose of prophecy, divination, and to make horoscopes! Astrology professes to discover certain connections between the position and movements of the planets and events which occur on earth. **This was practiced by the Babylonians, Egyptians, Lybians, Ethiopians, Indians, Arabians and Chinese.** From the rising and setting of the planets, their orbits and color, they predicted storms, heat, rain, comets, eclipses, earthquakes, and ordinary human affairs affecting both nations and individuals. To assist astrologers in making calculations from the planets, the heavens were divided into 12 equal parts called "houses". The various things affecting man were placed within these houses such as marriage, life, death, religion, etc. From the position of stars in these "houses" the calculations were made. Although it is a heathen and pagan practice, it is still popular today!

**"Star-gazers"** were those who endeavored to tell the future by the relative position of the stars. Isaiah 47:13/Jeremiah 10:2/Daniel 1:20/2:2, 10/4:7/5:7-15.

**"Monthly prognosticators"** were those who gave knowledge of events which might occur within the month, according to the various positions and shapes of the moon.

**"Observing times"** is the same thing as prognostication. Leviticus 19:26/2 Kings 21:6/2 Chronicles 33:6.

*"For all that do these things are an abomination* (disgusting) *unto the Lord: and because of these abominations the Lord thy God doth drive them out from before thee."* **Deuteronomy 18:12**

**Did you know that when God permits Satan to do so, he can control the elements and cause storms? So, why would you want to believe in the elements? Read: Job 1:18-19**

According to **Luke 12:29** people who practice star-gazing and charting new moons are of a "doubtful mind"! Following horoscope charts also causes a person to be anxious! It causes a person to be torn between hope and fear. Signs of the zodiac, **and horoscopes are a division of witchcraft, according to the Scriptures!** They are superstitions. They are forbidden! These are done under the guise of witchcraft and traffic with demons in the name of science! Read: **Jeremiah 10:2/Daniel 1:20/2:2, 10/4:7/5:7-15**

**The practice of charting your horoscope is very popular today along with conversations about one's personal sun sign. This is an abomination in God's eyes!** This demonic activity is called using "familiar spirits" in the Bible. All who forsake God's help and seek out these demons will be destroyed unless they repent and turn away from this forbidden practice! **Leviticus 19:31/20:6/Deuteronomy 18:11/1 Samuel 28/2 Kings 21:6/23:24/1 Chronicles 10:13/2 Chronicles 33:6/Isaiah 8:19/19:3/29:4/1 Timothy 4:1-8/2 Thessalonians 2:8-12/Matthew 24:24/Revelation chapter 13/16:13-16/19:20.**

137

(Continued)

Did you know that the increase in popularity of horoscopes and astrology is a sign of the last days before Christ returns? *"For there shall arise false Christs, and false prophets* (psychics, astrologers), *and shall shew great signs and wonders* (Satanic powers, ESP, Flying saucers, all occult things); *insomuch that, if it were possible, they shall deceive the very elect* (Jewish people).'' **Matthew 24:24**

God loves you and wants you to get saved! He wants you to turn away from any belief in horoscopes! But, if you willfully choose to stick with your astrological charts as a ''sorcerer'' you disobey God by following the occult! Therefore you will not be allowed to enter heaven! Read: Exodus 7:11/Jeremiah 27:9/Daniel 2:2/Revelation 21:8/22:15/1 Timothy 1:4.

Full Moon

**HOROSCOPES AND ASTROLOGY ARE A FORM OF IDOLATRY! IDOLATRY IS FORBIDDEN BY GOD!** Those who worship or reverence anyone or anything other than the One True Living God will not be allowed to enter heaven! Read: **1 Corinthians 5:10/6:9/10:7/Revelation 21:8/22:15/Romans 1:30.**

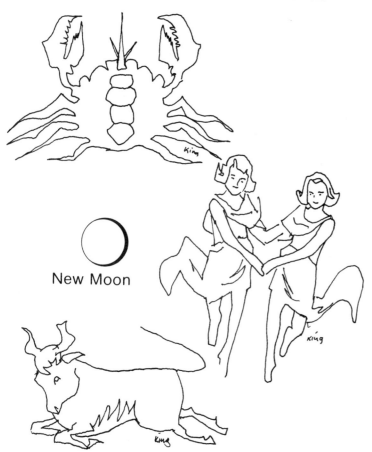

New Moon

*"You are wearied with your many counsels* (charts, astrologers, calculations, theories), *Let now the* **astrologers**, *Those who* **prophesy** *by the stars, Those who* **predict** *by the new moons,* **stand up and save you** *from what will come upon you.''* **Isaiah 47:13** (The Amplified Bible)

According to Deuteronomy 18:9-12 God said we are not to believe in fortune tellers, astrologers, spiritualists, magicians, hypnotists, psychics, nor attempt to communicate with the dead!

In the last days before Christ returns there will be signs in the sun, moon and stars. The purpose of this will be to utterly confound man because of his unbelief in God. *"And then there shall be signs in the sun, and in the moon, and in the stars; and upon the earth distress of nations, with perplexity; the sea and the waves roaring; mens hearts failing them for fear, and for looking after those things which are coming on the earth: for the powers of heaven shall be shaken. And then shall they see the Son of man* (Jesus) *coming in a cloud with power and great glory. And when these things begin to come to pass, then look up, and lift up your heads; for your redemption* (Christ) *draweth nigh.''* **Luke 21:25-28**

**IT MAKES SENSE THAT SINCE ASTROLOGY AND HOROSCOPES ARE FORBIDDEN WE SHOULD:** *"Abstain from all appearances of evil.''* **1 Thessalonians 5:22**

**PLEASE DON'T BE GULLIBLE. DON'T PURCHASE THOSE SILLY HOROSCOPE BOOKS! THEY ONLY BUILD YOU UP TO LET YOU DOWN! THERE IS NOT ONE WORD OF TRUTH IN THEM AS THE BIBLE CLEARLY INDICATES! THE WORLD IS FULL OF ''CHARLATANS'' OUT TO GET YOUR MONEY! THEY'LL PRINT ANYTHING TO SELL TO GULLIBLE PEOPLE! IT'S ALL FAKERY TO MAKE A FAST BUCK! DON'T GET CAUGHT UP IN THE OCCULT! ONLY JESUS CAN OFFER HAPPINESS, SECURITY AND ETERNAL LIFE! CAN ANY HOROSCOPE FULFILL THAT PROMISE? OF COURSE NOT!** JESUS SAID: *"Heaven and earth shall pass away, but my words shall not pass away.''* **Matthew 24:35**

**FOR A MORE COMPREHENSIVE STUDY READ: ''ASTROLOGY'' AND ''SORCERY'' CHAPTERS.**

### PRAYER

Dear God, Please forgive me for believing in astrology and for reading those silly **horoscope** books! Forgive me for spending my money so foolishly. Please forgive me for all my sins. I turn away from all occult teachings! I will study my Bible so I can gain proper wisdom! I know that You gave me free will to make my own choices. I choose to become a Christian! I turn away from those influences which are false and totally against Your Word! Please come into my life and cleanse me of all my sins. I will confess to others that I am a Christian! I will never be ashamed of You! I know You love me and want what's best for me! I want to be assured that my future is in Your hands! I turn away from sin. I turn my life over to You! In Jesus' name, I pray. AMEN!

# HOW TO BECOME A BORN-AGAIN CHRISTIAN

**FIRST:** The Bible says you must **ACKNOWLEDGE** that you are a **sinner!** *"For all have sinned and come short of the glory of God."* **Romans 3:23** *"God be merciful to me a sinner."* **Luke 18:13** *"As it is written, There is none righteous, no, not one."* **Romans 3:10**

**SECOND:** The Bible says: *"Except ye REPENT, ye shall all likewise perish."* **Luke 13:3, 5** *"Repent ye therefore, and be converted, that your sins may be blotted out."* **Acts 3:19**

**THIRD:** The Bible says we must **CONFESS** our sins to God. *"If we confess our sins, he (God) is faithful and just to forgive us our sins, and to cleanse us from all unrighteousness."* **1 John 1:9** *"If we say that we have not sinned, we make him a liar, and his word is not in us."* **1 John 1:10**

**FOURTH:** The Bible says we must **FORSAKE** our sinful ways. *"Let the wicked forsake his way, and the unrighteous man his thoughts: and let him return unto the Lord for he will abundantly pardon."* **Isaiah 55:7**

**FIFTH:** The Bible says we must **BELIEVE.** *"For God so loved the world, that he gave his only begotten Son (Jesus), that whosoever believeth in him should not perish, but have everlasting life."* **John 3:16**

**SIXTH:** The Bible says we must **RECEIVE** JESUS. *"He (Jesus) came unto his own (the Jews), and his own received him not. But as many as receive him, to them gave he power to become the sons of God, even to them that believe on his name."* **John 1:11-12**

**ROMANS 10:9 says:** *"If thou shalt confess with thy mouth the Lord Jesus, and shalt believe in thine heart that God hath raised him (Jesus) from the dead, thou shalt be saved."*

**GOD WANTS TO SAVE YOU! HE WILL NEVER TURN ANYONE AWAY!** *"For whosoever shall call upon the name of the Lord shall be saved."* **Romans 10:13** *"And it shall come to pass, that whosoever shall call on the name of the Lord shall be saved."* **Acts 2:21** *"For the wages of sin is death; but the gift of God is eternal life through Jesus Christ our Lord."* **Romans 6:23**

**A genuine born-again Christian turns his entire life over to Christ! He serves only Christ as his Lord and Master!** Christ longs to be a part of your thoughts, actions, relationships, finances, your health, etc.

A genuine born-again Christian wants above everything else to do God's will! He is not ashamed to witness to others and tell them how to become a born-again Christian!

A genuine born-again Christian does not renig on his COMMITMENT to Christ to GROW SPIRITUALLY each day. He honors his commitment by daily feeding on God's Word! He studies the Scriptures and ASKS GOD FOR WISDOM AND UNDERSTANDING! He spends his time with other Christian friends!

A genuine born-again Christian is WATER BAPTISED After he has become a born-again Christian. He knows that water does not wash away sins, but he is obedient in being baptised as an act of faith. he wants to let the world see and know that he is following Christ's example!

A genuine born-again Christian JOINS A BIBLE BELIEVING CHURCH and is REGULAR IN ATTENDANCE! He is being obedient in paying his TITHES and OFFERINGS. He PRAYS FOR THE SICK. HE SUPPORTS HIS PASTOR. He prays for the body of believers, his pastor, and for all people, including the Jews!

## PRAYER

Dear God, I want to become a born-again Christian. I confess to You that I am a sinner. I ask You to forgive me for my sins and to blot them out from Your memory. I believe You sent Your only son to die on the cross to pay for my sins. I believe Jesus lives today! Come into my life and I will live for You from this moment on. I turn away from my sins. I confess I am now a Christian. I will tell others how they too might be saved. Thank You for allowing me to become a born-again Christian through Your loving kindness. In Jesus' name, I pray. AMEN!

# HUMANISM

**Definition:** A doctrine, attitude, or way of life centered on human interests or values. A philosophy that asserts the dignity and worth of man and his capacity for self-realization through reason and that often rejects supernaturalism.

## WHAT DO HUMANISTS BELIEVE?

They deny the deity of God, Christ, the Holy Spirit, and the Bible! They deny that salvation exists! (QUOTE FROM MANIFESTO #1:) **"Promises of immortal salvation or fear of eternal damnation are both illusory and harmful."** They deny the existence of heaven and hell. They deny man has an eternal soul. (QUOTE—MANIFESTO #1:) **"There is no credible evidence that life survives the death of the body."** They deny the Biblical account of creation. They reject the principal of right and wrong (and truth and lies) as being absolute! They believe all moral values are situational which each person can determine for himself! They write: **"The traditional dualism of mind and body must be rejected."** They teach sexual freedom between consenting individuals (regardless of age) including pre-marital sex, homosexuality, lesbianism and incest! (QUOTE: Manifesto #2:) **"Individuals should be permitted to express their sexual proclivities and pursue their life-styles as they desire! We believe that intolerant attitudes, often cultivated by orthodox religions and puritanical cultures, unduly repress sexual conduct. The right to birth control, abortion, and divorce should be recognized."** They dissolve the distinction between male and female, confusing their roles and relationships! They seek a unisex society! They believe in the right of abortion (Manifest #2)! They believe in euthanasia (mercy killing) (Manifesto %2)! They believe in the right to suicide (Manifesto #2)! They believe in equal distribution of America's wealth to reduce poverty! They believe in the free enterprise system; in disarmament, and the creation of a socialist one-world government! They seek to remove all traces of American patriotism! They justify genicide (the systematic killing or termination of people)! Abortion and euthanasia fall in this category! They propose it would be beneficial to terminate (kill) millions of our elderly, terminally ill, crippled, retarded, insane, etc. Humanists see mankind as a mechanical machine. They totally deny God's divine purpose for man. (QUOTE: Manifesto #1:) **"But we can discover no divine purpose or providence for the human species."** They regard the universe as self-existing and not created! They believe that man is a part of nature, and that he has emerged as the result of a continuous process. (QUOTE: Manifesto #1:) **"Science affirms that the human species is an emergence from natural evolutionary forces."** They believe that our intellect will convince us that we are our own gods! They believe that man and science has all the answers to our problems! They teach that the distinction between the sacred and the secular can no longer be maintained! They only believe in the "HERE and NOW!" They teach that when man dies . . . that's all there is! They teach that personal life and social well-being should replace worship and prayer! They do not believe in the supernatural (such as God, Christ, the Holy Spirit, Satan, demons and resurrected saints). They teach man must learn to be satisfied with himself and his own accomplishments, rather than realizing the needs of others! They evaluate, transform, control and direct the humanist philosophy on our children and there is nothing that parents can do about it! The remedy for this cancer is to enroll your child in a Christian school! They believe a socialized and cooperative economic order must be established to equally distribute the means of life! Humanists demand a fair share of the world's goods. They say the faith and religion our fathers had is no longer adequate and must go! They teach man is alone in this world and must think only for himself and be responsible only to himself—not his parents or God! They do not believe in nuclear war nor biological and chemical weapons to defend our country from an invasion!

**THE AUTHOR OF SECULAR HUMANISM IS SATAN!** Satan lied to Adam and Eve in the garden of Eden when he told them they would not die if they ate the fruit from the forbidden tree. He said God didn't want them to eat it because they would become gods knowing (determining for themselves) good and evil **(Genesis 3:1-5)!** He enticed them to disobey God and challenged them to determine for themselves what was good and evil! When they ate of the tree, they became the first members of the humanist religion under its priest, Satan! QUOTE: Humanist Manifesto #1 **"As nontheists, we begin with humans not God, nature not deity."**

**HUMANISM IS A RELIGION WITHOUT GOD, JESUS, THE HOLY SPIRIT, THE BIBLE, OR A CHURCH BUILDING!** They teach man to become his own god. THEY ARE ATHEISTS! They teach man he is totally independent of any need of a god, parent or anyone else! They teach man to "do his own thing!"

## Humanism

**TO EMBRACE HUMANISM WILL COST YOUR SOUL!** Jesus said that prior to His return there would arise a one-world false religion. It's here and it's called humanism! Read: Revelation 3:14-18, 20. "Laodicea" in Greek means "human rights" from which our word humanism is derived. Humanism has invaded every area of society, government, our educational system, and even our churches! Manifesto #1 Rule #10 states: **"There will be no uniquely religious emotions and attitudes of the kind hitherto associated with belief in the supernatural."**

**HUMANISM DENIES WE ARE BORN INTO THIS WORLD A SINNER AND NEED TO ASK GOD TO FORGIVE US — IF WE PLAN TO SPEND ETERNAL LIFE WITH JESUS!** To embrace humanism is to cheat yourself out of the love, forgiveness and blessings of God! Most Americans are totally unaware of this one-world religion, which will continue to grow, until Jesus returns and sets up His kingdom!

(Continued)

**THE GOAL OF THE HUMANIST IS TO BRING ABOUT THE ESTABLISHMENT OF A ONE-WORLD GOVERNMENT AND AN ATHEISTIC ONE-WORLD RELIGION!** It will be a new world order totally controlled by the state, under the auspices of Satan! The varities of humanism include: scientific, ethical, democratic, religious and marxist. The roots of modern humanism trace back to ancient China, classical Greece, and Rome!

**DIRECT QUOTE . . . MANIFESTO #2 PREFACE:**
"As in 1933 (when humanist manifesto #1 was written), humanists still believe that traditional theism, especially faith in the prayer-hearing God, assumed to love and care for persons, to hear and understand their prayers, and to be able to do something about them, is an unproved and outmoded faith. Salvationism, based on mere affirmation, still appears as harmful, diverting people with false hopes of heaven hereafter. Reasonable minds look to other means for survival."

**THE HUMANIST ULTIMATE GOAL IS TO CREATE A MASTER RACE THROUGH EXPERIMENTAL HUMAN BREEDING!** This is exactly what Hitler tried. They plan to eventually place man in a highly regulated environment, in order to control him!

**THEY SEEK TO TAKE AWAY OUR GOD GIVEN FREEDOMS!** Their philosophy teaches that man is no more than a machine — a piece of trash to be discarded when no longer desirable!

**HUMANIST MANIFESTO #2 SAYS THAT CHRISTIANITY HAS LOST ITS SIGNIFICANCE AND IS POWERLESS TO SOLVE THE PROBLEMS OF HUMANITY IN THE 20TH CENTURY!** (QUOTE:) "Traditional moral codes and newer irrational cults both fail to meet the pressing needs of today and tomorrow. False theologies of hope and messianic ideologies, substituting new dogmas for old, cannot cope with existing world realities. They separate rather than unite peoples . . . No deity will save us; we must save ourselves. Promises of immortal salvation or fear of eternal damnation are both illusory and harmful."

HUMANISTS ARE TRYING TO TAKE AWAY THE TRUE MEANING OF CHRISTMAS BY MAKING IT SOLELY COMMERCIAL. THEY REPLACE EASTER WITH A CELEBRATION TO THE VITAL FORCES OF NATURE AND THE RENEWAL OF MAN'S OWN ENERGIES!

HUMANISM IN GOVERNMENT IS A DEADLY SATANIC CANCER! Our government is being used as an agent to administer their philosophy! They have crept into every office of our government, our world leaders, politicians, public schools and even the United Nations!

**OUR PUBLIC SCHOOL SYSTEM TEACHES HUMANISM — EVEN THOUGH OUR CONSTITUTION REQUIRES THE SEPARATION OF CHURCH AND STATE!** Bible believers pay the expenses for this religion without being able to stop the humanistic doctrines that are being implanted in our children's minds! **The teaching technique known as "VALUES CLARIFICATION" was developed by Pavlov, under Lenin and Stalin, and is being taught in our public schools!** It teaches children to ignore their parents' teachings and religious beliefs. They are taught in the same way as the Russians train their animals! **2 Timothy 3:2 says:** *"This know also, that in the last days perilous times shall come. For men shall be lovers of their own selves, covetous, boasters, proud, blasphemers, disobedient to parents, unthankful, unholy, without natural affections* (homosexuals, lesbians, abortionists, sado-masochists, rapists, arsenists, hired killers, etc.), *trucebreakers, false accusers, incontinent* (loss of self-control), *fierce, despisers of those that are good, traitors, heady* (headstrong), *highminded* (egotists), *lovers of pleasures more than lovers of God; having a form of godliness, but denying the power of the Holy Spirit) thereof: from such turn away."*

**THEY ARE DETERMINED TO GRADUALLY ALIENATE A CHILD FROM HIS PARENTS!** *"Children obey your parents in the Lord: for this is right."* **Ephesians 6:1 READ: Colossians 3:20.** *"For rebellion is as the sin of witchcraft, and stubbornness is as iniquity and idolatry. . ."* **1 Samuel 15:23**

**HUMANISTS BROUGHT THE THEORY OF EVOLUTION INTO THE CLASSROOM AND TOOK PRAYER OUT!**

**HUMANIST PHILOSOPHY TEACHES YOU TO IGNORE ANY RESPONSIBILITY TO ANYONE ELSE!** *". . .Woe to the inhabiters of the earth and of the sea! for the devil is come down unto you, having great wrath, because he knoweth that he hath but a short time."* **Revelation 12:12**

**SATAN HAS PLANTED HUMANIST AGENTS IN MANY CHURCHES!** Matthew 13:18-30 tells us that tares (false doctrines) will creep up among good wheat (true Bible doctrines)! **Matthew 7:15 says:** *"Beware of false prophets, which come to you in sheep's clothing* (pretending to be holy), *but inwardly they are ravening wolves."* **Ephesians 6:11-13 says:** *"Put on the whole armour of God, that ye may be able to stand against the wiles of the devil. For we wrestle not against flesh and blood, but against principalities, against powers, against the rulers of the darkness* (evil forces) *of this world, against spiritual wickedness in high places, wherefore take unto you the whole armour of God, that ye may be able to withstand in the evil day, and having done all, to stand."*

**HUMANISM IS CONCERNED ONLY WITH THE PRESENT . . . CHRISTIANITY IS CONCERNED WITH ETERNITY!** Humanism disregards the possibility of sin. Christianity sees sin as man's disobedience to God's perfect will for our lives. Humanism is not concerned about man's soul. They teach: "You only go around once in this life, so take all the gusto you can get!"

**HUMANISTS CONTROL THE TEXTBOOKS IN MOST OF OUR SCHOOLS!** In the past 20 years the suicide rate in the 10-14 year age group has doubled and in the 15-19 year age group it is 3 times as high! Violent crime by young people has doubled in this decade. Drug and alcohol offenses have increased by 37 percent. Assaults on teachers has increased by 77 percent. In 1976 there were 7,000 violent assaults on teachers. In the U.S.A., students are allowed to physically assault their teachers because there is no code of conduct! Teachers are never allowed to spank their students! In most cities it's more dangerous to be a school teacher than a policeman! People under the age of 21 commit 78 percent of all auto thefts and 74 percent of all burglaries (according to the U.S. News & World Report). This age group commits 65 percent of all arsen — 62 percent of larcenies — 60 percent of robberies — 40 percent of rapes — 36 percent of aggravated assault, and 29 percent of murders! When the public schools teach our young people they're no more than a machine (or piece of junk) they react accordingly! Humanists teach them to totally disregard the moral standards of the Bible, and the teachings of their parents, and the world reaps violence and crime as a reward! Humanism is a result of the last days just as Christ described it would be! It's the oldest and most dangerous religion in the world. It's subtly designed to bring in socialism, atheism, and one-world government! ALERT YOUR FRIENDS AND FAMILY TO THE DANGERS OF HUMANISM BEFORE IT'S TOO LATE! (QUOTE: Manifesto #2:) **"Destructive ideological differences among communism, capitalism, socialism, conservatism, liberalism, and radicalism should be overcome."**

**ONLY ALMIGHTY GOD COULD LOVE AND FORGIVE THESE EVIL EDUCATORS AND GOVERNMENT OFFICIALS WHO BROUGHT SECULAR HUMANISM DOWN ON US!** God offers each one personal salvation in spite of their plan to take over His creation! We should pray for our leaders, our government, our teachers, our children and our churches! **Please join me in prayer for the signers of the Humanist Manifesto #1 & 2.** Many are the leading professors of the world, physicians, rabbis, Russian scientists, ministers, and the list encompasses the world!

# HUSBANDS

*"And the Lord caused a deep sleep to fall upon Adam, and he slept: and He took one of his ribs, and closed up the flesh instead thereof; and the rib, which the Lord God had taken from man, made he a woman, and brought her unto the man. And Adam said, this is now bone of my bones, and flesh of my flesh: and she shall be called woman, because she was taken out of man. Therefore shall a man leave his father and his mother, and shall cleave unto his wife: and they shall be one flesh."* **Genesis 2:21-25**

**GOD COMMANDS A HUSBAND TO LOVE HIS WIFE AND TREAT HER WITH RESPECT!** *"Husbands, love your wives, and be not bitter* (hateful, angry) *against them."* **Colossians 3:19**

**GOD'S PLAN IS FOR THE HUSBAND TO BE HEAD OF HIS HOUSEHOLD!** *"For the* **husband** *is head of the wife, even as Christ is the head of the church: and he* (Christ) *is the saviour of the body. Therefore as the church is subject unto Christ, so let the wives be to their own* **husbands** *in every thing."* **Ephesians 5:23-24 NOTE:** Obedience to the husband in all things is based upon the husband loving his wife in the same way Christ loves the church (born-again Christians). This does not give a husband license to demand unlawful things of his wife that would cause her to lose her soul. Christ must come first in the husband or wife's life! Read: **Matthew 22:37/Luke 14:26-27.**

**THE HUSBAND IS PART OF HIS WIFE AND IS ONE FLESH WITH HER!** *"Husbands, love your wives, even as Christ also loved the church, and gave himself for it."* **Ephesians 5:25** *"So ought men to love their wives as* (they do) *their own bodies. He that loveth his wife loveth himself. For no man ever yet hated his own flresh* (body), *but nourisheth and cherisheth it, even as the Lord* (does) *the church: For we are members of his* (Christ's) *body, of his flesh, and of his bones. For this cause shall a man leave his father and mother, and shall be joined unto his wife, and they two shall be* **one flesh.** *"* **Ephesians 5:28-31** *"Nevertheless let everyone of you in particular so love his wife even as himself: and the wife see that she reverence her* **husband.** *"* **Ephesians 5:33**

A husband is commanded to be faithful to his wife and to give her no excuse to sin! A husband is commanded to honor his wife, using his mental, physical and spiritual strength to protect her! A husband and wife are heirs together in life! *"Likewise, ye* **husbands** *dwell* (live) *with them according to knowledge* (which God gives), *giving honour unto the wife, as unto the weaker* (less physically robust) *vessel* (person), *and as being heirs together of the grace of life; that your prayers be not hindered* (because of the unfaithfulness of either person)." **1 Peter 3:7**

**A HUSBAND IS COMMANDED TO BE:** 1. Sober 2. Serious 3. Temperate 4. A Christian 5. Loving 6. Patient! **Titus 2:2**

**GOD'S DESIRE IS FOR A PERSON TO REMAIN A VIRGIN UNTIL HE MARRIES! THE BIBLE SAYS IT'S BETTER TO MARRY THAN TO HAVE UNCONTROLLED PASSION!** *". . .It is good for a man not to touch a woman. Nevertheless, to avoid fornication* (sex without marriage) *let every man have his own wife, and let every woman have her own* **husband.** *Let the* **husband** *render* (give) *unto the wife due benevolence* (kindness): *and likewise also the wife unto the* **husband.** *"* **1 Corinthians 7:1-3** *"If they cannot contain* (stay sexually pure) *let them marry: for it is better to marry than to burn* (with erotic passion)." **1 Corinthians 7:9**

**A HUSBAND AND WIFE BELONG TO EACH OTHER. NEITHER OF THEM HAS ANY AUTHORITY TO REFUSE WHAT THE OTHER PARTNER NEEDS. ALL ACTS OF PERVERSION OR UNNATURAL AFFECTION MUST BE TOTALLY REJECTED!** *"The wife hath not power of her own body, but the* **husband** (does): *and likewise also the* **husband** *hath not power of his own body, but the wife* (does)." **1 Corinthians 7:4**

**A HUSBAND SHOULD DO HIS PROPER SHARE OF EVERYTHING WITHIN THE MARRIAGE! THIS INCLUDES HIS SHARE OF THE RESPONSIBILITIES, FINANCES, TIME, ATTENTION, LOVE, RESPECT, SEX, OR ANYTHING ELSE UNLESS — THERE IS A MUTUAL CONSENT BETWEEN THEM!** *"Defraud ye not one the other, except it be with consent for a time* (a mutual agreement perhaps to abstain from sexual intercourse for a time), *that ye may give yourselves to fasting and prayer; and* (then) *come together again that Satan tempt you not for your incontinency* (failure to restrain your sexual appetite)." **1 Corinthians 7:5**

Husbands and wives have equal rights in the Scriptures. A husband should not divorce his wife (whether she is a Christian or not) if she does not want or deserve a divorce! *"And unto the married I* (Paul) *command, yet not I, but the Lord, Let not the wife depart* (divorce) *from her* **husband:** *But if she depart, let her remain unmarried; or be reconciled to her* **husband:** *and let not the* **husband** *put away* (divorce) *his wife . . . If any brother* (Christian) *hath a wife that believeth not* (is not a Christian), *and she be pleased to dwell with him, let him not put her away* (divorce her). *And the woman which hath a* **husband** *that believeth not, if he be pleased to dwell with her, let her not leave him."* **1 Corinthians 7:10-13**

God ordained a legal and Scriptural reason for divorce and remarriage. If the unbeliever refuses to live with a wife (or a husband) because of Christianity, the Christian is not under further marriage bonds. He (or she) is not held responsible to remain single the rest of his (or her) life because of the rebellion of the other. The Christian is to submit to the dissolving of the marriage contract under such circumstances! *"But if the unbelieving depart* (separates, divorces), *let him* (or her) *depart* (get a divorce). *A brother or sister* (Christian) *is not under bondage in such cases: but* (nevertheless) *God hath called us to peace."* **1 Corinthians 7:15**

(Continued)

**IF A MAN LIVES WITH A WOMAN IN A COMMON LAW RELATIONSHIP, IN GOD'S EYES HE IS MARRIED TO HER!** *"What? know ye not that he which is joined to an harlot is one body? for two, saith he (God), shall be one flesh."* **1 Corinthians 6:16** *"Flee fornication (sex without marriage). Every sin that a man doeth is without (outside) the (his) body; but he that committeth fornication sinneth against his own body (soul, spirit)."* **1 Corinthians 6:18**

**8 COMMANDS FOR HUSBANDS: 1. Be head of your wife:** Ephesians 5:23. **2. Love your wife as Christ loves the church:** Ephesians 5:25. **3. Love your wife as your own body:** Ephesians 5:28, 33. **4. Nourish, care for, protect:** Ephesians 5:29. **5. Cherish, foster, warm her in your bosom:** Ephesians 5:29/1 Thessalonians 2:7. **6. Be joined as one flesh and equal partners:** Ephesians 5:30-31. **7. Leave parents for your wife:** Ephesians 5:31/Genesis 2:21-25. **8. Cleave to your wife:** Ephesians 5:31/Matthew 19:5.

**A REMINDER TO HUSBANDS:** *"Thou shalt not take the name of the Lord thy God in vain."* **Exodus 20:7** *"Remember the sabbath day, to keep it holy."* **Exodus 20:8**

# IF I HAVE TOLD YOU EARTHLY THINGS AND YE BELIEVE NOT, HOW SHALL YE BELIEVE, IF I TELL YOU OF HEAVENLY THINGS?
## St. John III: 12

**IN CLOSING:** *"Let us not be desirous of vain glory, provoking one another, envying one another."* **Galatians 5:26**

### PRAYER
Dear God, Please forgive me for all my sins. I want to be saved. I want to do right by my wife. I know the Bible says that when a man finds a wife he finds a good thing. Teach me to be the spiritual leader of my household. I will ask my wife to forgive me for anything I have done to offend or oppress her! I will make things right with You and my wife! **I will set a good example of being a loving Christian husband, from this moment on!** I will hold up my end of all the responsibilities in my marriage, including family worship! I want to be the kind of Christian husband You want me to be! I am so sorry I have disappointed You! The Bible says that when we repent that You are faithful and just to forgive our sins and to blot them out! I ask You to do this for me! I will go to church! I will lead my family in studying the Bible! I don't want my marriage to end up in divorce! I thank You for opening my eyes as to how a husband should properly treat his wife! In Jesus' name, I pray. AMEN!

**If a husband commits adultery, God will judge him! And unless he repents and turns away from sin, he will not be allowed to inherit the kingdom of God!** *"Marriage is honourable in all (people, even priests), and the bed undefiled: but whoremongers and adulterers God will judge."* **Hebrews 13:4** *"Thou shalt not commit adultery."* **Exodus 20:14**

**WOMAN WAS NOT TAKEN OUT OF MAN'S HEAD TO BE "LORDED" OVER BY HIM — NOR FROM HIS FEET TO BE TRAMPLED ON BY HIM — BUT FROM HIS SIDE TO BE EQUAL WITH HIM — FROM UNDER HIS ARM TO BE PROTECTED BY HIM — AND FROM HIS HEART TO BE LOVED BY HIM!**

# HYPOCRITES

**DEFINITION:** A feigning to be what one is not or to believe what one does not; the false assumption of an appearance of virtue or religion; one who affects virtues or qualities he does not have; an act to make others believe something which is genuine.

**The dreams and hopes of a hypocrite shall perish if he doesn't get right with God!** *"So are the paths of all that forget God; and the hypocrite's hope shall perish."* **Job 8:13**

**The joy of a hypocrite can only last a moment. Wicked people can only triumph for a short while! Job 20:5**

**A HYPOCRITE DESTROYS HIS NEIGHBOUR WITH HIS MOUTH!** *"An hypocrite with his mouth destroyeth his neighbour: but through knowledge* (of God) *shall the just be delivered."* **Proverbs 11:9**

**Jesus said that people honour Him with their lips — but the hypocrite's heart is far removed from Him! Mark 7:6/12:15**

**Did you know that the increase in hypocrisy is a sign of the last days before Christ returns to earth?** *"Now the* (Holy) *Spirit speaketh expressly, that in the **latter times** some shall depart from the faith* (in God), *giving heed to seducing spirits, and doctrines of devils; speaking lies in **hypocrisy;*** (and) *having their conscience seared with a hot iron."* **1 Timothy 4:1-2 JESUS SAID:** *". . .O ye hypocrites, ye can discern the face of the sky* (predict the weather); *but can ye not discern the **signs** of the times?"* **Matthew 16:3/Luke 12:56**

**A HYPOCRITE IS AN EVIL DOER!** *"Therefore the Lord shall have no joy in their young men,* (and) *neither shall* (the Lord) *have mercy on their fatherless and widows: for every one is an **hypocrite and an evildoer,** and every mouth speaketh folly. For all this his anger is not turned away, but his hand is stretched out still* (inviting sinners to repent and be saved)." **Isaiah 9:17**

**Did you know that the Bibles calls Israel a "hypocritical nation" because of their refusal to accept Christ as their messiah? Isaiah 10:1-6**

**IF YOU ARE A HYPOCRITE, THIS QUESTION IS FOR YOU!** *"For what is the hope of the **hypocrite,** though he hath gained, when God taketh away his soul? Will God hear his cry when trouble cometh upon him? Will he delight himself in the Almighty? Will he always call upon God?"* **Job 27:8-10**

**A hypocrite can find fault with the other person, but never see his own faults!** *". . . Why beholdest* (see) *thou the mote* (splinter, particle of dust, speck) *that is in thy brother's eye, but perceivest not the beam* (log) *that is in thine eye? how canst* (can) *thou say to thy brother, Brother, let me pull out the mote* (speck) *that is in thine eye, when thou thyself beholdest not the beam* (splinter) *that is in thine own eye? Thou **hypocrite,** cast* (take) *out first the beam out of thine own eye, and then shalt thou see clearly to pull out the mote* (speck) *that is in thy brother's eye."* **Luke 6:41-42/Matthew 7:3-5   HYPOCRITES = MOCKERS! Psalm 35:16**

**Hypocrisy starts in the heart and if allowed to grow it soon becomes a killer of the soul!** *". . .The **hypocrites in heart** heap up* (God's) *wrath: they cry not when he bindeth them."* **Job 36:13**

**Jesus said that hypocrites pray and give money to churches, in order to receive glory and praise from men!** *"Take heed that ye do not your alms* (give $, etc., for the needy or charity) *before men, to be seen of them: otherwise ye have no reward of your Father which is in heaven. Therefore when thou doest thine alms, do not sound a trumpet before thee* (don't brag about what you're going to give), *as the **hypocrites** do in the synagogues and in the streets, that they may have glory of men. Verily I* (Christ) *say unto you, They have their reward. But when thou doest alms, let not thy left hand know what thy right hand doeth. That thine alms may be in secret: and thy Father* (God) *which seeth in secret himself shall reward thee*

*openly. And when thou prayest, thou shalt not be as the **hypocrites** are: for they love to pray standing in the synagogues and in the corners of the streets, that they may be seen of men. Verily, I say unto you, They have their reward. But thou, when thou prayest, enter into thy closet* (seek a room by yourself), *and when thou hast shut thy door, pray to thy Father* (God) *which is in secret* (cannot be seen); *and thy Father which seeth in secret shall reward thee openly."* **Matthew 6:1-6**

**Jesus said hypocrites disfigure their faces so people will think they are fasting (when they aren't) and will feel sorry for them and give them extra attention!** *"Moreover when ye fast, be not as the **hypocrites,** of a sad countenance: for they disfigure their faces, that they may appear unto men to fast. Verily I say unto you, They have their reward* (the praise they receive from man is their full receipt — they'll get nothing from God for their trickery)." **Matthew 6:16**

**At least 8 times Jesus called the Pharisees and Scribes "hypocrites" because they tried to entangle Him and tempt Him! Never did he fall prey to their lies, and deceit! When Jesus says, "Woe unto you," it means you are in real trouble!** *". . .Woe unto you, scribes and Pharisees, hypocrites! for ye shut up the kingdom of heaven against men: for ye neither go in yourselves, neither suffer* (allow) *ye them that are entering to go in. **Woe unto you, scribes and Pharisees, hypocrites!** for ye devour* (rob) *widows' houses, and for a pretence make long prayer: therefore ye shall receive the greater damnation* (from God). ***Woe unto you, scribes and Pharisees, hypocrites!** for ye compass* (travel) *sea and land to make one* (newcomer) *proselyte* (turn away from being of Gentile religion to Judaism), *and when he is made* (has turned away from his religion over to yours), *ye make him twofold* (twice) *more the child of hell than yourselves."* **Matthew 23:13-15** *"**Woe unto you, scribes and Pharisees, hypocrites!** "for ye pay tithe of mint* (a sweet scented plant) *and anise* (dill) *and cummin* (exotic food seasonings), *and have omitted the weightier matters of the law, judgement, mercy and faith: these ought ye to have done, and not to leave the other undone."* **Matthew 23:23** *"**Woe unto you, scribes and Pharisees, hypocrites!** for ye make clean the outside of the cup and of the platter, but within they are full of extortion and excess."* **Matthew 23:25** *"**Woe unto you, scribes and Pharisees, hypocrites!** for ye are like unto whited sepulchres, which indeed appear beautiful outward, but are within full of dead men's bones, and all uncleanness. Even so ye also outwardly appear righteous unto men, but within ye are full of **hypocrisy** and iniquity* (sin). ***Woe unto you, scribes and Pharisees, hypocrites!** because ye build the tombs of the prophets, and garnish the sepulchres of the righteous, and say, If we had been* (alive) *in the days of our fathers, we would not have been partakers with them in the blood of the prophets. Wherefore ye be witnesses unto yourselves, that ye are ṇe children of them which killed the prophets."* **Matthew 23:27-31/Luke 11:47-48** *"**Woe unto you, scribes and Pharisees, hypocrites!** for ye are as graves which appear not, and the men that walk over them are not aware of them."* **Luke 11:44**

**How can a hypocrite overcome this sin? Acknowledge that you have sinned! Repent and ask God to forgive you! Resist the devil when he tempts you to say or do anything which you know in your heart makes you a hypocrite! Invite God to give you wisdom. Read your Bible daily. Pray for guidance and patience. Control your tongue! Learn to love others as you do yourself! When you wrong someone, ask their forgiveness! Lean on God and He will direct you! God loves the hypocrite but hates the sin he commits! God wants you to turn away from this sin. He will help you if you will just humble yourself and ask Him!**

**PRAYER**

Dear God, Please forgive me for being a **hypocrite.** I am very unhappy with myself at this moment. I want to become a born-again Christian. Will You forgive me? I know You love me and want me to be saved. I know I have done wrong. I repent from the bottom of my heart. Please come into my life and I will live for You. Please help me daily in my Christian walk. Create in me a clean heart and mind. Help me guard what I say, where I go. I will pray and study my Bible! I know I am now a Christian and I thank You for having mercy on me. In Jesus' name, I pray. AMEN!

# HYPNOSIS

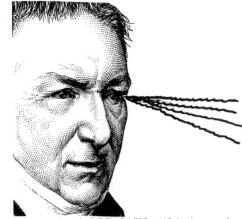

WHEN A PERSON **HYPNOTISES** HIS "SUBJECT" HE USES **MESMERISM**, WHICH IS DEFINED AS A **HYPNOTIC** INDUCTION USED TO INVOLVE **ANIMAL MAGNETISM** ... TO SPELLBIND ... FASCINATE ... MAKE IRRESISTABLE. THE HYPNOTIST ENTICES HIS SUBJECT TO HEAR AND OBEY ONLY HIS VOICE! **THE BIBLE SAYS THAT ANY PERSON WE SERVE AND OBEY (OTHER THAN THE ONE TRUE LIVING) GOD IS IDOLATRY! GOD HATES ALL FORMS OF IDOLATRY!**

**THE HYPNOTIST SAYS:** "Put your trust in me . . . you will listen to and obey my commands!" **GOD SAYS:** *"It is better to trust in the Lord than to put confidence in man."* **Psalm 118:8**

**THE HYPNOTIST SAYS:** "I have been trained in 'secret methods' the way to hypnotise you . . . I can implant new 'thought patterns' into your sub-consciousness!" **GOD SAYS:** *"The secret things belong unto the Lord our God: but those things which are revealed belong to us and to our children forever, that we may do all the words of this (God's) law."* **Deuteronomy 29:29**

**WHY WOULD ANYONE DELIBERATELY SURRENDER HIS SUB-CONSCIOUSNESS OVER TO A HYPNOTIST?** *"See, I have set before thee this day, life and good, and death and evil; in that I command thee this day to love the Lord thy God, to walk in his ways, and to keep his commandments and his statutes and his judgements, that thou mayest live and multiply: and the Lord thy God shall bless thee in the land whither thou goest to possess it. But if thine heart turn away, so that thou wilt not hear, but shalt be drawn away, and worship other gods, and serve them; I (God) denounce unto you this day, that ye shall surely perish, and that ye shall not prolong your days upon the land . . . I (God) call heaven and earth to record this day against you, that I have set before you life, and death, blessing and cursing: therefore choose life, that both thou and thy seed (descendants) may live."* **Deuteronomy 30:15-19**

**IF YOU HAVE A BAD PROBLEM . . . WHY GO TO A "SHRINK" OR A HYPNOTIST? ALL THE HELP YOU NEED IS JUST A PRAYER AWAY! (PRAY)** *"Wash me thoroughly from mine iniquity (wrongdoing), and cleanse me from my sin."* **Psalm 51:2**

**THE HYPNOTIST SAYS:** "Obey my voice!" He also says that your free will not allow you to say or do anything under **hypnosis** that is not natural and familiar to you. But, why would you want to surrender your free will? Especially when you don't have any way of knowing which master he serves? His master may be God or Satan! **GOD SAYS:** *"Stand fast therefore in the liberty (gospel) wherewith Christ hath made us free, and be not entangled again with the yoke of bondage."* **Galatians 5:1**

*"Know ye not, that to whom ye yield yourselves servants to obey; his servants ye are to whom ye obey: whether of sin unto death, or of obedience unto righteousness?"* **Romans 6:16**

**THE HYPNOTIST SAYS:** "I can help you overcome all your problems!" **GOD SAYS:** *"Our help is in the name of the Lord who made heaven and earth."* **Psalm 124:8**

**THE HYPNOTIST SAYS:** *"Relax, don't be afraid . . . No harm will come to you . . . You can trust me . . . You're falling deeper . . . deeper . . . deeper into sleep!"* **GOD TELLS US TO SAY:** *"What time I am afraid, I will trust in thee."* **Psalm 56:3**

**THE HYPNOTIST SAYS:** "Submit yourself into my hands . . . I will safely guide you into 'another dimension' . . . You will feel calm . . . You will be totally relaxed! **I don't know about you but if I'm going into another dimension, I want to know about it, and have something to say about where I go! I don't want to go** anyplace asleep or unconscious! **GOD SAYS:** *"Submit yourselves therefore to God. Resist the devil, and he will flee from you."* **James 4:7**

**THE HYPNOTIST SAYS:** "Don't be afraid . . . Look straight into my eyes . . . You are floating . . . You're getting sleepy . . . Your arms are so heavy you can't even lift them . . . You're floating . . . Trust me . . . I'll bring you back!" **GOD SAYS:** *"Cast all your cares upon Him; for he careth for you."* **1 Peter 5:7**

**THE HYPNOTIST SAYS:** "You are relaxed . . . You are falling, falling, falling . . . Sleep, sleep, sleep!" **GOD SAYS:** *"Be sober (awake), be vigilant (on guard); because your adversary the devil, as a roaring lion, walketh about, seeking whom he may devour."* **1 Peter 5:8**

**THE HYPNOTIST SAYS:** "You're getting drowsy . . . Sleep will be so peaceful . . . You can no longer open your eyelids . . . You cannot even lift your arm . . . You are totally under my power!" **GOD SAYS:** *"But the end of all things is at hand: be ye therefore sober (awake and serious), and watch unto prayer."* **1 Peter 4:7**

**THE HYPNOTIST SAYS:** "I am here to help you . . . You will hear and obey only the sound of my voice . . . I will safely lead you to say and do only the right things . . . I will help you with your problem!" **GOD SAYS:** *"For if a man think himself to be something when he is nothing, he deceiveth himself."* **Galatians 6:3**

**THE HYPNOTIST SAYS:** "Follow only my instructions!" **GOD SAYS:** *"Be ye therefore followers of God."* **Ephesians 5:1**

**THE HYPNOTIST SAYS:** "Everything is getting darker. . ." **GOD SAYS:** *"Have no fellowship with the unfruitful works of darkness, but rather reprove them."* **Ephesians 5:11**

**HYPNOSIS FALLS INTO THE CATEGORY OF THE OCCULT! ANYONE WHO "CASTS A SPELL" ON ANOTHER PERSON IS PRACTICING WITCHCRAFT! FOR A MORE DETAILED EXPLANATION READ: "ENCHANTMENTS".**

**A PERSON WHO USES A HYPNOTIST IS DOUBLE-MINDED!** He falsely thinks the hypnotist has special powers to help him! He thinks the **hypnotist** has all the answers! *"A double minded man is unstable in all his ways."* **James 1:8** *"Draw nigh to God, and he will draw nigh to you. Cleanse your hands, ye sinners; and purify your hearts, ye **double minded.**"* **James 4:8**

There may be many safe experts in this type of mind control. But I would not do anything deliberately to forfeit my own self-control! The choice is up to you, however!

**PRAYER**

Dear God, Please forgive me for all my sins. Please help me to never forget that You can and will give me all the help I need. I know I can trust You! I repent of all my sins. Help me with my problems and bad habits! I will do my part to make this happen! I want to be the kind of person You want me to be! In Jesus' name, AMEN!

# IDLENESS

**THERE IS AN AGE-OLD EXPRESSION WHICH SAYS: "IDLENESS IS THE DEVIL'S WORKSHOP!"**

**JESUS COMMANDS US TO OCCUPY (WORK, STAY BUSY) UNTIL HE RETURNS TO PLANET EARTH!** *"And he* (Jesus) *called his ten servants, and delivered them ten pounds* (or $17,000 ea.), *and said unto them,* **occupy** *till I come."* **Luke 19:13** *"Till I come, give attendance to* **reading,** *to* **exhortation,** *to* **doctrine."** **1 Timothy 4:13**

**WHAT CAN A PERSON DO TO DEFEAT IDLENESS? SPEND MORE TIME STUDYING THE SCRIPTURES! BECOME MORE GODLY!** *"But godliness with contentment is great gain."* **1 Timothy 6:6** *"Study to shew thyself approved unto God, a workman* (laborer) *that needeth not to be ashamed, rightly dividing* (interpreting) *the word of truth."* **2 Timothy 2:15**

**GOD SAID WOMEN SHOULD NOT BE IDLE EVEN WHEN THEY'RE AT HOME!** *"She looketh well to the ways of her household* (is a good manager, uses economy), *and eateth not the bread of* **idleness."** **Proverbs 31:27 NOTE:** That verse means that the woman uses her intelligence to see that her children behave and have the right kind of friends. All who are allowed to enter her house are decent. She teaches those in her house to have faith in God. She is well informed in timely events and how they relate to her family. She understands many things. She sets an example of godliness. **She knows that idleness leads to discontentment,** so she sees that each person has his own work to perform, his proper share of food, clothes, etc. She sees to it that good education comes next in importance to faith in God. She takes her family to church. She helps her children in their education. She excels as a wife, mother, religious leader. She is interested in the business world.

AN **IDLE PERSON** USUALLY RESORTS TO **IDLE CHATTER** INSTEAD OF FINDING SOMETHING CONSTRUCTIVE TO DO WITH HIS HANDS AND MIND! **GOD HATES IDLE CHATTER!** *"But shun profane* (vulgar) *and vain babblings: for they will increase unto more ungodliness."* **2 Timothy 2:16**

# IDLE CHATTER

Christians should be busy witnessing, praying for the sick, assisting in charitable work, visiting those in hospitals, and nursing homes, and teaching in church! Christians should never resort to idleness! *". . .And Let every one that nameth the name of Christ depart from iniquity* (wrong doing, **idleness, idle chatter**)." **2 Timothy 2:19**

**IDLENESS LEADS TO UNPRODUCTIVE DAY DREAMING!** *"Flee also youthful lusts: but follow righteousness, faith, charity, peace, with them that call on the Lord out of a pure heart. But foolish and unlearned questions avoid, knowing that they do gender strifes. And the servant of the Lord must not strive; but be gentle unto all men, apt to teach, patient, in meekness instructing those that oppose themselves; if God peradventure will give them repentance to the acknowledging of the truth; And* **that they may recover themselves out of the snare of the devil, who are taken captive by him at his will."** **2 Timothy 2:22-26**

**IDLENESS CAUSES A PERSON TO SLEEP A LOT. GOD SAYS DON'T DO THIS! HE SAYS STAY BUSY!** *"Slothfulness* (laziness, idleness) *casteth into a* **deep sleep;** *and an* **idle soul shall suffer hunger."** **Proverbs 19:15**

**GOD REFERS TO THE CITY OF SODOM AS HAVING BEEN FULL OF PRIDE, FOOD, AND AN ABUNDANCE OF IDLENESS!** *"And they were haughty, and committed abomination* (terrible sins) *before me: therefore I took them away* (by flood) *as I saw good* (the proper thing to do)." **Ezekiel 16:50**

According to the Scriptures, idleness is a result of laziness! Idleness is often referred to as being "slothful"! Not only does an idle man neglect to maintain his roof so it won't leak and the rafters rot and fall through, he probably doesn't maintain his spiritual life! *"By much* **slothfulness** (idleness, laziness) *the building decayeth; and through* **idleness of the hands** *the house droppeth through* (the roof)." **Ecclesiastes 10:18**

# IDLENESS

### PRAYER

Dear God, Please forgive me for feeling sorry for myself because I have too much time on my hands. I'm **idle** most of the time, as You know! Please forgive me for all my sins. Please give me new directions whereby I can overcome this condition. Tell me what You would like for me to do to stay busy! I want to work for You. I will read my Bible and pray. I need a Christian challenge to keep my mind occupied. **Please help me overcome being idle!** In Jesus' name, I pray. AMEN!

# IDOLATRY

*". . .we know that an idol is nothing in the world, and that there is none other God but one."* **1 Corinthians 8:4**

**GOD FORBIDS US TO WORSHIP IDOLS!** *"Thou shalt have no other gods before me."* **Exodus 20:3** *"Thou shalt not make unto thee any* **graven image,** *or any likeness of any thing that is in heaven above, or that is in the earth beneath, or that is in the water under the earth: Thou shalt not bow down thyself to them, nor serve them: for I the Lord thy God am a jealous God, visiting the iniquity of the fathers upon the children unto the third and fourth generation of them that hate me; And shewing mercy unto thousands of them that love me, and keep my commandments."* **Exodus 20:4-6** *"Turn ye not unto* **idols,** *nor make to yourselves* **molten gods:** *I am the Lord your God."* **Leviticus 19:4** *"Ye shall not make with me* **gods of silver,** *neither shall ye make unto you* **gods of gold."** **Exodus 20:23** *"Ye shall make you no* **idols nor graven image,** *neither rear you up a* **standing image,** *neither shall ye set up any* **image of stone** *in your land, to bow down unto it: for I am the Lord your God."* **Leviticus 26:1/Deuteronomy 5:7-10**

**SOME MODERN FORMS OF IDOLATRY WHICH MILLIONS OF PEOPLE WORSHIP TODAY ARE:** Money, drugs, sex, alcohol, politics, antiques, tranquilizers, gold, homosexuality, incest, sodomy, fast cars, fortune tellers, junk food, cigarettes, playing the stock market, switching marriage partners, gambling, forging checks, suing for profits, psychiatrists, Yoga, physical fitness, football, television, ouija boards, horoscopes, crystal balls, ESP, palmistry, reincarnation, pornographic movies and magazines, all false religions-cults, and the list goes on and on, with no end!

*"Cursed be the man that maketh any graven or molten image, an abomination unto the Lord, the work of the hands of the craftsman, and putteth it in a secret place. And all the people shall answer and say, amen (we agree)."* **Deuteronomy 27:15**

*"And what agreement hath the temple of God with idols? For ye are the temple of the living God; as God hath said, I will dwell in them, and walk in them; and I will be their God and they shall be my people. Wherefore come out from among them (idol worshippers), and be ye separate, saith the Lord, and touch not the unclean thing: and I (God) will receive you. And will be a father unto you, and ye shall be my sons and daughters, saith the Lord almighty."* **2 Corinthians 6:16-18**

Since the beginning of time idols have been worshipped by people of all races! They have been used as part of festivities, in black magic, in connection with human sacrifices, in the burning of incense, in connection with pagan prayers, music and dancing! They have been kissed and bowed down to. God hates idolatry.

Idols are the work of men's hands: Jeremiah 10:3. Idols may be plated with silver or gold: Jeremiah 10:4. Idols are usually secured in place to prevent them from falling: Jeremiah 10:4. Idols cannot move or speak: Jeremiah 10:4-5. Idols have to be carried around by man: Jeremiah 10:5. Idols cannot do good or evil - they are useless: Jeremiah 10:5. Idols have no breath of life: Jeremiah 10:14. Idols are a work of vanity: Jeremiah 10:8, 15. Idols are a work of many errors: Jeremiah 10:15. Idols defile you: Ezekiel 22:3-4/23:7/20:7, 18. Idols pollute you: Ezekiel 23:30/Acts 15:20. Idols are dumb: 1 Corinthians 12:2. Idols are useless! They cannot see, hear, walk, nor save you: Revelation 9:20.

**GOD PROMISES TO DESTROY ALL IDOLS:** Exodus 23:24/34:13/Leviticus 26:30/Numbers 33:52/Deuteronomy 7:5, 25/Isaiah 2:18

*"For thou shalt worship no other God: for the Lord, whose name is jealous, is a jealous God."* **Exodus 34:14**

*"If thou serve their gods* (idols), *it will surely be a snare* (trap) *unto thee."* **Exodus 23:33** *"Their land also is full of idols; they worship the work of their own hands, that which their own fingers have made."* **Isaiah 2:8** *"Thou shalt not bow down to their* **gods,** *nor serve them, nor do after their works: but thou shalt utterly overthrow them, and quite break down their images."* **Exodus 23:24** *"Neither be ye idolaters, as were some of them; as it is written, The people sat down to eat and drink, and rose up to play."* **1 Corinthians 10:7** *"My children, keep yourselves from idols."* **1 John 5:21**

*"Thy graven images also will I (God) cut off, and thy standing images out of the midst of thee; and thou shalt no more worship the work of thine hands."* **Micah 5:13**

**GOD COMMNANDS US TO FLEE FROM IDOLATRY!** *"Wherefore, my dearly beloved, flee from idolatry."* **1 Corinthians 10:14**

*"What profiteth the* **graven image** *that the maker thereof hath graven it; the* **molten image,** *and a teacher of lies, that the maker of his work trusteth therein, to make* **dumb idols?** *Woe unto him that saith to the wood, awake: to the* **dumb stone;** *arise, it shall teach! Behold, it is laid over with gold and silver, and* **there is no breath at all in the midst of it.** *But the Lord is in His holy temple: let all the earth keep silence before Him."* **Habakkuk 2:18-20**

People who worship any form of idolatry should repent, get saved, and turn away from this sin or he will not be allowed to enter heaven! *"Know ye not that the unrighteous shall not inherit the kingdom of God? Be not deceived, neither fornicators, nor* **idolaters,** *nor adulterers, nor effeminate, nor abusers of themselves with mankind, nor thieves, nor covetous, nor drunkards, nor revilers, nor extortioners, shall inherit the kingdom of God."* **1 Corinthians 6:9-10**

**PRAYER**

Dear God, I am guilty of worshipping other things instead of worshipping You! I am guilty of not putting You first and foremost in my life! Please forgive me. Come into my life and I will serve You. I know that everything I have worked and saved for could be taken away from me in a matter of seconds and that only my rewards in Heaven can last! From this moment on, I will serve You! I give You my total allegiance. I will live for You! I ask You to forgive all my sins. In Jesus' name, AMEN!

# INCEST

**DEFINITION:** Sexual intercourse with persons so closely related that they are forbidden by law to marry; also: the statutory crime of such a relationship.

Statistics tell us that today in **one out of every ten American homes incest has or is being committed!** WHAT CAUSES A PERSON TO INFLICT THIS SIN UPON ANOTHER PERSON? SATAN!

**INCEST RUINS LIVES!** The act of **incest** can even **kill** a small child! And it may cause a person to be suicidal even if he is the innocent victim! In any event, **incest** always leaves a person disillusioned and with feelings of guilt and shame. In many cases these feelings may never go away! It is so important for the person who has taken advantage of another person through **incest** to ask God to forgive him or her! God loves every person on this earth and He is totally forgiving!

**The rising increase in incest fulfills end time prophecy regarding the last days before Christ returns!** *"And ye shall be betrayed both by parents, and brethren, and kinsfolks, and friends; and some of you shall they cause to be put to death."* **Luke 21:16**

**INCEST = CONFUSION! READ: Leviticus 20:12**

*"None of you shall approach to any that is near of kin to him, to uncover their nakedness. . ."* **Leviticus 18:6**

### DO NOT HAVE SEX WITH YOUR:
**FATHER:** Leviticus 18:7/Genesis 19:31-38
**MOTHER:** Leviticus 18:7
**FATHER'S WIFE:** Leviticus 18:8/20:11/Deuteronomy 27:20/Genesis 35:22/2 Samuel 16:20-23/1 Kings 2:17/1 Corinthians 5:1-5
**SISTER:** Leviticus 18:9
**FATHER'S DAUGHTER:** Leviticus 18:9/Genesis 20:12/2 Samuel 13:12, 16, 20
**MOTHER'S DAUGHTER:** Leviticus 18:9
**MOTHER'S SON'S DAUGHTER:** Leviticus 18:10
**DAUGHTER'S DAUGHTER:** Leviticus 18:10
**FATHER'S WIFE'S DAUGHTER:** Leviticus 18:11
**FATHER'S SISTER:** Leviticus 18:12/Exodus 6:20
**FATHER'S BROTHER:** Leviticus 18:14
**BROTHER'S WIFE:** Leviticus 18:14
**DAUGHTER-IN-LAW:** Leviticus 18:15
**ANY IN-LAW'S:** Leviticus 20:12, 21

In the Old Testament there was a death penalty law for the crime of incest! Death was to be executed by burning or by hanging! Leviticus 20:11-14, 20 Jesus came to pay the penalty on the cross for our sins so we can be saved. **God wants to save the person who commits incest!** *"This I say them, Walk in the* (Holy) *Spirit, and ye shall not fulfil the lust of the flesh."* **Galatians 5:16**

**Unless a person repents, asks forgiveness, and turns away from committing incest, he will never see heaven!"** *". . .they which do such things **shall not inherit the kingdom of God.**"* **Galatians 5:21** *"Be not deceived: God is not mocked: for whatsoever a man* (person) ***soweth,** that shall he also **reap.**"* **Galatians 6:7** *"Know ye not that the unrighteous **shall not inherit the kingdom of God?** Be not deceived: neither fornicators, nor idolaters, nor adulterers, nor effeminate, **nor abusers of themselves with mankind*** (incest, rape, sex perverts, sodomy, homosexuality, etc.), *nor thieves, nor covetous, nor drunkards, nor revilers, nor extortioners shall inherit the kingdom of God."* **1 Corinthians 6:9-10/1 Timothy 1:10** *"For whosoever shall commit any of these abominations, even the souls that commit them shall be cut off* (totally separated from God) *from among their people. Therefore shall ye keep my ordinance, that ye commit not any one of these abominable customs, which were committed before you, and that ye*

*defile not yourselves therein: I am the Lord your God."* **Leviticus 18:29-30**

*"Now we know that God heareth not sinners: but if any man be a worshipper of God, and doeth His will, him He heareth."* **John 9:31**

*"For if ye forgive men their trespasses* (sins), *your heavenly father will also forgive you: but if ye forgive not men their trespasses, neither will your father* (God) *forgive your trespasses."* **Matthew 6:14-15**

If you have committed **incest,** or you're the **victim** of this terrible unmerciful act, don't seek vengeance! Vengeance and justice belongs only to Almighty God! **Jesus says we must forgive those who wrongfully use us.** He said we should forgive seventy times seven times! Even if you're a child, you can seek help from a minister, doctor, teacher, neighbor, or call the police! Pray, and ask God to forgive you and the other person! God promises He will and God cannot lie! He will also help you get out of that situation. And He will give you peace!

*"For the eyes of the Lord are over the righteous, and His ears are open unto their prayers: but the face of the Lord is against them that do evil."* **1 Peter 3:12**

### PRAYER FOR THE ASSAILANT:
Dear God, **I am guilty of committing incest!** I am so ashamed! Guilt is eating me up alive! I need to feel release from my shame! Please forgive me and help me. I desperately need Your help because I have messed everything up! Please come into my heart and forgive me. Please take away my guilt and replace it with peace. **I repent that I have sinned against You, myself, and another!** In Jesus' name, AMEN!

### PRAYER FOR THE VICTIM
Dear God, **I am a victim of incest!** I feel shame, hatred and vengeance! I feel dirty, helpless and ugly. I know that You love me! I am not guilty of having encouraged this crime against my body and soul! Please show me happiness in exchange for my sorrow! Please forgive me for all my sins! I forgive the person who did this to me! **I will not seek vengeance!** I will seek help from others so that I will not feel forced to live under the same roof with the person who did this terrible thing to me! Help me forget . . . Come very close to me . . . I need You! In Jesus' name, AMEN!

# INCOME TAX EVASION

**GOD CREATED HUMAN GOVERNMENT!** *"...we know that the law is good, if a man use it lawfully..."* **1 Timothy 1:8**

**GOD CREATED HUMAN GOVERNMENT FOR THE LAWLESS!** *"...the law is not made for a righteous man, but for the lawless and disobedient, for the ungodly and for sinners, for unholy and profane, for murderers of fathers and murderers of mothers, for manslayers (murderers, abortionists), for whoremongers, for them that defile themselves with mankind (rape, incest, all sex sins), for menstealers (kidnappers), for liars, for perjured persons, and if there be any other thing that is contrary to sound doctrine."* **1 Timothy 1:9-10**

In order to maintain peace and security, God commanded us to obey human government! *"Let every soul be subject unto the higher powers (from the president, king, or other ranks of government). For there is no power but (what is ordained) of God: the powers that be (that exist) are ordained of God. Whosoever therefore resisteth the power (of government, and God), resisteth the ordinance of God: and they that resist shall receive to themselves damnation."* **Romans 13:1-2**

The Bible says: the person who disobeys God's laws, and the laws of human government, should fear the consequences from God and man! *"For rulers are not a terror to good works, but to the evil. Wilt (won't) thou then not be afraid of the power (of God and human government)? do that which is good, and thou shalt have praise of the same (God and human government which He alone ordained)."* **Romans 13:3**

**GOD CREATED HUMAN GOVERNMENT SO INJUSTICE WOULD NOT GO UNPUNISHED!** *"Love worketh no ill to his neighbour: therefore love is the fulfilling of the law."* **Romans 13:10**

**LAW BREAKERS DO NOT HAVE THE HOLY SPIRIT ABIDING IN THEM!** *"And he that keepeth his (God's) commandments dwelleth in him, and he in him. And hereby we know that he abideth in us, by the (Holy) Spirit which he hath given us."* **1 John 3:24**

If you say you love God and transgress the laws of our land—you are a liar and a thief! God loves honesty, justice and fairness! Romans 13:13

To avoid paying income tax is to steal from the government and from God! Perhaps you'd never consider robbing a bank, or holding up a "Brinks" truck! But, when you don't pay your share of taxes you willfully disobey God and His laws for human government! Exodus 20:15 and Deuteronomy 5:19 say: *"Thou shalt not steal."* Deuteronomy 5:20 says: *"Neither shalt thou bear false witness against thy neighbour (anyone)."*

**JESUS SAID:** *"Render (pay) therefore unto Caesar (human government) the things which be (owed to) Caesar's and unto God the things which be God's."* **Luke 20:25**

**INCOME TAX EVASION IS A WILLFUL ACT TO DISOBEY GOD!** *"Whosoever committeth sin transgresseth also the law: for sin is the transgression of the law."* **1 John 3:4**

**A BORN-AGAIN CHRISTIAN SHOULD NEVER BE GUILTY OF NOT PAYING INCOME TAX!** *"He that committeth sin is of the devil: for the devil sinneth from the beginning. For this purpose the Son of God (Jesus) was manifested (made known to man), that he might destroy the works of the devil. Whosoever is born of God (a born-again Christian) doth not commit sin; for his seed remaineth in him: and he cannot sin, because he is born of God. In this the children of God are manifest (made known) and (also) the children of the devil: Whosoever doeth not righteousness is not of God, neither he that loveth not his brother."* **1 John 3:8-10**

*"Wherefore the law (of God and God ordained human government) is holy, and the commandment holy, and just, and good."* **Romans 7:12**

If you don't pay your share of income tax God says you won't have a clear conscience! *"For he (all government officials) is the minister (servant of the law) of God to thee for good (and not evil). But if thou do that which is evil (such as not paying income tax), be afraid; for he (those in authority) beareth not the sword in vain (punishment is authorized by God, even to the point of execution): for he is the minister (civil servant) of God, a revenger to execute wrath upon him that doeth evil. Wherefore ye must needs be subject (are commanded to obey), not only for wrath (to escape jail, prison, execution), but also for (your) conscience sake."* **Romans 13:4-5**

All enforcement officers who carry out the laws of the land and defend the just are to be supported by paying our share of taxes! This is God's plan for our lives! *"For this cause (to protect the community and to uphold the law abiding citizens in safety) pay ye tribute (fair share of taxes) also: for they are God's ministers (servants who uphold justice), attending continually upon this very thing (peace and safety). Render (pay) therefore to all their dues: tribute (tax money, salaries, etc.) to whom tribute is due; custom to whom custom; fear to whom fear; honour to whom honour."* **Romans 13:6-7**

God is not mocked! He sees and knows everything we do! And He ordained human government for our peace of mind, our safety, our school system, and the list is unending! God knows that there are law breakers in our civil system, but he will straighten out everything in the end! *"Not everyone that saith unto me, Lord, Lord, shall enter into the kingdom of heaven; but he that doeth the will of my Father which is in heaven."* **Matthew 7:21**

**IN CLOSING:** *"And whosoever will not do the law of thy God, and the law of the king (or president), let judgement be executed speedily upon him, whether it be unto death, or to banishment, or to confiscation of goods, or to imprisonment."* **Ezra 7:26**

### PRAYER

Dear God, Please forgive me for all my sins. **Please forgive me for stealing money from the government by not paying my income tax!** Please forgive me for those times **I cheated on my income tax** and when I failed to pay traffic tickets! Forgive me for every sin I have ever committed. I know You love me and want what's best for my life. I thank You for being merciful! I will obey Your laws because I know they are good and right for my life! I want to spend eternity with Jesus. Thank You for forgiving all my sins! In Jesus' name, I pray. AMEN!

# INDECISION

**INDECISION SEPARATES A PERSON FROM RECEIVING GOD'S BLESSINGS!** *"I call heaven and earth to record this day against you, that I have set before you life and death, blessing and cursing: Therefore choose life* (through becoming a born-again Christian), *that both thou and thy seed* (children) *may live: That thou mayest love the Lord thy God, and that thou mayest obey his voice, and that thou mayest cleave unto him: for he is thy life, and the length of thy days; That thou mayest dwell in the land which the Lord sware unto thy fathers . . . to give them."* **Deuteronomy 30:19-20**

**TODAY IS THE DAY TO MAKE THE MOST REWARDING DECISION YOU WILL EVER MAKE! WHY NOT CHOOSE TO FOLLOW GOD NOW, BEFORE IT'S TOO LATE?** *"Choose you this day whom ye will serve; . . . But as for me and my house, we will serve the Lord."* **Joshua 24:15**

**GOD COMMANDS US NOT TO CHOOSE SATAN. HE IS THE OPPRESSOR!** *"Envy thou not the oppressor* (Satan), *and choose none of his ways."* **Proverbs 3:31**

**WHAT HAPPENS IF YOU REMAIN NEUTRAL AND CHOOSE NOT TO FOLLOW GOD? IF YOU DON'T CHOOSE TO FOLLOW GOD . . . YOU AUTOMATICALLY CHOOSE TO FOLLOW SATAN! THE BIBLE SAYS THERE ARE ONLY 2 MASTERS!** *". . .Except ye repent, ye shall all likewise perish."* **Luke 13:3, 5** *"No man can serve two masters: for either he will hate the one, and love the other; or else he will hold to the one, and despise the other. Ye cannot serve God and mammon* (riches)." **Matthew 6:24**

**NO MAN IS AN ISLAND! EITHER HE SERVES GOD OR HE SERVES SATAN — THERE'S NOTHING IN BETWEEN!** *"For whosoever exalteth himself shall be abased; and he that humbleth himself* (and realizes that he needs God) *shall be exalted* (in God's kingdom)." **Luke 14:11**

**JESUS SAID:** *"Behold, I stand at the door* (your heart), *and knock: if any man hear my voice, and open the door* (to his heart), *I will come in to him, and will sup with him, and he with me.* **To him that overcometh will I grant to sit with me in my throne,** *even as I also overcame, and am set down with my Father in his throne."* **Revelation 3:20-21**

**GOD HATES INDECISION. HE WILL NOT TOLERATE IT!** *"I know thy works* (thoughts, actions), *that thou art neither cold nor hot* (neither love nor hate God): *I would* (wish) *thou wert* (were) *cold or hot. So then because thou art lukewarm, and neither cold nor hot, I will spue* (vomit) *thee out of my mouth."* **Revelation 3:15-16**

**THE RISING INCREASE IN INDECISION FULFILLS END TIME PROPHECY REGARDING THE LAST DAYS BEFORE CHRIST RETURNS!** *"This know also, that in the last days* (before Christ returns) *perilous times shall come. For men shall be lovers of their own selves* (indecisive and indifferent about following God), *covetous, boasters, proud, blasphemers, disobedient to parents, unthankful, unholy, without natural affection, trucebreakers, false accusers, incontinent* (uncontrolled), *fierce, despisers of those that are good, traitors, heady, highminded, lovers of pleasures more than lovers of God; having a form of godliness, but denying the power thereof: from such turn away."* **2 Timothy 3:1-5** *"For the time will come when they will not endure sound doctrine; but after their own lusts shall they heap to themselves teachers, having itching ears; and they shall turn away their ears from the truth, and shall be turned unto fables."* **2 Timothy 4:3-4**

**WHY ARE SO MANY PEOPLE INDECISIVE? BECAUSE THEY'RE ALWAYS DOING AND LEARNING WORLDLY THINGS! THEY STUDY FALSE THEORIES SUCH AS "I'M OKAY, YOU'RE OKAY!" THEY DON'T SPEND TIME LEARNING WHAT GOD, OUR CREATOR, HAS TO SAY FOR THEIR LIFE!** *"Ever learning, and never able to come to the knowledge of the truth."* **2 Timothy 3:7** *"But shun profane and vain babblings: for they will increase unto more ungodliness."* **2 Timothy 2:16**

**MANY PEOPLE STUDY THE WRONG MATERIALS! GOD SAYS WE MUST STUDY THE SCRIPTURES OR WE WILL BE ASHAMED WHEN WE STAND BEFORE HIM FACE TO FACE!** *"Study to shew thyself approved unto God, a workman* (student) *that needeth not to be ashamed, rightly dividing* (understanding) *the word of truth* (the scriptures)." **2 Timothy 2:15**

*"He that is not with me is against me: and he that gathereth not with me scattereth."* **Luke 11:23**

# indecision

### PRAYER

Dear God, I know that You created the universe and everything in it including me! I know that I cannot save myself. I ask You to forgive all my sins. I turn away from the confusion of being indecisive! I accept You as my Lord and Saviour. Come into my heart and live in me. In Jesus' name, I thank You for saving my soul! AMEN!

# INHERITANCE

*"Riches and honour are with me* (God); *yea, durable riches and righteousness. My fruit* (gift) *is better than gold, yea, than fine gold; and my revenue than choice silver. I lead in the way of righteousness, in the midst of the paths of judgement. That I may cause those that love me to inherit substance; and I will fill their treasures."* **Proverbs 8:18-21**

To receive an inheritance of wisdom (from God) is far better than receiving an inheritance of millions of dollars! *"Receive my instruction, and not silver; and knowledge rather than choice gold. For wisdom is better than rubies; and all the things that may be desired are not to be compared to it."* **Proverbs 8:10-11**

*"For what shall it profit a man, if he shall gain the whole world, and lose his own soul?"* **Mark 8:36**

Some of the richest people in the world are the most unhappy! This is because they don't put God first in their life or use their wealth to support God's work! When a person gives his inheritance (or a large part of it) to be used for the Lord's work, God promises him a reward for his consecration! *"And every one that hath forsaken houses, or brethren, or sisters, or father, or mother, or wife, or children, or lands, for my name's sake, shall receive an hundredfold, and shall* **inherit everlasting life.** *"* **Matthew 19:29** *"Then shall the King* (Jesus) *say unto them on his right hand, Come, ye blessed of my Father,* **inherit the kingdom** *prepared for you from the foundation of the world."* **Matthew 25:34**

No inheritance will last, unless a person freely gives it back to the Lord! If a person loves his money more than he loves God, he worships a false God which can never save him! *"Wealth gotten by vanity shall be diminished: but he that gathereth by labour shall increase."* **Proverbs 13:11** *"Every good gift and every perfect gift is from above, and cometh down from the Father of lights, with whom is no variableness, neither shadow of turning."* **James 1:17**

It's true that you can't take your money with you! It's also true that the wealth of a sinner will be used for the just . . . this is God's law of reciprocity! *"A good man leaveth an* **inheritance** *to his children's children: and the wealth of the sinner is laid up for the just."* **Proverbs 13:22**

**MONEY WON'T BUY YOU ANYTHING IN THE DAY OF GOD'S WRATH!** *"Riches profit not in the day of wrath: but righteousness delivereth from death* (eternal separation from God)." **Proverbs 11:4**

**HERE'S THE BEST KIND OF INHERITANCE A PERSON CAN EVER BE GIVEN!** *"Wisdom is good with an* **inheritance:** *and by it there is profit to them that see the sun* (remain alive). *For wisdom is a defence, and money is a defence: but the excellency of knowledge is, that wisdom giveth life to them that have it."* **Ecclesiastes 7:11-12**

*"In the day of prosperity by joyful, but in the day of adversity* (trouble, sorrow) *consider* (this): *God also hath set the one* (day) *over against the other, to the end* (extent) *that man should find nothing after him* (self apart from God)." **Ecclesiastes 7:14**

If you love your inheritance of land, oil, gold, money, or houses more than God, and if you are not using your inheritance to help spread the Gospel — then it will not comfort you when you stand among the heathens! You will be separated from the love and protection which only God can give! *"And thou shalt take thine* **inheritance** *in* (to) *thyself in the sight of the heathen, and thou shalt know that I am the Lord."* **Ezekiel 22:16**

**THE WISE SHALL INHERIT GLORY! Proverbs 3:35 THE MEEK SHALL INHERIT THE EARTH! Matthew 5:5** *"An* **inheritance** *may be gotten hastily at the beginning: But the end thereof shall not be blessed."* **Proverbs 20:21**

Every born-again Christian is given an inheritance more excellent than the angels receive! Hebrews 1:4

*"Go to now, ye rich men, weep and howl for your miseries that shall come upon you. Your riches are corrupted and your garments are moth-eaten. Your gold and silver is cankered; and the rust of them shall be a witness against you, and shall eat your flesh as* (if) *it were fire. Ye have heaped treasure together for the last days."* **James 5:3**

There is an inheritance which is incorruptible and undefiled. It's reserved just for you, when you become a born-again Christian! **READ: 1 Peter 1:4**

*"Love not the world, neither the things that are in the world. If any man* (person) *love the world, the love of the Father is not in him. For all that is in the world, the lust of the flesh, and the lust of the eyes, and the pride of life, is not of the Father, but is of the world. And the world passeth away, and the lust thereof: but he that doeth the will of God abideth forever."* **1 John 2:15-17**

### PRAYER

Dear God: I confess that because of my earthly **inheritance,** I have put my faith in my riches! I know this is wrong! I know this is selfish! I repent of this sin! I will give at least one tenth of my income to help support the Lord's work! I will help support Christian TV for those who are unable to attend church. I will go to church and will read my Bible. **I will no longer love my inheritance and serve it before I love and serve You!** I ask You to forgive all my sins. Please come into my life and fill me with Your love. I believe that every good and perfect gift comes from above! Thank You for opening my eyes so I can receive my share of rewards in heaven! I will release much of my money to do Your work! In Jesus' name, I pray. AMEN!

# INJUSTICE

*"Love worketh no ill to his neighbour: therefore love is the fulfilling of the law."* **Romans 13:10**

When a person suffers from an injustice he should take an honest look at himself to see if he is guilty! *"But ye should say, Why persecute we him, seeing the root of the matter is found in me?"* **Job 19:28**

*"Let love be without dissimulation* (genuine). *Abhor that which is evil;* (but) *cleave to that which is good. Be kindly affectioned one to another with brotherly love; in honour preferring one another."* **Romans 12:9-10**

Before you pray, make sure you have not done an injustice to anyone! Be sure your own prayer is pure! Read: Job 16:17

IN JOB 19-7 JOB CRIED OUT TO GOD: *"Behold, I cry out of wrong* (an injustice done me), *but I am not heard: I cry aloud, but there is no judgment* (justice)." **"DO YOU FEEL LIKE JOB?"**

If you are being unjust to another person — better pray as David did in Psalm 119:124 *"Deal with thy servant according unto thy mercy, and teach me thy statutes* (laws)."

If you are receiving unjust treatment and your conscience is clean that you are innocent of any wrong doing, pray: *"I have done judgment and justice: leave me not to mine oppressors. Be surety for thy servant for good: let not the proud oppress me."* **Psalm 119:121-122**

Always remember that any injustice comes from allowing Satan to "do his own thing" in our lives! He is the author of confusion! God calls Satan a thief! *"The thief* (Satan) *cometh not, but for to steal, and to kill, and to destroy: I* (Christ) *am come that they* (you, me) *might have life, and that they might have it more abundantly. I am the good shepherd: the good shepherd giveth his life for the sheep."* **John 10:10-11**

*"Whosoever hateth his brother is a murderer: and ye know that no murderer hath eternal life abiding in him."* **1 John 3:15**

*"For this is the message that ye heard from the beginning, that we should love one another."* **1 John 3:11**

NEVER RETALIATE IF YOU HAVE RECEIVED AN INJUSTICE! Jesus said: *"Ye have heard that it hath been said, An eye for an eye, and a tooth for a tooth: But I say unto you. That ye resist not evil: but whosoever shall smite thee on thy right cheek, turn to him the other also. And if any man will sue thee at the law, and take away thy coat, let him have thy cloke also. And whosoever shall compel thee to go a mile, go with him twain* (two). *Give to him that asketh thee, and from him that would borrow of thee turn not thou away."* **Matthew 5:38-42**

JESUS SAID THAT WE ARE TO FORGIVE AN INJUSTICE 70 x 7 TIMES! Matthew 18:21-22

*"But why dost thou judge thy brother? or why dost thou set at nought thy brother? For we shall all stand before the judgment seat of Christ."* **Romans 14:10** *"Let us not therefore judge one another any more: But judge this rather, that no man put a stumblingblock or an occasion to fall in his brother's way."* **Romans 14:13**

JESUS SAID: *". . .Love your enemies, do good to them which hate you. Bless them that curse you and pray for them which despitefully use you."* **Luke 6:27-28** *"Bless them which persecute you: bless, and curse not."* **Romans 12:14**

1 JOHN 3:16 SAYS WE OUGHT TO LAY DOWN OUR LIFE FOR OUR BROTHER. WE ARE NEVER TO DO HIM AN INJUSTICE!

. . .

### PRAYER

Dear God, I am guilty of dealing out **injustice** to others! I have also been dealt **injustices** from others! I know that judgement is Yours to pass out if we misbehave! Please forgive me for my sins. I will go to those I have treated unfairly and beg their forgiveness! When I am wronged, I will pray for my oppressor! Teach me what You would have me say and do! I repent for my wrongdoings! I praise You and thank You for extending me mercy. In Jesus' name, I pray. AMEN!

# INSOMNIA

It's the middle of the night . . . Every one is sound asleep . . . But your eyes are wide open! You feel as though you're the only conscious being in all creation . . . And God says *". . .commune with your own heart upon your bed, and be still."* **Psalm 4:4**

Between 20-30 percent of the population are **"INSOMNIACS"**. They often feel isolated. Insomniacs may spend 30 minutes in bed before falling asleep, or they may fall asleep rapidly, but they don't stay asleep.

**HERE IS A GOOD VERSE TO REPEAT BEFORE CLOSING YOUR EYES EACH NIGHT:** *"I will both **lay me down** in peace, and **sleep:** for thou, Lord, only makest me dwell in safety."* **Psalm 4:8**

If you need help getting to sleep more often than once or twice a week — try a glass of warm milk. Take a hot bath and then pray: *"I will not be afraid of ten thousands of people, that have set themselves against me round about."* **Psalm 3:6**

**THEN, WHEN YOU GET UP THE NEXT MORNING YOU CAN HONESTLY SAY:** *"I laid me down and slept; I awaked; for the Lord sustained me."* **Psalm 3:5**

If you use sleeping pills (or any chemical aids) you create your own sleepless problem! Instead, take authority over it! Defeat the devil! He makes you lose sleep! Don't take anything if your health is okay and you're sure there is no sin in your life that you need to ask Jesus to forgive, then make up your mind that you will get a good night's sleep and do it! Pray: *"Give ear to my words, O Lord, consider my meditation. Hearken unto the voice of my cry, my King, and my God: for unto thee will I pray. My voice shalt thou hear in the morning, O Lord; in the morning will I direct my prayer unto thee, and will look up."* **Psalm 5:1-3**

**ACCORDING TO PSALM 37:7** Sinners have trouble sleeping, because they haven't the **covering** of God's protection, **but the Christian can** *"Rest in the Lord"*!

It's not too important how many hours you sleep but it is important how you feel! If sleep-loss interferes with your vitality and contentment, take authority over Satan and overcome your insomnia! Before you lay down, read your Bible and pray! Never forget that Satan is the "author of confusion" and "the thief" who steals your sleep! He wants to destroy your body, and your mind! *"The **thief** cometh not, but for to steal, and to kill, and to destroy: I (Christ) am come that they might have life, and that they might have it more abundantly."* **John 10:10**

**TO TAKE AUTHORITY OVER SLEEPLESSNESS: 1. Pray. 2. Read your Bible. 3. Repeat 10 times a day:** *"Get thee behind me, Satan!"* **Matthew 16:23**

**TO TAKE AUTHORITY OVER INSOMNIA:** *"Cease from anger, and forsake wrath: fret not thyself in any wise to do evil. For evildoers shall be cut off* (eternally separated from God, unless they repent, and forsake their wicked ways): *but those that wait upon the Lord, they shall inherit the earth."* **Psalm 37:8-9**

**IF YOU ARE AN INSOMNIAC:** DON'T TAKE A NAP DURING THE DAY. DON'T DRINK TEA OR COFFEE AFTER DINNER! DON'T WATCH A SUSPENSEFUL TV SHOW OR YOU MIGHT BE IN FOR A WAKEFUL NIGHT! THANK GOODNESS GOD NEVER SLEEPS! HE'S ALWAYS READY TO LISTEN TO OUR PRAYERS AND TO TALK TO US WHEN WE CAN'T SLEEP! *". . .He that keepeth thee will not slumber."* **Psalm 121:3**

THE BORN-AGAIN CHRISTIAN, WHO IS LIVING IN GOD'S COMPLETE WILL FOR HIS LIFE, HAS THIS PROMISE: *"When thou **liest down**, thou shalt not be afraid: yea, thou shalt **lie down**, and thy sleep shall be sweet."* **Proverbs 3:24**

Don't take "downers" or sedatives! Let go of this problem. Let God help you! Stretch out on the couch at least an hour before you go to bed. Start counting your blessings . . . it will relax you! Praise God for all the wonderful things he has done for you! Never work on anything that requires concentration, just before you retire! *"For he shall give his angels charge over thee, to keep thee in all thy ways."* **Psalm 91:11**

**NEVER GO TO BED IRRITATED OR ANGRY!** *"Be ye angry, and sin not: let not the sun go down upon your wrath: Neither give place to the devil* (or he'll destroy your sleep, dreams)." **Ephesians 4:26-27**

**IF YOU'RE NOCTURNAL (A "NIGHT OWL") AND YOU WAKE UP FREQUENTLY IN THE NIGHT: OPEN YOUR BIBLE TO THE BOOK OF PSALMS . . . MEDITATE ON GOD'S WORD!** *"My help cometh from the Lord, which made heaven and earth. He will not suffer* (allow) *thy foot to be moved: he that keepeth thee will not slumber* (sleep)." **Psalm 121:2-3** *"The Lord shall preserve thee from all evil: he shall preserve thy soul. The Lord shall preserve thy going out and thy coming in from this time forth, and even for evermore."* **Psalm 121:7-8**

# Insomnia

### PRAYER

Dear God, Please forgive me for all my sins. Please help me to overcome **insomnia. I need to get a good night's sleep every night! I** want to wake up each morning and feel like saying, "This is the day the Lord hath made, I will rejoice and be glad in it."! **If there is something I am doing which prevents me from getting my rest, please make me aware of it so I can change!** Please create in me the kind of person You want me to be. I thank You from the bottom of my heart for the many blessings You have bestowed upon me. Thank You for saving my soul! I turn away from all sin. From this moment on I will live for You! In Jesus' name, I pray. AMEN!

# JAIL—PRISON

## *FBI Crime Clock*

One **violent crime** every **24 seconds**
One **murder** every **24 minutes**
One **forcible rape** every **six minutes**
One **robbery** every **56 seconds**
One **aggravated assault** every **48 seconds**
One **property crime** every **2.6 seconds**
One **burglary** every **eight seconds**
One **larceny-theft** every **4.5 seconds**
One **motor vehicle theft** every **20 seconds**
One **crime index offense** every **2.4 seconds**

**THE BIBLE SAYS:** *"Correction is grievous unto him that forsaketh the way. . ."* **Proverbs 15:10**

**THE PRAYER OF THE PRISONER SHOULD BE:** *"Lead me, O Lord, in thy righteousness because of mine enemies; make thy way straight before my face."* **Psalm 5:8**

God hates sin—but loves the sinner! If you are in jail or prison please know that God is with you. He will give you peace and companionship, if you will repent of your sins, and ask his forgiveness. Ask Him to live inside you! God goes into jails and prisons to save people. *"Attend unto my cry; for I am brought very low: deliver me from my persecutors; for they are stronger than I. Bring my soul out of prison, that I may praise thy name: the righteous shall compass (surround) me about; for thou shalt deal bountifully with me."* **Psalm 142:6-7**

God is not the one who puts a person in jail (or prison) to punish him for wrong doing! God wants each one of us to live a happy, godly, productive life! Satan is solely responsible for sickness, bondage, death! God calls Satan a "thief"! God has no part in the evil work that Satan does! God gives us a free will to follow him — or Satan! When a person follows Satan he does a terrible thing, because Satan is out to kill him! God is out to save him! *"The thief (Satan) cometh not (to planet earth), but for to steal, and to kill, and to destroy. I (Christ) am come that they might have life, and that they might have it more abundantly. I (Christ) am the good shepherd: the good shepherd giveth his life for the sheep."* **John 10:10-11**

When a person is in prison he feels isolated, unloved, and forsaken! But God promises He will never forsake you if you will repent and ask His forgiveness! He will comfort you and visit you! Then you can say: *"We are troubled on every side, yet not distressed; we are perplexed, but not in despair; persecuted, but not forsaken; cast down, but not destroyed."* **2 Corinthians 4:8-9**

**2 Corinthians 6:5-6** says we should not give offence to anyone, and that we should be patient even if we're in prison. **If you are in jail or prison, please repent, ask forgiveness from God and then repeat this verse 10 times a day:** *"The Lord is my helper, and I will not fear what man shall do unto me."* **Hebrews 13:6**

**LEST WE FORGET:** Some of the greatest soul winning people in the world are those who are confined to prison!

If you know anyone who is in jail or prison . . . never be guilty of judging him! Who are we to judge another? The Bible says all have sinned! Pray for those in jail and prison! Ask God to visit them and give them wisdom to know who their enemy is! Ask God to reveal himself to them and give them comfort! Pray for them! Visit them and take them a Bible! God will bless you!

**GOD'S WARNING:** *"Because sentence against an evil work is not executed speedily, therefore the heart of the sons of men is fully set in them to do evil."* **Ecclesiastes 8:11**

Though Jesus was never physically in jail (or prison) he related to the sorrow, grief, and mistreatment of people in prison that He had this to say: *"For I was an hungred and ye (Christians) gave me meat: I was thirsty and ye gave me drink: I was a stranger, and ye took me in: naked, and ye clothed me: I was sick, and ye visited me: I was in prison, and ye came unto me. Then shall the righteous answer him, saying, Lord when saw we thee hungred, and fed thee? or thirsty, and gave thee drink? when saw we thee a stranger, and took thee in? or naked, and clothed thee? or when saw we thee sick, or in prison, and came unto thee? And the King (Jesus) shall answer and say unto them, Verily I say unto you, In asmuch as ye have done it (anything godly) unto (for) one of the least of these my brethren, ye have done it unto (for) me. Then shall he say also unto them on the left hand, Depart from me, ye cursed, into everlasting fire, prepared for the devil and his angels: For I was an hungred, and ye gave me no meat: I was thirsty, and ye gave me no drink: I was a stranger, and ye took me not in: naked, and ye clothed me not: sick, and in prison, and ye visited me not. Then shall they also answer and say unto him, Verily I say unto you, Inasmuch as ye have done it (anything godly) unto (for) one of the least of these my brethren, ye shall he answer them, saying, Verily I say unto you, Inasmuch as ye did it not to one of the least of these, ye did it not to me. And these shall go away into everlasting punishment: but the righteous into life eternal."* **Matthew 25:35-46**

**WHY IS A PERSON EVER SENTENCED TO JAIL OR PRISON?** Because his master is NOT God, and he is not living in the perfect will of God in his life! **Satan is the oppressor!** God is all loving! God said that if we will all put on the **whole armour of God** that we will be able to stand against the devil. **It is the devil who sends people to jail or prison, by instructing them to disobey God's laws and man's laws!** You see, Satan hates everyone!

**GOD'S PROMISE:** *"Though a sinner do evil an hundred times, and his days be prolonged, yet surely I know that it shall be well with them that fear God, which fear before him: But it shall not be well with the wicked, neither shall he (God) prolong his days, which are as a shadow; because he feareth not before God."* **Ecclesiastes 8:12-13**

### PRAYER

Dear God, I am in **jail (or prison)**, but I know that I am not alone! I know that You are here with me and waiting patiently for me to call on You for comfort! I repent of my sins! Please come into my heart and cleanse me! I believe that Jesus died on the cross to pay the penalty for my sins, so I could receive forgiveness! Please help me to say and do the right things from this moment on. I will read my Bible daily! I will pray! I will turn the other cheek when some one offends me! I will give You the glory for saving my soul! I will never be ashamed to confess that You alone have spared me from going to hell! I love You because You first loved me! I praise You. I know I will never be alone again. I will witness to others around me. In Jesus' name, AMEN!

# JEALOUSY

In the Book of Numbers, Chapter 5, there was a ''jealousy law'' which protected an innocent wife from the insane jealousy of her husband. It became obvious to all that she was innocent of any wrong doing! If she were guilty . . . at least she was put into a position whereby the truth came out!

A spirit of jealousy is the work of a supernatural diabolic influence . . . or a passion stirred up, as the ''by-product'' of the imagination!

**Ecclesiastes 5:2 says:** *''Be not rash with thy mouth, and let not thine heart be hasty to utter anything before God: for God is in heaven, and thou upon earth: therefore let thy words be few.''*

**JEALOUSY IS THE RAGE OF A MAN!** *''For jealousy is the rage of a man: therefore he will not spare in the day of vengeance.''* **Proverbs 6:34**

**LOVE IS AS STRONG AS DEATH AND JEALOUSY IS AS CRUEL AS HELL!** *''. . .For love is strong as death; **jealousy is cruel** as the grave* (sheol-hell, the unseen world of departed conscious spirits): *the coals thereof are coals of fire, which hath a most vehement flame. Many waters cannot quench love* (it is totally indestructive), *neither can the floods drown it: if a man would give all the substance of his house for love, it would utterly be contemned* (condemned by the person whose love he attempted to buy, for real love cannot be bought at any price).'' **Song of Solomon 8:6-7**

**A WIFE SHOULD GIVE HER HUSBAND NO REASON TO BE JEALOUS OF HER!** *''The heart of her husband doth safely trust in her, so that he shall have no need of spoil. She will do him good and not evil all the days of her life.''* **Proverbs 31:11-12**

*''A virtuous woman is a crown* (an emblem of honor) *to her husband: but she that maketh ashamed is as rottenness in his bones. The thoughts of the righteous are right: but the counsels* (devices, schemes, actions) *of the wicked are deceit* (cheating, deception).'' **Proverbs 12:4-5**

**IT IS NEVER GOD'S PLAN FOR HUMANS TO BE JEALOUS OVER EACH OTHER, OR OVER THINGS! GOD, HOWEVER, IS A JEALOUS GOD! HE HAS THE RIGHT TO BE JEALOUS OVER HIS CREATION . . . FOR ALL CREATION SPEAKS OF HIS LOVE FOR US!** In the ten commandments the third commandment says: *''Thou shalt not bow down thyself to them* (idols), *nor serve them: for I the Lord thy God am a jealous God, visiting the iniquity of the fathers upon the children unto: the third and fourth generation of them that hate me; and shewing mercy unto thousands of them that love me, and keep my commandments.''* **Exodus 20:5-6** *''For thou shalt worship no other god: for the Lord, whose name is Jealous, is a jealous God.''* **Exodus 34:14 Also Read: Deuteronomy 4:24/6:15/Joshua 24:19/Ezekiel 39:25/Joel 2:18/Nahum 1:2/Zechariah 1:14/8:2/Ezekiel 36:5**

**VERY WELL PUT!** *''Wounds from a friend are better than kisses from an enemy!''* **Proverbs 27:6** (The Living Bible)

**THE BIBLE SAYS NO MAN EVER HATED HIS OWN FLESH (BODY)! Read: Ephesians 5:29**

JEALOUSY IS WRONG IN A MAN, WOMAN, BOY OR GIRL! JEALOUSY IS A FORM OF IDOLATRY! THE ONLY JEALOUSY WHICH IS GODLY IS THE JEALOUSY THAT GOD HAS OVER HIS CHILDREN! AND THIS IS A LOVING, PROTECTIVE JEALOUSY! *''For I am jealous over you with godly jealousy: for I have espoused you to one husband* (born again Christians will become the bride of Christ), *that I may present you as a chaste virgin to Christ.''* **2 Corinthians 11:2**

**ROMANS 3:4 SAYS:** *''. . .let God be true, but every man* (who practices sin) *a liar. . .''*

# JEALOUSY

### PRAYER

Dear God, Please forgive me for all my sins. I am guilty of being **jealous** over those I love. I know that this is not what You desire for my life! I know that You are my Creator and that I should give my first love to You! I know that **jealousy** is merely feelings of **insecurity.** I know that **jealousy is suspicion** and unfounded in most cases! I know that **jealousy is fear.** Please come into my heart and give me a total sense of security. Fill me with Your love so I will no longer desire to live in the flesh. **Please take away my suspicions of jealousy, for they hold me back from totally giving myself over to You for divine safekeeping.** I love You and I want to serve You. I will need help in walking the straight and narrow path. Please help me and I will praise You for ever! In Jesus' name, I pray. AMEN!

# JOKERS

THE WORDS OF THE JOKER ARE FOOLISH AND A SOURCE OF HIS OWN PRIDE AND EGO! WHEN HE TRIPS HIMSELF UP, IT'S LEFT UP TO THE WISE PERSON TO KEEP HIM FROM FALLING ON HIS FACE FROM EMBARRASSMENT, OR FROM RECEIVING SOME OF WHAT HE HAS ALREADY "DISHED-OUT"! *"In the mouth of the foolish is a rod of pride: but the lips of the wise shall preserve them."* **Proverbs 14:3**

INIQUITY (SIN) IS A SPORT TO THE JOKER . . . BUT A MAN WHO HAS REAL UNDERSTANDING HATES SIN! *"It is as sport to a fool to do mischief: But a man* (person) *of understanding hath wisdom."* **Proverbs 10:23**

Little children have fun playing jokes on everyone. They are usually harmless and kids have a vivid imagination! However, if their jokes are meant to hurt (or trick) anyone . . . then the parents, school teachers, friends, neighbours or church should investigate the real reason behind his tricks and then set down godly rules for proper conduct! When a person has a habit of playing practical jokes with full intent to trick, embarrass, or call attention to himself, he resorts to being a child again! *"When I was a child, I spake* (spoke) *as a child, I understood as a child, I thought as a child: but when I became a man* (grown person), *I put away childish things."* **1 Corinthians 13:11**

THE PRACTICAL JOKER IS CONFUSED! HE SAYS AND DOES THINGS JUST TO CONFUSE YOU! THIS DISPLEASES GOD. GOD DESIRES PEACE, NEVER CONFUSION, FOR OUR LIVES! *"For God is not the author of confusion, but of peace, . . ."* **1 Corinthians 14:33**

*"Th e tongue of the wise useth knowledge aright: but the mouth of fools poureth out foolishness."* **Proverbs 15:2**

You may think you are a clever practical joker, and that your jokes are harmless and cute! You may think those who don't appreciate your jokes are just "old sticks in the mud"! But are they? Is being a joker really worth the risk of saying or doing the wrong thing? Is it possible that your jokes may have hurt or embarrassed a person at some time? Take inventory! *"The eyes of the Lord are in every place, beholding the evil and the good."* **Proverbs 15:3**

A PRACTICAL JOKER IS VOID OF WISDOM! HE DOESN'T REALIZE THE EFFECTS OF HIS JOKES ON THOSE HE INFLICTS HIS HUMOR! *"Folly is joy to him that is destitute of wisdom: but a man* (person) *of understanding walketh uprightly."* **Proverbs 15:21**

GOD SAYS: *"Let all things be done decently and in order."* **1 Corinthians 14:40**

*"The heart of him that hath understanding seeketh knowledge: but the mouth of fools feedeth on foolishness."* **Proverbs 15:14**

A PRACTICAL JOKER HATES IT WHEN A PERSON PLAYS A JOKE ON HIM! HE WON'T ALLOW YOU TO TELL HIM WHEN HE DOES WRONG OR TO ASK HIM TO STOP PULLING SILLY JOKES! HE SHUTS HIS EARS! *"A scorner loveth not one that reproveth him; neither will he go unto the wise."* **Proverbs 15:12**

*"The crown of the wise is their riches* (wisdom): *but the foolishness of fools is folly."* **Proverbs 14:24**

THE WORLD HATES A PRACTICAL JOKER BECAUSE HE CAN'T BE TRUSTED TO BE HARMLESS! HE'S LIKELY TO EMBARRASS YOU, AND SAY OR DO THE WRONG THING! *"A man* (person) *of wicked devices* (jokes, tricks, deception, revealing a secret in order to get a laugh, etc.) *is hated."* **Proverbs 14:17**

A PRACTICAL JOKER CHATTERS ENDLESSLY! *"The wise in heart will receive* (God's) *commandments: but a prating fool* (practical joker) *shall fall."* **Proverbs 10:8** *"He that winketh with the eye causeth sorrow, but a prating fool shall fall."* **Proverbs 10:10** *". . .he that refraineth his lips is wise."* **Proverbs 10:19** *"A whip for the horse, a bridle for the ass, and a rod for the fool's back."* **Proverbs 26:3**

GOD'S ADVICE: *"Answer not a fool* (or joker) *according to his folly, lest thou also be like unto him."* **Proverbs 26:4**

A PRACTICAL JOKER CAN NOT BE TRUSTED! HE REPEATS WHAT YOU TELL HIM. YOU CAN NEVER BE ASSURED HE'LL TELL THE STORY STRAIGHT! *"The legs of the lame are not equal: so is a parable in the mouth of fools."* **Proverbs 26:7**

GOD SAYS THAT FOOLS (INCLUDES JOKERS) ARE NOT HONOURABLE PEOPLE! *"As snow in summer, and as rain in harvest, so honour is not seemly* (appropriate) *for a fool."* **Proverbs 26:1**

SINCE THE SCRIPTURES SAY THAT GOD DOES NOT LIKE CONFUSION . . . AND SINCE JOKERS DEAL IN CONFUSION . . . DOESN'T IT MAKE SENSE TO PUT AWAY ALL FORMS OF FOOLISHNESS?

### PRAYER

Dear God, Please forgive me for wasting so much time **kidding and joking** around with people! I may never know how foolish I have been or how many people I may have embarrassed! I may have hurt people's feelings without even knowing it. I know there are better things I should be doing. I know that my behavior has not been pleasing in Your sight. I ask You to forgive all my sins. **I want to be a person who doesn't talk excessively.** I want to be a person who can be trusted at all times. I no longer want to be a person who does the unexpected for "shock" value. Please come into my heart and take control over my tongue and thoughts. Help me see myself as others see me. Help me to remember to ask myself, "What would Jesus say or do if He were here at this very moment?" Thank You for caring for me and for loving me. In Jesus' name, I pray. AMEN!

# JUDGING ANOTHER

**JESUS SAID:** *"Judge not, that ye be not judged. For with what judgement ye judge, ye shall be judged: and with what measure ye mete* (give out), *it shall be measured to you again."* **Matthew 7:1-2**

*"For the Lord is our judge, the Lord is our lawgiver, the Lord is our king; He will save us."* **Isaiah 33:22**

*"Speak not evil one of another, brethren. He that speaketh evil of his brother, and judgeth his brother, speaketh evil of the law* (of God), *and judgeth the law: but if thou judge the law, thou art not a doer of the law* (of God), *but a judge. There is* (only) *one lawgiver* (God) *who is able to save and to destroy: who art thou that judgeth another?"* **James 4:11-12**

**INSTEAD OF JUDGING ANOTHER PERSON . . . PRAY FOR HIM!** *"Confess your faults one to another, and pray one for another, that ye may be healed. The effectual fervent prayer of a righteous man availeth much."* **James 5:16**

*". . . For He* (God) *cometh to judge the earth: with righteousness shall He judge the world, and the people with equity."* **Psalm 98:9**

*"Ye shall do no unrighteousness in judgement: thou shalt not respect the person of the poor, nor honour the person of the mighty: but in righteousness shalt thou judge thy neighbour."* **Leviticus 19:15**

**JESUS SAID:** *". . . Love your enemies, do good to them which hate you, bless them that curse you, and pray for them which despitefully use you."* **Luke 6:27-28**

**JESUS SAID:** *"Judge not, and ye shall not be judged: condemn not, and ye shall not be condemned; forgive, and ye shall be forgiven."* **Luke 6:37**

**JESUS SAID:** *". . . Out of thine own mouth will I judge thee, thou wicked servant. Thou knewest that I was an austere man, taking up that* (burden of our sins) *that I laid not down, and reaping that* (which) *I did not sow."* **Luke 19:22**

*" God judgeth the righteous, and God is angry with the wicked every day."* **Psalm 7:11** *"Therefore judge nothing before the time, until the Lord come, who both will bring to light the hidden things of darkness, and will make manifest* (known) *the counsels* (condition) *of the hearts: and then shall every man have praise of God."* **1 Corinthians 4:5**

*For we must all appear before the judgement seat of Christ* (in Heaven) *that every one may receive the things done in his body* (while he was in his flesh and blood body on earth), *according to that* (thoughts, actions, deeds which) *he hath done* (on earth), *whether it be good or bad."* **2 Corinthians 5:10**

**WHO DO WE THINK WE ARE TO JUDGE ANOTHER PERSON? ONLY GOD IS GOD!** *"But God is the judge: he putteth down one, and setteth up another."* **Psalm 75:7**

*"So speak ye, and so do, as they that shall be judged by the* (new) *law of liberty* (which Jesus gives us). *For he* (that judges another) *shall have judgement without mercy, that hath shewed no mercy; and mercy rejoiceth against judgement."* **James 2:12-13**

**TO JUDGE ANOTHER PERSON IS UNGODLY AND INEXCUSABLE!** *"Therefore thou art inexcusable, O man, whosoever thou art that judgest: for wherein thou judgest another, thou condemnest thyself; for thou that judgest doest the same things. But we are sure that the judgement of God is according to truth against them which commit such things. And thinkest thou this, O man, that judgest them which do such things, and doest the same, that thou shalt escape the judgement of God?"* **Romans 2:1-3**

**WARNING:** *"But if ye bite and devour one another, take heed that ye be not consumed one of another."* **Galatians 5:15**

**A PERSON WHO JUDGES ANOTHER PERSON IS A CONCEITED PERSON! GOD HATES CONCEIT! IT IS VANITY AND A SIN!** *"Be of the same mind one toward another, mind not high things, but condescend* (humble yourself) *to men of low estate: Be not wise in your own conceits. Recompense to no man evil for evil. Provide things honest in the sight of all men. If it be possible, as much as lieth in you* (to the very best of your ability), *live peaceably with all men."* **Romans 12:16-18**

*". . . Why dost thou judge thy brother* (anyone)? *or why dost thou set at nought* (discredit) *thy brother? For we shall all stand before the judgement seat of Christ. For it is written, as I live, saith the Lord, every knee shall bow to me, and every tongue shall confess to God. So then every one of us shall give account of himself to God. Let us not therefore judge one another any more: but judge this rather, that no man put a stumblingblock or an occasion to fall in his brother's way."* **Romans 14:10-13**

All Christians will be judged in heaven at the judgement seat of Christ! Read: Matthew 16:27/1 Corinthians 3:11-15

All the wicked will be judged on planet earth at the Great White Throne Judgement! Read: Revelation 20:11-15/Acts 10:42/17:31/Romans 2:16/John 5:27/Revelation 19:20/20:10-15/21:8/22:15

## PRAYER

Dear God, **Please forgive me for judging other people.** I know that I am not perfect! I realize I have been doing this out of my own conceit, and feelings of importance! Next to You, I know I am nothing! **I know that You love the people I have judged as much as You love me.** I thank You God, that all people on this earth are not like me or I would have no friend to turn to. You are the only person who is able to change me and to help me see myself as others see me! Please teach me to love others more, and to think about myself less! Create in me a humble spirit, to replace my haughty one! I will do my part. I will take control over my thoughts, and actions. Teach me to see kindness, instead of displeasure in others! Humble me, Lord, and I will lift You up. Forgive me for all my sins. Cleanse me. In Jesus' name, I pray. AMEN!

# KEEPING THE SABBATH

*"For all have sinned, and come short of the glory of God."*
**Romans 3:23**

*"Remember the sabbath day, to keep it holy."* **Exodus 20:8**

**GOD GAVE MAN A SABBATH DAY EACH WEEK WITH THE INSTRUCTIONS HE WAS TO REST FROM ALL UN-NECESSARY WORK, WORSHIP GOD, AND READ THE BI-BLE!** *"Six days shalt thou labour, and do all thy work: But the seventh day is the sabbath of the Lord thy God: in it **thou shalt not do any work**, thou, nor thy son, nor thy daughter, thy manservant, nor thy maidservant, nor thy cattle, nor thy stranger that is within thy gates: For in six days the Lord made heaven and earth, the sea, and all that in them is, and rested the seventh day: wherefore the Lord blessed the sabbath day, and hallowed it."* **Exodus 20:9-11**

To the Jew the sabbath starts Friday evening and ends Saturday at 6:00 p.m. To the Christian the sabbath is Sunday. The day of the week is not the important issue here! The fact that God asks us to rest and worship one day out of the 7 is an act of obedience on our part! God does not need rest, nor does God ever sleep! But, he specifically set aside a day of rest and worship for us. We need it for our body, our spirit, and to show obedience to Him! God rested on the seventh day — to set an example for us to follow! *"Ye shall keep my sabbaths, and reverence my sanctuary; I am the Lord."* **Leviticus 19:30**

*"For the Son of Man* (Jesus) *is Lord even of the sabbath day."* **Matthew 12:8**

*"And he* (Jesus speaking) *said unto them* (his disciples), *the sabbath was made for man, and not man for the sabbath: therefore the Son of Man* (Jesus) *is Lord also of the sabbath."* **Mark 2:27-28/Luke 6:5**

**SUNDAY, FOR MOST PEOPLE, IS A DAY TO GO TO CHURCH AND WORSHIP GOD!** *"I was glad when they said unto me, Let us go into the house of the Lord."* **Psalm 122:1**

Even if Sunday is not the day you call the sabbath, it does not excuse you from worshipping God on one day each week! This is not a commandment to take lightly! The sabbath was not given man to go fishing, water-skiing, or shopping! The sabbath is a time of visiting with the family, resting, watching a little Christian TV, reading and meditating on the Word of God. It is okay to cook lunch and do the dishes. Then you should rest and enjoy some peace and quiet! Mankind abuses the sabbath and this displeases God!

**WHAT'S SO HARD ABOUT OBSERVING THE SABBATH — IN THE WAY GOD ASKED YOU TO? THINK OF THE ADVANTAGES OF PLEASING GOD! GO TO CHURCH AND LEARN ABOUT THE WONDERFUL BLESSINGS GOD HAS IN STORE FOR YOU! GIVE YOUR TIRED BODY AND MIND A REST! WHAT'S SO HARD ABOUT READING THE BIBLE OR LISTENING TO SOME BEAUTIFUL GOSPEL SONGS ON THE STEREO?**

### PRAYER

Dear God, Please forgive me for all my sins. **Please forgive me for breaking the sabbath! I know You want me to go to church so that I will gain strength and knowledge about the Scriptures! I have been disobedient in this! I don't read the Bible as often as I should! I will begin to read the Scriptures this very moment. I will read my Bible at least thirty minutes each day! I know I will find the answers to life's problems. I ask You to forgive me for disobeying Your commandments! I know that I need to rest my body and mind one day a week! Please teach me to be still and quiet! Please help me take control of my thoughts and ac-tions, while resting and worshipping on the sabbath. I know that You are not capable of making mistakes! You lovingly designed the sabbath for my physical and spiritual welfare! I want to do what is right in Your eyes. Please help me to always obey Your Word in respect to the sabbath and all things! In Jesus' name, I pray. AMEN!**

# KIDNAP

WHY DOES A PERSON EVER KIDNAP ANOTHER PERSON? BECAUSE SATAN PLANTS THE IDEA IN HIS MIND THAT HE CAN MAKE SOME MONEY, OR FOR POLITICAL REASONS. IT IS A SIN FOR A PERSON TO KIDNAP ANOTHER PERSON, ANIMAL OR ANYTHING! A KIDNAPPER IS A THIEF! GOD SAYS SATAN IS THE INVENTOR OF LIES AND CONFUSION. GOD SAYS THAT SATAN IS A THIEF WHO COMES TO KILL, STEAL AND DESTROY! *"The thief* (Satan) *cometh not* (to planet earth), *but for to steal, and to kill, and to destroy: I* (Christ speaking) *am come* (to planet earth) *that they* (me, you) *might have life, and that they might have it more abundantly."* **John 10:10**

MANY TIMES A PERSON KIDNAPS ANOTHER PERSON HE DOESN'T EVEN KNOW! SOMETIMES IT'S FOR REVENGE THOUGH IT'S USUALLY A CASE OF GREED FOR MONEY! AND, IF RANSOM IS NOT PAID, THE KIDNAPPER OFTEN KILLS THE VICTIM SO HE WON'T BE IDENTIFIED AND FORCED TO SERVE A PRISON SENTENCE! SOMETIMES A PARENT WILL KIDNAP HIS OWN CHILD FOR REVENGE!

## Child Stealing

When a person kidnapped another person, in the Old Testament days, he was put to death! *"And he that stealeth* (kidnaps) *a man* (person), *and selleth him* (or collects money in exchange for the victim's life), *or if he be found in his hand* (if the kidnapper gets caught with the victim), *he shall surely be put to death."* **Exodus 21:16**

THANK GOD FOR SENDING JESUS TO PAY THE PENALTY FOR OUR SINS! OTHERWISE, A PERSON WOULD NOT HAVE A CHANCE TO BE SAVED WHETHER HE WAS A KIDNAPPER OR NOT! IN THE OLD DAYS THEY

JUST AUTOMATICALLY KILLED YOU! KIDNAPPING IS EVIL. IT IS WRONG! IT IS A SIN! JESUS LOVES THE KIDNAPPER AND WILL SAVE HIM IF HE WILL REPENT AND ASK FORGIVENESS, AND TURN FROM HIS SINFUL WAYS!

KIDNAPPING IS STEALING! *"If a man* (person) *be found stealing any of his brethren* (kidnapping) *of the children of Israel, and maketh merchandise of him* (holds him in bondage as security in lieu of money or favour as were our American hostages just a year ago), *or selleth him: then that thief shall die; and thou shalt put evil away from among you."* **Deuteronomy 24:7 NOTE:** The kidnapper who sold a person for ransom was put to death in the Old Testament times, so they could be sure they were doing away with every evil person! Jesus said that He came to give us life. If a person commits the sin of kidnapping, he can be forgiven by God! Then he must go and sin no more!

**Exodus 20:15 says:** *"Thou shalt not steal."* **Deuteronomy 5:19 says:** *"Neither shalt thou steal."*

*"Ye shall not steal, neither deal falsely, neither lie one to another."* **Leviticus 19:11**

THE BIBLE SAYS WE ARE NOT TO LAY UP TREASURES BECAUSE THERE ARE THIEVES AND KIDNAPPERS EVERYWHERE! AND RICHES WILL NOT SAVE US! WE ARE TO LAY UP TREASURES IN HEAVEN WHERE THIEVES CAN'T STEAL, AND WHERE GREEDY PEOPLE CAN'T KIDNAP IN ORDER TO TAKE AWAY OUR MONEY OR LIFE! *"Lay not up for yourselves treasures upon earth, where moth and rust doth corrupt, and where thieves break through and steal: But lay up for yourselves treasures in heaven, where neither moth nor rust doth corrupt, and where thieves do not break through nor steal: For where your treasure is, there will your heart be also."* **Matthew 6:19-21**

THE PERSON WHO KIDNAPS ANOTHER PERSON, ANIMAL OR THING, SERVES HIS MASTER WHOSE NAME IS SATAN! NO ONE DESERVES TO BE TAKEN AWAY AGAINST HIS WILL! KIDNAPPING CARRIES A STIFF PENALTY AND PERHAPS A PRISON SENTENCE! IT MAY EVEN CARRY THE DEATH PENALTY! IF YOU KNOW ANYONE WHO IS THINKING OF KIDNAPPING ANOTHER PERSON . . . TELL THEM TO GO TO CHURCH AND GET SAVED!

### PRAYER

Dear God, I ask You to forgive my sins and to blot them out of Your memory. I am guilty of planning to kidnap for money. I know this is wrong. I know that I enjoy my freedom and it would be wrong to rob another person of his! Please forgive me. Come into my life and live in me. In Jesus' precious name, I pray. AMEN!

# KILL—MURDER

  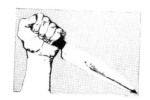

**ACCORDING TO STATISTICS ON LEGISLATIVE CRIME FIGHTING IN WASHINGTON: A MURDER OCCURS EVERY 24 SECONDS!**

**GOD SAYS:** *"Thou shalt not kill."* **Exodus 20:13/Deuteronomy 5:17**

**KILLING, WHETHER ACCIDENTAL OR BY DESIGN WAS REVENGED (IN THE OLD TESTAMENT) BY TAKING THE LIFE OF THE PERSON WHO WAS GUILTY OF THE CRIME.** *"Whoso sheddeth man's blood, by man shall his* (own) *blood be shed: for in the image of God made he man."* **Genesis 9:6** *"He that smiteth a man* (in malice, jealousy, hatred), *so that he die, shall be surely put to death."* **Exodus 21:12 NOTE:** The 2 verses above were old testament laws which did not prohibit killing as a punishment for crimes, or killing in war, which God Himself commanded these same people to do; but it does prohibit killing for malice, and premeditated and wilful destruction of man, who was made in the image of God! All **violence,** strategem (Exodus 21:14) **assault and battery** (Exodus 21:18), **hatred and anger** (Leviticus 19:14, 17) **vengeance** (Leviticus 19:18), and **danger to human life in general,** was forbidden (Deuteronomy 22:8) ALSO READ: Ezekiel 3:18, 20/33:6-8 Proverbs 28:17/Leviticus 24:17-18/24:21

**OLD TESTAMENT LAWS REGARDING WILFUL MURDER: Numbers 35:16-21/30-34**
**OLD TESTAMENT LAWS REGARDING INVOLUNTARY MURDER: Numbers 35:22-29**
**OLD TESTAMENT LAWS REGARDING INQUEST FOR THE SLAIN: Deuteronomy 21:1-9**

Jesus said that if we are angry with our brother without a just and lawful cause we are in danger of the judgment (Matthew 5:21-22) and this is just as much a sin in God's eyes as the person who kills another person!

*"Thou shalt not commit adultery, thou shalt not kill, thou shalt not steal, thou shalt not bear false witness, thou shalt not covet; and if there be any other commandments* (which a Christian is commanded to obey) *it is briefly comprehended in this saying, namely, thou shalt love thy neighbour as thyself."* **Romans 13:9**

*"Now the works of the flesh are manifest* (made known), *which are these: adultery, fornication, uncleanness, lasciviousness, idolatry, witchcraft, hatred, variance, emulations, wrath, strife, seditions, heresies, envyings, murders, drunkenness, revellings, and such like: of the which I tell you before, as I have also told you in time past; that they which do such things shall not inherit the kingdom of God."* **Galatians 5:19-21**

**IN JOSHUA 20:9 GOD ORDERED THAT ANY MURDERER RECEIVE A FAIR TRIAL!**

**THE BIBLE SAYS THAT A MURDERER KILLS BY DAY AND ROBS BY NIGHT: Job 24:14**

**MURDERERS SOMETIMES KILL INNOCENT PEOPLE THEY DON'T EVEN KNOW!** *"And they lay wait for their own blood; they lurk privily* (privately) *for their own lives. So are the ways of every one that is greedy of gain; which taketh away the life of the owners thereof."* **Proverbs 1:18-19**

*"We know that we have passed from death unto life, because we love the brethren.* **He that loveth not his brother abideth in death.** *Whosoever hateth his brother is a* **murderer:** *and ye know that no* **murderer** *hath eternal life abiding in him* (unless he repents)." **1 John 3:14-15**

**THE BIBLE SAYS NOT TO BE AFRAID OF ANYONE WHO CAN KILL YOUR PHYSICAL BODY!** *"And I say unto you my friends, Be not afraid of them that kill the body* (man can never kill the soul and spirit because they are immortal), *and after that have no more that they can do. But I will forewarn you whom ye shall fear: Fear him* (God), *which after he* (the murderer) *hath killed hath power to cast into hell; yea, I say unto you, Fear him."* **Luke 12:4-5**

**PEOPLE WHO KILL OTHERS UNLAWFULLY ARE NOT BORN-AGAIN CHRISTIANS! SATAN IS THEIR MASTER! WHETHER THEY KNOW IT OR NOT — SATAN IS A THIEF AND A KILLER! HE PLANTS THE IDEA IN THE MINDS AND HEARTS OF PEOPLE, TO KILL OTHERS!** *"The thief* (Satan) *cometh not* (to planet earth), *but for to steal, and to kill, and to destroy: I* (Christ) *am come that they might have life, and that they might have it more abundantly."* **John 10:10**

**ABORTION = MURDER! *READ: "ABORTION"** chapter.**

*"These six things doth the Lord hate: yea, seven are an abomination unto him. A proud look, a lying tongue, and hands that shed innocent blood. An heart that deviseth wicked imaginations, feet that be swift in running to mischief, a false witness that speaketh lies, and he that soweth discord among brethren."* **Proverbs 6:16-18**

**Make no mistake about it: murder is sin and usually carries a death penalty sentence! But, as sinful as murder is, God still loves the murderer and wants him to get saved! Even when a person is about to be executed, if he will repent and ask forgiveness, God will save him! Nothing can separate us from the love of God!**

Most good people think they will go to Heaven and all **murderers** will go to hell. But this is not scriptural! The good person must repent of his sins just as the **murderer** must repent of his! God is no respecter of persons! *"Except ye repent, ye shall all likewise perish."* **Luke 13:3** *"Repent ye therefore, and be converted, that your sins may be blotted out."* **Acts 3:19** *"And it shall come to pass, that whosoever shall call on the name of the Lord shall be saved."* **Acts 2:21**

*"For God so loved the world, that He gave His only begotten son, that whosoever believeth in Him should not perish, but have everlasting life."* **John 3:16**

### PRAYER
Dear God, I want to become a born-again Christian. I confess I am a sinner! **I am guilty of killing another person.** I ask You to forgive me for my sins and to blot them out from Your memory! I believe You sent Your only Son to die on the cross to pay for my sins. I believe He lives today. I believe Jesus is coming back! I want to be saved. Please come into my life and I will live for You, from this moment on! Thank You for making a way whereby I can be saved! I am now a born-again Christian! When I die I know I will go to heaven to be with You. In Jesus' name, I pray. AMEN!

# KISSING

**DID GOD (OR MAN) CREATE KISSING? WHAT WAS THE ORIGINAL PURPOSE OF KISSING?** God created kissing so mankind could show an outward expression of Christian love and affection . . . and as a way for families to greet each other! **Genesis 27:26-27/1 Kings 19:20**

**KISSING IS AN ANCIENT SHOW OF SUBJECTION, OBEDIENCE AND FRIENDSHIP. KISSING EVENTUALLY BECAME THE THING THAT EVERYONE DID WHETHER IT WAS A RESULT OF LOVE OR OTHERWISE! 1 Samuel 10:1/1 Kings 19:18/Hosea 13:2.**

**IT WAS A CUSTOM AMONG THE JEWS, GREEKS, AND ROMANS TO KISS THE FEET OF ANY PERSON THEY SOUGHT A SPECIAL FAVOR FROM . . . OR AS AN OUTWARD SHOW OF GRATITUDE FROM CONQUERED PEOPLE! THE KISS THEN BECAME THE ULTIMATE SIGN OF SUBJECTION AND OBEDIENCE. READ: Luke 7:36-50**
No doubt that's where the expression "**Kiss my foot**" came from! That expression calls for the other person to surrender and shows contempt! God doesn't like that expression! It's hateful!

**IT WAS AN ANCIENT CUSTOM THAT MEN GREET EACH OTHER WITH A KISS! Genesis 27:27/29:13/33:4/45:15/48:10/Exodus 4:27/18:7/1 Samuel 20:41/Luke 15:20/Acts 20:37.**

**KISSING WAS AN ANCIENT CUSTOM TO SHOW TRIBUTE TO ONE'S OWN MASTER! Psalm 2:12/1 Samuel 10:1/Job 31:27.**

**KISSING WAS ALSO AN ANCIENT CUSTOM (AMONG CHRISTIANS) AS A TOKEN OF PEACE, FRIENDSHIP AND BROTHERLY LOVE!** "*All the brethren greet you. Greet ye one another with an holy kiss.*" **1 Corinthians 16:20/2 Corinthians 13:12/1 Thessalonians 5:26/Romans 16:16.** People who greet each other with a holy kiss today are simply carrying on an oriental custom which is still being practiced among Eastern people, whether they are Christian or not! **2 Samuel 20:9**

There is a special kiss of congratulations a person gives another person, to show his satisfaction for a job well done . . . such as the kiss a child receives from his parents when he brings home good grades! **Proverbs 24:26**

There are **kisses of betrayal** which are sometimes called the "**kiss of death**" or "**Judas kiss**". **Judas betrayed Christ with such a kiss!** Read: **Matthew 26:48/Mark 14:44.**
Kissing is practiced as an act of genuine love. Kissing is sometimes a token of subjection! Moses kissed his father-in-law, and Naomi kissed her daughter-in-law! Good friends (male and female) kiss when they greet each other today, just as David and Jonathan did!

IT WAS AN ANCIENT CUSTOM TO KISS IDOLS, AND UNFORTUNATELY THIS IS STILL IN PRACTICE TODAY! A PERSON MAY **KISS THE DEED** TO A NEW CAR, **KISS THE DICE** BEFORE HE ROLLS THEM, **KISS A BIG INCOME TAX RETURN, KISS THE FOOTBALL** THAT WON THE GAME, **KISS A TROPHY** OR PAYCHECK. READ: 1 Kings 19:18

There is a **beautiful kiss** that results from mutual parent-child love! Read about the father and his prodigal son in **Luke 15:20.**
**THERE IS A SPECIAL "GOOD-BYE KISS" A PERSON GIVES A LOVED ONE WHO IS ON HIS DEATH BED!** Genesis 50:1-2

There are **holy** kisses, **loving** kisses, kisses of **comfort**, kisses of **greetings**, kisses meant to **manipulate**, **affectionate** kisses, the kisses relatives give each other in family love. People kiss animals and idols! People betray with kisses! People kiss in order to arouse their passions in an ungodly way . . . And the list goes on!
**LET'S DISCUSS THE KIND OF KISSES THAT ARE NOT PLATONIC! THESE ARE PASSIONATE AND SEXUAL KISSES WHICH ARE MEANT TO PORTRAY A DIRECT MESSAGE OR INVITATION TO GAIN SEXUAL FAVOR! ACCORDING TO THE BIBLE, WE ARE TO KEEP OUR BODY FREE FROM SIN AND TEMPTATION. OUR BODY IS THE TEMPLE OF GOD.** "*What? know ye not that your body is the temple of the Holy Ghost which is in you, which ye have of God, and ye are not your own? For ye are bought with a price: therefore glorify God in your body, and in your spirit, which are God's*" **1 Corinthians 6:19-20**

**MANY TIMES A YOUNG VIRGIN GIRL HAS SUCCOMBED TO TOO MANY KISSES AND LOST HER VIRGINITY!** The Bible says: "*Ye are bought with a price* (the death of Jesus on the cross to pay for our sins); *be not ye the servants of men.*" **1 Corinthians 7:23** The Bible says a person should remain a virgin until he is married. **1 Corinthians 7:25-26.** Doesn't it make sense to control your "**kissing**" so you won't be tempted to go too far? "*Nevertheless he that standeth stedfast in his heart, having no necessity, but hath power over his own will, and hath so decreed in his heart that he will keep his virgin* (virginity), *doeth well.*" **1 Corinthians 7:37**

**IF THERE IS A CHANCE THAT KISSING WILL LEAD YOU TO HAVE INTERCOURSE AND YOU'RE NOT MARRIED . . . ABSTAIN!** "*Let no man* (person) *deceive you with vain words: for because of these things cometh the wrath of God upon the children of disobedience.*" **Ephesians 5:6** "*And have no fellowship with the unfruitful works of darkness* (things that Satan will whisper for you to do), *but rather reprove them. For it is a shame even to speak of those things which are done of them in secret.*" **Ephesians 5:11-12**

**MANY TIMES A GIRL (OR BOY) WILL MISTAKE KISSES AND PETTING FOR LOVE!** Before you get into the "kissing game" so deep that you don't know when to stop and end up having intercourse . . . better guard your emotions and actions! "*Neither give place to the devil*" **Ephesians 4:27**

"*And walk in love, as Christ also hath loved us, and hath given himself for us an offering and a sweetsmelling savour. But fornication* (sex without marriage), *and all uncleanness* (oral sex, etc.) *or covetousness, let it not be once named among you, as becometh saints* (born-again Christians); *Neither filthiness, nor foolish talking, nor jesting, which are not convenient* (necessary); *but rather giving of thanks* (unto God).'' **Ephesians 5:2-4**

In closing: there is nothing wrong with kissing (if) the motive behind the kiss is Christian and pure! But, if the act of kissing is to deceive and gain some special favor (or) to arouse sexual appetites, outside of marriage, (or) to betray a person — stop it! God would not approve! "*Greet ye one another with a kiss of charity* (genuine love). *Peace be with you all that are in Christ Jesus.*" **1 Peter 5:14**

### PRAYER

Dear God, Please forgive me for all my sins. Please tell me if I use my **lips and tongue** in an ungodly manner! I want to please You. I don't want to ever sin again. **I know that kissing is wonderful when given out of a pure conscience.** I ask You to forgive me for any kiss which was not pure or genuinely felt! I don't want to be guilty of deceiving anyone with a kiss if I don't feel real love and concern for him! **Teach me when it is appropriate to kiss and when it is not!** Thank You for saving my soul! I now take complete charge of my body. When we meet face to face, You won't be disappointed in me! In Jesus' name. AMEN!

# LASCIVIOUSNESS

(Dirty old man — loose woman)

A person who is lascivious has **impure thoughts.** His conversations are full of **filthy** remarks. He is **shameless.** He may also be an **exhibitionist.** He uses **ribald gestures.** His actions are **suggestive and nasty.** He thinks **smut. Obscenities** are a very important part of his vocabulary. He loves **pornographic books and pictures.** He is called "**a dirty old man**". She is called a "**loose woman**"

**HE (OR SHE) IS A SEXUAL DELINQUENT!** He has a **roving eye.** He can't keep his hands to himself. He operates in **debauchery.** He uses **flattery and seduction** to win his "**easy mark**". He visualizes people as walking around naked. **He is lecherous.** He practices **fornication (sex without marriage). He (or she) is promiscuous.** He is called a **whore** in the Bible.

She is a **nymphomaniac!** The practice of adultery or **sex orgies** gives a lascivious person a special thrill. He believes in free love. He likes to have several **sex partners** at one time. He wants to own his own **concubines.** He is not above **rape or indecent assault. Sex crimes or even sex murder** is exciting to him!

A **lascivious** person is sometimes a **streetwalker or prostitute.** He is capable of being arrested for **indecent exposure.** He (or she) may be a **pimp or operate a white-slave market.** He operates or visits a **whore house.**

**MODERN DAY EXPRESSIONS WHICH TYPIFY LASCIVIOUSNESS ARE:** Over-sexed, sexed-up, woman-crazy, hot-pants, free, goatish, street-walker, hot, loose, gay, bed-hopping, switching, cuckold, fornicate, in heat, pimp, pander, violate, to be seduced, deflower, lay, and the list goes on and on!

**UNLESS A LASCIVIOUS PERSON REPENTS AND TURNS AWAY FROM SIN HE WILL NEVER SEE HEAVEN!** "*Now the works of the flesh are manifest* (made known), *which are these: Adultery, fornication, uncleanness,* **lasciviousness,** *idolatry, witchcraft, hatred, variance, emulations, wrath, strife, seditions, heresies, envyings, murders, drunkenness, revellings* (wild parties), *and such like: of the which I tell you before, as I have also told you in time past, that they which do such things shall not inherit the kingdom of God.*" Galatians 5:19-21/2 Corinthians 12:20-21

"*Let no man say when he is tempted, I am tempted of God: for God cannot be tempted with evil; neither tempteth he any man: but every man is tempted* (by Satan),*wh en he is drawn away of his own lust, and enticed. Then when lust hath conceived, it bringeth forth sin: and sin, when it is finished, bringeth forth death.*" James 1:13-15

**ACCORDING TO THE BIBLE, A LASCIVIOUS PERSON'S UNDERSTANDING OF GOD AND THE BIBLE IS DARKENED BY SATAN! HE IS ALIENATED FROM THE KNOWLEDGE OF GOD. HE IS IGNORANT. HIS HEART IS BLIND.** "*Who being past feeling* (conscience) *have given themselves over unto* **lasciviousness,** *to work* (do) *all uncleanness with greediness.*" **Ephesians 4:18-19** "*when we walked in* **lasciviousness,** *lusts, excess of wine, revellings, banquetings, and abominable idolatries:*" **1 Peter 4:3**

**THE CONDITION OF A LASCIVIOUS PERSON IS THE RESULT OF LISTENING TO THE VOICE OF SATAN . . . HE INVENTED LIES AND CONFUSION!** "*For from within, out of the heart of men, proceed evil thoughts, adulteries, fornications, murders, thefts, covetousness, wickedness, deceit,* **las c iviousness,** *an evil eye, blasphemy, pride, foolishness: All these evil things come from within, and defile the man.*" **Mark 7:21-23**

"*For it is written, As I live, saith the Lord, every knee shall bow to me, and every tongue shall confess to God. So then every one of us shall give account of himself to God.*" **Romans 14:11-12**

"*The night is far spent, the day is at hand: let us therefore cast off the works of darkness, and let us put on the armour of light* (Christ, the Bible, and truth). *Let us walk honestly, as in the day; not in rioting and drunkenness, not in chambering and* **wantonness,** *not in strife and envying. But put ye on the Lord Jesus Christ, and* **make not provision for the flesh, to fulfil the lusts thereof.**" **Romans 13:12-14**

**LASCIVIOUSNESS = WANTONNESS! 2 Peter 2:18**

**LASCIVIOUSNESS IS A SIN THAT GOD HATES, BUT HE LOVES THE SINNER! GOD WANTS HIM TO BE SAVED AND TURN AWAY FROM THIS EVIL CONDITION. GOD WILL LOVINGLY FORGIVE HIM AND WILL HELP HIM CLEAN UP HIS LIFE, HIS THOUGHTS AND HIS HEART WHEN HE REPENTS. IF THE PERSON WHO IS LASCIVIOUS DOES NOT REPENT AND TURN AWAY FROM ALL LUST AND SIN IN HIS LIFE, HE WILL NEVER BE ALLOWED TO ENTER HEAVEN! SATAN IS RESPONSIBLE FOR CONFUSING AND PUTTING THIS PERSON INTO BONDAGE. SATAN IS A THIEF!** "*The thief cometh not but for to steal, and to kill, and to destroy: I* (Christ) *am come that they might have life, and that they might have it more abundantly.*" **John 10:10**

"*This I say then, Walk in the* (Holy) *Spirit, and ye shall not fulfil the lust of the flesh.*" **Galatians 5:16**

**IF YOU ARE LASCIVIOUS, MEMORIZE AND REPEAT THIS VERSE 100 TIMES A DAY:** "*I can do all things through Christ which strengtheneth me.*" **Philippians 4:13**

### PRAYER

Dear God, **Please forgive me now for committing lustful sins in my body, mind and soul.** Please forgive me for **sinning against other people** through my **uncontrolled lust.** I know that Satan has been holding me in bondage. Satan doesn't want me to go to Heaven. I realize I have been serving Satan! I want to be free to make wholesome choices. **I don't want to be a slave to sex any more.** I want to feel good about myself. I must have Your loving help. I don't know how You could love me like I am but I know that You do! For this I thank You with all my heart! Please come into my life and live in me. Please forgive me for all sin in my life. I turn away from all sin in my life. I will read my Bible. I will pray each day. I will stay away from all people who would seek to entice me back into sin. I will go to church regularly so I can grow in wisdom. If Satan should come against me, I will also repeat "Get thee behind me, Satan!" I love You and I will serve only You! My flesh will no longer rule my heart. In Jesus' name, AMEN!

162

# LAW BREAKERS

*"Where there is no vision, the people perish: but he that keepeth the law, happy is he."* **Proverbs 29:18**

*". . .We know that **the law is good,** if a man use it lawfully; Knowing this, that the law is not made for a righteous man, but for the **lawless** and disobedient, for the ungodly and for sinners, for unholy and profane, for murderers of fathers and murderers of mothers, for manslayers, for whoremongers, for them that defile themselves with mankind, for menstealers, for liars, for perjured persons, and if there be any other thing that is contrary to sound doctrine."* **1 Timothy 1:8-10**

A debt is often referred to as a vow or promise in the Bible. The Bible says if you make a debt or promise, you are not to hesitate to pay it. If you hesitate then it is counted as sin to you. Whatever we say we will do is counted as a promise to God according to **Deuteronomy 23:21-23.** Read: **Leviticus 27.** *"If a man vow a vow unto the Lord, or swear an oath to bind his soul with a bond; he shall not break his word, he shall do according to all that proceedeth out of his mouth."* **Numbers 30:2**

**ROMANS 7:1 SAYS THAT THE LAW HAS DOMINION OVER A MAN AS LONG AS HE LIVES!**

**2 PETER 2:10 SAYS THAT PEOPLE WHO WALK AFTER THE FLESH DESPISE GOVERNMENT, ARE SELF WILLED, AND ARE NOT AFRAID TO SPEAK EVIL OF DIGNITARIES!**

**ROMANS 1:29-31 SAYS LAW BREAKERS ARE WITHOUT UNDERSTANDING. THEY'RE IMPLACABLE AND UNMERCIFUL. AND EVEN THOUGH THEY KNOW THE JUDGEMENT OF GOD . . . THEY NOT ONLY BREAK GOD'S LAWS AND MAN'S LAWS, BUT HAVE PLEASURE IN OTHERS THAT DO THE SAME THING!**

**CHRIST CAME TO FULFIL THE LAW!** **Matthew 5:17.** *"Bear ye one another's burdens, and so fulfil the law of Christ."* **Galatians 6:2**

*"For all the law is fulfilled in one word, even in this; thou shalt love thy neighbour as thyself."* **Galatians 5:14**

**THE PERSON WHO OBEYS GOD'S LAWS AND THE LAWS OF HUMAN GOVERNMENT IS BLESSED!** *". . .Whoso looketh into the perfect law of liberty, and continueth therein, he being not a forgetful hearer, but a doer of the work, this man shall be blessed in his deed (obedience)."* **James 1:25**

Ezekiel chapter 18 gives the description of a person who obeys God's laws and man's laws. He is not an idolator. He does not defile his neighbour's wife, does not oppress anyone. He pays his debts. He does not use violence. He feeds the poor and clothes the naked. He does not charge unusual and cruel interest. He does not discriminate between people. He deals fairly and believes in justice among all. God placed individual responsibility on each person for his own sins! The son shall not be held liable to bear the sins of the father and vice-versa!

**GOD CREATED HUMAN LAWS UNIVERSALLY FOR OUR BENEFIT, SECURITY, AND HAPPINESS!** *"And thou shalt **teach them ordinances and laws,** and shalt shew (show) them the way wherein they must walk, and the work that they must do. Moreover thou shalt provide out of all the people **able men such as fear God, men of truth, hating covetousness;** and place such over them to be **rulers of thousands, and rulers of hundred, rulers of fifties, and rulers of tens.** And let them judge the people at all seasons: and it shall be, that every great matter they shall bring unto thee, but every small matter they shall judge: so shall it be easier for thyself, and they shall bear the burden with thee. If thou shalt do this thing, and **God commanded thee** (to do) so, then thou shalt be able to endure, **and all this people shall also go to their place in peace."* **Exodus 18:20-23**

**GOD SAID HE WILL PUT HIS LAWS IN OUR HEARTS** (Hebrews 10:16), **AND IN OUR MINDS** (Hebrews 8:10). *"Put them in mind to be subject to **principalities and powers, to obey magistrates,** to be ready to (do) every good work. To speak evil of no man, to be no brawlers, but gentle, shewing all meekness unto all men."* **Titus 3:1-2**

**GOD SEES AND KNOWS THERE ARE CORRUPT LEADERS IN POWER!** He knows there are corrupt judges who will accept bribes, **Micah 3:11.** Nevertheless, God commands us to obey all human governmental laws because they are created for our safety and peace! God alone will straighten everything out with justice and fairness in His own way and in His own time! Just because there are corrupt leaders in every country of the world does not give mankind license to disobey God's laws or man's laws! *"For whosoever shall keep the whole law, and yet offend in one point, he is guilty of all."* **James 2:10**

**THE BIBLE SAYS THAT WHEN A PERSON BOASTS ABOUT BREAKING THE LAW HE DISHONORS GOD** (Romans 2:23). God calls the law that says: THOU SHALT LOVE THY NEIGHBOUR AS THYSELF," the "royal law"! **James 2:8** God said whatever we speak or do will be judged by the "law of liberty"! **James 2:12.**

God says the law is "righteous" **Romans 2:26.** God said He would put His law in our inward parts and write them in our hearts **Jeremiah 31:33.** *"Great peace have they which love thy law: and nothing shall offend them."* **Psalm 119:165**

*"For as many as have sinned without the law shall also perish without the law; and as many as have sinned in the law shall be judged by the law; for not the hearers of the law are just before God, but the doers of the law shall be justified."* **Romans 2:12-13**

**GOD'S LAWS ARE SPIRITUAL! Romans 7:14**

### PRAYER

Dear God, Please forgive me for all my sins. I have broken many **laws.** Please help me to become honest. I will pay my fines and taxes on time. I want to do what is right. I want to be a Christian. I don't like myself because of the sins I have committed. Please help me clean up my life. I will be obedient to Your laws and to man's laws from this moment on! Come into my heart to stay. Thank You for loving and forgiving me. In Jesus' name, I pray. AMEN!

# LAWSUITS

God created the establishment of lower and higher courts. God believes in justice and fairness! A person should always pray and seek God's will in legal matters, before he resorts to court action! *"Hearken now unto my voice, I will give thee counsel. and God shall be with thee: Be thou for the people to God-ward, that thou mayest bring the causes unto God: And thou shalt teach them ordinances and laws, and shalt shew* (show) *them the way wherein they must walk, and the work that they must do."* **Exodus 18:19-20**

*"Moreover thou shalt provide out of all the people able men, such as fear God, men of truth, hating covetousness; and place such over them, to be* **rulers of thousands, and rulers of hundreds, rulers of fifties, and rulers of tens.** *And let them judge the people at all seasons: and it shall be, that every great matter they shall bring unto thee, but every small matter they shall judge: so shall it be easier for thyself, and they shall bear the burden with thee. If thou shalt do this thing, and God command thee* (to do) *so, then thou shalt be able to endure, and all this people shall also go to their place in peace."* **Exodus 18:21-23**

**CHRISTIANS ARE FORBIDDEN TO GO TO COURT BEFORE NON-BELIEVERS!** *"Dare any of you, having a matter against another, go to law before the unjust* (sinners), *and not before the saints* (born-again Christians)?" **1 Corinthians 6:1**

**CHRISTIANS SHOULD SETTLE DIFFERENCES BETWEEN THEMSELVES WITHOUT A LAW SUIT!** *"Do ye not know that the saints* (born-again Christians) *shall judge the world* (during the Millennium)? *and if the world shall be* **judged** *by you, are ye unworthy to judge the* **smallest matters?** *Know ye not that we shall judge angels? how much more* (we should be able to judge the) *things that pertain to this life?"* **1 Corinthians 6:2-3**

**A CHRISTIAN DOES WRONG WHEN HE SUES ANOTHER CHRISTIAN! HE SHOULD WORK OUT A FAIR AND EQUITABLE SETTLEMENT OUT OF COURT! 1 Corinthians 6:4-8**

**JESUS SAID:** *"Agree with thine adversary quickly whiles thou art in the way with him; lest at any time the adversary deliver thee to the* **judge,** *and the judge deliver thee to the* **officer,** *and thou be cast into* **prison.** *Verily I say unto thee, Thou shalt by no means come out thence* (out of the courtroom, jail, or prison), *till thou hast* **paid** *the uttermost farthing* (the debt owed down to the very penny)." **Matthew 5:25-26**

**IF YOU SHOW ANY DEGREE OF PARTIALITY AND INJUSTICE YOU BREAK GOD'S LAW! THIS MAKES YOU A TRANSGRESSOR OF THE LAW.** *"For whosoever shall keep the whole law, and yet* **offend in one point, he is guilty of all.** *"* **James 2:10** *"Are ye not then* **partial** *in yourselves, and are become* **judges** *of evil thoughts?"* **James 2:4** *"If ye fulfil the* **royal law** *according to the scripture, Thou shalt love thy neighbour as thyself, ye do well: But if ye have* **respect to persons, ye commit sin, and are convinced of the law as transgressors."** James 2:8-9**

**TAKE INVENTORY OF YOUR HEART AND MOTIVES BEFORE YOU SUE ANYONE!** *"Also to punish the just is not good. . ."* **Proverbs 17:26**

**BEFORE YOU DECIDE TO GO TO COURT TO SUE ANOTHER PERSON: TAKE INVENTORY OF YOUR MOTIVES TO SEE IF YOU'RE GUILTY!** *"Withhold not good from them to whom it is due, when it is in the power of thine hand to do* (pay or return) *it."* **Proverbs 3:27** *"Devise not evil against thy neighbour, seeing he dwelleth securely by thee."* **Proverbs 3:29** *"Strive not with a man without cause, if he have done thee no harm."* **Proverbs 3:30**

*"He that turneth away his ear from hearing the law, even his prayer shall be abomination* (disgusting to God)." **Proverbs 28:9**

**IF A PERSON HAS A LEGITIMATE REASON TO SUE ANOTHER PERSON AND IT IS UNDERSTOOD THAT IT CANNOT BE SETTLED OUT OF COURT, MAKE SURE YOU HIRE ONLY A CHRISTIAN LAWYER! PLANS FAIL WHEN THERE ISN'T GOOD COUNSELLING. THEY SUCCEED WHEN WISE MEN COUNSEL! Proverbs 15:22** *"Rejoice not when thine enemy falleth, and let not thine heart be glad when he stumbleth: Lest the Lord see it, and it displease him, and he turn away his wrath from him* (and place it on you)." **Proverbs 24:17-18**

*"When the righteous are in authority, the people rejoice: but when the wicked beareth rule, the people mourn."* **Proverbs 29:2**

*"**Judges and officers** shalt thou make thee in all thy gates, which the Lord thy God giveth thee, throughout thy tribes: and they shall **judge the people with just judgement.** Thou shalt not wrest judgment: **thou shalt not respect persons, neither take a gift:** for a gift* (bribe) *doth **blind the eyes of the wise, and pervert the words** of the righteous."* **Deuteronomy 16:18-19**

**THE SCRIPTURES SAY THAT TWO OR THREE WITNESSES ARE REQUIRED FOR CONVICTION.** *"At the mouth of two witnesses, or three witnesses, shall he that is worthy of death be put to death: but at the mouth of one witness he shall not be put to death. The hands of the witnesses shall be first upon him to put him to death, and afterward the hands of all the people. So thou shalt put the evil away from among you."* **Deuteronomy 17:6-7 Read: Numbers 35:30/19:15/Matthew 18:16/2 Corinthians 13:1/1 Timothy 5:19/Hebrews 10:28**

**REGARDING THE USE OF SUPREME COURT:** *"If there arise a matter too hard for thee in judgment, between blood and blood, between plea and plea, and between stroke and stroke, being matters of controversy within thy gates."* **Deuteronomy 17:8** *"According to the sentence of the law which they shall teach thee, and according to the judgment which they shall tell thee, thou shalt do: thou shalt not decline from the sentence which they shall shew thee, to the right hand, nor to the left."* **Deuteronomy 17:11**

*"**Blessed is the man** (person) **that walketh not in the counsel of the ungodly, nor standeth in the way of sinners, nor sitteth in the seat of the scornful. But his delight is in the law of the Lord; and in His law** (of love and forgiveness) **doth he meditate day and night. And he shall be like a tree planted by the rivers of water, that bringeth forth his fruit in his season; his leaf also shall not wither; and whatsoever he doeth shall prosper."* **Psalm 1:1-3**

. . .

### PRAYER

Dear God, Please forgive me for all my sins. I do not like to go to court. I ask you to forgive me if I have wronged anyone. **Please give me proper guidance in the way You want me to handle my legal matters.** Please come into my life and live in me. Guide me in every area of my life and I will praise You forever. In Jesus' name, I pray. AMEN!

# LAZINESS

*"From the fruit of his lips a man is filled with good things as surely as the work of his hands rewards him."* **Proverbs 12:14** (New International Version)

**A PERSON WHO IS TOO LAZY TO WORK MAY STEAL TO GET WHAT HE WANTS!** *"Let him that stole steal no more: but rather let him labour, working with his hands the thing which is good (honest), that he may have to give to him that needeth."* **Ephesians 4:28**

*"Wealth gotten by vanity shall be diminished: but he that gathereth by* (his own) *labour shall increase."* **Proverbs 13:11**

*"Diligent hands will rule, but laziness ends in slave labour."* **Proverbs 12:24** (New International Version)

**LAZINESS CAUSES EXCESSIVE SLEEPINESS!** *"How long wilt thou* **sleep**, *O sluggard* (lazy person)? *When wilt thou arise out of thy* **sleep**? *Yet a little sleep, a little slumber, a little folding of the hands to* **sleep**: *So shall thy poverty come as one that travelleth and thy want as an armed man."* **Proverbs 6:9-11** *"The* **sleep of a labouring man** *is sweet, whether he eat little or much: but the abundance of the rich will not suffer* (allow) *him to* **sleep**.*"* **Ecclesiastes 5:12** *"Slothfulness casteth into a* **deep sleep**; *and an idle soul shall suffer hunger."* **Proverbs 19:15** *"He that gathereth* (his harvest) *in summer is a wise son: but he that* **sleepeth** *in harvest is a son that causeth shame."* **Proverbs 10:5** *"Love not sleep, lest thou come to poverty: open thine eyes, and thou shalt be satisfied with bread."* **Proverbs 20:13/9:9**

**A LAZY PERSON USES OTHER PEOPLE'S MONEY TO GET WHAT HE WANTS!** *"Let love be without dissimulation* (phony). *Abhor* (hate) *that which is evil; cleave to that which is good. Be kindly affectioned one to another with brotherly love; in honour preferring one another; not slothful in business; fervent in spirit; serving the Lord; rejoicing in hope; patient in tribulation; continuing instant in prayer."* **Romans 12:9-12**

**PARENTS . . . DON'T ALLOW YOUR CHILDREN TO DEVELOP A LAZY TRAIT! THE RESPONSIBILITY IS ON YOUR SHOULDERS!** *"Train up a child in the way he should go: and when he is old, he will not depart from it."* **Proverbs 22:6**

**A LAZY PERSON IS CONCEITED!** *"The sluggard* (lazy person) *(thinks he) is wiser in his own conceit than seven men that can render reason* (solve a problem).*"* **Proverbs 26:16**

**A LAZY PERSON IS TOO LAZY TO MOVE HIMSELF!** *"As the door turneth upon his hinges, so doeth the slothful* (lazy person) *upon his bed."* **Proverbs 26:14**

LAZY PEOPLE ARE **CARELESS AND UNPREDICTABLE** Proverbs 6:6-9

LAZY PEOPLE **IRRITATE OTHERS** Proverbs 10:26

LAZY PEOPLE **FOLD THEIR HANDS** INSTEAD OF WORKING Proverbs 24:33/26:15

LAZY PEOPLE **WON'T COOK FOR THEMSELVES** Proverbs 12:27

**LAZY PEOPLE ARE "WISHFUL THINKERS"!** *"The soul of the sluggard* (lazy person) *desireth, and hath nothing: but the soul of the diligent shall be made fat."* **Proverbs 13:4**

**A LAZY PERSON'S LIFE IS FULL OF TROUBLES!** *"The way of the slothful* (lazy) *man is as a hedge of thorns: but the way of the righteous is made plain."* **Proverbs 15:19**

LAZY PEOPLE **WASTE** EVERYTHING! *"He also that is slothful* (lazy) *in his work is* (a) *brother to him that is a great waster."* **Proverbs 18:9**

LAZY PEOPLE **REFUSE TO WORK!** *"The sluggard* (lazy person) *will not plow by reason of the cold; therefore shall he beg in harvest, and have nothing."* **Proverbs 20:4** *"The desire of the slothful killeth him; for his hands refuse to labour."* **Proverbs 21:25**

LAZY PEOPLE USE **SENSELESS EXCUSES** FOR THEIR LAZINESS! **Proverbs 22:13**

LAZY PEOPLE **DON'T WANT TO BE TAUGHT** ANYTHING! **Proverbs 24:30**

LAZY PEOPLE **SIT IDLY BY AND WATCH THEIR PROPERTY RUIN!** **Proverbs 24:31** *"By much slothfulness the building decayeth; and through idleness of the hands the house droppeth through."* **Ecclesiastes 10:18**

A LAZY PERSON **CAN NOT BE TRUSTED** (Read the parable of the talents: Luke 19:11/Matthew 16:27)

LAZY PEOPLE ARE USUALLY **TOO LAZY TO GET SAVED!** Hebrews 6:11-12

LAZY PEOPLE **LACK THE ABILITY TO CARRY ON IN THE BUSINESS WORLD!** Romans 12:11

LAZY PEOPLE CAN **LEARN A LESSON** IF THEY WILL WATCH HOW BUSY **ANTS** ARE!

# Laziness

**PRAYER**

Dear God, Please help me overcome my terrible habit of being lazy! From this moment on I will work eight hours a day! I will read my Bible. I will not spend so much time in front of a television set! I will pray several times a day for wisdom. I will do my part in all areas of housekeeping. I will not be a burden or embarrassment to others. I will hold up my end of the work load. I confess I have been a burden to others and myself. I need Your help to overcome. Please forgive me for all my sins and I will serve You as a good Christian should. In Jesus' name, I pray. AMEN!

# LIES

## *"Death and life are in the power of the tongue."* Proverbs 18:21

**GOD HATES LYING!** *"Lying lips are* (an) *abomination to the Lord: but they that deal truly are his delight."* **Proverbs 12:22**

**IS THIS ANYONE YOU KNOW?** *"Thou lovest evil more than good; and lying rather than to speak righteousness. Thou lovest all devouring words, O thou deceitful tongue."* **Psalm 52:3-4**

**YOU CAN LIE TO YOURSELF AND YOU CAN LIE TO EVERYONE ELSE ... BUT GOD HEARS YOUR LIES! YOU'RE IN REAL TROUBLE ... YOU NEED TO REPENT AND KICK THE HABIT!** *"Every word of God is pure: he is a shield unto them that put their trust in him. Add thou not unto his words, lest he reprove thee, and thou be found a liar."* **Proverbs 30:5-6**

**THE BIBLE SAYS THE LIPS OF TRUTH SHALL BE ESTABLISHED FOR EVER: BUT A LYING TONGUE IS BUT FOR A MOMENT Proverbs 12:19**

**THE BIBLE SAYS A LIAR LIKES TO LISTEN TO A PERSON WITH A NAUGHTY TONGUE! Proverbs 17:4**

**DAVID EXPRESSED MY SENTIMENTS WHEN HE SAID:** *"I hate and abhor lying: but thy* (God's) *law do I love."* **Psalm 119:163** *"He that worketh deceit shall not dwell within my house: he that telleth lies shall not tarry in my sight."* **Psalm 101:7**

**THE SCRIPTURES SAY THAT PEOPLE WHO DELIGHT IN LIES WILL BLESS YOU WITH THEIR MOUTH AND CURSE YOU INWARDLY! Psalm 62:4**

*"Let the lying lips be put to silence; which speak grievous things proudly and contemptuously against the righteous."* **Psalm 31:18**

**IF YOU ARE A LIAR YOU NEED TO PRAY THIS PRAYER. GOD WILL HELP YOU OVERCOME!** *"Deliver my soul, O Lord, from lying lips, and from a deceitful tongue."* **Psalm 120:2**

**A CHRISTIAN SHOULD NEVER BE GUILTY OF LYING! Colossians 3:9-10**

**Ephesians 4:25 SAYS TO PUT AWAY ALL LYING AND SPEAK THE TRUTH BECAUSE WE ARE MEMBERS ONE OF ANOTHER!**

**Exodus 23:1 SAYS NOT TO GIVE A FALSE REPORT OR SHAKE HANDS WITH A WICKED PERSON AND AGREE TO BE A LYING WITNESS FOR HIM!**

**THE BIBLE SAYS THAT THE PERSON WHO LIES IN-CREASES HIS LIES DAILY! Hosea 12:1**

*"A faithful witness will not lie: but a false witness will utter lies."* **Proverbs 14:5**

**PROVERB 10:18 SAYS PEOPLE HIDE HATRED WITH LYING LIPS!**

**MICAH 6:12 SAYS THAT RICH PEOPLE TELL LIES!**

**2 THESSALONIANS 2:9-12 SAYS THAT WHEN A PERSON REFUSES TO BELIEVE THE TRUTH OF GOD AND THE BIBLE, GOD WILL SEND HIM A STRONG DELUSION SO THAT HE WILL BELIEVE A LIE!**

# COULD YOU BE CONNED?

**TITUS 1:2 AND HEBREWS 6:18 SAYS GOD CANNOT LIE.** PRAISE GOD!

**PSALM 63:11** SAYS THAT THOSE WHO SPEAK **LIES** SHALL BE STOPPED!

**A LIAR CANNOT ENTER INTO THE ETERNAL CITY OF GOD Revelation 21:27/22:15**

*"A false witness shall not be unpunished, and he that speaketh lies shall not escape."* **Proverbs 19:5** *"A false witness shall not be unpunished, and he that speaketh lies shall perish."* **Proverbs 19:9**

### THE HISTORY OF A LIE

First somebody told it,
Then the room couldn't hold it,
So the busy tongues rolled it
Till they got it outside!

Then the crowd came across it,
And never once lost it,
But tossed it and tossed it,
Till it grew long and wide.

This lie brought forth others,
Evil sisters and brothers,
And fathers and mothers,
A terrible crew,
As headlong they hurried,
The people they flurried
And troubled and worried,
As lies always do.

So, evil-boded,
This monstrous lie goaded,
Till at last it exploded,
In sin and shame.

But from mud and from mire
The pieces flew higher,
Till they hit the sad liar,
And killed his good name.
· · ·

#### PRAYER:

Dear God, **Please forgive me for being a liar.** Please forgive all my sins! Help me to control my tongue. Help me to do and say the things that please You. In Jesus' name, AMEN!

# LONELINESS

*"Who shall separate us from the love of Christ? Shall tribulation, or distress, or persecution, or famine, or nakedness, or peril, or sword (trouble, war)?"* **Romans 8:35**

*"Nay (no), in all these things we are more than conquerors through him that loved us. For I am persuaded, that neither death, nor life, nor angels, nor principalities, nor powers, nor things present, nor things to come, nor height, nor depth, nor any other creature; shall be able to separate us from the love of God, which is in Christ Jesus our Lord."* **Romans 8:37-39**

**A PERSON CAN EXPERIENCE LONELINESS EVEN WHEN THERE ARE PEOPLE ALL AROUND!** Many people confuse loneliness with alone-ness. **Loneliness is feeling alone.** A person may have many friends or social contacts, yet he is lonely because he is not satisfied with his relationships.

**BECAUSE THE THEORY OF "DO YOUR OWN THING" HAS BECOME A WAY OF LIFE TODAY, IT HAS CREATED A NATIONAL EPIDEMIC OF LONELY PEOPLE!**

**LONELINESS IS A REAL PROBLEM. BUT WHAT CAUSES LONELINESS?** There are many reasons for loneliness. Social conditions or **personal crises** such as a **death of a spouse,** parent or child may cause **loneliness.**

**WE ARE CREATED IN THE IMAGE OF GOD. WE WERE CREATED TO HAVE FELLOWSHIP AS SOCIAL BEINGS. WE NEED EACH OTHER!** Analyze what causes you to be lonely. Has there been a recent death? Have you moved to a new town? Are you bored with too much time on your hands? Do you not feel loved by one special person? Is Christ living in your heart 24 hours a day in a very personal way? Do you constantly feel the presence of God in your life?

**LONELINESS CAN BE OVERCOME THROUGH CONSTANT PRAYER!** Without realize it, we become "victims" of loneliness, when we fail to visit with God throughout the day and night!

**GOD EXPECTS US TO DO OUR PART IN OVERCOMING LONELINESS! Ephesians 6:9** says that God is no respecter of persons. He doesn't want you to be unhappy! **Philippians 4:6 says:** *"Be careful for nothing; but in everything by prayer and supplication with thanksgiving let your requests be made known unto God."*

TV isn't very much comfort when you're lonely because **God created us with the built-in need to talk!** The best cure for loneliness is to become a born-again Christian. Then join (or organize) a prayer chain through your local church! There's always a shortage of volunteers. You could be a very important part of this much needed ministry! God would certainly bless you for caring about others. Think of the new friends you'd meet! *"Bear ye one another's burdens, and so fulfill the law of Christ."* **Galatians 6:2**

**A PERSON MAY FEEL LONELY BECAUSE HE'S AFRAID TO EXPRESS HIS INNERMOST FEELINGS!** He **fears** they will seem boring or he may appear weak to another person! He **fears** if he is not on top of every situation others will not enjoy his company!

**PEOPLE WHO ONLY SHARE "TALES OF WOE" WITH OTHERS — SET A TRAP FOR THEMSELVES! THEIR SAD TALES MAY BECOME THEIR "RECREATION," IF THEY DON'T TAKE ACTION TO CORRECT THEIR SITUATION! GOD WILL HELP YOU OVERCOME LONELINESS IF YOU JUST ASK!** *"My voice shalt thou hear in the morning, O Lord; in the morning will I direct my prayer unto thee, and will look up."* **Psalm 5:3**

**THE CURE TO OVERCOMING LONELINESS STARTS WHEN YOU GET RIGHT WITH GOD!** Pray several times a day. Fast one meal every other day. Read the Bible at least 30 minutes each day. Make a determination that **with God's help you will overcome!** Resolve to keep your thoughts, conversations, and body clean. **Be patient and God will direct you.** Don't expect a miracle overnight, but do expect God to reveal His desire for your life in this area! Change your hairstyle a little. It will lift your spirits! Repaint a small room in your house. Change the furniture and pictures around. **Do something, don't sit idle!** Don't **over-eat, don't tell everyone your problems!** God knows your hurts. Give Him a chance to work out His plan! Whatever you do **go to church twice a week** and make it a point to **speak to at least two people you don't know.** They might be lonely too and you might be the only person who notices them. Think of others in a loving and positive way, while God is working out His plan for you!

**EVERYONE HAS TEMPORARY PERIODS OF LONELINESS. EVEN JESUS WAS LONELY SOME OF THE TIME. BUT IF LONELINESS PERSISTS AND HAS BECOME A WAY OF LIFE — THEN YOU ARE DEFINITELY NOT LIVING IN GOD'S PERFECT WILL FOR YOUR LIFE!** Extreme or chronic loneliness is neither **normal or healthy.** Underneath, there are deep feelings of **inadequacy, isolation and insecurity!** Perhaps you need to see a good Christian counselor if you feel **worthless and unable** to maintain close relationships!

**DON'T LIVE IN THE PAST!** This is the most unproductive thing a person can ever do. God said we are to occupy (work) until He returns! If you are too old to work an outside job, work at locating good, clean, used clothing for the needy for your church, over the phone! Locate someone who will donate blankets, shoes, eyeglasses. If you don't know who to call, try calling the merchants where you trade and ask them if they will assist you on a one-time only basis. Then, call the church and ask if there are any needy families with children! Call around and find some people who are willing to donate a Bible to a needy family, jail or prison. **Keep yourself busy!** If you are living right, in the eyes of God, you will see your loved ones in time. If your spouse is dead and gone, get busy! He would want you to! **Don't live in the past!**

**LONELINESS IS NOT ALL BAD ... IT CAN BRING BENEFITS!** A person may be forced to analyze his life and "re-group!" He may find he is too **aggressive** and has driven off friends! Or, perhaps he's too **shy** to contribute to a good conversation! He may be too **dependent** on others! Ask God to reveal your shortcomings and tell you what you need to do to overcome them! The rewards of knowing far outweigh the pain of loneliness!

### PRAYER

Dear God, I need Your help! I acknowledge and confess that I am a sinner! I ask You to forgive all my past sins. I will sin no more! Come very near to me and give me a new direction for my life! I have been lonely long enough! Please put some happiness back into my life! I apologize that I have suffered this condition as long as I have without asking You to help me. With Your help I can make it! I will serve You! Instead of telling others how **lonely** I am, I will tell them how **loving** and **gracious** You are! I praise You! I know that when others have let me down, You are always there waiting for me to call on You and talk to You! Thank You for that. In Jesus' name, I pray! AMEN!

# LUKEWARM CHRISTIANS

**JESUS SAID:** *"I know thy works* (the condition of your heart, what you say, think, do), *that thou art neither cold* (hate me) *nor hot* (spiritually on fire): *I would* (wish) *that thou wert* (were) *cold or hot. So then because thou art* **lukewarm,** *and neither cold nor hot, I will spue* (vomit) *thee out of my mouth."* **Revelation 3:15-16**

**JESUS SAID:** *"Not every one that saith unto me, Lord, Lord, shall enter into the kingdom of heaven; but* (only) *he that doeth the will of my Father which is in heaven."* **Matthew 7:21**

## WHAT IS A LUKEWARM CHRISTIAN?

**1.** He is a person who thinks he is a Christian because his parents had him **SPRINKLED** as an infant. He has never had a personal born-again experience! He has never asked the Holy Spirit to come into his life! **WATER WILL NOT WASH AWAY SINS!**

**2.** He is a person who has been **BAPTISED** without having received a born-again experience! He falsely believes his brief "dunking" in water will save him! **WATER WILL NOT WASH AWAY SINS!** *Ye must be born again or you cannot see the kingdom of God.* **John 3:3**

**3.** He is only a **CHURCH MEMBER,** yet he calls himself a Christian. He could be listed on the membership roll of every church in the entire world, but until he has a born-again experience he will never see heaven! **Jesus said:** *"Whosoever committeth sin is the servant of sin."* **John 8:34 NO CHURCH MEMBERSHIP CAN GUARANTEE YOU WILL GO TO HEAVEN!**

**4.** He thinks that because he **gives to the poor, goes to Sunday school, pays tithes, and is a good person** that he is a Christian and will go to heaven. *"Not by works of righteousness which we have done, but according to his* (God's) *mercy he saved us."* **Titus 3:5**

**5.** He calls himself a Christian, though he does not believe that Christ died on the cross to pay for our sins and arose on the third day and is alive today! **Jesus said:** *"If God were your Father, ye would love me: for I proceeded forth and came from God; neither came I of myself, but he sent me."* **John 8:42** *"He that is of God* (has been born again) *heareth God's words: ye therefore hear them not, because ye are not of God."* **John 8:47**

**6.** He thinks he is a Christian while he worships **FALSE GODS** such as money, power, intellect, sports, drugs, alcohol, sex. *"For what shall it profit a man, if he shall gain the whole world, and lose his own soul?"* **Mark 8:36** *"Ever learning* (worldly things) *and never able to come to the knowledge of the truth* (the Bible)." **2 Timothy 3:7**

**7.** He thinks he is a Christian because he is a **MEMBER OF A CHURCH** which has an outstanding minister and large membership. *But if you attend a church that denies you must be born again, or that does not teach the entire Bible, you are practicing a false religion! There are no denominations in heaven . . . only born-again Christians! If you attend a church which teaches from writings of some person or group — you are worshipping the ideas of mortal man, and not God!* *"Beware of false prophets; which come to you in sheep's clothing* (pretending to be godly), *but inwardly they are ravening wolves."* **Matthew 7:15** *"It is better to trust in the Lord than to put confidence in man."* **Psalm 118:8 READ: 2 Timothy 3:5**

**8.** He is a person who embraces the **occult teachings such as: astrology, fortune telling, hypnosis, ESP, Humanism, man's psychology, reincarnation.** He may embrace **cult religions which are false teachings.** *"Heaven and earth shall pass away: but my* (God's) *words* (the Bible) *shall not pass away."* **Luke 21:33**

**9.** He falsely believes that because he was **BORN IN THE UNITED STATES** that he is a Christian, since it is often referred to as a "Christian Nation!"

**10.** He thinks he is a Christian just because he believes there is a **God** as opposed to believing in **evolution.** He is not a born-again Christian, yet he feels quite safe that he will go to heaven! **Jesus said:** *"I go my way, and ye shall seek me, and shall die in your sins: whither I go, ye cannot come."* **John 8:21** He falsely thinks that there's **plenty of time to get saved — perhaps on his death bed.** *"A double minded man is unstable in all his ways."* **James 1:8** *"Now is the accepted time* (to become a born-again Christian): *behold* (listen), *now is the day of salvation."* **2 Corinthians 6:2** *"Therefore to him that knoweth to do good, and doeth it not, to him it is sin."* **James 4:17**

. . .

## Lukewarm Christians

### PRAYER

Dear God, Please forgive me for all my sins. I want to become a born-again Christian right now. I acknowledge that I am a sinner. I confess to You that I have sinned. I am sorry for my sins. I ask You to save me and blot out my sins from Your memory. I believe that Jesus died on the cross for my sins and arose and is alive today. In Jesus' name, I pray. AMEN!

**A PERSON IS EITHER A GENUINE 100 PERCENT BORN-AGAIN CHRISTIAN, OR HE IS NOT A CHRISTIAN AT ALL! THERE'S NO SUCH THING AS A "HALF-WAY" CHRISTIAN!**

# LUST

*"But every man is tempted, when he is drawn away of his own lust, and enticed. Then when lust hath conceived, it bringeth forth sin: and sin, when it is finished, bringeth forth death* (eternal separation from God).*" James 1:14-15*

**LUST = SIN = WORKS OF THE FLESH! . . . HERE IS A PARTIAL LIST OF THE WORKS OF THE FLESH!** *"Now the works of the flesh are manifest* (made knwon), *which are these: ADULTERY* (sodomy, homosexuality, lesbianism, bestiality [sex with animals], rape, incest, pederasty [anal intercourse, especially with a child], masturbation, all sexual perversion), *LASCIVIOUSNESS* (read chapter by same name), *IDOLATRY* (worship of money, alcohol, power, false religions, etc.), *WITCHCRAFT, HATRED, VARIANCE* (debates, quarrels), *EMULATIONS* (jealousy, rivalry), *WRATH* (rage, turmoil), *STRIFE* (feelings of superiority, revenge), *SEDITIONS* (disorder, divisions, over-throwing homes, religion, government), *HERESIES* (cults, sects), *ENVYINGS, MURDERS, DRUNKENNESS, REVELLINGS* (riots, obscene talk, music, pictures, sex orgies, wild parties, booze, drugs, cursing, etc.), *and such like: . . . they which do such things shall not inherit the kingdom of God."* Galatians 5:19-21

According to **1 Peter 4:2** The Bible says we are to live out the rest of our time in the will of God, and should not live out our days in lust!

**LUST = LASCIVIOUSNESS! LUST = EXCESS OF WINE, WILD PARTIES, RIOTS, ORGIES, PRACTICING IDOLATRY OR WITCHCRAFT! 1 Peter 4:3-4**

**LUST OF THE FLESH = VANITY, LICENTIOUSNESS!** *"For when they* (we) *speak great swelling words of vanity, they allure through the lusts of the flesh, through much wantonness . . ."* 2 Peter 2:18

**LUST = UNGODLINESS AND WORLDLY LIVING AND THINKING!** The Scriptures say we should live **soberly, righteously, and godly** in this present world. We should look for that blessed hope (Christ), and His glorious appearing. **Titus 2:12-13**

**LUST COMES IN MANY FORMS!** Homosexuality, lesbianism, transvestites, bi-sexuals, bestiality, adultery, fornication, sado-masochism, ego, money, sex, power, intellect, etc., are all lust and a sin against our body and God!

**DID YOU KNOW THAT THE INCREASE IN LUST, WHICH IS RUNNING RAMPANT OVER THE WORLD, FULFILLS END TIME PROPHECY ABOUT THE LAST DAYS BEFORE CHRIST RETURNS TO EARTH?** *"This know also, that in the last days perilous times shall come. For men shall be lovers of their own selves, covetous, boasters, proud, blasphemers, disobedient to parents, unthankful, unholy, without natural affection, trucebreakers, false accusers, incontinent, fierce, despisers of those that are good, traitors, heady, highminded, lovers of pleasures more than lovers of God; having a form of godliness, but denying the power thereof: from such turn away. For of this sort are they which creep into houses, and lead captive silly women laden with sins, led away with divers* (different kinds of) *lusts, ever learning, and never able to come to the knowledge of the truth."* 2 Timothy 3:1-7 *"But evil men and seducers shall wax* (grow) *worse and worse, deceiving, and being deceived."* 2 Timothy 3:13

**JESUS SAID THAT IF A PERSON LUSTS FOR SEX (WHEN HE SEES ANOTHER PERSON) HE IS GUILTY OF COMMITTING ADULTERY IN HIS HEART!** *"But I say unto you, That whosoever looketh on a woman* (or man) *to lust after her* (or him) *hath committed adultery with her* (or him) *already in his heart."* Matthew 5:28

**LUST IS A DEADLY AND POWERFUL MAGNET DESIGNED BY SATAN TO DRAW PEOPLE INTO HIS NET! NO ONE IS EXEMPT, UNLESS THEY ARE LIVING IN THE PERFECT WILL OF GOD!**

**A SINNER IS FOOLISH, DISOBEDIENT, AND DECEIVED! HE SERVES DIFFERENT KINDS OF LUST AND PLEASURES! HE LIVES IN MALICE AND ENVY. HE IS HATEFUL AND HATES OTHERS, ACCORDING TO Titus 3:3!** Every sinner needs to become a born-again Christian. Then he will grow to love others. He will also turn away from his sins and serve God. Then he can be truly happy and at peace!

**THE WORLD IS CURRENTLY FULL OF LUST AND VANITY, JUST AS IT WAS DURING THE DAYS OF SODOM AND GOMORRAH! ONCE CHRIST RETURNS, LUST WILL PASS AWAY!** *"For all that is in the world, the LUST OF THE FLESH, and the LUST OF THE EYES, and the PRIDE OF LIFE* (vanity, ego, coveting), *is not of the Father* (God), *but is of the world* (and Satan is the prince of the world). *And the world passeth away, and the lust thereof: but he that death the will of God abideth for ever."* 1 John 2:16-17 *"He that committeth sin is of the devil: for the devil sinneth from the beginning. For this purpose the Son of God* (Jesus) *was manifested* (made known), *that he might destroy the works of the devil."* 1 John 3:8

**THE BIBLE SAYS WE ARE TO FLEE YOUTHFUL LUSTS!** *"Flee also youthful lusts: but follow righteousness, faith, charity* (love), *peace, with them that call on the Lord out of a pure heart."* 2 Timothy 2:22

**1 PETER 1:14 SAYS THAT AFTER WE ARE SAVED WE ARE TO BE AS OBEDIENT CHILDREN. WE ARE NOT TO ADHERE TO THE FORMER LUSTS THAT WE COMMITTED IN IGNORANCE!**

**THE CARNAL MIND = A LUSTING MIND AND IS AN ENMITY OF GOD!** *"For to be carnally minded is death* (eternally separated from God until a person gets saved); *but to be spiritually minded is life and peace."* Romans 8:6 *Read Romans chapter 8

**LUST = A FLESHLY MIND WHICH IS ALL "PUFFED-UP" WITH EGO! Colossians 2:18**

**SATAN PUTS LUST IN OUR BODY PARTS, WHICH ARE CALLED "MEMBERS"! THEN OUR BODY PARTS WAR AGAINST OUR LORD.** *"Ye lust, and have not; ye kill, and desire to have, and cannot obtain: ye fight and war, yet ye have not, because ye ask not. Ye ask, and receive not, because ye ask amiss, that ye may consume it upon your lusts."* James 4:2-3

**PRAYER**
Dear God, I confess I am a sinner. **I have been lusting all my life!** If it wasn't lust for money, it was for things, sex, power or something. I ask You to forgive me for all my sins. Please come into my life and clean up my heart, mind and actions. I trust You completely to create in me the kind of person You want me to be. I praise You for loving me when I was such a sinner! I will not let You down. From this moment on I will serve You and only You! In Jesus' name, I pray. AMEN!

# MARRIAGE

## MIXED MARRIAGES — RE-MARRIAGE COMMON LAW

*"And the Lord God said, It is not good that the man should be alone; I will make him an help meet for him."* **Genesis 2:18** *"And the Lord God caused a deep sleep to fall upon Adam, and he slept: and he took one of his ribs and closed up the flesh instead thereof; and the rib which the Lord God had taken from man, made he a woman, and brought her unto the man. And Adam said, This is now bone of my bones, and flesh of my flesh: she shall be called woman, because she was taken out of Man. Therefore shall a man leave his father and his mother, and shall cleave unto his wife: and they shall be one flesh."* **Genesis 2:21-24**

*"But from the beginning of the creation God made them male and female. For this cause (marriage) shall a man leave his father and mother, and cleave to his wife; and they twain (two) shall be one flesh: so then they are no more twain (two), but one flesh. What therefore God hath joined together, let not man put asunder."* **Mark 10:6-9**

**JESUS SAID:** *"For this cause shall a man leave father and mother, and shall cleave to his wife: and they twain (two) shall be one flesh? Wherefore they are no more twain (two), but one flesh. What therefore God hath joined together, let not man put asunder."* **Matthew 19:5-6/Ephesians 5:31**

**STAY A VIRGIN UNTIL YOU MARRY AND OBEY GOD'S COMMAND!** *"But if they cannot contain (remain sexually pure), let them marry: for it is better to marry than to burn (with passion)."* **1 Corinthians 7:9** *"But and if thou marry, thou hast not sinned: and if a virgin marry, she hath not sinned. . . ."* **1 Corinthians 7:28** *"Nevertheless he that standeth stedfast in his heart, having no necessity, but hath power over his own will, and hath so decreed in his heart that he will keep his virgin (virginity), doeth well."* **1 Corinthians 7:37/1 Timothy 5:2/1 Corinthians 6:9. Read Chapter: "FORNICATION"**

**Proverbs 18:22 SAYS:** *"Whoso findeth a wife findeth a good thing, and obtaineth favour of the Lord."*

**GENESIS 3:16 SAYS A WIFE'S DESIRE SHOULD BE ONLY TO HER HUSBAND!**

*"Marriage is honourable in all, and the bed undefiled: but whoremongers and adulterers God will judge."* **Hebrews 13:4**

*"Husbands, love your wives, even as Christ also loved the church* (body of born-again Christians), *and gave himself for it."* **Ephesians 5:25**

*"Wives, submit yourselves unto your own husbands, as it is fit* (proper) *in the Lord."* **Colossians 3:18/Ephesians 5:22**

*"Husbands, love your wives, and be not bitter against them."* **Colossians 3:19**

*"For the husband is the head of the wife, even as Christ is the head of the church* (born-again Christians): *and he is the saviour of the body. Therefore as the church is subject unto Christ, so let the wives be to their own husbands in everything."* **Ephesians 5:23-24**

*"So ought men to love their wives, as their own bodies. He that loveth his wife loveth himself."* **Ephesians 5:28**

**NOW THAT THERE ARE TWO OF YOU . . .**

*"Likewise, ye wives, be in subjection to your own husbands; that, if any obey not the word* (of God), *they also may without the word* (knowledge of the Bible) *be won by the conversation of the wives."* **1 Peter 3:1**

**1 Peter 3:7 says** husbands are to give honour to their wives as the weaker vessel. Together they are **heirs** of life!

God commanded the older women to teach the younger women to love their husbands, obey them, and to love their children **Titus 2:3-5!** *"Let the husband render (give) unto the wife due benevolence: and likewise also the wife unto the husband. The wife hath not power of her own body, but the husband (does): and likewise also the husband hath not power of his own body, but the wife (does). Defraud ye not one the other, except it be with consent for a time, that ye may give yourselves to fasting and prayer; and come together again, that Satan tempt you not for your incontinency."* **1 Corinthians 7:3-5**

**THERE ARE NO MARRIAGES IN HEAVEN!** *"For when they shall rise from the dead, they neither marry, nor are given in marriage; but are as the angels which are in heaven."* **Mark 12:25/Luke 20:34-36** *"For in the resurrection they neither marry, nor are given in marriage, but are as the angels of God in heaven."* **Matthew 22:30**

**FOR MARRIAGE INSTRUCTIONS TO CHRISTIANS READ: 1 Corinthians 7**

# Good Marriages Don't Just Happen —

(Continued)

# COMMON LAW

**THE BIBLE CLEARLY STATES THAT COUPLES ARE NOT TO HAVE SEX OR LIVE TOGETHER BEFORE MARRIAGE!** *"Now the spirit speaketh expressly, that in the later times some shall depart from the faith, giving heed to seducing spirits, and doctrines of devils; speaking lies in hypocrisy; having their conscience seared with a hot iron; forbidding to marry* (choosing not to marry), *and commanding to abstain from meats, which God hath created to be received with thanksgiving of them which believe and know the truth* (of God).'' **1 Timothy 4:1-3** *NOTE: Read: "FORNICATION"

*"Know ye not that the unrighteous shall not inherit the kingdom of God? Be not deceived: neither fornicators, nor idolaters, nor adulterers, nor effeminate, nor abusers of themselves with mankind, nor thieves, nor covetous, nor drunkards, nor revilers, nor extortioners shall inherit the kingdom of God.''* **1 Corinthians 6:9-10** *"Now the body is not for fornication, but for the Lord: and the Lord for the Body.''* **1 Corinthians 6:13** *"Know ye not that your bodies are the members of Christ? shall I then take the members of Christ, and make them the members of an harlot? God forbid.* **What? know ye not that he which is joined to an harlot is one body? for two, saith he** (God), **shall be one flesh.** *But he that is joined unto the Lord is one spirit. Flee fornication. Every sin that a man doeth is without the body,* **but he that committeth fornication sinneth against his own body.** *What? know ye not that your body is the temple of the Holy Ghost which is in you, which ye have of God, and ye are not your own? For ye are bought with a price: therefore glorify God in your body, and in your spirit, which are God's.''* **1 Corinthians 6:15-20**

**ACCORDING TO THE BIBLE, A CHRISTIAN SHOULD NOT MARRY AN UNBELIEVER!** *"Be ye not unequally yoked together with unbelievers: for what fellowship hath righteousness with unrighteousness? and what communion hath light* (truth) *with darkness* (wickedness)?'' **2 Corinthians 6:14**

If you are a Christian, and marry an unsaved person, how can you teach your children the importance of spiritual things and the necessity for them to put Christ first in their lives, if one parent denies such things? Can you be sure you will have God's blessings and guidance when you make major decisions when one partner is not willing to pray with you, attend church, or support you in bringing up the children in church? **NEVER LET LONELINESS PRESSURE YOU INTO A MARRIAGE YOU WILL REGRET LATER ON!** God loves you. Ask Him to deliver to you the proper marriage partner. Trust Him to do so! He will bring you a Christian who will love you and honor Christ in your marriage!

**WHEN YOU REPEAT THE MARRIAGE VOWS YOU DON'T PROMISE EMPTY WORDS! YOU MAKE A SOLEMN VOW TO GOD!** God's plan for every marriage is for it to last as long as both partners live. God permits divorce in extreme circumstances but it is not His perfect will for our lives. **Matthew 19:6, 9.**

**COMMIT YOUR MARRIAGE TO GOD!** There should be **three** partners in a marriage—the husband, the wife and God! Let God rule in your marriage. Each person should ask God for wisdom and strength to say and do only the right things. Ask God to keep each of you free from selfish feelings and desires. Each should concentrate on meeting the needs of the other. God can bless a marriage in ways that people could never accomplish! **God can turn a sour marriage into a loving one.** Nothing is impossible for God. Pray for each other. You can become a couple who honor and serve God throughout your marriage!

**FOR BLESSINGS UPON THE HOME, READ: Deuteronomy 11:18-20**

**IF YOUR MARRIAGE IS IN TROUBLE THE PLACE TO START TO MAKE IT A HAPPY ONE IS WITH GOD!** God is the one who designed marriage and He never intended it to be a battle zone! God's perfect will for our lives is for every marriage to be a source of happiness and contentment. A marriage only gets into difficulties when the people neglect to follow the guidelines God has set forth for marriage. Each partner needs to come together and face their problems squarely and get on their knees and ask God to restore or build a solid Christian marriage. Getting on the knees and humbling yourselves before the Lord is the only answer! Ask God to give you a brand new love for each other and for Him! Marriages begin to crumble when each person wants the other to do things his way. When this happens you place your own wishes and wants ahead of the needs of the other person. This is the opposite of true love. True love is not concerned about what it gets, but what it can give. Each partner should sit down and think of specific ways he can make the other partner happy and meet his needs.

**IF YOU REALLY WANT GOD'S BLESSINGS IN YOUR MARRIAGE, DON'T DWELL ON THE THINGS YOU DON'T LIKE ABOUT YOUR PARTNER!** Instead, ask God to recall to your memory the things that caused you to fall in love with each other! Begin to seek to please each other. Rid yourself of the things which harm your relationship. **Ephesians 5:33** says each one of you must love his wife as he loves himself, and the wife must respect her husband. **The answer for a troubled marriage is GOD!**

### INTER-RACIAL (MIXED) MARRIAGES

The Bible is totally silent on the subject of mixed marriages! God created all races in His image. So, we can only assume that God does not disapprove of mixed marriages or He would have been very specific. Most people have in their bloodline a mixture of Irish, English, Oriental, Indian, Scottish, etc. What kind of God would show favoritism when He created us all? God is love. The Bible says Satan is the author of confusion, not God! Because of the tricks of Satan, he has used a demonic system to divide the children of God in an all-out effort to conquer. Thousands of service men have gone overseas and brought back oriental wives and have excellent marriages and beautiful children. Why would God not bless them? Satan, in my opinion, has caused all the animosity that exists between God's beautiful black and white people! The Bible says Satan is a liar, thief and a murderer. **SHOULD A BLACK AND WHITE MARRY?** The Bible doesn't say they shouldn't! However, they should anticipate that there would be stares from the public and unkind remarks because Satan is our enemy and he wants to destroy goodwill between all men. If a couple really love each other and are willing to face a life together with these existing circumstances, it apparently is alright with God, because He didn't say for them not to!

### PRAYER

Dear God, please help my troubled marriage. I don't believe divorce is the answer. I believe if I humble myself before You and ask Your forgiveness for not doing my part to make a happy marriage, that You will help me. I repent of all my sins. I humble myself and ask You for help. Create in me the kind of wife (or husband) that You want me to be. I pray for my spouse. In my heart I still love him (or her). I need You to intercede. Bring us back to the loving relationship we had when we repeated our marriage vows. I believe You will restore my marriage. I will do my part. I will read my Bible. I will think before I speak. I will not forget to go to church and to praise You. In Jesus' name I pray, AMEN!

# MASTURBATION

**DEFINITION:** Stimulation of the genital organs to achieve orgasm by manual or other bodily contact exclusive of sexual intercourse.

**MASTURBATION (AUTOEROTICISM) IS SEXUAL GRATIFICATION OBTAINED SOLELY THROUGH ONE'S OWN ORGASM.**

**MASTURBATION IS A SEXUAL FANTASY!** To the unsaved person it may seem perfectly natural and okay!

It's sad but true that most Christians would be too embarrassed to offer advice to persons with this problem, because of their "hang-ups"! A Christian should never wear a cloke of "self-righteous" indignation! When Jesus was confronted with a prostitute who had been caught in the act of adultery and about to be stoned, He didn't offer her "self-righteous" indignation, nor did He condemn her! He witnessed to her through love and told her to go and sin no more!

The person who masturbates may feel his condition is totally out of control and that he has no one to turn to for Christian counselling. He may feel hopeless! It's high time for Christians to realize that their silence does not stop the problem. **Christians need to come out of the closet! A Christian's silence (or refusal) to speak out against masturbation plays right into the hands of secular writers who whole-heartedly endorse masturbation!**

God is not the author of confusion and masturbation is confusion and bondage! God lays down open and honest rules on purity and sexuality. Secular writers say your body is your own and that you shouldn't have any "hang-ups". They say masturbation is healthy, normal, and self-fulfilling! They say masturbation is the ultimate way to obtain correct sexual behavior in most cases through "self-gratification"! They say that any attempt to abstain is damaging. They teach from their own written materials instead of the Holy Bible, which has the answers for every area of our life!

**EVEN A CHRISTIAN MAY FALL PREY TO THE TRICKS OF SATAN AND THINK MASTURBATION IS OK!** He may assume that because Masters and Johnson said it's okay, then it has to be true! Their statistics may sound very medical and true, but the problem is a SPIRITUAL one! God has the answers and God cannot lie!

**MAN IS CREATED IN GOD'S IMAGE.** God made a distinct difference in man and animal. Man is a three part being composed of body, soul, and spirit! Man is unique! God created man to have holy fellowship with Him! God did not create humans to masturbate or He would have specifically told us to!

**IF MASTURBATION CAN'T HARM ME . . . WHY SHOULDN'T I DO IT?** Because it is not God's plan for us! It's not the form of sexual activity God has in mind for us. Common sense will tell you that anything which has shame or guilt attached to it is never God's plan for mankind! Despite any theories in favor of masturbation few people are happy who engage in it. And masturbation is not a substitute for fornication! Sin is sin! There are no degrees of sin! In **Matthew 5:28** Jesus said that if you **lust for sex** in your heart, you have **committed sex** in God's eyes!

**GOD WANTS US TO LIVE A SEXUALLY PURE LIFE! WE ARE NOT TO HAVE INTERCOURSE EXCEPT THROUGH THE SANCTION OF MARRIAGE!** It's hard to imagine that God would approve of masturbation since it is a counterfeit expression of intercourse!

**MASTURBATION DOES NOT PREVENT FORNICATION!** A person must discipline himself to say "NO" to his erotic impulses when he is alone. Then when he is tempted to have intercourse he will be strong enough to abstain until he is married!

**MASTURBATION IS VERY HABIT FORMING!** It promises instant sexual tension release. But, if a person does **not abstain** from masturbation, it will be **even harder to abstain** from fornication. It's a fact that masturbation is a "way of life" to many people regardless of age, social conditions or education!

*"I beseech (beg) you therefore, brethren, by the mercies of God, that ye* **present your bodies a living sacrifice, holy, acceptable unto God,** *which is your reasonable service (in appreciation for Christ's dying on the cross for your sins so you can be saved). And be not comformed to (the teachings of) this world: but be ye transformed by the* **renewing of your mind, that ye may prove what is that good, and acceptable, and perfect will of God."** Romans 12:1-2

**SELF DENIAL BUILDS PURITY AND SPIRITUAL MATURITY!** 1 Corinthians 6:15 says: *"Know ye not that your bodies are the members of Christ?. . ."* 1 Corinthians 6:18 says: *"Flee fornication. Every sin that a man (person) doeth is without the body, but he that committeth fornication sinneth against his own body!"*

**1 Corinthians 6:19-20 says:** *"What, know ye not that* **your body is the temple of the Holy Ghost which is in you,** *which ye have of God, and ye* **are not your own?** *For ye are* **bought with a price: therefore glorify God in your body,** *and in your spirit which are God's."*

**1 Corinthians 7:9 says:** *"But if they cannot contain (abstain from fornication) let them marry: for it is better to marry than to burn (with sexual passion). Nevertheless, to avoid fornication, let every man have his own wife, and let every woman have her own husband."*

God designed sex to be a loving relationship between a husband and wife **Ephesians 5:31.** Therefore, masturbation is a **cheap** substitute! So, when the temptation to masturbate comes into your mind, say **"NO"!**

**MASTURBATION IS "SELFISH LUST" DIRECTED TOWARDS "SELFISH SATISFACTION"! IT IS ONE-SIDED! IT BRINGS FRUSTRATION! PEOPLE WHO MASTURBATE, BEFORE MARRIAGE, WILL BE CONFRONTED WITH THE SAME HABIT AFTER MARRIAGE!**

Masturbation is not a satisfying release to the person who practices it. It is a recurring problem he faces! If not corrected, it worsens! Masturbation leaves a person feeling guilt and shame!

**MASTURBATION IS A CRUTCH MANY PEOPLE USE WHO ARE AFRAID TO ESTABLISH A NORMAL RELATIONSHIP WITH THE OPPOSITE SEX!** It supports their fear and builds up more fear, instead of building confidence and strength of character!

**ASK THE HOLY SPIRIT TO HELP YOU KEEP YOUR BODY INTACT FOR YOUR MARRIAGE PARTNER!** Your body needs all the **protection** that only the Holy Spirit can give, throughout your life! This is God's plan for us.

172

(Continued)

**MASTURBATION TENDS TO MAKE A PERSON BECOME NEUROTIC! SO . . . HOW CAN A PERSON BREAK THE HABIT OF MASTURBATING?** Determine today to **take control** of your mind and actions! Ask God to help you overcome! Don't be spiritually lazy! God can and will help you but You must do your part! God knows your problem and longs to help you, but He won't force Himself on you! He knows your tensions and He understands puberty! He has a perfect plan for your body, mind and soul! His perfect plan is for you to have a loving wife or husband and to reproduce, he never planned for humans to have any form of sexual activity other than through holy matrimony! God doesn't want us to do anything to our body that would make us ashamed or apprehensive! Sex is not evil! God designed sex to be a loving and beautiful relationship between a husband and wife.

**SATAN USES SEX AS A "POWER-TOOL" TO SEPARATE US FROM GOD . . . IF WE LET HIM!** Satan will destroy your body, mind, and soul ONLY if you allow him to! That's up to you!

**MASTURBATION IS A CHEAT!** Satan uses masturbation to bring a person into **bondage** by telling him that he doesn't have to be **pure or wait** for a permanent marital relationship to enjoy himself! **All sins are self-serving and a rebellion against God's plan for us!** If you do the things that Satan wants you to do, you follow the wrong road! If you do the things God wants you to do you will have a happy and fulfilled life! So, if you are tempted to masturbate — ask yourself this question out loud: **"What would God want me to do?"**

**James 1:14-15 says:** *"But every man* (person) *is tempted* (by Satan to sin), *when he is drawn away of **his own lust** and enticed. Then when **lust hath conceived**, it bringeth forth sin: and sin, when it is finished, bringeth forth death* (eternal separation from God).*"*

**SEXUAL FANTASIES BREED A DESIRE TO MASTURBATE OR FORNICATE!** Keep your thoughts pure! **Philippians 4:8 says:** *"Finally, brethren, whatsoever things are **true**, whatsoever things are **honest**, whatsoever things are **just**, whatsoever things are **pure**, whatsoever things are **lovely**, whatsoever things are of **good report**: if there be any virtue, and if there be any praise, think on these things."*

**A SPIRITUALLY WEAK PERSON IS "OPEN-PREY" FOR SINFUL DESIRES!** Burn all pornographic pictures and books! Don't go to movies that contain sex scenes or dialogue! Choose Christian fiends! Call Christian counselors for help! Be honest and confess your sin to God! Fast and pray. This is the very best way to learn self-control! Satan is a liar, a thief and the author of confusion! **Acknowledge that masturbation is a sin and that you will not be taken in by Satan's cheap tricks anymore! if you listen to Satan he will lead you to hell! He wants to spend eternity with you!** It's up to you. Stand fast on your decision not to masturbate. And, when Satan throws the temptation in your face, say "NO! NO! NO! NO! KEEP YOUR PROMISE TO YOURSELF AND TO GOD! **SOON SATAN WILL GET THE MESSAGE AND LEAVE YOU ALONE!** YOU WILL HAVE WON THE BATTLE! *"Therefore to him that knoweth to do good, and doeth it not, to him it is sin."* **James 4:17**

**MEMORIZE THIS VERSE:** *"Nevertheless he that standeth stedfast in his heart, having no necessity* (to masturbate or fornicate), *but hath power over his own will, and hath so decreed in his heart that he will keep his virgin* (virginity) *doeth well."* **1 Corinthians 7:37**

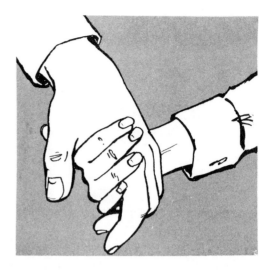

*If I have told you earthly things, and ye believe not, how shall ye believe, if I tell you of heavenly things?*

*"Ye have lived in pleasure on earth, and been wanton* (worldly, sinful); *ye have nourished your hearts, as in a day of slaughter."* **James 5:5**

**PRAYER**

Dear God, **I am guilty of masturbating.** I need Your help right now! Please give me strength to always do what is proper and pure in Your eyes. **I know that masturbation leaves me feeling guilt and shame.** I know that it is a trick of Satan to separate me from Your love and presence in my life. I know that I have to do my part. I know that I must say "NO" to my sinful desires! **I know that I must stay pure if I want to go to Heaven.** I love You and I know that You love me. Come into my heart and live in me. Please forgive me for all my sins. I want to please You and I want to live a happy, fulfilled life. I know that I must discipline myself and that You will see me through this problem. I praise You and I thank You, in advance, for all the help You are going to give me. In Jesus' name, I pray. AMEN!

# MATERIAL POSSESSIONS

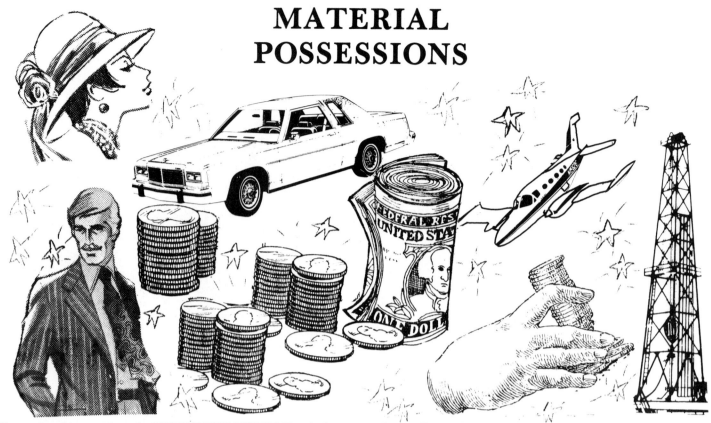

Remember the story about the **RICH YOUNG RULER?** He asked Jesus what **GOOD THING** he could do to inherit eternal life. Jesus told him to sell his riches and give to the poor and then he would have treasure in heaven. Then Jesus said, "Follow me!" *"But when the young man heard that saying, he went away sorrowful: for he had **great possessions.**"* **Matthew 19:22/Mark 10:22**

**SINCE THE BEGINNING OF TIME MANY PEOPLE HAVE LOVED THEIR MATERIAL POSSESSIONS MORE THAN GOD!**

**WARNING TO RICH PEOPLE:** *"Lay not up for yourselves **treasures** upon earth, where moth and rust doth corrupt, and where thieves break through and steal: But lay up for yourselves **treasures** in heaven where neither moth nor rust doth corrupt, and where thieves do not break through nor steal: **For where your treasure is, there will your heart be also.**"* **Matthew 6:19-21**

When one of the people surrounding Jesus asked him to speak to his brother to talk him into dividing his inheritance with him, here is what Jesus said: *"And he (Jesus) said unto them, Take heed, and beware of covetousness: for a man's life consisteth not in the **abundance** of the **things which he possesseth.**"* **Luke 12:15**

**JESUS SAID:** *"O generation of vipers (snakes), how can ye, being evil, speak good things? for out of the **abundance** of the heart (your wealth in things) the mouth speaketh. A good man out of the **good treasure** (God's blessings) of the heart bringeth forth good things: and an evil man out of the **evil treasure** bringeth forth evil things."* **Matthew 12:34-35/Luke 6:45**

**JESUS SAID IT IS REALLY HARD FOR A RICH MAN TO ENTER INTO THE KINGDOM OF GOD, BECAUSE HE LOVES HIS RICHES MORE THAN HE LOVES GOD!** Jesus said: *"It is easier for a camel to go through the eye of a needle, than for a **rich man** to enter into the kingdom of God."* **Mark 10:25/Luke 18:25**

**DID YOU KNOW THAT THE LOVE OF MONEY AND MATERIAL POSSESSIONS FULFILLS END TIME PRO-PHECY ABOUT THE LAST DAYS BEFORE CHRIST RETURNS?** *"Go to now, ye rich men, weep and howl for your miseries that shall come upon you. Your riches are corrupted, and your garments are*

*moth eaten. Your **gold and silver** is cankered (rusted); and the rust of them shall be a witness against you, and shall eat your flesh as (if) it were fire. Ye have heaped treasure together for the last days."* **James 5:1-3**

*"BUT GODLINESS WITH CONTENTMENT IS GREAT GAIN. **FOR WE BROUGHT NOTHING INTO THIS WORLD, AND IT IS CERTAIN WE CAN CARRY NOTHING OUT.** AND HAV-ING FOOD AND RAIMENT (CLOTHES) LET US BE THEREWITH CONTENT. BUT THEY THAT WILL BE **RICH** FALL INTO TEMPTATION AND A SNARE (TRAP), AND INTO MANY FOOLISH AND HURTFUL LUSTS, WHICH DROWN MEN IN DESTRUCTION AND PERDITION. **FOR THE LOVE OF MONEY IS THE ROOT OF ALL EVIL, WHICH WHILE SOME COVETED AFTER, THEY HAVE ERRED FROM THE FAITH** (IN GOD), AND PIERCED THEMSELVES THROUGH WITH MANY SORROWS . . . FLEE THESE THINGS: AND FOLLOW AFTER RIGHTEOUSNESS, GODLINESS, FAITH, LOVE, PATIENCE, MEEKNESS. FIGHT THE GOOD FIGHT OF FAITH, LAY HOLD ON ETERNAL LIFE. . ."* **1 Timothy 6:6-12**

God blesses people who obey His commandments in their business, marriage, home, health, and especially in finances! Money is a blessing when used to do God's work! There's always enough left over for the niceties in life. Put God first in your finances, and He will prosper you even more!

## PRAYER

Dear God, Please forgive me for I have paid more attention to my **material possessions** than I have to You! I repent of my sins. **I know that the love for money and things has separated me from doing Your will in my life. I know that money can't buy the peace and happiness that only You can give!** I repent of all my sins. Please help me to be more aware of this in the future. From this moment forward, I will pay at least ten percent of my income to do the Lord's work. I know that You command us not to love riches above You and that tithing is an act of faith on my part! Riches on earth are nice but I can live without them. What **I really want is to be rich in rewards in heaven.** I love You and I thank You for opening my eyes! I don't want to be separated from You! In Jesus' name, I pray. AMEN!

# MEANNESS

**DEFINITION OF MALICE:** Intent to commit an unlawful act or cause harm without legal justification or excuse; ill will, spite, grudge; a deep seated and often unreasonable dislike and a desire to see one suffer; an intense driving force of resentment or ill will that seeks satisfaction.

**MEANNESS OR MALICIOUSNESS IS A SIN AND GOD PLACES IT IN THE SAME CATEGORY AS MURDER!** *"And even as they did not like to retain God in their knowledge, God gave them over to a reprobate mind, to do those things which are not convenient* (natural); (who) *being filled with all unrighteousness, fornication, wickedness, covetousness,* **maliciousness;** *full of envy, murder, debate, deceit, malignity; whisperers* (gossips), *backbiters, haters of God, despiteful, proud, boasters, inventors of evil things, disobedient to parents, without understanding, covenantbreakers, without natural affection* (homosexuals, lesbians, all sex sins), *implacable, unmerciful: Who knowing the judgment of God, that they which commit such things are worthy of death, not only do the same, but have pleasure in them that do them."* **Romans 1:28-32**

**MEANNESS STOPS SPIRITUAL GROWTH!** *"Wherefore laying* (lay) *aside all* **malice,** *and all guile* (spite), *and hypocrisies, and envies, and all evil speakings, as newborn babes, desire the sincere milk of the word* (of God), *that ye may grow thereby."* **1 Peter 2:1-2 PAUL SAID:** *"Brethren, be not children in understanding; howbeit in* **malice** *be ye children, but in understanding be men."* **1 Corinthians 14:20**

**CHRISTIANS ARE COMMANDED NOT TO BE MALICIOUS!** *"For so is the will of God, that with well doing ye may put to silence the ignorance of foolish men: as free* (born-again Christians), *and not using your liberty for a cloke of* **maliciousness,** *but as the servants of God. Honour all men. Love the brotherhood* (of Christian believers). *Fear God. Honour the king* (president and governmental officials)." **1 Peter 2:15-17**

**IT GRIEVES THE HOLY SPIRIT WHEN A CHRISTIAN IS MALICIOUS!** *"And grieve not the Holy Spirit of God, whereby ye are sealed unto the day of redemption. Let all bitterness, and wrath, and anger, and clamour* (loud threats), *and evil speaking, be put away from you, with all* **malice:** *and be ye kind one to another, tenderhearted, forgiving one another, even as God for Christ's sake hath forgiven you."* **Ephesians 4:30-32** *"But now ye also put off all these; anger, wrath,* **malice,** *blasphemy, filthy communication out of your mouth."* **Colossians 3:8**

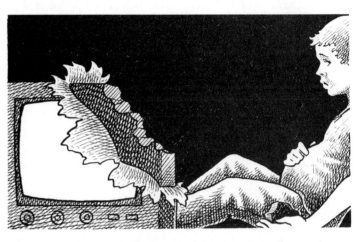

*PAUL WROTE: "Put them in mind to be subject to principalities and powers, to obey magistrates, to be ready to* (do) *every good work, to speak evil of no man, to be no brawlers, but gentle, shewing all meekness unto all men. For we ourselves also were sometimes foolish, disobedient, deceived, serving divers* (various) *lusts and pleasures,* **living in malice** *and envy, hateful, and hating one another. But after that the kindness and love of God our Saviour toward men appeared."* **Titus 3:1-4**

**1 Peter 2:21-24 says:** *". . .because Christ also suffered for us, leaving us an example that ye should follow his steps:* (Christ) *who did no sin, neither was guile* (meanness) *found in his mouth: who, when he was reviled, reviled not again; when he suffered, he threatened not; but committed himself to him that judgeth righteously; who his own self bare our sins in his own body on the tree* (cross), *that we, being dead to sins, should live unto righteousness; by whose stripes ye were healed."*

**THE BIBLE SAYS ALL MEAN PEOPLE WILL BE BROUGHT DOWN AND HUMBLED!** *"And the* **mean** (common) *man shall be brought down, and the mighty* (the great or famous) *man shall be humbled, and the eyes of the lofty* (vain, proud) *shall be humbled."* **Isaiah 5:15** *"Seest thou a man diligent in his business? he shall stand before kings; he shall not stand before* **mean** *men."* **Proverbs 22:29**

**IN CLOSING:** *"Finally, be ye all of one mind, having compassion one of another, love as brethren, be pitiful, be courteous: not rendering evil for evil, or railing for railing: but contrariwise blessing; knowing that ye are thereunto called, that ye should inherit a blessing. For he that will love life, and see good days, let him refrain his tongue from evil, and his lips that they speak no guile* (meanness): *Let him eschew* (put off) *evil, and do good: let him seek peace, and ensue it. For the eyes of the Lord are over the righteous, and his ears are open unto their prayers: but the face of the Lord is against them that do evil. And who is he that will harm you, if ye be followers of that which is good?"* **1 Peter 3:8-13**

### PRAYER

Dear God, Please forgive me for all my sins. I humble myself and ask You to forgive me for being a **malicious and mean** person! I have hurt the very people I love the most. I will not do this any more. I will do my part to overcome this evil sin. I need Your help every day in every way. Please come into my heart to stay. I know that You love me and want what's best for me. Help me to think before I open my mouth. I want to please You and to win back those I have mistreated. In Jesus' name, I pray. AMEN!

# MISTRESS
## (Sexual)

*". . .It is good for a man not to touch a woman. Nevertheless, **to avoid fornication** (sex without marriage), **let every man have his own wife**, and let every woman have her own husband."* **1 Corinthians 7:1-2**

**NO MARRIED PERSON HAS THE RIGHT TO GIVE HIS BODY IN A SEXUAL ACT TO ANOTHER PERSON! IT DOESN'T BELONG TO HIM!** *"The wife hath not power of (over) her own body, but the husband (does): and likewise also the husband hath not power of (over) his own body, but the wife (does). Defraud ye not one the other, except it be with consent for a time, that ye may give yourselves to fasting and prayer; and come together again (continue to have sexual intercourse), that Satan tempt you not for your incontinency."* **1 Corinthians 7:4-5**

**PAUL WROTE:** *". . .therefore to the unmarried and widows, It is good for them if they abide even as I (celibate). But if they cannot contain (their sexual passions), let them marry: for it is better to marry than to burn (with passion)."* **1 Corinthians 7:8-9**

*"But she that liveth in pleasure is dead (separated from God until she repents and forsakes living in sin) while she liveth."* **1 Timothy 5:6**

**GOD'S PLAN FOR ALL MEN AND WOMEN IS FOR THEM TO REMAIN A VIRGIN UNTIL THEY MARRY!** *"I will therefore that the younger women marry, bear children, guide the house, give none occasion to the adversary (enemy, demon forces) to speak reproachfully. For some are already turned aside after Satan."* **1 Timothy 5:14-15**

*"Lay hands suddenly on no man, neither be partaker of other men's sins: keep thyself pure."* **1 Timothy 5:22** *"Ye have lived in pleasure on earth, and been wanton (worldly, sinful); ye have nourished your hearts, as in a day of slaughter."* **James 5:5**

*"While they promise them liberty, they themselves are the servants of corruption; for of whom a man is overcome (taken in by), of the same is he brought into bondage."* **2 Peter 2:19**

**THE BIBLE SAYS NOT TO KEEP COMPANY WITH FORNICATORS. 1 Corinthians 5:9** *"But now I have written unto you not to keep company, if any man that is called a brother be a **fornicator,** or covetous, or an idolater, or a railer, or a drunkard, or an extortioner; with such an one no not to eat."* **1 Corinthians 5:11**

**PEOPLE WHO COMMIT SEX SINS WILL NOT INHERIT THE KINGDOM OF GOD UNLESS THEY REPENT AND FORSAKE THEIR WAYS! NO PERSON KNOWS WHEN HE WILL DIE. THEREFORE ALL SHOULD REMAIN SEXUALLY PURE AND ONLY HAVE INTERCOURSE WITH THEIR MARRIAGE PARTNER!** *"Know ye not that the unrighteous shall not inherit the kingdom of God? Be not deceived: neither **fornicators,** nor idolaters, nor **adulterers,** nor effeminate, nor **abusers of themselves with mankind,** nor thieves, nor covetous, nor drunkards, nor relivers, nor extortioners shall inherit the kingdom of God."* **1 Corinthians 6:9-10**

**OUR BODY IS THE TEMPLE OF GOD! WE ARE COMMANDED TO KEEP IT PURE. MARRIAGE IS THE ONLY PERMISSABLE WAY TO HAVE SEX!** *"Know ye not that ye are the temple of God, and that the Spirit of God dwelleth in you? If any man (person) defile the temple of God, him shall God destroy; for the temple of God is holy, which temple ye are."* **1 Corinthians 3:16-17**

*"And (they) shall receive the reward of **unrighteousness,** as they that count it pleasure to riot in the day time. **Spots** they are and **blemishes,** sporting themselves with their own deceivings while they feast with you; having **eyes full of adultery, and that cannot cease from sin; beguiling unstable souls;** an heart they have exercised with covetous practices; cursed children: which have forsaken the right way, and are gone astray. . . ."* **2 Peter 2:13-15**

**AFTER A PERSON BECOMES A CHRISTIAN, IF HE THEN COMMITS SIN THE END RESULT IS WORSE FOR HIM THAN BEFORE HE BECAME A CHRISTIAN! IT NEVER PAYS TO TURN YOUR BACK ON GOD!** *"For if **after** they have escaped the pollutions of the world through the knowledge of the Lord and Saviour Jesus Christ, they are **again entangled** therein, and **overcome** (give in), the latter end is worse with them than the beginning. For it had been better for them not to have known the way of righteousness, than, after they have known it, to turn from the holy commandment delivered unto them. But it is happened unto them according to the true proverb, The dog is turned to his own vomit again; and the sow that was washed to her wallowing in the mire."* **2 Peter 2:20-22** *"Ye therefore, beloved, seeing ye know these things before, beware lest ye also, being led away with the error of the wicked (sin), fall from your own stedfastness. But grow in grace, and in the knowledge of our Lord and Saviour Jesus Christ. To him be glory both now and for ever."* **2 Peter 3:17-18**

**ALL SEXUAL SIN IS WICKEDNESS!** *"There is no peace saith the Lord unto the wicked."* **Isaiah 48:22**

**DID YOU KNOW THAT THE INCREASE IN SEX SINS FULFILLS END TIME PROPHECY ABOUT THE LAST DAYS BEFORE CHRIST RETURNS TO EARTH?** *"This know also, that in the **last days** perilous times shall come. For men shall be lovers of their own selves, covetous, boasters, proud, blasphemers, disobedient to parents, unthankful, unholy. Without natural affection, trucebreakers, false accusers, incontinent, fierce, despisers of those that are good, traitors, heady, highminded, lovers of pleasures more than lovers of God; having a form of godliness, but denying the power thereof: from such turn away."* **2 Timothy 3:1-5**

**MOST PEOPLE DON'T WANT TO BE PURE THEREFORE THEY DON'T WANT CHRIST TO RETURN 1 John 3:2-3.**

### LETTER TO ANY MISTRESS WHO IS IN LOVE WITH A MARRIED MAN

Never expect to see him on Sundays or holidays. Never call him at his home. Never expect him to take you to public places because he will be ashamed to be seen with you. Do expect to entertain him at your place. Occasionally he will furnish the food for you to cook. But in actual dollars and cents, you will spend more on him than he'll spend on you. Never depend on him in times of personal crisis. Don't believe him when he tells you that his wife is cold, doesn't love him, is too fat, or hasn't slept with him in five years! Don't expect his wife to divorce him if she ever catches him. She knows that you are not his first mistress and won't be his last! She is not about to give up her social status, home, financial security and retirement income because of you! When she discovers about you he will likely terminate his affair with you. So be prepared to start all over circulating to find another man whose wife is cold, homely, too fat, and hasn't slept with him in over in over five years.

**IF YOU ARE A MISTRESS — ASK GOD TO FORGIVE YOU! GOD LOVES YOU. HE WILL FORGIVE AND FORGET YOUR SINS! THEN TURN AWAY FROM ALL SEXUAL SIN AND TURN YOUR LIFE OVER TO GOD!**

### PRAYER

Dear God, I have been living in **sexual sin.** I know that Your will for my life is to be married and bear children in the admonition of the Lord. I repent of all my sins. I turn away from them forever. Please come into my life and live in me. I will change every area of my life which caused me to sin in the first place! I will read my Bible. I will go to church. I will not let Satan tempt me to commit **sexual sin** again. I will need Your help daily to overcome! I want to be pure in Your eyes. Thank You for setting me straight. I give You all the glory. In Jesus' name, I pray. AMEN!

# MONEY

**PROVERBS 11:28 SAYS:** *"He that trusteth in his riches shall fall: but the righteous shall flourish as a branch."*

**GOD GIVES MANY RIGHTEOUS PEOPLE RICHES . . . BUT, IF A PERSON LOVES MONEY ABOVE GOD, HE WILL RECEIVE MANY SORROWS!** *"For the love of money is the root of all evil: which while some coveted after, they have erred from the faith, and pierced themselves through with many sorrows."* **1 Timothy 6:10**

**IF YOU DON'T HAVE ENOUGH MONEY TO SUPPLY YOUR NEEDS — HERE'S HOW YOU CAN HAVE PLENTY! FIRST: REPENT OF YOUR SINS AND LIVE A HOLY LIFE. THEN GOD WILL SUPPLY ALL YOUR NEEDS!** *"Every one that thirsteth, come ye to the waters (the living Word of God), and he that hath* **no money***: come ye, buy, and eat; yea, come, buy wine and milk* **without money and without price***. Wherefore (why) do ye spend money for that which is not bread? and your labour for that which satisfieth not? hearken (listen) diligently unto me, and eat ye that which is good, and let your soul delight itself in fatness. Incline your ear, and come unto me: hear, and your soul shall live; and I will make an everlasting covenant with you. . . ."* **Isaiah 55:1-3**

*"For wisdom is a defence, and* **money is a defence***: but the excellency of knowledge is, that wisdom giveth life to them that have it."* **Ecclesiastes 7:12**

**GOD BENEFITS BORN-AGAIN CHRISTIANS IN THE AREA OF OUR FINANCES! HE PLUGS UP THE HOLES WHERE OUR MONEY RUNS OUT!** *". . . Consider your ways. Ye have sown much, and bring in little; ye eat, but ye have not enough; ye drink, but ye are not filled with drink; ye clothe you, but there is none warm; and he that earneth wages earneth wages to put it into a bag with holes."* **Haggai 1:5-6**

**WHEN PEOPLE FORGET GOD THEIR MONEY SEEMS TO GO THROUGH GIGANTIC HOLES IN THEIR POCKET! GENESIS 47:15-16 SAYS THAT MONEY FAILS! BUT WE KNOW THAT GOD CAN NEVER FAIL! THEREFORE, IF YOU HAVEN'T ENOUGH MONEY TO MEET YOUR NEEDS, TAKE INVENTORY OF YOUR HEART AND LIFE. SEE IF THERE IS ANY AREA IN YOUR LIFE THAT NEEDS FORGIVENESS. GOD PROMISES TO TAKE CARE OF THE RIGHTEOUS! ARE YOU RIGHTEOUS? THE PSALMIST DAVID WROTE:** *"I have been young, and now am old; yet have I not* **seen the righteous forsaken, nor his seed begging bread***. He (God) is merciful, and lendeth; and his seed (born-again Christians) is blessed."* **Psalm 37:25-26**

**NOT ENOUGH MONEY**

**BEFORE YOU GO TO A RELATIVE (OR A BANK) TO BORROW MONEY, GET RIGHT WITH GOD AND WITH YOUR RELATIVES AND NEIGHBOURS! GOD WILL SUPPLY YOUR NEEDS! HE IS OUR REFUGE!** *"The Lord also will be a refuge for the oppressed, a refuge in times of trouble."* **Psalm 9:9**

**MONEY SEPARATES FAMILIES AND FRIENDS!** Only God can be totally trusted when you need financial help! He will never leave you to beg for what you need! *"And they that know thy name will put their trust in thee (God); for thou, Lord, hast not forsaken them that seek thee."* **Psalm 9:10**

**MOST OF THE POPULATION OF THE WORLD NEVER THINK THEY HAVE ENOUGH MONEY! THE SEARCH FOR MONEY NEVER ENDS! ALL THE MONEY IN THE WORLD CAN NEVER MAKE A PERSON HAPPY IF HE DOES NOT KNOW AND WORSHIP THE LORD!** *"For what shall it profit a man, if he shall gain the whole world, and lose his own soul?"* **Mark 8:36**

**GOD WILL TEACH US TO BE MORE PROFITABLE WHEN WE OBEY HIS COMMANDMENTS AND CALL ON HIM BEFORE WE COMMIT OURSELVES IN FINANCIAL VENTURES!** *"Thus saith the Lord, thy Redeemer, the Holy One of Israel;* **I am the Lord thy God which teacheth thee to profit***, which leadeth thee by the way that thou shouldest go."* **Isaiah 48:17**

**THE ANSWER TO ANYONE WHO HAS A FINANCIAL DIFFICULTY IS TO ASK GOD FOR WISDOM TO HANDLE MONEY!** *"But the wisdom that is from above is first* **pure, then peaceable, gentle, and easy** *to be intreated (understood and used), full of mercy and good fruits, without partiality, and without hypocrisy."* **James 3:17** *"And whatsoever we ask, we receive of him, because we keep his commandments, and do those things that are pleasing in his sight."* **1 John 3:22**

### PRAYER

Dear God, Please forgive me of all my sins. Help me in every area of my life and in my finances and I will praise You forever! In Jesus' name I pray. AMEN!

# MOTHER
# MOTHER-IN-LAW

*"Who can find a virtuous woman? For her price is far above rubies. The heart of her husband doth safely trust in her, so that he shall have no need of spoil. She will do him good and not evil all the days of her life. She seeketh wool, and flax, and worketh willingly with her hands. She is like the merchants' ships; she bringeth her food from afar. She riseth also while it is yet night, and giveth meat to her household, and a portion to her maidens. She considereth a field, and buyeth it: with the fruit of her hands she planteth a vineyard. She girdeth her loins with strength, and strengtheneth her arms. She perceiveth that her merchandise is good: her candle goeth not out by night. She layeth her hands to the spindle, and her hands hold the distaff. She stretcheth out her hand to the poor; yea, she reacheth forth her hands to the needy. She is not afraid of the snow for her household; for all her household are clothed with scarlet. She maketh herself coverings of tapestry; her clothing is silk and purple. Her husband is known in the gates, when he sitteth among the elders of the land. She maketh fine linen, and selleth it; and delivereth girdles unto the merchant. Strength and honour are her clothing; and she shall rejoice in time to come. She openeth her mouth with wisdom, and in her tongue is the law of kindness. She looketh well to the ways of her household, and eateth not the bread of idleness. Her children arise up, and call her blessed; her husband also, and he praiseth her. Many daughters have done virtuously, but thou excellest them all. Favour is deceitful, and beauty is vain: but a woman that feareth the Lord, she shall be praised. Give her of the fruit of her hands; and let her own works praise her in the gates."* **Proverbs 31:10-31**

*"A virtuous woman is a crown to her husband: but she that maketh (him) ashamed is as rottenness in his bones."* **Proverbs 12:4**

*"Children, **obey your parents** in the Lord: for this is right. Honour thy father and **mother**; which is the first commandment with promise; that it may be well with thee, and thou mayest live long on the earth."* **Ephesians 6:1-3** *"Honour thy father and thy **mother**, as the Lord thy God hath commanded thee; that thy days may be prolonged, and that it may go well with thee, in the land which the Lord thy God giveth thee."* **Deuteronomy 5:16**

**IN THE OLD TESTAMENT DAYS THERE WAS A DEATH PENALTY FOR PARENTAL DISRESPECT!** *"And he that smiteth his father, or his **mother**, shall be surely put to death."* **Exodus 21:15**

**WE ARE COMMANDED NEVER TO CURSE OUR PARENTS!** *"And he that curseth his father, or his **mother**, shall surely be put to death."* **Exodus 21:17** *"For every one that curseth his father or his **mother** shall be surely put to death: he hath cursed his father or his **mother**; his blood shall be upon him."* **Leviticus 20:9** *"For God commanded, saying, Honour thy father and **mother**; and, He that curseth father or **mother**, let him die the death."* **Matthew 15:4/Mark 7:10** *"Whoso curseth his father or his **mother**, his lamp shall be put out in obscure darkness."* **Proverbs 20:20**

*"Honour thy father and thy **mother**: and, thou shalt love thy neighbour as thyself."* **Matthew 19:19**

*"Thou knowest the commandments, Do not commit adultery, Do not kill, Do not steal, Do not bear false witness, Defraud not, Honour thy father and **mother**."* **Mark 10:19/Luke 18:20**

**EVE IS THE MOTHER OF ALL LIVING PEOPLE!** *"And Adam called his wife's name Eve; because she was the **mother** of all living."* **Genesis 3:20**

**THE BIBLE SAYS WE ARE NEVER TO TURN OUR BACK ON OUR MOTHER WHEN SHE IS OLD!** *"Hearken unto thy father that begat thee, and despise not thy **mother** when she is old."* **Proverbs 23:22**

**WE ARE COMMANDED TO FEAR AND RESPECT OUR MOTHER!** *"Ye shall fear every man his **mother**, and his father, and keep my sabbaths: I am the Lord your God."* **Leviticus 19:3**

**GOD GAVE GOVERNMENTAL LAWS TO PROTECT MOTHERS!** *"But we know that the law is good, if a man use it lawfully; knowing this, that the law is not made for a righteous man, but for the lawless and disobedient, for the ungodly and for sinners, for unholy and profane, for murderers of fathers and murderers of **mothers**, for manslayers, for whoremongers, for them that defile themselves with mankind, for menstealers, for liars, for perjured persons, and if there be any other thing that is contrary to sound doctrine."* **1 Timothy 1:8-10**

**CHRISTIANS ARE COMMANDED TO TREAT OLDER WOMEN AS MOTHERS AND YOUNGER WOMEN AS SISTERS WITH ALL PURITY.** 1 Timothy 5:2

**WHEN A PERSON GETS MARRIED GOD'S PLAN IS FOR THE PERSON TO LEAVE HIS FATHER AND MOTHER AND TO CLEAVE TO HIS SPOUSE.** Genesis 2:24/19:5/Mark 10:7/Ephesians 5:31

**SARAH WAS BLESSED WHEN GOD GAVE HER A SON AT 90 YEARS OF AGE! GOD CALLED SARAH THE "MOTHER OF ALL NATIONS"!** Genesis 17:15-16

**JOHN THE BAPTIST WAS FILLED WITH THE HOLY GHOST IN HIS MOTHER'S WOMB!** *"For he shall be great in the sight of the Lord, and shall drink neither wine nor strong drink; and he shall be filled with the Holy Ghost even from his **mother's** (Elisabeth's) womb."* **Luke 1:15**

# MOTHER-IN-LAW

**ONE OF THE MOST BEAUTIFUL STORIES IN THE BIBLE IS THE STORY OF RUTH AND HER MOTHER-IN-LAW NAOMI. TREAT YOURSELF AND READ THE ENTIRE BOOK OF RUTH!** *"And Ruth said, Intreat me not to leave thee, or to return from following after thee: for whither thou goest, I will go; and where thou lodgest, I will lodge; thy people shall be my people, and thy God my God: where thou diest, will I die, and there will I be buried: the Lord do so to me, and more also, if ought but death part thee and me."* **Ruth 1:16-17**

**THE BIBLE PROPHESIED THERE WOULD BE DISCORD BETWEEN A DAUGHTER-IN-LAW AND HER MOTHER-IN-LAW IN THE LAST DAYS BEFORE CHRIST RETURNS TO EARTH!** *"For the son dishonoureth the father, the daughter riseth up against her **mother**, the daughter in law against her **mother in law**; a man's enemies are the men (people) of his own house."* **Micah 7:6** *"The father shall be divided against the son, and the son against the father; the **mother** against the daughter, and the daughter against the **mother**; the **mother in law** against her daughter in law, and the daughter in law against her **mother in law**."* **Luke 12:53**

### PRAYER

Dear God, As a **mother** I have made many mistakes. I ask You to forgive me for all my mistakes and many sins. Make me the kind of person You want me to be. I have not always been the best wife or **mother**. I have not always been the best **mother-in-law**. Take away all animosity from my heart toward my **mother** and **mother-in-law**. I know that none of us are perfect. Only Jesus is perfect. I want to be more like Him and I need Your help! In Jesus' name, AMEN!

# MOURNING

ANY PERSON WHO IS NOT HAVING A DAILY WALK WITH GOD IS MORE APT TO MOURN FOR A LONGER PERIOD OF TIME! GOD IS OUR COMFORTER. HE WILL SEE YOU THROUGH YOUR PERIOD OF MOURNING! *"Draw nigh to God, and he will draw nigh to you. Cleanse your hands (of sins), ye sinners; and purify your hearts, ye double minded. Be afflicted and* **mourn,** *and weep: let your laughter be turned to* **mourning,** *and your joy to heaviness. Humble yourselves in the sight of the Lord, and he shall lift you up."* **James 4:8-10**

IF WE NEVER HAD AN OCCASION TO MOURN AND BE SAD WE MIGHT NEVER CALL ON GOD! HE'S ALWAYS WAITING TO GIVE US COMFORT WHEN WE CALL ON HIM! *"Blessed are they that* **mourn:** *for they shall be comforted."* **Matthew 5:4**

NO MATTER HOW SEVERE YOUR HEARTACHE, WITH GOD'S HELP HE CAN TURN YOUR MOURNING INTO DANCING! *"Hear O Lord, and have mercy upon me: Lord, be thou my helper. Thou hast turned for me my* **mourning into dancing** . . . *and girded me with gladness. To the end that my glory may sing praise to thee, and not be silent. O Lord my God, I will give thanks unto thee for ever."* **Psalm 30:10-12**

THE REMEDY FOR SHAKING OFF MOURNING IS TO COMMIT YOUR CAUSE TO GOD! JOB WROTE: *"I would seek unto God, and unto God would I commit my cause."* **Job 5:8**

GOD PROMISES HE WILL SET ON HIGH THOSE THAT ARE LOW! AND THOSE WHO MOURN WILL BE EXALTED TO SAFETY! Job 5:11

GOD PROMISES HE WILL RESTORE COMFORT TO THE PERSON WHO MOURNS! Isaiah 57:18

HERE ARE SOME VERSES YOU SHOULD MEMORIZE IF YOU ARE READY FOR YOUR MOURNING TO GO AWAY! *"Cast thy burden upon the Lord, and he shall sustain thee: he shall never suffer (allow) the righteous to be moved."* **Psalm 55:22** *"What time I am afraid, I will trust in thee."* **Psalm 56:3** *"Evening, and morning, and at noon, will I pray, and cry aloud: and he shall hear my voice."* **Psalm 55:17** *"God is our refuge and strength, a very present help in trouble."* **Psalm 46:1** *"Make haste, O God, to deliver me; make haste to help me, O Lord."* **Psalm 70:1** *"O God, be not far from me: O my God, make haste for my help."* **Psalm 71:12** *"I cried unto God with my voice, even unto God with my voice; and he gave ear unto me."* **Psalm 77:1** *"In the day of my trouble I will call upon thee: for thou wilt answer me."* **Psalm 86:7** *"For the Lord God is a sun and shield: the Lord will give grace and glory: no good thing will he withhold from them that walk uprightly."* **Psalm 84:11**

MOURNING GIVES A PERSON TIME TO REFLECT ON HIS LIFE AND TO SEE IF THERE IS UNFORGIVENESS IN HIS HEART! THE CURE FOR MOURNING IS TO HUMBLE YOURSELF TO GOD AND ASK HIM TO FORGIVE YOU FOR ALL YOUR SINS. THEN ASK HIM TO TAKE YOUR BURDEN TOTALLY OFF YOUR SHOULDERS! BE WILLING TO LET GO! LIFE MUST GO ON! GOD WANTS US TO BE HAPPY AND TO LIVE A PRODUCTIVE LIFE! HIS WILL IS FOR US TO LIVE AN ABUNDANT LIFE! HE IS OUR ONLY HELP! LET GO AND LET GOD HAVE THE BURDEN! THEN, GET BUSY DOING THE LORD'S WORK! HE WILL HELP YOU EACH DAY IF YOU ASK HIM AND WILL ACCEPT HIS HELP!

*" '. . .if God be for us, who can be against us?"* Romans 8:31

Thank God when we get to heaven, there will be no more death, sorrow, tears or reason to mourn. Why not let go of your sorrow and let God step in and give you peace? He's just waiting to hear from you!

## "Mercy unto you, and peace, and love, be multiplied." Jude 2

### PRAYER

Dear God, I have been sad for too long. I humble myself and ask You to forgive all my sins. Please come into my heart and life. Create in me a happy person who is eager to do Your will in every area of my life! **I know that too much mourning is never productive!** Give me a new lease on life and I will serve You. Give me new energy to do Your work. Help me to take my mind off myself and to put it on You. Thank You in advance for an answer to my prayer. I will serve You and work for You from this moment on. In Jesus' name, AMEN!

# NECROMANCY

**DEFINITION:** Conjuration of the spirits of the dead for purposes of magically revealing the future or influencing the course of events; magic, sorcery.

Our English word **OBITUARY** comes from the word **NECROLOGY** which means a list of the recent dead. **NECROPHAGIA** is the act or practice of eating corpses.

Our English word **CEMETERY** is translated from **NECROPOLES** which means city of the dead. **NECROPHILIA** means those that are dead.

**GOD FORBIDS THE PAGAN AND HEATHEN PRACTICE OF NECROMANCY!** *"There shall not be found among any one that maketh his son or his daughter to pass through the fire* (in a idol worship ceremony), *or that useth divination* (fortune telling),*or an observer of times* (astrology), *or an enchanter, or a witch, or a charmer, or a consulter with familiar spirits, or a wizard* (male witch), *or a necromancer* (one who attempts to communicate with the dead). *For all that do these things are an abomination unto the Lord: and because of these abominations the Lord thy God doth drive them out from before thee. Thou shalt be perfect with the Lord thy God."* **Deuteronomy 18:10-13**

NEVER BE GUILTY OF PAYING A VISIT TO A PSYCHIC MEDIUM TO HAVE YOUR FORTUNE TOLD! GOD UTTERLY FORBIDS ANY ATTEMPT TO COMMUNICATE WITH THE DEAD! FORTUNE TELLERS (PSYCHIC MEDIUMS) GET THEIR INFORMATION FROM FAMILIAR SPIRITS WHICH ARE SPIRITS FROM HELL! THE SPIRITS OF DECEASED BORN-AGAIN CHRISTIANS RESIDE IN HEAVEN AND THEY HAVE NO PART IN THE EVIL WORK OF PSYCHIC MEDIUMS! ANY PRETENDED OR ACTUAL COMMUNICATION WITH THE DEAD CAN ONLY COME FROM DECEASED SPIRITS IN HELL! *"And when they shall say unto you, Seek unto them that have **familiar spirits** (spirits out of hell), and unto wizards that peep, and that mutter (as in seances or trances): should not a people seek unto their God? for the living (rather than) to the dead? To the law (of God) and to the testimony (of God): if they speak not according to this word (the Scriptures), it is because there is no light (truth of God) in them. And they shall pass through it, hardly bestead and hungry: and it shall come to pass, that when they shall be hungry, they shall fret themselves, and curse their king and their God, and look upward. And they shall look unto the earth; and behold trouble and darkness, dimness of anguish; and they shall be driven to darkness (lies, deceit, satanic oppression)."* **Isaiah 8:19-22**

FORTUNE TELLERS READ PALMS, CARDS, AND GAZE INTO CRYSTAL BALLS. THEY PRACTICE NECROMANCY! SEANCES ARE A CEREMONY TO THE DEAD AND THIS IS ALSO NECROMANCY. PSYCHIC MEDIUMS AND HEALERS PRACTICE NECROMANCY. OUIJA BOARDS AND GAMES LIKE "DUNGEONS AND DRAGONS" ARE A FORM OF NECROMANCY. MAGIC IS A FORM OF NECROMANCY. ANYTHING TO DO WITH CONJURING UP DECEASED SPIRITS IS OF SATAN! HE IS THE AUTHOR OF CONFUSION AND LIES! THEORIES OF PYRAMIDOLOGY, AUTOMATIC WRITING, ASTRAL PROJECTION, SILVA MIND CONTROL, TRANSCENDENTAL MEDITATION, EDGAR CAYCE WRITINGS, ROSICRUCIANS, AND YOGA ARE ALL DEVICES OF SATAN TO BRING YOU INTO BONDAGE AND TO EVENTUALLY TAKE YOU TO HELL! ANYTHING THAT IS DESIGNED TO TAKE CONTROL OF YOUR MIND IS DANGEROUS AND A FORM OF POSSESSION!

READ: 1 Samuel 28:7-25/1 Chronicles 10:13/Deuteronomy 14:1/Leviticus 21:5, 27/20:6/19:26/Exodus 22:18/1 Timothy 4.

DRUGS ARE KNOWN TO CAUSE PEOPLE TO HAVE VISITATIONS FROM "SPIRIT GUIDES" WHICH ARE DEMON SPIRITS! Drugs can cause a person to hallucinate and communicate with these spirits. We should never turn our free will over to anything or anyone but God! He created us in His image and He longs to guide us in truth and wisdom! God loves you. He wants only what's best for your mental, physical, and spiritual well being. Why would you ever want to turn your mind over to demon spirits? They will eventually take you to hell, if you allow them to take possession of your mind and actions!

READ: ENCHANTMENTS — FAMILIAR SPIRITS — ASTROLOGY — PSYCHIC MEDIUMS — OCCULT ACTIVITY — WITCHCRAFT!

THERE IS NO "GIVE OR TAKE" WITH GOD, REGARDING THE SUBJECT OF ANY OCCULT ACTIVITY! GOD WILL NOT TOLERATE THIS SIN! HE LOVES EACH ONE OF US. GOD IS NO RESPECTOR OF PERSONS! HE WANTS TO SAVE EACH OF US. HE WILL FORGIVE YOUR PARTICIPATION IN ANY OCCULT ACTIVITY! HE INSISTS THAT ONCE A PERSON REPENTS AND IS FORGIVEN OF THIS SIN, HE IS TO TURN AWAY FROM IT, FOREVER! FAILURE TO TURN AWAY FROM SIN BRINGS DEATH (TOTAL AND ETERNAL SEPARATION FROM GOD)! *"And the soul that turneth after such as have **familiar spirits**, and after wizards, to go a whoring after them, I will even set my face against that soul, and will cut him off from among his people. Sanctify yourselves therefore, and be ye holy: for I am the Lord your God."* **Leviticus 20:6-7**

## PRAYER

Dear God, I am guilty of practicing various forms of the occult! Please forgive me and take away my fascination with the occult. I know that occult teachings are a form of idolatry and You said we should have no other god but You! I repent of all my sins. Fill my mind and heart with You. I am now a born-again Christian! In Jesus' name, I pray. AMEN!

# NERVES

**HAVE YOU EVER FELT LIKE THIS?** *"I am feeble and sore broken: I have roared by reason of the* **disquietness** *(nervousness) of my heart."* **Psalm 38:8**

**OUR HEALTH AND PEACE OF MIND IS EQUAL TO OUR OBEDIENCE TO GOD! Jesus said:** *"But I say unto you, love your enemies, bless them that curse you, do good to them that hate you, and pray for them which despitefully use you, and persecute you."* **Matthew 5:44**

**NERVOUSNESS BRINGS FEAR, LOSS OF SLEEP, AND TREMBLING!** *"In thoughts from the* **visions** *of the night, when deep* **sleep** *falleth on me,* **fear** *came upon me, and* **trembling,** *which made all my bones to shake."* **Job 4:13-14**

**IF YOU ARE A BORN-AGAIN CHRISTIAN YOU CAN PUT YOUR TRUST IN THE LORD. HE WILL HELP YOU WITH YOUR NERVOUS CONDITION! IF YOU'RE A SINNER, NO ONE CAN HELP YOU!** *"The Lord also will be a refuge for the oppressed, a refuge in times of trouble. And they that know thy name will put their trust in thee: for thou, Lord, hast not forsaken them that seek thee."* **Psalm 9:9-10**

**DAVID PRAYED:** *"I am feeble and sore broken: I have roared by reason of the* **disquietness** *of my heart. Lord, all my desire is before thee; and my groaning is not hid from thee. My* **heart** *panteth* (beats too fast), *my* **strength faileth me:** *as for the light of mine eyes, it also is gone from me."* **Psalm 38:8-10**

David committed adultery and had Bathsheba's husband killed. But, he humbled himself and sincerely begged God to forgive him for his sins, and God lovingly took him back into the fold. *"Knowing this, that the trying of your faith worketh patience. But let patience have her perfect work, that ye may be perfect and entire, wanting nothing."* **James 1:3-4**

*"Be patient therefore, brethren, unto the coming of the Lord. . ."* **James 5:7**

*"Be ye also patient; stablish* (establish) *your hearts: for the coming of the Lord draweth nigh."* **James 5:8**

**IF YOU'RE NERVOUS ALTHOUGH YOU'RE GETTING ENOUGH SLEEP AND EATING PROPERLY . . . TAKE INVENTORY OF YOUR HEART TO SEE IF THERE'S ANY UNFORGIVENESS FOR ANOTHER PERSON!** *"Is any* **sick** *among you? let him call for the elders of the church; and let them pray over him, anointing him with oil in the name of the Lord. And the prayer of faith shall save the* **sick,** *and the Lord shall raise him up; and if he have committed sins, they shall be forgiven him. Confess your faults one to another, and pray one for another, that ye may be healed. The effectual fervent prayer of a righteous man* (person) *availeth much."* **James 5:14-16**

**JESUS SAID:** *"And when thou prayest, thou shalt not be as the hypocrites are: for they love to pray standing in the synagogues and in the corners of the streets, that they may be seen of men. Verily I say unto you, They have their reward. But thou, when thou prayest, enter into thy closet* (any private place), *and when thou hast shut thy door, pray to thy Father which is in secret* (heaven); *and thy Father which seeth in secret shall reward thee openly. But when ye pray, use not vain repetitions, as the heathen do: for they think that they shall be heard for their much speaking. Be not ye therefore like unto them: for your Father* (God) *knoweth what things ye have need of before ye ask him."* **Matthew 6:5-8**

**IF YOU HAVE ANYTHING AGAINST ANOTHER PERSON, THE BIBLE SAYS YOU MUST FIRST FORGIVE THAT PERSON! THEN THE LORD WILL FORGIVE YOU AND ANSWER YOUR PRAYER. JESUS SAID WE MUST LOVE OUR NEIGHBOR AS WE LOVE OURSELF!** *"Behold, thou* (God) *hast instructed many, and thou hast* **strengthened the weak hands.** *Thy words have upholden him that was* **falling,** *and thou hast* **strengthened the feeble knees."** **Job 4:3-4**

**PSALM 46:10 SAYS:** *"Be still, and know that I am God: I will be exalted among the heathen, I will be exalted in the earth."* **Psalm 46:10**

**IF YOU HOPE IN THE LORD . . . AND YOU HAVE FAITH THAT GOD CAN AND WILL ANSWER YOUR PRAYER . . . AND IF YOU HAVE COMPLETELY FORGIVEN ANYONE WHO HAS HURT OR DISAPPOINTED YOU . . . GOD WILL HEAL YOUR NERVOUS CONDITION!** *"Why art thou cast down, O my soul? and why art thou* **disquieted** *(uneasy, nervous) within me? hope in God: for I shall yet praise him, who is the* **health** *of my countenance, and my God."* **Psalm 43:5/42:5, 11.**

# Nerves

### PRAYER

Dear God, Please forgive me for all my sins. If there is any unforgiveness in my heart I repent of it here and now! Please come into my heart to stay! I need Your help, dear God! I have a nervous condition which I know You can heal. I ask You to heal me now, dear God! I will praise You and serve You as long as I live. In Jesus' name, I pray. AMEN!

# NUDITY

**WHEN GOD CREATED ADAM AND EVE THEY WERE IN-NOCENT. AND, THEY WERE NAKED BEFORE THEY SINNED AND ATE OF THE FORBIDDEN FRUIT!** *"And they were both **naked,** the man and his wife, and were not ashamed."* **Genesis 2:25**

**THEY WILLFULLY DISOBEYED GOD AND SINNED:** *"And the eyes of them both were opened* (they realized what they had done), *and they knew that they were **naked;** and they sewed fig leaves together, and made themselves aprons."* **Genesis 3:7** *"And he* (Adam) *said, I heard thy* (God's) *voice in the garden, and I was afraid, because I was **naked;** and I hid myself. And he* (God) *said, Who told thee that thou wast **naked?** Hast thou eaten of the tree, whereof I commanded thee that thou shouldest not eat? And the man* (Adam) *said, The woman whom thou gavest to be with me, she gave me of the tree, and I did eat."* **Genesis 3:10-13**

**EXODUS 28:42 SAYS WE ARE TO COVER OUR NAKEDNESS!**

**THE BIBLE SAYS WE ARE NOT TO LOOK AT ANOTHER PERSON'S NAKEDNESS!** Leviticus 18:6-19/20:10-21/ Deuteronomy 22:30/Genesis 9:22-23

**1 SAMUEL 5:9 AND ISAIAH 3:17 REFERS TO THE PRIVATES ON A PERSON AS "SECRET" PARTS!**

THE BIBLE SAYS OUR **NAKEDNESS IS A SHAME!** Revelation 3:18/16:15/Jeremiah 13:26/Nahum 3:5

**THE BIBLE SAYS A PERSON IS RESPONSIBLE NOT TO LET OTHERS DISCOVER HIS OWN NAKEDNESS!** Ezekiel 16:36-37

*"Who shall separate us from the love of Christ? shall tribulation, or distress, or persecution, or famine, or **nakedness,** or peril, or sword? As it is written, For thy sake, we are killed all the day long; we are accounted as sheep for the slaughter. Nay* (no), *in all these things we are more than conquerors through him* (Christ) *that loved us. For I am persuaded, that neither death, nor life, nor angels, nor principalities, nor powers, nor things present, nor things to come, nor height, nor depth, nor any other creature, shall be able to separate us from the love of God, which is in Christ Jesus our Lord."* **Romans 8:35-39**

When Moses came down from Mount Sinai, with the tablets containing the Ten Commandments, he found the people **naked and exposing their shame** to their enemies in their idol worship ceremonies. **Exodus 32:25**

**HELL IS NAKED (EXPOSED) BEFORE GOD!** Job 26:6

**IF A PERSON IS POOR, NEEDY, OR NAKED, THE BIBLE SAYS WE ARE TO COVER HIM!** Isaiah 58:7 *"If a brother or sister be **naked,** and destitute of daily food, and one of you say unto them, Depart in peace, be ye warmed and filled; notwithstanding ye give them not those things which are needful to the body; what doth it profit? Even so faith, if it hath not works, is dead, being alone."* **James 2:15-17**

**WE CANNOT HIDE ANYTHING FROM GOD!** ALL THINGS ARE **NAKED** (REVEALED) AND OPEN TO GOD'S EYES! HE CREATED US AND HE KNOWS THE EXACT NUMBER OF HAIRS THAT ARE ON OUR HEAD! **Hebrews 4:13**

When a person becomes demon oppressed he may resort to exposing his **nakedness,** according to **Acts 19:16!**

**JESUS SAID:** *"I know thy works* (thoughts, actions), *that thou art neither cold nor hot* (neither love me or hate me): *I would* (wish) *thou wert cold or hot. So then because thou art lukewarm* (indifferent), *and neither cold nor hot, I will spue* (vomit) *thee out of my mouth. Because thou sayest, I am rich, and increased with goods, and have need of nothing; and knowest not that thou art wretched, and miserable, and poor, and blind, and **naked:** I counsel thee to buy of me gold tried in the fire, that thou mayest be rich; and white raiment, that thou mayest be clothed, and that the shame of thy **nakedness** do not appear; and anoint thine eyes with eye-salve, that thou mayest see. As many as I love, I rebuke and chasten: be zealous therefore, and repent. Behold, I stand at the door, and knock: if any man hear my voice, and open the door, I will come in to him, and will sup with him, and he with me. To him that overcometh will I grant to sit with me in my throne, even as I also overcame, and am set down with my Father in his throne."* **Revelation 3:15-21**

**IF YOU KNOW A PERSON WHO IS PRE-OCCUPIED WITH GOING AROUND NAKED:** PRAY FOR HIM AND COUNSEL WITH HIM. GOD WOULD WANT YOU TO! IF THIS PERSON DOES NOT OVERCOME THIS SINFUL HABIT, TALK WITH A GOOD CHRISTIAN PASTOR. IT'S POSSIBLE HE MAY HAVE A DEMON SPIRIT WHICH WILL NEED TO BE CAST OUT BEFORE HE CAN BE TOTALLY FREE FROM THIS SIN!

**GOD WOULD NOT APPROVE OF NUDIST COLONIES!** GOD WOULD NOT APPROVE OF PARENTS EXPOSING THEMSELVES IN FRONT OF THEIR CHILDREN! GOD LOVES PURE AND HOLY PEOPLE! GOD LOVES DECENCY! NUDITY IS A WAY OF DELIBERATELY DEFYING GOD! DON'T FALL FOR THIS TRICK FROM SATAN! DON'T UNDRESS FOR ANY REASON (DOWN TO THE BARE SKIN) UNLESS YOU ARE BEING EXAMINED BY A MEDICAL DOCTOR, OR YOU ARE BEFORE YOUR OWN MARRIAGE PARTNER!

### PRAYER

Dear God, Please forgive me for all my sins. Please forgive me for **flaunting my nakedness.** I know that You do not approve. I know that You want me to live a pure and holy life! I want to live for You. I want to be decent and good in Your eyes. Please forgive me and blot my sins from Your memory. I will praise You and love You as long as I live! In Jesus' name, I pray. AMEN!

# NYMPHOMANIA

**DEFINITION;** Excessive sexual desire by a female; a frenzy of sexual emotion by a female.

*"Know ye not that the unrighteous **shall not** inherit the kingdom of God? Be not deceived: neither **fornicators** (those who engage in sex without marriage), **nor idolaters** (people can worship and serve sex as an idol), **nor adulterers** (sex with one who you are not married to), **nor effeminate** (boys on the way to becoming hard-core homosexuals), **nor abusers of themselves with mankind** (kinky sex, rape, incest, homosexuals, lesbians, bestiality, etc.), **nor thieves, nor covetous** (lust for sex falls into this category), **nor drunkards, nor revilers, nor extortioners,** shall inherit the kingdom of God."* 1 Corinthians 6:9-10

**GOD DID NOT CREATE US TO LIVE ONLY FOR SEX! SEX IS A SIN WHEN IT IS DONE OUTSIDE THE BOUNDS OF LEGAL MARRIAGE!** *". . .Now the body is not for **fornication**, but for the Lord: and the Lord for the body."* **1 Corinthians 6:13**

**OUR BODY DOESN'T BELONG SOLELY TO US! IT BELONGS TO OUR CREATOR, GOD!** *"Know ye not that your bodies are the members of Christ? shall I then take the members of Christ, and make them the members of an **harlot** (whore, prostitute)? God forbid . . . know ye not that he which is joined to an **harlot** is one body? for two, saith he (God), shall be one flesh. But he that is joined unto the Lord is one spirit. **Flee fornication.** Every sin that a man (person) doeth is without the body; but he that committeth **fornication** sinneth against his **own body** . . . **know ye not that your body is the temple of the Holy Ghost** which is in you, which ye have of God, and ye are not your own? For ye are bought with a price* (through the death and resurrection of Christ on the cross to pay for our sins so we can be saved and forgiven): *therefore glorify God in your body, and in your spirit, which are God's."* **1 Corinthians 6:15-20**

*". . .To avoid fornication, let every man have his own wife, and let every woman have her own husband."* **1 Corinthians 7:2**

**THE BIBLE CLEARLY STATES THAT IF A PERSON HAS TROUBLE CONTROLLING HIS SEXUAL PASSIONS HE IS TO GET MARRIED! GOD BLESSES MARRIAGE. GOD WANTS US TO HAVE A HAPPY AND HOLY FAMILY LIFE!** *"But if they cannot contain (control their passions), let them marry: for it is better to marry than to burn* (not be able to control passion by committing sexual sins)." **1 Corinthians 7:9**

**WE ARE COMMANDED NOT TO SERVE MEN WITH OUR BODIES! OUR BODIES ARE TO BE HOLY IN GOD'S EYES!** *"Ye are bought with a price; be not ye the servants of men."* **1 Corinthians 7:23**

*"For this is the will of God, even your sanctification, that ye should **abstain from fornication**: that every one of you should know how to possess his vessel* (body) *in sanctification and honour."* **1 Thessalonians 4:3-4** *"For God hath not called us unto **uncleanness**, but unto holiness."* **1 Thessalonians 4:7**

*"Having therefore these promises, dearly beloved, let us cleanse ourselves from all filthiness of the flesh and spirit, perfecting holiness in the fear of God."* **2 Corinthians 7:1**

If you know someone who is a nymphomaniac **pray** for her and witness to her about the love of God. God loves this person and wants to cleanse her and set her on the right path! If Christian counseling is not enough to make her want to change, then one must consider that Satan (or his demon spirits) has possessed her! In this case you should consult a spirit-filled minister of God and have the unclean spirit cast out! Then she can worship and serve God. She will be free, at last!

*The Lord knoweth how to deliver the godly out of temptations, and to reserve the unjust unto the day of judgment to be punished."* **2 Peter 2:9**

**DID YOU KNOW THAT PEOPLE WHO HAVE RECEIVED CHRIST, AS THEIR PERSONAL SAVIOUR, ARE THE LEAST LONELY?** All mankind needs intimacy! And intimacy depends upon finding, knowing, and sharing God's love in your own life, and with others! **We need each other, but without the love of God, intimacy can never be satisfying or fulfilling!**

**FOR MORE DETAILED CHAPTERS ON SEX SINS, READ: FORNICATION/ BESTIALITY/ HARLOT-WHORE-PROSTITUTE/ LASCIVIOUSNESS/ MASTURBATION/ MISTRESS/ HOMOSEXUALS-LESBIANS/ ADULTERY/ SADO-MASOCHISM/ SODOMY.**

**PRAYER**

Dear God, please forgive me for all my sins. I repent of every sin I have ever committed. Please forgive me. I will live a godly life to the very best of my ability. I know that You love me and really want me to set my life straight. I know that I want to serve You from this moment on! I will not fail You! I thank You for loving a person like me. I love You in return. I praise You for being merciful to me. In Jesus' name, AMEN!

# OBEDIENCE

**SINNERS LIVE IN DIRECT DISOBEDIENCE TO GOD!**
*"Know ye not, that to whom ye yield yourselves servants to obey, his servants ye are to whom ye obey; whether of sin unto death, or of obedience unto righteousness? But God be thanked, that ye were the servants of sin, but ye have obeyed from the heart that form of doctrine which was delivered you. Being then made free from sin, ye became the servants of righteousness."* **Romans 6:16-18**

*"For the weapons of our warfare are not carnal, but mighty through God to the pulling down of strong holds, casting down imaginations, and every high thing that exalteth itself against the knowledge of God, and bringing into captivity every thought to the obedience of Christ; and having in a readiness to revenge all disobedience, when your obedience is fulfilled."* **2 Corinthians 10:4-6**

*"Honour thy father and thy mother, as the Lord thy God hath commanded thee; that thy days may be prolonged, and that it may go well with thee, in the land which the Lord thy God giveth thee."* **Deuteronomy 5:16**

*"For it is better, if the will of God be so, that ye suffer for well doing, than for evil doing. For Christ also hath once suffered for sins, the just for the unjust, that he might bring us to God, being put to death in the flesh, but quickened by the Spirit: By which also he went and preached unto the spirits in prison: which sometime were disobedient. . .* **1 Peter 3:17-20**

**BORN-AGAIN CHRISTIANS HAVE THE LORD TO TURN TO SO THEY WON'T BECOME DISOBEDIENT!** *"The Lord knoweth how to deliver the godly out of temptations, and to reserve the unjust unto the day of judgment to be punished."* **2 Peter 2:9**

*"FOR AS BY ONE MAN'S DISOBEDIENCE (SPEAKING OF ADAM) MANY WERE MADE SINNERS, SO BY THE OBEDIENCE OF ONE (SPEAKING OF CHRIST) SHALL MANY BE MADE RIGHTEOUS."* **Romans 5:19**

**TO BE DISOBEDIENT IS TO BE REBELLIOUS TO GOD!**
*"For rebellion is as the sin of witchcraft, and stubbornness is as iniquity and idolatry."* **1 Samuel 15:23**

**IN ORDER TO BE 100 PERCENT OBEDIENT TO GOD WE MUST WALK IN THE HOLY SPIRIT!** *"This I say then, Walk in the (Holy) Spirit, and ye shall not fulfil the lust of the flesh."* **Galatians 5:16** *"For if ye live after the (desires of the) flesh, ye shall die: but if ye through the (Holy) Spirit do mortify the deeds of the body, ye shall live. For as many as are led by the Spirit of God, they are the sons of God."* **Romans 8:13-14**

**DISOBEDIENCE TO GOD BRINGS CONFUSION! SATAN IS THE AUTHOR OF CONFUSION!** *"For God is not the author of confusion, but of peace, as in all churches of the saints."* **1 Corinthians 14:33**

**TO OBEY GOD IS BETTER THAN ANY SACRIFICE! 1 Samuel 15:22**

**HAD CHRIST NOT BEEN OBEDIENT TO GOD THERE WOULD BE NO HOPE FOR US! HELL WOULD BE OUR FINAL RESTING PLACE THROUGHOUT ETERNITY!** *"Though he (Christ) were a Son, yet learned he obedience by the things which he suffered; and being made perfect, he became the author of eternal salvation unto all them that obey him."* **Hebrews 5:8-9**

**CHILDREN ARE COMMANDED TO BE OBEDIENT TO THEIR PARENTS AND TO GOD! 1 Peter 1:14**

**WOMEN ARE COMMANDED TO BE OBEDIENT TO THEIR OWN HUSBANDS! Titus 2:5**

**SERVANTS ARE COMMANDED TO BE OBEDIENT TO THEIR OWN MASTERS! Titus 2:9**

**CHRISTIANS ARE COMMANDED TO BE OBEDIENT TO GOD!** *"If ye be willing and obedient, ye shall eat the good of the land: But if ye refuse and rebel, ye shall be devoured with the sword: for the mouth of the Lord hath spoken it."* **Isaiah 1:19-20**

*"Let this mind be in you, which was also in Christ Jesus: who, being in the form of God, thought it not robbery to be equal with God: but made himself of no reputation, and took upon him(self) the form of a servant, and was made in the likeness of men: and being found in fashion as a man, he humbled himself, and became obedient unto death, even the death of the cross. Wherefore God also hath highly exalted him, and given him a name which is above every name: that at the name of Jesus every knee should bow, of things in heaven, and things in earth, and things under the earth. And that every tongue should confess that Jesus Christ is Lord, to the glory of God the Father."* **Philippians 2:5-11**

# OBEDIENCE
### PRAYER
Dear God, please forgive me for being **disobedient** to Your commandments. I repent of every sin I have ever committed. Please forgive me. I want to do right and live the way You designed me to live. Come into my life and live in me. Thank You for loving me and for being merciful to me. In Jesus' name, I pray. AMEN!

# OBESITY

**OVERWEIGHT OR OBESITY, AS IT IS KNOWN BY THE MEDICAL PROFESSION, IS A VERY COMMON DISORDER OF THE HUMAN RACE WHICH CAN BE CORRECTED WITHOUT RIGID DIETING!** An overweight condition may be a disease in itself as well as a symptom of some other disease.

Obesity is a disorder of metabolism (the change of food intake to body energy) which is characterized by an excessive accumulation of body fat. Approximately 600,000 Americans are grossly overweight. They are classified as potentially ''morbid'' because their extra poundage is a risk to life! Their death rate from heart disease, stroke, and diabetes is 12 times the rate for persons of normal weight!

**GOD DOES NOT DELIVER ANYONE FROM OVERWEIGHT!** Overweight is **not** a matter for deliverance. **It's a matter of self-discipline, self-control!** God does not change His laws regarding obedience and disobedience. God gave us a land of plenty but He expects us to discipline our appetites, whether they are for money, food, sex, power, etc.

**GOD GAVE US FREE WILL TO MAKE OUR OWN CHOICES!** We shouldn't ask or expect God to take away our fat anymore than we would expect Him to take years off of our life and make us a child again! If food is a weapon that makes you fat, then you must deny your appetite and eat only small amounts while fasting and praying. Talk to the food while you eat and say, *''No weapon that is formed against thee* (me) *shall prosper.''* **Isaiah 54:17**

**IF YOU ARE OBESE WHY NOT PRAY FOR GOD TO HELP YOU WITH YOUR TEMPTATION TO OVER-INDULGE?** *''The Lord knoweth how to deliver the godly out of temptations, and to reserve the unjust unto the day of judgment to be punished.''* **2 Peter 2:9**

**TAKE CONTROL OF YOUR LIFE AND APPETITE! DON'T BE A SERVANT TO FOOD AND DRINK! THE ANSWER IS IN SELF-DISCIPLINE! FOOD WILL BE YOUR MASTER — UNLESS YOU DECIDE NOT TO LET IT BE!** *''Know ye not, that to whom* (or what) *ye yield yourselves servants to obey, his servants ye are to whom ye obey, whether of sin unto death* (and food can bring on your death), *or of obedience unto righteousness? But God be thanked, that ye were the servants of sin, but ye have obeyed from the heart that form of doctrine which was delivered you. Being then made free from sin, ye became the servants of righteousness.''* **Romans 6:16-18**

**GOD WANTS US TO CONQUER OUR APPETITES AND TO RULE THEM — RATHER THAN LETTING THEM RULE US!** He will help us control our appetites, but He won't deliver us from them through the Holy Spirit. *''. . .Be not conformed to this world: but be ye transformed by the renewing of your mind. . .''* **Romans 12:2**

**FAT CAN BECOME TRIM ONLY THROUGH THE RENEWING OF THE MIND!** If you wish to change your weight, something NEW has to occur in your mind. Habits are hard to break and the remedy for breaking them has to start in the heart and in the mind. God does not make us change our habits any more than He makes us become a Christian when we are a sinner! Each obese person has to make up his own mind that he will no longer **LIVE TO EAT.** Fasting and prayer, every other day, is a good way to take control of your mind. *''But I keep under my body, and bring it into subjection: lest that by any means, when I have preached to others, I myself should be a castaway.''* **1 Corinthians 9:27**

**WHEN YOU BRING YOUR BODY UNDER SUBJECTION THINGS WILL BEGIN TO HAPPEN!** Your subconscious mind is very receptive. It will do as you command it to do. Order your

flesh to eat only enough food to make your body function properly! Our attitude toward food is a real measure of the place Jesus holds in our life. If food is more important to us than Jesus is, well you know what that says about our commitment to Him! If we put food first then Christ is not first in our life and all our witnessing of His being our Lord and Master becomes senseless and empty! If you mean business put Him ahead of food! There's no need of asking God for help or deliverance if we're going to continue putting food ahead of Him! Only we can deliver ourselves from taking in those extra calories! God will never stop us from being disobedient. He gave us free will, remember?

**SO WHAT IF YOUR STOMACH HURTS WHEN IT IS HUNGRY? CHRIST LEARNED THE MEANING OF OBEDIENCE THROUGH HIS SUFFERING. ARE WE ANY BETTER THAN HIM?** *''Though he were a son* (of God), *yet learned he obedience by the things which he suffered; and being made perfect, he became the author of eternal salvation unto all them that obey him.''* **Hebrews 5:8-9** *''Furthermore we have had fathers of our flesh which corrected us, and we gave them reverence: shall we not much rather be in subjection unto the Father of spirits, and live?''* **Hebrews 12:9**

**Judges 3:17-22** tells about a fat man. **Genesis 41:2-18** talks about fat flesh. **Job 36:16** talks about fatness. **1 Samuel 4:18** talks about a man who was heavy. **Isaiah 58:7, 10** says to deal out bread to the hungry. *''For he satisfieth the longing soul, and filleth the hungry soul with goodness.''* **Psalm 107:9**

**THE SOONER YOU START AN EFFECTIVE SELF-CONTROL PROGRAM OF TREATMENT . . . THE SOONER YOU WILL SEE RESULTS!**

**OVERWEIGHT PEOPLE ARE MORE SUSCEPTIBLE TO DISEASE!** Too much fat interferes with physical activity. Obesity puts a burden on the heart by increasing the load it is expected to carry. OBESITY AFFECTS THE PERSONALITY!

(Continued)

**LOSS OF UNSIGHTLY FAT GIVES A PERSON A MENTAL STIMULUS THAT IS SO UPLIFTING THAT IT'S HARD TO DESCRIBE, FOR IT'S SO WONDERFUL!!** Count your blessings. Obesity is not to be pitied or compared to paralysis, deadly cancer, or blindness! You can whip the overweight problem when you make up your own mind that you want to!

**BALANCED MEALS ARE ESSENTIAL DURING AND AFTER WEIGHT LOSS!** Starvation diets cause skin flabbiness. A gradual reduction of 3-6 pounds a month is best according to most doctors.

**YOU KNOW YOUR EATING HABITS . . . AND YOU KNOW WHAT YOU SHOULD DO . . . BUT WHAT ARE YOU GOING TO DO ABOUT IT?** You can (and should) take control and change your obese condition. I personally challenge you to rise above the obesity problem that you have gotten yourself into! You can be the ultimate winner! You don't have to be a weak-willed glutton or a person who can't overcome . . . unless you are a quitter! Just make up your mind to do it and then do it! You can help others, too! Peace of mind is yours when you alone decide to use your own free will which God gave you! It's up to you! God will bless you as you conquer the overeating habit!

# What will you do...

**HERE ARE SOME SIMPLE GUIDELINES THAT MAY HELP YOU TAKE WEIGHT OFF!**

1. Admit to yourself that you let food manage your life.
2. Believe that God can help you control the temptation to overeat.
3. Make a decision to turn your will and life over to God.
4. Take inventory of your habits which cause you to crave food.
5. Confess your faults honestly to God.
6. Determine to let God remove your faults while you do your part.
7. Humble yourself to God. Ask His help in your project to lose all the extra pounds.
8. Make a list of every person you have harmed, and be willing to make amends to them all. Make amends as much as is possible!
9. Continue to take personal inventory of your thoughts and actions each day. When you are wrong, promptly admit it and correct it. Ask God to help you with this.
10. Study the Bible, and pray only for knowledge for His will in your life. Ask Him to end your overweight condition, safely.
11. Witnes to others how they too can break the bondage of compulsive eating.
12. Don't complain. Praise God for helping you. Be patient. Don't indulge in self-pity. Free yourself of guilt and self-condemnation.

# The five most dangerous words in the English language.

# Maybe it will go away

**PRAYER**

Dear God, Please forgive me for all my sins. Please forgive me for abusing my own body. I know You created me in Your image and I am destroying Your image! I need Your help in resisting the temptation to overeat. I know You won't make my fat vanish, like magic! I will have to exercise my own free will and take control over this situation! I know You will always help me when I do all I can to help myself! Thank You for that. In Jesus' name, I pray. AMEN!

# OCCULT ACTIVITY

**ALL OCCULT ACTIVITY IS CREATED BY SATAN AND FORBIDDEN BY GOD!**

**IN THESE APOCALYPTIC TIMES IT'S ONLY NATURAL THAT SATAN IS STAGING AN ALL-OUT CAMPAIGN TO RECRUIT PEOPLE!** This is a fact not to be dismissed as a casual observation. Every day more and more people are being drawn into occult doctrines, music, games, and the powers of evil!

**IT'S TIME FOR CHRISTIANS TO STOP YAWNING THEIR LIFE AWAY!** They need to wake up from their deep sleep and look around them at the zodiac charms on their neighbor's bracelets. They need to witness to them about the dangers of flirting with any area of the occult. They need to wake up to the message on many rock-n-roll records and realize that games like "Dungeons and Dragons" and ouija boards are Satan's tools!

**TO DABBLE IN OCCULTISM IN THE NAME OF CURIOSITY, SOPHISTICATION, OR ENLIGHTENMENT IS TO OPEN YOURSELF UP TO THE VERY ONE WE ARE URGED TO RESIST . . . AND THAT IS SATAN!** Belief in astrology, transcendental meditation, witchcraft, levitation, sorcery, ESP, evolution, palmistry, familiar spirits, pyramid power, astral projection, voodoo, tarot cards, tea leaves, fortune telling, mind control, automatic writing, ouija boards, seances, idols, sex orgies, reincarnation, magic, theories of Atlantis, poltergeists, I-Ching, Edgar Cayce, cabala, gematria, theosophy, yogism, alchemy, chiromancy, clairvoyance, mesmerism (hypnosis), crystal balls, thought transference, Buddhism, ectoplasm, telekinesis, planchettes, Rosicrucian, seers, prophets, water diviners, dream analysis, predestination, dowsing, omens, card readers, dice, crystal mirrors, gypsies, horoscopes, fairies, gnomes, leprechauns, genies, banshees, giants, bogeyman, vampires, werewolves, abominable snowman, elves, illusions, necromancy, witch doctors, incantations, jinxs, love-potions, talisman, amulets, lucky charms, swastikas, wishing wells, wonder-workers, snake charming, wands, magic rings, Witch of Endor, Freud, Cassandra, Jung, Delphic, Gestalt, Pythias, etc., is to court "the god of this world" . . . "the prince of the power of the air " whose name is Satan!

**WHEN A PERSON TOTALLY COMMITS HIS LIFE TO JESUS AND ASKS HIM TO POSSESS EVERY AREA OF HIS LIFE, HE WILL NOT BE GUILTY OF DABBLING IN THE OCCULT!** He serves the one true living God. He will have no fear that Satan will take control of his life. He will not fear the temptation to submit to any occult activity. He consciously determines to follow Christ. He looks to Him for strength.

**TODAY OCCULTISM IS SWEEPING EVERY NATION AND IT'S TOO LATE FOR A CASUAL CHRISTIAN STAND!** To live a total Christian life means you must understand who Satan is and seriously believe what the Scriptures say at face value. **1 John 5:19** says the whole world is in the power of the evil one. **Matthew 13:19** says Satan snatches away the truth of the Gospel. **Revelation 12:9** says Satan deceives the whole world. **Acts 8:9-11** says Satan is able to counterfeit the genuine power of God. **Luke 22:31** says Satan is out to get us. **Luke 13:16** says Satan binds men spiritually.

**THE SCRIPTURES ARE VERY CLEAR THAT JESUS CHRIST TRIUMPHS OVER SATAN!** Jesus saw Satan fall like lightning from heaven. **Luke 10:18**

**Born-again Christians consciously build one another up in the faith.** They strengthen, counsel, and pray for one another! **1 Peter 5:8-9** says to be sober and watchful because our adversary, the devil, prowls around like a roaring lion seeking whom he may devour.

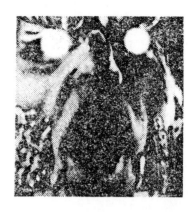

Born-again Christians share Christ! Any church who teaches the entire Holy Bible is equipped to do this. **While the secular world is doing everything in its power to cause people to drift into the occult, the body of born-again believers are giving their all to obey the Great Commission.** Christians are obedient to God. They have no fear they will be overrun by Satan and his occult teachings. Dedicated Christians do not worry about their own well-being. They obey God out of an overwhelming love and desire to please Him!

**Born-again Christians totally yield themselves to Christ.** They do not just give lip service on Sunday mornings! They are daily aware of God in their lives! They listen to Him through prayer and reading the Scriptures! **1 Corinthians 6:20** says we are not our own. We are bought with a price. Jesus shed his blood on the cross and paid for our sins so we could be saved.

**Born-again Christians are not afraid of Satan's temptations! God gives them a special armor that cannot be overcome by the powers of darkness. God teaches, loves, heals and liberates those who have been caught in the forces controlled by Satan.**

**Christ is our victory—our freedom!** Satan will soon be burned alive in the eternal lake of fire throughout eternity! Christ is our island of rescue in a rough storm or sea! **Christ offers the demon-possessed person the only way to become whole!** Christians offer a helping hand just as Christ does. The Christian has a light that Satan can never put out in this age of Aquarius or any other age!

**Thousands of people have spent their dollars to see "The Exorcist," "The Omen," "Carey," "Rosemary's Baby," and other occult films which only guarantee another deluge of satanic films for the years to come. Christians need to speak up! Tell them they play right into the hands of Satan! They open themselves up for demon oppression and possibly possession!**

**AN EFFECTIVE CHRISTIAN DOES NOT NEED TO HAVE HAD A FIRST-HAND OCCULT EXPERIENCE TO WITNESS!** He does need to have some wisdom about the devices Satan uses. He needs to witness about God's power in overcoming the enemy! He must understand and deal with the evil powers of Satan. If you want to live with Christ throughout eternity, stay close to Him and away from ALL OCCULT ACTIVITY! THAT IS AN ORDER FROM GOD!

### PRAYER

Dear God, please forgive me for all my sins. I turn away from all interest and participation in the **occult!** I didn't realize that horoscopes, fortune tellers, reincarnation or pyramids were tricks of Satan to get me interested in the **occult.** I will not play any games that have demons, dragons or space invaders in the game rules. I will read my Bible to see what Your perfect will for my life is. From this moment on I will never dabble in any form of the **occult.** Thank You for saving my soul. In Jesus' name, I pray. AMEN!

# OLD AGE

**FEAR OF OLD AGE = THE FALSE ASSUMPTION THAT I STILL HAVE MANY YEARS OF LIFE AHEAD OF ME!** *"So teach us to number our days, that we may apply our hearts unto wisdom."* **Psalm 90:12** *"O satisfy us early with thy mercy; that we may rejoice and be glad all our days."* **Psalm 90:14**

**QUESTION:** *"What man is he that desireth life, and loveth many days* (wants to live a ripe old age), *that he may see good?"* **ANSWER:** *"Keep thy tongue from evil, and thy lips from speaking guile. Depart from evil, and do good; seek peace, and pursue it. The eyes of the Lord are upon the righteous, and his ears are open unto their cry."* **Psalm 34:12-15**

**OLD PERSON: "YOU DON'T WANT TO DIE AND BE FOREVER FORGOTTEN, DO YOU?"** *"The face of the Lord is against them that do evil* (are sinners), *to cut off the remembrance of them from the earth."* **Psalm 34:16**

**GOD COMMANDS US TO REVERENCE OLDER PEOPLE!** *"Thou shalt rise up before the hoary head* (grey haired person), *and honour the face of the old man* (or woman) *and fear thy God: I am the Lord."* **Leviticus 19:32**

**IF YOU OBEY GOD'S COMMANDMENTS YOU WILL LIVE TO A RIPE OLD AGE!** *"And thou shalt go to thy fathers in peace; thou shalt be buried in a good old age."* **Genesis 15:15**

**IT'S DANGEROUS TO WAIT ONE MOMENT LONGER TO BECOME A BORN-AGAIN CHRISTIAN!** *"Go to now, ye that say, Today or tomorrow we will go into such a city, and continue there a year, and buy and sell, and get gain: whereas ye know not what shall be on the morrow. For what is your life? It is even a vapour, that appeareth for a little time, and then vanisheth away. For that ye ought to say, If the Lord will, we shall live, and do this, or that. But now ye rejoice in your boastings: all such rejoicing is evil. Therefore to him that knoweth to do good, and doeth it not, to him it is sin."* **James 4:13-17**

**OLD AGE IS PROMISED TO YOU IF . . .** *"If they obey and serve him* (God), *they shall spend their days in prosperity, and their years in pleasures. But if they obey not, they shall perish by the sword, and they shall die without knowledge."* **Job 36:11-12** *"Thou shalt know also that thy seed shall be great, and thine offspring as the grass of the earth. Thou shalt come to thy grave in a full age* (and die a natural death), *like as a shock of corn cometh in in his season."* **Job 5:25-26**

**THESE SCRIPTURES ARE FOR ANYONE WHO IS OLD OR APPROACHING OLD AGE!** *"Cast me not off in the time of old age; forsake me not when my strength faileth."* **Psalm 71:9** *"Remember not the sins of my youth, nor my transgressions: according to thy mercy remember thou me for thy goodness sake, O Lord."* **Psalm 25:7** *"Now also when I am old and greyheaded, O God, forsake me not; until I have shewed* (showed) *thy strength unto this generation, and thy power to every one that is to come."* **Psalm 71:18** *". . .Days should speak, and multitude of years should teach wisdom."* **Job 32:7**

**DO YOU WANT TO LIVE TO A RIPE OLD AGE?** *"Hearken unto thy father that begat thee, and despise not thy mother when she is old!"* **Proverbs 23:22** *"The fear of the Lord prolongeth days: but the years of the wicked shall be shortened."* **Proverbs 10:27**

**GREY HAIR IS BEAUTIFUL AND A BLESSING OF LIFE!** *"The glory of young men is their strength: and the beauty of old men is the grey head."* **Proverbs 20:29** *"The hoary head* (grey hair) *is a crown of glory, if it be found in the way of righteousness."* **Proverbs 16:31**

**NOT ALL OLD PEOPLE ARE WISE, BUT THAT DOESN'T GIVE US LICENSE TO BE DISRESPECTFUL! Jesus said:** *"Verily I say unto you, except ye be converted, and become as little children, ye shall not enter into the kingdom of heaven."* **Matthew 18:3** *"Great men are not always wise: neither do the aged understand judgment."* **Job 32:9** *"The fear of the Lord is the beginning of wisdom: and the knowledge of the holy is understanding. For by me thy days shall be multiplied, and the years of thy life shall be increased."* **Proverbs 9:10-11**

**HERE IS A PROMISE AND A BLESSING TO AN OLDER PERSON WHO HAS LIVED A RIGHTEOUS LIFE!** *"I have been young, and now am old; yet have I not seen the righteous forsaken, nor his seed* (descendants) *begging bread."* **Psalm 37:25**

**HERE IS SOMETHING PRODUCTIVE AN OLDER PERSON CAN DO INSTEAD OF FOLDING HIS HANDS!** *"I remember the days of old; I meditate on all thy works; I muse on the work of thy hands. I stretch forth my hands unto thee: my soul thirsteth after thee, as a thirsty land* (longs for rain)." **Psalm 143:5-6**

## *Old Age*
**PRAYER**

Dear God, Please forgive me for every sin I ever committed. I repent I have not spent my entire lifetime obeying and serving You! I want to spend eternity with You. Please be my friend, my heavenly Father, and my companion. I praise You and I love You. If I can be an effective witness in leading another person to Christ, please use me. In Jesus' name, I pray. AMEN!

# OPPRESSION

**DEFINITION:** To suppress; to crush or burden by abuse of power or authority; to burden spiritually or mentally as if by pressure; weigh down; unjust or cruel exercise of authority or power; a sense of heaviness or obstruction in the body or mind; depression.

**WE ARE COMMANDED NOT TO OPPRESS ANY STRANGER!** *"Thou shalt neither **vex** (aggravate) a stranger, nor **oppress** him. . ."* **Exodus 22:21** *"And if a stranger sojourn with thee in your land, ye shall not **vex** him."* **Leviticus 19:33/Deuteronomy 10:19**

**WE ARE COMMANDED NOT TO OPPRESS A WIDOW OR ORPHAN!** *"Ye shall not **afflict any widow or fatherless child** (orphan). If thou **afflict** them in any wise, and they cry at all unto me, I will surely hear their cry; And my wrath shall wax (grow) hot, and I will kill you with the sword (of righteousness); and your wives shall be **widows**, and your children **fatherless** (orphans)."* **Exodus 22:22-24 ALSO READ: Matthew 23:14**

**GOD SAID WE ARE NOT TO OPPRESS ANIMALS!** **Deuteronomy 22:6-7**

**WE ARE COMMANDED NOT TO OPPRESS OUR NEIGHBOURS!** *"Thou shalt not **defraud** thy neighbour, neither rob him. . ."* **Leviticus 19:13** *"And if thou sell ought unto thy neighbour, or buyest ought of thy neighbour's hand, **ye shall not oppress one another.**"* **Leviticus 25:14**

**WE ARE COMMANDED NOT TO OPPRESS THE DEAF OR BLIND!** *"Thou shalt not **curse the deaf**, nor put a **stumbling block** before the blind, but shalt fear thy God: I am the Lord."* **Leviticus 19:14**

*"Ye shall not therefore oppress one another; but thou shalt fear thy God: for I am the Lord your God."* **Leviticus 25:17**

*"The Lord also will be a refuge for the oppressed, a refuge in times of trouble."* **Psalm 9:9**

**WE ARE COMMANDED NOT TO OPPRESS ANYONE!** *"Be merciful unto me, O God: for man would swallow me up; he **fighting daily oppresseth me.** Mine enemies would daily swallow me up; for they be many that **fight** against me, O thou most High. What time I am afraid, I will trust in thee."* **Psalm 56:1-3**

**ROBBERY IS OPPRESSING ANOTHER PERSON OF HIS OWN GOODS. EVEN IF A PERSON IS NEEDY, HE SHOULD NEVER OPPRESS ANYONE!** *"The people of the land have used **oppression**, and exercised robbery, and have **vexed** the poor and needy: yea, they have **oppressed** the stranger wrongfully."* **Ezekiel 22:29**

**IF YOU ARE GUILTY OF OPPRESSING ANYONE, YOU NEED TO PRAY THE PRAYER THAT DAVID PRAYED!** *"Look thou upon me, and be merciful unto me, as thou usest to do unto those that love thy name. Order my steps in thy word: and let not any iniquity (wrong doing) have dominion over me. **Deliver me from the oppression of man:** so will I keep thy precepts. Make thy face to shine upon thy servant; and teach me thy statutes."* **Psalm 119:132-135**

**GOD IS MERCIFUL TO TAKE CARE OF THE OPPRESSED!** *"The Lord executeth righteousness and judgment for all that are **oppressed.**"* **Psalm 103:6**

*"Thou shalt not oppress an hired servant that is poor and needy, whether he be of thy brethren, or of thy strangers that are in thy land within thy gates."* **Deuteronomy 24:14**

**NEVER FORGET THAT SATAN IS THE AUTHOR OF OPPRESSION. IT IS SATAN THAT WHISPERS IN EVERY PERSON'S EAR TO DO SOMETHING WRONG! THE CHOICE IS YOURS WHETHER TO OBEY HIM OR NOT!**

### PRAYER

Dear God, Please forgive me for all my sins. Please forgive me for **oppressing** others. I will do everything in my power to make full restitution to those I have **oppressed.** Thank You for loving and forgiving me! In Jesus' name, I pray. AMEN!

# PARENTS

*"Train up a child in the way he should go: and when he is old, he will not depart from it."* **Proverbs 22:6**

**IT IS THE DUTY OF PARENTS TO TALK ABOUT GOD WHEN THEY SIT, WALK, GO TO BED, AND WHEN THEY WAKE UP!** *"And these words, which I command thee this day, shall be in thine heart: And thou shalt teach them diligently unto thy children, and shalt talk of them when thou sittest in thine house, and when thou walkest by the way, and when thou liest down, and when thou risest up."* **Deuteronomy 6:6-7**

**JESUS SAID WE ARE TO TAKE OUR CHILDREN TO CHURCH SO THEY WILL LEARN ABOUT CHRIST!** *"Suffer* (allow) *little children, and forbid them not, to come unto me: for of such is the kingdom of heaven."* **Matthew 19:14**

**PARENTS ARE COMMANDED TO NOT USE PROFANITY!** *"Thou shalt not take the name of the Lord thy God in vain: for the Lord will not hold him guiltless that taketh his name in vain."* **Deuteronomy 5:11**

**PARENTS ARE COMMANDED TO NEVER COMMIT ADULTERY!** **Deuteronomy 5:18**

**PARENTS ARE COMMANDED TO NEVER STEAL!** **Deuteronomy 5:19**

**PARENTS ARE COMMANDED TO NEVER BEAR FALSE WITNESS AGAINST THEIR NEIGHBORS!** **Deuteronomy 5:20**

**PARENTS ARE COMMANDED TO TEACH THEIR CHILDREN TO LOVE GOD!** *"O that there were such an heart in them, that they would fear* (and respect) *me, and keep all my commandments always, that it might be well with them, and with their children for ever!* **Deuteronomy 5:29**

**PARENTS ARE COMMANDED TO TEACH THE BIBLE TO THEIR CHILDREN!** *"And thou shalt teach them diligently unto thy children. . . ."* **Deuteronomy 6:7**

**WE ARE COMMANDED NEVER TO DESPISE OUR ELDERLY PARENTS!** **Proverbs 23:22**

**GRANDCHILDREN ARE A CROWN TO THE ELDERLY IF THEY HAVE BEEN REARED PROPERLY!** *"Children's children* (grandchildren) *are the crown of old men; and the glory of children are their fathers."* **Proverbs 17:6**

**THE PUNISHMENT FOR NOT BRINGING UP CHILDREN IN THE LORD IS THAT THEY WILL BRING YOU GRIEF!** *"A foolish son is a grief to his father, and bitterness to her that bare him."* **Proverbs 17:25**

**JESUS SAID:** *"If ye then, being evil, know how to give good gifts unto your children, how much more shall your Fther which is in heaven give good things to them that ask him?"* **Matthew 7:11**

**PARENTS SHOULD PREPARE AHEAD FOR THEIR CHILDREN'S WELFARE AND UPKEEP!** *". . .for the children ought not to lay up for the parents, but the parents for the children."* **2 Corinthians 12:14**

**PARENTS ARE COMMANDED TO NOT PROVOKE THEIR CHILDREN TO WRATH!** *"And ye fathers, provoke not your children to wrath: but bring them up in the nurture and admonition of the Lord."* **Ephesians 6:4**

**PARENTS SHOULD TEACH THEIR CHILDREN, WITHOUT GETTING ANGRY OR MAKING THEM ANGRY!** *"Fathers, provoke not your children to anger, lest they be discouraged."* **Colossians 3:21**

*"Ye shall fear* (and respect) *every man his mother, and his father, and keep my sabbaths: I am the Lord your God."* **Leviticus 19:3**

*"Honour thy father and thy mother: that thy days may be long upon the land which the Lord thy God giveth thee."* **Exodus 20:12**

*"A wise son maketh a glad father: but a foolish son is the heaviness of his mother."* **Proverbs 10:1**

**GOD COMMANDED PARENTS TO DISCIPLINE THEIR CHILDREN IN LOVE!** *"He that spareth his rod* (switch) *hateth his son: but he that loveth him chasteneth* (corrects) *him betimes* (when needed)."* **Proverbs 13:24**

**IF YOU DO NOT BRING UP YOUR CHILDREN PROPERLY, YOU WILL PAY THE PRICE!** *"The father of a fool has no joy.* **Proverbs 17:21**

### PARENT'S PRAYER

Dear God, teach me to be a better parent. Help me to understand my children, to listen patiently to what they have to say, and to answer all questions kindly! Teach me not to interrupt them. Teach me to be as courteous to them as I want them to be to me. Give me the courage to ask their forgiveness when I know that I have done wrong. Teach me not to vainly hurt the feelings of my children. Forgive me for laughing at their mistakes, and for resorting to shame and ridicule as punishment. Teach me not to tempt a child to lie and steal. Please guide me hour by hour to demonstrate, by all I say, and do, that honesty produces happiness! Please reduce any meanness or short temper in me! Teach me not to nag. And when I am out-of-sorts, help me! Teach me to hold my tongue! Teach me to overlook insignificant errors of my children. Help me to see the good things that they do. Give me a ready word of honest praise. Help me to treat my children as those of their own age. Teach me not to exact of them the judgments and conventions of adults. Teach me not to rob them of the opportunity to wait upon themselves, to think, to choose, and to make their own decisions! Teach me to not punish them for my own selfish satisfaction. Teach me to grant their wishes if they are reasonable ones, and to have the courage to withhold a privilege that I know will do them harm! Teach me to be a fair and just companion to my children so they will have genuine esteem for me. Prepare me to be loved and imitated by my children. Teach me to be calm, poised, and in self-control, while You guide me all the way. Thank You for the blessing and privilege of being a parent. I love my children but I will not put them before my love for You! I will do every thing in my power and wisdom to train them in the way that You want me to! As long as I live I will serve You. In Jesus' name. AMEN!

# PATIENCE

*"Wait on the Lord, and keep his way, and he shall exalt thee to inherit the land: when the wicked are cut off, thou shalt see it."* **Psalm 37:34**

**THE END RESULT OF PATIENCE IS PEACE!** *"Mark the perfect man, and behold the upright: for the end of that man is peace."* **Psalm 37:37**

**PATIENCE TRULY MAKES ONE PERFECT!** *"Now the God of peace, that brought again from the dead our Lord Jesus, that great shepherd of the sheep, through the blood of the everlasting covenant, make you perfect in every good work to do his will, working in you that which is well pleasing in his sight, through Jesus Christ; to whom be glory for ever and ever."* **Hebrews 13:20-21**

*"Be **patient** therefore, brethren, unto the coming of the Lord. Behold, the husbandman (Christ) waiteth for the precious fruit of the earth (born-again Christians), and hath **long patience** for it, until he receive the early and latter rain (complete and entire harvest of souls). Be ye also **patient**; stablish your hearts: for the coming of the Lord draweth nigh."* **James 5:7-8**

**JOB WAS A CLASSIC EXAMPLE OF LEARNING PATIENCE!** *"Take (consider) my brethren, the prophets, who have spoken the name of the Lord, for an example of suffering affliction, and of **patience**. Behold, we count them happy which endure. Ye have heard of the **patience** of Job, and have seen the end of the Lord; that the Lord is very pitiful, and of tender mercy."* **James 5:10-11**

**THE BIBLE SAYS WE ARE TO BE PATIENT IN TRIBULATION!** *"Let love be without dissimulation. Abhor that which is evil; cleave to that which is good. Be kindly affectioned one to another with brotherly love; in honour preferring one another; not slothful in business; fervent in spirit; serving the Lord: rejoicing in hope; **patient in tribulation**; continuing instant in prayer; distributing to the necessity of saints; given to hospitality. Bless them which persecute you: bless, and curse not. Rejoice with them that do rejoice, and weep with them that weep. Be of the same mind one toward another. Mind not high things, but condescend to men of low estate. Be not wise in your own conceits. Recompense to no man evil for evil. Provide things honest in the sight of all men. If it be possible, as much as lieth in you, live peaceably with all men."* **Romans 12:9-18**

**WHY NOT START NOW TO LET PATIENCE HAVE A PERFECT WORK IN YOU?** *"Knowing this, that **the trying of your faith worketh patience. But let patience have her perfect work,** that ye may be perfect and entire, wanting nothing. If any of you lack wisdom, let him ask of God, that giveth to all men liberally, and upbraideth not; and it shall be given him. But let him ask in faith, nothing wavering. For he that wavereth is like a wave of the sea driven with the wind and tossed. For let not that man think he shall receive anything of the Lord. A double minded man is unstable in all his ways."* **James 1:3-8**

**BLESSED IS THE PERSON WHO ENDURES TEMPTATION, YIELDS NOT, AND LEARNS PATIENCE FROM IT!** *"Blessed is the man that endureth temptation: for when he is tried, he shall receive the crown of life, which the Lord hath promised to them that love him. Let no man say when he is tempted, I am tempted of God: for God cannot be tempted with evil, neither tempteth he any man: But every man is tempted when he is drawn away of his own lust, and enticed. Then when lust hath conceived, it bringeth forth sin: and sin, when it is finished, bringeth forth death (eternal separation from God)."* **James 1:12-15**

### *A merry heart doeth good like a medicine (Prov. 17:22)*

*". . .But we glory in tribulations also: knowing that **tribulation worketh patience; and patience, experience;** and experience, hope: and hope maketh not ashamed; because the love of God is shed abroad in our hearts by the Holy Ghost which is given unto us. For when we were yet without strength, in due time Christ died for the ungodly."* **Romans 5:3-6**

# PATIENCE
#### PRAYER

Dear God, please come into my heart and give me wisdom and understanding so I may be better able to cope with my problems! Cleanse me. Cleanse all my sins. I repent of every thing I have ever done that was not Christ-like! **Please teach me patience.** I need all the help You can give me, since I am usually a nervous and anxious person. Give me peace in time of troubles. Give me strength to laugh in the face of temptations. I praise You and love You. In Jesus' name, AMEN!

# PEER PRESSURE

**PEER PRESSURE RESULTS WHEN A WEAK PERSON BECOMES EASILY INFLUENCED BY OTHERS!** He doesn't want to be singled out as different. He fears he will be known as square, weird or different, so he goes along with the crowd in their pursuit of ideas. **He does what his peers say to do, whether they are right or wrong, rather than be left out!** He eventually loses his own self-identity. He forfeits his own ideas and better judgment. He is a follower, not a leader! He puts the wishes of his **peers** above those of his own, his parents, and everyone else!

**TO BECOME AWARE OF THE PEER PRESSURE PROBLEM GIVES A PERSON A CHANCE TO DO SOMETHING TO CORRECT IT!** If you don't learn to resist peer pressure, it will harm you as a person and possibly get you into a great deal of difficulty!

**PROVERBS 13:20 SAYS:** *"He that walketh with wise men (people) shall be wise: but a companion of fools shall be destroyed* (as a result of following their example).*"*

**PEER PRESSURE MAY SEEM THE ONLY WAY TO GO ... BUT IT'S THE WRONG WAY!** *"There is a way which seemeth right unto a man* (person), *but the end thereof are the ways of death (eternal separation from God)."* **Proverbs 14:12**

**PEER PRESSURE IS A TRAP!** Anyone who falls into this trap accepts every word and does every thing his **peers** tell him, without asking a question! He lowers himself to become a sponge that soaks up whatever is spilled on him. He becomes an imitator. He could be an intelligent person, but because he willingly sought out the peer pressure trap (and fell in) he now becomes a simpleton! *"The simple believeth every word: but the prudent man* (person) *looketh well to his* (own) *going. A wise man feareth, and departeth from evil: but the fool rageth* (on), *and is confident."* **Proverbs 14:15-16**

**PEER PRESSURE WILL TAKE YOU DOWN ALL THE WRONG ROADS BECAUSE YOU RELINQUISH YOUR OWN RIGHT TO CHOOSE!** *"Folly is joy to him that is destitute of wisdom: but a man* (person) *of understanding walketh uprightly."* **Proverbs 15:21**

**THE FIRST STEP TO GET FREE FROM PEER PRESSURE IS TO COMMIT YOUR LIFE TO CHRIST!** He will forgive all your sins. He longs to come into your life and to be your personal friend. Since you're accustomed to being a follower, why not follow the real leader, instead of the losers? Jesus will give you the wisdom and strength to do what ever is necessary to get free! He will help you resist any temptation you face, each day! **Jesus said:** *"Take heed lest any man* (person) *deceive you."* **Mark 13:5**

**TO FALL INTO THE PEER PRESSURE TRAP IS TO GIVE UP YOUR IDENTITY AND BECOME DOUBLE MINDED!** *"A double minded man* (person) *is unstable in all his ways."* **James 1:8**

**GOD IS NO RESPECTER OF PERSONS ... SO WHY SHOULD YOU BE?** If you're afraid to get out of the **peer pressure trap** because you think you'll have no friends left, you're mistaken! *"But rather seek ye the kingdom of God; and all these things shall be added unto you."* **Luke 12:31**

**PEER PRESSURE = DECEPTION (PLUS) THE TEMPTATION TO FORGET YOUR "THING" AND DO THEIR "THING"!** *"For if a man* (person) *think himself to be something, when he is nothing, he deceiveth himself. But let every man* (person) *prove his own work, and then shall he have rejoicing in himself alone, and not in another."* **Galatians 6:3-4**

**WHEN YOU SUBMIT TO PEER PRESSURE, YOU SHOW PARTIALITY TO THOSE LEFT BEHIND ... AND WHEN THE PEER PRESSURE GROUP TIRES OF YOU, THEY WILL DROP YOU!** *"Are ye not then partial in yourselves, and are become judges of evil thoughts?"* **James 2:4**

**JESUS MAKES YOU A PROMISE THAT NO OTHER PERSON CAN MAKE!** *"But as many as received him, to them gave he power to become the sons of God...."* **John 1:12**

**PEER PRESSURE = A FORM OF IDOLATRY!** Idolatry is anything or anyone that is put above a person's love and service to God! *"Wherefore, my dearly beloved, flee from idolatry."* **1 Corinthians 10:14**

**SATAN IS THE AUTHOR OF PEER PRESSURE ... AND HE NEVER HAS YOUR BEST INTEREST IN MIND!** *"For nothing is secret* (to God), *that shall not be made manifest* (known); *neither any thing hid, that shall not be known..."* **Luke 8:17**

**IF YOU ARE AFRAID TO BREAK AWAY FROM A GROUP FOR FEAR OF REJECTION: REMEMBER THAT GOD WILL GIVE YOU STRENGTH TO BREAK AWAY ... HE WILL MAKE A WAY TO ESCAPE AND IT WON'T BE HARD FOR YOU TO BEAR!** *"There hath no temptation taken you but such as is common to man* (other people): *but God is faithful, who will not suffer* (allow) *you to be tempted above that* (which) *ye are able* (to stand): *but will with the temptation also make a way to escape, that ye may be able to bear it."* **1 Corinthians 10:13**

**YOU CAN BREAK THE CHAINS OF BONDAGE THAT COME FROM PEER PRESSURE AND BE YOUR OWN PERSON AGAIN!** *"But every man* (person) *is tempted, when he is drawn away of his own lust, and enticed. Then when lust hath conceived, it bringeth forth sin: and sin, when it is finished, bringeth forth death* (eternal separation from God)."* **James 1:14-15**

**WHEN YOUR "SO-CALLED" FRIENDS DROP YOU, GOD WILL GIVE YOU NEW AND BETTER ONES!** Read your Bible regularly and pray. You can turn to God any time of the day or night! Live right and when you ask God to give you new friends, he will special order them and send them to you! He knows what you need to make you happy and he wants what's best for you! He will never let you down!

**TAKE PRACTICAL STEPS TO AVOID ANY PRESSURE!** You will need to go to church and attend classes and socials with your own age group. Meet other Christians. Avoid situations where you know you can be tempted with the **peer pressure** groups!

**MAKE A RESOLUTION TO FREE YOURSELF FROM PEER PRESSURE!** Resolve to please Christ! Don't worry about what others may think of you. **You got yourself into the peer pressure trap, and it's up to you to get yourself out!** But, you won't have to do it alone because God will help you every step of the way!

## PRAYER

Dear God, Please forgive me for all my sins. I know that You love me and I love You! I need to have friends who will love me and accept me, without trying to make me do their "thing"! I want to be free to make my own choices. I also want to please You! I don't want to be a sponge for others to use. I know I will lose some old friends, but I trust You to supply me with new friends. I thank You for forgiving my sins. In Jesus' name, I pray. AMEN!

# PHILOSOPHY

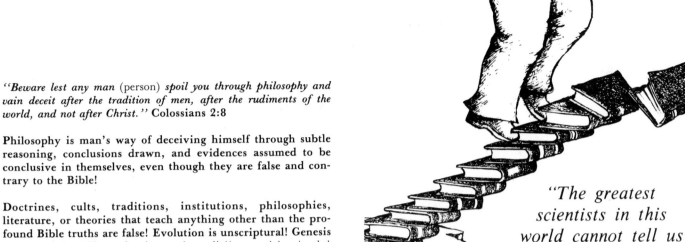

*"Beware lest any man* (person) *spoil you through philosophy and vain deceit after the tradition of men, after the rudiments of the world, and not after Christ."* Colossians 2:8

Philosophy is man's way of deceiving himself through subtle reasoning, conclusions drawn, and evidences assumed to be conclusive in themselves, even though they are false and contrary to the Bible!

Doctrines, cults, traditions, institutions, philosophies, literature, or theories that teach anything other than the profound Bible truths are false! Evolution is unscriptural! Genesis 1:3-26/Job 38:4 Humanism is unscriptural! *". . .much learning doth make thee mad."* Acts 26:24

IN THESE LAST DAYS BEFORE CHRIST RETURNS, THERE ARE HUNDREDS OF PHILOSOPHIES BEING BORN EACH YEAR. BUT THERE IS ONLY ONE TRUE RELIGION, ONE HOPE, ONE LORD, ONE FAITH, ONE BAPTISM! Ephesians 4:5/Corinthians 4:13. *"But foolish and unlearned questions avoid, knowing that they do gender strifes. And the servant of the Lord must not strive; but be gentle unto all men, apt to teach* (the Bible), *patient, in meekness instructing those that oppose themselves; if God peradventure will give them repentance fo the acknowledging of the truth; and that they may recover themselves out of the snare of the devil, who are taken captive by him at his will."* 2 Timothy 2:23-26

TRUE CHRISTIANITY IS RECOGNIZED BY ITS FRUIT! Matthew 7:19-20/Luke 6:43-44/John 15:8

THERE ARE MANY PHILOSOPHIES, SECTS, CULTS, AND RELIGIONS — SO HOW CAN YOU IDENTIFY THE REAL TRUTH? Jesus foretold the time of unity of true worshipers. John 4:23-24 In he last days true servants of God will be made known. Matthew 13:37-39, 41, 43 True religion is recognized by its fruits. Malachi 3:18/Matthew 7:20

DIFFERENCES SHOULD NOT PREVENT BIBLE DISCUSSION! We are encouraged to set matters straight. Isaiah 1:18/Psalm 25:4-5 Christians must have unity of mind. 1 Corinthians 1:10/Ephesians 4:5, 13 The Bible is the basis for all truth. 2 Timothy 3:16-17 Discovering the truth brings eternal life and proves what is right. John 17:3/1 Thessalonians 5:21/1 John 4:1

TO GET ALL YOUR QUESTIONS ANSWERED, GO TO THE BIBLE! True seekers of God know the Bible is true. John 7:16-17 Compare your questions with the Bible, not with man's word. Acts 17:11/Psalm 146:3 All things are set straight by the Bible. 2 Timothy 3:16-17/John 5:39 Knowledge is a protection which leads to eternal life. Ecclesiastes 7:12/Proverbs 3:13-18

*"Study* (the Bible) *to shew thyself approved unto God, a workman* (student) *that needeth not to be ashamed, rightly dividing the word of truth. But shun profane and vain babblings: for they will increase unto more ungodliness."* 2 Timothy 2:15-16

FALSE DOCTRINES WERE CONDEMNED BY JESUS! Matthew 23:15, 29-31/15:4-9 The truth makes you free. John 8:31-32 People are destroyed for lack of knowledge. Hosea 4:1-2, 6 God must be true though all men are liars. Romans 3:3-4/Proverbs 30:6 False doctrines, cults, and philosophies must be exposed. Ezekiel 34:2, 8-10 The person who tells the Bible truths is not your enemy. Galatians 4:16-17

*"The greatest scientists in this world cannot tell us at this moment what life is all about.*

THE WHOLE WORLD IS BEING DECEIVED THROUGH FALSE RELIGIONS, PHILOSOPHIES AND CULTS! WE MUST TURN TO THE TRUE TEACHINGS CONTAINED IN THE BIBLE. Revelation 12:9/Romans 12:2 Accurate knowledge should be welcomed! Acts 18:25-26/Proverbs 1:5

IT IS NOT TRUE THAT THERE IS "GOOD" IN ALL TEACHINGS (OR) RELIGIONS! God sets the standard for worship. John 4:23-24/James 1:27 No theory is valid if it is not contained in God's Word. Romans 10:2-3/Proverbs 28:9/John 14:15 Good "works" alone are rejected as being able to save you. Matthew 7:21-23/Isaiah 1:15. The Bible says to test all works with the Bible truths. Matthew 7:20/Malachi 3:18/Isaiah 1:18

BECAUSE THERE ARE MANY PHILOSOPHIES AND FALSE RELIGIONS DOES NOT PROVE THAT NO ONE TRUE RELIGION EXISTS! Those who teach for dishonest gain are condemned. Titus 1:10-11 False teachers, like Satan, blind people from knowing the truth. Matthew 23:13/15:7-9, 14 The truth is available for those who are searching!

TRUE SCIENCE AGREES WITH THE BIBLE! The earth is round and suspended in space. Isaiah 40:22 Earth's cycles of operation are stable. Ecclesiastes 1:5-9/Genesis 8:22 Science cannot save mankind. Isaiah 43:11/Matthew 6:10/Revelation 21:3-5 Science cannot cure delinquency and world troubles. 2 Timothy 3:1-5/Luke 21:25 Science and philosophy cannot save a person from death. John 5:28-29/11:23-25/Psalm 49:7

PHILOSOPHY TURNS MAN AWAY FROM BEING SPIRITUAL! Colossians 2:8 The Bible helps avoid being caught unaware. Luke 21:36/1 Thessalonians 5:4 *"Professing themselves to be wise, they became fools."* Romans 1:22

THE SOLUTION TO WORLD DISTRESS IS IMPOSSIBLE WITH MEN! Men are fearful and perplexed. Luke 21:25-26/2 Timothy 3:1-5/Isaiah 13:8 Men's peace efforts are doomed to failure. Isaiah 33:7/8:9-13/Jeremiah 23:17 Men's philosophy and teachings will not succeed. God's Word will! Daniel 2:44/Matthew 6:10 God provides deliverance for the obedient. John 3:16/Hebrews 2:14-15

(Continued)

193

DON'T GET CAUGHT UP IN THE TEACHINGS OF OUR WORLD SYSTEM ... BECAUSE IT WILL BE DESTROYED! LASTING PEACE IS SOON TO ARRIVE! **Psalm 37:10-11** *". . .your faith should not stand in the wisdom of men, but in the power of God."* **1 Corinthians 2:5**

IT'S TIME TO REACH A DECISION THAT THE BIBLE IS TRUE — BECAUSE WE ARE NEAR THE END OF THIS WORLD SYSTEM! Our world leaders are no help, they're confused. **Luke 21:25-26/Micah 3:6-7** The Bible gives a clear-cut warning. **Zephaniah 2:2-3/Revelation 18:4/Luke 21:20-22** Christ will not accept a neutral position from you. **Matthew 25:31-34, 41, 46**

DO NOT HESITATE — DECIDE NOW FOR THE REAL TRUTH AND FOR ETERNAL LIFE WITH JESUS! **1 Kings 18:21** *"I call heaven and earth to record this day against you, that I have set before you life and death, blessing and cursing: therefore choose life, that both thou and thy seed may live."* **Deuteronomy 30:19**

# WISDOM

HERE IS PRACTICAL WISDOM FOR THIS AGE OF AD-VANCED LEARNING! God is our Creator, our source. **Proverbs 2:6-9/James 3:17/1 Corinthians 2:6-8** God is revealed through Christ. **Ephesians 1:3, 8/1 Corinthians 1:30/Colossians 2:2-3** Christ reveals God's will for His kingdom's administration. **Ephesians 1:9-10** The world's wisdom is demonic and impractical. **James 3:15-16/1 Corinthians 3:19** To receive eternal life we must receive divine wisdom. **Proverbs 3:21-26/John 17:3** Our spiritual needs must receive our highest value. **Matthew 4:4/6:25-26, 33** To ignore our spiritual needs is impractical and dangerous. **Luke 10:40-42/Matthew 13:22** To ignore the warnings and signs of these last days is fatal. **Luke 21:34-35/Matthew 24:37-39** Eternal life depends on knowing God and accepting Jesus as our personal Savior. **John 17:3/Hosea 4:6**

# HIDE GOD'S WORD IN YOUR HEART.

PEOPLE WHO ACCEPT PHILOSOPHY (INSTEAD OF THE HOLY BIBLE) ARE IGNORANT OF THE TRUTH! THEY ARE SUSPICIOUS. THEY ARGUE. THEY SPLIT HAIRS. THEY STRIVE AND ARE DESTITUTE OF THE TRUTH! *"If any man teach otherwise* (other than the Bible), *and consent not to wholesome words, even the words of our Lord Jesus Christ, and to the doctrine which is according to godliness; he is proud, knowing nothing, but doting about questions and strifes of words, whereof cometh envy, strife, railings, evil surmisings, perverse disputings of men of corrupt minds, and destitute of the truth, supposing that gain is godliness: from such withdraw thyself."* **1 Timothy 6:3-5**

# Knowing of God doesnt mean you know him

PHILOSOPHY ONLY CONFUSES AND SIDE-TRACKS PEOPLE! *"Ever learning, and never able to come to the knowledge of the truth."* **2 Timothy 3:7**

**1 Timothy 6:19-20** says we are to store up a good foundation (in the scriptures) to prepare ourselves for the days to come! In doing so, we can lay hold on eternal life! We are to keep the teachings in our mind and heart and to trust in the commandments! It says we are to avoid profane and vain babblings, and **oppositions of science** which are false! *"Till I come, give attendance to reading* (the Bible), *to exhortation, to doctrine. Meditate upon these things; give thyself wholly to them; that thy profiting may appear to all. Take heed unto thyself, and unto the doctrine; continue in them: for in doing this thou shalt both save thyself, and them that hear thee."* **1 Timothy 4:13, 15-16.**

# Philosophers

### PRAYER

Dear God, please forgive me for all my sins. **Please forgive me for being taken in by the philosophy of man.** I know the Bible is the Living Word of God! I will study to make myself approved! I am not ashamed of You and I don't want You to be ashamed of me! I love You! Thank You for setting me straight! In Jesus' name, I pray. AMEN!

# PHOBIAS

MANY PEOPLE ARE AFRAID TO FLY ... AFRAID TO LEAVE THEIR HOUSE ... AFRAID TO LIVE AND AFRAID TO DIE! THEY TRY TO HIDE THEIR FEARS AND GUILT FEELINGS BUT THEY'RE UNSUCCESSFUL! THEY HATE TO BE IN THIS CONDITION BUT THEY DON'T KNOW THE WAY OUT.

**Phobias can cause disorder, unbalance, delirium, obsessions, alienism, neurosis, epilepsy, vertigo, nervousness, hysteria, paranoia, delusions, hallucinations, depression, melancholia, schizophrenia, kleptomania, insanity and suicide!**

**PHOBIAS ARE THE RESULT OF WHAT SATAN DOES TO A PERSON, WHETHER HE REALIZES IT OR NOT! GOD SAID SATAN IS A THIEF AND A DESTROYER OF PEOPLE!** *"The thief cometh not* (to planet earth), *but for* (these reasons) *to steal, and to kill, and to destroy: I* (Christ speaking) *am come that they might have life, and that they might have it more abundantly."* **John 10:10**

**A PERSON WHO IS AFRAID TO LEAVE HIS HOUSE IS AN AGORAPHOBIC!** He has a fear of public places and open spaces. He feels dizzy and nauseated at the thought of going outside. He feels paralyzed.

**MILLIONS OF MEN AND WOMEN ARE VICTIMS OF PHOBIAS. THEY'VE LOST CONTROL OF SOME VITAL ASPECT OF THEIR LIVES!** At times their fears are so intense that their free will is suppressed. They can no longer resolve simple questions or make decisions.

**FEAR OF OTHER HUMANS IS ANTHROPHOBIA. FEAR OF MEN IS ANDROPHOBIA. FEAR OF WOMEN IS GYNEPHOBIA. FEAR OF CHILDREN IS PEDIOPHOBIA.**

**IT'S NORMAL TO HAVE SOME REALISTIC FEARS!** They alert us to the dangers on the highways. They tell us to protect ourselves by driving safely. But, phobics imagine danger where none exists! They react with a fear so paralyzing that they become unable to defend themselves from whatever they encounter. They seek constant ways to escape. *"The Lord is my light and my salvation; whom shall I fear? the Lord is the strength of my life; of whom shall I be afraid?"* **Psalm 27:1**

**FEAR OF CROWDS IS OCHLOPHOBIA. FEAR OF YOURSELF IS AUTOPHOBIA. CLAUSTROPHOBIA IS FEAR OF ENCLOSED SPACES.** He feels as though he'll suffocate so he panics!

**ACROPHOBIA IS FEAR OF HIGH ALTITUDES.** They are afraid to fly and become panic-stricken when they look out upper-story windows in skyscrapers. They become nauseated and panic or faint!

**WHAT REALLY FRIGHTENS PHOBICS ISN'T A PARTICULAR OBJECT SUCH AS BLOOD, SNAKES, EATING IN PUBLIC, AN ELEVATOR, OR AIRPLANE! THEY FEAR THEIR OWN REACTION ... THEY FEAR THE FEAR ITSELF!** *"Be not afraid of sudden fear, neither of the desolation of the wicked, when it cometh."* **Proverbs 3:25**

**FEAR CAUSES PHOBICS TO LIE — IN AN EFFORT TO CONCEAL THEIR TRUE CONDITION!** Doctors don't know what causes most phobias. Only occasionally will a traumatic experience explain someone's terror. Doctors agree that phobias are born out of stressful situations. Anxiety first arises from a particular situation. Then the anticipation of being terrified actually produces

the physical sensation all over again. The phobic then begins shaking, sweating, and grows dizzy. Lastly, the feelings of physical discomfort comfirm the phobic's fear and panic is then inevitable. The urge to escape takes over like a car out of control that's speeding downhill and the phobic is unable to apply the brakes. **Fear is acutely painful.**

**PHOBIAS ARE AN ILLNESS WHICH GOD CAN (AND WILL) CURE WHEN A PERSON TOTALLY SUBMITS HIMSELF OVER TO GOD!** Many intelligent people have phobias. Dumb people are less likely to be able to grapple with abstract fear. Smart people are highly imaginative and their senses respond more to suggestion. They are more apt to identify with fictional characters in novels and films. They're hypersensitive and vulnerable to potentially frightening situations. **God is the only answer in overcoming phobias!** He longs for you to repent of your sins and call on him for help. He will never leave you nor forsake you!

**PHOBIAS CAUSE GUILT!** They're afraid they'll lose their jobs and marriage partner. They are insecure and embarrassed! *"In God have I put my trust: I will not be afraid what man can do unto me."* **Psalm 56:11** *"What time I am afraid, I will trust in thee."* **Psalm 56:3**

**ALL FEAR COMES FROM SATAN! FEAR IS THE OPPOSITE OF FAITH!** When a person becomes a born-again Christian, he can conquer the fear which causes his phobias! He can build up his faith in God by studying the Bible and praying. God will protect him and free him of this terrible condition when he believes and exercises his total faith in God! God loves us. He doesn't want us to be fearful and oppressed! **Phobias are a manifestation of how evil Satan is to mankind. GOD IS LOVE!** *"There is no fear in love; but perfect love casteth out fear; because fear hath torment. He that feareth is not made perfect in love. We love him* (God) *because he first loved us."* **1 John 4:18-19**

*"Be sober, be vigilant; because your adversary the devil, as a roaring lion, walketh about, seeking whom he may devour* (with a phobia, sickness, or death)." **1 Peter 5:8**

**"TO KEEP A PHOBIA OR TO GET RID OF IT?" THAT IS THE QUESTION! IT'S UP TO YOU! Jesus said:** *"... Why are ye fearful, O ye of little faith."* **Matthew 8:26**

**FEAR OF DEATH = THANATOPHOBIA!** *"Yea* (yes), *though I walk through the valley of the shadow of death, I will fear no evil: for thou art with me; thy rod and thy staff they comfort me."* **Psalm 23:4** Fear of death is only an evil trick of Satan to scare you. *"For I am persuaded, that neither death, nor life, nor angels, nor principalities, nor powers, nor things present, nor things to come, nor height, nor depth, nor any other creature, shall be able to separate us from the love of God, which is in Christ Jesus our Lord."* **Romans 8:38-39**

195

(Continued)

# There's a first time for every thing.

NO MATTER HOW TRIVIAL OR TRAUMATIC — PHOBIAS ARE ENEMIES! GOD WILL DESTROY YOUR PHOBIA WHEN YOU BECOME A BORN-AGAIN CHRISTIAN AND SEEK DELIVERANCE! *"For he (God) hath delivered me out of all trouble: and mine eye hath seen his desire upon mine enemies."* **Psalm 54:7**

IF YOU HAVE A PHOBIA ABOUT DARKNESS (OR DEMONS) GOD CAN DELIVER YOU! *"(God) hath delivered us from the power of darkness, and hath translated us into the kingdom of his dear Son (Jesus)."* **Colossians 1:13** *"When thou liest down, thou shalt not be afraid: yea, thou shalt lie down, and thy sleep shall be sweet."* **Proverbs 3:24**

TO OVERCOME ANY PHOBIA: FIRST, YOU MUST REPENT OF ALL YOUR SINS! SECOND: YOU MUST PUT YOUR TOTAL TRUST IN GOD. HE WILL CURE YOU WHEN YOU GET SERIOUS WITH HIM! *"In God have I put my trust: I will not be afraid what man can do unto me."* **Psalm 56:11** *"What time I am afraid, I will trust in thee."* **Psalm 56:3** Jesus said: *". . . Be not afraid, only believe."* **Mark 5:36**

WHEN FEAR ENTERS YOUR MIND — TALK TO IT! SAY: "FEAR, I DO NOT RECEIVE YOU! I REJECT YOU IN THE NAME OF JESUS, BY THE AUTHORITY GIVEN ME THROUGH THE DEATH AND RESURRECTION OF JESUS CHRIST! FEAR BE GONE! THANK YOU, JESUS!"

IF YOU HAVE A PHOBIA: RIGHT NOW IS THE PERFECT TIME TO SEEK THE LORD'S HELP! *"I sought the Lord, and he heard me, and delivered me from all my fears."* **Psalm 34:4**

*"Having therefore these promises, dearly beloved, let us cleanse ourselves from all filthiness* (phobias, for example) *of the flesh and spirit, perfecting holiness in the fear* (respect) *of God."* **2 Corinthians 7:1**

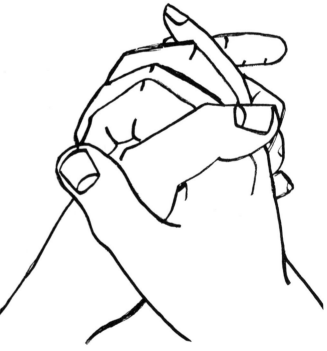

### PRAYER

Dear God, I humble myself and repent of every sin I ever committed. Please accept my sincere apology and forgive me. I turn away from all sin. I turn my life over to You. Please come into my heart to live forever. I will do my part to grow in faith by reading my Bible daily and praying! I will talk to fear, if it arises, and I will refuse to accept it because I know that fear is a gift from Satan! I take authority over fear in the name of Jesus! I thank You for giving me life. And, as of this moment, I will live life to the fullest! In Jesus' name, I pray. AMEN!

# PORNOGRAPHY

**PORNOGRAPHY IS A MORAL DISEASE, WHICH IS RUNNING RAMPANT IN OUR SOCIETY! IT IS A MALIGNANT SOCIAL CANCER THAT SPREADS INTO A COMMUNITY, WITH FULL INTENT TO TAKE IT OVER, AND THEN SEND IT TO HELL!** It is the symptom of other social ills. Vice, crime, prostitution, and drugs move in, and a general deterioration of the surrounding neighborhood and businesses can be expected. *"For this cause God gave them up unto vile affections: for even their women did change the natural use into that which is against nature* (they became lesbians, committed incest, bestiality): *and likewise also the men, leaving the natural use of the woman, burned in their lust one toward another; men with men working that which is unseemly* (became homosexuals), *and receiving in themselves that recompence* (just reward) *of their error which was meet* (only appropriate they receive). *And even as they did not like to retain God in their knowledge, God gave them over to a reprobate mind, to do those things which are not convenient; being filled with all unrighteousness, fornication* (sex without marriage), *wickedness, covetousness, maliciousness; full of envy, murder, debate, deceit, malignity; whisperers, backbiters, haters of God, despiteful, proud, boasters, inventors of evil things* (sex, drug and tortue devices), *disobedient to parents, without understanding* (of God), *covenantbreakers, without natural affection, implacable, unmerciful: Who knowing the judgment of God, that they which commit such things are worthy of death, not only do the same, but have pleasure in them that do them."* **Romans 1:26-32**

**GOD HELP US! THE FIRST AMENDMENT GUARANTEES FREEDOM OF SPEECH AND EXPRESSION — THE RIGHT TO SEE AND HEAR ANYTHING WE DESIRE!** The First Amendment really works when it comes to pornography. Other kinds of speech and expressions can be amended. Consider all the slander and liable suits, and false advertising! The Supreme Court, of the United States, blatantly states that pornography is NOT protected by the Constitution! *"But chiefly them that walk after the flesh in the lust of uncleanness, and despise government. Presumptuous are they, selfwilled, they are not afraid to speak evil of dignities."* **2 Peter 2:10**

**DOES ANY CENSOR HAVE THE RIGHT TO TELL CONSENTING ADULTS WHAT THEY CAN OR CANNOT READ OR SEE?** Note the increase in sex films, literature, and sex clinics that spring up? They use carefully selected erotic films in their therapy to treat sexual dysfunctioned people and hard-core perverts. Though they may be successful some of the time, **the negative aspect is that these tactics can also teach sexual deviants new avenues of erotic stimulus! Pornographic films and literature are a work of Satan to destroy and separate mankind from God!** Jesus said: *"But I say unto you, That whosoever looketh on a woman to **lust** after her hath committed adultery with her already in his heart."* **Matthew 5:28**

**WE LEARN BY WHAT WE HEAR AND SEE . . . WE ARE AFFECTED BY WHAT WE EXPERIENCE!** No person, regardless of age, is exempt! If we feed our mind vulgar trash, it will accept it. If we feed our mind God's Word, it accepts God's Word! *"But every man* (person) *is tempted, when he is drawn away of his own lust, and enticed. Then when lust hath conceived, it bringeth forth sin: and sin, when it is finished, bringeth forth death."* **James 1:14-15**

**AS A RESULT OF EXPOSURE TO PORNOGRAPHY, SOME INDIVIDUALS ACT OUT THEIR SEXUAL AGGRESSION AGAINST A WOMAN OR CHILD! THROUGH PORNOGRAPHIC IDEAS THEY BECOME INSPIRED TO COMMIT ADULTERY, BRUTAL RAPE, OR ASSAULT, TO FREE THEIR FRUSTRATIONS!**

*"Seek ye the Lord while He may be found, call ye upon Him while He is near. Let the wicked forsake his way, and the unrighteous man his thoughts: and let him return unto the Lord, and He will have mercy upon him; and to our God, for He will abundantly pardon."* **Isaiah 55:6-7**

**EXPOSURE TO PORNOGRAPHY CAN WARP A PERSON, AS THE EXPOSURE INCREASES! EACH NEW VIEWING INCREASES THE RISK! SOON, THE REPEATER IS "HOOKED", BECAUSE OF THE EROTIC HIGH HE EXPERIENCES. 2 Peter 1:4 SAYS THE WORLD IS BEING CORRUPTED THROUGH LUST.**

**AN APPETITE FOR PORNOGRAPHY OFTEN STARTS WITH AN ACCIDENTAL EXPOSURE TO A PICTURE, SEXUAL JOKE, OR CONVERSATION. REPEATED EXPOSURE PRODUCES A CONDITIONING EFFECT. THE MORE PORNOGRAPHY IS PRESENT IN A COMMUNITY, THE GREATER THE RISK OF PEOPLE BEING EXPOSED AND INFECTED!** *"He that committeth sin is of the devil; for the devil sinneth from the beginning. For this purpose the Son of God was manifested* (made known), *that he might destroy the works of the devil. Whosoever is born of God* (a born-again Christian) *doth not commit sin; for his* (Christ's) *seed* (the Holy Spirit) *remaineth in him: and he cannot sin, because he is born* (again through repentance) *of God."* **1 John 3:8-9**

**SEXUAL DEVIANCY IS NOT INHERITED . . . IT IS LEARNED!** It may be impossible to view graphic sexual acts, which are meant to stimulate, without recurring fantasies! **The fantasy may lead one to experience the actual act by molesting a child, committing incest or rape!** *"For all that is in the world, the lust of the flesh, and the lust of the eyes, and the pride of life, is not of the Father* (God), *but is of the world. And the world passeth away, and the lust thereof: but he that doeth the will of God abideth for ever."* **1 John 2:16-17**

**PORNOGRAPHY IS ADDICTIVE!** A person gets "hooked" just as he would on drugs, or alcohol, and he keeps coming back for more and more! As time goes by, he needs more and rougher explicit material, in order to get his "fix"! Eventually, what was once shocking or distressing becomes only tolerable. He is conditioned for more hard-core materials. He begins to rationalize incest, rape, sex with animals, injury to women and children to achieve new sexual excitement!

**EVENTUALLY, HE ACTS OUT HIS FANTASIES! HE MAY URGE HIS PARTNER, WIFE, OR OTHER MEMBERS TO ENGAGE, ALSO! HE IS NOW "DOING" WHAT HE SAY DEPICTED IN PORNOGRAPHIC DETAIL!** *"And why wilt thou, my son, be ravished with a strange woman, and embrace the bosom of a stranger? For the ways of man are before the eyes of the Lord, and he pondereth all his goings. His own iniquities shall take the wicked himself, and he shall be holden with the cords of his sins. He shall die without instruction; and in the greatness of his folly he shall go astray."* **Proverbs 5:20-23**

**GOD LOVES THE SEXUAL DEVIANT AND WANTS TO HELP HIM AND SAVE HIM!** *"For God so loved the world, that he gave his only begotten Son* (Jesus), *that whosoever believeth in him should not perish, but have everlasting life."* **John 3:16**

(Continued)

**THE SEXUAL DRIVE IN HUMANS SHOULD BE HEALTHY . . . JUST AS GOD DESIGNED IT TO BE!** Sex can be a great healing bond between a husband and wife. Pornography gives false ideas about sex. Most sex education is sex ''mis-education''! Pornography does not promote healthy sexual relations. It disturbs the relationship between men, women, and children. The sexual drive should be healthy, happy, healing and therapeutic in marriage. But, to people who are vulnerable, pornography is highly self-destructive! It produces negative effects on the other partner who may become the next victim! Impulses get out of control and then. . .? *"Can a man take fire in his bosom, and his clothes not be burned? Can one go upon hot coals, and his feet not be burned? So he that goeth in to his neighbour's* (anyone's) *wife: whosoever toucheth her shall not be innocent.''* **Proverbs 6:27-29**

**PORNOGRAPHY OFTEN LEADS TO ADULTERY, ASSAULT, BRUTAL RAPE AND MURDER!** It teaches the weak person exactly what to do and how to go about it. Many a tormented person or dead child would testify to this! Exposure to pornography is almost always the contributing factor to these crimes. Most offenders constantly seek new materials in order to discover new methods to torture and molest people, while having sex with them! After an offender kills two or three people after sexually molesting them, murder doesn't bother him any more! *"But whoso committeth adultery with a woman lacketh understanding: he that doeth it destroyeth his own soul.''* **Proverbs 6:32**

**GOD SAYS THAT WE SHOULD PROSECUTE OFFENDERS THROUGH THE LEGAL SYSTEM!** This would curb the effects of pornography. Concerned citizens should become more aroused about the quality of life in their community and unite their efforts with their neighbors in opposition to this problem. If we really believe in democracy, we should do all we can to help enforce laws for self-protection against all forms of pornography. *Read: GOVERNMENT/CAPITAL PUNISHMENT

**PARENTS: IT IS YOUR RESPONSIBILITY TO TRAIN YOUR CHILDREN PROMPTLY SO THEY WILL NOT BE ENTICED BY PORNOGRAPHY! YOU MUST SET THE EXAMPLE BEFORE THEM, NEVER BEING GUILTY OF HAVING ANY SEXUALLY EXCITING MATERIALS IN YOUR HOME, OR IN YOUR CONVERSATIONS! YOU DON'T WANT TO BE THE MOTHER, OR FATHER, OF A PERVERT ONE DAY, DO YOU?** *"Train up a child in the way he should go: and when he is old, he will not depart from it.''* **Proverbs 22:6**

# Child Pornography

**CHILD PORNOGRAPHY IS A SIN AGAINST GOD, THE CHILD, AND THE PERSON WHO DOES THIS EVIL DEED! EVERYONE PAYS A TERRIBLE PRICE! NO GOOD CAN EVER COME FROM CHILD PORNOGRAPHY!**

Over 100,000 innocent children are used, and perhaps abused each year, in pornographic pictures and articles in America, alone!

The world is full of sick, perverted people! The world is also full of decent, God-fearing people!

**CHILD PORNOGRAPHERS ARE NOT NECESSARILY ALCOHOLICS, DRUG ADDICTS, OR HOMOSEXUALS! MEN AND WOMEN WHO ARE SEXUALLY DRAWN TO YOUNG BOYS AND GIRLS MAY NOT BE AT ALL INTERESTED IN AN ADULT SEXUAL PARTNER!**

**WHERE DO THE CHILDREN COME FROM WHO BECOME THE VICTIMS OF PORNOGRAPHY?** They are: hitch-hikers, run-aways, children left with new babysitters, kids left alone in parked cars while parents are shopping, kids left to fend for themselves while parents work. They are kids picked up in large parks and crowds! Because of the love of money, some parents give their consent to let their children pose. Some parents seek out those in the pornography trade so they can make money off their children. Some parents pose with their own children. They are all sick, and we need to pray for them!

**LITTLE CHILDREN NEVER PROVOKE SEX OFFENCES! LITTLE CHILDREN DO NOT SEEK TO HAVE THEIR PICTURES TAKEN NAKED, NOR PARTICIPATING IN SEX ACTS!** Jesus said: *"Suffer* (allow) *little children, and forbid them not, to come unto me: for of such is the kingdom of heaven.''* **Matthew 19:14**

**WHAT HAPPENS TO THE CHILDREN WHO WERE FORCED, AGAINST THEIR WILL, TO POSE OR PARTICIPATE IN PORNO FILMS WHEN THEY ARE FINISHED WITH THEM, OR THE CHILD GETS SICK?** Some are killed, some are sold into prostitution rings. Some are dumped on the side of the road. Some are never seen or heard from again.

### PRAYER

Dear God, Please forgive me for all my sins. I especially beg You to forgive me for taking **pictures of a child** for the purpose of exciting lust in myself or others! I have exploited myself and children  by doing this. I knew it was wrong. I am so sorry I have sinned. I sincerely beg You from the bottom of my heart to forgive me! I want to start my life all over again, but I know this is impossible. However, I know that I can begin a new life with Your divine help. Please help me forget what I have done, so it won't hold me back from living a Christian life. Please help erase those terrible memories. I will fast and pray daily. I will read my Bible, and go to church. I will not dwell on my sordid past! I will think of my future with You! I will live for You! I will serve You! I will witness to others of Your loving kindness and forgiveness. I will tell others how they too can become a Christian. **I will never let Satan tempt me in this area again.** I will love You and serve You as long as I live! In Jesus' precious name, I pray and praise You. AMEN!

# POVERTY

*"And he* (Jesus) *lifted up his eyes on his disciples, and said,* **blessed be ye poor:** *for yours is the kingdom of God.* **Blessed are ye that hunger now: for ye shall be filled.** *Blessed are ye that weep now: for ye shall laugh."* **Luke 6:20-21**

*"If a brother or sister be naked, and* **destitute** *of daily food, and one of you say unto them, Depart in peace, be ye warmed and filled; notwithstanding ye give them not those things which are* **needful** *to the body; what doth it profit* (them or you)? *Even so faith, if it hath not works, is dead, being alone."* **James 2:15-17**

*"Blessed is he that considereth the poor: the Lord will deliver him in* (his) *time of trouble."* **Psalm 41:1**

*"For this is the message that ye heard from the beginning, that we should love one another."* **1 John 3:11**

*"But whoso hath this world's good, and seeth his brother have* **need,** *and shutteth up his bowels of compassion from him, how dwelleth the love of God in him? My little children, let us not love in word, neither in tongue; but in deed and in truth."* **1 John 3:17-18**

**IF YOU ARE POOR AND NEEDY, PRAY THIS VERSE AND ASK GOD TO HELP YOU:** *"Bow down thine ear, O Lord, hear me: for I am* **poor and needy.**" **Psalm 86:1** *"Give ear, O Lord, unto my prayer: and attend to the voice of my supplications. In the day of my trouble I will call upon thee: for thou wilt answer me."* **Psalm 86:6-7**

**AS CHRISTIANS, WE ARE COMMANDED TO LOVE OUR NEIGHBOUR AS WE LOVE OURSELVES! WE SHOULD HAVE GREAT COMPASSION ON THE NEEDY AND DO EVERYTHING WE CAN TO GET THEM SAVED, FED AND HEALTHY ... SO THEY CAN WORK.** *"The people of the land have used oppression, and exercised robbery, and have vexed the* **poor and needy:** *yea, they have oppressed the stranger wrongfully."* **Ezekiel 22:29**

## POVERTY

## not just a handout!

**Each night threatens the very life of every one of the broken men on the Bowery. If he "flops down" and dozes off in a doorway, he may wake up without out shoes.**

*"Whoso mocketh the poor reproacheth his maker* (God): *and he that is glad at calamities shall not be unpunished."* **Proverbs 17:5**

*"Poverty and shame shall be to him that refuseth instruction: but he that regardeth reproof shall be honoured."* **Proverbs 13:18**

**IF A PERSON IS NEEDY BECAUSE HE REFUSES TO WORK ... GOD HAS NO COMPASSION ON HIM!** *"The righteous eateth to the satisfying of his soul: but the belly of the wicked shall want."* **Proverbs 13:25**

*"The poor is hated even of his own neighbour; but the rich hath many friends. He that despiseth his neighbour sinneth: but* **he that hath mercy on the poor, happy is he.**" **Proverbs 14:20-21**

**A CHRISTIAN WOMAN SHOULD NEVER TURN HER BACK ON THE POOR!** *"She stretcheth out her hand to the* **poor;** *yea, she reacheth forth her hands to the* **needy.**" **Proverbs 31:20**

*"Wealth maketh many friends; but the* **poor** *is separated from his neighbour."* **Proverbs 19:4**

*"He that hath pity upon the* **poor** *lendeth unto the Lord; and that which he hath given will he* (God) *pay him again."* **Proverbs 19:17**

**NEVER ABUSE, MISTREAT, OR HATE ANYONE THAT IS POOR. BECAUSE, JUSTICE BELONGS TO GOD AND HE WILL REPAY!** *"There is a generation, whose teeth are as swords, and their jaw teeth as knives, to devour the* **poor** *from off the earth, and the* **needy** *from among men."* **Proverbs 30:14**

*"Whoso stoppeth his ears at the cry of the poor, he also shall cry himself, but shall not be heard."* **Proverbs 21:13**

### PRAYER

Dear God, please forgive me for all my sins. I have not done my part in aiding the **poor and needy.** I ask You to forgive me. The Bible says that when we do anything for a **needy** person we do it for Christ. I will do more to help those less fortunate than myself. In Jesus' name I pray. AMEN!

# PREDESTINATION

**DEFINITION:** To foreordain to an earthly or eternal lot or destiny by divine decree; predetermine.

**MAN PREDETERMINES AND SEALS HIS OWN FATE BEFORE HE DIES!** While he lives, every person is given a free will choice to spend eternity with God, or with Satan. After his death, he can not make that decision! The choice is his, and he alone must decide. He prearranges his future home for all eternity! If he accepts Christ as his personal savior, he receives forgiveness for his sins. Then, he must turn away from all sin and live a godly life. If he is guilty of backsliding, he must ask forgiveness! If he dies while living a life of sin, he is not entitled to spend eternity with Jesus. There will be no corrupted people in heaven, and we certainly wouldn't want there to be!

**GOD PREDESTINED THAT MAN SHOULD BE CREATED IN HIS OWN IMAGE AND WOULD WANT TO LOVE HIM AND RECEIVE SALVATION!** *"And we know that all things work together for good to them that love God, to them who are THE CALLED according to his* (divine) *purpose. For whom he* (God) *did FOREKNOW, he also did PREDESTINATE to be conformed to the image of his Son* (Jesus), *that he might be the first born among many brethren* (Christians). *Moreover whom he did predestinate, them he also called: and whom he called, then he also justified: and whom he justified, them he also glorified* (give an incorruptible body just as Christ has)." **Romans 8:28-30**

**GOD FOREKNEW US BEFORE WE WERE BORN! HE PREDETERMINED THAT ALL HUMANS WOULD BE GIVEN THE OPPORTUNITY TO RECEIVE SALVATION. BUT, HE LEAVES THE CHOICE TO ACCEPT OR DENY HIM TO THE FREE-WILL OF EACH INDIVIDUAL!** Only those who freely accept salvation, through the repentance of their sins and obey His commandments, are the special "called ones" who will receive eternal life. They must meet the terms as outlined in the Bible! **Who accepts salvation . . . and who rejects salvation is not predestined!** That's left up to each individual according to **John 3:16/1 Timothy 2:4/2 Peter 3:9/Revelation 22:17/Mark 16:16/Acts 2:38/3:19.** All things depend upon meeting the conditions God spelled out in the Holy Bible. **Romans 8:1-13, 28**

**WARNING:** *"Ye therefore, beloved, seeing ye know these things before, beware lest ye also, being led away with the error of the wicked, fall from your own stedfastness."* **2 Peter 3:17**

It is **predetermined** by God's divine law of love, mercy, and grace, that once a person repents of his sins and receives salvation, he will receive eternal life with God! If a person (of his own volition) turns away from living a godly life and goes back into a life of sin, he then nullifies God's original plan for him. He can lose his salvation!

God **predestined** that He would have to send a Savior to redeem man from sin. No single individual is selected to be saved or lost without his personal choice and responsibility in the matter. **John 3:16/1 Timothy 2:4/2 Peter 3:9/Revelation 22:17**

**GOD IS NO RESPECTOR OF PERSONS. HE IS NOT CRUEL OR UNJUST. HE WOULD NEVER SHOW PARTIALITY. GOD DOES NOT REGARD ONE PERSON AND DISREGARD ANOTHER PERSON! GOD DOES NOT SAVE ONE PERSON AND DAMN ANOTHER. WE DECIDE OUR OWN DESTINY WHETHER IT'S HEAVEN OR HELL! GOD LEAVES THAT UP TO US!** God offers salvation to everyone. He keeps His promises. All men are invited to choose eternal life with God. All are given warning of eternal punishment, if they deny or reject Him! God is incapable of choosing to save some and not to save all! *"With the precious blood of Christ, as a lamb* (sacrifice) *without blemish* (fault) *and without spot* (sin): *who verily was foreordained before*

the foundation of the world, but was manifest (made known) in these last times for you, who by him (Jesus) do believe in God, that raised him (Jesus) up from the dead (death on the cross), and gave him glory (an incorruptible body, soul), that your faith and hope might be in God." **1 Peter 1:19-21** *"Being born again* (through repentance and forgiveness), *not of corruptible seed* (as living descendants of Adam), *but of incorruptible* (being born again through forgiveness and being spiritually "washed" in the blood of Christ), *by the Word of God* (the Bible), *which liveth and abideth for ever."* **1 Peter 1:23**

**GOD FOREKNEW IT WAS NECESSARY TO SEND A SAVIOR FOR MEN OR HIS ETERNAL PLAN FOR MANKIND WOULD COME TO NAUGHT! GOD PROVIDED A SACRIFICE TO SAVE MANKIND. HE PERMITTED THE WICKED HANDS OF MEN TO SLAY CHRIST (WHO IS GOD IN HUMAN FLESH)!** *"Him* (Jesus), *being delivered by the determinate counsel and foreknowledge of God, ye have taken, and by wicked hands have crucified and slain: whom God hath raised up, having loosed the pains* (finality) *of death: because it was not possible that he* (Jesus) *should be holden* (held down) *of it."* **Acts 2:23-24**

**GOD PREDESTINATED US TO BE HIS SONS — IF WE WILL ONLY ACCEPT HIM!** *"According as he* (God) *hath chosen us* (to be) *in him before the foundation of the world, that we should be holy and without blame* (sin) *before him* (Jesus) *in love. Having predestinated us unto the adoption of children by Jesus Christ to himself, according to the good pleasure of his will."* **Ephesians 1:4-5**

**GOD GAVE US AN INHERITANCE WHEN HE PREDESTINED SALVATION FOR ALL WHO WOULD ACCEPT IT!** *"In whom also we have obtained an inheritance* (the gift of eternal life with Jesus), *being predestinated according to the purpose of him who worketh all things after the counsel of his own will."* **Ephesians 1:11**

*". . . We speak the wisdom of God in a mystery, even the hidden wisdom, which God ordained before the world unto our glory."* **1 Corinthians 2:7**

. . .

### PRAYER

Dear God, please forgive me for all my sins. I have reached the age to know the difference between right and wrong. I know that I am accountable for my sins. I ask You to forgive me for all my sins and to blot them from Your memory. I turn away from all sins. **Thank You for setting me straight on the subject of predestination!** I know Your will, for my life, is for me to receive salvation. I receive it, now! Thank You for saving my soul! I want to spend eternity with Jesus! Thank You for coming into my life and for loving me! In Jesus' name, I pray. AMEN!

# PRE-MARITAL SEX

**GOD COMMANDS SEXUAL PURITY BEFORE MARRIAGE AND MANY YOUNG PEOPLE DON'T WANT TO HEAR THIS.** They deliberately disobey their own conscience, God and any other authority figure!

**TO HAVE SEXUAL INTERCOURSE (OR ANY OTHER SEXUAL ACT) WITHOUT MARRIAGE IS TO DELIBERATELY DEFY GOD'S LAWS!**

**SEX ACTS BETWEEN TWO PEOPLE WHO HAVE NO MARRIAGE PARTNER IS FORNICATION. SEX ACTS COMMITTED BY A PERSON WHO IS MARRIED, WITH ANYONE WHO IS NOT HIS LEGAL MARRIAGE PARTNER, IS ADULTERY! 1 Corinthians 6:18** says to flee from all sexual immorality. All other sins a person commits are outside his body; but when he sins sexually, **he sins against his own body!**

**DESPITE THE FACT THAT SOCIETY SEEMS TO CONDONE PRE-MARITAL SEX, IT DOES NOT CHANGE GOD'S LAWS!** God gave us healthy restrictions for our own good. He loves us and knows what's best for us. He knows **promiscuous** living destroys an individual and society!

**MANY YOUNG PEOPLE FALSELY BELIEVE THAT SEX IS THE MOST IMPORTANT THING IN A RELATIONSHIP BETWEEN TWO PEOPLE! THAT'S A LIE DREAMED UP BY SATAN!** Sex should be a beautiful experience between a man and wife. This is God's plan! Sex is not only the means by which children are brought into the world, it's also the means by which two people express their love for each other. This is only possible with a commitment of marriage!

**PRE-MARITAL SEX MAY END UP IN PREGNANCY, DISEASE, OR ABORTION!** As soon as a young man (or any age) finds that a girl (or woman) is ''loose with her body'', he loses respect for her. Having sex becomes habit forming and soon the conscience becomes tolerant and craves for more. Boys (men) having sex with girls (women) soon tire of the ''same old stuff'', and drop you and look for ''new stuff''. Don't lower yourself to a whore and forfeit spending eternity with Jesus over sexual sin! It's not worth it, ever! Eventually, it becomes hard to say ''no'', and soon you are a promiscuous person!

*''AND EVEN AS THEY DID NOT LIKE TO RETAIN GOD IN THEIR KNOWLEDGE, GOD GAVE THEM OVER TO A REPROBATE MIND, TO DO THOSE THINGS WHICH ARE NOT CONVENIENT: BEING FILLED WITH ALL UNRIGHTEOUSNESS, FORNICATION, WICKEDNESS, COVETOUSNESS, MALICIOUSNESS: FULL OF ENVY, MURDER, DEBATE, DECEIT, MALIGNITY, WHISPERERS, BACKBITERS, HATERS OF GOD, DESPITEFUL, PROUD, BOASTERS, INVENTORS OF EVIL THINGS, DISOBEDIENT TO PARENTS, WITHOUT UNDERSTANDING, COVENANT-BREAKERS, WITHOUT NATURAL AFFECTION, IMPLACABLE, UNMERCIFUL: WHO KNOWING THE JUDGEMENT OF GOD, THAT THEY WHICH COMMIT SUCH THINGS ARE WORTHY OF DEATH, NOT ONLY DO THE SAME, BUT HAVE PLEASURE IN THEM THAT DO THEM.''*
**Romans 1:28-32**

**THE BIBLE SAYS WE ARE FEARFULLY AND WONDERFULLY MADE! WE SHOULD PRAISE GOD FOR BEING CREATED IN HIS IMAGE! Psalm 139:14**

*You are not tempted because you are evil; you are tempted because you are human.*

**NOTE: FOR A MORE DETAILED DISCUSSION ON THE SUBJECT OF SEX, PLEASE READ THE CHAPTERS: ADULTERY — ABORTION — CARNAL — FORNICATION — MISTRESS — LASCIVIOUSNESS — MASTURBATION — HOMOSEXUALS — LESBIANS — PROSTITUTES**

## Pre-Marital Sex
### PRAYER

Dear God, please forgive me for having sex without marriage. Please forgive me for all my sins. I repent of my sins and I turn away from them. I will pray and read my Bible. I will keep myself sexually pure from this moment on. I know You designed me in Your image and Your will for my life is for me to have a marriage partner. I know sex without marriage is wrong, and I will not be guilty of repeating this sin. I want to spend eternity with Jesus, therefore I will clean up my body, mind and spirit. Thank You for loving me and for giving me another chance! In Jesus' name, I pray. AMEN!

# PRIDE

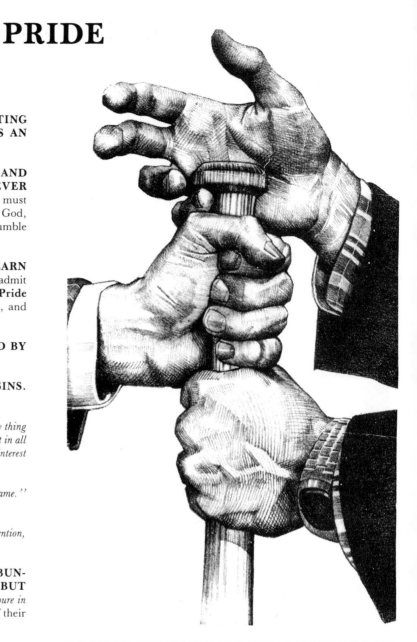

**PRIDE KEEPS MANY PEOPLE FROM ACCEPTING CHRIST AS THEIR PERSONAL SAVIOR. PRIDE IS AN ENEMY TO GOD!**

**Matthew 18:3-4 SAYS THAT UNLESS YOU CHANGE AND BECOME LIKE LITTLE CHILDREN, YOU WILL NEVER ENTER THE KINGDOM OF HEAVEN!** This means you must humble yourself and let your heart be open and receptive to God, just as a little child's is! You must destroy **pride** and humble yourself before God!

**PRIDE TELLS US WE ARE GOOD ENOUGH TO EARN GOD'S FAVOR JUST AS WE ARE! Pride** tells us not to admit we are sinners. **Pride** says we are not unclean in God's eyes. **Pride** says we don't need to admit that our only hope is in Christ, and without Him we are heading straight to hell!

**PRIDE CAUSED ADAM AND EVE TO BE DECEIVED BY SATAN! Genesis 3:5**

**A "PROUD LOOK" IS ONE OF THE SIX DEADLY SINS. Proverbs 6:17**

**PAUL SAID:** *"As for me, God forbid that I should boast about any thing except the cross of our Lord Jesus Christ. Because of that cross my interest in all the attractive things of the world was killed long ago, and the world's interest in me is also long dead."* **Galatians 6:14** (The Living Bible)

**PRIDE BRINGS SHAME!** *"When **pride** cometh, then cometh shame."* **Proverbs 11:2**

**PRIDE BRINGS CONTENTION!** *"Only by **pride** cometh contention, but with the well advised is wisdom."* **Proverbs 13:10**

**THIS GENERATION IS GUILTY OF AN OVER ABUNDANCE OF PRIDE, EGO, VANITY! GOD LOVES US BUT HATES THIS TRAIT IN US!** *"There is a generation that are pure in their own eyes, and yet is not washed from their filthiness* (forgiven of their sins)." **Proverbs 30:12**

*"Pride goeth before destruction, and an haughty spirit before a fall."* **Proverbs 16:18**

*"A man's **pride** shall bring him low: but honour shall uphold the humble in spirit."* **Proverbs 29:23**

*"For from within, out of the heart of men, proceed evil thoughts, adulteries, fornications, murders, thefts, covetousness, wickedness, deceit, lasciviousness, an evil eye, blasphemy, **pride**, foolishness. All these evil things come from within, and defile the man."* **Mark 7:21-23**

**WHEN PRIDE LIFTS YOU UP, YOU FALL INTO THE CONDEMNATION OF THE DEVIL! 1 Timothy 3:6**

**PRIDE = SELF DECEPTION!** *"There is a way which seemeth right unto a man, but the end thereof are the ways of death* (eternal separation from God)." **Proverbs 14:12**

**THE BIBLE SAYS WE ARE NOT TO RESPECT THE PROUD!** *"Blessed is that man that maketh the Lord his trust, and respecteth not the **proud**, nor such as turn aside to lies."* **Psalm 40:4** *"The Lord shall cut off all flattering lips, and the tongue that speaketh **proud things**: Who have said, With our tongue will we prevail; our lips are our own: Who is lord over us?"* **Psalm 12:3-4**

**DID YOU KNOW THAT THE INCREASE IN PRIDE (EGO) DURING OUR GENERATION IS A SIGN OF THE LAST DAYS BEFORE CHRIST RETURNS?** *"This know also, that in the last days perilous times shall come. For men shall be **lovers of their own selves**, covetous, **boasters**, **proud**, blasphemers, disobedient to parents, unthankful, unholy, etc."* **2 Timothy 3:1-2**

**GOD RESISTS THE PROUD AND GIVES GRACE TO THE HUMBLE! James 4:6/1 Peter 5:5** *"An high look, and a proud heart* (ego), *and the plowing of the wicked, is sin."* **Proverbs 21:4** *"Proud and haughty scorner is his name, who dealeth in **proud wrath**."* **Proverbs 21:24**

**FOR ADDITIONAL SCRIPTURES ON PRIDE READ: Psalm 10:2/73:6/119:21/Proverbs 28:25/1 John 2:16**

## PRIDE

### PRAYER

Dear God, please forgive me for all my sins. Forgive me for letting **pride** get in the way of my loving and serving You! I love You. I repent for being guilty of having an excessive ego! I turn away from this sin and all other sins! I will serve only You. Thank You for saving my soul! In Jesus' name, I pray. AMEN!

# PROCRASTINATE

*" Boast not thyself of to morrow; for thou knowest not what a day may bring forth. "* **Proverbs 27:1**

ANOTHER TIME . . . NEXT WEEK . . . WAIT TILL A MORE CONVENIENT SEASON . . . NOT NOW . . . I'M NOT READY JUST YET . . . PERHAPS LATER ON . . . BEFORE I DIE I WILL! These are just a few of the excuses people give for not getting saved! *"Wherefore (as the Holy Ghost saith), To day if ye will hear his voice, harden not your hearts . . ."* **Hebrews 3:7-8, 15** *"But exhort one another daily, while it is called To day; lest any of you be hardened through the deceitfulness of sin."* **Hebrews 3:13**

**PROCRASTINATION HAS SECRET PAYOFFS FOR LAZY PEOPLE!** It lets them avoid doing what they don't like (or want) to do! *"Slothfulness (laziness, idleness)) casteth into a deep sleep; and an idle soul shall suffer hunger."* **Proverbs 19:15**

**HABITUAL PROCRASTINATION CAN LEAD TO CRITICAL FEELINGS OF DEPRESSION, GUILT, AND ANXIETY!** Procrastinators tend to think of themselves as worthless. They feel they have lost all control over their own life! *"By much slothfulness (laziness, idleness), the building decayeth; and through idleness of the hands the house (rots and) droppeth through."* **Ecclesiastes 10:18**

**PROCRASTINATION CAN SERIOUSLY CAUSE YOU TO DENY REALITY AND INVOLVEMENT WITH OTHER PEOPLE! IDLENESS IS THE DEVIL'S WORKSHOP!**

**PROCRASTINATION BECOMES AN ESCAPE TRAP!** It prevents a person from living life to the fullness God wants for each of us! It teaches one to accept limitations, whenever possible. **JESUS SAID:** *"The thief (Satan) cometh not, but for to steal, and to kill, and to destroy: I am come that they might have life, and that they might have it more abundantly."* **John 10:10**

**PROCRASTINATION MAY CAUSE A PERSON TO ESCAPE INTO FANTASY!** It tells you that you'll get things done eventually, when circumstances are different! When a person stops procrastinating and determines to do a task, he usually surprises himself at how much energy he has!

**JESUS SAID WE ARE TO WORK UNTIL HE RETURNS!** *"And he called his ten servants, and delivered them ten pounds and said unto them, occupy (work) till I come."* **Luke 19:13**

**PROCRASTINATION MAKES A PERSON FEEL INFERIOR, FOOLISH, KNOCKED-DOWN AND DRAGGED-OUT!** Everyone owes it to himself to feel alive, warm and energized. God can help you like yourself again when you're willing to change your image, humble yourself, repent of your sins, and seek His help!

**PROCRASTINATION IS HARD WORK!** Taking action and reaching a decision usually proves easier! **JESUS SAID:** *"Till I come, give attendance to reading, to exhortation, to doctrine."* **1 Timothy 4:13**

**DON'T WORK YOURSELF UP INTO A DEPRESSED STATE OVER THINGS YOU'VE LEFT UNDONE!** It serves no useful purpose! Forgive yourself for your past "sins" of procrastination. Self-punishment and guilt are a form of idolatry, and not honest regret!

**A SMALL AMOUNT OF ANXIETY AND SUSPENSE CAN BE A HEALTHY MOTIVATOR!** Doing a small job well is a valuable experience.

**DEMAND MORE OF YOURSELF!** Get angry at that part of you which habitually procrastinates! You have control over most of what you do, or don't do! The choice is yours!

**IT'S TIME TO TAKE STOCK OF YOUR LIFE!** Are you a Christian? What are you waiting for? You don't even know whether you'll be alive tomorrow and neither does anyone else! The very first thing you should do is fall on your knees and ask God to come into your life! Admit that you are a sinner and ask forgiveness for your sins. Then get up and get busy! Read a chapter in the Bible and pray before you start. Ask God to give you an understanding of what you read. When you get up, do something constructive and keep it up. It's high time to reassess your life, friends, job, etc. Don't force yourself to go on doing anything that you know is wrong for your life! Ask God for wisdom, daily! He will be glad to give it to you!

**RECOGNIZE THAT PROCRASTINATION IS SELF-DECEPTION!** When, where, and how did it take root? Look for evidence of much deeper concerns, such as your low self-esteem, fear of failure, fear of success, hostility, denial or spite, passiveness, aggressiveness, anger and resentment. Ask God to create a clean heart in you! *"Create in me a clean heart, O God: and renew a right spirit within me."* **Psalm 51:10**

**IT'S YOUR RESPONSIBILITY TO DEAL DIRECTLY WITH YOUR FEELINGS. GOD WANTS TO HELP YOU! ASK HIM TODAY (AFTER) YOU REPENT OF YOUR SINS AND RECEIVE SALVATION! GOD'S ONLY A PRAYER AWAY!**
**GET ON WITH THE PRESENT!** Just because you haven't done something as yet, does not mean you're a failure! You're a person with many positive, and negative characteristics, who has things he needs to start doing, today! If you really can't (or don't want to) do something, be honest with yourself and other people, so they can act without you! At times we all need to put something off. Then it's best to give a specific time extension. If you inconvenience someone . . . offer to compensate him in some other way! *"So teach us to number our days, that we may apply our hearts unto wisdom."* **Psalm 90:12**

**SET PRIORITIES ACCORDING TO IMPORTANCE — AND THEN DO THEM!** If your life is disorganized, write out a schedule that is realistic. It will make your life and routines a lot easier! You'll be able to keep track of your responsibilities and accomplishments. Set goals that will prompt you to work, instead of procrastinating! Break down big tasks into smaller manageable ones! Set short term intervals and keep your promises!

**ANALYZE YOUR BEHAVIOR!** What do you like to do? What do you dislike? Discover what feelings you have about doing uncompleted tasks. Wouldn't it be better to get them over with than to stew over your regrets? Don't keep putting things off or you'll end up hating yourself and those who fuss at you for being so lazy! You've no one to blame but youself! God loves you very much, but He would never approve of someone staying in a rut instead of getting himself out! God wants to help you! Call on him!

## PRAYER

Dear God, please forgive me for every sin I have committed. Clean up my heart and life. Help me restore confidence in myself. Help me to get my life organized. Remind me to never **procrastinate** when it's within my power to work! Forgive me for being lazy and for wasting precious time. I will study my Bible and pray, daily! I turn away from all negative thoughts about myself, my work, and anything else! Teach me to be productive, instead of wasting my time! Help me restore those relationships that I have torn down! Teach me to love myself and others, just as You love me! Thank You for coming into my heart and giving me new directions for my life. In Jesus' name. AMEN!

# PROSTITUTE

**DEFINITION:** A prostitute; a lewd or promiscuous woman; to offer indiscriminately for sexual intercourse especially for money; a person who engages in promiscuous sexual intercourse deliberately debases himself for consideration (as money); to practice unlawful intercourse for hire; to pursue a faithless, unworthy, or idolatrous desire; to corrupt your own body and soul by lewd intercourse;

**LISTED BELOW ARE SEVEN SINS OF A HARLOT . . . WHORE . . . PROSTITUTE!**
1. A harlot (whore) **flatters with her lips:** Proverbs 2:16
2. She **forsakes her parents' guidance:** Proverbs 2:17
3. She forgets God's covenant and **renounces true religion or marriage vows:** Proverbs 2:17
4. **Prostitution shortens her life:** Proverbs 2:18
5. She **leads others to hell:** Proverbs 2:18
6. She **destroys men utterly:** Proverbs 2:19
7. **Her sin leads to permanent ruin:** Proverbs 2:19
*"To deliver thee from the strange woman, even from the stranger which **flattereth with her words;** Which **forsaketh the guide** (guidance) of her youth (parents, teachers), and forgeteth the **covenant** of her God. For her house (body) inclineth unto **death,** and her **paths unto the dead** (she shortens her life span). **None that go unto her** (have sex with her) **return** (sinless) again, neither take they hold of the paths of life (which is through Jesus)."* **Proverbs 2:16-19**

**ANY HARLOT (PROSTITUTE) CAN RECEIVE SALVATION IF SHE (OR HE) WILL JUST ASK GOD TO RECEIVE AND FORGIVE HER (OR HIM)!** *"Wherefore I say unto you, All manner of sin and blasphemy shall be forgiven unto men* (all people): *but the blasphemy against the Holy Ghost shall not be forgiven unto men. And whosoever speaketh a word against the Son of man* (Jesus), *it shall be forgiven him: but whosoever speaketh against the Holy Ghost, it shall not be forgiven him, neither in this world, neither in the world to come."* **Matthew 12:31-32**

**JESUS WAS BORN, CRUCIFIED, AND RESURRECTED IN ORDER TO MAKE INTERCESSION FOR ALL WHO SIN! THIS INCLUDES PROSTITUTES AND THOSE WHO HAVE SEX WITH THEM! THE BIBLE SAYS WE HAVE ALL SINNED! Hebrews 7:25** *"If we say we have no sin, we deceive ourselves, and the truth is not in us. If we confess our sins, he* (God) *is faithful and just to forgive us our sins, and to cleanse us from all unrighteousness. If we say that we have not sinned, we make him* (God) *a liar, and his word is not in us."* **1 John 1:8-10**

**HARLOTS . . . PROSTITUTES . . . WHORES CONSTANTLY CHANGE THEIR ALLUREMENTS TO TRAP YOU! THEY SEEM TO APPEAR AND DISAPPEAR OVERNIGHT! THEIR WAYS ARE UNPREDICTABLE! UNLESS SHE (OR HE) REPENTS AND TURNS AWAY FROM ALL SIN, WHEN SHE (OR HE) DIES, HELL WILL BE THEIR ETERNAL HOME! AND YOU WHO FREQUENTLY VISIT A PROSTITUTE, IF YOU DO NOT REPENT YOU WILL GO THERE, TOO!** *"For the **lips of a strange woman** drop as an honeycomb, and her **mouth is smoother than oil:** But her **end is bitter** as wormwood* (a bitter plant which is offensive and makes you vomit), *sharp as a two-edged sword. **Her feet go down to death; her steps take hold on hell.** Lest thou shouldest ponder the path of life, **her ways are moveable, that thou canst not know them.**"* **Proverbs 5:3-6**

**15 REASONS TO STAY AWAY FROM A HARLOT . . . PROSTITUTE . . . WHORE:**
1. She is an **apostate:** Proverbs 5:3
2. She is **deceptive:** Proverbs 5:3
3. She is a **flatterer:** Proverbs 5:3
4. Her **end is bitter:** Proverbs 5:4
5. Her **end is destructive:** Proverbs 5:4-5

6. **Her feet go down to death:** Proverbs 5:5
7. **Her steps lay hold of hell:** Proverbs 5:5
8. **Her ways are unpredictable:** Proverbs 5:6
9. **She will ruin your reputation:** Proverbs 5:9
10. She **will cause you years of trouble:** Proverbs 5:9
11. She **will bring you material ruin:** Proverbs 5:10
12. She **will ruin your health:** Proverbs 5:11
13. She **will bring remorse:** Proverbs 5:12-13
14. She **will reduce herself and you to wickedness:** Proverbs 5:14
15. She **will cause eternal ruin:** Proverbs 5:23.

*"Listen to me, my son! I know what I am saying; listen! Watch yourself, lest you be indiscreet and betray some vital information. For **the lips of a prostitute** are as sweet as honey, and smooth **flattery is her stock in trade.** But afterwards only a bitter conscience is left to you, sharp as a double-edged sword. **She leads you down to death and hell.** For she does not know the path to life. She staggers down a crooked trail, and doesn't even realize where it leads. young men, listen to me and never forget what I'm about to say: **Run from her! Don't go near her house, lest you fall to her temptation and lose your honor,** and give the remainder of your life to the cruel and merciless: lest strangers obtain your wealth, and you become a slave of foreigners. **Lest afterwards you groan in anguish and in shame, when syphilis consumes your body,** and you say, "Oh, if only I had listened! If only I had not demanded my own way! Oh, why wouldn't I take advice? Why was I so stupid? For now I must face public disgrace." Drink from your own* (water) *well, my son — be faithful and true to your wife. Why should you beget children with women of the street? Why share your children with those outside your home? Let your manhood be a blessing; rejoice in the wife of your youth. Let her charms and tender embrace satisfy you. Let her love alone fill you with delight. **Why delight yourself with prostitutes, embracing what isn't yours? For God is closely watching you, and he weighs carefully everything you do.** The wicked man* (anyone who sins) *is doomed **to hell unless he repents**) by his own sins; they are ropes that catch and hold him. **He shall die because he will not listen to the truth; he has let himself be led away into incredible folly.**"* **Proverbs chapter 5** (The Living Bible)

**WHY TURN ALL YOUR HARD EARNED MONEY OVER TO A PROSTITUTE? THE END RESULT WILL BRING CONFUSION, BITTERNESS AND SUFFERING IN YOUR BODY! EVENTUALLY YOU WILL CONTACT SYPHILIS OR SOME OTHER INFECTIOUS DISEASE, WHICH CAN LEAD TO YOUR DEATH! HELL IS A TERRIBLE PLACE TO SPEND ETERNITY IN EXCHANGE FOR A LIFE OF DEBAUCHERY! UNLESS YOU REPENT, YOU ARE NOT BETTER THAN THE COMMON STREET WHORE WHO IS SURELY HEADED FOR HELL! GOD LOVES YOU! HE MADE A WAY WHERE BY YOU CAN BE SAVED AND DELIVERED! ONLY GOD CAN GIVE YOU PEACE AND LASTING HAPPINESS! WHAT DO YOU HAVE TO LOSE TO TRY GOD? HE WOULD LOVE TO HAVE YOU JOIN HIS BODY OF BELIEVERS!**

**A HARLOT . . . WHORE . . . PROSTITUTE IS CALLED A "FOOLISH" WOMAN IN THE BIBLE!**
1. She is **clamourous** (loud mouth) and in a continual uproar, noisy, boisterous: Proverbs 9:13/7:11. She tells her clients that unlawful pleasures are sweeter than lawful ones.
2. She is **simple, silly and easily seduced:** Proverbs 9:13/2 Timothy 3:6.
3. She **knows nothing, knows no shame, she's utterly ignorant and depraved:** Proverbs 9:13
4. She **watches for victims to commit sin with:** Proverbs 9:14/ Genesis 38:14/Jeremiah 3:2
5. She is **impudent or bold to call to any stranger and tempt the innocent to sin:** Proverbs 9:15-17

(Continued)

WHEN A MARRIED PERSON HAS INTERCOURSE WITH ANYONE WHO IS NOT HIS SPOUSE, HE COMMITS ADULTERY! LISTED BELOW ARE SEVEN GOOD REASONS TO STAY AWAY FROM A . . . PROSTITUTE!

1. She is **evil**: Proverbs 6:24
2. She uses **flattery to trap you**: Proverbs 6:24
3. You will **lust** after her and lust will trap you: **Proverbs 6:25**
4. She will **captivate you** with her eyelids: **Proverbs 6:25**
5. **The cost of her sex will reduce you to poverty**: Proverbs 6:26
6. Being with her is to choose **death** over life: **Proverbs 6:26**
7. You **commit sin** when you have **sex** with her: **Proverbs 6:27-29**

"*. . .keep thee* (away) *from the **evil woman**, from the flattery of the tongue of a strange woman. Lust not after her beauty in thine heart; neither let her take thee* (captive) *with her eyelids. For by means of a **whorish woman** a man is brought to a piece of bread: and the **adulteress** will hunt for the precious life* (take away your money to get what she wants). *Can a man take fire in his bosom* (become hot with passion), *and his clothes not be burned? Can one go upon hot coals, and his feet not be burned? So he that goeth in to his neighbour's wife* (has intercourse); ***whosoever toucheth her shall not be innocent.*** **Proverbs 6:24-29** "*But whoso committeth **adultery** with a woman lacketh understanding; **he that doeth it destroyeth his own soul.** A wound* (sex disease) *and dishonour shall he get, and his reproach* (sorrow) *shall not be wiped away. For jealousy is the rage of a man: therefore he will not spare in the day of vengeance.*" **Proverbs 6:32-34**

**BELOW ARE 10 CHARACTERISTICS OF PROSTITUTES:**
1. Their clothes, makeup, jewelry, etc., advertise them for hire: Proverbs 7:10/Genesis chapter 38
2. Their subtility of heart: Proverbs 7:10
3. Their boisterous and loud disposition: Proverbs 7:11-12
4. Their "gad-about" disposition: Proverbs 7:11-12
5. Their stubbornness and persistence in seducing innocent victims: Proverbs 7:11. They have no respect for the good of men, married or unmarried, innocent or guilty of immoral crimes. They gloat over causing young men to fall into sin and husbands to go astray.
6. They are bold, unashamed, impudent and unlawfully familiar: Proverbs 7:13
7. They are flatterers: Proverbs 7:5, 14-21
8. They are deceitful of heart: Proverbs 7:13-21
9. They are liars: Proverbs 7:14-21
10. They are tempters and seducers: Proverbs 7:13-21

A PROSTITUTE WILL ENTICE A MAN (OR BOY) WITH KISSES, WHILE SHE MAKES KNOWN HER INTENTIONS! Proverbs 7:12-13. SHE WILL MAKE HER FACE LOOK FRIENDLY, CONFIDENT, AND SINCERE IN ORDER TO TRAP HER VICTIMS! "*Follow my advice, my son; always keep it in mind and stick to it. Obey me and live! Guard my words as your most precious possession. Write them down, and also keep them deep within your heart. Love wisdom like a sweetheart; make her a beloved member of your family.* **Let her** (wisdom) **hold you back from visiting a prostitute,** *from listening to her flattery. I was looking out the window of my house one day, and saw a simple-minded lad, a young man lacking common sense, walking at twilight down the street to the house of this wayward girl, a prostitute. She approached him, saucy and pert, and dressed seductively.* **She was the brash, coarse type, seen often in the streets and markets, soliciting at every corner for men to be her lovers.** *She put her arms around him and kissed him, and with a saucy look she said, "I've decided to forget our quarrel! I was just coming to look for you and here you are! My bed is spread with lovely colored sheets of finest linen imported from Egypt, perfumed with myrrh, aloes and cinnamon. Come on, let's take our fill of love until morning, for my husband is away on a long trip. He has taken a wallet full of money with him, and won't return for several days."* **So she seduced him with her pretty speech, her coaxing and her wheedling, until he yielded to her. He couldn't resist her flattery.** *He followed her as an ox going to the butcher, or as a stag* (deer) *that is trapped, waiting to be killed with an arrow through its heart. He was as a bird flying into a snare, not knowing the fate awaiting it there. Listen to me, young men, and not only listen but obey;* ***don't let yourself think about her. Don't go near her; stay away from where she walks, lest she tempt you and seduce you. For she has been the ruin of multitudes — a vast host of men have been her victims. If you want to find the road to hell, look for her house.***" **Proverbs chapter 7** (The Living Bible)

"*A prostitute is loud and brash, and never has enough of **lust and shame**. She sits at the door of her house or stands at the street corners of the city, **whispering to men going by** and to those minding their own business. "Come home with me", she urges simpletons. "Stolen melons* (water) *are the sweetest; stolen apples* (food) *taste the best!" But they don't realize that her former guests are now citizens of hell.*" **Proverbs 9:13-18** (The Living Bible)

DID YOU KNOW THE INCREASE IN PROSTITUTION FULFILLS END TIME PROPHECY ABOUT THE LAST DAYS BEFORE CHRIST RETURNS? THAT YOUNG PEOPLE NO LONGER RESPECT THE DISCIPLINES OF THEIR PARENTS OR AUTHORITIES? THAT MANY PEOPLE LOVE PLEASURE MORE THAN GOD? THAT UNNATURAL SEX ACTS ARE ON THE INCREASE? YES, THESE ARE SIGNS WE ARE SEEING FULFILLED TODAY! MEANS JUST ONE THING . . . CHRIST WILL RETURN VERY SOON! 2 Timothy 3:2-5 says: "*This know also, that in the last days perilous times shall come. For men shall be **lovers of their own selves**, covetous, boasters, proud, blasphemers, disobedient to parents, unthankful, unholy. **Without natural affection,** trucebreakers, false accusers, incontinent, fierce, despisers of those that are good, traitors, heady, highminded, **lovers of pleasures more than lovers of God;** having a form of godliness, but denying the power* (of the Holy Spirit) *thereof; from such* (people) *turn away.*"

**FIRST:** You need to realize why God wants to forgive you of your sins. Then realize what He has already done to make your forgiveness possible. God wants to forgive you of your sins for one basic reason. HE LOVES YOU! He knows that sin hurts you — whether you realize it or not! Sin, if not repented of, will cut you off from God and the blessings he has in store for you! **God cannot be mocked!** A person does sow what he reaps! When a person sows to please his sinful nature, that same nature will grow to reap his own destruction. **Galatians 6:7-8** Sin also hurts you because it cuts you off from God eternally, unless you, of your own free will, repent and turn away from sin! God loves you so much and he wants you to live in Heaven with Him, forever! He wants you to know the joy of having a loving and personal relationship with Him right now. That's only possible if you choose to let God forgive your sins. God has already done everything necessary to make forgiveness possible. God cannot sin. God is just, and because of that sin must be punished! In other words, God could not simply decide to forgive everyone — because if He did, sin would not be punished! God came down to this earth, in the person of His Son (Jesus). He allowed His Son to undergo the punishment for sin that you and I deserve! Christ died in your place . . . and in mine! He took upon himself the pain and death that you and I deserve! This is why forgiveness is possible, because Jesus Christ has paid the price for you and me on the cross! Why not trust what Jesus Christ has done on the cross for us all? Commit your life to Him in repentance and faith. Ask Him to come into your life as your Lord and Savior. If you do, you have God's promise that you are forgiven! Then, thank God and praise Him everyday of your life! Live for Him and serve Him! Never be ashamed of God or He will be ashamed of you!

**PRAYER**

Dear God, I confess that I am a sinner. I know that I will never be a truly happy person until I am forgiven of my sins. I humbly ask You to forgive all my sins! Please blot them out from Your memory! Come into my life and cleanse me through the precious shed blood of Jesus. I want to be forgiven! I want to change my life! I know You love me or You wouldn't have sent Jesus to take my place on the cross. I believe Jesus is alive and is coming back! I want to be ready when He does. I repent and want to receive everything You have in store for me! I will not be ashamed of You! I confess with my mouth that I am now a Christian! I will tell others how to become a born-again Christian! I will read my Bible! I will go to church, regularly! I will change my life-style and my friends, if necessary! I will do anything to safeguard my salvation! I praise You and I thank You with all my heart for turning my life around before I ended up in hell! Now, I am saved! I'm free! Now with Your help I will grow daily as a Christian! In Jesus' name, I pray. AMEN!

# PSYCHIC MEDIUMS

**DEFINITION:** An individual held to be a channel of communication between the earthly world and a world of spirits, a go-between.

**MEDIUMS POSSESS "FAMILIAR SPIRITS" WHICH, ACCORDING TO THE HOLY BIBLE, ARE DEMON SPIRITS!** Mediums submit their free will over to demon spirits so they can imitate dead beings and give predictions, advice and teachings. Psychic mediums frequently use a **trumpet** to conjure up these demon spirits. The spirits speak through it to give the medium's voice more volume. **CHRISTIANS ARE ABSOLUTELY FORBIDDEN TO PRACTICE ANY OCCULT ACTIVITY!** People who practice Transcendental Meditation, Yoga and Silva Mind Control are taught to mumble a sound while meditating. They leave themselves wide open for familiar spirits to enter through their vocal cords. **READ: "ENCHANTMENTS"**

*"And the soul that turneth after such as have **familiar spirits**, and after wizards* (male witches), *to go a whoring after them, I will even set my face against that soul, and will cut him off* (separate him) *from among his people."* **Leviticus 20:6**

**IN THE OLD TESTAMENT DAYS, MEDIUMS AND OCCULT TEACHERS WERE STONED TO DEATH!** *"A man also or woman that hath a **familiar spirit**, or that is a wizard, shall surely be put to death: they shall stone them with stones: their blood shall be upon them."* **Leviticus 20:27/Exodus 22:18**

Jesus paid the price for our sins on the cross. And because He did, even spirit mediums, occult teachers, witches, wizards, etc., can repent of their sins and be forgiven!

**GOD STRICTLY WARNS US NEVER TO HAVE ANYTHING TO DO WITH ANY FORM OF THE OCCULT!** *"Regard not them that have **familiar spirits**, neither seek after wizards, to be defiled by them: I am the Lord your God."* **Leviticus 19:31**

SATAN IS A FALLEN ANGEL WHO USES AN UNSAVED PERSON'S MIND AND VOICE TO TRANSMIT HIS LIES AND TRICKERY! HE USED THIS DEVICE TO TRICK EVE IN THE GARDEN OF EDEN. HE IS STILL USING THIS TECHNIQUE TO OCCUPY A PERSON'S VOICE BOX! PEOPLE SPEND FORTUNES GOING TO PSYCHIC MEDIUMS FOR ANSWERS. GUESS WHO IS REALLY GIVING THE ANSWERS TO THEIR QUESTIONS FROM BEYOND? WHAT A FOOL SOME PEOPLE CAN BE . . . AND HOW IGNORANT OF THEM NOT TO SEEK THE TRUTH FROM THE HOLY BIBLE! Read: **Genesis 3:1**

**GOD COMMANDS US NOT TO LEARN OR PRACTICE THESE EVIL PAGAN THINGS!** *"When thou art come into the land which the Lord thy God giveth thee, thou shalt not learn to do after the abominations of those nations. There shall not be found among you any one that maketh his son or his daughter to pass through the fire* (a pagan worship to an idol god), *or that useth **divination**, or an **observer of times*** (astrology) *or an **enchanter**, or a **witch**, or a **charmer**, or a **consulter with familiar spirits**, or a **wizard**, or a **necromancer**. For all that do these things are an abomination unto the Lord: and because of these abominations the Lord thy God doth drive them out from before thee."* **Deuteronomy 18:9-12**

Saul died because he sought the **counsel of a medium with a familiar spirit** instead of seeking counsel from the Lord. Because of his unpardonable sin the kingdom was turned over to David. Read: **1 Chronicles 10:13-14**

*"And when they shall say unto you, Seek unto them that have **familiar spirits**, and unto wizards that peep, and that mutter* (mantras): *should not a people seek unto their God? for the living* (instead of) *to the dead? To the law*

*and to the testimony* (of God): *if they speak not according to this word* (the scriptures), *it is because there is no light* (truth, knowledge, wisdom, God) *in them. And they shall pass through it, hardly bestead and hungry: and it shall come to pass, that when they shall be hungry, they shall fret themselves, and curse their king and their God, and look upward. And they shall look unto the earth; and behold trouble and darkness, dimness of anguish; and they shall be driven to darkness."* **Isaiah 8:19-22**

**DID YOU KNOW THAT THE INCREASE IN OCCULT ACTIVITY TODAY FULFILLS END TIME PROPHECY ABOUT THE LAST DAYS BEFORE CHRIST RETURNS TO EARTH?** *"Now the* (Holy) *Spirit speaketh expressly, that in the **latter times** some shall depart from the faith* (in God), *giving heed to **seducing spirits**, and **doctrines of devils**; speaking lies in hypocrisy; having their conscience seared with a hot iron."* **1 Timothy 4:1-2**

King Manasseh was involved in **astrology, enchantments, witchcraft, wizards** and he had a **familiar spirit.** He did much evil in the sight of the Lord! Read: **2 Chronicles 33**

**EGYPT, DURING THE WRITING OF THE BIBLE, WAS TOTALLY SOLD OUT TO FALSE GODS, IDOLS, FAMILIAR SPIRITS AND WIZARDS. READ: Isaiah 19:1-10**

**Isaiah 29:4** says that the voice of **familiar spirits** comes out of the ground. You can be assured that the voice which comes from mediums who possess a **familiar spirit** is not coming from a heavenly being!

**SOME FORBIDDEN HEATHEN PRACTICES WHICH ARE STILL IN PRACTICE TODAY INCLUDE:** Enchantments, witchcraft, sorcery, sooth-saying, divination (fortune tellers), wizardry (male and female witches), necromancy (fortune telling through communication with the dead), magic, using charms, prognostication (predicting by signs, omens), observing times, astrology and star gazing. **All who practice the above mentioned heathen practices are in contact with demon spirits whether they know this or not!** All occult activity is under the leadership of demon spirits which are called familiar spirits. **UNLESS A PERSON REPENTS AND FORSAKES THESE FORBIDDEN PRACTICES, HE WILL NOT BE ALLOWED TO ENTER HEAVEN!**

(Continued)

Luke 12:29 REFERS TO PEOPLE WHO PRACTICE OR TEACH ANY OCCULT ACTIVITY AS HAVING A "DOUBTFUL MIND"!

# OUIJA BOARD Tarot Cards Tea Leaves

# Free advice

GOD WILL NOT TOLERATE OCCULT ACTIVITY IN THE LIFE OF A CHRISTIAN! SO, IF YOU WANT TO SPEND ETERNITY WITH GOD, AND NOT SATAN, GIVE UP ANYTHING THAT HAS TO DO WITH ASTROLOGY, WITCHCRAFT, FORTUNE TELLING, MEDIUMS, PALMISTRY, AUTOMATIC WRITING, ASTRAL PROJECTION, HYPNOSIS, ETC. THE CHOICE IS YOURS. WILL IT BE ETERNITY WITH GOD OR SATAN? YOU CAN'T HAVE THE CHOICE WHERE YOU WANT TO SPEND ETERNITY AFTER YOU DIE!

**SURELY YOU'VE GOTTEN GOD'S MESSAGE BY NOW! SORCERY CAN'T POSSIBLY SAVE YOU, BECAUSE IT ALL COMES FROM SATAN!**

**JESUS SAID:** *"For there shall arise false Christs, and false prophets, and shall shew* (show) *great signs and wonders* (satanic manifestations will run rampant during the seven year tribulation periods after the Christians have been raptured to heaven with Jesus); *insomuch that, if it were possible, they shall deceive the very elect* (Jews)." **Matthew 24:24** NOTE: For more information about the demon occult activity during the tribulation period, read **2 Thessalonians 2:7-12/Revelation 13:1-18/16:13-16/19:20/Daniel 8:24.**

**FOR MORE INFORMATION ABOUT FAMILIAR SPIRITS, READ: 2 Kings 21/23:24.**

**FINAL WARNING TO MEDIUMS AND THOSE WHO BELIEVE IN, OR PRACTICE, ANY OCCULT ACTIVITY!**
*"**Defile** not ye yourselves in any of these things: for in all these the nations are **defiled** which I cast out before you: And the land is **defiled:** therefore I do visit the iniquity thereof upon it, and the land itself vomiteth out her inhabitants. Ye shall therefore keep my* (God's) *statutes* (laws) *and my judgments, and shall not commit any of these abominations; neither any of your own nation, nor any stranger that sojourneth* (travels) *among you: For all these abominations have the men of the land done, which were* (born) *before you, and the land is **defiled;** That the land spue not you out also, when ye **defile** it, as it spued out the nations that were before you. For whosoever shall commit any of these abominations, even the souls that commit them shall be cut off from among their people. Therefore shall ye keep mine ordinance* (absolute laws), *that ye commit not any one of these abominable customs, which were committed before you, and that ye **defile** not yourselves therein: I AM THE LORD YOUR GOD."* **Leviticus 18:24-30**

# MEDIUMS
### PRAYER

Dear God, Please forgive me for my interest in **horoscopes, astrology, and psychic research.** I know the Bible says that anyone who practices or believes in any form of occult activity separates himself eternally from You, unless he repents and forsakes it! I repent of all my sins. **I turn away forever from any form of occult activity in my life!** I turn my life over to You! I will **burn all literature, charms, zodiacs and records** that are in my possession! I will not communicate with anyone who is interested in occult activity so Satan cannot tempt me to fall back into it! I will not believe in the power of **pyramids,** either! From this moment on, I will serve and worship only You! I will read my Bible diligently and pray daily for guidance, truth and wisdom! In Jesus' name, I pray. AMEN!

# RAPE

**WHAT IS RAPE?** Rape is forcing a person to engage in sexual intercourse against their will. Rape is forcing sexual penetration without consent such as the attack on a child by an adult!

**THE BEST WAY TO PREVENT RAPE FROM OCCURING IS TO AVOID ANY SITUATION WHICH MIGHT BE CONDUCIVE TO IT!** Shun dark streets, deserted cars, don't open your door to strangers, don't hitchhike!

**RAPE IS THE WORST FOUR-LETTER WORD OF THEM ALL!** Criminologists consider forcible rape as a sex-related offense. It's really a "hate-related" crime. Rape has little to do with carnal gratification! The rapist often selects an aging person instead of a young beauty.

**GOD HELP THE VIOLATER IF HE DOESN'T REPENT AND TURN AWAY FROM HIS SINS!** The victim of rape is sometimes robbed or killed before the offender gets through. Some people who've been raped become so despondent and full of shame and guilt that they commit suicide!

**OUR NATION'S POPULATION INCREASES LESS THAN 1 PERCENT PER YEAR. RAPE INCREASED 15 PERCENT IN 1981!** As a nation, we're returning to the wickedness of Sodom and Gomorrah, Rome and others, where empires were raped and robbed. Women were a part of the spoils of conquest then and still are! Society teaches the "have-nots" to go take a share of what the "haves" have!

**RAPE IS A WORD MOST MEN NEVER ENTIRELY UNDERSTAND AND FEW WOMEN FULLY COMPREHEND!** In the old testament there was a uniform death penalty code for rape in an effort to put away all sin **Deuteronomy 22:20-29.** Thank God a rapist can now be forgiven if he humbles himself and repents of his sin. Jesus paid the ultimate price for our sins when He died on the cross and was resurrected. Had He not done this for us we would all be lost forever! Even the rapist is promised eternal life with Jesus, if he repents! God loves the rapist but hates all sin. God wants to forgive him, but he must make the decision to repent for himself!

**RAPE IS THE FASTEST GROWING AND LEAST REPORTED CRIME IN THE U.S. IT IS THE MOST MISUNDERSTOOD OF ALL VIOLENT CRIMES!** Rape is almost always done by someone a person knows or is related to. Studies have shown that rape is almost always premeditated . . . and not by mentally ill or sexually perverted persons! Rape is an act of violence, not uncontrollable sexual urges! The rapist's motivation is usually hostility toward women in general!

**52 PERCENT OF ALL RAPES OCCUR IN THE HOME!** Most rapes do not occur in isolated places at night. They also occur in buses, subways, stairwells, parking lots, parks, cars and offices!

**RAPED VICTIMS DO NOT INVITE THE ATTACK!** It's time to stop shifting the blame from offender to victim! Eighty year old women, nuns, children, and unattractive women do not invite rape!

**A WOMAN'S BEST DEFENSE IS GOD!** First she should become a born-again Christian! She should always dress decently. She should grow in prayer and reading the Bible. She should memorize verses each day! *"No weapon that is formed against thee shall prosper. . ."* **Isaiah 54:17** Jesus said: *"Behold, I give unto you power to tread on serpents and scorpions, and over all the power of the enemy, and nothing shall by any means hurt you."* **Luke 10:19** Some women fight . . . some claim to have venereal disease or be in a menstrual period. Some pretend to be pregnant. Some faint, urinate or vomit. Wouldn't it be better to **BIND SATAN** and run the attacker off? If a rapist came near me, I would begin instantly praying to God and for the offender. I would quote scripture after scripture. I would tell him Jesus loves him, no matter how frightened I might be, because

that's the only thing I know that works! **Jesus said:** *"Verily I say unto you, whatsoever ye shall bind on earth shall be bound in heaven: and whatsoever ye shall loose on earth shall be loosed in heaven."* **Matthew 18:18**

**STAND YOUR GROUND! SCREAM THIS MESSAGE AT THE TOP OF YOUR VOICE:** "Satan, I bind you in the name of Jesus! I am a child of God. Take your filthy body off my property. Your hands will not touch this child of God! You will not rape me or God will punish you as long as you live. I command you to leave me alone. Father, God, send thousands of angels to protect me!" And if the offender still persists — kick his genitals! God would give us permission to fight sex offenders with His scriptures, and to also guard our body. Because, it is His temple!

**WARNING TO YOUNG GIRLS:** Don't become overly familiar with boys and men! Friendliness is nice but you never know where another person is coming from! Without meaning to do so, you could be sending out "vibes" that you are loose, if you're overly friendly! Be more aware of the messages you send out! Dress decently and be on good behavior so boys will clearly understand you are a Christian! Command respect and decent conversations, wherever you go!

**PARENTS: PROTECT YOUR CHILDREN BY FOLLOWING GOD'S RULES AND COMMON HORSE SENSE!** *"Train up a child in the way he should go: and when he is old he will not depart from it."* **Proverbs 22:6** Children respond to authority so teach him to obey all your rules! Tell your child that no one has the right to invade his privacy or body. Tell them never to let anyone fondle them. Teach them who they can and cannot talk to! Conversations with your child about sex should not be frightening. If your child has been raped, tell him that he did nothing wrong to bring this about. Alleviate his guilt! Children should know their full name, address, phone number, numbers of neighbors and emergency numbers. Children should be invited to discuss with their parents any incident that has confused them. They should be told that if any one exposes himself they are to report it to the parents, and then to the police! They should be told never to tell a stranger they are at home alone when they answer the phone, or that mother is next door! Never let them take shortcuts through vacant lots or parks. Let them know that they are always to come straight home after school, unless they have permission otherwise! Take them to public restrooms, don't send them off alone! If they ever get lost tell them to approach a woman, rather than a man, to ask for assistance! Teach them to pray and read their Bible and to trust in God!

**IF YOU OR YOUR CHILD IS RAPED:** Report it to the police and prosecute whenever possible, in order to get the offender off the streets! God created human government to protect the just from the unjust! Rapists can be forgiven by God!

## PRAYER

Dear God, please forgive me for all my sins. I will read my Bible and pray daily. I will memorize those verses which will strengthen and protect me! Help me to teach my children how to grow up without fear of rape while teaching them the safeguards against it. Help me to always show good conduct to those I encounter. Please forgive me if I have ever said or done anything that would cause a person to think I'm an easy mark for sex! Help me to keep my body pure in Your sight! In Jesus' name, I pray. AMEN!

## PRAYER FOR THE RAPIST

Dear God, please forgive all my sins. I am a rapist. I am so sorry, I repent from the bottom of my heart! Please forgive me because I don't want to go to hell! I turn away from all forms of sexual perversion. From this moment on, I will lead a good clean life. I will attend church. I will mind my own business. I will keep my thoughts and actions clean! If You could forgive the thief on the cross, I know You can forgive me. I accept Your forgiveness. I will live for You and serve You from this moment on. In Jesus' name, I pray. AMEN!

# REBELLION

**WARNING TO ATHEISTS, FALSE TEACHERS, OCCULT TEACHERS:** *"Therefore thus saith the Lord; Behold, I will cast thee from off the face of the earth: this year thou shalt die, because thou hast taught* **rebellion** *against the Lord."* **Jeremiah 28:16** *". . .he shall not have a man to dwell among this people; neither shall he behold the good that I will do for my people, saith the Lord; because he hath taught* **rebellion** *against the Lord."* **Jeremiah 29:32**

**REBELLION IS A SIN AGAINST YOURSELF, AGAINST ANOTHER PERSON, AND AGAINST GOD! SATAN WAS THE INVENTOR OF REBELLION AND BECAUSE OF HIS REBELLION, HE WAS THROWN OUT OF HEAVEN! IF YOU DO NOT FORSAKE YOUR REBELLIOUS SPIRIT AGAINST GOD, YOUR PARENTS, OR ANYONE ELSE — YOU WILL MISS OUT ON GOD'S BLESSINGS AND WILL SUFFER THE CONSEQUENCES FOR YOUR SINS!**

**GOD LOVES THE PERSON . . . BUT HATES ALL FORMS OF REBELLION!**

**ALL OCCULT ACTIVITY IS A DIRECT REBELLION AGAINST THE TEACHINGS OF GOD!** *"For rebellion is as the sin of* **witchcraft**, *and stubbornness is as iniquity and idolatry. Because thou hast rejected the word of the Lord. . ."* **1 Samuel 15:23**

**ALL EVIL PEOPLE ARE REBELLIOUS!** *"An evil man seeketh only* **rebellion**: *therefore a cruel messenger* (from Satan) *shall be sent against him."* **Proverbs 17:11**

**IN THE OLD TESTAMENT, WHEN PARENTS HAD A REBELLIOUS SON THEY WOULD TAKE HIM INTO THE CITY AND THE ELDERS WOULD STONE HIM TO DEATH! Deuteronomy 21:18-21** Aren't we glad that Jesus went to the cross and was resurrected, so that we can pray and receive forgiveness for our sins? Until we get saved, we are all in rebellion to God!

## *Unlawful . . . . Unruly*

**PSALM 78:8 SAYS WE ARE A REBELLIOUS GENERATION WHOSE HEART AND SPIRIT IS NOT RIGHT WITH GOD!** *"But this people hath a revolting and a* **rebellious** *heart; they are revolted and gone."* **Jeremiah 5:23**

**THERE ARE MANY HOUSES THAT ARE REBELLIOUS!** *"And they, whether they will hear, or whether they will forbear, (for they are a* **rebellious** *house), yet shall (they) know that there hath been a prophet among them. And thou, son of man, be not afraid of them, neither be afraid of their words, though briers and thorns be with thee, and thou dost dwell among scorpions: be not afraid of their words, nor be dismayed at their looks, though they be a* **rebellious** *house. And thou shalt speak my words unto them, whether they will hear, or whether they will forbear: for they are most* **rebellious.**" **Ezekiel 2:5-8/3:9, 26-27/12:2-9/17:12/24:3**

**REBELLION IS ALWAYS AN ENEMY TO GOD!** *"For there is no faithfulness in their mouth; their inward part* (heart) *is very wickedness; their throat is an open sepulchre* (tomb); *they flatter with their tongue. Destroy thou them, O God; let them fall by their own counsels; cast them out in the multitude of their transgressions; for they have* **rebelled** *against thee. But let all those that put their trust in thee rejoice: let them ever shout for joy, because thou defendest them: let them also that love thy name be joyful in thee."* **Psalm 5:9-11**

**WARNING: GOD WILL PUNISH EVERY REBELLIOUS PERSON WHO DOES NOT TURN AWAY FROM SIN AND RECEIVE GOD'S FORGIVENESS! GOD LOVES EVERY PERSON BUT HE WILL NOT BE MOCKED!** *"He* (God) *ruleth by his power for ever; his eyes behold the nations: let not the* **rebellious** *exalt themselves."* **Psalm 66:7**

**HOW CAN YOU BREAK A REBELLIOUS SPIRIT?** *"Wash you, make you clean; put away the evil of your doings from before mine eyes; cease to do evil; Learn to do well; seek judgment, relieve the oppressed, judge the fatherless, plead for the widow. Come now, and let us reason together, saith the Lord: though your sins be as scarlet, they shall be as white as snow; though they be red like crimson, they shall be as wool. If ye be willing and obedient, ye shall eat of the good of the land: But if ye refuse and* **rebel**, *ye shall be devoured with the sword: for the mouth of the Lord hath spoken it."* **Isaiah 1:16-20**

**Invite Jesus into your life. Tell Him you want Him to be your Savior, personal guide and friend throughout your life. He loves you so much! You are very special to Him! He even knows exactly how many individual hairs are on your head! Luke 12:7**

### PRAYER

Dear God, please forgive me for all my sins. I am guilty of having a **rebellious** heart and spirit. As a result of this, I had cut myself off from You and others that I love. Please forgive me and cleanse me. Make me into the kind of person You want me to be. I turn away from all forms of **rebellion.** I submit my own free will over to You! Mold me and make me worthy of being called Your child! Thank You in Jesus' name. AMEN!

# REINCARNATION

...

**DEFINITION:** Rebirth in new bodies or forms of life; rebirth of a soul in a new human body.

**THOSE WHO BELIEVE IN REINCARNATION FALSELY BELIEVE THAT WHEN THEY DIE THEY WILL COME BACK TO EARTH IN THE FORM OF A NEW BODY OR ANIMAL.** They wholeheartedly believe they will inhabit new bodies, time and time again, until they have conquered all their mistakes and have learned from them! They are confident they will have many chances to come back from the grave! They deny the finality and reality of heaven and hell! They believe that eventually they will know all things.

**YOU CAN'T BELIEVE THE BIBLE IS 100 PERCENT TRUE AND STILL BELIEVE IN REINCARNATION!**

**REINCARNATION IS REFERRED TO AS:** prospective time, womb of time, time to come, days and years to come, fate, destiny, distant future, future generations, future state, doomsday, afterlife, life to come, hereafter, in the fullness of time, in due course, in the long run . . . and the list is unending!

**REINCARNATION IS AN OCCULT TEACHING OF SATAN!** Satan must get a big laugh every time a person falls for that line of malarkey!

**THE BIBLE TELLS US WE LIVE ON THIS EARTH ONLY ONCE. AND WHEN WE DIE WE GO TO WHICHEVER ETERNITY WE SELECTED WHILE WE LIVED! WE ONLY HAVE TWO CHOICES, HEAVEN OR HELL!** *"And as it is appointed unto men once to die, but after this the judgment."* **Hebrews 9:27**

**REINCARNATION IS NOT TAUGHT IN THE BIBLE — BECAUSE IT DOESN'T EXIST!** It is taught in certain religions from the Far East. The basic idea is that a person, through a succession of reincarnations, can eventually become more and more perfect until he is finally free from sin and "one" with the universe! **THE THEORY OF REINCARNATION IS A LIE!** Neither man, nor animal, returns from the grave to inhabit another person or animal's body!

*"For all flesh is as grass, and all the glory of man as the flower of grass. The grass withereth, and the flower thereof falleth away* (dies): *But the word of the Lord endureth for ever. And this is the word which by the gospel is preached unto you."* **1 Peter 1:24-25**

**THE BIBLE CLEARLY TELLS US THAT OUR GREATEST PROBLEM IS SIN!** Man could do nothing to save himself until Christ died on the cross, and was resurrected, in order that we could repent and receive forgiveness for our sins! We cannot solve sin by ourselves! Sin is like an incurable cancer that we cannot destroy, without God's help!

**THE BIBLE SAYS:** *"As it is written, There is none righteous, no, not one:"* **Romans 3:10** So, what good would it be to come back from the grave again and again, when you could never be free from sin?

**HERE IS THE WONDERFUL TRUTH!** What we could never do for ourselves, God has done for us! Christ died on the cross for us. He took upon himself our sin and guilt. *"In whom we have redemption through his blood, the forgiveness of sins, according to the riches of his grace."* **Ephesians 1:7** We could never rid ourselves of sin and guilt, so God provided the way for us in Christ! By trusting Christ as our Lord and Savior, we can become a born-again Christian! Therefore, there is no need for reincarnation, and neither is there any such thing! What we do during this life will determine our eternal destiny. God left the choice up to us where we will spend eternity! *"For by grace are ye saved through faith; and that not of yourselves: it is the gift of God: Not* (a gift) *of* (good) *works, lest any man should boast."* **Ephesians 2:8-9**

**MATTHEW 22:32 SAYS GOD IS NOT THE GOD OF THE DEAD . . . BUT OF THE LIVING!**

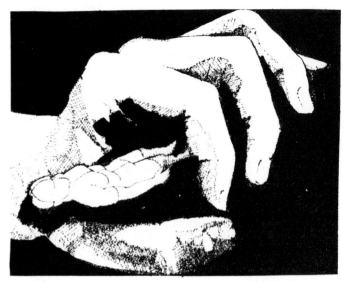

**DEATH WILL BE DESTROYED AND LIFE RESTORED! 1 Corinthians 15:26/Revelation 21:4**

**MOST OF OUR DIFFICULTIES CAN BE TRACED TO THE WAYS IN WHICH WE HAVE DISOBEYED GOD!** We must face the consequences of our disobedience. If we deliberately turn our back on Him and sin against Him, we will eventually pay the price for our rebellion! God loves us and wants us to spend eternity with Him, but we make our own choice . . . heaven or hell!

**THE BIBLE SAYS:** *"Be not deceived: God is not mocked: for whatsoever a man soweth, that shall he also reap. For he that soweth to his* (lusts of the) *flesh shall of the flesh reap corruption; but he that soweth to the* (Holy) *Spirit shall of the* (Holy) *Spirit reap life everlasting."* **Galatians 6:7-8**

**DEATH IS CERTAIN!** *"Then shall the dust return to the earth as it was* (before God created man out of it): *and the spirit* (of man), *shall return unto God who gave it."* **Ecclesiastes 12:7**

*"For we must needs die, and are as water spilt on the ground, which cannot be gathered up again; neither doth God respect any person: yet doth he devise means, that his banished be not expelled from him."* **2 Samuel 14:14**

**REINCARNATION WAS DREAMED UP BY SATAN TO DECEIVE PEOPLE INTO THINKING THEY DON'T HAVE TO BECOME BORN-AGAIN CHRISTIANS . . . AND TO CONVINCE THEM THERE'S NO HEAVEN OR HELL! HE'LL DO ANYTHING TO KEEP PEOPLE FROM KNOWING THE TRUTH!** THE THEORY OF REINCARNATION WOULD HAVE YOU BELIEVE THAT YOU NEED NOT REPENT OF YOUR SINS! THE TRUTH IS THAT IF YOU DON'T REPENT, YOU WILL GO TO HELL WHEN YOU DIE! PLEASE GET SAVED SO YOU CAN SPEND ETERNITY WITH JESUS, INSTEAD OF WITH SATAN!

### PRAYER

Dear God, please forgive me for all my sins. Forgive me for believing in reincarnation. I realize that it is a lie dreamed up by Satan! I confess I am a sinner and I ask You to forgive me for my sins. I know that no person can come back to life, from the grave, and inhabit another person or animal. I know that the only way to spend eternity with You is for me to be forgiven of my sins and to accept Jesus as my Savior and Lord. I want to spend eternity with You. I love You because You first loved me. Thank You for urging me to break through and receive the truth about reincarnation! I will serve You and only You! In Jesus' name, I pray. AMEN!

# REPUTATION

*"A good name is rather to be chosen than great riches, and loving favour rather than silver and gold."* **Proverbs 22:1**

# Who could ask for anything more

*"A good reputation is more valuable than the most expensive perfume..."* **Ecclesiastes 7:1** (The Living Bible)

*Reputation*

A HUMBLE SPIRIT IS BETTER THAN A FAMOUS REPUTATION! *"Let nothing be done through strife or vainglory; but in lowliness of mind let each esteem other better than themselves. Look not every man on his own things, but every man also on the things of others. Let this mind be in you, which was also in Christ Jesus: Who, being in the form of God, thought it not robbery to be equal with God: But made himself of no reputation, and took upon him the form of a servant, and was made in the likeness of men: and being found in fashion as a man, he humbled himself, and became obedient unto death, even the death of the cross. Wherefore God also hath highly exalted him, and given him a name which is above every name: That at the name of Jesus every knee should bow, of things in heaven, and things in earth, and things under the earth: And that every tongue should confess that Jesus Christ is Lord, to the glory of God the Father."* **Philippians 2:3-11**

### GUARD IT WISELY
· · ·

You got your name from your father.
It was all he had to give.
So, it's yours to use and cherish
For as long as you may live.

If you lose the watch he gave you,
it can always be replaced.
But a black mark on your name,
can never be erased!

It was clean the day you took it
And a worthy name to bear.
When he got it from his father,
There was no dishonor there!

So, make sure you guard it wisely.
After all is said and done
You'll be glad the name is spotless
When you give it to your son!

### PRAYER

Dear God, please forgive me for all my sins. Help me establish a good reputation. Forgive me if I have let my ego and vanity get in the way. Help me to be more aware of what I say and do and to try to emulate Jesus! Teach me how to have a humble spirit. Teach me to keep my mind on You at all times. Help me to curb my curiosity about what others think of me. Teach me not to be pre-occupied with my own intellect, looks, successes and thoughts. I want my reputation to be that of a follower of Christ and not for my own glory! I will strive for this. I thank You for loving me when I was a sinner. Thank You for saving my soul, because I know my good name does not merit my salvation, I know that Jesus died on the cross for my sins and lives today. I want to spend eternity with You and I thank You for the privilege. In Jesus' name, I pray. AMEN!

*"The memory of the just is blessed: but the name of the wicked shall rot."* **Proverbs 10:7**

# REVENGE

*"For if ye forgive men their trespasses, your heavenly Father will also forgive you. But if ye forgive not men their trespasses, neither will your Father (God) forgive your trespasses."* **Matthew 6:14-15**

*". . .Today if ye will hear his (God's) voice, harden not your hearts. . ."* **Hebrews 3:7-8, 15**

*"Moreover if thy brother (another Christian) shall trespass against thee, go and tell him his fault between thee and him alone: if he shall hear thee, thou hast gained thy brother. But if he will not hear thee, then take with thee one or two more, that in the mouth of two or three witnesses every word may be established. And if he shall neglect to hear them, tell it unto the church: but if he neglect to hear the church, let him be unto thee as an heathen (stranger) man and a publican."* **Matthew 18:15-17**

## HOW MANY TIMES SHOULD WE FORGIVE A PERSON?
*"Then came Peter to him (Jesus), and said, Lord, how oft (often) shall my brother sin against me, and I forgive him? till seven times? Jesus saith unto him, I say not unto thee, Until seven times: but Until seventy times seven."* **Matthew 18:21-22**

**JESUS SAID:** *"But I say unto you which hear, Love your enemies, do good to them which hate you, Bless them that curse you, and pray for them which despitefully use you. And unto him that smiteth thee on the one cheek offer also the other; and him that taketh away thy cloke forbid not to take thy coat also. Give to every man that asketh of thee; and of him that taketh away thy goods ask them not again. And as ye would (wish) that men should do to you, do ye also to them likewise. For if ye love them which love you, what thank (thanks) have ye? for sinners also love those that love them. And if ye do good to them which do good to you, what thank (thanks) have ye? for sinners also do even the same. And if ye lend to them of whom ye hope to receive, what thank (thanks) have ye? for sinners also lend to sinners, to receive as much again. But love ye your enemies, and do good, and lend, hoping for nothing again; and your reward shall be great, and ye shall be the children of the Highest: for he is kind unto the unthankful and to the evil. Be ye therefore merciful, as your Father (God) also is merciful. Judge not, and ye shall not be judged; condemn not, and ye shall not be condemned: forgive, and ye shall be forgiven: Give, and it shall be given unto you; good measure, pressed down, and shaken together, and running over, shall men give into your bosom. For with the same measure that ye mete (do to others) withal it shall be measured to you again."* **Luke 6:27-38**

### God hears prayer because he is a compassionate Father

# Some Shocking Facts You May Not Know

*"Take heed to yourselves: If thy brother trespass against thee, rebuke him; and if he repent, forgive him. And if he trespass against thee seven times in a day, and seven times in a day turn again to thee, saying, I repent; thou shalt forgive him."* **Luke 17:3-4**

**JESUS SAID:** *"Ye have heard that it hath been said, An eye for an eye, and a tooth for a tooth: But I say unto you, That ye resist not evil: but whosoever shall smite thee on thy right cheek, turn to him the other also. And if any man will sue thee at the law, and take away thy coat, let him have thy cloke also. And whosoever shall compel thee to go a mile, go with him twain (two). Give to him that asketh thee, and from him that would borrow of thee turn not thou away. Ye have heard that it hath been said, Thou shalt love thy neighbour, and hate thine enemy. But I say unto you, Love your enemies, bless them that curse you, do good to them that hate you, and pray for them which despitefully use you, and persecute you; That ye may be the children of your Father (God) which is in heaven: for he maketh his sun to rise on the evil and on the good, and sendeth rain on the just and on the unjust. For if ye love them which love you, what reward have ye? do not even the publicans (do) the same? And if ye salute your brethren only, what do ye more than others? do not even the publicans so? Be ye therefore perfect, even as your Father which is in heaven is perfect."* **Matthew 5:38-48**

*"Say not thou, I will recompense evil: but wait on the Lord, and he shall save thee."* **Proverbs 20:22**

### PRAYER
Dear God, please forgive me for all my sins. Forgive me for seeking revenge when I get my feelings hurt. Teach me to be more forgiving and loving. Teach me to emulate the love Christ had for me when He died on the cross to pay for my sins. Thank God, He is alive today and I will spend eternity with Him! Help me keep my thoughts and actions pure. Forgive me if I have caused another person to stumble. May my expression and language always tell the world that I am a Christian. In Jesus' name, I pray. AMEN!

# ROCK-N-ROLL
## Country Music — Operas
## TV — Movies

**IT HAS BEEN SAID THAT MUSIC IS THE UNIVERSAL LANGUAGE!** God created music as an integral part of praise and worship. **Ezekiel 28:13** tells us that Satan was the first musician prior to being cast out of heaven because of his ego! Ever since then, he has taken deliberate steps to corrupt people and music!

**ROCK & ROLL IS AN EXPRESSION WHICH MEANS "TO HAVE SEX"!** Satan created a pulsating beat to correspond with body rhythms in a sexual act! To many secular writers and musicians, the word "love" means to have sex! I will hasten to say that not all rock music has pornographic lyrics! Country music and operas are not "lily-white". Both contain oppressive lyrics! **According to Frank Zappa: "Rock music is sex. . . the big beat matches the body rhythm!"**

**LOOK AT THE JACKET COVERS AND TITLES ON MOST ROCK RECORDS:** Some picture nudity, sado-masochism, death, shades of bestiality, occult themes, Satan's lightning bolt, pentagrams, 666 (the number of antichrist), crystal balls, the Christian cross upside down, pyramids, satanic monoliths (used to conjure up evil spirits), the all-seeing eye of Lucifer, Egyptian Ank, tea-leaf readers, tarot cards, Confucius, violent acts, fire, blood, genitals, bulls and goats. **Hebrews 10:4 says:** *"For it is not possible that the blood of bulls and goats should take away sins."* **NOTE:** Goats blood is used in satanic rituals and is often featured on jacket covers. The Rolling Stones posed as witches on the cover of their album, "Their Satanic Majesties Request." "Sympathy For The Devil" has become a theme song for Satan followers! "Goat Head Soup" was recorded at a Haitian voodoo ritual as you hear the screams of people supposedly becoming demon possessed. "Dancing With Mr. D" portrays a graveyard romp with Satan! Did you know that the universal symbol for Satan worship is a GOAT'S HEAD.

**THE GROUP "BLACK SABBATH" SINGS: "WE SOLD OUR SOUL FOR ROCK-N-ROLL" (AND) "MY NAME IS LUCIFER, PLEASE TAKE MY HAND!"** AC/DC Says: "I'm going to take you to hell . . . If you're into evil, you're a friend of mine!" Pink Floyd's album "Animals" quotes verses from the Satanic Book of Shadows (a diabolical version of the 23rd Psalm). John Lennon called the Holy Trinity: "Father, Sock, and Mickey Most!"

**SATAN IS THE INSTIGATOR OF SEX, VIOLENCE AND OCCULT LYRICS!** Rock-N-Roll has become a tool that Satan uses to program people into accepting sinful suggestions! **Music can be hypnotic!** Some rock artists commission witches to cast spells and perform voodoo rituals before they record and altar calls to Satan have occurred during some rock concerts! One of the prominent themes in rock lyrics is to promote death (both physical and eternal separation from God). **SOME ROCK GROUPS CLAIM DEATH IS THE ULTIMATE TRIP!**

**NATAS = SATAN SPELLED BACKWARDS.** The current trend is to record backwards. This is called backward masking! Again, this is Satan's subtle way of invading a person's subconscious mind! Since God recommended music as a vital part of worship and praise, He must be heartsick at what Satan has done to music!

**THE MUSIC IS REVERSIBLE . . . TURN BACK . . . TURN BACK!** In "Fire On High" by ELO the lyrics say: "The music is reversible, turn back, turn back." In "Eldorado" the lyrics say: "He (Christ) is the nasty one . . . Christ, you're infernal" (when played backwards!) In "Race With The Devil", the lyrics (backwards) say: "Satan . . . Satan . . . Satan . . . He Is God" (with wild demoniac laughter in the background)! The pulsating beat of rock and roll is so thick you could slice it with a knife!

**LISTEN BELOW ARE A FEW OF THE MANY RECORDS, ARTISTS AND GROUPS THAT PROMOTE SATANIC THEMES!** Kiss (Iron Maiden) — **Wilie Hutch** (Mark of The Beast) — **Todd Rungren** (Healing / Tiny Demons) — **Meat Loaf** (Bat Out of Hell) — **Judius Priest** (Sad Wings of Destiny) — **Godz** (Nothing Is Sacred) — **Rush** (2112 / Moving Pictures) — **Rolling Stones** (Goathead Soup / Sympathy For The Devil / Mr. D.) — **ELO** (Eldorado / Discovery) — **Plasmatics** (Metal Priestess) — **Fleetwood Mac** (Rumors) — **Lucifer's Friend** (Mean Machine) — **The Flesh Eaters** (A Minute To Pray A Second To Die) — **Pink Floyd** (Off The Wall / Animals) — **Scorpions** (The Virgin Killers) — **Alice Cooper** (Welcome To My Nightmare / Cold Ethel / Alice Cooper Goes To Hell) — **AC/DC** (Highway to Hell / If You Want Blood / Hell Ain't A Bad Place To Be) — **Blue Oyster Cult** (Agents of Fortune / Some Enchanted Evening) — **Beatles** (Sgt Peppers Lonely Hearts Band /Revolution #9) — **Ozzie Osbourne** (Blizzard of Oz / Diairy Of A Mad Man) — **Black Sabbath** (We Sold Our Soul For Rock N Roll / Sabbath Bloody Sabbath / Mob Rules) — **The Eagles** (Hotel California) — **Led Zepplin** (Presence) — **Blondie** (Stay Pretty, Die Young) — **Black Oak Arkansas** (The Day Electricity Came To Arkansas).

**NO PARENT WANTS HIS CHILD TO BECOME A HOMOSEXUAL, LESBIAN, ALCOHOLIC, DRUG ADDICT, SATAN WORSHIPPER OR SEX PERVERT!** No parent wants his child to imagine what suicide would be like. Yet, many lyrics promote these things! Better investigate all lyrics to see if you're doing your part as a proper parent! **The Bible says to train up a child in the way he should go, Proverbs 22:6!** Paul Kantner said: "Our music is intended to broaden the generation gap . . . to alienate children from their parents and to prepare people for the revolution!" Parents should search their children's rooms to see if there are satanic bibles, porno material, drugs, paraphernalia, ouija boards, candles or incense! Encourage your child not to listen to music of any artist or group who advocates drugs, sex, violence, reincarnation, witchcraft, suicide, Buddhism, Egyptian rites, pyramidology, astral projection, fortune telling, cursing, fornication, etc.! **Ephesians 6:1 and Colossians 3:20 says children are to obey their parents! 2 Timothy 3:2** says that in the last days, before Christ returns, children will be disobedient to their parents! Satan attempts to poison their minds! Take inventory of your child's record collection and find out who they listen to on the radio! Encourage your child to have a bonfire to get rid of these evil messages, while there is still time! The Bible says that disobedience = rebellion and is kin to the sin of witchcraft and idolatry, **1 Samuel 15:23! Deuteronomy 7:26 says:** *"Neither shalt thou bring an abomination into thine house lest thou be a cursed thing like it; but thou shalt utterly detest it and thou shalt utterly abhor (hate) it; for it is a cursed thing."* Now that most rock and roll has become so polluted, why not follow the good advice found in **Amos 5:23** which says: *"Take thou away from me the noise of thy songs; for I will not hear the melody of thy viols (string instruments)."* **READ: Amos 6:5**

**MANY ROCK-N-ROLL RECORDS CONTAIN SEXUAL GROANS — PROMOTE DRUGS — BOOZE — SUICIDE AND OCCULT ACTIVITY!** Funky refers to sex odors. Gig = sex orgies. Groovy = the ideal position for intercourse. Groupies = prostitutes who give sex freely to rock stars. Get-off = orgasm. **1 Timothy 4:1** says that in the last days, before Christ returns, some will give heed to seducing spirits and doctrines of demons!

213

(Continued)

**BEHIND CLOSED DOORS:** David Bowie and Elton John are bi-sexuals. Joan Baez is a lesbian! (Queen Bitch / Make up). Olivia Records markets lesbian albums (Gay & Proud / Women Loving Women). Daryl Hall and John Oates promote homosexual lyrics. The Tubes lead singer calls himself "Quay Lewd" (from the drug Quaalude). They recorded "Don't Touch Me There" and it is LEWD! Alice Cooper (I Love The Dead) simulates sex onstage with mannequins. John Lennon said: "Woman Is The Nigger Of The World." (AND) "Christianity will go . . . We're more popular than Jesus now!"

**DRUGS ARE A STEADY PART OF THE DIET OF MANY ROCK STARS!** Most live ungodly hours and have many mood swings. Some snort cocaine while signing contracts and being arrested for drug violations increases their popularity! Mick Jagger and Gregg Allman were famous for this! Linda Rondstadt says she sings better after shooting "smack" (Heroin). The Doobie Brothers derived their name from "doobie's" (joints of marajuana). The Bee Gee's are known to brag about their drug intake. Canned Heat / Uriah Heep / Sha Na Na / The Who / Little Feat / Deep Purple / Sex Pistols / Average White Band (and others) have lost a member of their group through death, as a result of drug overdose! There are thousands who still worship Elvis Presley more than Jesus Christ! David Gilmore says: "There's no way out of here . . . When you come in — you're in for good!"

**"SHIVA'S HEADBAND" GROUP IS NAMED AFTER THE HINDU GOD OF DESTRUCTION!** Many rock stars believe in astral projection, pyramid power, Yoga, transcendental meditation, voodoo, karma, chanting, tarot cards, witchcraft, suicide and drugs. "Santana" conducts business under the auspices of guru's. The proceeds from George Harrison's records go to support the Hare Krishna cult, Hinduism, drugs and acupuncture practices.

**THE THEME OF "WITCHY WOMAN" AND "ONE OF THESE NIGHTS" IS A SEARCH FOR THE DAUGHTER OF THE DEVIL!** "Hotel California" has a diabolical theme. The members of Deep Purple hold seances and worship Baal (mentioned many times in the Bible). They promote black magic (Star Gazer / Tarot Woman). Jimmy Page (lead guitarist for Led Zeppelin) and Daryl Hall own occult bookstores and are followers of the late British spiritualist, Aliester Crowley, who was known for murder and sex perversion. Mr. Crowley called himself "The beast—666". Jimmy Page lives in Mr. Crowley's mansion and claims to hear chains dragging and footsteps! Many rock stars are fascinated with Lucifer and Beelzebub! Fleetwood Mac dedicated his album "Rheannon" to a witch. Many groups dedicate their recordings to "All The Witches Of The World!" Earth, Wind & Fire promotes mysticism, astrology, Buddhism and the martial arts! Todd Rundgren's album "RA" is dedicated to the Egyptian sun god. He believes in pyramid power, astral projection and reincarnation. America recorded "God Of The Sun" about sun worship. Genesis recorded a song about tarot cards called "Voyage Of The Acolyte." Jackson Browne, Van Morrison and Stevie Wonder promote astrology. The director of the movie "Exorcist" was inspired by the satanic sounds of "Tangerine Dream" and used them for the movie called "The Sorcerer." Cat Stevens is a convert of Islam. Meat Loaf (Bat Out Of Hell) features demons and he claims to be possessed! Nazareth, Savoy Brown, Santana, Queen, and Uriah Heep feature demons, astral projection, and hexes! Paul McCartney wrote: "None of us believe in God"! Yoko Ono said: "We're aiming for a world of no money, no police, no government."! John Lennon was a believer in Marx and Lenin. He believed in atheism, socialism, drugs and revolution!

**GOD HATES ALL FORMS OF OCCULT ACTIVITY!** Christians should never purchase the devil's tools! John Lennon wrote: "Jesus is a garlic eating, stinking, little, yellow, greasy, fascist, bastard, Catholic, spaniard!"

**THE GROUP "KISS" DRESSES IN CHAINS AND LEATHER (TOOLS OF SADO-MASOCHISM)! BLUE OYSTER CULT HAS A THEME OF TEENAGE LOVE-PACK SUICIDE IN "DON'T FEAR THE REAPER!"**

**TV AND MOVIES ARE 100 PERCENT GUILTY!** EXAMPLE: ET / TEN / Victor-Victoria / Cat People / Exorcist / Omen / Deathtrap / On Golden Pond / A Little Sex / Reds / Arthur / Close Encounters Of The Third Kind / Poltergeists / and the list could reach to the moon and back! Many TV programs (during prime time) contain profanity, swearing, lying, extra-marital affairs, adultery, abortion, suicide, murder, blaspheming the Lord, rape, incest, homosexuality, sleeping pills, blackmail and death. Soap operas reek of despair, loneliness, betrayal, confusion and hopelessness!

**COUNTRY ARTISTS AND LYRICS ARE ALSO GUILTY!** EXAMPLE: Conway Twitty (Hot Legs / You've Never Been This Far Before) — Barbara Mandrell (Married But Not To Each Other) — Tammy Wynette (D-I-V-O-R-C-E) — David Houston (No Tell Motel) — Jeannie Seely (Take Me To Bed) — Johnny Paycheck (Take This Job & Shove It) and the list is unending!

**GOD LOVES ABBA, THE BEACHBOYS, BLACK SABBATH, BLUE OYSTER CULT, ERIC CLAPTON, ALICE COOPER, THE GRATEFUL DEAD, JEFFERSON STARSHIP, KISS, LED ZEPPELIN, ROD STEWART, THE WHO . . . & EVERYONE IN THE WORLD!** He wants all people to acknowledge they are sinners who need to ask forgiveness in order to spend eternal life with Jesus! God gives everyone the choice to decide whether he will go to heaven or hell! After you die you have no more choices! The Bible says after we die we face the judgment, **Hebrews 9:27!** I feel confident that if any deceased rock star (who rejected God) could talk to us now, he would warn us about hell and ask us to get straight with God, before it's too late!

**WHY NOT ADMIT YOU ARE A SINNER AND ASK GOD TO COME INTO YOUR HEART? GOD PROMISES HE WILL NOT TURN ANYONE AWAY!** He promises He will forgive and blot out your sins from His memory! Then you can have peace, contentment, and eternal life with Jesus! We've established that rock music is a tool that Satan uses to program your mind in an effort to turn you away from God and the Bible. God says Satan is the father of lies and confusion! **Ephesians 5:18-19 says:** *"And be not drunk with wine, wherein is excess; but be filled with the* (Holy) *Spirit; speaking to yourselves in psalms and hymns and spiritual songs, singing and making melody in your heart to the Lord."* **Psalm 98:1 says:** *"O sing unto the Lord a new song. . ."*

**PRAYER**

Dear God, please forgive me for all my sins. I humble myself. I need Your help! I didn't know there was anything wrong with the music I listened to! I don't want to do anything that will separate me from You. No record (or group) is worth jeopardizing my relationship with You! I will destroy all my records which contain questionable lyrics or covers! I won't be guilty of financially supporting the tools of Satan's trade! I will go to a church that teaches the entire Bible. I will study my Bible to learn what You have to say for my life! I believe You love me and want what's best for me. Thank You for opening my eyes about the music of today! In Jesus' name, I pray. AMEN!

# RUNAWAY KIDS

**A NEW WAVE OF PROSTITUTION BY TEENAGERS AND YOUNG CHILDREN HAS INVADED MOST LARGE CITIES AND SMALL TOWNS, ACROSS THE WORLD!** Many of these kids are the products of broken homes and brutality. Many are children of alcoholic or drug addicted parents. So they run away. And, with no other means of survival . . . they offer their bodies. They are beaten by pimps to bring them into total subjection and to rid them of their last trace of self-esteem. They live in fear when they think of any attempt to escape the racket! *"All we like sheep have gone astray; we have turned every one to his own way; and the Lord hath laid on him* (self) *the iniquity of us all* (when Jesus was crucified on the cross to pay the penalty for our sins)." Now we can repent and receive forgiveness for our sins. We are entitled to spend eternity with Him, if we obey His commandments! **Isaiah 53:6**

**MANY KIDS ARE BROUGHT TO CUSTOMERS NAKED AND EXHIBITED LIKE LIVESTOCK!** Rings of girls and boys as young as 12 years of age are working! Some earn as much as $200 nightly for their pimps. **In Los Angeles and Houston the police estimate that over 3,000 kids are engaged in prostitution, as a result of running away from home!** The average age of runaway kids is 15!

**The Mafia has lucrative interests in crime, drugs, loan-sharks, topless and bottomless bars, prostitution, quick turnover hotels, massage parlors, and child pornography.** Pimps recruit girls and boys, from all over the world, and then move them from one area to another to stay ahead of the police. Many are moved to New York, which has become a magnet for runaways, and are then forced to turn 5-6 "tricks" each night.

**Pimps buy these kids a meal and then take them to an apartment. They make the kids work the streets and teach them to steal from their customers. They plant them in front of luxury hotels. When they try to leave their pimp they usually get their jaw broken!** Many kids try to kill themselves and only a few are ever able to escape! Before this happens, they have usually provided their pimp with thousands of dollars in just a few short weeks! Many pimps won't let the kids go to bed until they have brought in at least $150 a day. Most are beaten up so badly that they end up in hospitals. Then they are thrown back on the streets. Many suffer still more abuse from their perverted customers who practice "kinky" sex on them! Upon any attempt to escape, many are held prisoner or maimed with broken bottles.

**Many police departments are cracking down on "pimps" and "Johns"! They are charging them with felony crimes of "soliciting for a juvenile prostitute" and for transporting across state lines for immoral purposes!** There are no simple answers for these kids who desperately need care and counselling. The penalty for those adults who exploit kids for sexual pleasure is not uniformly enforced, nor severe enough to slow them down!

*"For the Son of man* (Jesus) *is come to save that which was lost . . . if a man have an hundred sheep, and one of them be gone astray, doth he not leave the ninety and nine, and goeth into the mountains, and seeketh that which is gone astray? And if so be that he find it, verily I say unto you, he rejoiceth more of that sheep, than of the ninety and nine which went not astray. Even so it is not the will of your Father which is in heaven, that one of these little ones should perish."* **Matthew 18:11-14**

# Do You Know Where You're Going?

(Continued)

# MAKING IT AS A DROPOUT

**JESUS SAID:** *"The thief (Satan) cometh not (to planet earth), but for to steal, and to kill, and to destroy: I am come that they might have life, and that they might have it more abundantly. I am the good shepherd: the good shepherd giveth his life for the sheep."* **John 10:10-11**

**Many parents know what their kids are doing and their greatest fear is that their child will be arrested and their name will end up in the newspaper!**

**TO THE PARENTS OF A RUNAWAY CHILD:** It seems the best thing to do would be to make every effort to find your child. Keep on keeping on! And if you are fortunate enough to find him, sit down and ask him what was on his mind. Tell him over and over again that you love him and God loves him! Find out what was troubling him. After you've talked, try to change the things he didn't like! Compromise! Let him know that he is special in your eyes and in God's! Let him know that he'll never again be hungry, cold or naked! Let him know he'll never have to steal, lie, or feel helpless, again! Let him know that he is not a bum but a child who can be forgiven! Let him know he will never need to feel pain and humiliation again with God's help! Dry his tears and he'll dry yours! Never stop praying for God's help!

**HOW CAN WE ALL HELP?** There are shelters for runaways financed by governmental and private sources which provide temporary housing and food to homeless children. You can get in touch with those in your community through the National Runaway Hotline (1-800-231-6946) or the National Runaway Switchboard (1-800-621-4000). Or write the National Youth Work Alliance, Dept 9. 1346 Connecticut Ave. N.W., Washington D.C. 20036

**These precious runaway kids wander the streets and sleep in fleabag hotels!** For many of them donut shops are the only place they have to go to stay out of view from the police. Some of these same kids could be from your neighborhood or mine! Many of them, as young as 10 years old, can't go home because dad drinks and beats on them! **Most parents never discussed the Biblical rules on sex, at home, before they ran away!** Many kids drink before they have sex so they can escape reality! Many turn to mud wrestling and after each match they are auctioned off to the highest bidder. These kids feel they have no choices, no identity, and nobody tries to help them! Police cars cruise by and so do pimp cars, both looking for kids to pick up! Such a waste of precious children . . . God have mercy on our generation!

**Up to 1 million children in the U.S. run away from home each year, according to the Federal Health and Human Services Administration! More than ½ of the runaways are girls who were victims of child abuse, incest or rape! THE MAJORITY ARE NEVER REPORTED AS MISSING BY THEIR PARENTS, according to social workers!** The men who have sex with these children are mostly middle-class, married, and with children at home about the same age as the children they violate! They rarely get arrested. The children are lonely, hungry, cold, homeless, weak and defenseless. And for them, it's a "do or die" situation! Some youngsters run away from home merely for adventure or because they hate school. Then, after they are raped, while hitch-hiking, they become too frightened to tell anyone. So they continue on in their desperate search for drugs, food, and an aching need to belong somewhere, to somebody! These poor kids sleep in bus depots, parks, abandoned cars and empty houses. They are shy and suspicious. They often have bruised faces and cuts. Most can never go home again because they were kicked out. For most kids, the desire to run away stemmed from their parents' divorce or the death of one parent. Many young girls run away when they get pregnant and are forced to abort their baby or be sent away to a reformatory. **What a vicious trap Satan has set for these once innocent children! Don't you hate him? . . . I do!**

### PRAYER

Dear God, please forgive our nation for not bringing up all children in the nurture and admonition of the Lord. God, I know that not a single sparrow falls to the ground but what You see and care about it! I know that You love all the runaway children. Please comfort them as they turn to You for help. I know it saddens You for parents to mistreat their children and cause them to runaway! I know it saddens You when these children are violated and mistreated! I know that You stand at the door of every heart just waiting for parents, children, and offenders to repent and seek Your help and guidance. Forgive us, Lord, for not doing our best in our schools, neighborhoods, and churches to teach the world about Your precious love for us all! I know that Jesus died on the cross so that we could receive salvation when we humble ourselves and repent of our sins. I thank You for that! Please help all the parents who are grieving over their runaway children and the children who feel they can never go home! Help us all. In Jesus' precious name, I pray. AMEN!

# SADIST

**DEFINITION:** The infliction of pain (as upon a love object) as a means of obtaining sexual release; delight in excessive cruelty.

**THE SADIST IS A PHYSICAL ABUSER!** He takes out his frustrations violently, and only on weaker people. His victims are usually women and children.

**THE SADIST IS PUBLIC ENEMY #1!** You wouldn't know by looking at him that he's a wife beater. He looks like a regular guy. He appears quiet and contained. He may reek of traits you would admire.

**HE USUALLY HITS WHERE IT DOESN'T SHOW AND WHEN NO ONE CAN SEE HIM!** He socks you, twists arms, pulls hair, locks you in the closet. He works behind closed doors. Only his victims know his secret. He may offer extravagant apologies or threaten you with further abuse if he thinks you will tell! *"And whosoever shall offend one of these little ones that believe in me* (Christ), *it is better for him that a millstone were hanged about his neck, and he were cast into the sea."* **Mark 9:42/Matthew 18:6/Luke 17:2**

**THE SADIST HAS A THEORY THAT IF HE IS "MORE OF A MAN" IT WILL MAKE YOU "MORE OF A WOMAN"!** He is a pervert! He doesn't think of women as something he could possibly like. A woman, to him, is something you use for sex and as a servant!

**IF YOU'RE DATING (OR MARRIED TO) A SADIST . . . PRAY FOR HIM AND TRY TO GET HIM SAVED! BUT, IF HE REFUSES . . . LEAVE HIM AT ANY COST OR YOU COULD GET KILLED! HE HAS A DEMON SPIRIT AND UNLESS HE GETS DELIVERED THE DEMON WILL TRY EVERYTHING TO KILL YOU!** The sadist doesn't know his own boundaries. Once he starts beating you, he'll go as far as he is physically able. He rarely changes anymore than a leopard changes its spots! The police, battered-wife centers, hot lines, social workers, safe houses are available and all can help! Never threaten to leave him or you may get your jaw broken. If he is not willing to get Christian counselling . . . leave him! *"And these* (un-repenting sadists, for example) *shall go away into everlasting punishment: but the righteous into life eternal* (with Christ)." **Matthew 25:46**

**HELL IS A PLACE OF TORMENT RESERVED FOR PEOPLE WHO DO NOT REPENT OF THEIR SINS AND TURN AWAY FROM THEM!** **Luke 16:28** If the sadist doesn't repent before he dies, he will spend eternity in hell! **Luke 16:23-28/Isaiah 66:22-24/Matthew 8:29/Mark 5:7/Luke 8:28** *"The same shall drink of the wine of the wrath of God, which is poured out without mixture into the cup of his indignation; and he shall be tormented with fire and brimstone in the presence of the holy angels, and in the presence of the Lamb* (Christ). *And the smoke of their torment ascendeth up for ever and ever: and they have no rest day or night. . ."* **Revelation 14:10-11** *"And the devil that deceived them was cast into the lake of fire and brimstone, where the beast* (Satan) *and the false prophet are, and shall be tormented day and night for ever and ever."* **Revelation 20:10**

**JESUS COMMANDS US TO LOVE ONE ANOTHER!** *"These things I command you, that ye love one another."* **John 15:17** *"Herein is love, not that we loved God, but that he loved us, and sent his Son* (Jesus) *to be the propitiation for our sins. Beloved, if God so loved us, we ought also to love one another."* **1 John 4:10-11**

**WHERE THERE IS FEAR — THERE IS TORMENT . . . BUT THERE IS NO FEAR IN PERFECT LOVE!** *"There is no fear in love; but perfect love casteth out fear: because fear hath torment. He that feareth is not made perfect in love. We love him because he first loved us. If a man say, I love God, and hateth his brother* (anyone), *he is a liar: for he that loveth not his brother whom he hath seen, how can he love God whom he hath not seen? And this commandment have we from him, That he who loveth God love his brother* (anyone) *also."* **1 John 4:18-21**

**IF YOU ARE THE VICTIM OF TORMENT AND TORTURE BY A SADIST:** First, you must repent of your own sins and become a born-again Christian! Then, you will be able to exercise the authority, which Jesus gives you, to ward off the evil powers of Satan in the sadist's life! **JESUS SAID:** *"Verily I say unto you, whatsoever ye shall bind on earth shall be bound in heaven: and whatsoever ye shall loose on earth shall be loosed in heaven."* **Matthew 18:18** *"Behold I give you power to tread on serpents and scorpions, and over all the power of the enemy, and nothing shall by any means hurt you."* **Luke 10:19**

**NEVER FORGET THAT GOD LOVES THE SADIST . . . BUT HATES HIS SIN! GOD WANTS TO SAVE HIM AND MAKE HIM A NEW PERSON!** *"For God so loved the world that he gave his only begotten Son* (Jesus), *that whosoever believeth in him should not perish, but have everlasting life* (with God)." **John 3:16**

### PRAYER

Dear God, please forgive me for all my sins. **I am a sadist. I am guilty of inflicting pain on others!** Please forgive me. I am truly sorry for what I have done! Never again will I be guilty of hurting or abusing anyone! I don't want to go to hell. I want to live to be with Jesus, through all eternity! Please believe me and accept my forgiveness. I turn away from all sin. Teach me to love others as You love me. In Jesus' name, I pray. AMEN!

# SADO-MASOCHIST

**DEFINITION:** The derivation of pleasure from the infliction of physical or mental pain either on others or on oneself.

**THE SADO-MASOCHIST WANTS TO BE WHIPPED AND ABUSED!** He will pay whatever it costs to be flogged with whips, chains, etc. He is perverted and bound by Satan. Therefore it takes this kind of stimulation and pain for him to become sexually aroused! God calls Satan a thief and a destroyer. *"The thief* (Satan) *cometh not, but for to steal, and to kill, and to destroy: I* (Christ) *am come that they might have ife, and that they might have it more abundantly."* **John 10:10**

**DUNGEONS FULL OF RACKS, CAGES, WHIPPING POSTS, SHACKLES, AND WOOD CROSSES (FOR SPREAD-EAGLE CLIENTS) ARE CROPPING UP IN MAJOR CITIES ACROSS THE U.S.!** Masochists need pain. They thrive on it. They may be judges, doctors, and executives who want to be bound, gagged, stretched, beaten and understood. They are not God fearing people or they would be free from this satanic oppression! They thrive on fantasies. Their "trip" is mental! They love bruises and welts! Their so-called "therapists" claim to provide mental relief to their clients. They too are perverted because they refer to themselves as social workers! *"And even as they did not like to retain God in their knowledge, God gave them over to a reprobate mind, to do those things which are not convenient* (natural); (who) *being filled with all unrighteousness, fornication, wickedness, covetousness, maliciousness; full of envy, murder, debate, deceit, malignity; whisperers, backbiters, haters of God, despiteful, proud, boasters, inventors of evil things* (sado-masochistic devices, treatment), *disobedient to parents, without understanding, covenantbreakers, without natural affection* (homosexuals, lesbians, sadists, sado-masochists, sex with animals, etc.), *implacable, unmerciful: Who knowing the judgment of God, that they which commit such things are worthy of death, not only do the same, but have pleasure in them that do them."* **Romans 1:28-32**

**SOME ROCK GROUPS PROMOTE SADO-MASOCHISM MESSAGES IN THEIR SONGS!** Fashion photographers consider it to be high chic to handcuff mannequins and decorate them with black garter-belts, etc.! Blindfolds, harnesses, ankle and wrist restraints are in demand in large city boutiques.

**SOME SADO-MASOCHIST HOUSES PROVIDE PROSTITUTES (AS WELL AS ABUSE) AROUND THE COUNTRY!** In Dallas, almost all of the city's nude modeling studios have installed sado-masochist rooms and offer stomping and whomping. The bored are looking for new taboos to break and new ways to shock the sexually square. They are all under bondage to Satan! They say, "If it pleases us, where is the harm?" How can they possibly think that all this bashing and thrashing is affection? It's sad, but true, that many couples try spanking each other as a part of sexual foreplay. They are neurotic! *". . .be ye all of one mind, having compassion one of another, love as brethren* (Christians), *be pitiful, be courteous: not rendering evil for evil, or railing for railing: but contrariwise blessing; knowing that ye are thereunto called, that ye should inherit a blessing. For he that will love life, and see good days, let him refrain his tongue from evil, and his lips that they speak no guile. Let him eschew* (put off) *evil, and do good; let him seek peace, and ensue it. For the eyes of the Lord are over the righteous, and his ears are open unto their prayers: but the face of the Lord is against them that do evil. And who is he that will harm you, if ye be followers of that which is good?"* **1 Peter 3:8-13**

**GOD IS ANGERED WITH ANYONE WHO HITS OR ABUSES ANOTHER PERSON!** *"Cursed be he that smiteth* (hits, beats-up) *his neighbour* (anyone) *secretly."* **Deuteronomy 27:24**
**SADO-MASOCHISM IS A FORM OF IDOLATRY AND RITUAL!** Satan is the inventor of all idol practices. Sado-masochism is predominantly an activity for males. Women mostly do so to humor a husband or boyfriend. Homosexuals often engage in sado-masochism. *"The heart is deceitful above all things, and desperately wicked: who can know it?"* **Jeremiah 17:9**

*"For it is a shame even to speak of those things which are done of them in secret."* **Ephesians 5:12**

**COUPLES WHO DABBLE IN SADO-MASOCHISM EXPRESS RESENTMENTS AND ANGER — UNDER THE GUISE OF A FANTASY OR GAME!** Satan has twisted their minds until they find sex boring or impossible without pain or humiliation! Many secular psychiatrists think resistance, tension or problems between partners always enhances sex. They are wrong! They need to get saved and read their Bible! Meek perverted men pretend to be Tarzan and the power broker and politician often request bondage, humiliation, and pain, once they are away from their office! Satan has really done a number on them! God said that when a person hits, mistreats, abuses or offends another person, it would be better for him if a millstone were hung around his neck and he was thrown in a sea to drown. **Matthew 18:5-7/Mark 9:42/Luke 17:1**

**GOD SAID LOVE SHOULD BE NATURAL — NOT ARTIFICIAL!** *"Let love be without dissimulation* (artificial). *Abhor* (hate) *that which is evil; cleave* (hang-on) *to that which is good. Be kindly affectioned one to another with brotherly love; in honour preferring one another; not slothful* (lazy) *in business; fervent* (energetic) *in spirit; serving the Lord; rejoicing in hope; patient in tribulation* (troubles); *continuing instant in prayer."* **Romans 12:9-12**

**PRAYER**

Dear God, Please forgive me for all my sins. I want to change my life. I want to become a born-again Christian. Forgive me, Lord, for being perverted. I realize I have been under bondage from Satan. Help me clean up my life. I will change my image and heart, with Your help! I will not go to the places were I have done this terrible thing. I will read my Bible and pray each day. Create in me a new person and I will thank You for ever! In Jesus' name, I pray. AMEN!

# SATAN

**WHERE DID SATAN COME FROM?** Satan was created by Christ along with other beings, principalities and powers in heaven and earth. **Job 38:4-7/Ezekiel 28:11-17/Colossians 1:15-18**
**HE WAS ORIGINALLY NAMED LUCIFER!** Isaiah **14:12-14/Jeremiah 4:23-26/Ezekiel 28:11-17/Luke 10:18** Lucifer had a kingdom on earth long before the 6 days of Genesis 1:3-30 and the creation of Adam! These verses reveal that he led an invasion into heaven and was defeated. Because of this the earth was cursed, and all life destroyed by the first flood. **Genesis 1:2** Satan regained rulership over the earth in Adam's day, usurping man's dominion by causing his fall. His relationship to man through the ages has been that of a usurper. And, as long as man tolerates Satan's dictatorship, that long will he remain subject to Satan! Each person can, by the power of the gospel, defeat Satan and rid himself of all demon relationship! This is what God demands and He has provided the means whereby it can be attained **Mark 16:17-18/Luke 10:19/24:49/Acts 1:8/Ephesians 6:10-18/James 4:7/1 Peter 5:8-9.** Satan's present position as ruler of this world's system, and as the prince of this world, will be ended forever when Christ comes **Revelation 19-20** and man will again inherit the earth and live in it forever.

In the beginning, God made intelligent creatures free moral agents **Genesis 1:26-27.** Satan, however, entertained selfish thoughts and brought sin upon this earth **James 1:14-15.** Because of Adam's sin, physical death was brought to all offspring **Romans 5:12.**

**GOD FORBIDS SPIRITISM BECAUSE IT IS A WORK OF SATAN AND HIS DEMONS** Isaiah 8:19-20/Leviticus 19:31/20:6, 27/Deuteronomy 18:10-12. Spiritism leads to destruction, **Galatians 5:19-21/Revelation 21:8/22:15/18:23.** Fortune telling is demonic and controlled by Satan, **Acts 16:16-18/1 Samuel 28:3. God forbids astrology** because it ensnares a person and is authored by Satan, **Jeremiah 10:2.**
**SATAN WAS JEALOUS OF GOD AND THIS CAUSED HIS OVERTHROW!** Through pride over his own beauty, **Ezekiel 28:11-17/1 Timothy 3:6** and trying to exalt himself above God, **Isaiah 14:12-14.**

**SATAN IS VERY MUCH ALIVE AND WORKING DAILY TO OPPOSE GOD WHENEVER POSSIBLE!** He is the deceiver of all men, **2 Corinthians 11:14/Revelation 12:9/20:1-10.** He is the leader of all sinners and backsliders, **1 John 3:8-10/1 Timothy 5:15** and all spirit rebels, **Matthew 9:34/Ephesians 6:10-18.** He causes all sickness, disease, physical, and mental maladies in the human race, **Luke 13:16/Acts 10:38.** He takes advantage of all adversities of men to further their rebellion and to hold them captive, **2 Corinthians 2:11/1 Timothy 1:20/5:11-15.** He tempts men, **Mark 1:13/1 Corinthians 7:5.** He provokes people to sin, **1 Chronicles 21:1.** He causes offense, **Matthew 16:23.** He transforms himself into an angel of light, **2 Corinthians 11:14.** He resists others, **Zechariah 3:1-2.** He enters into union with people against God, **Luke 22:3/John 13:2.** He sends demon messengers to defeat Christians, **2 Corinthians 12:7/1 Thessalonians 2:18.** He hinders the gospel, **Acts 13:10.** He steals the Word of God from men lest they should believe it, **Matthew 13:19/Luke 8:12.** He works fake miracles, **2 Thessalonians 2:9.** He contends with messengers of God, endeavoring to hold them captive, **Daniel 10:12-21/Jude 9.** He hinders answers to our prayers, **Daniel 10:12-21.** He sets snares for men to fall into sin, **1 Timothy 3:7/2 Timothy 2:26.** He causes diversion and blinds men to the gospel, **2 Corinthians 4:4.** He causes double-mindedness, **James 1:5-9.** He causes doubt and unbelief, **Genesis 3:4-5/Romans 14:23.** He causes darkness and oppression, **2 Corinthians 4:4/2 Peter 1:4-9.** He causes delay and compromise, **Acts 24:25/26:28.** He causes divisions and strife, **1 Corinthians 3:1-3/1 Peter 5:8.** He makes war on the saints, **Ephesians 6:10-18.**

Satan

**SATAN'S PRIMARY CHALLENGE TODAY IS TO COUNTERFEIT THE DOCTRINES OF GOD IN ORDER TO DECEIVE CHRISTIANS!** 2 Corinthians 11:14-15/Ephesians 6:10-18/1 Timothy 4:1-7/Revelation 12:9-12. God commands men to prove and test all doctrines and experiences in the supernatural realm to see if they are of God or of Satan, **1 Corinthians 2:12-16/Philippians 1:9-10/1 Thessalonians 5:21-22/1 John 4:1-6.** It is certain that not every religion, doctrine, and experience among men comes from God! We must therefore judge them by the true written Word of God. The knowledge of truth is the first essential in warfare against demons and error. **Great is the danger when believers accept anything and everything, in the realm of the supernatural, as being from God!** The fact that the believer is a child of God does not stop Satan from trying in every conceivable way to imitate God to him! Believers are the primary ones Satan concentrates on and wars against! There are definite ways outlined in Scripture whereby one can detect what kind of spirit is seeking to control him. But if one neglects to study the Word of God, he may fall prey to Satan or his demons, through his own ignorance! Ignorance is no guarantee against workings of evil spirits. In fact, this is one of the chief means by which Satan and his forces try to control men! It accounts for Satan's widespread success in getting men to accept his suggestions, doctrines, ideas and guidance.

**AMONG THE GUIDING PRINCIPLES USEFUL IN DETECTING GOOD AND EVIL SPIRITS, THEIR OPERATIONS AND DOCTRINES, THE OUTSTANDING ONES ARE THESE: 1.** Any **doctrine** that denies or causes doubt and unbelief concerning anything taught in Scripture, is from Satan and his demons, **1 Timothy 4:1-8. 2.** Any **religion** denying the inspiration of the Bible; the **reality of God** as a person; the **virgin birth and divinity of Christ:** His miraculous power and supernatural ministry; the **death, burial, bodily resurrection,** and bodily manifestation of Christ **after** His resurrection; the bodily **ascension to heaven and coming again of Jesus Christ** to set up a kingdom in the world forever; **the necessity of the new birth;** cleansing from sin and living free from sin; and any religion denying these fundamental truths is yielding to the "spirit of error" and not to "the

219

(Continued)

spirit of truth'', **1 John 4:1-6. 3.** Any power, influence, or doctrine that causes one to become passive, inactive, submissive, and unresisting to the workings of supernatural spirits, seeking to control his life, is contrary to the teachings of Scripture and is not of God! The Bible says, *''Resist the devil.''* **James 4:7/1 Peter 5:8-10!** Any inclination to **approve of sin,** and to **ignore** the necessity of repentance and holy living, or doubt that **hell is literal and eternal,** is promoted by Satan! **Just as God requires the true working of the Holy Spirit in a life . . . the devil plants lies in the minds of men to hold them in bondage, 1 Corinthians 6:9-11/10:12-13/2 Corinthians 11:3-15/Galatians 5:19-21/6:7-8/Ephesians 6:10-18/1 Timothy 4:1-9/James 1:22/2:10. 4.** The Holy Spirit can be recognized by the fruits of the Spirit, which are love, joy, peace, long suffering, gentleness, goodness, faith, meekness, temperance, **Galatians 5:22-23.**

### THE NATURE AND PERSONALITY OF SATAN:

He is the **enemy and accuser** of God and man, **Revelation 12:9-12/Ezekiel 28:11-17.** He is the **father of lies, John 8:44.** A **murderer, John 8:44.** A **sower of discord, Matthew 13:39.** The **adversary, 1 Peter 5:8-9.** The **first sinner, the first rebel,** and the first to consecrate himself to self-gratification and to wage war against all society, **Isaiah 14:12-14/Ezekiel 28:11-17/Revelation 12:9/20:7-10.** He is **cunning, 2 Corinthians 2:11/11:14/Ephesians 6:11-12.** Wicked, **Matthew 13:18, 38/John 8:44/1 John 3:8/5:18.** Malignant, **Luke 8:12/2 Corinthians 4:4/1 Peter 5:8-9.** Cowardly, **James 4:7.** A tempter, **Matthew 4:1-11.** A thief, **John 10:10. Without principle** in taking advantage of men in their weak moments, **Matthew 4:1-11/Luke 22:40/2 Corinthians 2:11/11:3** in tempting men after great success, **John 6:15;** in suggesting the use of right things in a wrong way and at a wrong time, **Matthew 4:1-11; in slandering God** to man — and man to God, **Genesis 3:1-10/Job 1:6-12/2:1-7. In appearing as an angel of light** (truth) to deceive, **2 Corinthians 11:14.** In deluding his followers as to their eternal end, **2 Thessalonians 2:8-12/Revelation 12:9/20:7-10.** He is **presumptuous, Job 1:6-12/2:1-7. Proud, Ezekiel 28:17/1 Timothy 3:6. Deceitful, 2 Corinthians 11:14/Revelation 12:9/20:10. Fierce and cruel, Luke 8:29/9:39/1 Peter 5:8-9. Aggressive, Ephesians 4:27/6:10-18/1 Peter 5:8-9.** Satan has never been known to be merciful, good, loving, kind, gentle, pitiful, patient, or to have any of the graces of God — since he became the enemy of God and man! He is compared to a **FOWLER, Psalm 91:3. FOWLS, Matthew 13:4, 19. A WOLF, John 10:12. A DESTROYER, John 10:10. A ROARING LION, 1 Peter 5:8-9, A SERPENT, Revelation 12:9/20:3. A DRAGON, Revelation 12:3-12.**

### WHY DOES GOD ALLOW SATAN TO CONTINUE?

To develop **character and faith in the believer, James 1:12/1 Peter 1:7-13/5:8-9/2 Peter 1:4-9/Jude 20:24.** To keep the believer **humble, 2 Corinthians 12:7.** To provide a **conflict** for saints that they may be rewarded through overcoming, **1 John 2:13/4:1-6/Revelation 2:7, 11, 17, 26-28/3:5, 12, 21. To demonstrate the power of God over the power of Satan, Mark 16:17-20/1 Corinthians 4:9/Ephesians 2:7/3:10.** To use him in afflicting people to bring them to repentance, **1 Corinthians 5:1-6/2 Corinthians 2:5-11/Job 33:14-20.** To purge man of all possibility of falling in the eternal future, **Revelation 21.**

### WILL SATAN EVER BE DESTROYED?

It is predicted in Genesis 3:15, and accomplished at the first advent, **John 19:30/Colossians 2:14-17.** And at the second advent, **Revelation 20:1-3.** And at the battle of Gog and Magog, **Revelation 20:7-10.** The purpose of the 1000 year reign of Christ after the second advent (return of Christ to planet earth) will be to suppress all rebellion, **1 Corinthians 15:24-28.** The final defeat of Satan, and his hosts, at the end of that period (called the Millennium) must be accomplished before the earth is entirely rid of rebels. They must be confined to the **lake of fire** forever before rebellion is finally and eternally overcome. The earth will be purified by fire and made perfect for the third time. At last the kingdom of God will be as it was before rebellion was started by Satan and Adam in their respective kingdoms.

### METHODS SATAN USES:

He uses every conceivable means to hold men in subjection to himself and to keep them from turning to God. If he fails in this, he **tries to kill** the believer's testimony and ruin his influence for God. **If one falls, Satan tries to make him stay fallen or commit suicide.** He endeavors to cause men to end their lives by insisting it is the best way out. Satan hides the true fact that this will be only the beginning of real torment in eternal hell. Satan tries to get others in a **lukewarm condition.** And, if he succeeds, he urges them to stay in that condition so that God will cut them off in the end! He dares people to do many things they would not do under ordinary circumstances! And some are foolish enough to think they are not brave if they do not accept his dares! **He makes people think they are missing everything in life if they do not go into all kinds of sins, which in the end will damn their souls!** He emphasizes sin and sinful pleasures as innocent enjoyment. He stirs unholy passions in men and women, causing them to throw away all restraint and live a life of revelry. **He tries to make people think there is no joy in serving the Lord.** This is one of his greatest errors!! **Serving God, and winning souls to Christ, pays the greatest dividends and affords the greatest pleasures known to mankind!** Satan preaches to the diligent in business that he needs to take all his time to get rich before serving the Lord. The fact is that if one will truly serve the Lord, he can be abundantly prosperous, with God's help! He urges churches, and their leaders, to make religion a paying proposition by appealing to the rich and influential through lowering the standards of holy living, making salvation easy for all. He compromises the essentials of faith. He feeds the people messages on current events or book reviews, instead of the infallible Word of God!

# SATAN

### MORE FACTS ABOUT WHO SATAN IS:

He is a person whose personal acts and plans are to oppose God through every attempt to destroy mankind, **Job 1:6-12/2:1-8!** He **roams the earth** from one end to the other, **Job 1:7/2:2/1 Peter 5:8.** He has access to heaven, **Job 1:1/2:1/Revelation 12:9-12. He is responsible for temptations to man, Matthew 4:3. He is the accuser of all Christians, Job 1:9-11. He is the author of sickness and disease, Job 2:7/7:5, 13/16:8/19:17/Acts 10:38. He goes from place to place, Job 1:6-7/2:1-2. He associates with angels, Job 1:6/2:1. He appears before God, Job 1:6/2:1. He carries on conversations with God, Job 1:7-12/2:2-6. He singles out individuals hoping to destroy them, Job 1:8, 12/2:4-6. He hates good men, Job 1:8-12/2:3-6. He envies the blessing of God on others, Job 1:10/2:4-5. He seeks to destroy the fellowship between God and His children, Job 1:10-11/2:4-6. He seeks to destroy men to curse God and deny Him, Job 1:11/2:5. He is limited by God in touching His children, Job 1:12/2:6. He can destroy riches of men, Job 1:12-19. He destroys to the limit of his ability through God's permission, Job 1:12-19/2:6-10. He has many agents on earth who do his bidding, Job 1:15, 17. He can send fire down from heaven, Job 1:16. He can control the elements and cause storms when God permits, Job 1:18-19. He never gets tired of efforts to destroy good men, Job 2:1-8. All world distress is caused by Satan, Revelation 12:12/2 Corinthians 4:4/1 Peter 5:8. His ruling power causes all our troubles, Proverbs 29:2/28:28. He is the enemy of God, 2 Corinthians 4:4/1 John 5:19/John 12:31. SATAN'S TIME IS RUNNING OUT, Revelation 12:9, 12/16:14, 16. Soon Satan will be bound and endless peace will follow, Revelation 20:1-3/21:3-4/Isaiah 14:15-18.** Christ foretold the evil conditions that would be brought about because of Satan, **Luke 21:7, 10-11/21:25-26/Matthew 24:3, 7-8, 29. Satan challenges the loyalty of all creatures to God, Job 1:11-12,** and the faithful are given an opportunity to prove loyal, **Romans 9:17/Proverbs 27:11. Satan is a proven liar, John 12:40/Nahum 1:11,** and the faithful are rewarded with everlasting life, **Romans 2:6-7/Revelation 21:3-5/John 3:16. SATAN EVEN TEMPTED JESUS! Matthew 4:1-11/Mark 1:12-13/Luke 4:1-13.**

(Continued)

## SATAN IS CALLED:

THE TEMPTER, 1 Thessalonians 3:5/Mark 1:13/1 Corinthians 7:5/2 Corinthians 2:11/11:14. LUCIFER, Isaiah 14:12-14. THE CREATURE, Romans 1:25. THE WICKED ONE, Matthew 13:19/1 John 5:18. THE SON OF PERDITION, John 17:12. THE DRAGON, Revelation 12:7-9. THE GOD OF THIS WORLD, 2 Corinthians 4:4. THE SERPENT, Revelation 12:9/20:2/2 Corinthians 11:3. A MURDERER, John 8:44/10:10. THE ANOINTED CHERUB, Ezekiel 28:11-17. A LIAR AND THE FATHER OF LIES, John 8:44. ANGEL OF LIGHT, 2 Corinthians 11:14. A THIEF, John 10:10. PRINCE OF DEVILS, Matthew 12:24. A DESTROYER, John 10:10. PRINCE OF THIS WORLD, John 12:31. KING OVER ALL THE CHILDREN OF PRIDE, Job 41:34. PRINCE OF THE POWER OF THE AIR, Ephesians 2:1-3. THE ENEMY, Matthew 13:13/Luke 10:19. ACCUSER OF THE BRETHREN, Job 1:6-13/2:1-7/Revelation 12:10. LEVIATHIN, Job 41:1/Isaiah 27:1. BEELZEBUB, Matthew 10:25/12:24. DECEIVER OF THE WHOLE WORLD, Revelation 12:9. A ROARING LION, 1 Peter 5:8. A WOLF, John 10:12.

## A CHRISTIAN'S PROTECTION FROM THE EVIL POWERS OF SATAN:

When one is "born again" he enters the realm of the supernatural and spiritual. He should begin to study the Bible to see what it teaches, regarding how he should walk and conduct himself in spiritual warfare with Satan and demons! Christians are commanded to put on the whole armour of God, Ephesians 6:11-18. To know Satan's devices, 2 Corinthians 2:11. To give him no place in their lives, Ephesians 4:27. To resist him, James 4:7/1 Peter 5:8-9. To be sober and vigilant lest he devour them, 1 Peter 5:8-10. To overcome him by the blood of Christ, Revelation 12:11. To overcome him by Christ and His name, Ephesians 1:19-22/2:6/2 Corinthians 2;15. To overcome him by birth of the Spirit and faith, 1 John 2:29/3:9/5:1-4, 18. To overcome him by the Holy Spirit, Romans 8:1-13/Galatians 5:15-26.

## CAN SATAN AND HIS DEMONS READ YOUR MIND?

A person must think evil before he commits evil. A thought is the father to the deed. How can Satan tempt anyone without first knowing what is going on in his mind? Temptation begins in the mind and the Bible describes Satan as **"THE TEMPTER"** Matthew 4:3/1 Thessalonians 3:5. *"Every man is tempted when he is drawn away of his lusts and enticed."* **James 1:14**

**OUR MIND IS A BATTLEFIELD!** If Satan is able to enter our body and heart, what would stop him from entering our mind? He is a spirit that roams the earth seeking whom he may devour. God has limited him to the spirit-realm. Our thoughts are spirit! No one can see a thought. Our thoughts are where the Holy Spirit works, also! The difference is that the Holy Spirit works to stir us to do what is right and Godly. **Satan is an unholy spirit!** He works long and hard to get us to do evil. Paul describes the contest between Satan and the Holy Spirit as a **WAR. Romans 7:23 says:** *". . .I see . . . another law in my members* (body parts), *WARRING against the law of my mind, and bringing me into the captivity to the law of sin which is in my members* (body parts)." **YES, THERE ARE TWO GREAT POWERS WARRING IN OUR THOUGHT LIFE!** Each strives to change our life. While Satan appeals to our flesh, the Holy Spirit encourages us to come close to God! All this battle takes place in our mind!

**NEVER FORGET THAT SATAN (AND HIS DEMONS) ARE AS REAL AS GOD! SATAN HATES YOU AND WILL DESTROY YOU IF YOU LET HIM!** God could have easily destroyed Satan in the beginning but he chose instead to use him to bring us to a mature dependency on God our Father. Satan is a tool that God uses. The Bible calls him **"THE PRINCE OF THE POWER OF THE AIR"** because he operates in the spirit realm, **Ephesians 2:2.** Satan only has one nature and personality, and it is to destroy! He has no mercy! He knows his time is running out.

Therefore, he works 24 hours a day to wreck, ruin, and kill people! There's no stopping him until a person chooses of his own free will to turn his life over to God and take authority over Satan. **Christians are to resist Satan, James 4:7.** We are to **FIGHT** him with the spiritual weapons God gives to born-again Christians. **Ephesians 6:12-17/2 Corinthians 10:4** *"When any one heareth the word of the kingdom, and understandeth it not, then cometh **the wicked one**, and catcheth away that which was sown in his heart. . ."* **Matthew 13:19**

**JESUS TOLD US TO SOW GOD'S WORD IN OUR HEARTS!** That means that when a person doesn't understand the Word of God Satan snatches it away from his mind. It's important to pray and read the Bible every day to learn how you can overcome Satan and take hold of the true power that God gives you to use with all authority against him! Now, if Satan couldn't read a person's mind, how could he know whether a person understood the Word of God, or not? He must know a person's thoughts, reasonings and feelings. Is it possible that our entire thought process is open to the devil's eyes? If the Holy Spirit is able to discern between the thoughts and intentions of our heart, then the great imposter (Satan) must be able to do the same thing, Hebrews 4:12. Man has FREE WILL to choose between these two warring spirits, and that makes his mind a spiritual battlefield!

**IT'S DANGEROUS TO ASSUME THAT SATAN DOESN'T EXIST OR IS POWERLESS!** Jesus said: *"Watch and pray, that ye enter not into temptation: the spirit indeed is willing, but the flesh is weak."* **Matthew 26:41** Jesus said that verse right after He had prayed. He endured a battle in His mind that was so intense it actually caused Him to sweat droplets of blood, **Luke 22:44!** Jesus knew, by experience, how Satan works in a person's thoughts when he prays!

**HAVE YOU EVER NOTICED HOW MANY TIMES YOUR MIND TENDS TO WANDER WHEN YOU PRAY?** You surely don't do this deliberately! This is why Jesus said to "WATCH" even before we pray. Satan tries hard to distract us when we pray! He tries to make our prayers ineffective!

**IF SATAN CAN'T READ OUR MIND — HOW CAN HE KNOW HOW (OR WHEN) TO DROP IN HIS SUGGESTIONS — OR WHAT WILL SPECIFICALLY WORK ON EACH INDIVIDUAL?** He's a master at implanting his ideas while making you think they're your own! His suggestions are always evil! We tend not to give him credit for the awful notions that enter our head when we know we didn't deliberately put them there! Satan is a genius when it comes to making his suggestions flow smoothly with our own thoughts! Many people are deceived and not even suspicious when Satan is influencing them! If Satan can't read our minds, he couldn't influence us! We're free to accept his ideas or reject them. God gave us that free will!

**FEW CHRISTIANS REALIZE THE POWER OF THIS UNSEEN ENEMY!** Many people believe in the power of the Holy Spirit but do not believe in the power of Satan! **Many people simply don't believe that Satan even exists!** Because of this, Satan leads them around by the nose. He will lead you into debt through your craving for material things. He will split up marriages by suggesting faults in each other. He may cause you to over-eat by putting pressure on your appetite. He puts mischief and disobedience in your children's hearts. He will tell you to watch TV programs and movies that are not wholesome! He says you should cheat on your income tax. He says it's okay to argue over Bible doctrines. He causes you to worry till you become ill. He plants unclean thoughts and pictures in your imagination. He encourages anger, temper, bitterness, illicit sex, jealousy, and the list goes on and on!

# SEDUCING SPIRITS

(Continued)

**CHRISTIANS NEED TO LEARN HOW TO RECOGNIZE SATAN'S ATTACKS ON THEM AND HOW TO DEAL WITH THEM!** It is a comfort to know that all the evil things that go on in our minds are NOT a result of our being totally wicked! Satan is the source!! You can't make Satan flee by only reading your Bible and praying. We've already established that Satan uses our prayer time as one of his favorite targets! As a Christian who believes every word of the Bible, you know that God commands you to take authority over Satan and his demons!

**SATAN IS A DEFEATED ENEMY!** Because Christ died on the cross for our sins and was resurrected, we now have the authority, as born-again believers, to overcome him! Aren't you tired of having Satan manipulate your thoughts? Tired of having him interrupt your sleep? You can truly have victory over him . . . HE IS YOUR ENEMY! *". . .I give you power to tread on serpents and scorpions, and over all the power of the enemy: and nothing shall by any means hurt you."* **Luke 10:19**

**ALL OF THIS HAS BEEN THE BAD NEWS . . . NOW FOR THE GOOD NEWS:** Ultimately we know that good WILL triumph over evil! Christ will return to planet earth soon to rule with love and righteousness. When He does, Satan will be destroyed and every evil will be judged. In the meantime, we live in a world full of evil forces . . . but God is busy at work, also! *"For we wrestle not against flesh and blood, but against principalities, against powers, against the rulers of the darkness of this world, against spiritual wickedness in high places."* **Ephesians 6:12.** There are times when it looks as if evil is winning out and good is not being rewarded. We must always take Satan and his demons very seriously! We need to depend on Christ 24 hours a day to supply our needs, while we continue to live a holy life! God guarantees that evil, sickness, and death will be destroyed and we must trust Him to keep His Word! Those of us who belong to Jesus Christ are called to obey Him above all else! We should never repay evil for evil **Romans 12:17, 19.** Read your Bible daily and pray without ceasing! Jesus is coming very soon! *". . .In my name shall they cast out devils. . ."* **Mark 16:17**

## *"Be sober, be vigilant; because your adversary the devil, as a roaring lion, walketh about, seeking whom he may devour."*

## 1 Peter 5:8

### PRAYER

Dear God, please forgive me for all my sins. Forgive me for my complacence in not realizing that Satan does exist. I know it's impossible to read the Bible and believe in You, without believing what You say about Satan! I believed Christ died for my sins so I could receive forgiveness. I believe He is alive today and is coming back. I want to be ready for the soon-to-come rapture. From this moment on, I will rebuke Satan with the authority You have given me, in the name of Jesus! I will not give him any opportunity to invade my thoughts or actions! I will resist him by living a holy life. I hereby take authority over all the powers of darkness. I will not accept anything Satan tries to put in my mind. I will read my Bible and pray daily! I will go to a church that teaches that all are sinners and must be born again, and that Christ is coming soon. I believe that Satan will be cast into the eternal lake of fire and that I will be allowed to spend eternity with You. I repent of all my sins. I turn away from any evil influence in my life. Thank You for setting me straight regarding how evil Satan is, and how loving and forgiving You are! I look forward to the blessings You have in store for my life, now that I have accepted Christ as my Lord and Savior! In Jesus' name, I pray. AMEN!

# SCOFF—SCORN—SWEAR—SLANDER SPITE

**DID YOU KNOW THAT THE INCREASE IN SCOFFING AND SCORNING CHRISTIANS, GOD, THE BIBLE, AND THE SECOND COMING OF CHRIST FULFILLS END TIME BIBLE PROPHECY?** *". . .there shall come in the last days scoffers, walking after their own lusts. . ."* **2 Peter 3:3**

*"A scorner seeketh wisdom, and findeth it not: but knowledge is easy unto him that understandeth."* **Proverbs 14:6**

**JOB WROTE:** *"I am as one mocked of his neighbour, who called upon God, and he answereth him: the just upright man is laughed to scorn."* **Job 12:4**

**BECAUSE THE SINNERS OF THE WORLD HAVE REJECTED, SCOFFED, AND SCORNED GOD . . . DURING THE SOON-TO-COME TRIBULATION PERIOD . . . GOD WILL LAUGH AT THEIR MISERY WHICH THEY BROUGHT UPON THEMSELVES!** *"He that sitteth in the heavens shall laugh: the Lord shall have them in derision."* **Psalm 2:4** *"But thou, O Lord, shalt laugh at them: thou shalt have all the heathen in derision."* **Psalm 59:8**

**WHEN JESUS HEALED A WOMAN WITH AN ISSUE OF BLOOD FOR 12 YEARS AND RESURRECTED A LITTLE GIRL FROM THE DEAD, THE PEOPLE LAUGHED HIM TO SCORN!** Matthew 9:24

*"A scorner loveth not one that reproveth him: neither will he go unto the wise."* **Proverbs 15:12**

*"An ungodly witness scorneth judgment: and the mouth of the wicked devoureth iniquity."* **Proverbs 19:28**

*"Judgments are prepared for scorners, and stripes for the back of fools."* **Proverbs 19:29**

*"How long, ye simple ones, will ye love simplicity? and the scorners delight in their scorning, and fools hate knowledge?"* **Proverbs 1:22**

*"The thought of foolishness is sin: and the scorner is an abomination to men."* **Proverbs 24:9**

*"Cast out the scorner, and contention shall go out; yea, strife and reproach shall cease."* **Proverbs 22:10**

*"If thou be wise, thou shalt be wise for thyself: but if thou scornest, thou alone shalt bear it."* **Proverbs 9:12**

*"When the scorner is punished, the simple is made wise: and when the wise is instructed, he receiveth knowledge."* **Proverbs 21:11**

*"Proud and haughty scorner is his name, who dealeth in proud wrath."* **Proverbs 21:24**

**JESUS SAID:** *". . .Swear not at all; neither by heaven; for it is God's throne: nor by the earth; for it is his footstool; neither by Jerusalem, for it is the city of the great King. Neither shalt thou swear by thy head, because thou canst not make one hair white or black. But let your communications be Yea, yea (yes-yes); Nay, nay (no-no); for whatsoever is more than these (yes or no) cometh of evil."* **Matthew 5:34-37**

**FOUL LANGUAGE WAS TRADITIONALLY USED ONLY BY MALES!** Men invented dirty talk. Today some men, women, boys, and girls **swear** like real troopers. They curse like sailors, and this is sad! The coarser the words the more power a person feels. No one should ever use rough language! In today's society, it has become fashionable to use gutter talk, blue language, dirty words and four-letter words. God have mercy on our generation!!

**NOT ONLY ARE PEOPLE USING MORE AND MORE WORDS TO SWEAR AND SLANDER . . . BUT THEY'RE USING THEM MORE AND MORE FREQUENTLY . . . WHY?** Some people **swear** because they feel less tense, miserable and frustrated after **swearing!** They think it lets off steam. Some **swear** as an act of hostility! They begin many phrases with "you----". **Swearing is a way to vent poisonous feelings, but God said we must never do this!** It's unconstructive and God never approves. **Swearing** is a requirement to show "progress" in a peer pressure situation! Many teenagers feel **swearing** makes them appear macho and very adult. *"But above all things, my brethren, swear not, neither by heaven, neither by the earth, neither by any other oath: but let your yea be yea (yes); and your nay, nay (no); lest you fall into condemnation."* **James 5:12**

*"Even so the tongue is a little member (of our body), and boasteth great things. . ."* **James 3:5** *"And the tongue is a fire, a world of iniquity: so is the tongue among our members, that it defileth the whole body, and setteth on fire the course of nature; and it is set on fire of hell. For every kind of beasts, and of birds, and of serpents, and of things in the sea, is tamed, and hath been tamed of mankind. But the tongue can no man tame; it is an unruly evil, full of deadly poison. Therewith bless we God, even the Father: and therewith curse we men, which are made after the similitude (likeness) of God. Out of the same mouth proceedeth blessing and cursing. My brethren, these things ought not so to be."* **James 3:5-10**

**IF YOU KNOW SOMEONE WHO SWEARS — USES SPITE — OR SLANDERS ANOTHER PERSON . . . PRAY CONSTANTLY FOR HIM . . . HE MAY BE UNDER DEMONIAC OPPRESSION!** God says He will judge every thought, word and action of us all! *"And I will come near to you to judgment; and I will be a swift witness against the sorcerers, and against the adulterers, and against false swearers. . ."* **Malachi 3:5** *"And if a soul sin, and hear the voice of swearing, and is a witness, whether he hath seen or known of it; if he do not utter it, then he shall bear his iniquity."* **Leviticus 5:1** *"Or if a soul swear, pronouncing with his lips to do evil, or to do good, whatsoever it be that a man shall pronounce with an oath, and it be hid from him; when he knoweth of it, then he shall be guilty in one of these. And it shall be, when he shall be guilty in one of these things, that he shall confess that he hath sinned in that thing."* **Leviticus 5:4-5**

**WHEN A PERSON SWEARS — HE USUALLY TELLS LIES!** **Leviticus 6:3-5** *"You must not steal nor lie nor defraud. You must not swear to a falsehood, thus bringing reproach upon the name of your God, for I am Jehovah."* **Leviticus 19:11-12** (The Living Bible)
*"Wherefore, my beloved brethren, let every man be swift to hear; slow to speak, slow to wrath: for the wrath of man worketh not the righteousness of God. Wherefore lay apart (away) all filthiness and superfluity (excessive) of naughtiness, and receive with meekness, the engrafted word (God's Bibical truths), which is able to save your souls."* **James 1:19-21**

**SLANDER IS AN UNMERCIFUL THING TO DO TO ANOTHER PERSON!** Words can truly hurt more than sticks or stones! David wrote: *"For I have heard the slander of many: fear was on every side: while they took counsel together against me, they devised to take away my life."* **Psalm 31:13** *"Whoso privily slandereth his neighbour, him will I cut off (from me): him that hath an high look (is an egotist) and a proud heart will not I suffer (allow)."* **Psalm 101:5** *"He that hideth hatred with lying lips, and he that uttereth a slander, is a fool."* **Proverbs 10:18**

**PRAYER**

Dear God, please forgive me for all my sins. I want to become a Christian. I repent of every unkind thing I have ever thought, said or done! Help me change my image. **Forgive me for swearing and slandering and spiting others!** I am truly sorry. I will not do these things again! Come into my life and heart and live in me. In Jesus' name, I pray. AMEN!

223

# SECRETS

**GOD KNOWS OUR SECRET SINS!** *"Thou (God) hast set our iniquities (wrong doings) before thee, our secret sins in the light (truth) of thy countenance."* **Psalm 90:8**

*"For it is a shame even to speak of those things which are done of them in secret."* **Ephesians 5:12**

**GOD SEES EVERYTHING AND HEARS EVERYTHING!** *"For he looketh to the ends of the earth, and seeth under the whole heaven."* **Job 28:24**

*"For if our heart condemn us, God is greater than our heart, and knoweth all things. Beloved, if our heart condemn us not, then have we confidence toward God."* **1 John 3:20-21**

**GOD WILL JUDGE ALL THE SECRETS OF MEN!** *"In the day when God shall judge the secrets of men by Jesus Christ according to my gospel."* **Romans 2:16**

*"For nothing is secret that shall not be made manifest (known); neither anything hid, that shall not be known and come abroad."* **Luke 8:17** *". . .for he knoweth the secrets of the heart."* **Psalm 44:21**

**NEVER BETRAY A PERSON'S CONFIDENCE BY REVEALING A SECRET HE SHARED ONLY WITH YOU!** *". . .discover not a secret to another lest he that heareth it put thee to shame, and thine infamy (evil reputation) turn (go) not away."* **Proverbs 25:9-10**

**GOD'S SECRET TRUTHS HAVE BEEN REVEALED TO US THROUGH JESUS CHRIST!** *"All these things spake Jesus unto the multitude in parables; and without a parable spake he not unto them: That it might be fulfilled which was spoken by the prophet, saying, I will open my mouth in parables (an earthly story with a heavenly meaning); I will utter things which have been kept secret from the foundation of the world."* **Matthew 13:34-35** *"Now to him that is of power to stablish you according to my gospel, and the preaching of Jesus Christ, according to the revelation of the mystery, which was kept secret since the world began, but now is made manifest (known), and by the scriptures of the prophets, according to the commandment of the everlasting God made known to all nations for the obedience of faith."* **Romans 16:25-26**

**IF YOU HAVE A SECRET, ASK GOD TO REVEAL TO YOU IF IT IS WHAT GOD WOULD WANT YOU TO THINK OR DO!** *"Search me, O God, and know my heart: try me, and know my thoughts: and see if there be any wicked way in me, and lead me in the way everlasting."* **Psalm 139:23-24**

### Revealing a secret

**"There is a way which seemeth right unto a man (person), but the end thereof are the ways of death (eternal separation from God)." Proverbs 14:12**

**GOD DOESN'T BETRAY OUR CONFIDENCE WHEN WE SHARE OUR SECRETS WITH HIM!** *"I love the Lord, because he hath heard my voice and my supplications. Because he hath inclined his ear unto me, therefore will I call upon him as long as I live."* **Psalm 116:1-2**

**IF YOU SHARE YOUR INNERMOST SECRETS WITH ANOTHER PERSON AND YOU THINK HE CAN HELP YOU, YOU ARE WRONG!** *"Our help is in the name of the Lord, who made heaven and earth."* **Psalm 124:8**

**NEVER KEEP YOUR REQUESTS A SECRET FROM GOD! TELL HIM WHAT YOUR NEEDS ARE. TELL HIM YOUR SINS, FAULTS, MISTAKES, AND REGRETS! HE LONGS TO HEAR FROM YOU. HE WANTS TO BE YOUR BEST FRIEND. HE WILL NEVER BETRAY YOU — LEAVE YOU — OR FORSAKE YOU!** *"Therefore I say unto you, What things soever ye desire, when ye pray, believe that ye receive them, and ye shall have them. And when ye stand praying, forgive, if ye have ought against any: that your Father also which is in heaven may forgive you your trespasses. But if ye do not forgive, neither will your Father which is in heaven forgive your trespasses."* **Mark 11:24-26**

### PRAYER

Dear God, please forgive me for all my sins and blot them from Your memory. I repent of every sin I have ever committed. I humbly ask you to forgive me for those times I betrayed another person's confidence by revealing his **secrets!** Forgive me for holding back my **secret** thoughts and actions from You! I was not aware that You see and hear everything that I do. From this moment on, I will try to emulate what Jesus would say or do! Thank You for being so loving, understanding, and forgiving! In Jesus' name, I pray. AMEN!

# SELFISH — STUBBORN

*"For rebellion is as the sin of witchcraft, and stubbornness is as iniquity and idolatry. Because thou hast rejected the word of the Lord, he hath also rejected thee. . ."* **1 Samuel 15:23**

*"That they might set their hope in God, and not forget the works of God, but keep his commandments. And might not be as their fathers, a **stubborn and a rebellious** generation; a generation that set not their heart aright, and whose spirit was not stedfast with God."* **Psalm 78:7-8**

**THE GOLDEN RULE:** *"And as ye would (wish) that men should do to you, do ye also to them like wise. For if ye love them which love you, what thank (thanks) have ye? for sinners also love those that love them. And if ye do good to them which do good to you, what thank (thanks) have ye? for sinners also do even the same. And if ye lend to them of whom ye hope to receive, what thank (thanks) have ye? For sinners also lend to sinners, to receive as much again. But love ye your enemies, and do good, and lend, hoping for nothing again; and your reward shall be great, and ye shall be the children of the Highest: for he is kind unto the unthankful and to the evil. Be ye therefore merciful, as your Father also is merciful."* **Luke 6:31-36**

**IT NEVER PAYS TO BE SELFISH WITH GOD OR ANYONE ELSE!** *"But this I say, He which soweth sparingly (selfishly) shall reap also sparingly; and he which soweth bountifully shall reap also bountifully. Every man according as he purposeth in his heart, so let him give; not grudgingly, or of necessity: for God loveth a cheerful giver. And God is able to make all grace abound toward you; that ye, always having all sufficiency in all things, may abound to every good work."* **2 Corinthians 9:6-8**

*"Be not deceived: God is not mocked: for whatsoever a man soweth, that shall he also reap."* **Galatians 6:7**

**CHURCH LEADERS ARE COMMANDED NOT TO BE STUBBORN (SELF-WILLED)!** Titus 1:7

*"The Lord knoweth how to deiver the godly out of temptations, and to reserve the unjust unto the day of judgment to be punished. But chiefly them that walk after the flesh in the lust of uncleanness, and despise government. Presumptuous are they, **selfwilled,** they are not afraid to speak evil of dignities."* **2 Peter 2:9-10**

**TOO MUCH PROSPERITY MAY CAUSE A PERSON TO BE SELFISH, ACCORDING TO PSALM** 30:6 *"Be not thou afraid when one is made rich, when the glory of his house is increased; for when he dieth he shall carry nothing away: his glory shall not descend after him."* **Psalm 49:16-17** *"For if a man think himself to be something, when he is nothing, he deceiveth himself."* **Galatians 6:3**

*Selfishness*

In the old testament, when parents had a stubborn and rebellious son, the elders of the city would stone him to death, in an effort to cleanse the land of all wickedness! Deuteronomy 21:18-21

**GOD HATES SELFISHNESS AND STUBBORNNESS!** Deuteronomy 9:27 *"Put away from thee a froward (sullen) mouth, and perverse lips put far from thee."* **Proverbs 4:24**

**THE BIBLE SAYS A SEXUALLY "LOOSE" WOMAN IS STUBBORN!** Proverbs 7:11

# stubborness

**LISTED BELOW ARE 6 THINGS GOD HATES!** *"These six things doth the Lord hate: yea seven are an abomination unto him: **a proud look,** a lying tongue, and hands that shed innocent blood. An heart that deviseth wicked imaginations, feet that be swift in running to mischief, a false witness that speaketh lies, and **he that soweth discord** among brethren."* **Proverbs 6:16-19**

**GOD SAID THE NATION OF ISRAEL IS STUBBORN AND REBELLIOUS . . . HE CALLED THEM "STIFFNECKED"!** *"Ye stiffnecked and uncircumcised in heart and ears, ye do always resist the Holy Ghost: as your fathers did, so do ye."* **Acts 7:51** *"For they are impudent children and stiffhearted. . ."* **Ezekiel 2:4/Exodus 32:9/33:3-5/34:9/Deuteronomy 9:6, 13/10:16/2 Chronicles 30:8**

**GOD HATES A SELFISH AND STUBBORN DISPOSITION IN A PERSON, BUT HE LOVES THE PERSON! HE CAN HELP YOU OVERCOME THIS PROBLEM AND BRING YOU PEACE AND HAPPINESS!** *"For God so loved the world, that he gave his only begotten Son, that whosoever believeth in him should not perish but have everlasting life."* **John 3:16** *"Whosoever therefore shall confess me before men, him will I confess also before my Father which is in heaven. But whosoever shall deny me before men, him will I also deny before my Father which is in heaven."* **Matthew 10:32-33**

### PRAYER

Dear God, please forgive me for all my sins. I have been **stubborn, and selfish,** to others and certainly to You! I repent of all the unkind things I have said, done and thought! Please forgive me and help me clean up my life. I want to please You and I want others to be able to love me and trust me! I thank You for saving my soul and for giving me a new lease on life. In Jesus' name, I pray. AMEN!

# SEX PERVERT

*"There is a way which seemeth right unto a man* (person), *but the end thereof are the ways of death* (eternal separation from God).*"* **Proverbs 14:12**

**DID YOU KNOW THAT SEXUAL PERVERSIONS AND ALL TYPES OF SEX SINS AND DISEASES ARE PROPHESIED TO BE A SIGN OF THE LAST DAYS BEFORE CHRIST RETURNS TO EARTH?** *"Now the* (Holy) *Spirit speaketh expressly, that in the latter times some shall depart from the faith, giving heed to* **seducing spirits,** *and doctrines of devils; speaking lies in hypocrisy; having their conscience seared with a hot iron; forbidding* (choosing not) *to marry, and commanding* (preferring) *to abstain from meats* (being vegetarians), *which God hath created to be received with thanksgiving of them which believe* (in God) *and know the truth."* **1 Timothy 4:1-4** *"But evil men and* **seducers** *shall wax* (grow) *worse and worse, deceiving, and being deceived. . ."* **2 Timothy 3:13**

**BEWARE OF THE COMPANY YOU KEEP!** *"The righteous is more excellent* (preferred with God) *than his neighbour: but the way of the wicked seduceth them* (to sin).*"* **Proverbs 12:26**

**A CHRISTIAN'S BODY IS NOT HIS OWN! HE IS TO GLORIFY GOD IN HIS BODY!** *"What? know ye not that your body is the temple of the Holy Ghost which is in you, which ye have of God, and ye are not your own? For ye are bought with a price: therefore glorify God in your body, and in your spirit, which are God's."* **1 Corinthians 6:19-20**

**GOD COMMANDS US TO BE A VIRGIN WHEN WE MARRY!** *"Ye are bought with a price: be not ye the servants of men."* **1 Corinthians 7:23** *"But if they cannot contain, let them marry: for it is better to marry than to burn* (with sexual passion).*"* **1 Corinthians 7:9**

**ALL ACTS WE DO IN OUR BODY WILL BE JUDGED!** *"For we must all appear before the judgment seat of Christ; that every one may receive the things done in his body, according to that* (which) *he hath done, whether it be good or bad."* **2 Corinthians 5:10**

**WE MUST DISCIPLINE OUR BODY AND KEEP IT UNDER SUBJECTION! Paul wrote:** *"But I keep under my body and bring it into subjection: lest that by any means, when I have preached to others, I myself should be a castaway."* **1 Corinthians 9:27**

**IF A PERSON WILLFULLY REJECTS GOD . . . HE MAY RELEASE HIM OVER TO A REPROBATE MIND!** *"For the wrath of God is revealed from heaven against all ungodliness and unrighteousness of men, who hold the truth in unrighteousness. Because that which may be known of God is manifest* (made known) *in them: for God hath shewed it unto them. For the invisible things of him from the creation of the world are clearly seen, being understood by the things that are made, even his eternal power, and Godhead: so that they are without excuse: Because that, when they knew God, they glorified him not as God, neither were thankful: but became vain in their imaginations, and their foolish heart was darkened. Professing themselves to be wise, they became fools. And changed the glory of the uncorruptible God into an image made like to corruptible man, and to birds, and fourfooted beasts and creeping things. Wherefore God also gave them up to* **uncleanness** (they became **sex perverts**) *through the* **lusts** *of their own hearts, to dishonour their own bodies between themselves: Who changed the truth of God into a lie, and worshipped and served the creature* (their body lusts) *more than the Creator* (God), *who is blessed for ever. For this cause God gave them up unto* **vile affections:** *for even their women did change the natural use into that which is against nature* (became **lesbians**). *And likewise also the men, leaving the natural use of the woman, burned in their* **lust** *one toward another* (became **homosexuals**): *men with men working that which is unseemly, and receiving in themselves that recompence* (penalty) *of their error which was meet* (only fitting they receive). *Being filled with all unrighteousness,* **fornication** (sex without marriage), *wickedness,*

*covetousness, maliciousness, full of envy, murder, debate, deceit, malignity, whisperers, backbiters, haters of God, despiteful, proud, boasters, inventors of evil things, disobedient to parents, without understanding, covenantbreakers* (law breakers), *without natural affection* **(sex perverts),** *implacable, unmerciful: Who knowing the judgment of God, that they which commit such things are worthy of death, not only do the same, but have pleasure in them that do them."* **Romans 1:18-32**

**GOD SAID WE ARE NEVER TO HAVE SEX WITH ANIMALS!** SEX WITH ANIMALS = BESTIALITY! **Exodus 22:19/Leviticus 18:23/20:15-16/Deuteronomy 27:21**

**HOMOSEXUALITY, LESBIANISM, AND SODOMY ARE FORBIDDEN BY GOD!** *"Thou shalt not lie with mankind, as with womankind: it is abomination."* **Leviticus 18:22/20:13**

**GOD FORBIDS ADULTERY! Leviticus 18:20/Exodus 20:14**

**INCEST IS FORBIDDEN!** Leviticus 18:6-18, 24-30/Deuteronomy 22:20

**RAPE IS FORBIDDEN! Deuteronomy 22:22-26/23:17**

**PROSTITUTION IS FORBIDDEN! Deuteronomy 23:18, 27/Proverbs 5:3-23/6:24-29/2:16/7:5-27/9:13-18**

**GOD FORBIDS ANYONE TO PROSTITUTE HIS DAUGHTER TO CAUSE HER TO BE A WHORE! Leviticus 19:29/Deuteronomy 23:17**

*"And many of them that sleep in the dust of the earth shall awake* (be resurrected), *some to everlasting life, and some to shame and everlasting contempt."* **Daniel 12:2**

*"I beseech* (beg) *you therefore, brethren, by the mercies of God, that ye present your bodies a living sacrifice, holy, acceptable unto God, which is your reasonable service. And be not conformed to this world: but be ye transformed by the renewing of your mind, that ye may prove what is that good, and acceptable, and perfect will of God."* **Romans 12:1-2**

*"This I say then, Walk in the* (Holy) *Spirit, and ye shall not fulfil the lust of the flesh."* **Galatians 5:16**

**WE SHOULD ALWAYS EXERCISE SELF-CONTROL, IN ALL MATTERS, JUST AS JESUS DID WHEN HE WAS TEMPTED BY SATAN!** Jesus was taken before Pilate to be sentenced. He was hit, spit on, bruised, lied about, and ridiculed. Yet, He never lost His self-control! *"And when he* (Jesus) *was accused of the chief priests and elders, he answered nothing."* **Matthew 27:12/26:59-75/Mark 14:53/Luke 22:63/John 18:12, 19**

**HERE ARE SEVEN WAYS TO STAY PURE IN GOD'S EYES: 1.** REPENT OF YOUR SINS AND TURN AWAY FROM THEM! **2.** DO NOT HAVE SEX WITH ANYONE WHO IS NOT YOUR HUSBAND (OR WIFE). **3.** DO NOT DRINK, USE FOUL LANGUAGE, OR MISTREAT ANYONE! **4.** GO TO CHURCH! **5.** USE SELF-CONTROL! **6.** READ YOUR BIBLE AND PRAY! **7.** LOVE YOUR NEIGHBOR

### PRAYER

Dear God, I have committed many sins. I repent and ask You to forgive me. I turn away from all sin in my life. To the very best of my ability, I will live a godly life! Please blot out all my sins and bring me peace and happiness. I know with Your help I will be able to forget my past sins! I will not let the memory of what I've done hold me back from worshipping and serving You. Teach me the proper way to live, talk and think and I will give You all the praise! In Jesus' name, I pray. AMEN!

# SMOKING

**SMOKING IS ADDICTIVE — SO DON'T START . . . IF YOU ALREADY SMOKE, WE'LL HELP YOU BREAK THE HABIT!**
Current cigarette smokers have 70 percent greater chance of dying from disease than non-smokers and on an average will die 8 years sooner than a non-smoker. Pregnant women who smoke risk spontaneous abortion and neonatal death. Young women between 17 and 24 are now outsmoking their male peers. Women who use the pill for birth control have a greater risk of heart attack. Cigarettes can cause cancer. You can become a slave to cigarettes!

**THERE'S NO SUCH THING AS A SAFE LOW TAR NICOTINE CIGARETTE!**
**PROVERBS 10:26 SAYS SMOKE BURNS THE EYES!**

**MESSAGE TO THE SMOKER:** *"My breath is corrupt, my days are (almost) extinct, (and because of my smoking) the graves are ready for me."* **Job 17:1**
**SMOKING SHOWS A WILLFUL DISRESPECT FOR GOD'S INSTRUCTIONS FOR YOUR BODY!** *"What? know ye not that your body is the temple of the Holy Ghost which is in you, which ye have of God, and ye are not your own? For ye are bought with a price: therefore glorify God in your body, and in your spirit, which are God's."* **1 Corinthians 6:19-20**
**SMOKING HURTS YOUR TESTIMONY WHEN YOU WITNESS TO OTHERS ABOUT BEING SAVED!** *"But take heed lest by any means this liberty of yours become a stumblingblock to them that are weak."* **1 Corinthians 8:9**
**CIGARETTES ARE WICKED . . . DON'T LIGHT UP AND THEY WON'T KILL YOU!** *"For my mouth shall speak truth; and wickedness (includes cigarettes) is an abomination to my lips."* **Proverbs 8:7**
**IT'S FOOLISH TO DISREGARD THE WARNING ON CIGARETTE LABELS. THE BIBLE SAYS TO FORSAKE FOOLISHNESS!** *"Forsake the foolish, and live; and go in the way of (God's) understanding."* **Proverbs 9:6**
**THE BIBLE SAYS WE ARE TO FEAR AND RESPECT WHAT GOD SAYS!** *"The fear of the Lord is the beginning of wisdom . . ."* **Proverbs 9:10**
**SMOKING MAKES YOUR TONGUE AND BREATH STINK . . . OTHERS SMELL IT, TOO!** *"The tongue of the just (person who lives a godly life) is as choice silver."* **Proverbs 10:20**
*"In the lips of him that hath understanding wisdom is found (not a cigarette)."* **Proverbs 10:13**
**SINCE YOUR BODY IS THE TEMPLE OF GOD, IF YOU SMOKE YOU NOT ONLY SIN AGAINST YOUR OWN BODY — YOU SIN AGAINST GOD!** *"But he that sinneth against me wrongeth his own soul: all they that hate me (by disobeying me) love death."* **Proverbs 8:36**

**SATAN WANTS TO DESTROY AND KILL YOU. THAT'S WHY HE INVENTED CIGARETTES, PIPES, SNUFF AND DRUGS!** *"The lips of the righteous know what is acceptable: but the mouth of the wicked (Satan) speaketh frowardness (opposition-disobedience)."* **Proverbs 10:32**
**HOW DO YOU STOP SMOKING?** First you make up your mind that you're going to stop! Then you throw your cigarettes away! Now, get down on your knees and ask God to change your taste buds so that you will not crave them. Ask Him to give you strength to keep your promise never to smoke again. Take authority over Satan! Announce to him that you will never go back on your promise to God! You started smoking, but God will help you stop! Repeat to yourself 100 times a day: *"I can do all things through Christ which strengtheneth me."* **Philippians 4:13**

**TOBACCO/DRUGS ENSLAVES YOU!** *". . .For of whom (or what) a man (person) is overcome, of the same is he brought in(to) bondage."* **2 Peter 2:19** *"All things are lawful unto me, but all things are not expedient: all things are lawful for me, but I will not be brought under the power of any."* **1 Corinthians 6:12**

**CHRISTIANS ARE COMMANDED TO CLEANSE OURSELVES OF ALL FILTHINESS OF THE FLESH AND SPIRIT!** *"Having therefore these promises, dearly beloved, let us cleanse ourselves from all filthiness of the flesh and spirit, perfecting holiness in the fear of God."* **2 Corinthians 7:1**

**CHRISTIANS ARE COMMANDED TO CRUCIFY ANY UNHOLY PASSIONS, AFFECTIONS AND LUSTS!** *"And they that are of Christ's have crucified the flesh with the affections and lusts."* **Galatians 5:24** *"Let not sin therefore reign in your mortal body, that ye should obey it in the lusts thereof."* **Romans 6:12** *"Dearly beloved, I beseech (beg) you as strangers and pilgrims, abstain from fleshly lusts, which war against the soul."* **1 Peter 2:11**

**CHRISTIANS ARE NOT TO BE STUMBLINGBLOCKS!** *". . . that no man put a stumblingblock or an occasion to fall in his brothers way."* **Romans 14:13** *"It is good neither to eat flesh, nor to drink wine, nor any thing (includes cigarettes) whereby thy brother stumbleth, or is offended, or is made weak."* **Romans 14:21** *"But when ye sin so against the brethren, and wound their weak conscience, ye sin against Christ. Wherefore, if meat (or cigarettes) make my brother to offend, I will eat no flesh (or smoke) while the world standeth, lest I make my brother to offend."* **1 Corinthians 8:12-13**

**THERE ARE REWARDS FOR "KICKING THE HABIT"!** *"If a man (person) therefore purge himself from these, he shall be a vessel unto honour, sanctified, and meet (fit) for the master's use, and prepared unto every good work."* **2 Timothy 2:21**

**A CHRISTIAN WHO SMOKES HURTS THE INFLUENCE OF THE CHURCH!** The church if the body of Christ. **Ephesians 1:22-23** *"And whether one member suffer, all the members suffer with it; or one member be honoured, all the members rejoice with it. Now ye are the body of Christ, and members in particular."* **1 Corinthians 12:26-27**

**ALL CHRISTIANS ARE COMMANDED TO BE EXAMPLES AND SMOKING HURTS THEIR INFLUENCE!** *"Let your light so shine before men, that they may see your good works, and glorify your Father (God) which is in heaven."* **Matthew 5:16**

**PARENTS SHOULD NOT SMOKE BEFORE THEIR CHILDREN!** *"Train up a child in the way he should go: and when he is old, he will not depart from it."* **Proverbs 22:6**

**DON'T BE EMBARRASSED TO ASK GOD TO HELP YOU STOP SMOKING!** *". . .for your Father (God) knoweth what things ye have need of, before ye ask him."* **Matthew 6:8**

### PRAYER
Dear God: please forgive me for all my sins. I don't know if smoking would cause me to go to hell or not, but I'm not willing to take any chances. I know that smoking can kill me and that Jesus came so that I might have life, abundantly! I turn away from all sin in my life. Please give me the strength to say "no" when someone offers me a cigarette. Please change my taste buds so that I will not crave cigarettes. I will bind Satan when he tempts me to smoke. I take authority over this evil habit and with Your help I will overcome! In Jesus' name. AMEN!

# SODOMY
## (Oral or Anal Sex)

**DEFINITION:** Non-coital carnal copulation with a member of the same or opposite sex, or with an animal.

"Sodomites" does not refer to the inhabitants of Sodom during the old testament days. It refers to the people who practiced oral sex as a pagan religious rite! This was an abomination to God. Sodomy is a sin to God and man! **It is the unnatural act of oral or anal sex from which the inhabitants of Sodom and Gomorrah derived their infamous reputation!**

**SODOMY IS FORBIDDEN BY GOD!** Genesis 19/Exodus 22:19/Leviticus 18:22/20:13/Deuteronomy 23:17/1 Corinthians 6:9-10/1 Timothy 1:10/Isaiah 3:9/Judges 19:22/20:13/Romans 1:18-32

The city of Sodom was located on what is now called the Dead Sea. Water probably covers the remains! Lot lived there **Genesis 13:1-13.** It was destroyed because of its wickedness **Genesis 13.** Sodom was a symbol of vice, infamy, and judgment Isaiah 1:9-10/3:9/Jeremiah 23:14/Lamentations 4:6/Ezekiel 16:46/Matthew 10:15/Revelation 11:8/Romans 9:29.

**ACCORDING TO DEUTERONOMY 23:17 SODOMY WAS FORBIDDEN BY LAW.** It became prevalent in Israel **1 Kings 14:24,** and the ancient heathen world **Romans 1:26,** and was practiced even in the temple **2 Kings 23:7.**

**THE PRACTICE OF SODOMY IS A DIABOLICAL INVENTION OF SATAN TO DAMN MAN'S SOUL AND BRING HIM INTO TOTAL SUBMISSION!** Satan knows that the unrighteous will never enter heaven. Satan always uses man's baser passions to bring him into bondage and slavery!

**SODOMY = HOMOSEXUALITY = LESBIANISM = PEDERASTY!** Genesis 19:5/Leviticus 20:13/Deuteronomy 23:17/1 Kings 14:24/15:12/22:46/2 Kings 23:7/Joel 3:3/2 Timothy 3:3, 13/2 Peter 2:7-22/Jude 7:19/Romans 1:26-27

**BECAUSE OF THE SIN OF SODOMY AND DELIBERATE DISOBEDIENCE, GOD GAVE MEN AND WOMEN UP TO DEFILE THEIR BODY AND SOUL! HE TOOK GREAT DISPLEASURE AT THEIR REFUSAL TO ACKNOWLEDGE HIM AND OBEY HIM!** Romans 1:20-32

**IN THE OLD TESTAMENT DAYS, THE EGYPTIANS WERE GUILTY OF HOMOSEXUALITY AND BESTIALITY (SEX WITH ANIMALS)!** Leviticus 18:23

**ORAL OR ANAL SEX IS A WORK OF THE FLESH!** Galatians 5:19-21

**SODOMY IS CALLED UNCLEANNESS:** 2 Corinthians 12:21/Galatians 5:19/Ephesians 4:19/5:3, 5/Colossians 3:5/1 Thessalonians 4:7/2 Peter 2:10. Sodomy (uncleanness) is a scriptural term for homosexuality, lesbianism, bestiality and all other sexual perversions.

**ALL DEMON, MORAL, AND PHYSICAL, UNCLEANNESS MUST BE CLEANSED FROM THE BODY AND SPIRIT IF YOU WANT THE PROMISES OF GOD, INSTEAD OF THE JUDGMENTS!** *"Wherefore come out from among them, and be ye separate, saith the Lord, and touch not the unclean thing: And I* (God) *will receive you."* **2 Corinthians 6:17**

**SODOMY = VILE AFFECTIONS:** Romans 1:26/Colossians 3:5

**SODOMY = SHAME:** 1 Corinthians 11:14

**SODOMY = A REPROBATE MIND:** Romans 1:28

**SODOMY IS NOT FITTING OR PROPER:** Romans 1:28

**SODOMY IS A DEPRAVED SEX ACT AND IS CALLED WICKEDNESS:** Romans 1:29

**SODOMY = LUST:** 1 Thessalonians 4:5

**SODOMY = PEDERASTY:** Genesis 19:5/Leviticus 20:13/Deuteronomy 23:17/1 Kings 14:24/15:12/22:46/2 Kings 23:7/Joel 3:3/2 Timothy 3:3, 13/2 Peter 2:7-22/Jude 7:19

**SODOMY = UNSEEMLY (INDECENT) ACTIVITY:** Romans 1:27

**A PERSON WHO PRACTICES ORAL SEX IS DESTITUTE OF NATURAL AFFECTION.** Romans 1:24-31

**IF YOU DO NOT REPENT AND TURN AWAY FROM ORAL (OR ANAL SEX, OR SEX WITH ANIMALS) . . . YOU WILL NOT GO TO HEAVEN!** *"Know ye not that the unrighteous shall not inherit the kingdom of God? Be not deceived: neither fornicators* (sex without marriage), *not idolaters, nor adulterers, nor effeminate, nor abusers of themselves with mankind, Nor thieves, nor covetous, nor drunkards, nor revilers, nor extortioners, shall inherit the kingdom of God."* **1 Corinthians 6:9-10**

**ORAL SEX = AN ABUSER OF YOURSELF AND ANOTHER!** Any person who is guilty of unnatural sex offenses is a sex pervert! 1 Corinthians 6:9/1 Timothy 1:10/Romans 1:27

**A CATAMITE = A MALE WHO SUBMITS HIS BODY TO UNNATURAL SEX ACTS!** 1 Corinthians 6:9/Joel 3:3

**AN EFFEMINATE MAN IS A PRIME TARGET FOR SATAN TO TURN INTO A HOMOSEXUAL!** He has womanlike traits which become inappropriate to his masculinity. He lacks in manly strength or aggressiveness. He is usually weak, soft, and loves ease. He is over-emotional or over-delicate. Oral Sex is one of the worst immoralities and sins a person can commit! But God has forgiven all who repent and ask forgiveness! *"And such were some of you: but ye are washed* (forgiven through the shedding of the blood of Jesus to pay for your sins), *but ye are sanctified, but ye are justified in the name of the Lord Jesus, and by the* (Holy) *Spirit of our God."* **1 Corinthians 6:11**

(Continued)

When Satan (Lucifer) was cast out of heaven, he took with him myriads of fallen angels. Upon their arrival to earth they began committing all types of sex perversions. They had sex with earthly women and produced a race of giants. Genesis 6:1-4 They are now bound in chains in Tartarus (a compartment in hell) until the Great White Throne Judgment. 2 Peter 2:4/Jude 6-7

According to Genesis 19:1-11, the sin of sodomy is an evil condition of living contrary to nature! Both men, women, and angels broke through the sex bounds that God set for them!

According to Jude 7 and Romans 1:24-32 strange flesh = homosexuality (men with men) and fallen angels with women, and women with women! *"Even as Sodom and Gomorrha, and the cities about them in like manner, giving themselves over to fornication, and going after strange flesh, are set forth for an example, suffering the vengeance of eternal fire."* **Jude 7. NOTE:** other examples of the suffering and vengeance of God upon those who do not repent of their sin are: Isaiah 66:24/Matthew 25:46/Mark 9:43-49/Revelation 14:9-11/20:10-15.

GOD'S JUDGMENT IS ALWAYS THE RESULT OF SIN IN PEOPLE'S LIVES!

The sin of oral sex, anal sex, or bestiality, always causes God to act in His hurt, anger, and wrath! God puts forth every effort to rid the world of such corruption (Deuteronomy 29:23) and as an example to others (2 Peter 2:6).

**WARNING TO YOU AND THE PERSON WHO ENTICES YOU TO HAVE ORAL OR ANAL SEX, OR SEX WITH ANIMALS:** *"While they promise them* (you) *liberty* (sexual freedom), *they themselves are the servants of corruption: for of whom a man* (person) *is overcome, of the same is he brought in* (to) *bondage."* **2 Peter 2:19**

**ISRAEL WAS AT ONE TIME FULL OF THE SIN OF SODOMY!** Deuteronomy 32:32/Isaiah 3:9 During the soon-to-come reign of Mr. Anti-Christ (during the 7-year tribulation period) Jerusalem will become known as the world headquarters for sodomites and whoredoms. **Isaiah 1:9-10/Ezekiel 16:46, 53/23:3, 8, 19, 27** During the last 3½ years the Gentiles will control the city **Revelation 11:1-2.** Sex and religious perversions will run rampant and this will bring a close to this age **Matthew 24:37-39/Luke 17:26-30.**

**LISTED BELOW ARE SIX SINS THAT CARRY A DEATH (ETERNAL SEPARATION FROM GOD) PENALTY!**

1. **INCEST:** Leviticus 18:6-18, 24-30
2. **ADULTERY:** Leviticus 18:20/Exodus 20:14
3. **IDOLATRY:** Exodus 20:4
4. **BLASPHEMY:** Leviticus 18:21/Exodus 20:7
5. **HOMOSEXUALITY-LESBIANISM:** Leviticus 18:22/20:13
6. **BESTIALITY** (sex with animals) Leviticus 18:23

**IF YOU ARE GUILTY OF PRACTICING ORAL SEX, ANAL SEX, OR BESTIALITY — STOP NOW AND REPENT!** God loves you so much that He gave His only Son to die on the cross to pay the penalty for your sins! He will forgive you and forget your sins, if you will humble yourself and ask His forgiveness! God will give you peace!

# Have You Experienced Being BORN AGAIN?

*"Finally, brethren, whatsoever things are true, whatsoever things are honest, whatsoever things are just, whatsoever things are pure, whatsoever things are lovely, whatsoever things are of good report: if there be any virtue, and if there be any praise, think on these things."* **Philippians 4:8**

# GOOD NEWS

You have been made in God's image; created to have power and authority over all the circumstances of your life.

**ONLY THE WICKED PERISH FOREVER!** Isaiah 26:10, 14/Proverbs 10:7/Psalm 9:5

### PRAYER

Dear God, I confess I am a sinner! I repent and humbly ask Your forgiveness! Come into my heart and live in me. From this moment on I will not be guilty of committing any sex sin! I will study my Bible to learn what Your promises, blessings and judgments are. In Jesus' name, I pray. AMEN!

# SOUL—SPIRIT

**WHAT IS MAN'S SOUL?** A person is a soul! A soul has appetites, mental faculties, feelings, emotions, desires and passions. The soul of man feels and the spirit knows **1 Corinthians 2:11.** A soul is a living, breathing, creature. *"And the Lord God formed man (out) of the dust of the ground, and breathed into his nostrils the breath of life; and man became a living soul."* **Genesis 2:7** *"And so it is written, the first man Adam was made a living soul; the last Adam (Christ) was made a quickening spirit.* **1 Corinthians 15:45** It takes both soul and spirit to make the inner man with his individual will, knowledge and intellect! Our soul contains our mind and heart. **God has a soul (Matthew 12:18/Hebrews 10:38). A soul can be lost (Mark 8:36),** or saved **(Hebrews 10:39/James 1:21/1 Peter 1:9).** God wants both our soul and body to be healthy **(3 John 2/1 Peter 2:24).** Soul and spirit of man are distinguished **(1 Thessalonians 5:23/Hebrews 4:12).** Our soul leaves our body at death **(2 Corinthians 5:8/Philippians 1:21-24/James 2:26/Hebrews 12:23/Revelation 6:9-11).** We are commanded to win souls to Christ **(Proverbs 11:30/14:25).** A soul can see, and be seen, after leaving the body at death **(Matthew 17:3/Luke 16:19-31/Hebrews 12:22-23/Revelation 6:9-11).** Our soul is immortal. **Man cannot kill the soul (Matthew 10:28). Soul and spirit at death (of the born-again Christian) go to heaven (2 Corinthians 5:8/Philippians 1:21-24/Hebrews 12:22-23/Revelation 6:9-11).** If unsaved the soul and spirit go to hell **(Isaiah 14:9/Luke 16:19-31/Revelation 20:11-15).** Lower animals also have souls! **(Numbers 31:28/Revelation 16:3).** Every soul has blood, eats and can die **(Jeremiah 2:34/Leviticus 7:18/Ezekiel 18:4).** *"For the life of the flesh is in the blood. . .for it is the blood that maketh an atonement for the soul."* **Leviticus 17:11**

**IF YOU ARE ALIVE — YOU HAVE A SOUL!** *"For what shall it profit a man, if he shall gain the whole world, and lose his own soul? Or what shall a man give in exchange for his soul?"* **Mark 8:36-37**

# soul

**THE LIFE FORCE THAT ACTIVATES OUR SOUL IS CALLED "SPIRIT"!** *"His (our) breath goeth forth, he (we) returneth to his earth: in that very day his thoughts perish."* **Psalm 146:4** *"Thou hidest thy face, they are trouble: thou takest away their breath, they die, and return to their dust."* **Psalm 104:29**

# spirit

**WHEN ONE DIES: THE FORCE OF LIFE "SPIRIT" RETURNS TO GOD!** *"Then shall the dust return to the earth as it was (before man was created): and the spirit shall return unto God who gave it."* **Ecclesiastes 12:7** *"And the Lord God formed man (out) of the dust of the ground, and breathed into his nostrils the breath of life; and man became a living soul."* **Genesis 2:7** Only God is able to put our life force into action **Revelation 11:11.**

**WHAT'S THE DIFFERENCE BETWEEN MAN'S SOUL AND HIS SPIRIT?** Our spirit is the breath of life which God gave us. Our soul is our entire person, body, personality, looks, etc.

**WHAT IS THE HOLY SPIRIT?** He is God's active force in our life. He is an extension of God. He is a real person in the Godhead, which is composed of God the Father, Jesus Christ, and The Holy Spirit! **These three combined are known as the TRINITY.** The Holy Spirit dwells with us, and in us, when we become born-again Christians **John 14:16-17.** The Holy Spirit was used in creation and in inspiring the Bible. *"And the earth was without form, and void; and darkness was upon the face of the deep. And the Spirit of God (Holy Spirit) moved upon the face of the waters."* **Genesis 1:2/Ezekiel 11:5 JESUS SAID:** *". . .Verily, verily, I say unto thee, Except a man be born of water and of the (Holy) Spirit, he cannot enter into the kingdom of God. That which is born of the flesh is flesh; and that which is born of the Spirit is spirit. Marvel not that I said unto thee, Ye must be born again. The wind bloweth where it listeth, and thou hearest the sound thereof, but canst not tell whence it cometh, and whither it goeth: so is every one that is born of the (Holy) Spirit."* **John 3:5-8/Isaiah 61:1.** The Holy Spirit created man. *"The spirit of God hath made me, and the breath of the Almighty hath given me life."* **Job 33:4** The Holy Spirit is still leading God's people today with power and love! *"This I say then, Walk in the (Holy) Spirit, and ye shall not fulfil the lust of the flesh. For the flesh lusteth against the (Holy) Spirit, and the (Holy) Spirit against the flesh: and these are contrary the one to the other: so that ye cannot do the things that ye would (should). But if ye be led of the (Holy) Spirit, ye are not under the law (of sin and death)."* **Galatians 5:16-18** *"For they that are after the (sins of the) flesh do mind the things of the flesh; but they that are after the (Holy) Spirit (do mind) the things of the (Holy) Spirit. For to be carnally minded is death; but to be spiritually minded is life and peace."* **Romans 8:5-6** *"For as many as are led by the (Holy) Spirit of God, they are the sons of God."* **Romans 8:14** *"The (Holy) Spirit itself beareth witness with our spirit, that we are the children of God. And if children, then heirs; heirs of God, and joint-heirs with Christ; . . ."* **Romans 8:16-17 NOTE:** YOU CANNOT BECOME A BORN-AGAIN CHRISTIAN WITHOUT THE ASSISTANCE OF THE HOLY SPIRIT!

**OUR HUMAN LIFE FORCE IS CALLED "SPIRIT" . . . AND OUR BREATH SUSTAINS IT!** *"For as the body without the spirit (breath) is dead, so faith without works is dead also."* **James 2:26** *"All the while my breath is in me, and the spirit of God is in my nostrils."* **Job 27:3**

**ALL LIFE FORCE . . . (HUMANS AND BEASTS) . . . BELONGS TO GOD!** Man and animals die but their spirits go to different places. Both return to the dust, but the spirit of humans goes either to God in heaven (if they were born-again Christians) or to hell (if they were unsaved)! *"All go unto one place; all are of the dust, and all turn to dust again. Who knoweth the spirit of man that goeth upward, and the spirit of the beast that goeth downward to the earth."* **Ecclesiastes 3:20-21**

. . .

**PRAYER**

Dear God, please forgive me for all my sins. I repent and turn away from all sin in my life. I want to be ready to meet Christ in the air when the rapture takes places. I declare with my own mouth that I am now a born-again Christian. If I should die before the rapture takes place, I know that my spirit will go to heaven to be with Jesus. I thank You for that! I love You for first loving me. Thank You for giving me life so that I can turn my life back over to You in service and obedience. In Jesus' name, I pray. AMEN!

# STEAL/SHOPLIFT

*"In the dark they dig through houses, which they had marked for themselves in the daytime. They know not the light. For the morning is to them even as the shadow of death. If one know them, they are in the terrors of the shadow of death."* **Job 24:16-17**

*"Thou shalt not **steal**."* **Exodus 20:15/Deuteronomy 5:19**

*"The **robbery** of the wicked shall destroy them; because they refuse to do judgment."* **Proverbs 21:7**

*"The people of the land have used oppression, and exercised **robbery**, and have vexed* (mistreated) *the poor and needy: yea, they have oppressed the stranger wrongfully."* **Ezekiel 22:29** *"Woe to the bloody city! It is all full of lies and **robbery**; the prey departeth not."* **Nahum 3:1**

**PEOPLE WHO ROB USUALLY HAVE A PARTNER IN THEIR CRIME:** *"Whoso is **partner** with a **thief** hateth his own soul: he heareth cursing, and bewrayeth* (betrayeth) *it not."* **Proverbs 29:24** *"Whoso **robbeth** his father or his mother, and saith, It is no transgression; the same is the **companion** of a destroyer."* **Proverbs 28:24**

*"Rob not the poor, because he is poor: neither oppress the afflicted in the gate. For the Lord will plead their cause, and spoil the soul of those that spoiled them."* **Proverbs 22:22-23**

**WHATEVER YOU GET THROUGH ROBBERY OR SHOP-LIFTING WILL NEVER MAKE YOU HAPPY!** *"Better is a little with righteousness than great revenues without right."* **Proverbs 16:8**

*"Let him that stole steal no more: but rather let him labour, working with his hands the thing which is good, that he may have to give to him that needeth."* **Ephesians 4:28**

**SATAN WAS THE FIRST THIEF! HE IS STILL ROBBING PEOPLE AND CONVINCING THEM TO ROB OTHERS!** *"The thief cometh not, but for to **steal**, and to kill, and to destroy: I* (Christ) *am come that they might have life, and that they might have it more abundantly."* **John 10:10**

**THE URGE TO STEAL — ROB OR SHOP-LIFT — STARTS IN THE HEART!** *"For out of the heart proceed evil thoughts, murders, adulteries, fornications, **thefts**, false witness, blasphemies."* **Matthew 15:19**

*"For from within, out of the heart of men, proceed evil thoughts, adulteries, fornications, murders, **thefts**, covetousness, wickedness, deceit, lasciviousness, an evil eye, blasphemy, pride, foolishness. All these evil things come from within, and defile the man."* **Mark 7:21-23**

*"If the **theft** be certainly found in his hand alive, whether it be ox, or ass, or sheep,* (or anything else) *he shall restore double."* **Exodus 22:4** *"If a man shall deliver unto his neighbour money or stuff to keep, and it be **stolen** out of the man's house; if the **thief** be found, let him pay double."* **Exodus 22:7**

*"Ye shall not steal, neither deal falsely, neither lie one to another."* **Leviticus 19:11**

*"Men do not despise a **thief**, if he **steal** to satisfy his soul when he is hungry; but if he be found, he shall restore sevenfold; he shall give all the substance of his house."* **Proverbs 6:30-31**

**GOD CREATED HUMAN GOVERNMENT TO PUNISH PEOPLE WHO STEAL — ROB AND SHOP-LIFT!** *"And whosoever will not do the law of thy God, and the law of the king* (human government), *let judgment be executed speedily upon him, whether it be unto death, or to banishment, or to confiscation of goods, or to imprisonment."* **Ezra 7:26**

**GOD HATES FOR PEOPLE TO STEAL — BUT HE LOVES THE SINNER AND WANTS TO FORGIVE HIM! REMEMBER THE THIEF ON THE CROSS? HE ASKED WHAT HE COULD DO TO BE SAVED AND JESUS FORGAVE HIS SINS AND HE WENT TO HEAVEN!**

*"Then it shall be, because he hath sinned, and is guilty, that he shall restore that which he took violently away, or the thing which he hath deceitfully gotten, or that which was delivered him to keep, or the lost thing which he found."* **Leviticus 6:4**

*"In the house of the righteous is much treasure: but in the revenues of the wicked is trouble."* **Proverbs 15:6**

**PRAYER**

Dear God, please forgive me for all my sins. I am guilty of stealing things that belonged to others. I repent and humbly ask You to forgive me. **I will never steal again.** I promise You that from this moment on, I will never be guilty of repeating my sinful acts. Thank You for forgiving my sins. I am now a born-again Christian. AMEN!

# SUICIDE

**THE SUICIDAL PERSON IS PRE-OCCUPIED WITH THIS THOUGHT:** *"What is my strength, that I should hope? and what is mine end, that I should prolong my life?"* **Job 6:11**
In the past 10 years the suicide rate in the U.S. has increased by 17 percent. Many kids kill themselves even though they may be high achievers and socially adept, but obviously emotionally fragile. Sometimes it only takes a devastating experience or a slight setback to trigger suicide. Among kids who commit suicide there is usually the influence of alcohol and drugs, or unwed pregnancies. **Whether they go to heaven or hell — only God knows!**

**AN INSATIABLE FASCINATION WITH BIZARRE RELIGIOUS CULTS AND SATANIC ACTIVITIES IS ALSO RESPONSIBLE FOR MANY SUICIDES.** Children of prominent and famous parents suffer a relentless assault on their identity because they are only noticed because they are "so-and-so's kids".

**MANY PEOPLE WHO DO NOT LIVE IN THE WILL OF GOD BECOME DEPRESSED AND SUICIDE-PRONE!** They lack identity, accomplishments, and peace of mind, which only God can give! They may also suffer from peer-pressure! They may gravitate toward cultic teachings in their search for a reason for being.

**DEMONS CAN CAUSE SUICIDAL MANIA TENDENCIES!**
Demons can cause dumbness, deafness, foaming at the mouth, fits, gnashing of teeth, lifelessness, prostrations, suicidal tendencies, screaming, tearing of the flesh, and insanity, according to **Mark 9:14-29/Matthew 17:15-18/Luke 9:37-43**

**THIS COULD NEVER BE THE STATEMENT OF A BORN-AGAIN CHRISTIAN WHO LIVES IN THE PERFECT WILL OF GOD!** *". . .my soul chooseth strangling, and death rather than my life. I loathe it; I would not* (wish to) *live alway* (always); *let me alone; for my days are vanity."* **Job 7:15-16**

**GOD IS NOT WILLING THAT ANY OF US PERISH!** *"The Lord is not slack concerning his promise, as some men count slackness; but is longsuffering to us-ward, not willing that any should perish, but that all should come to repentance."* **2 Peter 3:9**

**SATAN WANTS TO KILL US . . . HE WILL EVEN CONVINCE US TO KILL OURSELVES . . . HE WANTS LOTS OF COMPANY TO BE WITH HIM IN HELL!** *"The thief* (Satan) *cometh not, but for to steal, and to KILL, and to DESTROY: I* (Christ) *am come that they* (we) *might have life* (now and throughout eternity with him) *and that they* (we) *might have it more abundantly."* **John 10:10**

**THE BIBLE SAYS IT IS APPOINTED UNTO MEN ONCE TO DIE . . . BUT THIS DOES NOT GIVE US LICENSE TO KILL OURSELVES!** *"And as it is appointed unto men once to die, but after this the judgment."* **Hebrews 9:27**

**SUICIDE IS MURDER!** *"Thou shalt not kill."* **Exodus 20:13**
*"There remaineth therefore a rest to the people of God. For he that is entered into his rest, he also hath ceased from his own works, as God did from his."* **Hebrews 4:9-10** *This verse tells us that when a born-again Christian dies, he is at peace in the presence of the Lord! When a person commits suicide he breaks God's commandment which says, "Thou shalt not kill"!

**IF YOU KNOW ANYONE WHO IS SUICIDAL:** Pray for him. Intercede to God in his behalf, because he may be unable to pray! Visit him and read scriptures to him. Tell him that Christ died on the cross to pay for his sins, and doesn't want him to take his own life! Bind Satan by exercising the authority Christ gives you as a born-again Christian! Rebuke Satan from tormenting him. Cast Satan out so your friend can be free from oppression, or possibly possession! Then he must turn his life over to God by receiving salvation. **Luke 16:19-31** says there is an impassable gulf between those who die and go to heaven and those who die and go to hell!

**SATAN DECEIVES MANY PEOPLE INTO THINKING THAT IF THEY COMMIT SUICIDE, THEY WILL FIND PEACE AND TRANQUILITY AND GO TO BE WITH JESUS. GOD SAYS SATAN IS A LIAR AND THE INVENTOR OF LIES! WHO ARE YOU GOING TO BELIEVE?**

**MANY PEOPLE THINK THAT IF THEY KILL THEMSELVES THEY'LL PUNISH THOSE WHO SLIGHTED AND REJECTED THEM OR BROKE THEIR HEART!** They think they'll receive satisfaction from the other person's regrets. *"For in death there is no remembrance of thee: in the grave who shall give thee thanks?"* **Psalm 6:5**

**A SUICIDAL PERSON SHOULD PRAY THIS PRAYER:**
*"Consider and hear me, O Lord my God: lighten mine eyes, lest I sleep the sleep of death; lest mine enemy say, I have prevailed against him; and those that trouble me rejoice when I am moved* (gone)." **Psalm 13:3-4**

**MANY ROCK GROUPS ENCOURAGE YOU TO TAKE THE "ULTIMATE TRIP" — MEANING SUICIDE!** Satan gives them the lyrics and kids are very impressionable! But to kill anyone or yourself is still murder! *"He that committeth sin is of the devil: for the devil sinneth from the beginning. For this purpose the Son of God* (Jesus) *was manifested* (made known), *that he might destroy the works of the devil. Whosoever is born of God* (becomes a born-again Christian) *doth not commit sin; for his* (God's) *seed remaineth in him: and he cannot sin, because he is born of God."* **1 John 3:8-9**
*"But the fearful, and unbelieving, and the abominable, and* **murderers,** *and whoremongers, and sorcerers, and idolaters, and all liars shall have their part in the lake which burneth with fire and brimstone: which is the second death."* **Revelation 21:8**

**IF YOU ARE SUICIDAL:** First, you need to become a born-again Christian! Then you will be an overcomer! You will inherit God's blessings. And best of all, when you die you can be assured you will *spend eternity with Jesus! "He that overcometh shall inherit all things; and I will be his God, and he shall be my son."* **Revelation 21:7**

*"There is a way which seemeth right unto a man* (such as suicidal thoughts), *but the end thereof are the ways of death* (eternal separation from God)." **Proverbs 14:12**

**JOB WAS SUICIDAL — BUT HE OVERCAME — AND SO CAN YOU!** He wrote: *"Wherefore is light given to him that is in misery, and life unto the bitter in soul: which long for death, but it cometh not; and dig for it more than for hid treasures, which rejoice exceedingly and are glad, when they can find the grave?"* **Job 3:20-22** *"The paths of their way are turned aside: they go to nothing, and perish."* **Job 6:18**

**IT'S A SHAME AND PITY FOR SOMEONE TO KILL HIMSELF — WHEN GOD WANTED TO HELP HIM WITH HIS PROBLEMS AND GIVE HIM PEACE!** *"They are destroyed from morning to evening: they perish for ever without any regarding it. Doth not their excellency which is in them go away? they die, even without wisdom* (which only God can give)." **Job 4:20-21**

**THE SCRIPTURES TELL US THAT SAUL, AHITHOPHEL, ZIMRI AND JUDAS COMMITTED SUICIDE!** 1 Samuel 31:4-5/2 Samuel 17:23/1 Kings 16:18/Matthew 27:5/Acts 1:18

**A PERSON NEED NEVER COMMIT SUICIDE . . . IF SOMEONE WILL JUST TAKE THE TIME TO TELL HIM HOW MUCH GOD LOVES HIM!** *"And it shall come to pass, that whosoever shall call on the name of the Lord shall be saved* (and will spend eternity with God and Jesus)." **Acts 2:21**

**DO PEOPLE WHO COMMIT SUICIDE EVER GO TO HEAVEN?** Only God knows for sure! He knows the condition of each heart. he alone knows who has reached the age of accountability and who has not! God is loving and just! *"And many of them that sleep in the dust of the earth shall awake, some to everlasting life, and some to shame and everlasting contempt* (hell)." **Daniel 12:2**

### PRAYER
Dear God, please forgive me for all my sins. I want to be a born-again Christian. Come into my heart. Give me peace and many reasons to want to live. I forgive those who have hurt me. And I will ask them to forgive me, also! Your Word says we are to forgive and love one another. I will read my Bible and pray daily! I want to grow close to You! You know my heart. Give me courage and strength in my daily walk. In Jesus' name, I pray. AMEN!

# TEENAGERS

**GOD COMMANDS TEENAGERS TO OBEY THEIR PARENTS!** *"Honour thy father and thy mother: that thy days may be long upon the land which the Lord thy God giveth thee."* **Exodus 20:12**

**TEENAGERS ARE COMMANDED TO REMAIN SEXUALLY PURE UNTIL THEY MARRY!** *". . .He that standeth stedfast in his heart, having no necessity* (for sex), *but hath power over his own will, and hath so decreed in his heart that he will keep his virgin* (virginity) *doeth well."* **1 Corinthians 7:37** *"It is good for a man not to touch a woman. Nevertheless, to avoid fornication* (sex without marriage) *let every man have his own wife, and let every woman have her own husband."* **1 Corinthians 7:1-2**

**TEENAGERS SHOULD NOT DRINK ALCOHOL!** *"Be sober, be vigilant; because your adversary* (enemy) *the devil, as a roaring lion, walketh about, seeking whom he may devour."* **1 Peter 5:8**

**TEENAGERS SHOULD CONTROL THEIR ANGER!** *"Cease from anger, and forsake wrath; fret not thyself in any wise to do evil."* **Psalm 37:8**

**TEENAGERS SHOULD NOT COVET ANYTHING THAT BELONGS TO SOMEONE ELSE!** *"Thou shalt not covet. . ."* **Exodus 20:17**

**FRIENDS WILL OFTEN DISAPPOINT YOU . . . SO ALWAYS PUT GOD FIRST IN YOUR LIFE!** *"My friends scorn me: but mine eye poureth out tears unto God."* **Job 16:20**

**TEENAGERS SHOULD ALWAYS TRUST GOD. HIS WORDS ARE PURE. CAN WE SAY THAT ABOUT ANYONE ELSE?** *"The words of the Lord are pure words: as silver tried in a furnace of earth, purified seven times."* **Psalm 12:6**

**TEENAGERS SHOULD ASK GOD TO HELP THEM MAKE EVERY DECISION!** *". . .For your Father* (God) *knoweth what things ye have need of, before ye ask him."* **Matthew 6:8**

**ALL TEENAGERS SHOULD BECOME BORN-AGAIN CHRISTIANS!** *"Marvel not that I said unto thee, Ye must be born again."* **John 3:7**

**TEENAGERS SHOULD NOT BE JUDGMENTAL!** *"Judge not, that ye be not judged."* **Matthew 7:1**

**TEENAGERS SHOULD LEARN TO DISTINGUISH BETWEEN GODLY ADVICE AND FALSE TEACHERS (AND FALSE RELIGIONS)!** *"Beware of false prophets* (theories, psychology, cult religions), *which come to you in sheep's clothing* (pretending to be Christ like), *but inwardly they are ravening wolves."* **Matthew 7:15**

**TEENAGERS SHOULD BE FORGIVING OF OTHERS!** *"For if ye forgive men their trespasses, your heavenly Father will also forgive you. But if ye forgive not men their trespasses, neither will your Father* (God) *forgive your trespasses."* **Matthew 6:14-15**

**TEENAGERS SHOULD NOT BE SELFISH!** *"Therefore all things whatsoever ye would* (wish) *that men should do to you, do ye even so to them. . ."* **Matthew 7:12**

**TEENAGERS SHOULD WITNESS TO THEIR FRIENDS!** *". . .the harvest truly is plenteous* (you have many friends who need to get saved), *but the labourers* (those willing to witness) *are few."* **Matthew 9:37**

**TEENAGERS SHOULD NEVER BE ASHAMED OF GOD, THE BIBLE, OR OTHER CHRISTIANS!** *"Whosoever therefore shall confess me* (Christ) *before men, him will I confess also before my Father* (God) *which is in heaven. But whosoever shall deny me before men, him will I also deny before my Father which is in heaven."* **Matthew 10:32-33**

**TEENAGERS SHOULD KNOW THAT IT'S IMPOSSIBLE TO KEEP SECRETS FROM GOD!** *". . .For there is nothing covered, that shall not be revealed; and hid, that shall not be known* (to God)." **Matthew 10:26**

**TEENAGERS SHOULD STRIVE TO KEEP THEIR CONVERSATIONS PURE!** *". . .Every idle word that men* (people) *shall speak, they shall give account thereof in the day of judgment. For by thy words thou shalt be justified, and by thy* (own) *words thou shalt be condemned."* **Matthew 12:36-37**

**TEENAGERS SHOULD BE PREPARED FOR DEATH SINCE YOUNG AND OLD ALIKE, DIE!** Did you know that a person's eternal destiny is determined according to the condition of his heart and life at the point of his death? *"And as it is appointed unto men once to die, but after this the judgment."* **Hebrews 9:27** Therefore since it is appointed that each living person is going to die, then it is also determined that the exact state of your life, at the point of your death, is the same state you will personally spend in eternity — whether with God or Satan! So, if you die as an alcoholic, homosexual, drug addict, etc., that's the eternal state you will have wilfully chosen while you were alive! That state cannot be altered since God gave you a free will to choose good or evil (God or Satan). Repent of your own sins to God while you are alive because after you die it's too late! And, even God won't turn things around! *"He that is unjust* (a sinner when he dies), *let him be unjust still* (eternity): *and he which is filthy* (when he dies), *let him be filthy still* (in eternity): *and he that is righteous* (when he dies), *let him be righteous still* (in eternity): *and he that is holy, let him be holy still."* **Revelation 22:11** Since no person knows the exact moment he will die, and since the condition of your life and heart determine where you will spend eternity (heaven or hell), and since Jesus promised He would come back to earth quickly . . . This should be warning enough for each of us to get our lives in order. Time is short, so get saved now! **Jesus said:** *"And, behold, I come quickly; and my reward is with me, to give every man* (person) *according as his work shall be."* **Revelation 22:12** *"Blessed are they that do his commandments, that they may have right to the tree of life* (eternity with Jesus), *and may enter in through the gates into the city* (of God). *For without* (excluded) *are dogs* (homosexuals, adulterers, fornicators, alcoholics, liars, etc.), *and sorcerers* (occult teachers and believers), *and whoremongers* (prostitutes, pimps, sex sinners), *and murderers, and idolaters* (those who worship money, power, sex, false religions, anything other than Almighty God), *and whosoever loveth and maketh a lie."* **Revelation 22:14-15**

**TEENAGERS SHOULD OBEY ALL LAWS OF HUMAN GOVERNMENT!** *"Wherefore ye must needs be subject* (to the laws of the land, and of God), *not only for wrath, but also for* (your) *conscience sake."* **Romans 13:5**

**TEENAGERS SHOULD NOT STEAL!** *"Thou shalt not steal."* **Exodus 20:15**

**TEENAGERS SHOULD NOT CURSE!** *"Thou shalt not take the name of the Lord thy God in vain, for the Lord will not hold him guiltless that taketh his name in vain."* **Exodus 20:7**

**TEENAGERS SHOULD DO EVERYTHING IN THEIR POWER TO HELP KEEP THEIR PARENTS TOGETHER!** *"And if a house be divided against itself, that house cannot stand."* **Mark 3:25**

**TEENAGERS SHOULD KNOW THAT WHEN THEY BORROW ANYTHING THEY SHOULD PAY IT BACK!** *"Withhold not good from them to whom it is due, when it is in the power of thine hand to do it. Say not unto thy neighbour, go, and come again, and tomorrow I will give; when thou hast* (have) *it by* (with) *thee."* **Proverbs 3:27-28**

**TEENAGERS SHOULD KNOW, THAT EVEN IF THE WORLD CONDEMNS THEM, THAT JESUS DIED ON THE CROSS TO PAY FOR THEIR SINS SO THEY COULD ASK AND RECEIVE FORGIVENESS FOR THEIR OWN SINS!** *"For God sent not his Son* (Jesus) *into the world to condemn the world: but that the world through him might be saved. He that believeth on him is not condemned: but he that believeth not is condemned already, because he hath not believed in the name of the only begotten Son of God."* **John 3:17-18**

## PRAYER

Dear God, even though I'm a teenager, I realize that I must answer for my own sins! I repent of every sin I have ever committed. Come into my life and live in me. I declare with my mouth that I am now a born-again Christian. I will never be ashamed to let people know that through Your love and forgiveness I became a Christian! I will witness to others and attempt to lead them to Christ to the very best of my ability! Thank You for loving me. In Jesus' name, I pray. AMEN!

# TEMPTATION

**JESUS SAID:** *"Watch ye and pray, lest ye enter into temptation. The spirit truly is ready* (to serve God), *but the flesh is weak."* **Matthew 26:41/Mark 14:38/Luke 22:40** This means that our spirit is always ready but our flesh must be whipped into line with the will of God and then kept into subjection so it won't sin and fall away from God's commands for our life! **Paul wrote:** *"But I keep under my body, and bring it into subjection: lest that by any means, when I have preached to others, I myself should be a castaway."* **1 Corinthians 9:27**

**THE BIBLE SAYS WE ARE TO MORTIFY (PUT TO DEATH) OUR TEMPTATION TO SIN!** *"Mortify* (put to death) *therefore your members* (body parts, evil thoughts) *which are upon the earth; fornication* (sex outside marriage), *uncleanness* (all sexual sins, thoughts, fantasies), *inordinate affection, evil concupiscence* (lust, sexual desire), *and covetousness, which is idolatry. For which things' sake the wrath of God cometh on the children of disobedience."* **Colossians 3:5-6**

**IF WE GIVE IN TO TEMPTATION WE OBEY SATAN, AND THUS SEPARATE OURSELVES FROM GOD! IF WE DO THIS WE MUST ASK GOD TO FORGIVE US AND THEN TURN AWAY FROM ALL TEMPTATION AND SIN!** *"For if ye live after the flesh* (give in to temptation and commit sin) *ye shall die* (be eternally separated from God): *but if ye through the* (Holy) *Spirit do mortify* (kill) *the* (sinful) *deeds of the body, ye shall live* (eternally with God). *For as many as are led by the* (Holy) *Spirit of God, they are the sons of God."* **Romans 8:13-14**

**JESUS SAID THAT MANY PEOPLE RECEIVE THE SCRIPTURES WITH JOY. THEY BELIEVE AND SERVE GOD FOR A WHILE, BUT WHEN TEMPTATION, RICHES, OR PLEASURES (OF A SINFUL NATURE) COMES ALONG, THEY SOON FALL AWAY. Luke 8:13**

**GOD PROMISED US THAT WHEN TEMPTATIONS COME, HE WILL PROVIDE A WAY OF ESCAPE FOR US, IF WE WILL ONLY ACCEPT IT!** *"There hath no temptation taken you but such as is common to man: but God is faithful, who will not suffer* (allow) *you to be tempted above that* (which) *ye are able* (to stand): *but will with the temptation also make a way to escape, that ye may be able to bear it* (overcome and not sin)." **1 Corinthians 10:13**

# *"This I say then, Walk in the (Holy) Spirit, and ye shall not fulfil the lust of the flesh."* Galatians 5:16

*"LET NO MAN SAY WHEN HE IS **TEMPTED**, I AM **TEMPTED** OF GOD: FOR GOD CANNOT BE **TEMPTED** WITH EVIL, NEITHER **TEMPTETH** HE ANY MAN: BUT EVERY MAN IS **TEMPTED** WHEN HE IS DRAWN AWAY OF HIS OWN LUST, AND ENTICED. THEN WHEN LUST HATH CONCEIVED, IT BRINGETH FORTH SIN: AND SIN, WHEN IT IS FINISHED, BRINGETH FORTH DEATH* (ETERNAL SEPARATION FROM GOD)." **James 1:13-15**

*"BLESSED IS THE MAN THAT ENDURETH **TEMPTATION** (WITHOUT GIVING IN TO SIN): FOR WHEN HE IS TRIED, HE SHALL RECEIVE THE CROWN OF LIFE, WHICH THE LORD HATH PROMISED TO THEM THAT LOVE HIM."* **James 1:12**

**JESUS SAID WE ARE TO PRAY:** *"And lead us not into temptation, but deliver us from evil."* **Matthew 6:13** *This means we should ask God not to permit us to be overcome by the evil works of Satan! God will deliver us!

**RICHES SOMETIMES CAUSES A PERSON TO FALL INTO TEMPTATION!** Riches are wonderful when they're used to further the gospel. But to love money above God is idolatry! *"But they that will be rich fall into temptation and a snare* (trap set by Satan), *and into many foolish and hurtful lusts, which drown men in destruction and perdition. For the love of money is the root of all evil: which while some coveted after, they have erred from the faith, and pierced themselves through with many sorrows. But thou, O man of God, flee these things: and follow after righteousness, godliness, faith, love, patience, meekness. Fight the good fight of faith, lay hold on eternal life. . ."* **1 Timothy 6:9-12**

**IF WE OVERCOME TEMPTATION, JESUS WILL CONFESS US TO HIS FATHER, AND WE WILL ESCAPE THE TERRIBLE SEVEN YEAR TRIBULATION PERIOD. Revelation 3:10 WE WILL ALSO BE ENTITLED TO SPEND ETERNITY WITH JESUS. Revelation 3:5**

**SATAN IS THE "TEMPTER"!** He even tried to tempt Jesus . . . but he failed miserably **Matthew 4:1-11.**

**TEMPTATIONS START IN THE HEART, BUT IT'S UP TO US NOT TO GIVE IN!** *"For from within, out of the heart of men, proceed evil thoughts, adulteries, fornications, murders, thefts, covetousness, wickedness, deceit, lasciviousness, an evil eye, blasphemy, pride, foolishness: all these evil things come from within, and defile the man."* **Mark 7:21-23**

**HOW CAN A PERSON OVERCOME TEMPTATION?** *"This I say then, Walk in the* (Holy) *Spirit, and ye shall not fulfil the lust of the flesh."* **Galatians 5:16**

### PRAYER

Dear God, please forgive me for all my sins. I turn away from every form of temptation and sin! I take responsibility for my actions. I refuse to let Satan dictate to me what sinful things I should say or do! **When Satan comes to whisper temptations in my ear, I will quickly recognize the source as being him, and I will say, "Get thee behind me, Satan!"** From this moment on, I will live for You and serve You to the very best of my ability! Thank You for saving my soul. In Jesus' name, I pray. AMEN!

# THE TONGUE

**OUR TONGUE HAS TO BE TAUGHT WHAT IT CAN OR CANNOT SAY!** *"Teach me, and I will hold my tongue: and cause me to understand wherein I have erred (done wrong)."* **Job 6:24**

**HERE IS A VERSE WE SHOULD REPEAT EACH MORNING WHEN WE GET OUT OF BED!** *"My lips shall not speak wickedness, nor my tongue utter deceit."* **Job 27:4**

**1 Corinthians 10:10 says WE ARE NOT TO MURMUR!**

**PAUL WROTE IN Ephesians 5:4 THAT WE ARE TO ABSTAIN FROM FILTHINESS, FOOLISH TALKING AND JESTING! AND THAT WE SHOULD GIVE THANKS TO GOD!**

**VAIN TALK MAKES GOD VERY ANGRY WITH US!** *"Let no man deceive you with vain words: for because of these things cometh the wrath of God upon the children of disobedience."* **Ephesians 5:6** *"Wherefore laying (lay) aside all malice, and all guile, and hypocrisies, and envies and all evil speaking."* **1 Peter 2:1**

**IF YOU LOVE LIFE AND WANT TO LIVE TO A "RIPE OLD AGE" HERE IS THE RECIPE!** *"For he that will love life, and see good days, let him refrain his tongue from evil, and his lips that they speak no guile:"* **1 Peter 3:10**

**JESUS COMMANDED US NEVER TO SWEAR!** Matthew 5:33-36

**JESUS COMMANDED OUR CONVERSATIONS TO BE A CLEAR "YES" OR "NO"!** *". . .let your communication be, Yea, yea (yes); Nay, nay (no): for whatsoever is more than these cometh of evil."* Matthew 5:37

**WE ARE COMMANDED NEVER TO CURSE ANYONE!** *"Bless them which persecute you: bless, and curse not."* Romans 12:14

*"Therewith bless we God, even the Father; and therewith curse we men, which are made after the similitude of God. Out of the same mouth proceedeth blessing and cursing. My brethren, these things ought not so to be."* **James 3:9-10**

**WE ARE NEVER TO BLASPHEME THE WORD OF GOD! OUR SPEECH SHOULD BE ABOVE REPROACH!** *"In all things shewing (show) thyself a pattern of good works: in doctrine shewing uncorruptness, gravity, sincerity, sound speech, that cannot be condemned; that he that is of the contrary part may be ashamed, having no evil thing to say of you."* Titus 2:7-8

*"Wherefore, my beloved brethren, let every man be swift to hear, slow to speak, slow to wrath."* James 1:19

**THE NATURE OF THE TONGUE IS TO BOAST!** *"Even so the tongue is a little member (of our body), and boasteth great things. Behold, how great a matter a little fire kindleth!"* James 3:5

**THE TONGUE DEFILES THE WHOLE BODY!** *"And the tongue is a fire, a world of iniquity (sin): so is the tongue among our members, that it defileth the whole body, and setteth on fire the course of nature; and it is set on fire of hell."* James 3:6

**THE TONGUE IS UNCONTROLLABLE! NO MAN CAN TAME HIS OWN TONGUE. ONLY GOD CAN!** *"For every kind of beasts, and of birds, and of serpents, and of things in the sea, is tamed, and hath been tamed of mankind: But the tongue can no man tame; it is an unruly evil, full of deadly poison."* James 3:7-8

**THE CHRISTIAN ALWAYS HAS GOD TO HELP HIS CONTROL HIS TONGUE—IF HE WILL JUST REMEMBER TO PRAY FOR WISDOM TO KNOW HOW!** *"Who is a wise man and endued (gifted) with knowledge among you? let him shew (show) out of a good conversation his works with meekness of wisdom."* James 3:13

**WE SPEAK WORDS OF VANITY! WE FLATTER! WE HAVE A DOUBLE HEART! WE HAVE A SURPRISE COMING!** *"They speak vanity every one with his neighbour: with flattering lips and with a double heart do they speak. The Lord shall cut off all flattering lips, and the tongue that speaketh proud things: Who have said, With our tongue will we prevail; our lips are our own: who is lord (owner, master) over us (the tongue and lips)?"* Psalm 12:2-4

**MEMORIZE THIS VERSE AND REPEAT IT AT LEAST 10 TIMES EACH DAY!** *"Keep thy tongue from evil, and thy lips from speaking guile."* Psalm 34:13

**WHAT IS BETTER THAN LIFE ITSELF?** *"Because thy (God's) lovingkindness is better than life, my lips shall praise thee."* Psalm 63:3

**WHEN YOU'RE TEMPTED TO "LASH-OUT" . . . "WHISPER" — INSTEAD!** *"A soft answer turneth away wrath: but grievous words stir up anger."* Proverbs 15:1

**FOOLISH TALK COMES FROM FOOLS!** *"The tongue of the wise useth knowledge aright: but the mouth of fools poureth out foolishness."* Proverbs 15:2 *"The heart of him that hath understanding seeketh knowledge; but the mouth of fools feedeth on foolishness."* Proverbs 15:14

**A WHOLESOME TONGUE = PLEASANT WORDS!** *"The thoughts of the wicked are an abomination to the Lord: but the words of the pure are pleasant words."* Proverbs 15:26

**EVIL PEOPLE SPEAK EVIL THINGS!** *"The heart of the righteous studieth to answer (they think before they speak): but the mouth of the wicked poureth out evil things."* Proverbs 15:28

235 (Continued)

**THE TONGUE IS LIKE A RAZOR!** *"The tongue devises mischiefs; like a sharp razor, working deceitfully. Thou (the tongue) lovest evil more than good; and lying rather than to speak righteousness. Thou lovest all devouring words, O thou deceitful tongue. God shall likewise destroy thee for ever, he shall take thee away, and pluck thee out of thy dwelling place, and root thee out of the land of the living."* **Psalm 52:2-5**

**SHAME! SHAME! SHAME! SHAME!** *"Thou givest thy mouth to evil, and thy tongue frameth deceit. Thou sittest and speakest against thy brother; thou slanderest thine own mother's son."* **Psalm 50:19-20**

**MODEL PRAYER—FOR THE PERSON "PLAGUED" WITH A LIAR:** *"Deliver my soul, O Lord, from lying lips, and from a deceitful tongue."* **Psalm 120:2** *"Let the lying lips be put to silence: which speak grievous things proudly and contemptuously against the righteous."* **Psalm 31:18**

*"A word fitly spoken is like apples of gold in pictures of silver."* **Proverbs 25:11** *"The tongue of the just is as choice silver: the heart of the wicked is little worth. The lips of the righteous feed many: but fools die for want of wisdom."* **Proverbs 10:20-21**

**HAVE YOU HEARD THE EXPRESSION, "IF YOU WANT TO GO ON LIVING, YOU'D BETTER KEEP YOUR MOUTH SHUT!"?** *"He that keepeth his mouth keepeth his life; but he that openeth wide his lips shall have destruction."* **Proverbs 13:3** *"The wise in heart shall be called prudent: and the sweetness of the lips increaseth learning."* **Proverbs 16:21**

**A WISE PERSON TEACHES HIS LIPS WHAT THEY SHOULD SAY!** *"The heart of the wise teacheth his mouth, and addeth learning to his lips. Pleasant words are as an honeycomb, sweet to the soul, and health to the bones."* **Proverbs 16:23-24**

*"An ungodly man diggeth up evil: and in his lips there is as a burning fire."* **Proverbs 16:27** *"The words of the wicked are to lie in wait for blood: but the mouth of the upright shall deliver them."* **Proverbs 12:6**

**TRUTH = RIGHTEOUSNESS!** *"He that speaketh truth sheweth forth righteousness: but a false witness (shows) deceit. There is that speaketh like the piercings of a sword: but the tongue of the wise is health. The lip of truth shall be established for ever: but a lying tongue is but for a moment."* **Proverbs 12:17-19** *"Lying lips are abomination to the Lord: but they that deal truly are his delight."* **Proverbs 12:22**

**HERE IS A FORMULA FOR KEEPING YOUR SOUL FROM TROUBLES:** *"Whoso keepeth his mouth and his tongue keepeth his soul from troubles."* **Proverbs 21:23**

# We touch God through prayer, praise, obedience, witnessing, fasting, speaking the Word. God, in turn, reaches out and touches people through us.

## PRAYER

Dear God, I deserve to have my **tongue** cut out of my head. I am guilty of saying mean and hurtful things! I am also guilty of telling lies! I am guilty of falsely accusing others! I ask You to please forgive me for all my sins. I repent that I have done these things! I need Your forgiveness! **My tongue is my worst enemy!** Please help me clean up my act! Please teach me how to **control my tongue!** Please hear my prayer and forgive me. In Jesus' name, AMEN!

# TRANSVESTITE
# TRANSSEXUAL

**DEFINITION:** Adoption of the dress and often behavior of the opposite sex.

Transvestites are persons who cross-dress on various occasions. The majority of transvestites identify themselves as males, but get an erotic or emotional kick out of wearing women's clothing or in passing as a member of the opposite sex! Some can function sexually only after doing so. This distorted emotional condition can often be traced back to early repeated cross-dressing by parents or by the children themselves! Cross-dressing can produce emotional or sexual responses that when repeated become natural! **SATAN INVENTED THIS ABNORMAL CONDITION TO DEFY GOD'S PLAN FOR MANKIND!**

**GOD COMMANDED THAT WOMEN AND GIRLS NOT WEAR THAT WHICH PERTAINS TO A MAN AND THAT MEN SHOULD NOT PUT ON A WOMAN'S GARMENT. GOD SAID TO DO SO WAS AN ABOMINATION (DISGUSTING) TO HIM. GOD ALSO GAVE US THIS WARNING TO DISCOURAGE TRANSEXUALITY! Deuteronomy 22:5**

**TRANSSEXUALS MAY BE MALE OR FEMALE.** They feel they have the mind and emotions of the opposite sex and are trapped in the wrong physical body. Often this can be traced back to early childhood when someone depreciated or ignored a child's true sex and caused him to value only the feelings and emotions of the opposite sex! Effeminate mannerisms in males may be due to being reared in an almost exclusive female environment. Effeminate mannerisms may also be a way of portraying non-aggressiveness. Effeminacy is harmful because it damages a male's proper leadership and thinking in a family unit. Another word for effeminacy is "catamite" which refers to a boy being kept for unnatural (sexual) purposes. *"Know ye not that the unrighteous shall not inherit the kingdom of God? Be not deceived: neither fornicators, nor idolaters, nor adulterers, nor **effeminate**, nor abusers of themselves with mankind, nor thieves, nor covetous, nor drunkards, nor revilers, nor extortioners, shall inherit the kingdom of God."* **1 Corinthians 6:9-10**

**GOD SAYS WE MUST KEEP OUR BODY AND PASSIONS UNDER CONTROL — BECAUSE WE WILL HAVE TO ANSWER FOR THOSE ACTS WE HAVE DONE IN OUR BODY!** *"For we must all appear before the judgment seat of Christ; that every one may receive the things done in his body, according to that* (which) *he hath done, whether it be good or bad."* **2 Corinthians 5:10**

**A TRANSVESTITE WOULD FALL UNDER THE CATEGORY OF "UNCLEAN" IN THE SCRIPTURES! 2 Corinthians 12:21** *"Let not sin therefore reign in your mortal body, that ye should obey it in the lusts thereof."* **Romans 6:12**

**ALL MANNER OF SEXUAL SIN IS ALSO REFERRED TO AS "INFIRMITY" OF THE FLESH!** *". . . for as ye have yielded your members* (body parts) *servants to uncleanness* (sexual sins, thoughts, actions, clothes) *and to iniquity unto iniquity; even so now yield your members servants to righteousness unto holiness."* **Romans 6:19**

**TRANSVESTITES AND TRANSSEXUALS ARE OPPRESSED . . . BY PUBLIC ENEMY NUMBER 1 . . . SATAN!** *"Who being past feeling* (sexually corrupt) *have given themselves over unto lasciviousness* (lust, sex sins) *to work* (commit sexual sins, fantasies) *all uncleanness* (homosexuality, lesbianism, all sex sins) *with greediness."* **Ephesians 4:19**

*"But fornication* (sex outside marriage), *and all uncleanness* **(includes transvestites),** *or covetousness, let it not be once named among you, as becometh saints* (born-again Christians); *Neither filthiness, nor foolish talking, nor jesting, which are not convenient* (godly): *but rather, giving* (give) *of thanks* (to God for what He has done for you). *For this ye know, that no whoremonger, nor unclean person* (transvestite), *nor covetous man, who is an idolater, hath any inheritance in the kingdom of Christ and of God."* **Ephesians 5:3-5**

**ACCORDING TO EPHESIANS 5:12 SOME PEOPLE DO THINGS THAT ARE TOO OBSCENE TO EVEN DESCRIBE!**

**WILL BEING A TRANSVESTITE OR TRANSSEXUAL KEEP A PERSON FROM GOING TO HEAVEN?** I believe it will but why would he want to take a chance when God loves him and wants him to repent and be free of this condition? God gave us the Bible so we could know the true spiritual causes of human problems and what we can do to change them. Satan is responsible for the condition of transvestism. He delights in confusing people. He hates all people and will do anything to destroy us.

**IF YOU ARE A TRANSVESTITE OR KNOW ANYONE WHO IS — TELL HIM THAT JESUS WILL FREE HIM IF HE TRULY WANTS TO BE FREE. HE MUST REPENT OF ALL HIS SINS AND THEN RENOUNCE SATAN'S INFLUENCE IN HIS LIFE. HE CAN ALSO TAKE AUTHORITY OVER SATAN, IN THE NAME OF JESUS, AND CAST HIM OUT OF HIS LIFE AND BE FREE!**

### PRAYER

Dear God, Please forgive all my sins. **I take authority over Satan. I will no longer obey him by being a transvestite!** With Your help I will remain a Christian and free from this evil condition for the remainder of my life! I refuse to be in bondage to Satan any longer! **From this moment on, I declare I am a Christian and free from my desire to cross-dress and pretend to be the opposite sex!** I know I am not trapped in my body as a different sex than what You created me. I realize this is a vicious lie that Satan has told me! I take charge of my own life and actions. I am now free because of what Jesus did for me when He died on the cross and was resurrected. I realize He is coming back very soon and I want to be ready! Thank You God for loving me when I've disappointed You! I will repay You by being the kind of person You want me to be. In Jesus' name, I pray. AMEN!

# U.F.O.'s
## (Unidentified Flying Objects)

**FLYING SAUCERS HAVE BEEN FREQUENTLY REPORTED TO MAKE 90 DEGREE DIRECTIONAL CHANGES WHILE TRAVELLING AT EXTREMELY HIGH RATES OF SPEED. ACCORDING TO THE LAWS OF PHYSICS THIS IS PHYSICALLY IMPOSSIBLE. THEREFORE, FLYING SAUCERS ARE PHYSICALLY IMPOSSIBLE AND MUST BE ILLUSIONS FROM SATAN AND HIS ORGANIZATION OF DEMONS.**

**SATAN IS ,THE MASTER AND INVENTOR OF ILLUSIONS!** If flying saucers were visions from God they would not be seen doing things which are contrary to God's laws! *". . .This is what the Lord says: If I have not established my covenant with day and night and the fixed laws of heaven and earth, then I will reject the descendants of Jacob and David my servant and will not choose one of his sons to rule over the descendants of Abraham, Isaac and Jacob. For I will restore their fortunes and have compassion on them."* **Jeremiah 33:25** (New International Version)

**2 Corinthians 11:14 SAYS SATAN HIMSELF IS TRANSFORMED INTO AN ANGEL OF LIGHT!**

The Holy Bible, which has stood the test of time as being authentic, records only very few things that fly above the earth. My research revealed these few things that fly: fowls, God, The Holy Spirit, flying creatures that sting such as bees, locusts, angels which are messengers of God, demonic spirits, our own personal spirit (if it ascends to heaven), our thoughts, and dreams!

**THE U.S. GOVERNMENT SAYS IT KEEPS NO RECORDS ON UNIDENTIFIED FLYING OBJECTS, BECAUSE THEY DON'T EXIST!**

**U.F.O.'S HAVE THEIR OWN CULT FOLLOWERS!** Christians should never get nervous or have their faith in God shaken. **The Bible speaks about evil supernatural forces and beings.** In Old Testament times the scriptures speak of supernatural occurrences which had nothing to do with God. Ancient Hindu and Roman literature refers to U.F.O.'s and even Columbus reported a sighting in his notes. No one is able to say with certainty that these incidents are only a hoax, or hallucination, or whether these beings from outer space were instrumental in building the great pyramids, Mayan culture and Nazca lines. **Satan certainly has the intelligence, ability, and imagination to manifest extraterrestial space-craft in visions. He delights in confusion!**

**OUR GOVERNMENT HAS REACHED THE CONCLUSION THAT ALL U.F.O. SIGHTINGS WHICH CANNOT BE EXPLAINED THROUGH NATURAL PHENOMENA ARE PARA-PHYSICAL MANIFESTATIONS SIMILAR TO THOSE EXPERIENCED IN OCCULT SPIRITISM.** God absolutely forbids all forms of occult activity since it comes from Satan. People underestimate the devious powers of Satan by pretending he doesn't exist! They err in not believing what God says throughout the scriptures. U.F.O.'s cannot be explained or verified as being manufactured spacecraft from other planets. They are most likely deceiving spirits playing devilish games on real people! While there are only sparse reports of U.F.O. sightings, there have been multitudes of reports of demon manifestations ever since Satan entered the world scene!

**U.F.O. "BEINGS" SEEM TO HAVE NO CONSISTENT FORM AND THE BIBLE DESCRIBES FAMILIAR SPIRITS (DEMON SPIRITS) IN JUST THE SAME WAY!** Familiar spirits are what psychic mediums claim to see and converse with! U.F.O. beings (if they exist) seem to travel at tremendous speed and the maneuvers they perform with their space craft defy all known natural laws. Science cannot conceive of any natural being or material substance that can survive gravity shock at 90 degree turns made at 5,000 mph. Uri Geller (the occult key-bender) claims to receive his occult powers from extra-terrestial beings. Mediums with familiar spirits, trances, hypnotism, astral projection, thought transferrence, automatic writing, dreams and visions, are all tools used by Satan to confuse, deceive, and prepare mankind for the coming of the anti-christ . . . so are U.F.O.'s!

**Satan is the prince of the power of the air only until Jesus returns during the Second Advent!** Myriads of angels were cast out of heaven with Lucifer (Satan) when he was defeated in his attempt to overthrow God. They were confined to the atmospheric heavens of earth to await God's final judgment **Ezekiel 28:11-19/Revelation 12:7-12/Isaiah 14:12-17/Ephesians 2:2).** These same beings, no doubt, are the beings people claim to see in shining spacecraft.

**GOD INSTRUCTED CHRISTIANS TO PUT ON GOD'S WHOLE ARMOR SO WE CAN STAND UP AGAINST ALL THE TRICKS OF THE DEVIL!** The Bible says we **aren't** wrestling with flesh and blood but we **are** wrestling against demon spirits, and powers, and rulers of darkness which fight against the spirit forces of God in the heavenly (supernatural) sphere. **Ephesians 6:11-12**

(Continued)

# THE LAST DAYS BEFORE CHRIST RETURNS TO EARTH ARE PROPHESIED

*"Now the (Holy) Spirit speaketh expressly, that in the latter times some shall depart from the faith, giving heed to **seducing spirits,** and doctrines of devils; speaking lies in hypocrisy; having their conscience seered with a hot iron; forbidding (choosing not) to marry, and commanding (preferring) to abstain from meats (being vegetarians), which God hath created to be received with thanksgiving of them which believe (in God) and know the truth."* 1 Timothy 4:1-4

**BORN-AGAIN CHRISTIANS ARE GIVEN FULL AUTHORITY OVER ALL EVIL SPIRITUAL BEINGS! Luke 10:19.** Christians are told not to believe every spirit but to test them to see whether they are from God or Satan. **HOW DO YOU TEST THE SPIRITS?** Every spirit that confesses that Jesus Christ is the living Son of God who came down to earth and became a flesh and blood man, and died on the cross to pay the penalty for our sins and is coming back to earth to rule and reign forever is from God **1 John 4:1-3.** Every spirit which refuses to acknowledge and confess that Christ has come in the flesh is not of God! These are called the spirits of anti-christ and they run rampant in our world.

**U.F.O. "BEINGS" SUPPOSEDLY CLAIM TO SPAN THOUSANDS OF YEARS AND TO BE IMMORTAL! THEY CLAIM THEIR ADVANCED CIVILIZATION IS PERFECT.** God says Satan is a liar and the father of lies. These intergalactic visitors predict warnings of doom for earth. They deny a super-natural all-powerful God who works in saving individual lives. Their non-confession of Christ and God's plan of salvation classifies U.F.O.'s as evil spirits doing the devil's work! In my opinion, I believe they are merely seeking to divert man from receiving God's spiritual blessings and forgiveness by providing them with fantasies and fear tactics. They attempt to trick man into thinking they may come from heaven!

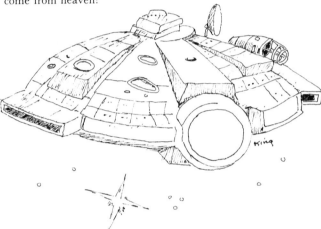

**NO ONE CAN ACTUALLY PROVE THAT U.F.O.'S EVEN EXIST!** However, historical evidence has proven that Jesus lived, died, and was resurrected! And thousands of Bible data can be verified and seen today! While U.F.O.'s maneuver the skies spreading doom and gloom, Jesus is spreading the skies teaching love, peace, prosperity, honesty, forgiveness, and love! God does not resort to playing games . . . Satan does! God offered Himself for us and gave us legal right to inherit His perfect kingdom if we will believe, repent, and accept Him! It's that simple! No one can answer the U.F.O. question with certainty. I personally think they do exist and are demoniac manifestations aimed to divert man's attention.

**When the Christians are raptured to heaven to enjoy seven years of peace and safety, Satan may try to convince the rest of the world (who rejected Jesus), into believing we were abducted by flying saucers!** Never put it past Satan to try to counteract the evacuation of Christians to Heaven, by presenting them with sightings of U.F.O.'s! Don't we have better things to do such as witnessing to a lost world about the true love of God, instead of spending so much time being pre-occupied with U.F.O.'s?

## PRAYER

Dear God, please forgive me for all my sins. Forgive me for being so interested in U.F.O.'s because I don't really believe they have anything to do with You! From this moment on I will spend my time reading the Bible. I know it has the answers to all our questions and problems. I know that You love me and want me to think on godly things rather than things that are not proven to be sound! I will study my Bible and pray so I can live a full life! Thank you for forgiving my sins. In Jesus' name, I pray. AMEN!

# UNFORGIVENESS

**JESUS SAID:** *"...Love your enemies, do good to them which hate you. Bless them that curse you, and pray for them which despitefully use you. And unto him that smiteth thee on the one cheek offer also the other; and him that taketh away thy cloke forbid* (him) *not to take thy coat also. Give to every man that asketh of thee; and of him that taketh away thy goods ask them not again. And as ye would that men should do to you, do ye also to them likewise. For if ye love them which love you, what thank* (thanks) *have ye? for sinners also love those that love them. And if ye do good to them which do good to you, what thank* (thanks) *have ye? for sinners also do even the same. And if ye lend to them of whom ye hope to receive, what thank* (thanks) *have ye? for sinners also lend to sinners, to receive as much again. But love ye your enemies, and do good, and lend, hoping for nothing again; and your reward shall be great, and ye shall be the children of the Highest: for he is kind unto the unthankful and to the evil. Be ye therefore merciful, as your Father* (God) *also is merciful. Judge not, and ye shall not be judged: condemn not, and ye shall not be condemned:* **forgive,** *and ye shall be* **forgiven."** Luke 6:27-37

*"And be ye kind one to another, tenderhearted,* **forgiving one another,** *even as God for Christ's sake hath forgiven you."* **Ephesians 4:32**

*"Forbearing one another, and* **forgiving one another,** *if any man have a quarrel against any: even as* **Christ forgave you,** *so also do ye."* **Colossians 3:13**

**JESUS SAID WE ARE TO FORGIVE 70 X 7 TIMES! Matthew 18:21-22**

*"If my people, which are called by my name, shall humble themselves, and pray, and seek my face, and turn from their wicked ways; then will I hear from heaven, and will* **forgive** *their sin, and will heal their land."* **2 Chronicles 7:14**

*"For if ye forgive men their trespasses, your heavenly Father will also forgive you: but if ye forgive not men their trespasses, neither will your Father* (God) *forgive your trespasses."* **Matthew 6:14-15**

*"And when ye stand praying,* **forgive,** *if ye have ought against any: that your Father also which is in heaven may* **forgive** *you your trespasses. But if ye do not* **forgive,** *neither will your Father which is in heaven* **forgive** *your trespasses."* **Mark 11:25-26**

*"Blessed is he whose transgression is* **forgiven,** *whose sin is covered."* **Psalm 32:1**

*"And you, being dead in your sins ... hath he quickened together with him* (Christ), *having* **forgiven you** *all* (your) *trespasses."* **Colossians 2:13**

*"To the Lord our God belong mercies and* **forgivenesses,** *though we have rebelled against him."* **Daniel 9:9**

*"Bless the Lord, O my soul, and forget not all his benefits: who* **forgiveth** *all thine iniquities; who healeth all thy diseases, who redeemeth thy life from destruction; who crowneth thee with lovingkindness and tender mercies."* **Psalm 103:2-4**

*"The Lord is longsuffering, and of great mercy,* **forgiving** *iniquity and transgression, and by no means clearing the guilty . . ."* **Numbers 14:18**

UNFORGIVENESS—

**Romans 8:12-14 says:** *"Therefore, brethren, we are debtors* (to God), *not to the flesh* (to sin with), *to live after the flesh. For if ye live after the flesh* (sin with your body), *ye shall die* (be forever separated from God): *but if ye through the* (Holy) *Spirit do mortify* (discipline your sinful nature) *the deeds of the body, ye shall live. For as many as are led by the Spirit of God, they are the sons of God."*

**WHEN A CHRISTIAN REALIZES THAT HE DOES (IN FACT) HAVE AN ENEMY, HE SHOULD LEAN ON THE LORD AND TRUST HIM MORE THAN EVER!** *"trust in the Lord with all thine heart; and lean not unto thine own understanding. In all thy ways acknowledge him, and he shall direct thy paths. Be not wise in thine own eyes: fear the Lord, and depart from evil."* **Proverbs 3:5-7**

**JESUS IS COMING BACK VERY SOON AND NO MAN KNOWS THE HOUR!** *"But of that day and hour knoweth no man, no, not the angels of heaven, but my Father* (God) *only."* **Matthew 24:36** *"Watch therefore, for ye know neither the day nor the hour wherein the Son of man* (Jesus) *cometh."* **Matthew 25:13** *"But of that day and that hour knoweth no man, no, not the angels which are in heaven, neither the Son* (Jesus), *but the Father* (only). *Take ye heed, watch and pray: for ye know not when the time is."* **Mark 13:32-33** *"Watch ye therefore: for ye know not when the master of the house cometh, at even* (evening), *or at midnight, or at the cockcrowing* (3-4:00 a.m.), *or in the morning."* **Mark 13:35-36**

**THE MODEL PRAYER READS:** *"...Our Father which art in heaven, Hallowed be thy name. Thy kingdom come. Thy will be done in earth, as it is in heaven. Give us this day our daily bread. And* **forgive** *us our debts, as we* **forgive** *our debtors. And lead us not into temptation, but deliver us from evil: For thine is the kingdom, and the power, and the glory, for ever, Amen."* **Matthew 6:9-13/Luke 11:2-4**

**THINK ABOUT THIS:**
A Christian is not one who is seeking God's forgiveness; he is one who has found it!

# unforgiveness
### PRAYER

Dear God, Please **forgive** me for all my sins. I repent of every one of them and I humble myself before You. Teach me to love others more. Let others see a reflection of Jesus in my face. **Thank You for forgiving and loving me when I was so unlovely!** In Jesus' name I pray. AMEN!

# UNPARDONABLE SIN

**MANY PEOPLE LIVE IN CONSTANT FEAR THAT THEY HAVE ALREADY COMMITTED THE UNPARDONABLE SIN AND WILL NOT BE ALLOWED TO GO IN THE RAPTURE, OR TO HEAVEN WHEN THEY DIE!** Let's see what the Bible says about the unpardonable sin and then it's up to you to accept by faith that what the Bible says is true! Many people believe they have already committed it when in reality they have not! Satan puts this suggestion in a person's mind in order to make him feel hopelessly defeated and on his way to hell. **Not many people are guilty of committing the unpardonable sin!**

**JESUS SAID:** *"Verily I say unto you, all sins shall be forgiven unto the sons of men, and* **blasphemies** *wherewith soever they shall* **blaspheme:** *But he that shall* **blaspheme** *against the Holy Ghost hath never forgiveness, but is in* **danger** *of eternal damnation: Because they said, He* (Jesus) *hath an unclean* (demon) *spirit."* **Mark 3:28-30**

**HOW CAN YOU KNOW IF YOU HAVE ALREADY COMMITTED THE UNPARDONABLE SIN?** If you are guilty of attributing the divine works of God, Jesus, or the Holy Spirit, as having come from Satan, you have committed the unpardonable sin. In other words, if God heals a person and you believe (or say) He didn't heal anyone, or that the healing was a fake, or that God cannot heal or perform miracles, you commit the unpardonable sin. If you believe and say that Jesus is dead, or not the Son of God, you commit the unpardonable sin. In God's eyes, you deny Him and slap Him in His face! Jesus performed many miracles yesterday and continues to perform many today always working through the precious Holy Spirit. *"Jesus Christ the same yesterday, and to day, and for ever."* **Hebrews 13:8** When a person says God is no longer in the miracle or healing business, he blasphemies God. And, unless he repents and receives forgiveness, he is wilfully committing the unpardonable sin. Only after he repents and finds forgiveness is he assured he will go to heaven!

**WHEN A PERSON WILFULLY REJECTS AND REFUSES TO ACCEPT GOD, JESUS, AND THE HOLY SPIRIT (CALLED THE DIVINE TRINITY) HE BLASPHEMES GOD!** If he dies in this same condition, he has already committed the unpardonable sin. After we die, we are not in a position to plead our own case! God will forgive you if you speak against Christ, but not if you claim the works of the Holy Spirit are not real, or they're fakes, or they're from Satan. For instance, if you say and believe in your heart that the gift of speaking in tongues comes from Satan (or mere man) rather than from the Holy Spirit, you totally disregard and reject what the scriptures say even though they tell us that this gift is from the Holy Spirit! In this case you blaspheme the Holy Spirit!

**IF A PERSON BLASPHEMES AGAINST THE HOLY SPIRIT IN IGNORANCE HE CAN BE FORGIVEN — IF HE ASKS GOD!** Paul described himself in this way: *"Who was before a* **blasphemer,** *and a persecutor, and injurious: but I obtained mercy, because I did it* (blasphemed) *ignorantly in unbelief* (before I repented and became a believer and follower of Christ)." **1 Timothy 1:13**

---

## It is strange that we prepare for everything except meeting God

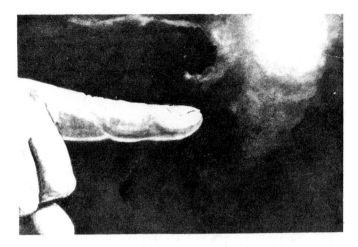

**DID YOU KNOW THAT THE SIN OF BLASPHEMY IS PROPHESIED AS A SIGN OF THE LAST DAYS BEFORE CHRIST RETURNS TO EARTH?** *"This know also, that in the last days perilous times shall come. For men shall be lovers of their own selves, covetous, boasters, proud,* **blasphemers,** *disobedient to parents, unthankful, unholy, without natural affection* (homosexuals, lesbians, rapists, incest, etc.), *truce breakers* (lawbreakers), *false accusers, incontinent* (failure to restrain sexual appetites), *fierce, despisers of those that are good, traitors, heady, highminded, lovers of pleasures more than lovers of God, having a form of godliness* (psychology, man made religions, humanism, self-help theories, science, etc.), *but denying the power* (of the Holy Spirit) *thereof: from such turn away."* **2 Timothy 3:1-5**

**THE PURPOSE OF THE HOLY SPIRIT IS TO CONVINCE PEOPLE OF THE TRUTH ABOUT JESUS!** Jesus said: *"And when he* (the Holy Spirit) *is* (has) *come, he will reprove* (convince) *the world of sin, and of righteousness, and of judgment; Of* **sin,** *because they believe not on me* (Jesus); *of* **righteousness,** *because I go to my Father, and ye see me no more* (until I return to earth at the Second Advent); *of judgment, because the "prince of this world"* (Satan) *is judged."* **John 16:8-11**

**THE UNPARDONABLE SIN IS TO WILFULLY REJECT THE HOLY SPIRIT WHEN HE "WOOS" YOU TO REPENT OF YOUR SINS AND TO ASK GOD TO FORGIVE YOU!** To commit this sin one must consciously, persistently and maliciously reject the Holy Spirit. And if a person continues to do this until his death, then he has **no** hope of forgiveness and eternal life with God!

**JESUS SAID:** *"He that is not with me* (believes, repents and accepts me as his savior) *is against me* (you can't remain neutral); *and he that gathereth not with me scattereth abroad. Wherefore I say unto you, all manner of sin and* **blasphemy** *shall be forgiven unto men: but the* **blasphemy** *against the Holy Spirit shall not be forgiven unto men. And whosoever speaketh a word against the Son of man* (Jesus), *it shall be forgiven him: but whosoever* **speaketh against the Holy Ghost, it shall not be forgiven him, neither in this world, neither in the world to come."** **Matthew 12:30-32**

**PSALM 74:18 SAYS IT'S FOOLISH TO BLASPHEME GOD!** If you blaspheme God, Jesus, or the Holy Spirit, you obey your master whose name is Satan, whether you realize it or not! God said Satan is a liar and the inventor of lies! Why listen to any suggestion this evil liar plants in your head? Satan wants you to burn in hell with him but you don't have to! Choose eternal life with Jesus by acknowledging that you are a sinner, repent, and ask forgiveness! God loves you very much and wants you to spend eternity in perfect peace and safety with Him!

(Continued)

**ONLY GOD CAN FORGIVE YOUR SINS!** *"Why doth this man thus speak* **blasphemies?** *who can forgive sins but God only?"* **Mark 2:7**

**GOD HEARS EVERY WORD OF BLASPHEMY SPOKEN BY A PERSON!** *"And thou shalt know that I am the Lord, and that I have heard all thy* **blasphemies** *which thou hast spoken . . . thus with your mouth ye have boasted against me, and have multiplied your words against me: I have heard them."* **Ezekiel 35:12-13**

**BLASPHEMEY STARTS IN THE HEART AND IS A GIFT FROM SATAN . . . BUT YOU DON'T HAVE TO ACCEPT THE GIFT!** *"But those things which proceed out of the mouth come forth from the heart; and they defile the man. For out of the heart proceed evil thoughts, murders, adulteries, fornications, thefts, false witness,* **blasphemies:**'*These are the things which defile a man: but to eat with unwashen hands defileth not a man."* **Matthew 15:18-20**

# ALL ACTS WE DO IN OUR BODY WILL BE JUDGED! *"For we must all appear before the judgment seat of Christ; that every one may receive the things done in his body, according to that* (which) *he hath done, whether it be good or bad."* **2 Corinthians 5:10**

**RIGHT NOW IS THE PERFECT TIME TO GET DOWN TO BUSINESS AND GET YOUR SINS FORGIVEN! IT'S POSSIBLE YOU HAVE COMMITTED THE UNPARDONABLE SIN IN IGNORANCE, BUT NOW YOU HAVE NO EXCUSE NOT TO GET RIGHT WITH GOD! TOMORROW MAY BE TOO LATE!** Since no person knows the exact moment he will die, and since the condition of your life and heart determines where you will spend eternity (heaven or hell), and since Jesus promised He would come quickly, this should be warning enough for every person to get his life in order. Time is marching on while you're reading this! **Jesus said:** *"And, behold, I* (will) *come quickly; and my reward is with me, to give every man according as his work shall be."* **Revelation 22:12** *"He that is unjust* (when he dies), *let him be unjust still* (in eternity): *and he which is filthy* (a sinner when he dies), *let him be filthy still* (in hell): *and he that is righteous* (when he dies), *let him be righteous still: and he that is holy, let him be holy still."* **Revelation 22:11**

**IF YOU THINK YOU HAVE COMMITTED THE UNPARDONABLE SIN, AND YOU'RE NOT A BORN-AGAIN CHRISTIAN, AND IGNORANT OF ALL THE SCRIPTURES HAVE TO SAY ON THE SUBJECT, BE ASSURED THAT GOD WILL FORGIVE YOU IF YOU HUMBLE YOURSELF, REPENT, AND ASK HIS FORGIVENESS! THEN TURN AWAY FROM ALL SIN IN YOUR LIFE! STUDY THE BIBLE! PRAY AND ATTEND CHURCH! LIVE FOR JESUS IN EVERYTHING YOU DO! GOD LOVES YOU AND WANTS YOU TO KNOW THE TRUTH! THE TRUTH WILL SET YOU FREE!**

# PRAYER
Dear God, I have committed many sins. I repent and ask You to forgive me. I turn away from all sin in my life. To the very best of my ability, I will live a godly life! Please blot out all my sins and bring me peace and happiness. I know with Your help I will be able to forget my past sins! I will not let the memory of what I've done hold me back from worshipping and serving You. Teach me the proper way to live, talk and think and I will give You all the praise! In Jesus' name, I pray. AMEN!

# VANITY
# (EGO)

**GOD HATES VANITY!** *"Woe unto them that are wise in their own eyes, and prudent in their own sight!"* **Isaiah 5:21**

**ECCLESIASTES 6:2 SAYS VANITY IS AN EVIL DISEASE!**

*". . .he that followeth vain persons is void of understanding."* **Proverbs 12:11**

*". . .every man at his best state is altogether vanity."* **Psalm 39:5**

**PSALM 39:11 SAYS EVERY PERSON IS VAIN!**

*"Surely men of low degree are vanity, and men of high degree are a lie: to be laid in the balance they are altogether lighter than vanity."* **Psalm 62:9**

*"THE LORD KNOWETH THE THOUGHTS OF MAN, THAT THEY ARE VANITY."* **Psalm 94:11/119:113/Ephesians 4:17**

*"Man is like to vanity: his days are as a shadow that passeth away."* **Psalm 144:4**

*"Vanity of vanities, saith the Preacher, vanity of vanities; all is vanity."* **Ecclesiastes 1:2/3:19/12:8**

**CONVERSATIONS CAN BE VAIN!** *"Let no man deceive you with vain words: for because of these things cometh the wrath of God upon the children of disobedience."* **Ephesians 5:6** **ALSO READ: 1 Peter 1:18/Exodus 5:9/Job 16:3/2 Kings 18:20.**

**TITUS 1:10 SAYS THERE ARE MANY VAIN TALKERS AND DECEIVERS!**

**Galatians 5:26 says:** *"Let us not be desirous of vain glory, provoking one another, envying one another."*

**JEREMIAH 13:15 SAYS BE NOT PROUD!**

*"The getting of treasures by a lying tongue is a vanity tossed to and fro of them that seek death (eternal separation from God)."* **Proverbs 21:6**

**TITUS 3:9 SAYS TO AVOID FOOLISH QUESTIONS, GENEALOGIES, CONTENTIONS AND STRIVINGS ABOUT THE LAW BECAUSE THEY ARE UNPROFITABLE AND VAIN!**

**AN INTELLECTUAL MAY BECOME VAIN! Job 15:2** *"Professing themselves to be wise, they became fools."* **Romans 1:22** *". . .The Lord knoweth the thoughts of the wise, that they are vain."* **1 Corinthians 3:20**

**IMAGINATIONS CAN BE VAIN! Romans 1:21**

**BEAUTY IS VAIN!** *"Favour is deceitful, and beauty is vain: but a woman that feareth the Lord, she shall be praised."* **Proverbs 31:30 BEAUTY IS ONLY SKIN DEEP! Jeremiah 4:30**

*"Let not him that is deceived trust in vanity: for vanity shall be his recompence."* **Job 15:31**

**PEOPLE SOMETIMES ENTICE LUST IN OTHERS WITH GREAT SWELLING WORDS OF VANITY! 2 Peter 2:18**

*"He that soweth iniquity shall reap vanity. . ."* **Proverbs 22:8** *"He that is of a proud heart stirreth up strife: but he that putteth his trust in the Lord shall be made fat (prosperous)."* **Proverbs 28:25**

*"Wealth gotten by vanity shall be diminished: but he that gathereth by labour shall increase."* **Proverbs 13:11**

**WE SHOULD MAKE A CONSCIOUS EFFORT TO OVERCOME VANITY BECAUSE GOD IS NO RESPECTER OF PERSONS! Acts 10:34**

**WILD PLEASURES ARE VANITY! Ecclesiastes 2:1-3**

**TO HATE WORK IS VANITY! Ecclesiastes 2:17/8:16-17**

**TO TRUST IN RICHES IS VANITY! Ecclesiastes 2:11/5:10**

**TO HATE LIFE IS VANITY! Ecclesiastes 2:17/11:8**

**LUST AND PASSION = VANITY! Ecclesiastes 2:10-11**

**TO NEVER HAVE YOUR DESIRES SATISFIED = VANITY! Ecclesiastes 6:7-9**

**TO DWELL ON GRIEF AND SORROW = VANITY! Ecclesiastes 2:23**

**TO BE JEALOUS OF ANOTHER PERSON'S REWARDS = VANITY! Ecclesiastes 8:14**

**OPPRESSION AND SIN = VANITY! Ecclesiastes 8:9-10**

**BRINGING UP A LARGE FAMILY AND DYING A PAUPER = VANITY! Ecclesiastes 6:3-6**

**INJUSTICE = VANITY! Ecclesiastes 4:13-16**

*"They conceive mischief, and bring forth vanity, and their belly prepareth deceit."* **Job 15:35**

### PRAYER

Dear God, please forgive me for all my sins. I humble myself before You. I need Your love and forgiveness! **I am guilty of being a vain person with vain thoughts!** I have revelled in my looks, my intellect, my job, etc. I repent for being vain! Help me to become the kind of person that You desire I should be! Help me to think before I open my mouth! Help me to overcome thinking about myself so much and to think and do for others! Help me to remember to pray for others, more than I seek Your favor for myself! **Thank You for loving me and for helping me to understand what the scriptures have to say on the subject of vanity!** In Jesus' name, I pray. AMEN!

# VENEREAL DISEASE (VD)

**SECULAR WRITERS WILL TELL YOU THAT LOVE = DESIRE = SEX!** They don't care what God says!

**DAVID SINNED AGAINST GOD. HE COMMITTED ADULTERY AND AS A RESULT OF HIS SIN HE CONTRACTED A VENEREAL DISEASE.** He repented and cried out to God and God forgave him and He'll forgive you! **David wrote:** *"My wounds stink and are corrupt because of my foolishness. I am troubled; I am bowed down greatly; I go mourning all the day long. For my loins are filled with a loathsome (burning) disease: and there is no soundness in my flesh. I am feeble and sore broken. I have roared by reason of the disquietness of my heart."* **Psalm 38:5-8** *"My lovers and my friends stand aloof from my sore; and my kinsmen stand afar off."* **Psalm 38:11**

**HERPES IS A VIRAL INFECTION SIMILAR TO A COLD SORE YOU MIGHT GET ON YOUR MOUTH!** It affects the vagina, vulva, cervix and pelvic organs. **THERE IS NO CURE FOR IT!** According to the American Social Health Association 5-20 million people have herpes in the U.S. today and the number is growing upwards to 500,000 new cases each year! Sores break out on the external genitals and vagina. The lymph nodes in the groin become swollen. Fever, chills, headache and muscle-pain set in. Colds and illnesses can trigger recurrences. VD can be transferred without a person even knowing he has it! The disease is so serious that if a pregnant woman contracts it, a cesarean section is usually performed. Otherwise, the baby may be born with the infection which is often fatal.

*"What? know ye not that your body is the temple of the Holy Ghost which is in you, which ye have of God, and ye are not your own? For ye are bought with a price: therefore glorify God in your body, and in your spirit, which are God's."* **1 Corinthians 6:19-20**

**HOW DO YOU AVOID GETTING HERPES — SYPHILIS — GONORRHEA?** Don't have sex without being married! This is God's plan! If you're married, be sexually faithful to your marriage partner. **Sexually active boys and girls totally disobey God's plan for their lives!** God requires us to remain chaste until our legal marriage.

*". . .It is good for a man not to touch a woman. Nevertheless, to avoid fornication, let every man have his own wife, and let every woman have her own husband."* **1 Corinthians 7:1-2**

**VD may disguise its ugly self as appendicitis or food poisoning!** VD can cause permanent damage in the reproductive organs. In some cases it becomes necessary to have a female's ovaries and womb removed!

**THE WORLD "VENEREAL" IS DERIVED FROM "VENUS" — THE MYTHICAL GODDESS OF LOVE!** VD is a particular threat to women.

**LACK OF INFORMATION CAN BE DANGEROUS!** VD causes pain, blindness, arthritis, infertility, brain damage, heart disease, paralysis and even death! There were 4 million new cases of Gonorrhea and Syphilis in the U.S. in 1981. These 2 diseases are more widespread than measles, scarlet fever, mumps, strep throat, hepatitis and TB combined! Crab lice, venereal warts and thousands of other germs affect the genitals, eyes, throat and blood.

**Romans 12:1 SAYS WE ARE TO PRESENT OUR BODIES AS A LIVING SACRIFICE, HOLY, AND ACCEPTABLE UNTO GOD, AS A REASONABLE SERVICE FOR WHAT HE HAS DONE FOR US!**

**VD HAS NO AGE OR RACE BARRIERS!** Syphilis at any stage can attack any organ of an unborn baby and cripple it for life. Gonorrhea can blind a newborn. In Los Angeles, New York and other big cities, it is estimated that the 12-20 age group triples the rest of the population in acquiring VD!

*"For we must all appear before the judgment seat of Christ; that every one may receive the things done in his body, according to that (which) he hath done, whether it be good or bad."* **2 Corinthians 5:10**

**1 Corinthians 9:27 SAYS WE ARE TO KEEP OUR BODY UNDER SUBJECTION!**

**SATAN IS RESPONSIBLE FOR TRICKING PEOPLE INTO THINKING THAT FREE-LOVE, PROMISCUITY, PENICILLIN AND THE PILL IS THE ONLY WAY TO GO!** Because of the increase in VD, the National Commission of Venereal Diseases has recommended a $68 million federal budget per year. *"For to be carnally minded is death* (eternal separation from God); *but to be spiritually minded is life and peace."* **Romans 8:6**

**AS A CHRISTIAN, I DON'T BELIEVE WE SHOULD HIDE OUR FACE AND LOWER OUR VOICE AGAINST THE CONSEQUENCES OF SEXUAL SINS! I BELIEVE WE SHOULD WARN OUR CHILDREN THAT SATAN WANTS TO DECEIVE AND DESTROY THEM! HE WANTS THEM TO BE DISEASED AND UNPURE IN GOD'S EYES. HE INVENTED SEXUAL PROMISCUITY . . . PASS THE WORD ON TO THEM ABOUT SATAN!**

**PARENTS: TEACH YOUR CHILDREN ABOUT VENEREAL DISEASE SO THEY WON'T BE IGNORANT! TELL THEM HOW THESE DISEASES ARE TRANSMITTED, WHAT THE CONSEQUENCES ARE, AND WHAT GOD SAYS ABOUT PURITY!** Teach them that crab lice may be contracted by sleeping on contaminated bedsheets or by hugging in the nude. Herpes simplex can survive in clothing and on toilet seats long enough to be transmitted! Children should be taught that they can contract VD without having sexual intercourse. Any opening in the body, including the lips, throat, eyes and skin can become infected! They should be told that drug abusers and alcoholics have more sexually transmitted diseases than those who refrain from drugs and alcohol! They should be warned that homosexuals, travel and tatooing are prime targets for acquiring VD. **WARN THEM THAT TO PLAY AROUND SEXUALLY IS JUST AS DANGEROUS AS PLAYING RUSSIAN ROULETTE!** *"Train up a child in the way he should go: And when he is old, he will not depart from it* (your training). **Proverbs 22:6**

**DID YOU KNOW THAT IF YOU DO NOT GIVE UP HAVING SEX (WITHOUT MARRIAGE) AND REPENT AND TURN AWAY FROM SIN — YOU WILL NOT BE ALLOWED TO ENTER HEAVEN?** *"Know ye not that the unrighteous shall not inherit the kingdom of God? Be not deceived: neither fornicators, nor idolaters, nor adulterers, nor effeminate, nor abusers of themselves with mankind, Nor thieves, nor covetous, nor drunkards, nor revilers, nor extortioners, shall inherit the kingdom of God."* **1 Corinthians 6:9-10**

*"For if ye live after the flesh, ye shall die: but if ye through the (Holy) Spirit do mortify the deeds of the body, ye shall live."* **Romans 8:13**

**1 Corinthians 6:13-18 SAYS OUR BODY IS NOT FOR FORNICATION (SEX WITHOUT MARRIAGE)!**
*"Know ye not that ye are the temple of God, and that the (Holy) Spirit of God dwelleth in you? If any man (person) defile the temple of God, him (you) shall God destroy; for the temple of God is holy, which temple ye (you) are."* **1 Corinthians 3:16-17**

### PRAYER
Dear God, I repent of all my sins and I ask You to forgive me. I humble myself before You. Teach me to take control over my passions! I want to be clean and pure in Your eyes! I want to go to heaven. I want to please You in all that I think, say and do. Come into my life and teach me how to resist temptations. Thank You for saving my soul. In Jesus' name, I pray. AMEN!

# VIOLENCE

**BECAUSE THERE IS SATAN . . . THERE IS VIOLENCE!**
*"The earth also was corrupt before God, and the earth was filled with violence."* **Genesis 6:11**

Jesus was sacrificed for our transgressions. he was buried among criminals and among the rich. He never did any **violence** and deceit never entered his mouth! **Isaiah 53:8-9**

**Matthew 11:12 says violent people take what they want by force!**

**JESUS SAID:** *". . .Do violence to no man, neither accuse any falsely; and be content with your wages."* **Luke 3:14**

Throughout the Bible, there have been great men and women of God who have quenched the violence of fire, escaped the edge of the sword, and out of weakness have been made strong. They grew valiant in fight and were able to turn to overthrow the armies of the aliens! **Hebrews 11:33-34**

*"He (God) delivered me from mine enemies: yea (yes), thou (God) liftest me up above those that rise up against me: thou (God) hast delivered me from the violent man."* **Psalm 18:48**

**THE BIBLE SAYS THAT IF YOU DEAL IN VIOLENCE IT WILL COME BACK AND FALL ON YOUR OWN HEAD!**
*"His (your) mischief shall return upon his own head, and his (your) violent dealing shall come down upon his own pate (scalp, skull)."* **Psalm 7:16**

*"Shall I (God) count them pure with the wicked balances, and with the bag of deceitful weights? For the rich men thereof are full of violence, and the inhabitants thereof have spoken lies, and their tongue is deceitful in their mouth."* **Micah 6:11-12**

**READ ABOUT MOB VIOLENCE IN ACTS 19:28-32**

*"A man that doeth violence to the blood of any person shall flee to the pit; let no man stay him."* **Proverbs 28:17**

*"Blessings are upon the head of the just: but violence covereth the mouth of the wicked. The memory of the just is blessed: but the name of the wicked shall rot."* **Proverbs 10:6-7**

*"There is no peace, saith my God, to the wicked."* **Isaiah 57:21**

**DID YOU KNOW THAT A PERSON'S ETERNAL DESTINY IS DETERMINED ACCORDING TO THE CONDITION OF HIS HEART AND LIFE AT THE POINT OF HIS DEATH?**
*"And as it is appointed unto men once to die, but after this the judgment."* **Hebrews 9:27** . . . Therefore since it is determined that each living person is going to die, then it is also determined that the exact state of your life and heart when you die is the same state you will spend in eternity! With this in mind, it is certain that you will spend eternity with God in Heaven, or with Satan in hell! So, if you die as an adulterer, alcoholic, homosexual, or guilty of any unforgiven **violent** action, you will have wilfully chosen (while you were alive) to spend eternity in hell, unless you repent and get saved while you're alive! God gave each person free will to choose good or evil while he is alive. After you die it's too late to turn things around! While you are alive you must choose because no one knows whether he'll be alive tomorrow or not! *"He that is unjust (when he dies), let him be unjust still (in eternity): and he which is filthy (when he dies), let him be filthy still: and he that is righteous (when he dies), let him be righteous still (in eternity): and he that is holy, let him be holy still (in eternity)."* **Revelation 22:11**

*"The mouth of a righteous man is a well of life: but violence covereth the mouth of the wicked."* **Proverbs 10:11**

*"But thine eyes and thine heart are not but for thy covetousness, and for to shed innocent blood, and for oppression, and for violence to do it."* **Jeremiah 22:17**

**1 PETER 5:8 SAYS:** *"Be sober, be vigilant; because your adversary the devil, as a roaring lion, walketh about, seeking whom he may devour."*

**THOSE WHO SHAME — MOCK — CURSE GOD — DISHONOR ANOTHER'S BELIEF IN GOD — ABUSE CHURCH BUILDINGS (OR CHRISTIANS) WILL BE JUDGED IN THE GREAT WHITE THRONE JUDGEMENT ACCORDING TO ROMANS 1:30! THEY WILL BE CAST INTO THE ETERNAL LAKE OF FIRE, TO BURN FOREVER!**
*Excerpts from "The Impending Hour" by Lu Ann Bransby

**PRAYER**

Dear God, violence seems to be on the increase and I hardly know how to protect my loved ones, myself, my property. Sometimes I become so frightened and discouraged that I imagine what it would be like to take the law into my own hands, in order to see that justice is done! Then, I'm stopped short because the Bible says we are not to judge others. I realize that it isn't more laws that are needed, it's a personal knowledge of Jesus Christ! Help me to be an example of a good law abiding citizen and a follower of Jesus. I repent of all my sins. I sincerely believe You will forgive me and will blot out my sins from Your memory. Help me guard my actions and conversations so that others will see Jesus in my life. I will no longer be guilty of doing violence to any person's character, property, privacy or time! As long as I live, I will not be afraid for I know You are on the side of all born-again believers! I confess You are the Lord of my life and my personal savior. I thank You for saving my soul and for never giving up on me! In Jesus' name, I pray. AMEN!

# VIRGINITY

**JESUS DIED ON THE CROSS TO PAY THE PENALTY FOR OUR SINS SO WE CAN REPENT, AND RECEIVE FORGIVENESS AND ETERNAL LIFE WITH HIM!**

**THE BIBLE TELLS US IT'S BETTER TO MARRY THAN TO BURN WITH PASSION AND GIVE IN TO SIN!** *"But if they cannot contain* (stay sexually pure), *let them marry: for it is better to marry than to burn* (with passion or give in to having intercourse)." **1 Corinthians 7:9**

*"What? know ye not that your body is the temple of the Holy Ghost which is in you, which ye have* (been given) *of God, and ye are not your own? For ye are bought with a price: therefore glorify God in your body, and in your spirit, which are God's."* **1 Corinthians 6:19-20**

**DID YOU KNOW THAT THE INCREASE IN SEXUAL SINS IS A SIGN OF THE LAST DAYS BEFORE CHRIST RETURNS TO EARTH?** *"Now the* (Holy) *Spirit speaketh expressly, that in the latter times some shall depart from the faith* (fear and respect of God), *giving heed to seducing spirits, and doctrines of devils; Speaking lies in hypocrisy; having their conscience seared with a hot iron; Forbidding to marry* (choosing not to marry and having sex anyway), *and commanding* (preferring) *to abstain from meats* (finding it preferable to be a vegetarian rather than to obey God's commandments), *which God hath created to be received with thanksgiving of them which believe and know the truth. For every creature of God is good, and nothing to be refused, if it be received with thanksgiving."* **1 Timothy 4:1-4**

*"Who can find a virtuous woman? for her price is far above rubies."* **Proverbs 31:10**

**PAUL WROTE:** *"Now concerning the things whereof ye wrote unto me: It is good for a man not to touch a woman. Nevertheless, to avoid fornication* (sex without marriage), *let every man have his own wife, and let every woman have her own husband."* **1 Corinthians 7:1-2**

**YOUR BODY DOES NOT BELONG ONLY TO YOU TO DO WHATEVER YOU WISH WITH IT. YOU ARE BOUGHT WITH A PRICE (THROUGH THE DEATH AND RESURRECTION OF JESUS TO PAY FOR OUR SINS!)**

# GOD COMMANDS US TO BE A VIRGIN WHEN WE MARRY!

*"Ye are bought with a price: be not ye the servants of men."* **1 Corinthians 7:23** *"But if they cannot contain, let them marry: for it is better to marry than to burn* (with sexual passion)." **1 Corinthians 7:9**

**IN THE OLD TESTAMENT, IF IT WAS DISCOVERED THAT A GIRL WAS NOT A VIRGIN SHE COULD BE STONED TO DEATH, IN AN EFFORT TO PUT AWAY ALL SIN IN ISRAEL! Deuteronomy 22:13-21**

*"Flee fornication. Every sin that a man doeth is without the body; but he that committeth fornication sinneth against his own body."* **1 Corinthians 6:18**

**FORNICATION IS FORBIDDEN!** *". . .Now the body is not for fornication* (sex without marriage), *but for the Lord: and the Lord for the body."* **1 Corinthians 6:13**

**1 Timothy 5:2 SAYS ELDER WOMEN ARE TO BE REVERENCED AND TREATED AS MOTHERS AND YOUNGER WOMEN ARE TO BE TREATED AS SISTERS WHO ARE SEXUALLY PURE!**

**Revelation 14:4 SAYS MEN SHOULD ALSO BE VIRGINS PRIOR TO MARRIAGE!**

**CHRISTIANS ARE SYMBOLIZED AS CHASTE VIRGINS WHO ARE ENGAGED TO CHRIST. AND, WHEN CHRIST RETURNS FOR US WE WILL CELEBRATE WITH HIM AT THE MARRIAGE SUPPER! CHRIST WILL BE THE HUSBAND AND CHRISTIANS WILL BE HIS BRIDE! 2 Corinthians 11:2**

*"For we must all appear before the judgment seat of Christ; that every one may receive the things done in his body, according to that* (which) *he hath done, whether it be good or bad."* **2 Corinthians 5:10**

**IF YOU HAVE COMMITTED A SEX SIN AND LOST YOUR VIRGINITY:** God still loves you and wants to forgive you! However, He will not force Himself on you! You must repent of your sins to God and ask His forgiveness! He will forgive you and then you must turn away from all sin! He loves you very deeply and wants to hear from you, today!

### PRAYER

Dear God, please forgive me for sinning against my own body and against You. I want to be forgiven! Come into my life and fill me with Your love. I will no longer have sex with anyone who is not my husband (or wife)! Please blot out my sins from Your memory and teach me to forgive myself. I want to live a Christian life and to please You in every way! I will study my Bible for I know it has all the answers to life's problems. I love You, because You first loved me! Thank You for forgiving me even though I disappointed You! I will serve You and I will praise You as long as I live! In Jesus' name, I pray. AMEN!

# WEALTH

JESUS WARNED US AGAINST LAYING UP TREASURES ON EARTH. THEY ARE NEVER SAFE. THEY DO NOT LAST. THEY DO NOT EVER FULLY SATISFY. YET, MOST PEOPLE THINK THAT HAPPINESS COMES FROM THINGS THAT WE OWN. THINGS CAN ROB US OF THE ONLY JOY THAT REALLY LASTS. *"For we brought nothing into this world, and it is certain we can carry nothing out. And having food and raiment (clothes) let us be therewith content. But they that will be* **rich** *fall into temptation and a snare (trap), and into many foolish and hurtful lusts, which drown men in destruction and perdition. For the* **love of money** *is the root of all evil: which while some coveted after, they have erred from the faith, and pierced themselves through with many sorrows. But thou, O man of God, flee these things; and follow after righteousness, godliness, faith, love, patience, meekness."* **1 Timothy 6:7-11**

*"Hell and destruction are never full; so the eyes of man are never satisfied."* **Proverbs 27:20**

*"For riches are not for ever: and doth the crown endure to every generation?"* **Proverbs 27:24**

*"For what shall it profit a man, if he shall gain the whole world, and lose his own soul?"* **Mark 8:36**

**WEALTH CAN BE WONDERFUL!** *"Behold that which I have seen: it is good and comely for one to eat and to drink, and to enjoy the good of all his labour that he taketh under the sun all the days of his life, which God giveth him: for it is his portion. Every man also to whom God hath given* **riches and wealth,** *and hath given him power to eat thereof, and to take his portion, and to rejoice in his labour; this is the gift of God."* **Ecclesiastes 5:18-19**

**WEALTH CAN STAND BETWEEN A MAN AND GOD . . . IF MAN CHOOSES TO LOVE WEALTH ABOVE GOD!** *"So is he that layeth up* **treaasure** *for himself, and is not* **rich** *toward God."* **Luke 12:21**

*ALL MEN DIE ALIKE AND LEAVE THEIR WEALTH TO OTHERS! Psalm 49:10*

*GOD GIVES US THE POWER TO BECOME WEALTHY! "And thou say in thine heart, My power and the might of mine hand hath gotten me this* **wealth.** *But thou shalt remember the Lord thy God: for it is he that giveth thee power to get* **wealth.** *. ."* **Deuteronomy 8:17-18**

**A GIFT OF WISDOM, AND HONOR, FROM GOD IS MUCH PREFERRED TO WEALTH!** *"And God said to Solomon, Because this was in thine heart, and thou hast not asked* **riches, wealth,** *or honour, nor the life of thine enemies, neither yet hast asked long life; but hast asked wisdom and knowledge for thyself, that thou mayest judge my people, over whom I have made thee king: wisdom and knowledge is granted unto thee; and I will give thee* **riches, and wealth,** *and honour, such as none of the kings have had that have been before thee, neither shall there any after thee have the like."* **2 Chronicles 1:11-12** *"For wisdom is better than rubies; and all the things that may be desired are not to be compared to it."* **Proverbs 8:11**

*"Lay not up for yourselves treasures upon earth, where moth and rust doth corrupt, and where thieves break through and steal: But lay up for yourselves treasures in heaven, where neither moth nor rust doth corrupt, and where thieves do not break through nor steal: For where your treasure is, there will your heart be also."* **Matthew 6:19-21**

*"Wealth gotten by vanity shall be diminished: but he that gathereth by labour shall increase."* **Proverbs 13:11**

**THE RICH VERSUS THE POOR:** *"The rich man's* **wealth** *is his strong city; the destruction of the poor is their poverty."* **Proverbs 10:15** *"**Wealth** maketh many friends; but the poor is separated from his neighbour."* **Proverbs 19:4**

**WHEN GOD GIVES WEALTH TO A GODLY PERSON . . . THERE IS NO SORROW WITH IT!** *"The blessing of the Lord, it maketh rich, and he addeth no sorrow with it."* **Proverbs 10:22**

**GOD SAYS A GIFT OF WISDOM IS BETTER THAN SILVER AND GOLD!** *"Receive my instruction, and not* **silver;** *and knowledge rather than choice* **gold!"** **Proverbs 8:10** *"**Riches** and honour are with me (God); yea, durable* **riches** *and righteousness. My fruit (blessings) is better than* **gold,** *yea, than fine* **gold;** *and my revenue than choice* **silver."** **Proverbs 8:18-19** *"That I (God) may cause those that love me to inherit substance (wealth); and I will fill their treasures."* **Proverbs 8:21**

*"A faithful man shall abound with blessings: but he that maketh haste to be* **rich** *shall not be innocent."* **Proverbs 28:20**

*"He that hasteth to be* **rich** *hath an evil eye, and considereth not that poverty shall come upon him."* **Proverbs 28:22**

**TO LOVE MONEY AND WEALTH MORE THAN GOD IS IDOLATRY! GOD FORBIDS IDOLATRY!** *"Thou shalt have no other gods before me."* **Exodus 20:3**

### PRAYER

Dear God, please forgive me for all my sins. I repent and turn away from all sinful thoughts, actions, and words in my life! I want to serve You! I want to receive Your blessings and wisdom more than wealth, which vanishes in time! I have all I need for this day in my life. Teach me to labor to make my own way, and not to covet, or be envious of others who have wealth! I know that money can't buy love, peace, or happiness! Help me to get my priorities straight! Help me put You in the center of my life! Thank You for saving my soul. In Jesus' name, I pray. AMEN!

# WIFE / WIDOW

## --WIDOW

*"Wives, submit yourselves unto your own husbands, as unto the Lord. For the husband is the head of the wife, even as Christ is the head of the church: and he (Christ) is the saviour of the body (of born-again believers). Therefore as the church is subject unto Christ, so let the wives be (subject) to their own husbands in every thing."* **Ephesians 5:22-24**

*"Wives, fit in with your husbands' plans; for then if they refuse to listen when you talk to them about the Lord, they will be won by your respectful, pure behavior. Your godly lives will speak to them better than any words. Don't be concerned about the outward beauty that depends on jewelry, or beautiful clothes, or hair arrangement. Be beautiful inside, in your hearts, with the lasting charm of a gentle and quiet spirit which is so precious to God. That kind of deep beauty was seen in the saintly women of old, who trusted God and fitted in with their husband's plans. Sarah, for instance, obeyed her husband Abraham, honoring him as head of the house. And if you do the same, you will be following in her steps like good daughters and doing what is right; then you will not need to fear (offending your husbands)."* **1 Peter 3:1-6** (The Living Bible)

**THE ABOVE VERSES TELL YOU HOW TO BE A MODEL WIFE AND EIGHT WAYS TO HELP IN WINNING YOUR HUSBAND TO CHRIST! 1.** Wives should submit. **2.** Wives should obey the WORD. **3.** Wives should have chaste conversations. **4.** Wives should not be pre-occupied with clothes, jewelry, hair to the extent of not taking care of their husbands. **5.** Wives should make sure their inner self is beautiful. **6.** Trust in God. **7.** Do right. **8.** Be faithful to your husband and he will know your conduct is above reproach!

**MANY TIMES A HUSBAND WILL NOT GO TO CHURCH, READ THE BIBLE, OR PRAY . . . SO YOU HAVE TO LET HIM SEE CHRIST IN YOUR BEHAVIOR, DRESS CODE, AND CONVERSATION!**

**Titus 2:3-5** says women are to behave and live a holy life. They are not to accuse or slander anyone. They are not to drink intoxicating beverages. They are to be teachers of good things. They are to be discreet, chaste, a good person, obedient to their husbands, and especially to God!

*"And be ye kind one to another, tenderhearted, forgiving one another, even as God for Christ's sake hath forgiven you."* **Ephesians 4:32**

**1 Timothy 2:9-15** says women should be quiet and sensible in manner and clothing. Christian women should be noticed for being kind and good, not for the expensive clothes they wear, how they fix their hair, and how many jewels they wear! Women should listen and learn quietly and humbly. They should never try to usurp authority over men or lord what they know over their husband. Women should continue in faith to God, and to their husbands! They should be charitable, holy and sober!

It was Jesus who gave dignity to women and a place of significance in what had been a man's world! Until Jesus came, women were not important in any community. They had few rights and certainly no place in the counsels of the world! Jesus understood the world's great need for the talents and gifts women have to offer. He wants all women to be feminine, gentle, understanding, with a keen sense of insight in exercising concern for humanity.

*"The church should take loving care of women whose husbands have died, if they don't have anyone else to help them. But if they have children or grandchildren, these are the ones who should take the responsibility, for kindness should begin at home, supporting needy parents. This is something that pleases God very much. The church should care for widows who are poor and alone in the world, if they are looking to God for his help and spending much time in prayer; but not if they are spending their time running around gossiping, seeking only pleasure and thus ruining their souls. This should be your church rule so that the Christians will know and do what is right. But anyone who won't care for his own relatives when they need help, especially those living in his own family, has no right to say he is a Christian. Such a person is worse than the heathen. A widow who wants to become one of the special church workers should be at least sixty years old and have been married only once. She must be well thought of by everyone because of the good she has done. Has she brought up her children well? Has she been kind to strangers as well as to other Christians? Has she helped those who are sick and hurt? Is she always ready to show kindness? The younger widows should not become members of this special group because after awhile they are likely to disregard their vow to Christ and marry again. And so they will stand condemned because they broke their first promise. Besides, they are likely to be lazy and spend their time gossiping around from house to house, getting into other people's business. So I think it is better for these younger widows to marry again and have children, and take care of their own homes; then no one will be able to say anything against them. For I am afraid that some of them have already turned away from the church an been led astray by Satan. Let me remind you again that a widow's relatives must take care of her, and not leave this to the church to do. Then the church can spend its money for the care of widows who are all alone and have nowhere else to turn."* **1 Timothy 5:5-16** (The Living Bible)

**There are 10 million widows in America alone and 75 percent became widows by the time they were 44 years old. The chances of a woman becoming a widow are 5 times greater than her husband! Widowhood is a terrible loss for a woman. It sometimes results in emotional problems. Fear of being alone may arise. She has to adjust to a different lifestyle. When crises arise she must handle them alone. Widows are usually mistreated, despised or neglected, by the world.**

248

(Continued)

# Endurance

**HOW TO OVERCOME GRIEF WHEN YOU BECOME A WIDOW?** You have to start quickly to overcome grief. Because if grief isn't relinquished, it can kill you! If a widow's husband was a Christian when he died, then she should praise God and make a diligent effort to rejoice, knowning her husband is happily with God in heaven! Every church should encourage widows to participate in teaching! Churches should not neglect to visit widows in their afflictions. You are a person and your time is not up. Don't give in to grief because God wants you to live a full life in good health! He wants you to be happy and secure in the knowledge that He cares for you! Make your requests known to God. He is our real source! Become vitally interested and active in helping others. Volunteer to work in the nursery, teach a class or visit shut-in's. Donate 1 day each week to visit church members who are hospitalized. Don't sit in a rocking chair and look sad! **Your life isn't over!** Serve God with prayer and fasting. Do good works in the name of your husband. Be strong. Don't give up and quit! Find something you like to do and give it all you've got. Don't expect people to feel sorry for you. Even in your sorrow you can bless others if you don't turn all your attention inwards! God can heal your grief! God can and will help you enjoy the wonderful things of life, if you'll let him! Rise and shine! Your life's not over!

*"AND WHERE THE SPIRIT OF THE LORD IS THERE IS LIBERTY."* **2 Corinthians 3:17**

**GOD WROTE LAWS AGAINST INJUSTICE TO WIDOWS!**
Deuteronomy 24:17/Matthew 23:14/Mark 12:40/Luke 20:47

**IT IS ALRIGHT WITH GOD IF WIDOWS REMAIN SINGLE AS LONG AS THEY ABIDE IN GOD AND OBEY HIS COMMANDMENTS. BUT, IF THEY CANNOT REMAIN SEXUALLY PURE, THEY SHOULD MARRY. 1 Corinthians 7:8-9**

**JAMES 1:27 SAYS WE SHOULD VISIT ORPHANS AND WIDOWS IN THEIR AFFLICTION!**

**NEVER FORGET: GOD IS NOT THE GOD OF DEAD, BUT OF THE LIVING! Matthew 22:32**

Whether going from wife to widow was an expected or unexpected experience it continues to be one of the greatest crises you will ever face. Don't be overwhelmed with the realization that now suddenly all the decisions are yours alone to make. There are practical considerations such as assessing your financial status, a possible relocation and seeking competent legal advice. The Mental Health Association is a non-profit education and advocacy organization supported by voluntary contributions. They offer a WIDOW'S EXCHANGE and there are no fees for attending the meetings. They are a support group for women who are recently widowed and have a common experience to share with each other. Don't forget your church. They can offer experienced counsellors to help see you through your grief!

*"I beseech (beg) you therefore, brethren, by the mercies of God, that ye present your bodies a living sacrifice, holy, acceptable unto God, which is your reasonable service. And be not conformed to this world: but be ye transformed by the renewing of your mind, that ye may prove what is that good, and acceptable, and perfect will of God."* **Romans 12:1-2**

**PRAYER**
Dear God, please forgive me for all my sins. I repent and turn away from them. Please forgive me and come into my heart. Clean up my life, my thoughts, my actions. Make me into the kind of person You desire I should be. Thank You for loving me and for never giving up on me. I will go to church and read my Bible and pray each day. Teach me patience. Let me feel Your presence in everything I say, or do, and I will praise You as long as I live! In Jesus' name, I pray. AMEN!

# WITCHCRAFT

**IN THE OLD TESTAMENT — THERE WAS A DEATH PENALTY FOR WITCHES!** *"Thou shalt not suffer a witch to live."* **Exodus 22:18**

**WITCHCRAFT IS A WORK OF THE FLESH! WITCHES, WIZARDS, AND ANYONE WHO PARTICIPATES IN WITCHCRAFT MUST REPENT AND FORSAKE ALL OCCULT ACTIVITY OR HE WILL NOT BE ALLOWED TO ENTER HEAVEN!** God loves you and wants you to repent and forsake all demon activity. He wants to save you! It's up to you, though! The choice is yours! *"Now the works of the flesh are manifest* (made known), *which are these; Adultery, fornication, uncleanness, lasciviousness* (sex perverts, 'abnormal sex drive), *idolatry,* **WITCH CRAFT,** *hatred, variance, emulations, wrath, strife, seditions, heresies, envyings, murders, drunkenness, revellings, and such like: of the which I tell you before, as I have also told you in time past, that* **they which do such things shall not inherit the kingdom of God.**" **Galatians 5:19-21**

**THE BIBLE SAYS NOT TO SEEK OUT WITCHES AND WIZARDS!** *"Ye shall not eat anything with the blood* (still in it): *neither shall ye use enchantment* (magic spells, hypnosis), *nor observe times* (sun-moon signs, omens in the skies)." **Leviticus 19:26**

**THE BIBLE SAYS NOT TO LISTEN TO WITCHES, WIZARDS OR PSYCHIC MEDIUMS!** *"Regard not* (don't listen to) *them that have familiar spirits* (psychic mediums possess them), *neither seek after wizards to be defiled by them: I am the Lord your God."* **Leviticus 19:31**

**THE BIBLE SAYS ALL FORMS OF WITCHCRAFT ARE FORBIDDEN!** *"There shall not be found among you any one that maketh his son or daughter to pass through the fire* (in worship to pagan gods), *or that useth divination* (fortune telling), *or an observer of times* (omens, signs, lucky-unlucky days, numerology, etc.), *or an enchanter* (hypnotist), *or a witch, or a charmer* (one who casts spells), *or a consulter* (psychic medium, palm reader, fortune teller) *with familiar* (demon) *spirits, or a wizard* (male witch), *or a necromancer* (one who communicates with deceased spirits). *For all that do these things are an abomination* (disgusting) *unto the Lord: and because of these abominations the Lord thy God doth drive them out from before thee."* **Deuteronomy 18:10-12**

**SAUL SOUGHT ADVICE FROM A WITCH WHO HAD A FAMILIAR SPIRIT AT ENDOR. HE LATER REPENTED AND GOD FORGAVE HIM!** 1 Samuel 28 chapter

**TO REBEL AGAINST GOD'S WORDS IS AS BAD AS THE SIN OF WITCHCRAFT!** *"For rebellion is as the sin of witchcraft, and stubbornness is as iniquity* (wicked determination) *and idolatry. Because thou hast rejected the word of the Lord. . ."* **1 Samuel 15:23**

**AFTER CHRIST RETURNS TO EARTH DURING THE SECOND ADVENT THERE WILL BE NO MORE WITCHCRAFT!** *"And I will cut off witchcrafts out of thine hand; and thou shalt have no more soothsayers."* **Micah 5:12**

**WARNING TO ANYONE WHO PRACTICES OR BELIEVES IN WITCHCRAFT:** *"And I will come near to you* (personally and visibly) *to* (do) *judgment; and I will be a swift witness against the* **SORCERERS,** *and against adulterers, and against false swearers, and against those that oppress the hireling* (employees) *in his wages, the widow, and the fatherless* (orphans), *and that turn aside the stranger from his right hand, and* (those who) *fear not me* (God), *saith the Lord of hosts. For I am the Lord, I change not. . ."* **Malachi 3:5-6**

**ALL FORMS OF OCCULT ACTIVITY ARE CALLED "WORKS OF DARKNESS!"** *"The night is far spent* (time is running out to get saved), *the day* (today) *is at hand: let us therefore* **CAST OFF THE WORKS OF DARKNESS** (witchcraft), *and let us put on the armour of light* (God's truths). *Let us walk honestly, as in the day* (we will stand before God), *not in rioting and drunkenness, not in chambering* (prostitution, sex sins) *and wantonness* (sex perverts), *not in strife and envying. But put ye on the Lord Jesus Christ, and make not provision for the flesh to fulfil the lusts thereof."* **Romans 13:12-14**

**IN THE SCRIPTURES, DARKNESS IS SYMBOLIC OF SATAN AND HIS DEMONS! LIGHT IS SYMBOLIC OF CHRIST!**

**ONLY WHEN A PERSON PUTS ON THE WHOLE ARMOR OF GOD CAN HE BE SAFE FROM THE EVIL EFFECTS OF WITCHCRAFT!** *"Put on the whole armour of God, that ye may be able to stand against the wiles of the devil. For we wrestle not against flesh and blood, but against principalities* (governments of evil spirits), *against* (evil spirit) *powers, against the rulers of the darkness of this world, against spiritual wickedness in high places. Wherefore take unto you the whole armour of God, that ye may be able to withstand in the evil day, and having done all, to stand. Stand therefore, having your loins girt about with truth, and having on the breastplate of righteousness; and your feet shod with the preparation of the gospel of peace. Above all, taking the shield of faith, wherewith ye shall be able to quench all the fiery darts of the wicked* (spirits, Satan). *And take the helmet of salvation, and the sword of the* (Holy) *Spirit, which is the word of God."* **Ephesians 6:11-17**

**HOW DO YOU BREAK AWAY FROM PARTICIPATION (OR BELIEF) IN WITCHCRAFT?** *"Giving* (give) *thanks unto the Father* (God), *which hath made us meet* (qualified to be) *partakers of the inheritance of the saints in light. Who hath delivered us from the power of darkness* (Satan, demons, familiar spirits, witches, witchcraft), *and hath translated* (removed and delivered) *us into the kingdom of his* (God's) *dear Son* (Jesus)." **Colossians 1:12-13**

**WHAT ARE SOME THINGS ASSOCIATED WITH WITCHCRAFT?** Witches, warlocks, magicians, hypnotists, E.S.P., auras, fortune telling, sorcery, sooth-saying, love potions, talisman, guides, astrology, divination, palmistry, thought transference, astral projection, seances, crystal balls, voodoo, levitation, necromancy, star gazing, hexes, automatic writing, ouija boards, hexagrams, fairies, witch doctors, superstitions, psychomancy, ghosts, omens, chants, jinxs, amulets, pentacles, scarobs,, caldrons, divining rods, seers, swastikas, alchemist, wonder-workers, exorcists, snake charmers, imps, vampires, horoscopes, incantations, table tapping, spirit rapping, planchettes, psychic research, gypsies, clairvoyance, telepathy, precognition, reincarnation, transcendental meditation, cabala, yoga, metaphysics, esoteric science, ectoplasms, telekinesis, Rosicrucians, mesmerize, trances, rituals, cults, disembody, sleeping-sickness, evolution, parapsychology, psychometry, deja-vu, gambling, dark horses, secret society, pyramidology, bats, Black Mass, cloven hooves, apollo, abaddon (angel of the bottomless pit), goblins, leprechauns, apparitions, banshees, giants, Buddhism, Inner Government of the World, Great White Lodge, Lord of the World Organization, (color) Black, etc.

**HERE IS A LIST OF WORDS MOST CHILDREN ARE FAMILIAR WITH THAT HAVE TO DO WITH WITCHCRAFT!** Wishing wells, wish-bone, Pied Piper, hag, hellcat, vampires, fairy godmother, wicked fairy, an evil eye, say the magic word, haunted house, sixth sense, spooky, tantalize, magnetism, ringleader, Mother Nature, Sleeping Beauty, Rip Van Winkle, nigger in the woodpile, snake in the grass, off the record, top-secret, underhand, behind the scenes, Santa Claus, Zombi's, pandemonium, spooks, phantoms, genies, bogeyman, Frankenstein, monsters, werewolves, nightmares, nymphs, mermaids, Old man of the sea, abominable snowman, lucky charms, birth stones, bell book and candle, witches broomstick, magic recipe, magic wand, magic rings, Aladdins lamp, magic mirror, flying carpet, seven league boots, love-potion, black sabbath, witching hour, black arts, incantations, open sesame, abraccadabra, hocus-pocus, mumbo jumbo, fee-faw-fum.

## PRAYER

Dear God, please forgive me for my involvement in occult activities. I repent of all my sins. I ask You to forgive me. I will never be guilty of believing in or practicing any form of the occult again. I will live for You. I will read my Bible and pray to You. Thank You for saving my soul. In Jesus' name, I pray. AMEN!

# WORRY

**WORRY CAUSES WRINKLES AND A LEAN, LONG FACE!**
Job 16:8

**WORRY IS THE WORST THIEF OF ALL . . . SATAN IS THE INVENTOR OF WORRY!** Worry robs us of peace and fulfillment. Worry brings physical consequences. Sometimes medicine removes the symptoms but it cannot remove the real cause! **WORRY IS AN INSIDE JOB!** We can buy sleeping pills but we can't buy rest. **JESUS SAID:** *"Come unto me, all ye that labour and are heavy laden (worried), and I will give you rest. Take my yoke upon you, and learn of me: for I am meek and lowly in heart: and ye shall find rest unto your souls. For my yoke is easy, and my burden is light."* **Matthew 11:28-30**

**WHY WORRY ABOUT YOUR FINANCES?** *"But my God shall supply all your need according to his riches in glory by Christ Jesus."* **Philippians 4:19**

**WHY WORRY ABOUT INSOMNIA?** *"I will both lay me down in peace, and sleep: for thou, Lord only makest me dwell in safety."* **Psalm 4:8**

**WHY WORRY ABOUT ACCIDENTS?** *"For he shall give his angels charge over thee, to keep thee in all thy ways."* **Psalm 91:11**

**WHY WORRY ABOUT YOUR BACK?** Luke 13:11-13

**WHY WORRY ABOUT ULCERS?** *"And ye shall serve the Lord your God, and he shall bless thy bread, and thy water; and I will take sickness away from the midst of thee."* **Exodus 23:25**

**WHY WORRY ABOUT A SKIN DISORDER?** *"Why art thou cast down, O my soul? and why art thou disquieted (worried) within me? hope thou in God: for I shall yet praise him, who is the health of my countenance, and my God."* **Psalm 42:11**

**WHY WORRY ABOUT STUTTERING?** *"The heart of the rash shall understand knowledge, and the tongue of the stammerers shall be ready to speak also plainly."* **Isaiah 32:4**

**WHY WORRY ABOUT BEING BARREN OR HAVING A MISCARRIAGE?** *"He maketh the barren woman to keep house, and to be a joyful mother of children. Praise ye the Lord."* **Psalm 113:9** *"Thy wife shall be as a fruitful vine by the sides of thine house: thy children like olive plants round about thy table."* **Psalm 128:3** *"There shall nothing cast their young, nor be barren, in thy land: the number of thy days I will fulfil."* **Exodus 23:26** *READ: Isaiah 65:20-23/Psalm 147:13

**WHY BE AFRAID OF DEATH?** *"I shall not die, but live, and declare the works of the Lord."* **Psalm 118:17**

**CHRISTIANS SHOULD NEVER WORRY ABOUT WHAT WORDS TO SAY TO DEFEND THEMSELVES!** *"But when they deliver you up, take no thought how or what ye shall speak: for it shall be given you in that same hour what ye shall speak. For it is not ye that speak, but the (Holy) Spirit of your Father (God) which speaketh in you."* **Matthew 10:19-20/Luke 12:11/Mark 13:11**

**WORRY MAKES YOU WEAK!** Psalm 6:2/Mark 14:38

**WHY WORRY IF YOU'LL LIVE A LONG LIFE?** *"For by me (Jesus) thy days shall be multiplied, and the years of thy life shall be increased."* **Proverbs 9:11**

**WHY WORRY ABOUT YOUR HEART?** *"Be of good courage, and he shall strengthen your heart, all ye that hope in the Lord."* **Psalm 31:24**

**WHY WORRY ABOUT WEIGHT CONTROL?** Luke 21:34/Romans 6:6-7, 14/14:17-18/Galatians 5:1, 16/2:21/6:8-9/2 Corinthians 10:4-5/Matthew 4:4/5:6/6:25, 33/Psalm 23/Proverbs 25:16/23:1-3/13:20, 25/Job 23:12/1 John 5:21/1 Corinthians 6:12-13

**WORRIED ABOUT HOW TO STOP SMOKING OR DRINKING?** 2 Corinthians 7:1/Philippians 4:13/Psalm 27:1/Romans 8:35-37

**WHY BE AFRAID YOU'LL HAVE A PRE-MATURE BABY?** READ: Isaiah 65:20

**WHY WORRY ABOUT CANCER?** *"There shall no evil befall thee, neither shall any plague come nigh thy dwelling."* **Psalm 91:10** *READ: Exodus 23:25/1 Peter 2:24/Matthew 8:17/Isaiah 53:4-5

**WHY WORRY ABOUT YOUR EARS?** *"And straightway his ears were opened, and the string of his tongue was loosed, and he spake plain."* **Mark 7:35/Proverbs 20:12**

**1 Peter 5:7 says to cast all our cares upon the Lord because He cares for us!**

251 (Continued)

*"Be careful for nothing; but in every thing by prayer and supplication with thanksgiving let your requests be made known unto God. And the peace of God, which passeth all understanding shall keep your hearts and minds through Christ Jesus."* **Philippians 4:6-7**

**WHY WORRY ABOUT A FIRE OR FLOOD?** *"When thou passest through the waters, I will be with thee; and through the rivers, they shall not overflow thee: when thou walkest through the fire, thou shalt not be burned; neither shall the flame kindle upon thee."* **Isaiah 43:2**

**WHY WORRY ABOUT YOUR EYES?** *"Then the eyes of the blind shall be opened, and the ears of the deaf shall be unstopped."* **Isaiah 35:5** *READ: Psalm 146:8/Proverbs 20:12/Mark 8:23/Deuteronomy 34:7

**WORRIED ABOUT WHETHER (OR NOT) TO MARRY AN UNSAVED PERSON? READ: 2 Corinthians 6:14-18**

**WHY WORRY ABOUT A GLANDULAR DEFICIENCY? Philippians 4:19/Exodus 23:25**

**WHY WORRY ABOUT YOUR KNEES?** *"Strengthen ye the weak hands, and confirm the feeble knees."* **Isaiah 35:3/Hebrews 12:12**

**WHY WORRY ABOUT EMERGENCIES OR FAMINE?** *"Behold the eye of the Lord is upon them that fear him, upon them that hope in his mercy: To deliver their soul from death, and to keep them alive in famine."* **Psalm 33:18-19**

**WHY WORRY ABOUT BECOMING SENILE? Luke 4:18-19/Isaiah 54:14, 17/35:3-4/Psalm 31:22-24/42:5, 11/9:9-10/146:8/Hebrews 12:12-13/Jeremiah 29:11-13/2 Timothy 1:7/1 Corinthians 2:16**

**WHY WORRY ABOUT PLAGUES?** *"There shall no evil befall thee, neither shall any plague come nigh thy dwelling."* **Psalm 91:10**

**WHY WORRY ABOUT A LEARNING DISABILITY? 1 Corinthians 2:16/Proverbs 4:13/Nehemiah 9:20/John 14:26/2 Timothy 1:7/Exodus 31:3, 6/Daniel 1:17/Psalm 19:7/Isaiah 54:13/Psalm 138:8/Job 32:8**

*Christians
are
like tea:
their
strength
is not
drawn out
until they
get into
hot water.*

**WORRY IS SINFUL AND WORTHLESS! JESUS SAID:**
*"Therefore I say unto you, Take no thought for your life, what ye shall eat, or what ye shall drink; nor yet for your body, what ye shall put on. Is not the life more than meat, and the body (more) than raiment (clothes)? Behold (look at) the fowls of the air: for they sow (plant) not, neither do they reap, nor gather into barns; yet your heavenly Father feedeth them. Are ye not much better than they? Which of you by taking thought can add one cubit (approx 25 inches) unto his stature (height)? And why take ye thought for raiment (clothes)? Consider the lilies of the field, how they grow; they toil not, neither do thy sin: and yet I say unto you, That even Solomon in all his glory was not arrayed like one of these. Wherefore, if God so clothe the grass of the field, which to day is, and tomorrow is cast into the oven, shall he not much more clothe you, O ye of little faith? Therefore take no thought, saying, What shall we eat? or What shall we drink? or Wherewithal shall we be clothed? For after all these things do the Gentiles seek: for your heavenly Father knoweth that ye have need of all these things. But seek ye first the kingdom of God, and his righteousness; and all these (other) things shall be added unto you. Take therefore no thought for the morrow (tomorrow); for the morrow shall take thought for the things of itself. Sufficient unto the day is the evil thereof."* **Matthew 6:25-34/Luke 12:22/Philippians 4:6/1 Peter 5:7**

**REMEDY FOR WORRY:** First acknowledge that you are a sinner and ask God to forgive all your sins. **Ask Him to help you overcome worry and He will!** Be sure to pray and read your Bible each day for wisdom and peace. Attend a church which teaches the entire Bible. Let go of **worry** and let God take control of your life. He is not capable of making a mistake! If, for some reason, you still **worry** then go to a spirit-filled minister and ask him to exercise his faith in casting out a demon of fear that may be oppressing you! God can't fail if you do your part. **GOD BLESS YOU AS YOU OVERCOME THE WORRY PROBLEM!**

WORRY **PRAYER**

Dear God, please forgive all my sins and cleanse me. I turn away from all sin and temptation. From this moment on I will put my trust in You to work out my problems whether they are real or imaginary! Take control of my life and give me peace and happiness. I want to be free from all worry. I will pray each day and read my Bible. Open my understanding to what the scriptures say. Please forgive me for worrying so much instead of putting my trust in You! I know You love me and have all the answers to life's problems. Thank You for forgiving my sins. In Jesus' name, I pray. AMEN!

*"For what shall it profit a man, if he shall gain the whole world, and lose his own soul?"* Mark 8:36

*"Therefore to him that knoweth to do good, and doeth it not, to him it is sin."* James 4:17

**"This I say then, Walk in the Spirit, and ye shall not fulfil the lust of the flesh."** **Galatians 5:16**

*". . . All things are naked and opened unto the eyes of him . . ."* Hebrews 4:13

*". . . Every one of us shall give account of himself to God."* Romans 14:12

*''Mercy unto you, and peace, and love, be multiplied.''*
**Jude 2**

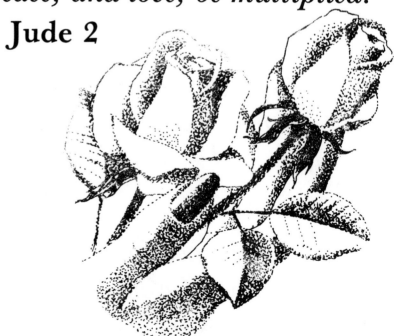